# MOUNTAINEERING

## THE FREEDOM OF THE HILLS

**6TH EDITION**

# MOUNTAINEERING

## THE FREEDOM OF THE HILLS

### 6TH EDITION

## Editors: Don Graydon and Kurt Hanson

THE
MOUNTAINEERS

Published by
The Mountaineers
1001 SW Klickitat Way
Seattle, WA 98134

10 9 8 7
5 4 3 2 1

Published by The Mountaineers
1001 SW Klickitat Way, Suite 201, Seattle, WA 98134

Published simultaneously in Great Britain by Swan Hill Press, an imprint of Airlife Publishing Ltd., 101 Longden Road, Shrewsbury, England, SY3 9EB
Manufactured in the United States of America

Library of Congress Cataloging-in-Publication Data
Mountaineering : the freedom of the hills / edited by Don
    Graydon and Kurt Hanson. -- 6th ed.
      p.  cm.
    Includes bibliographical references (p.    ) and index.
    ISBN 0 -89886-426-7 (cloth). -- ISBN 0-89886-427-5 (paper)
    1. Mountaineering. 2. Rock Climbing. 3. Snow and ice
    climbing. I. Graydon, Don. II. Hanson, Kurt. III. Mountain-
    eers (Society)
GV200.M688  1997
796.52'2--DC21
                                        97-11920
                                             CIP

Edited by Dana Lee Fos
Illustrations by Bob Cram, Nick Gregoric, Marge Mueller, and Ramona Hammerly
Cover design by Watson Graphics
Book design, art direction, typography, and layout by Gray Mouse Graphics

*Cover photograph:* Khumbu region, Nepal (Ama Dablam in background) ©Gordon Wiltsie; *Back cover:* Rock climbing at Palisade Head ©Ed Wargin/Corbis

*Frontispiece:* Needles, California © Uli Wiesmeier/ Adventure Photo. *Title page:* ©Heather Paxton

The following trademarks and brand names appear in this book: Air Traffic Controller, Avon Skin-so-Soft, Band-Aids, Benadryl, Benzoin, Big Bro, Cassin Dragon Fly, Clog, Cordura, Crazy Creek, Dachstein, Dacron, Diamox, DMM Predator, Friends, Frogwear, Gamow, Gemini, Gibbs, Gore-Tex, Grivel 2F, Hexentrics, Ice Scream, Jumars, Kevlar, La Sportiva K2, LiteLoft, Loctite, Lowe Footfang, Lowe Tri-Cam, Lowe Tuber II, Lycra, Masonite, Molefoam, Moleskin, North Wall, Petzl Grigri, Polarguard, PowerBar, Raptor, Ridge Rest, RURP (Realized Ultimate Reality Piton), Scarpa Eiger, Second Skin, Single Rope Controller, Spectra, Stoddard, Stokes, Stopper, Stubai Eiger Hammer, Stubai FKW, Styrofoam, Tabasco, Teflon, Therm-a-Rest, Thermos, Trango Pyramid, Trango-8, Variable Rope Controller, Velcro, Vibram, Yates Belay Slave, Yates Screamer

Printed on recycled paper

## A Note About Safety

Safety is an important concern in all outdoor activities. No book can alert you to every hazard or anticipate the limitations of every reader. Therefore, the descriptions of equipment and techniques in this book are not representations that a particular tool or technique will be safe for you or your party. When you participate in the activities described in this book, you assume the responsibility for your own safety. Keeping informed on current conditions and exercising common sense are the keys to a safe, enjoyable outing.

The Mountaineers

# CONTENTS

# PREFACE

**M**ountaineering: *The Freedom of the Hills* is intended as both an introductory and advanced text on the sport of mountaineering. This sixth edition continues the tradition established by the previous five editions of being the leading English-language text on mountaineering.

Each chapter from the fifth edition has been revised, rewritten, and, where necessary, expanded, and a section on the mountain environment has been added. These revisions reflect the rapid changes in mountaineering that have accompanied its increased popularity, the development of new techniques, and the introduction of new and improved equipment. Increased attention has been given to the issue of climber impact on the environment and methods to minimize it.

This edition maintains the format and style established by the fifth edition. The content was prepared by many contributors, all knowledgeable in mountaineering and especially knowledgeable in the area on which they wrote. A professional writer edited the material, bringing the various parts and chapters together to form a comprehensive and consistent text.

## Scope of the Book

As in previous editions, *Freedom* provides sound, clear, and current coverage of the concepts, techniques, and problems involved in the pursuit of mountain climbing. Individual topics, such as rock climbing or aid climbing, are detailed enough to be useful to readers with specific interests in those topics. The book provides a fundamental understanding of each topic.

Opposite: *Mt. Arapiles, Australia ©Uli Wiesmeier/ Adventure Photo*

It is not intended, however, to be exhaustive or encyclopedic. In addition to presenting information for the novice, much of the material in this book can help experienced climbers review and improve their skills.

Sport climbing—making use of artificial climbing walls or developed rock-climbing areas—is increasingly popular. While many techniques of sport climbing are interchangeable with those of mountain and rock climbing, there are differences. Those solely interested in sport climbing should also consult specialized texts.

Mountaineering cannot be learned just by studying a book. *Freedom* was originally written as a textbook for students and instructors participating in organized climbing courses. The context of learning that is provided in a course of instruction, given either individually or in groups, and by competent instructors, is essential for beginning climbers.

Of necessity, climbing requires continual awareness of the situation and environment at hand. Varying conditions, routes, and individual abilities all mean that the techniques used and decisions made must be based on the particular circumstances. To any situation, the individual climber and climbing team bring their knowledge, skills, and experience and then make their own judgment. To reflect this process, *Freedom* presents a variety of widely used techniques and practices and then outlines both their advantages and limitations. Material is presented not as dogma or the final word but as the basis for making sound judgments. To climb safely, one must view mountaineering as a problem-solving process and not as a rote application of techniques.

The type of climbing described in *Freedom* is frequently experienced (and most people would say best

7

experienced) in the wilderness. Any person who becomes a wilderness mountaineer must accept the responsibility to help preserve the wilderness environment for present and future generations. Walking softly so as to leave no trace of your passing in your own travels is a fair start. But the dwindling and finite mountain regions of the world are also our responsibility. We can all help educate other mountaineers in the techniques of low-impact mountaineering, and we can support organizations that preserve the wilderness both locally and globally.

## Origins of the Book

*Freedom*'s direction and emphasis originated from the development of climbing in the Pacific Northwest. The wild and complex character of the mountains in this region, with their abundance of snow and glaciers throughout the year, furthered the mountaineering challenge. Access was inherently difficult. There were few roads, and the initial explorations were themselves expeditions, often with native guides.

When The Mountaineers club was organized in 1906, one of its major purposes was to explore and study the mountains, forests, and watercourses of the Northwest. The journey to the mountain summit was a long and difficult one, and it required a variety of skills. With the knowledge of these skills, the competence that comes from their practice, and the experience gained through climbing mountains, more than a few had the exhilarating experience of the freedom of the hills.

As interest in mountaineering in the region grew, so did a tradition of tutelage. Increasingly, experienced climbers took novices under their wings to pass on their knowledge and skills. The Mountaineers formalized that exchange by developing a series of climbing courses. This book grew out of more than six decades' worth of teaching mountaineering and conducting climbs in the Northwest and throughout the world.

## Legacy of the Sixth Edition

Isaac Newton said, "If I see farther than others, it is because I stood on the shoulder of giants." The previous editions of *Freedom* represent a tradition of bringing together and sorting through the knowledge, techniques, opinions, and advice of a large number of practicing climbers. Students, both in training and

on actual climbs, have been a pivotal source of information.

Prior to publication of the first edition of *Freedom* in 1960, The Mountaineers climbing courses had used European works, particularly Young's classic *Mountaincraft,* as required reading. These works did not cover various subjects unique and important to American and Pacific Northwest mountaineering. To fill in the gaps, course lecturers prepared outlines, which they distributed to students. Eventually these outlines were fleshed out and gathered together as the *Climber's Notebook,* subsequently published, in 1948, as the *Mountaineers Handbook.* By 1955, tools and techniques had changed so drastically, and the courses had become so much more complex, that the new and more comprehensive textbook was needed.

Members of the first-edition editorial committee were Harvey Manning (chairman), John R. Hazle, Carl Henrikson, Nancy Bickford Miller, Thomas Miller, Franz Mohling, Rowland Tabor, and Lesley Stark Tabor. A substantial portion of the then relatively small Puget Sound climbing community participated— some seventy-five as writers of preliminary, revised, advanced, semifinal, and final chapter drafts, and another one or two hundred as reviewers, planners, illustrators, typists, proofreaders, financiers, promoters, retailers, warehousemen, and shipping clerks. At the time, there were few Mountaineers climbers who did not have a hand in making or selling the book. Those donating their time were rewarded by their accomplishment while those donating their money were repaid by the success of the book. *Freedom of the Hills* became the first title published by the now very successful Mountaineers Books.

Efforts leading to the publication of the second edition (in 1967) began in 1964. Members of the second edition editorial committee were John M. Davis (chairman), Tom Hallstaff, Max Hollenbeck, Jim Mitchell, Roger Neubauer, and Howard Stansbury. Even though much of the first edition was retained, the task force was, again, of impressive proportions, numbering several dozen writers, uncounted reviewers, and helpers. Survivors of the previous committee, notably John R. Hazle, Tom Miller, and Harvey Manning, provided continuity to the effort. As he had with the first edition, Harvey Manning once again edited the entire text and supervised production.

The third-edition editorial committee was formed in 1971 and headed by Sam Fry. Initially, a planning committee analyzed the previous edition and set guidelines for its revision. A steering committee, consisting of Jim Sanford, Fred Hart, Sean Rice, Howard Stansbury, and Sam Fry, directed the revision and had overall responsibility for the text. A large number of climbers contributed to individual chapters; the reviewing, revising, editing, and collation of chapters and sections was a true community effort. Peggy Ferber edited the entire book, which was published in 1974.

The fourth edition of *Freedom* (1982) involved a major revision and included complete rewrites of many chapters, most notably the entire section on ice and snow. A cast of hundreds was guided by a team of technical editors: Ed Peters (chairman), Roger Andersen, Dave Enfield, Lee Helser, John Young, Dave Anthony, and Robert Swanson. A large number of climbers submitted comments to the committee. Small teams of writers prepared a series of drafts for review by the technical editors. In addition to the substantial contribution of such writers, many others provided valuable help through critiques of subsequent and final drafts not only for technical accuracy and consistency but also for readability and comprehension.

Efforts on the fifth edition began in late 1987. Chaired by Paul Gauthier and, later, Myrna Plum, the committee undertook a major revision. Content was brought up to date and the layout and illustrations were redone to a more contemporary and readable format. Editorial coordinator Ben Arp and section coordinators Marty Lentz, Margaret Miller, Judy Ramberg, and Craig Rowley worked with volunteer contributors to develop the book's content. A professional editor/writer, Don Graydon, blended the volunteers' efforts into a consistent and readable style for the edition published in 1992.

## The Sixth Edition

Planning for a sixth edition began in the summer of 1994 with discussions between members of the Mountaineers climbing program and Mountaineers Books. That autumn, the Mountaineers Board chartered Kurt Hanson to lead an effort to develop a new edition. A structure similar to that used in prior years was used. Section coordinators were recruited, with Jo Backus for Outdoor Fundamentals, Myron Young for Climbing Fundamentals, Myrna Plum for Rock Climbing, Tom Hodgman for Snow, Ice, and Alpine Climbing, Marcia Hanson for Emergency Prevention and Response, and Myron Young for Mountain Environment, with Don Heck coordinating the illustrations.

What sets *Freedom* apart from other climbing texts is the process by which its content is prepared. The contributors are all active climbers who are regularly using and teaching the information and techniques about which they are writing. The collaborative effort distills the knowledge and experience of the many contributors into a whole. While one individual has responsibility for preparing the initial draft of a chapter, the other contributors comment and share their opinions on the material. After multiple iterations, the resulting text, again edited by Don Graydon, captures the shared knowledge of all of the contributors.

The five chapters on outdoor fundamentals were prepared by Teresa Soucie, First Steps; Brian Booth, Clothing and Equipment; Bert Daniels, Virginia Felton, and Teresa Soucie, Camping and Food; Bob Burns, with Mike Burns, Navigation; and Bert Daniels, Wilderness Travel.

The three chapters on climbing fundamentals were prepared by John Wick, Ropes, Knots, and Carabiners; Ken Small, Belaying; and Chuck Gorder, Rappelling.

Contributors for the four chapters on rock climbing were Barb McCann and Justin Davis, Rock-Climbing Technique; Karen Close, Rock Protection; Brad Berdoy, aided by Bill Doyle, Leading on Rock; and Jeff Johnson, with input from Mike Heil, John Medosch, and Gordon Warmouth, Aid Climbing.

Preparing the four chapters on snow, ice, and alpine climbing were Paul Russell, Ron Eng, and Paul Campbell, Snow Travel and Climbing; Tom Hodgman, Glacier Travel and Crevasse Rescue; Ron Eng and Dave Collins, Ice Climbing; and Gail McClary, Jim Tweedie, and Dave White, Alpine, Winter, and Expedition Climbing.

Contributors for the four chapters on emergency prevention and response were Cebe Wallace and Andy Dunning, Leadership; Steve Cox and Don Goodman, with help from Natala Goodman and Mike Burns, Safety; Margaret Cashman and Teresa Soucie, First Aid; and Mike Maude and Vera Dewey, Alpine Rescue.

The four chapters on the mountain environment

were the work of Ellen Bishop, with the help of Donna Calhoun, Mountain Geology; Sue Ferguson, The Cycle of Snow; Jeff Renner, Mountain Weather; and Marcia Hanson and Dave LeBlanc, Minimum Impact.

Additional valuable input was provided by Bill Serantoni and Ray Smutek.

---

THE MOUNTAINEERS, founded in 1906, is a non-profit outdoor activity and conservation club. Its purposes are:

- To explore, study and enjoy the mountains, forests and watercourses of the Northwest and beyond.
- To gather into permanent form the history and traditions of these regions and explorations.
- To preserve by example, teaching, and the encouragement of protective legislation or otherwise the beauty of the natural environment.
- To make expeditions and provide educational opportunities in fulfillment of the above purposes.
- To encourage a spirit of good fellowship among all lovers of outdoor life.

Based in Seattle, Washington, the club is now the third largest such organization in the United States, with 15,000 members and five branches throughout Washington State.

The Mountaineers sponsors both classes and year-round outdoor activities in the Pacific Northwest, which include hiking, mountain climbing, ski-touring, snowshoeing, bicycling, camping, kayaking and canoeing, nature study, sailing, and adventure travel. The club's conservation division supports environmental causes through educational activities, sponsoring legislation, and presenting informational programs. All club activities are led by skilled, experienced volunteers, who are dedicated to promoting safe and responsible enjoyment and preservation of the outdoors.

The Mountaineers Books, an active, nonprofit publishing program of the club, produces guidebooks, instructional texts, historical works, natural history guides, and works on environmental conservation. All books produced by The Mountaineers are aimed at fulfilling the club's mission.

If you would like to participate in these organized outdoor activities or the club's programs, consider a membership in The Mountaineers. For information and an application, write or call The Mountaineers, Club Headquarters, 300 Third Avenue West, Seattle, WA 98119; (206) 284-6310. e-mail: clubmail@mountaineers.org.

---

Opposite: *North Cascades ©Cliff Leight;* overleaf: *White River National Forest, Aspen, Colorado ©Tony Demin/Adventure Photo;* overleaf inset: *©David Schultz/Adventure Photo;*

# PART ONE

# OUTDOOR FUNDAMENTALS

# FIRST STEPS

Mountaineering is more than climbing, panoramic views, and wilderness experience. It is also challenge, risk, and hardship. And it is not for everyone. Those drawn to the mountains can find them exhilarating and irresistible, as well as frustrating and sometimes even deadly. There are qualities to mountaineering that bring inspiration and joy in a pursuit that is more than a pastime, more than a sport—a passion, certainly, and sometimes a compulsion.

"What was the force that impelled me?" asks American mountaineer Fred Beckey. "Something complex and undefinable, the attraction of uncertainty." British climber George Leigh Mallory, many years earlier, offered another version of mountaineering's attraction: "What we get from this adventure," he said, "is just sheer joy."

Distant views of mountains may speak of adventure, but they seldom more than hint at the joys and hardships that await. If you want to climb mountains, be prepared for the totality of nature—storms as well as soft breezes, tangled brush as well as alpine flowers, biting insects as well as singing birds. Climbing mountains is a tough way to spend your spare time, and anyone who does it knows what Polish climber Voytek Kurtyka meant when he said that "alpinism is the art of suffering." Mountaineering takes place in an environment indifferent to human needs, and not

Opposite: *Mount Rainier ©Carl Skoog*

everyone is willing to pay the price in hardship for its rich physical and spiritual rewards.

## Freedom of the Hills

"Freedom of the hills" is a concept that combines the simple joy of being in the mountains with the skill, equipment, and strength to travel without harm to ourselves, others, or the environment.

This book, with its roots in the mountains of the Pacific Northwest, champions this freedom by providing information for climbers of all levels, from novice to advanced. It represents the combined experiences of many climbers, who have traveled most of the major mountain ranges of the world. However, the great knowledge behind this book does not make it gospel. We benefit from the experiences of others, but often over time as we learn our own lessons in the mountains, we become teachers to those who first taught us.

As you read, remember that new techniques and technical advances occur so frequently that any attempt to document the "state of the art" is quickly outdated. With this caution in mind, this book can serve as your general passport to the freedom of the hills.

## Caring for the Wilderness

The beauty of wild places frequently becomes their undoing as they attract visitors—leaving the landscape touched by human hands and eventually less than wild. We are consuming wilderness at an alarming rate, using it and changing it as we do so.

Though we sometimes act otherwise, the mountains

don't exist for our amusement. They owe us nothing and they require nothing from us. Hudson Stuck wrote that he and the other members of the first party to climb Mount McKinley felt they had been granted "a privileged communion with the high places of the earth." As mountaineers traveling in the wilderness, our minimum charge for this privilege is to leave the hills as we found them, with no sign of our passing. We must study the places we visit and become sensitive to their vulnerability, then camp and climb in ways that minimize our impact.

The privileges we enjoy in the mountains bring the responsibility to help preserve this environment we love. The facts of mountaineering life today include permit systems that limit access to the backcountry, road and trail closures, environmental restoration projects, legislative alerts, and the clash of competing interest groups. While we tread softly in the mountains, it's also time to speak loudly back in town for support of wilderness preservation and sensitive use of our wild lands. As mountaineers, we need to be active wilderness advocates if we want our children to be able to enjoy what we take for granted.

## Knowledge and Skills

As part of our passport to travel the mountains, we need the skills for safe, enjoyable passage. For our sake and the sake of everyone we climb with, we learn the tools and techniques of minimum impact camping, navigation, belaying, rappelling, glacier travel, safety, wilderness first aid, rescue, and climbing on rock, snow, and ice. This book is a guide to this learning.

## Physical Preparation

Mountaineering is a demanding activity, both physically and mentally. Rock climbing, in particular, has become increasingly athletic, especially at the higher levels of difficulty. Climbers today accomplish what was considered impossible only a few years ago. Many serious rock climbers spend long hours on the climbing walls of specialized gyms, and the sport features international competitions. In the world of alpine climbing, the highest peaks are commonly climbed without supplementary oxygen, in record times, and by more and more difficult routes.

Most of us, however, appreciate such world-class performance from the sidelines. It's not necessary to devote your daily life to mountaineering in order to enjoy the activity at a level that provides personal satisfaction.

Levels of performance are rising even among recreational climbers and mountaineers. Good physical conditioning is one of the keys and can make the difference between enjoying an outing and merely enduring it. More important, the safety of the whole party may hinge on the strength—or weakness—of one member.

Many mountaineers dedicate an hour or two daily to keeping in shape. Running, cycling, swimming, and stair climbing are popular aerobic activities that pay off in better physical conditioning if they are done at least three days a week. Nearby hiking trails can serve as training grounds for mountaineers who hike uphill with heavy packs, while winter offers cross-country skiing, telemark skiing, and snowshoeing. In addition to aerobic conditioning, many climbers lift weights to build muscle strength and perform stretching exercises for flexibility.

Fitness centers provide workout equipment such as stationary bikes, treadmills, and stairway and rowing machines that make it convenient to establish a regular exercise program. Athletic trainers can be helpful in advising on exercises directed toward climbing. Optimal physical fitness is the foundation for all the strenuous activities of mountaineering.

## Mental Preparation

Just as important as physical conditioning, our mental attitude often determines success or failure. Once physical fitness is adequate, the "mind games" we play with ourselves are what really get us past a difficult move or help us decide to back off.

We need to be positive, realistic, and honest with ourselves. There is a personal balance required here. A "can do" attitude may turn into dangerous overconfidence if it isn't tempered with a realistic appraisal of our limitations and of the situation.

Many a veteran mountaineer says the greatest challenges are mental. Perhaps this is one of mountaineering's greatest appeals: while seeking the freedom of the hills, we come face to face with ourselves.

## Judgment and Experience

This book outlines the basics of equipment and techniques and suggests how to learn from practice. But the mountains serve up challenges that require not only technical competence but also the ability to solve problems and make decisions. Sound judgment, the most important of all mental qualities in climbing, develops from how we integrate our knowledge and experience.

Much of what we need are coping skills and problem-solving skills—the ability to deal with adverse weather, long hikes, thick brush, high exposure, mountain accidents, and the like. As we experience these situations, we become better decision-makers, and the knowledge we gain will be useful for comparison the next time the going gets tough.

However, mountaineering tends to provide plenty of new situations that require careful judgment rather than automatic responses. In this uncertainty lies much of the allure and challenge of mountaineering—as well as the potential for tragedy.

Many years ago, The Mountaineers devised a set of guidelines to help people conduct themselves safely in the mountains. Based on careful observation of the habits of skilled climbers and a thoughtful analysis of accidents, it has served well for not only climbers but, with slight adaptation, for all wilderness travelers. It is not inflexible doctrine, but the following climbing code has proven to be a sound guide to practices that minimize risk.

## A Climbing Code

- A climbing party of three is the minimum, unless adequate prearranged support is available. On glaciers, a minimum of two rope teams is recommended.
- Rope up on all exposed places and for all glacier travel. Anchor all belays.
- Keep the party together, and obey the leader or majority rule.
- Never climb beyond your ability and knowledge.
- Never let judgment be overruled by desire when choosing the route or deciding whether to turn back.
- Carry the necessary clothing, food, and equipment at all times.
- Leave the trip itinerary with a responsible person.
- Follow the precepts of sound mountaineering as set forth in textbooks of recognized merit.
- Behave at all times in a manner that reflects favorably upon mountaineering, with minimum impact to the environment.

This code is by no means a step-by-step formula for reaching summits but, rather, a set of guidelines to safe and sane mountaineering. Climbers sometimes question the need for such standards for a sport in which much of the appeal lies in the absence of formal rules. But many serious accidents could have been avoided or their effects minimized if these simple principles had been followed. This climbing code is built on the premise that mountaineers want a high probability for safety and success, even in risk-filled or doubtful situations, and that they want an adequate margin of safety in case they have misjudged their circumstances.

Experienced mountaineers often modify the code in practice, taking an independent course that combines an understanding of risk with the skill to help control it. The code is recommended especially for beginners, who have not yet developed the necessary judgment that comes only from years of experience.

If we learn to climb safely and skillfully, body and spirit in tune with the wilderness, we will be able to accept the lifetime invitation that John Muir extended to us many years ago.

"Climb the mountains," he told us, "and get their good tidings. Nature's peace will flow into you as sunshine flows into trees. The winds will blow their own freshness into you and the storms their energy, while cares will drop off like autumn leaves."

# CLOTHING AND EQUIPMENT

In packing for a wilderness trip, it's a simple matter of take it or leave it. The idea is to take what you need and to leave the rest at home. With thousands of choices widely available in outdoor clothing and equipment, it's no longer a question of how to find what you need but, rather, of limiting your load to just the items that will keep you safe, dry, and comfortable.

To strike a balance between too much and too little, monitor what you take with you. After each trip determine what was used, what was genuinely needed for a margin of safety, and what items were unnecessary. As you buy equipment, go for lightweight alternatives if the weight reduction does not jeopardize the item's performance or durability.

If you're new to mountaineering, you don't have the experience yet to know what will work best for you. So don't buy all your basic gear right away. Take it one trip at a time, one purchase at a time. Whether it's boots, packs, or sleeping bags, wait until you have enough experience to make intelligent decisions before spending your money. Rent, borrow, or improvise during your early outings until you learn what you need and what you don't need. Get advice by talking to seasoned climbers, by window-shopping at outdoor stores, and by reading mountaineering magazines.

This chapter provides information on basic wilderness gear, including guidelines on what constitutes good equipment. It won't tell you which brands to purchase, but it will help you find high-quality items among the many choices.

## CLOTHING

Clothing helps you stay comfortable by creating a thin insulating layer of warm air next to your skin. The enemies of comfort—rain, wind, and cold—work against this protective air layer.

"Comfort" is usually a relative term for mountaineers. Inclement mountain weather often forces climbers to endure conditions that deteriorate far below most people's concept of comfortable. In climbing, the key to maintaining relative comfort is to stay dry—or when wet, to stay warm and to get dry quickly.

But mountaineering clothing serves a much greater purpose than mere comfort. In the wilderness, safety is the primary role served by clothing. When you venture into remote territory, you sacrifice the option of quickly dashing back to civilization to escape foul weather. Instead, you must deal with the difficult conditions for however long they last.

Prolonged periods of dampness, even in moderately cool temperatures, can cause the body's warm air layer to fail. For many unfortunate individuals, substandard clothing has led to hypothermia—a dangerous, uncontrolled drop in body temperature that is one of the most frequent causes of death in the mountains. Your clothing system should be carefully selected to assure your survival through sustained exposure to the cold and wet.

Conversely, your clothing system must be able to protect you from overheating on hot days. Ventilation and breathability are the key considerations in order to prevent excessive sweating, which can dampen your clothing from within and can also lead to severe dehydration.

As you shop for clothing at outdoor equipment stores, you'll be faced with an overwhelming variety of garments, high-tech fabrics, and brand names, each proclaiming superior performance. Keep in mind that no single garment or fabric is ideal for all climbers or all situations. One climber may select a clothing system markedly different from that chosen by a climber with a different body structure or metabolism. And an individual climber won't always utilize the same clothing system. Vastly different clothing may be worn depending on the season and type of ascent. The best way to select an outdoor wardrobe is to gain experience and judgment by trial and error, sticking with the clothing strategies that keep you the most comfortable. Start with the following general guidelines and suggestions, and take it from there.

## Layering

You can optimize the effectiveness and versatility of your clothing by wearing it in a system of layers. Layering makes it easy to adapt to the fluctuating temperatures in the mountains. To adjust to changing conditions, add or subtract layers of clothing one by one.

The basic outdoor clothing system consists of three types of layers: a layer next to the skin, insulating layers, and an outer shell layer.

**The layer next to the skin** (underwear) should allow perspiration to pass through and evaporate without absorbing the moisture, keeping your skin dry. This "wicking" process can be vital to keeping you warm, because wet garments in contact with the skin cause twenty-five times more heat loss then dry ones.

**Insulating layers** should trap warm air next to the body. The thicker the layer of trapped, or "dead," air, the warmer you'll be. You can usually stay warmer by wearing several light, loosely fitting layers rather than one thick garment, because the multiple layers trap more layers of air.

**The shell layer** should provide protection from wind and rain, which can cause heat to be drawn away at an alarming rate.

## Fabrics

Clothing for the outdoors is made from a variety of fabrics, each with its particular advantages and drawbacks. Various features of outdoor fabrics are detailed in the following section and summarized in Figure 2-1.

### Natural Fibers

In the early days of mountaineering, natural-fiber clothes were worn exclusively. Natural fibers share the characteristic of readily absorbing water. They are becoming obsolete for the same reason.

**Cotton** is comfortable to wear when dry—but it loses its insulating qualities when wet, absorbs many times its weight in water, wicks perspiration very poorly, and takes a long time to dry. Because of these characteristics, cotton has virtually no business being worn in most mountain climates. Cotton's common role in hypothermia tragedies has earned it the nickname "death cloth" among many not-so-cynical climbers. In hot weather, however, cotton ventilates and cools well. Wet down a cotton T-shirt on a hot day, and the evaporating water will cool you off.

**Wool** is far less absorbent than cotton, so it holds less water when wet and requires far less heat to dry. When wet, wool does not collapse as much as cotton; therefore, it retains much of its dead-air space and still works very well as an insulating layer. This non-collapsing feature also makes wool a good material for socks. The main drawbacks of wool are weight and bulkiness. Wool garments vary in their processing— the lighter the processing (that is, the closer the wool resembles "raw" wool), the better the garment will shed water. But even the best wool is too absorbent (and too scratchy) to wear against the skin.

### Synthetic Fibers

Modern, high-tech synthetic fibers have virtually replaced natural fibers in mountaineering clothing. Synthetic fibers are generally hydrophobic, which means they tend not to absorb moisture. Garments made of synthetic fibers do absorb some moisture, but mainly only in the vacant spaces between the fibers

| Fabric | Advantages | Disadvantages | Uses |
|---|---|---|---|
| Polyester | Dries quickly. Comfortable. Lightweight. Some types retain insulating qualities when wet. | Expensive. Some types retain odors. | T-shirts and long underwear against skin. Insulating layers (long underwear, fleece jackets and pants). Hats, gloves, socks. |
| Polypropylene | Dries quickly. Lightweight. | Expensive. Somewhat scratchy. Retains odors. | Same as polyester. |
| Nylon | Strong and durable. Lightweight. Inexpensive. Various styles offer wind or abrasion resistance. | Fairly absorbent. Dries fairly slowly. | Parkas, wind garments, rain pants, overmitts, vapor-barrier socks. |
| Spandex | Stretchiness. | Compromises durability. Compromises wicking performance. Dries slowly. | Used as a blend element in many garments. |
| Wool | Retains some insulating qualities when wet. Fair wind and abrasion resistance. Inexpensive. | Dries slowly. Heavy and bulky. Scratchy. | Insulating layers (sweaters, shirts, pants). Caps, gloves, outer socks. |
| Cotton | Breathes well. Good in hot weather. Comfortable when dry. Inexpensive. | Absorbs a lot of water. Loses insulating qualities when wet. Dries very slowly. | Generally inappropriate. Exceptions: T-shirts for hot weather, sun-protection hats, bandannas. |

Fig. 2-1. Fabrics for outdoor clothing

rather than inside the individual fibers themselves. When wet, most of the moisture can be wrung out; the rest evaporates quickly.

**Polyester and polypropylene fabrics** are good at wicking perspiration, so they are well suited for use next to the skin. Polypropylene underwear performs excellently but is somewhat scratchy and tends to give off an offensive odor after having wicked sweat for a while, hence the nickname "polypew." Polyester has largely replaced polypropylene, offering a softer feel against the skin and less of an assault to the olfactory senses.

The packaging for different types of synthetic underwear commonly displays fancy-sounding brand names. It is easy to become confused trying to compare them. Often, brand names merely refer to different fabric treatments, and different-looking garments may actually be quite similar. Reading the garment tags and consulting a salesperson can help you sort through the confusion.

In addition to use against the skin, polypropylene and polyester work well as insulating layers. You can select from a number of different weights of long underwear. Or consider jackets and pants of different weaves, such as thick and fluffy polyester pile or fleece.

**Nylon** is manufactured in many, many forms, making it one of the world's most versatile fabrics. In the outdoor clothing industry, nylon fabrics find their main uses in shell garments. Characteristics vary widely from one style of nylon to another. Some nylons provide good wind resistance, others feel slick or soft, but virtually all are known for strength and durability. One shortcoming is that, unless specially treated, nylon absorbs a fair amount of water and dries fairly slowly.

**Spandex** is a very stretchy synthetic. Lycra is perhaps the most familiar example. Spandex is generally used only as a blending element to add stretchiness to another fabric, such as polyester or nylon.

When two fibers are blended together, the resulting fabric offers characteristics in-between the two materials. For example, a jacket that is 80 percent polyester blended with 20 percent spandex will offer more stretchiness but poorer wicking than plain polyester.

## Waterproof/Breathable Fabrics

Rain parkas and rain pants are generally made of nylon. Nylon itself is not waterproof, so rain garments derive their waterproofness from a number of different fabrication methods and treatments applied to the nylon.

The simplest method is to cover the nylon garment with a waterproof, nonbreathable coating, such as polyurethane. Polyurethane coatings are lightweight and relatively inexpensive, but they are not very resistant to abrasion or mildew.

Although polyurethane keeps rain out, it also seals in sweat and water vapor. If you're working hard, the sweat you generate can dampen your insulating layers from within. Think of a Styrofoam cup of hot coffee. If you put a plastic lid on the top, water from the coffee's steam will condense on the inside of the lid. In a way, your body is like that coffee: if your sweat doesn't have a way to escape through your shell layer, you won't stay dry.

Waterproof/breathable coatings were designed to attack this problem. These coatings, applied to the inside of the nylon shell, have billions of microscopic pores per square inch. Moisture vapor from your skin is emitted in the form of individual water molecules, which are much smaller than droplets of rain. The holes in the waterproof/breathable coating are large enough to let vapor escape but too small for raindrops to get in, so the coating breathes while staying waterproof. As you might expect, high-tech coatings like these are more expensive than polyurethane. Like much mountaineering equipment, waterproof/breathable coatings

go by a variety of brand names, and you often have to talk to a salesperson to understand what you're purchasing.

You also have the choice of garments with a laminated waterproof/breathable membrane instead of a coating. These membranes–Gore-Tex is the best known–are also perforated with microscopic pores. Membranes work on the same theory as coatings but are instead fabricated as a separate layer inside the nylon shell. Gore-Tex garments are typically even more expensive than those with waterproof/breathable coatings, but they have a longer functional life if they are cared for properly.

Although the waterproof/breathables are a marked improvement over old-style coated nylons, they are not perfect. If you work hard, you will exceed the garment's ability to blow off steam, and sweat will condense inside the shell. Once in liquid form, the sweat can no longer escape through the garment, and you're back to the original problem. Thus it is important to go for the right amount of breathability.

Most waterproof/breathables work reasonably well at being waterproof, but they can vary considerably in their breathability, depending on construction techniques and ventilation features, such as zippers under the arms. Extra breathability often demands a higher price.

How much breathability do you need? That's a question that only you can answer, and it takes experience to make a good judgment. Basically, the right amount of breathability depends on your personal body structure and metabolism and on your level of exertion while climbing.

### Care of Waterproof/Breathable Fabrics

Waterproof/breathable shells–whether they utilize a coating or a laminated membrane–depend on relatively delicate components in order to function. Don't expect even the most expensive rain parka to last for long if you abuse it.

First, grime and sweat can clog and contaminate fabric pores, reducing breathability. Keeping the shell clean helps keep it functioning up to its capability. Certain types of detergents can chemically break down shell elements, so read the tags and follow your garment's recommended washing and drying procedures.

It's usually not a good idea, however, to toss your

parka in the washer after every use. The churning motion of a washing machine will gradually remove the water-repellent finish on the exterior of the shell. Water-repellent finishes are applied in order to make rainwater bead up on the shell surface. If this exterior finish wears off, the waterproof/breathable coating or membrane on the inside of the shell will still function to keep water from reaching your inside garments—but the nylon fabric can now become saturated by rain, which degrades breathability and gives the parka a cold, clammy feel against the skin.

Regardless of the care you give your shell, the water-repellent finish will eventually wear off due to simple wear and tear. When water no longer beads on the surface, the shell can be restored somewhat with a wash-in or spray-on agent.

## Insulating Fills

Down, although a natural material, is still ounce for ounce the warmest insulating fill available. It is also the most compressible, so it packs away small yet

quickly regains its loft—and therefore its warmth—when unpacked. These qualities make down an excellent filling for cold-weather jackets and sleeping bags. Unfortunately, down loses all its insulating value when wet and is almost impossible to dry in the mountains, making it a poor choice in wet climates.

Synthetic insulations do not collapse when wet, as down does. Therefore they provide better insulation in moist climates. Although not as warm for their weight as down, and less compressible, they are cheaper and more easily cleaned. Again, brand names for these fillings can be confusing, so read the tags to figure out what you're looking at.

## Putting the Clothing System Together

Armed with a knowledge of outdoor fabric characteristics and the strategy of layering, you can assemble your mountaineering clothing system. Figure 2-2 shows typical examples how the various articles

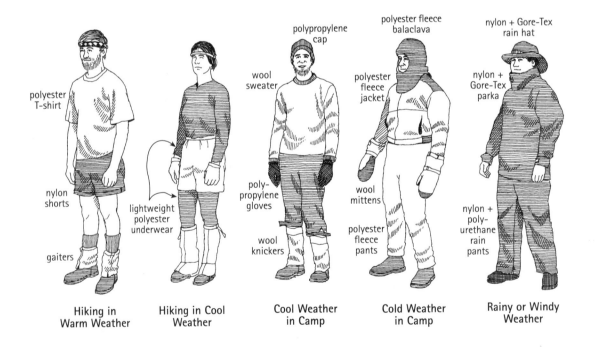

polypropylene cap

polyester fleece balaclava

nylon + Gore-Tex rain hat

polyester T-shirt

wool sweater

polyester fleece jacket

nylon + Gore-Tex parka

nylon shorts

lightweight polyester underwear

polypropylene gloves

wool mittens

nylon + polyurethane rain pants

gaiters

wool knickers

polyester fleece pants

polyester fleece pants

**Hiking in Warm Weather**    **Hiking in Cool Weather**    **Cool Weather in Camp**    **Cold Weather in Camp**    **Rainy or Windy Weather**

*Fig. 2-2. Typical examples of a clothing layering system*

in a complete clothing system can be mixed and matched to function well over a wide spectrum of weather conditions. The exact items that are chosen will vary significantly from climber to climber. The point is to make the system comprehensive and versatile. Following are some specific guidelines for each clothing layer.

### Layer Next to the Skin

Protection from the cold begins with appropriate long underwear. Wicking fabrics like polypropylene and polyester are the best for this purpose.

Dark-colored long underwear absorbs more heat—keeping you warmer—and dries more quickly in sunlight. Light colors, absorbing less heat from the sun, are better on hot days, when you may choose to wear long underwear as protection from sunburn or insects.

Spandex-blended polyester tights are occasionally used in place of straight polyester long underwear for rock climbing, as their stretchiness permits fuller range of motion. But their absorbency makes them a poor choice for traveling through wet brush or for use when perspiring heavily.

#### T-Shirts and Shorts

Although T-shirts, shorts, underwear, and sports bras do not really constitute a "layer," they should be chosen to perform basically the same function as long underwear. In other words, they should allow perspiration to pass through.

For hot weather, wicking away sweat is unnecessary, so a cotton T-shirt or tank top will suffice. But for cooler mountain climates, cotton won't cut it. On a moderately cool and breezy day, you could soak a cotton T-shirt with sweat while ascending a steep hill and then get a deep chill when stopping for a break. Synthetic fabric shirts are much better than cotton in this situation. T-shirts should be light-colored for coolness and moderately baggy for good ventilation.

For shorts, ventilation and abrasion resistance are the key requirements. A loose-fitting pair of nylon shorts, fitted with an integral nylon mesh brief, usually works well. Cotton shorts are not commonly worn by climbers, as they can cause uncomfortable chafing when dampened with perspiration. A popular clothing combination on a mild day is lightweight polyester long underwear topped with a pair of nylon shorts.

### Insulating Layers

In cold weather, you'll need to carry several insulating layers for both your torso and legs. Upper-body layers can include heavyweight long underwear, wool shirts, sweaters, or synthetic fleece jackets. For the legs, choose heavyweight long underwear or wool or fleece pants. There are many choices; the main objective is retaining warmth when wet. Leave the cotton sweatshirts and jeans at home.

Shirts and sweaters should be long in the torso so they tuck into or pull over the waist of the pants. Gaps between the pants and upper body layer(s) let valuable heat escape. Turtleneck underwear and sweaters can also provide a significant warmth benefit with little extra penalty in weight.

Insulating pants should be loose-fitting or stretchy for freedom of movement and made of a closely woven fabric with a hard finish for resistance to wind and abrasion. Wool and wool/polyester blends work well. Fleece pants are lighter but are not as abrasion- or wind-resistant as wool. Look for pants with reinforced seats and knees and with long side zippers that allow you to put the pants on while wearing boots.

Some climbers prefer knee-length knickers to long pants for freedom of movement and better ventilation and to avoid saturating pant legs from contact with snow or dew. Obviously, knickers are not the best choice for extremely cold weather.

### Shell Layer

The ideal shell is uninsulated, windproof, completely waterproof, and completely breathable. There is no single garment that can achieve all these objectives, but there are various strategies that come as close as possible.

One strategy is to have a single multifunctional shell layer, such as Gore-Tex rain pants and rain parka, or rain gear with a waterproof/breathable coating. If this single shell layer provides sufficient breathability for you, it is probably the best way to go.

An alternative strategy is to carry two shell layers: a breathable layer of wind gear plus a nonbreathing set of rain gear. With this strategy, the wind gear is worn in breezy and possibly lightly drizzling conditions; the rain gear goes on when it rains more heavily. This two-shell strategy can be cheaper, and the wind gear allows for better ventilation in dry conditions. But the nonbreathing layer will be more uncomfortable in rain than waterproof/breathable rain gear, and the additional shell layer carries a weight penalty.

Rain parkas come in different styles (fig. 2-3). Standard parkas feature a full front zipper, with a ventilation adjustment capability. Anoraks (pullover jackets without full front zippers) don't provide as much adjustment but are considered to be more reliable by some climbers because they cannot fail due to a jammed or broken zipper.

Many of the qualities you should look for when shopping for a rain parka are the same whether or not the fabric breathes:

- A size large enough to allow for additional insulating layers of clothing underneath without compressing your insulation or restricting your movement.

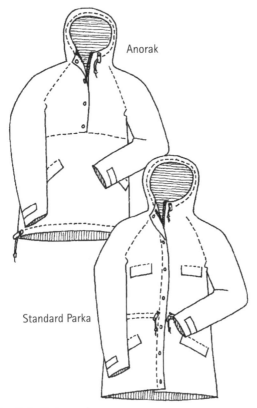

*Fig. 2-3. Rain parkas*

- A hood with a brim, neck flap, and good drawstrings to keep water from dribbling down your face and neck. The hood should be large enough to accommodate a hat (or climbing helmet) and should not impair vision when you glance to the side.
- Adjustable openings at the front, waist, underarms, sides, and cuffs that allow you to open up for ventilation or shut tight for trapping warm air next to your body.
- Zippers with large, durable teeth and with good flaps that keep the zipper dry.
- A dual front zipper that allows you to unzip from either the top or bottom. This can be useful for putting on a climbing harness or for belaying.
- Well-bonded, tape-sealed seams.
- Pockets that are easily accessible with gloved hands and with a pack on. Pockets also need good rain flaps that keep water out.
- A coat length that extends below your hips, and a drawstring at the waist that allows you to seal off the bottom of the coat.
- Sleeves that cover the wrists. Snaps, elastic, or Velcro should keep the sleeve in place at the wrist.

Rain pants should come with long zippers. Breathability is typically not as critical for the legs as for the torso. You may find that a nonbreathing pair of rain pants is comfortable, even if a similar type of parka is not. If so, you're probably better off with the cheaper, nonbreathing rain pants, as they tend to get easily trashed from bushwhacking through brush or glissading down snow.

Some climbers use waterproof/breathable bib pants, held up with suspenders, as a lower-body shell layer. Some bibs contain insulating fills and are best suited to cold-weather expeditions, ice climbs, and ski mountaineering. They are considerably warmer than rain pants because they cover much of the torso and keep snow from melting around the waistline, but they are too warm for most summer uses.

## Headgear

The old adage says, "If your feet are cold, put on a hat." Without a hat, your head acts like a radiator and can account for more than half of your body's heat loss. There is some truth to the old saying, because as the body gets cold, it reduces blood flow to the arms and legs in an attempt to warm more vital areas, such as the head. Putting on a hat will help reverse the effect.

Climbers usually carry several different types of hats. Warm insulating caps come in wool, polypropylene, or polyester fleece. Balaclavas (fig. 2-4) are versatile insulators because they can cover both your face and neck or can be rolled up to allow ventilation of your collar area. Consider carrying two insulating hats; an extra hat affords almost as much warmth as an extra sweater while weighing much less.

(Rolled up)

*Fig. 2-4. Balaclava*

A rain hat is useful, as it provides more ventilation and is often more comfortable than a parka hood. Some rain hats are available in waterproof/breathable fabrics, allowing further ventilation.

Cotton sun-protection hats, with protective shades draping over the neck and ears, are popular for glacier climbs. A baseball cap with a bandanna pinned on it can accomplish the same purpose.

A small arsenal of hats in a convenient pocket provides a quick method of adapting to changing temperatures. It's wise to carry one cap that is thin enough to fit beneath a climbing helmet.

To prevent the misfortune of having a hat blow off and sail over the edge of a cliff, sew leashes onto your headgear.

## Gloves and Mittens

Activities such as handling wet rope and scrambling on wet rock can saturate gloves or mittens, even in dry weather. Fingers are perhaps the most difficult part of the body to keep warm because of the body's tendency to sacrifice blood flow to the extremities in very cold weather. Unfortunately, this altered blood flow can inhibit tasks that involve the fingers—such as pulling zippers and tying knots—which may slow your party's progress at the very time you need to move the fastest to find shelter from the cold.

It can take considerable experience to wisely select the mittens and gloves that have such crucial impact on your comfort and safety during a trip. The decision usually entails a compromise between dexterity and warmth. In general, bulk equates with increased warmth and reduced dexterity. The more technical a climb, the more significant the compromise.

The layering concept for clothing also applies to your hands, although layer upon layer cannot be added without impairing blood circulation in your fingers and thumbs. The first layer may be a pair of gloves; additional layers will usually have to be mittens. Mittens are warmer than gloves because they allow your fingers to share warmth. A layered system of thin glove liners topped with mittens and overmitts usually works well.

As with other insulating garments, mittens and gloves should be made of fabrics that retain warmth when wet. Synthetic fabrics, with their low absorbency, can be very beneficial on snow climbs. Polyester fleece mitts can be wrung out when soaking wet and still retain most of their insulating loft. Gloves and mittens also come in wool/synthetic blends, offering more durability and wind resistance but taking longer to dry.

Overmitts constitute the shell layer for hands. The backhand side of the overmitt should be made of a waterproof/breathable fabric only. The palm side should be waterproof, but it does not have to be breathable. A nonslip coating on the palm will improve your grip on snow and ice tools. The overmitt cuff should overlap your parka sleeve some 4 to 6 inches, and elastic or Velcro closures can cinch the overmitt around your forearm.

As with hats, sew security cords onto mittens and overmitts. You'll find it well worth the effort when you need to pull off your mittens to climb rock or apply sunscreen.

In camp, wearing thin glove liners or fingerless gloves inside your mittens can permit good dexterity for delicate chores without exposing the entire hand. In very cold temperatures (around 0 degrees Fahrenheit), keeping your fingers from freezing to metal is the objective, and glove liners are better than fingerless gloves. But when you are rock climbing in cold weather and don't want a layer of fabric between your fingers and the rock, fingerless gloves are best.

Leather gloves can be worn for rope handling while rappelling or belaying, providing a better grip and preventing rope burns in the event of a fall. Leather gloves are difficult to waterproof and they soak up water, so they are not utilized for warmth.

## Clothing Considerations

There are many factors to keep in mind when establishing your outdoor clothing system. With the dazzling matrix of high-tech fabrics vying for your purchase, assembling a clothing system for the first time can be a daunting and confusing task.

If you are new to wilderness travel, it's probably best to start out carrying what seems like more than enough layers to keep yourself warm and dry. Delete items from your pack once you gain enough experience to confidently know you can survive without them.

When shopping for clothing, ask questions and read tags to help you make informed decisions. Evaluate garments for their functionality—will they work when wet? In addition to cost, consider durability, versatility, and reliability.

Try to minimize the weight of the clothing you carry, but not at the expense of compromising safety. After all, an additional lightweight underwear top may weigh a mere 4 ounces.

Finally, before heading out to the peaks, get a weather forecast. Think ahead about what temperatures and conditions you will encounter, and prepare accordingly. Then, relax and enjoy yourself climbing.

## FOOTGEAR

### Boots

Historically, almost all mountaineering boots were made of leather. Then came the advent of modern materials offering alternatives to leather. The classic leather boot has now been joined by plastic boots and by lightweight boots incorporating fabric panels as common footgear for wilderness travelers, although leather is still the first choice for general-purpose mountaineering.

### Leather Boots

A major factor in mountaineers' enduring respect for leather boots is their versatility. A general mountaineering boot must strike a balance of being tough enough to withstand the scraping of rocks, stiff and solid enough for kicking steps in hard snow, yet comfortable enough for the approach hike. In a single day of climbing, boots may have to contend with mud, streams, gravel, brush, scree, hard snow, and steep rock. Leather functions well at all these tasks and is very durable, to boot.

The classic leather mountaineering boot (fig. 2-5) has the following features:

- High uppers ($5\frac{1}{2}$ to $7\frac{1}{2}$ inches) to support and protect the ankles in rough terrain.
- Vibram-type soles for traction on slippery vegetation, mud, and snow.
- A fairly stiff shank.

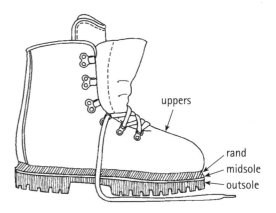

*Fig. 2-5. Classic leather mountaineering boot*

Other desirable boot features include the following:

- A minimum number of seams, to decrease the places water can leak through.
- A gusseted tongue, or a bellows tongue, to keep water from easily entering the boot.

- Rubber rands sealing the soles to the uppers, to aid in waterproofing and to simplify boot maintenance.
- Beefed-up toes and heels, with double- or triple-layered leather, for durability when scuffed.
- Hard toe counters (interior stiffeners) to protect the feet, reduce compression caused by crampon straps, and facilitate stepkicking in hard snow.
- Heel counters (interior stiffeners) to increase foot stability and facilitate plunge-stepping down steep snow slopes.
- Tops that open wide so the boots can be put on easily even when wet or frozen.

## Leather/Fabric Boots

*Fig. 2-6. Leather/fabric boot*

Advances in boot technology have led to boots that incorporate synthetic fabric panels that partially replace leather. Sometimes referred to as "lightweight boots," leather/fabric boots (fig. 2-6) provide a number of advantages over all-leather boots, including:

- Reduced weight.
- Improved comfort and shorter break-in time.
- Faster drying time.
- Lower cost.

However, leather/fabric boots also have significant drawbacks compared with all-leather boots:

- Less stability on difficult off-trail terrain.
- Less waterproofness.
- Less durability.

- Insufficient weight/stiffness for stepkicking in firm snow or for wearing with crampons.

If you are buying leather/fabric boots for climbing, check that the uppers are high enough for ankle protection and rigid enough for decent ankle support, that stiff counters wrap the heel and toe, and that abrasion areas are reinforced.

Some leather/fabric boots feature Gore-Tex liners, which can help keep your feet drier in the rain. Gore-Tex is no panacea for boots, however: if water enters the boot over the cuff, the waterproof/breathable laminate will be defeated. Gore-Tex also adds to the cost of a boot, and it may make your feet more uncomfortable during hot weather.

## Plastic Boots

Plastic boots (fig. 2-7) consist of hard plastic outer shells with inner insulating boots. They were originally designed for cold-weather expeditions and ice climbing but have since found a much wider market among general mountaineers interested in snow routes.

The plastic shells of the boots are very stiff—and thus excellent for climbing steep ice. The stiffness of plastic boots makes them good for use with crampons or snowshoes, as they permit straps to be cinched tightly without impairing circulation in the feet.

Being waterproof, plastic boots are also great for

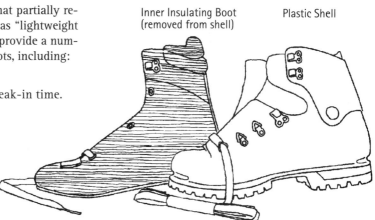

Inner Insulating Boot (removed from shell)     Plastic Shell

*Fig. 2-7. Plastic boots*

long trudges through snow. The inner insulating boot remains free of melted snow and keeps your feet warm. In camp, the inner boot can be removed, which helps in drying out perspiration. Unfortunately, the very factors that make plastic boots ideal for snow and ice (rigidity, waterproofness, and warmth) make them a poor choice for general trail use.

## The Right Support

Outdoor equipment stores typically carry a wide array of footwear, from trail shoes and cross-trainers to light- and heavy-duty backpacking boots to full-scale mountaineering boots. The degree of rigidity—controlled by selection of materials for uppers, midsoles, and shanks—is the primary characteristic that distinguishes the various categories. The best choice of boot materials depends on how the boot will be used and is largely a compromise between the boot's comfort and its technical capability.

For trails and easy snow or rock routes, boots with moderate stiffness provide sufficient support while being acceptably flexible and comfortable. Both leather and leather/fabric boots work well for these applications, provided their soles are reasonably firm.

For technical alpine rock climbing, leather/fabric boots are not sufficient. You have little choice for this type of climb but to sacrifice some comfort to achieve technical capability, and a sturdy all-leather boot will be necessary. (For information on specialized rock shoes, see Chapter 9, Rock-Climbing Technique.) The stiffer soles make walking somewhat harder, but they greatly reduce leg fatigue when you're standing on small rock nubbins. The more challenging the rock, the stiffer the boot you should seek. Look for soles strong enough to permit standing on narrow rock edges (fig. 2-8). Rigid soles are minimum equipment for the most difficult climbs.

For traveling on hard snow, either by kicking steps or by wearing crampons, leather/fabric boots are, again, too flexible. Sufficient stiffness and safety with crampons requires all-leather boots, with plastic boots also being an option.

Ice climbing demands a higher level of boot performance, and completely rigid soles are a minimum requirement. Here, plastic boots are the best, with extremely stiff leather boots providing an alternative.

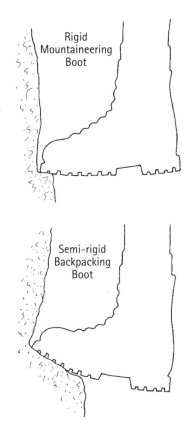

*Fig. 2-8. The stiffness of a boot affects its technical capability.*

## The Proper Fit

Whether you're looking at leather, leather/fabric, or plastic boots, the fit is critical. Try on several makes and styles. Some brands are available in multiple widths; others offer both men's and women's options—so shop around.

When heading to the stores to compare boots, take along socks similar to the ones you will wear on a climb, as well as any orthotic devices, insoles, or other inserts you plan to use. Most people's feet swell during the course of the day, so consider shopping in the evening.

After lacing up the boots in the store, try standing on a sharp edge or rocking side to side to test stability. Stand and walk in the boots for several minutes, with a heavy pack on if possible, to allow the boots' inner liners to conform to your feet. Then note whether the boots have any uncomfortable seams or creases or whether they pinch against your foot or Achilles' tendon. In boots that fit properly, your heels will feel firmly anchored in place while your toes will have plenty of room to wiggle and will not jam against the toe box when you press forward. Try standing on a downward incline for the most critical test of toe space.

Boots that are too tight will constrict circulation, which causes cold feet and increases susceptibility to frostbite. Tight boots, as well as excessively loose boots, can cause blisters. Given the choice between boots that are a bit too big and ones that are a bit too small, go with the larger boots. You can fill the space with thicker socks, and boots can shrink as much as a half size over time (because the toe of a boot has a tendency to curl).

Plastic boots need to fit well from the start because their rigid shape will not mold around your feet over time like the lining of a leather or leather/fabric boot. When fitting plastic boots, check extra carefully that they do not constrict the feet. Feet swell at high altitude, and plastic boots are frequently used for high-altitude expeditions.

### Boot Care

With proper care, good boots can last several years. Keep mildew at bay by frequently washing both the insides and outsides of the boots. After washing, stuff them with a boot tree or newspaper, and dry them in a warm (not hot) ventilated area. Avoid exposing boots to high temperatures, as heat can damage leather, linings, and sole adhesives. Boots dried over a campfire are likely to be the ones that fall apart on a future trip.

During an outing, water can seep into boots through the uppers and seams. Waterproofing agents can help limit the entry of water. Waterproofing is a process that needs to be repeated regularly.

There are several types of boot waterproofing products. The appropriate type for your boots depends on how the leather uppers were tanned, so follow the manufacturer's recommendations. Fabric panels in leather/fabric boots cannot be completely waterproofed, but they can be made more water-resistant by applying silicone-based sprays. Whatever you use on your boots, apply it frequently if you expect your feet to stay dry.

Before waterproofing, boots must be clean and dry, with any wax removed. Clean them with a mild soap, such as saddle soap, that will not damage the leather. It is difficult to remove every speck of grime, so waterproofing will usually not last as long on used boots as on new. Work in the waterproofing product, following instructions on the container.

With plastic boots, remove the inner boots after use and allow them to dry. Shake out any debris in the inner boots or plastic shells to prevent abrasion and excessive wear.

## Specialized Footwear

Depending on the trip, a climber may wear one kind of boot for the approach hike, another type of footwear in camp, and yet another on the climb. If you can afford additional footgear and are willing to carry the extra weight, consider these options:

- Lightweight, flexible trail shoes for easy approaches. They are less likely to cause blisters and are less fatiguing to wear than leather boots. However, these lightweight shoes may not provide the support you need when carrying a heavy pack, especially on descents.
- Running shoes, tennis shoes, sandals, neoprene socks, or booties, for comfort in camp and to give boots a chance to dry. They can also be used for stream crossings.
- Insulated booties and/or fleece socks for warmer sleeping.
- Special rock-climbing shoes for technical rock (see Chapter 9).

## Socks

Socks cushion and insulate the feet and reduce friction between the boot and the foot. Socks made of wool or synthetic materials can perform these functions; those made of cotton cannot. Cotton socks will get saturated, collapse, and stick to your feet, softening the skin and leading to blisters.

Socks must also absorb perspiration. Because boot uppers do not breathe appreciably, the sweat generated by your feet collects and builds up until you get the opportunity to remove your boots. Synthetic sock materials (including polyester, nylon, and acrylic) dry faster than wool.

Most climbers wear two pairs of socks. Next to the skin, a smooth and thin polyester sock transports perspiration from the foot and stays somewhat dry in the process. The outer sock is thicker and rougher in order to absorb the moisture passing through the inner sock and to abrade against the boot lining.

Of course, there are many exceptions to this two-sock guideline. A rock climber wants flexible rock shoes to fit like a glove and so usually wears only one thin pair of socks. A hiker using trail shoes on a warm day may keep feet cooler by wearing just a single pair of socks, whereas a winter climber may wear three pairs of socks inside oversized boots. If opting for this latter strategy, keep your toes free enough to wiggle; an additional pair of socks will not improve warmth if they constrict circulation.

Before donning socks, consider putting protective moleskin or tape on your feet at places prone to blisters, such as the back of the heel. Moleskin is especially valuable when breaking in new boots or early in the climbing season before your feet have toughened up. Another blister fighter is foot powder sprinkled on your socks and in your boots.

Waterproof/breathable Gore-Tex socks can improve comfort in extremely wet conditions. Worn over an inner pair of standard socks, the Gore-Tex socks function much like boots with Gore-Tex liners, while providing a higher and snugger cuff.

On expeditions or in cold weather, a vapor-barrier sock may be worn between the two main sock layers. Vapor-barrier socks are waterproof and nonbreathing, which may seem at first to be contradictory to clothing strategies outlined previously. However, think of the example of the hot coffee in the Styrofoam cup: although putting the plastic lid on the cup keeps the moisture trapped inside, it also keeps the coffee hot. Vapor-barrier socks apply the same principle to your feet: the feet get damp, but they stay warm. Vapor-barrier socks are best suited for extreme cold, where they reduce the danger of frostbite.

The obvious drawback of vapor-barrier socks is that they prevent your inner socks from wicking away sweat. That may be acceptable to you if your thicker, outer socks stay dry as a result. Or in wet, mushy snow, the dampness in the inner socks may be minor compared to the soaking they would get without the vapor-barrier socks. However, if the internal moisture

is allowed to continue for long, the serious condition of trench foot can develop. If you use vapor-barrier socks, dry your feet thoroughly at least once each day.

Insoles added to the inside of your boots provide extra insulation and cushioning. Synthetic insoles are nonabsorbent, do not become matted when damp, and have a loose structure that helps ventilate your foot. Insoles made of felt, leather, and lambskin all absorb moisture and must be removed when drying boots.

## Gaiters

During an outing, water and snow can get into your boots by going in over the cuff. Gaiters (fig. 2-9) are used to seal the boundary between your pant legs and boots. Climbers often carry gaiters both summer and winter, as rain, dew, mud, and snow provide year-round opportunities for water to saturate pant legs, socks, and boots.

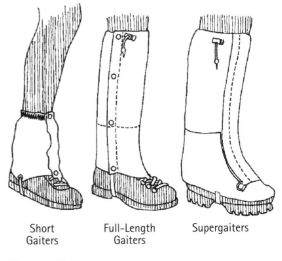

Short Gaiters　　Full-Length Gaiters　　Supergaiters

*Fig. 2-9. Gaiters*

Short gaiters, extending 5 or 6 inches over the top of the boot, are adequate for keeping corn snow and gravel out of your boots in summer. The deep snows of winter, however, usually call for standard gaiters that extend up to the knee.

Supergaiters completely cover the boot from the welt up, leaving the lug soles exposed for good traction. Insulation built into these gaiters covers the boots and reduces the chance of frostbite during cold-weather climbs.

The portion of the gaiter covering the boot should be made of a heavy-duty fabric coated with a water repellent. Higher-performance gaiters feature an additional waterproof membrane inside the heavy-duty fabric. The fabric covering the calf should be breathable or waterproof/breathable, to allow perspiration to escape. Gaiters are usually held closed with Velcro, snaps, or zippers, with Velcro offering the easiest fastening in cold weather. If selecting gaiters with zippers, be sure the teeth are heavy-duty. A flap that closes over the zipper with snaps or Velcro protects it from damage and can keep the gaiter closed and functional even if the zipper breaks.

A drawstring at the top of the gaiter keeps it from sliding down. A snug fit around the calf helps prevent crampon points from catching on the gaiters.

A tight fit around the boot is essential to prevent snow from entering under the gaiter, especially when plunge-stepping during descents. A strap runs under the foot to help the gaiter hug your boot. The strap under the foot will wear out during the life of the gaiter, so look for gaiters designed for easy replacement of straps. Neoprene straps work well in snow but wear quickly on rock, whereas heavy cord survives rock better but sometimes balls up with snow.

## PACKS

Climbers usually own at least two packs: a day pack to hold enough paraphernalia for a single-day climb and a full-size backpack to carry gear for camping in the backcountry. All packs should allow you to carry weight close to your body and to center the load over your hips and legs.

### Internal-Frame Versus External-Frame Packs

Internal-frame packs (fig. 2-10) are by far the most popular packs among climbers and ski mountaineers. A rigid frame within the pack helps it maintain its shape and hug your back, assisting you in keeping your balance as you climb or ski. When you shoulder an internal-frame pack, the weight is carried relatively low on your body, which is another plus for maintaining balance. A moderate drawback of this feature is that the weight is not carried high enough to be completely transferred to your hips. Instead, some burden must be carried by your shoulders and back. The body-hugging nature of internal-frame packs also makes them somewhat uncomfortable in hot weather.

The volume of most internal-frame packs can be easily adjusted with compression straps, and this is a significant advantage for climbing. A full-size pack can be used on the approach and then emptied of tent and sleeping bag at camp and transformed into a compact summit pack. The clean, narrow profile of internal-frame packs allows them to be taken through heavy brush or hauled up rock pitches with a minimum of snags.

External-frame packs (fig. 2-11) were once the only type of pack in use, but they now see only limited service with mountaineers. The pack contents are suspended from a ladderlike frame, which is held away from the back by taut nylon back bands. External-frame packs provide some advantages, like holding the load high (transferring the load more ideally to your hips) and keeping you cooler. Some climbers use them for long, easy approaches, carrying a small day pack inside for the summit day. But external frames are mainly limited to trail use. On the more challenging and uneven terrain encountered in climbing, they tend to shift without warning. The sudden movement of 40 pounds or so across your shoulder blades can easily make you lose your balance. It is also difficult to self-arrest on snow while wearing an external-frame pack.

### Buying an Internal-Frame Pack

Before shopping for a full-size internal-frame pack, decide what capacity is right for your intended uses. Overnight trips typically require packs of 3,000 to 5,000 cubic inches capable of carrying 30 to 55 pounds, depending on the demands of the climb. Longer trips and winter climbs require up to 6,000 cubic inches; expedition climbs can demand even more. (For special considerations in buying day packs, see the next section.)

The most important objective is to buy a pack that fits your body. The pack's adjustment range must be compatible with your back length. Some packs adjust to a wide range of sizes; others don't. Virtually no

Fig. 2-10. Internal-frame pack

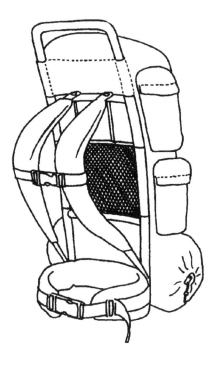

Fig. 2-11. External-frame pack

individual backpack provides a good fit for everyone, so don't place all your faith in endorsements from acquaintances or outdoor equipment magazines. Try on various packs and be your own judge.

Don't be in a hurry when fitting a pack. Load it up, as you would on an actual climb; bring your own gear to the store, if you like. Without a typical load, you can't tell how the pack rides or if the adjustments provide a good fit.

Loosen all the adjustment straps before putting the pack on, then tighten up the straps in the order recommended by the salesperson. Check yourself in a mirror, or ask someone, to see if the frame correctly follows the curve of your back. If it doesn't, check whether the stays or frame can be bent to improve the fit. (Some frames are made of composite materials that can't be reshaped.) The shoulder straps should attach to the pack about 2 or 3 inches below the crest of your shoulders and leave little or no gap behind your back.

Once the pack is adjusted to your liking, check the head clearance. Can you look up without hitting your head on the frame or top pocket? Can you look up if you're wearing a helmet? Next, check for adequate padding wherever the pack touches your body. Pay particular attention to the thickness and quality of padding used in the shoulder straps and hip belt. The hip belt should be substantial; its padding should cover the hip bones by good margins. For proper load transfer to the hips, ensure that the hip belt wraps directly onto the top of your hip bones, not around the sides of the hip bones or around the waist.

Here are some additional questions to consider when shopping for a pack (see Figure 2-12 for illustrations of common pack features):

- How is the suspension system designed? Does it look durable, or does it look like it could fail at weak spots?
- How sturdy is the pack's stitching?
- Does the pack rely on zippers to retain the contents?

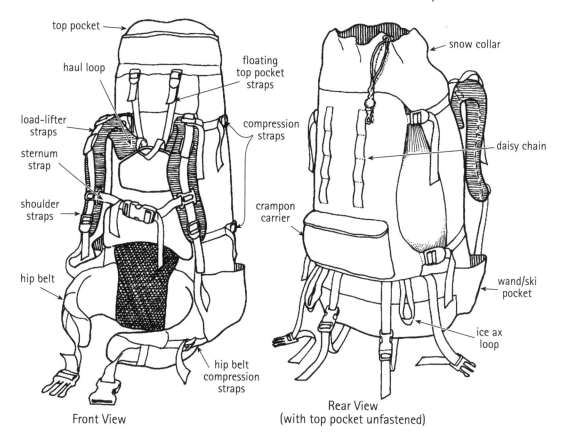

*Fig. 2-12. Common features of internal-frame packs*

If the zippers fail, can you still use the pack?

- How convenient is it to store, arrange, and access your gear in the pack?
- Does the pack provide means of carrying special items like crampons, skis, snowshoes, shovels, and wands?
- Does the pack have haul loops and ice ax loops?
- Are there compression straps to reduce the pack's volume or to prevent the load from shifting while climbing or skiing?
- Is there a means of increasing the pack's capacity for extended trips, such as an expandable snow collar with a floating top pocket or separate side pocket accessories?
- Does the pack have a sternum strap to help prevent the pack from shifting on difficult terrain?

- Does the pack have a smooth profile, or will it get tangled up during bushwhacks through heavy brush?

## Buying a Day Pack

Day packs for climbing usually have volumes of between 1,800 and 2,500 cubic inches, enough to carry 20 to 30 pounds. You can find a wide selection of day packs on the market, varying over a wide spectrum in terms of sturdiness. Some are designed without a rigid frame or a padded hip belt and are too flimsy for serious climbing.

Keep in mind that, as a climber, you will be carrying heavy items like rope, carabiners, a helmet, an ice ax, and crampons in your day pack. Seek a pack with a sturdy internal frame and a hip belt that is at least

2 inches wide at the buckle and 4 inches wide where it covers the hips. Narrow your selection by eliminating day packs that lack climbing features such as ice ax loops, haul loops, and crampon carriers.

Many of the questions of sturdiness, convenience, and utility that you should consider in choosing a full-size pack are also applicable to day packs. Does the pack offer a sternum strap, compression straps, sturdy stitching, convenient storage and access, and a smooth profile? Try on and compare day packs as thoroughly as you would a full-size backpack.

## Tips on Packing

Strategically loading the items in your internal-frame pack can dramatically influence your speed, endurance, and enjoyment of an outing. Generally, you will feel best if you can concentrate the load on your hips and avoid loading your back and shoulders.

On trails, the load should be carried high and fairly close to the back, as this will allow your hips to take the majority of the weight (fig. 2-13a) To implement this strategy, load your lightest, fluffiest articles (sleeping bag and extra clothing) in the bottom; place the densest items (water, food, stove fuel, rope) up top, near the shoulder blades.

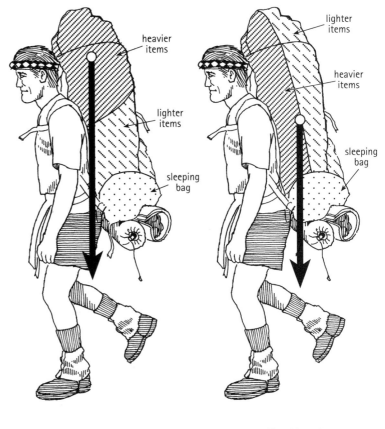

a) Trails           b) Off-Trail

*Fig. 2-13. Strategically loading your pack can dramatically influence your climbing endurance. The black arrow shows approximate center of gravity and weight distribution.*

For more difficult terrain, revise your trail-packing strategy. Pack the heavy items slightly lower, and ensure they are as close to the back as possible (fig. 2-13b). This will force more of the load onto your back and shoulders but will lower your center of gravity and allow you to more easily keep your balance.

Along with arranging items in your pack for optimum weight distribution, organize them for quick access. Articles like gloves, hats, sunglasses, maps, and insect repellent, which are sometimes needed at a moment's notice, are ideally carried in side and top pockets. Such gear can also be kept handy in jacket pockets or in a "fanny pack" that is worn on the abdomen in combination with the main pack.

Determine a strategy to keep your pack contents dry in rainy weather, because even packs constructed from waterproof materials are not necessarily waterproof. Water can leak through seams, zippers, pockets, the top opening, and places where the coating has worn off. Individual plastic bags or good stuff sacks can help protect pack contents, especially when you have to set up or break camp in the rain.

Most pack manufacturers offer waterproof pack covers as accessories. You may also choose to simply use a large plastic trash bag as a waterproof liner inside your pack.

## ESSENTIAL EQUIPMENT

There is a small selection of critical items that deserve a place in almost every pack in addition to normal supplies of clothes, water, and food. You won't use every one of these items on every trip, but they can be lifesavers in an emergency, insurance against the unexpected.

Exactly how much "insurance" you should carry is a matter of debate. Some respected minimalists argue that weighing down your pack with insurance items causes you to climb slower, making it more likely you'll get caught by a storm or nightfall and be forced to bivouac. "Don't carry bivy gear unless you plan to bivy," they argue.

The majority of climbers, however, take along carefully selected safety items to survive the unexpected. They sacrifice some speed but argue they will always be around tomorrow to attempt again what they failed to climb today.

### The Ten Essentials

The special items most climbers believe should always be with you have become known as the Ten Essentials. They are listed here and then described in more detail. A memory aid is provided as well.

| | |
|---|---|
| 1. Map | Mom's |
| 2. Compass | cafe |
| 3. Sunglasses and sunscreen | serves |
| 4. Extra food | everyone |
| 5. Extra clothing | extra |
| 6. Headlamp/flashlight | helpings of |
| 7. First-aid supplies | French |
| 8. Fire starter | fries, |
| 9. Matches | mustard, and |
| 10. Knife | ketchup |

### 1. Map

Always carry a detailed topographic map of the area you are visiting, in a protective case or plastic covering. (Chapter 4, Navigation, gives details about topographic maps.)

### 2. Compass

A compass is an essential tool of navigation and routefinding. It is necessary for each member of the party to carry a map and compass, in case the group accidentally gets separated. (Chapter 4, Navigation, explains the workings of the compass and other navigation instruments.)

### 3. Sunglasses and Sunscreen

The harsh brilliance of mountain skies can make sun protection necessary on any trip. Above timberline, the sun is difficult to avoid. Ultraviolet rays at an altitude of 10,000 feet are 50 percent stronger than at sea level, and reflection of the rays by snow can magnify their power even more.

**Sunglasses** are critical items in alpine country. Subjecting your unprotected eyes to bright sunlight reflecting off a field of snow, even briefly, can bring on headache and distract you from focusing on the route. The eyes are particularly vulnerable to radiation, and the corneas of unprotected eyes can be easily burned before any discomfort is felt, resulting in the excruciatingly painful condition known as snow blindness. Ultraviolet rays can penetrate some cloud layers, so don't let cloudy conditions fool you into leaving your eyes uncovered.

Sunglasses should filter 95 to 100 percent of the ultraviolet light. They should also be tinted so that only a fraction of the visible light is transmitted through the lens to your eyes. For glacier glasses, you want a lens with a 5 to 10 percent transmission rate. Look in a mirror when trying on sunglasses: if you can easily see your eyes, the lenses are much too light. Lens tints should be gray or green if you want the truest color or yellow if you want better visibility in overcast or foggy conditions.

There is little proof that infrared rays (heat-carrying rays) harm the eyes unless you look directly at the sun, but any product that filters out a high percentage of infrared, as most sunglasses do, is added eye insurance.

The frames of sunglasses should have side shields that reduce the light reaching your eyes yet allow adequate ventilation to prevent fogging. Problems with fogging can be reduced by using an anti-fog lens-cleaning product.

Groups should carry at least one pair of spare sunglasses in case a pair is lost or forgotten. If no spare is available, eye protection can be improvised by cutting small slits in an eye cover made of cardboard or cloth.

Many climbers who need corrective lenses prefer using contact lenses instead of glasses. Contacts improve visual acuity, don't slide down your nose, don't get water spots, and allow the use of nonprescription sunglasses. Contacts do have some problems, however. Blowing dust, sweat, and sunscreen can irritate your eyes. Backcountry conditions make it difficult to clean and maintain contacts. Whether choosing contacts or glasses, a climber who depends on corrective lenses should always carry a backup, such as a spare pair of normal glasses or prescription sunglasses.

**Sunscreen** creams for the skin are also vital to your well-being in the mountains. Although individuals vary widely in natural pigmentation and the amount of screening their skin requires, the penalty for underestimating the protection needed is so severe, including the possibility of skin cancer, that you must always protect your skin.

While climbing, use a sunscreen that blocks both UVA and UVB rays and has a sun protection factor (SPF) of 15 or more. The SPF number—15, for example—means that the sunscreen is formulated to permit the average individual to stay in the sun 15 times longer without burning than if the person had applied no protection. Sunscreens are available up to SPF 40 or more, although their protection is limited by their ability to remain on your skin while you are sweating. Some sunscreens are advertised as waterproof and will protect longer than regular products, but regardless of the claims on the label reapply the sunscreen frequently.

Cover all exposed skin with sunscreen, including the undersides of your chin and nose and the insides of your nostrils and ears. Even if you are wearing a hat, apply sunscreen to all exposed parts of your face and neck to protect against reflection from snow. Apply sunscreens half an hour before stepping out in the sun, as they usually take time to start working.

Zinc oxide paste or actor's grease paint (clown white) can be used on your nose as an alternative to regular sunscreens, as they ensure complete protection and will not wash off. One application lasts the entire climb, except where fingers or equipment rub the skin bare. The disadvantages of these creams is that they are messy and so difficult to remove that you may need help from a cold-cream cleanser.

Clothing offers more sun protection than sunscreen. Light-colored, breathable long underwear or wind garments are frequently worn on sunny glacier climbs. The discomfort of long underwear, even under blazing conditions, is often considered a minor nuisance compared to the hassle of regularly smearing on sunscreen.

Lips are skin, too, and require protection to prevent peeling and fever blisters. Cover your lips with a total-blocking lip balm that resists washing, sweating, and licking. Zinc oxide and lip balms containing para-aminobenzoic acid (or PABA) are both good. Reapply lip protection frequently.

(Chapter 19, First Aid, also includes information on sunburn and snow blindness.)

## 4. Extra Food

A one-day supply of extra food is a reasonable emergency stockpile in case you are delayed by foul weather, faulty navigation, injury, or other reasons. The food should require no cooking, be easily digestible, and store well for long periods. A combination of jerky, nuts, candy, granola, and dried fruit works well. If a stove is carried, cocoa, dried soup, and tea can be added. There are many possibilities. Some climbers only half-jokingly point out that pemmican bars and U.S. Army Meals Ready to Eat (or MRE) packs serve well as emergency rations because no one is tempted to eat them except in an emergency.

## 5. Extra Clothing

How much extra insulation is necessary for an emergency? The garments used during the active portion of a climb and considered to be your basic climbing outfit include inner and outer socks, boots, underwear, pants, shirt, sweater or fleece jacket, hat, mittens or gloves, and rain gear. The term "extra clothing" refers to additional layers that would be needed to survive the long, inactive hours of an unplanned bivouac.

Extra clothing should be selected according to the season. Ask yourself this question: What do I need to survive the worst conditions I could realistically encounter?

An extra layer of underwear can have great warmth value while adding negligible weight to your pack. Underwear that gets soaked with sweat during a strenuous climb should be stripped off at camp and replaced with dry underwear, allowing you to stay much warmer while you cook and sleep. It is also wise to pack extra hats or balaclavas, as they provide more warmth for their weight than any other clothing article. For the feet, bring an extra pair of heavy socks; for the hands, an extra pair of polyester or fleece mitts. For winter and expedition climbing in severe conditions, you'll need more insulation for the torso as well as insulated overpants for the legs.

In addition to your rain shell, carry some sort of extra shelter from the rain, such as a plastic tube tent or a jumbo plastic trash bag. The possibility of cold-related injuries in the mountains makes it wise to bring a reflective emergency blanket. It can be used in administering first aid to a hypothermia victim or can double as a means of shelter. Carry an insulated pad to reduce heat loss while sitting or lying on snow (some packs can double for this purpose).

Some climbers carry a bivouac sack as part of their survival gear and compensate for the extra weight (about a pound) by going a little lighter on their insulating clothing layers. It can be a good strategy. A bivy sack protects your insulating layers from the weather, minimizes the effects of wind, and traps much of the heat escaping from your body inside its cocoon. (See Chapter 3, Camping and Food, for details on bivouacs and bivy sacks.)

## 6. Headlamp/Flashlight

Even if you plan to return to the car before dark, it's essential to carry a headlamp or flashlight, just in case. Batteries and bulbs don't last forever, so carry spares of both at all times.

Headlamps are much more convenient than flashlights for lighting a predawn ascent route or traveling after dark. Headlamps are also much more useful in camp because they allow freedom of both hands.

Lights are important enough and temperamental enough to make it worthwhile to invest in only quality equipment. At a minimum, get a light that is moistureproof (designed to keep out rain). Or, for extra insurance, purchase a fully waterproof light (designed to operate even if submerged in water). Waterproof lights often merit their extra expense, as they function reliably in any weather and the contacts or batteries won't corrode even if stored for months in a moist basement or garage.

All lights need durable switches that cannot turn on accidentally in the pack, a common and potentially serious problem. Switches tucked away in a recessed cavity are excellent. So are rotating switches in which the body of the flashlight must be twisted a half turn. If it looks like your light switch could be tripped accidentally, guard against this danger by taping the switch closed, removing the bulb, or reversing the batteries.

Adjustable focus is an excellent feature available on some lights. Wide floodlighting is good for chores close at hand; concentrated spotlighting assists in viewing objects far away, letting you see farther than with a brighter light lacking this feature.

The spare flashlight bulbs you carry don't have to be identical to the bulb that comes with your light. If you have a standard vacuum bulb, you can get a brighter beam with a replacement bulb filled with a gas, such as halogen, krypton, or xenon. These gases allow filaments to burn hotter and brighter than in vacuum bulbs, though they also draw more current and shorten battery life. You can get an idea of relative battery life by comparing bulb current ratings, usually marked on the base.

**Alkaline batteries** perform the best of general-purpose batteries commonly available at mass merchandisers. They pack more energy than cheaper lead-zinc batteries. The major problems with alkalines are that voltage (hence brightness) drops significantly as they discharge and their life is drastically shortened by cold temperatures (they operate at only 10 to 20 percent efficiency at 0 degrees Fahrenheit).

**Nickel-cadmium batteries** (nicads) can be recharged up to a thousand times, maintain their voltage and brightness throughout most of their discharge, and function well in the cold (about 70 percent efficient at 0 degrees Fahrenheit). However, they don't store as much energy as alkalines. For climbing, look for high-capacity nicads, which pack two to three times the charge of standard nicads and are worth the added expense.

**Lithium batteries** offer higher performance at a higher price. One lithium cell packs more than twice the amp-hours of two alkalines. The voltage remains almost constant over the life of a lithium battery, and its efficiency at 0 degrees Fahrenheit is nearly the same as at room temperature. Lithium batteries have twice the voltage of their standard counterparts, so you'll need to rewire your light to run off half as many batteries.

## 7. First-Aid Supplies

The very nature of climbing—steep terrain, slick surfaces, loose rocks, sharp tools, heavy loads, fatigue—makes it essential to carry a first-aid kit. However, don't let a first-aid kit give you a false sense of security. It cures very few ills. Doctors say that in the field there is often little they can do for a serious injury or affliction except initiate basic stabilizing procedures and evacuate the patient. The best course of action is to always take the steps necessary to avoid injury or sickness in the first place.

Your first-aid kit should be small, compact, and sturdy, with the contents wrapped in waterproof packaging. Commercial first-aid kits are widely available, though many are inadequate.

At a minimum, your kit should include gauze pads in various sizes, roller gauze, small adhesive bandages, butterfly bandages, triangular bandages, battle dressing (or Carlisle bandage), moleskin, adhesive tape, scissors, cleansers or soap, latex gloves, and paper and pencil.

Carry enough bandages and gauze to absorb a significant quantity of blood. Severe bleeding wounds are a common backcountry injury, and sterile absorbent material cannot be readily improvised.

Consider the length and nature of your trip in deciding whether to add to the basics of the first-aid kit. If you are traveling on a glacier, for example, tree branches won't be available for improvised splints, so a wire ladder splint would be extremely valuable in the event of a fracture. For a climbing expedition, you may need to consider appropriate prescription medicines.

See Chapter 19, First Aid, for a more detailed listing of contents of a basic first-aid kit for one person. Two of the best sources of additional information on first-aid kits are *Medicine for Mountaineering and Other Wilderness Activities* (1992), James A. Wilkerson, M.D., editor, and *Mountaineering First Aid: A Guide to Accident Response and First Aid Care* (1996), by Jan D. Carline, Martha J. Lentz, and Steven C. Macdonald, both published by The Mountaineers. See Appendix B, Supplementary References, at the back of this book for other suggested references on first aid (discussed under Chapter 19).

## 8. Fire Starter

Fire starters, supplying a much more sturdy flame than a match or lighter, are indispensable for igniting wet wood quickly to make an emergency campfire. They can even be used to warm a cup of water or soup, if you have a metal cup to heat it in.

Common fire starters include candles, chemical heat tabs, and canned heat. On a high-altitude snow or glacier climb, where firewood is nonexistent and heat tabs may be grossly insufficient, you may choose to carry a stove as an additional emergency heat source (see Chapter 3, Camping and Food, for information concerning stoves).

## 9. Matches

An emergency supply of matches, stored in a watertight container, should be carried on every trip in addition to the matches or butane lighter used routinely. Matches—not lighters—should serve as the emergency backup because matches are considered to be slightly less susceptible to failure. Storing the matches in a film canister, along with a strip of sandpaper, makes for a good emergency system.

Matches are available in different varieties, including wooden, windproof, and waterproof. Whatever type you carry, try them out ahead of time in windy or wet conditions to make sure they will work well for you in an emergency situation.

## 10. Knife

Knives are so useful in first aid, food preparation, repairs, and even rock climbing that every climber needs to carry one. The knife should have two folding blades, plus a screwdriver, an awl, and a pair of folding scissors (unless these items are already part of your first-aid or repair kit). The tools and the inside of the casing should be made of stainless steel. A cord attached to the knife and secured to your belt or harness lets you keep the knife in your pocket for ready access without danger of losing it.

## Other Important Items

There are, of course, many backpack items necessary for the climbing of peaks in addition to the Ten Essentials. The items discussed in the following section are also quite often considered to be "essentials," depending on the nature of the climb.

Every climber has his or her own opinion about what items are necessary. With experience, you will develop your own preferences. However, regardless of the "essentials" you select or don't select, it's always essential to engage your brain while mountain climbing. Think ahead. Take time periodically to envision scenarios of possible accidents and unexpected circumstances. What would you do in those situations? What equipment would you need to be prepared? And what risks are you willing to accept?

### Water and Water Containers

Wide-mouthed polyethylene water bottles are the most popular drinking-water containers because they can be easily refilled and impart no flavor to the water. Commonplace plastic soda bottles are cheaper, and surprisingly strong and durable, but their narrow tops make them painstaking to fill. Some water sacks are designed to be stored in the top of your pack and feature a long plastic straw that allows you to take a sip without even slowing your pace. (See Chapter 3, Camping and Food, for information on water, its relationship to climbing endurance, and water purification methods.)

### Ice Ax

An ice ax is indispensable on snowfields and glaciers and is very useful on snow-covered alpine trails in spring and early summer. An ice ax is a versatile tool, coming in handy for traveling in steep heather, scree, or brush, crossing streams, and digging sanitation holes. (For details on ice axes and their uses, see Chapter 5, Wilderness Travel, and Chapter 13, Snow Travel and Climbing.)

### Repair Kit

It's helpful to carry an emergency repair kit for your equipment. It could include any of the following items:

- Stove tools and spare parts.
- Duct tape.
- Patches.
- Safety pins.
- Heavy-duty thread.
- Awl and/or needles.
- Cord and/or wire.
- Small pliers.

This kit will probably grow over time as you add items you wished were along on a previous trip.

### Insect Repellent

The wilderness is an occasional home for people but the permanent habitat of insects. Some of them—mosquitoes, biting flies, "no-see-um" gnats, ticks, chiggers—want to feast on your body. For winter trips or for snow climbs any time of year, insect repellent may be unnecessary; for a low-elevation summer approach, thwarting mosquitoes may be essential.

One way to protect yourself from voracious insects is with heavy clothing, including gloves and head nets in really buggy areas. In hot weather, long shirts and pants made of netting may prove worthwhile. If it's too hot to wear much clothing, insect repellents serve as a good alternative.

Repellents with $N,N$-diethyl-metatoluamide (DEET) claim to be effective against all the principal biting insects but really perform best against mosquitoes. One application of a repellent with a high concentration of DEET will keep mosquitoes from biting for several hours, though they will still hover about annoyingly. Mosquito repellents come in liquid, cream, spray, and stick form and are available in various strengths.

Be aware that DEET is a potent toxin and can dissolve plastics and synthetic fabrics. You may choose to use a less toxic repellent like citronella or Avon Skin-so-Soft, but test it out first and make sure it works for you. In many situations, DEET is the only effective compound.

DEET is not very effective at repelling biting flies. Products with ethyl-hexanediol and dimethyl phthalate are much more effective against black flies, deer flies, and gnats. Unfortunately, fly repellents don't do much to ward off mosquitoes.

Ticks are a potential health hazard because they can carry Lyme disease or Rocky Mountain spotted fever. In tick country, especially when thrashing through brush, check clothing and hair frequently during the day, and give your clothes and body a thorough inspection at night.

## Signaling Devices

Flares, mirrors, whistles, and radios may be life-savers in some situations but useless in others. It's largely a matter of luck, discounting the misfortune of getting into an emergency in the first place. As all signal devices share the trait of being unreliable or ineffectual under certain circumstances, they should never be carried with absolute faith that they will actually communicate your emergency message.

Flares obviously won't do much good in daylight, and they are short-lived. Their main purpose is to shine a nighttime alert to any plane passing overhead. If you buy flares, be sure they're waterproof. Conversely, a mirror will help only when the day is sunny, which is not the type of weather typically associated with climbing emergencies.

A whistle, though limited in its scope, is probably the most reliable signaling device you can carry. A whistle's shrill, penetrating blast greatly exceeds the range of your voice and can serve as a crude means of communication in situations where shouts for help cannot be heard—such as being trapped in a crevasse or becoming separated from your party in fog, darkness, or thick forest. Whistles will prove much more useful if your party designates certain signals before the trip, such as one sound of the whistle for "Where are you?" two for "I'm here and OK," and three for "Help!"

Snow climbs, especially during winter, can require the carrying of an avalanche rescue beacon, used to locate a buried victim of a snow slide. (See Chapter 13, Snow Travel and Climbing, for detailed instructions on using avalanche rescue beacons.)

A hand-held citizens band (CB) radio, ham radio, or walkie-talkie may be worth its weight on some climbs. On an expedition, radios can greatly ease communication between climbers or from climbers to base camp, and they could save critical hours in getting help for an injured person. Local ranger stations or logging trucks may monitor specific CB channels, although their policies often vary from region to region. Radios are by no means foolproof; their range is limited, and in jagged terrain a peak or ridge can easily block transmission.

An increasing number of wilderness enthusiasts are carrying cellular phones as an emergency communication device. A telephone can be useful even in situations other than emergencies. For instance, if your party gets delayed, you can call home simply to say that you will be late. But cell phones, like radios, frequently exhibit shortcomings in the mountains. These phones depend on relay stations that may be blocked by a peak or ridge or may be too far away to pick up the phone's signal. And the convenience of cellular phones can give a party a false sense of security. Carrying a phone in order to compensate for a lack of planning or skill is recklessness that can lead to tragedy.

Bring signaling devices with you on a climb if you decide they are worth the burden of carrying, but never depend on them to get you out of a jam. Successful climbers prepare for the wilderness and act safely to minimize the chance they will ever need to send an emergency signal.

## ——— EQUIPMENT CHECKLIST ———

Experienced climber or not, it's easy to forget an important item in the rush to get ready for the next trip. Seasoned climbers have learned that using a checklist is the only sure way to avoid an oversight. The following list is a good foundation for formulating your own personal checklist. Add to or subtract from this list as you see fit; then get in the habit of checking your own list before each trip.

# A Sample Equipment List

*Pack*
*ice axe*

### ALL TRIPS

#### The Ten Essentials
1. Map
2. Compass
3. Sunglasses and sunscreen
4. Extra food
5. Extra clothing
6. Headlamp/flashlight
7. First-aid supplies
8. Fire starter
9. Matches (in waterproof container)
10. Knife

#### Clothing
Boots
Socks (inner and outer)
[T-shirt/tank top]
[Shorts]
Long underwear (top and bottom)
Insulating shirts, sweaters, or jackets (synthetic or wool)
Insulating pants (synthetic or wool)
Rain parka
[Windbreaker]
Rain pants
[Wind pants]
Insulating hats (synthetic or wool)
[Rain hat]
[Sun-protection hat]
[Balaclava]
Mittens
Gloves
[Glove liners]
[Overmitts]
[Gaiters]
[Stream-crossing footwear]
[Waterproof/breathable socks]

#### Other
Toilet paper
[Signaling device: whistle, mirror, etc.]
[Insect repellent]
[Spare eyeglasses]
[Cup]
[Moleskin]
[Nylon cord]
[Altimeter]
[Camera and film]
[Binoculars]
[Bandannas]

### ADDITIONAL ITEMS FOR OVERNIGHT TRIPS

Internal- or external-frame pack
Sleeping bag and stuff sack
Sleeping pad
*Tent or tarp
*Ground cloth
*Food
*Water container
*Repair kit
*Stove, fuel, and accessories
*Pots (and cleaning pad)
Spoon
[Fork]
[Bowl]
[Toiletries]
[Alarm clock or alarm watch]
[Camp clothing]
[Camp footwear]
[Pack cover]
[Candle lantern]

### ADDITIONAL GEAR FOR GLACIER OR WINTER CLIMBS

Crampons
Carabiners
Seat harness
Chest sling or harness
Prusik slings
Rescue pulley
Additional warm clothing, such as mittens, mitten shells, socks, balaclava, insulated parka, insulated bib pants, long underwear
*Climbing rope
*Spare sunglasses
*Snow shovel
*Group first-aid kit
[Plastic boots]
[Helmet]
[Runners]
[Supergaiters]
[Snowshoes or skis]
[Avalanche rescue beacon]
*[Avalanche probe]
*[Flukes, pickets, ice screws]
*[Wands]
*[Snow saw]
[Handwarmer]
[Thermos bottle]

### ADDITIONAL GEAR FOR ROCK CLIMBS

Helmet
Seat harness
Carabiners
Runners
Belay/rappel device
Leather belay gloves
Prusik sling
*Climbing rope
*Rack: chocks, stoppers, etc.
*Chock pick
[Rock-climbing shoes]
[Chalk]

[ ] = Items are optional, depending on your own preference and the nature of the trip.

* = Items can be shared by the group.

# 3
# CAMPING AND FOOD

*trailhead bar*

Camping, like mountaineering in general, is part ecstasy, part drudgery. You can make life easier on yourself by learning the art of camping and alpine cookery. Setting up a temporary home in the wilds ought to be quick work and provide cozy shelter, a warm bag, and good food.

Camping has another critical component: respect for the wilderness. In fact, that's number one. Let's face it: our comfort is secondary to preserving the mountain environment. The peaks aren't there for us, they're just there, and it's really not hard to do the things that show our respect for the places that bring us such happiness. That's why this chapter includes a lot of tips on camping clean in addition to camping easy.

## LOW-IMPACT CAMPING

A short list of tips on careful camping basically sums up the responsible approach to spending time in the wilderness. (Chapter 24, Minimum Impact, reviews this subject and includes further information.) Here are eight principles of low-impact camping:

- Stay on established trails; do not cut switchbacks.
- Camp in established campsites whenever possible.
- Properly dispose of human waste away from water, trails, and campsites.
- Use a camp stove instead of building a fire.
- Wash well away from camps and water sources.
- Leave flowers, rocks, and other natural features undisturbed.

- Keep wildlife healthy and self-reliant by not feeding them; leave pets at home.
- Pack out all party garbage, plus any litter left by others.

## The Campsite

Mountain climbers don't always set up camp in the most comfortable places. They may walk right past an idyllic spot in the forest in favor of a windy mountain ledge because that puts them closer to the summit. What other reasons might there be for picking a particular campsite? Because it's comfortable? Scenic? Environmentally sound? Sometimes you can have it all, but at other times you need to give a little to help preserve the wilderness.

Let's look at camps from the standpoint of the wilderness to see which sites are least damaging to the environment. From best to worst, they are:

**Established, fully impacted campsite:** You can't hurt it further by staying in the impacted area.

**Snow:** The snow will melt and show no sign of your tenancy.

**Rock slab:** Solid rock resists most damaging effects of a campsite.

**Sandy, dirt, or gravelly flat:** Most signs of your presence can be swept away.

**Duff in deep forest:** Duff and other decaying matter are only lightly impacted by your presence.

**Grass-covered meadow:** Meadows are fragile ecosystems. A tent left on a grass-covered meadow for a week can wipe out an entire growing season for the covered patch. Moving a long-term camp every few days reduces the harm to any one spot. The higher the meadow, the more sensitive it will be to trampling.

**Plant-covered meadow above timberline:** Alpine plants grow very slowly, and woody plants are more sensitive to impact than grasses, such as sedges. Heathers, for example, have only a couple of months to bloom, seed, and add a fraction of an inch of growth. They could take many years to recover from the damage of a brief encampment.

**Waterfront:** Waterside plant life is especially delicate, and water pollution is a growing problem as more people head into the backcountry. A large proportion of long-established campsites in American mountains are on the banks of lakes and streams, but many areas now ban camping within 200 feet of the water.

The proper use of an established, fully impacted campsite—one worn down to mineral earth—is just the opposite of proper use of a pristine site. At an established campsite, your tent can stay long-term in one spot, and your party can camp together, trod existing paths repeatedly, and use an established toilet. But at a pristine site, the tent stay must be short-term, and the party's tents should not be grouped together. A pristine area calls for dispersed toilet sites and for varied walkways so that no single path gets trampled to where the vegetation can't recover. Contrary to first instinct, it's often better to camp in a "leave no trace" fashion at a pristine spot than at a slightly impacted one where your use may degrade it beyond the point where it can naturally recover.

Honestly visualize your impact before selecting a campsite. Look for a resilient, naturally bare site. Camp away from water, meadows, trails, and other campers. Select an acceptable established campsite rather than setting up a new one. Walk lightly, and switch to lightweight shoes that will do less damage around camp. Sit on existing rocks and logs instead of moving more in. Try to find a spot that has just the right natural slope, because you should not level it or dig channels for drainage.

From the standpoint of comfort, wind is a big consideration in choosing a campsite. Alpine breezes are capricious. An upslope afternoon breeze may reverse at night to an icy downslope draft from snowfields. Cold air, heavier than warm air, flows downward during settled weather, following valleys and collecting in depressions. Thus there is often a chill breeze down a creek or dry wash and a pool of cold air in a basin. Night air is often several degrees cooler near a river or lake than on the knolls above.

Consider wind direction in pitching your tent. In good weather, facing an opening into the wind will distend the tent, minimizing flapping. But alpine winds are reversible without warning. In foul weather, orient your tent so that the storm does not blow directly inside.

## Campfires

The old romantic days of cooking over an open fire and lounging around a big campfire in the backcountry are long past. The price is too high in old scarce trees, especially at higher elevations. And no matter where, campfire scars are a blemish. Mountaineers now cook almost exclusively on lightweight stoves they carry with them even where campfires are permitted, a big step toward low-impact, no-trace camping. Stoves provide more consistent heat for cooking than firewood does, and you can't always count on finding wood.

Some simple rules apply in case you do build a campfire. Keep it small, within an existing fire ring, and only where and when it's safe and legal. Stay there until the fire is dead and the ashes cold. For firewood, use only dead or downed wood from outside the camp area; never cut a standing tree or snag. In high-elevation, sparsely forested areas, even taking fallen, dead branches from beneath a healthy tree can be harmful, because the decomposing branches are an important energy source for the tree.

## Washing

You can keep dishes reasonably clean without soap. By taking moderate care in cleaning pots with hot water after each meal, parties commonly remain healthy on week-long trips without so much as a pinch of soap or biodegradable detergent. Fill pots with water as soon as they are empty, and clean them right away or leave them to soak. Woven plastic or metal scouring pads are handy for cleaning the pots, and they weigh next to nothing. Teflon-coated pots are easy to clean, but of course they can be easily damaged with metal or abrasive cleaners. Using sand, gravel, or grass to clean pots can leave unsightly bits of food to attract flies and rodents.

Be sure to get rid of the cleaning water downwind from your campsite and a long way from water sources. If you do use soap, use a biodegradable product and keep it off the plant life. If you're only out for a single night, it can be easiest to carry dishes and pots home dirty. Carry leftovers out with you, and try to do better meal planning next time.

For bringing water to camp, it helps to have a large container, like a water bag or the plastic liner from a wine box, to save yourself a lot of trips to the water source and to reduce your impact on the terrain. If you need to wash yourself or your clothing, stay at least 200 feet from natural water sources. Go without soap, or use only biodegradable soap in very small quantities.

## Sanitation

The rule about food containers and packaging is that if you can carry them into the wilderness full, you can carry them out empty. Keep a heavy-duty plastic bag on hand to carry out the garbage. Clean up every bit of garbage, down to the foil-flecks, and pack out anything you find in camp or on the trail, no matter who left it. Never bury garbage or dump it in latrines. Pick up trash before it gets covered with new-fallen snow that will hide it until the spring thaw. The golden rule of camping: Leave the campsite cleaner than you found it.

For carrying garbage and for many other uses, mountaineers soon learn the value of plastic bags. They use them to package food, as emergency mini-tents, and sometimes on their feet to keep water out. A large, heavy-duty plastic bag makes a good pack cover for a wet night. Kitchen trash-compactor bags are strong and fit nicely into the main compartments of a pack to keep contents dry.

Heavily used campsites usually have a pit toilet, set away from water. If no pit toilet is available, go at least 200 feet from any open water (allowing for maximum level around lakes). Using a small trowel or an ice ax, dig a "cat hole" into the humus, 8 to 10 inches in diameter and no more than 8 inches deep (and not deeper than the humus, for maximum decomposition rate). After use, fill the hole with loose soil and tamp it back in place. Sometimes instead of digging a hole, you can lift out a rock that is 8 to 12 inches in diameter, use its depression as a cat hole,

and then set the rock back without leaving a visible disturbance.

It is possible to use natural materials—such as leaves, pine cones, rocks, or snow—for cleaning, instead of toilet paper. Any toilet paper should be neutral-colored; pack out the used paper, if practical. It does no harm to urinate in random locations away from streams and not directly on fragile plants, although it is courteous to cover yellow snow.

On tundra and sparsely vegetated alpine areas, surface deposition of solid waste and use of the smear technique is the method least harmful to the sensitive terrain. Select a site well away from the usual route and exposed to the full sun. Use a rock to smear the waste out as thinly as possible for maximum rapid decomposition by the sun.

In deep snow, find an unobtrusive toilet area, such as a clump of trees well away from camp, and bury the waste just below the snow surface. On lightly traveled glacier routes, you can dig a community pit with a snow-block privacy wall in an area away from the route and then later dispose of the solids in a deep, narrow crevasse. On heavily traveled glacier routes, you may be required to pack out all solid human waste in heavy-duty double bags (the "blue-bag" system). Pack out used nonbiodegradable items of personal hygiene, such as bandages and sanitary napkins, in airtight containers. Refer to Chapter 24, Minimum Impact, for more information on solid waste disposal in mountaineering, including the blue-bag system, use of the "poop tube," and special considerations for various types of climbs and terrain.

## Wilderness Encounters

Most people go into the wilderness to be alone or to be with just a few companions. There are ways we can help keep it that way—for example, by choosing less popular routes or days. We can contribute to the wilderness experience of others by camping away from them, traveling through their space only if it's necessary, keeping noise to a minimum, and practicing "leave no trace" mountaineering. When mountaineers cross paths, everyone is usually happy to simply greet each other, perhaps converse briefly, and move on. Personal radios, tape players, and CD players can be distracting for the users and for those around them and often aren't welcome in the wilderness or on a climb. Leave your pets at home.

When you encounter animals on your route, move slowly and allow them plenty of time to drift away. Try to pass on their downhill side; they typically head uphill to escape. Give them some elbow room. An animal rushing from a close encounter with a human is in danger of stress or injury; too many of these encounters, and it may feel forced to abandon its home grounds for poorer terrain.

In bear country, stay out of the "personal space" of bears. Try not to surprise them. Make a lot of noise on the trail and in your tent if you see or hear bears. If people get too close, black bears often climb trees to escape—but they may attack, especially to protect their young. Brown bears, especially grizzlies, are more likely to attack (and polar bears think everything they see is food). If confronted directly by a bear, do not run; this will almost surely provoke it to attack. Grizzlies are not known to attack parties of four or more persons, so this should be the minimum group size in grizzly country—and everyone should stay together. Sleep in a tent rather than in the open.

## Animals and Food

Bears have an acute sense of smell; in bear country, your kitchen area and food stash should be at least 100 yards downwind from your tent. Wash all cookware well, using no soap or detergent. Burn or triple-bag everything with odor attractive to the bear, especially fish or meat residue and used feminine hygiene articles. Special bear-resistant, unbreakable plastic containers are very effective for storing food, and they are required in some areas.

Bears and rodents will tear and gnaw through plastic bags, packs, and even tents for food. A food sack or pack hung by a cord from a tree or suspended from a pole must be farther from the tree trunk and higher from the ground than a bear can reach. A high horizontal "bear wire" is often provided in more popular camping spots. It may be necessary to run the cord through a rat guard—a 10-inch-diameter metal disc—to keep mice from walking the line and dropping down to the food. If you suspect raccoons are in the area, it may be wise to tie your food down as well as up, because they can go out on a limb and pull the food *up* by its hanging line.

Hanging food 4 feet from the tree trunk and 12 feet from the ground gives you a fighting chance against animals. If there is no way to hang the food and you do not have intrusion-resistant containers, divide the food into dispersed hiding places so that if one is broken into, your party still won't go hungry.

Some other tips: Always keep the cooking area and food storage well away from where you sleep (hanging food above your tent is an invitation to being stepped on). Package food in containers with tight lids or in sealed plastic bags to conceal the smell. Never feed wildlife.

Hiding a food cache for your party in the wilderness is generally not acceptable and often not permitted. Animals can get into an improperly protected food cache and leave a big mess, which will only draw more animals, who will then get in the habit of seeking people out for food.

## SHELTER

When you settle in for a night in the mountains, your home away from home will be a tent, bivy sack, tarp, snow shelter, or hut. We will take a close look here at the kinds of shelters you can carry on your back.

Tents are the most common shelter because of their many virtues. They are relatively quick and easy to put up, rainproof, private, usable almost anywhere, a refuge from wind or sun, and often roomy enough for you *and* your gear. Tents are usually the best shelter above timberline and for glacier camps, for winter camping, in moderate winds, and in mosquito country. Alpine climbers in a hurry can get nighttime protection from a lightweight bivy sack, though the sack is not much help in heavy rain and has limited room inside for gear and for changing clothes. A tarp in combination with a bivy sack increases protection from the elements. The rain fly of some tents can be set up alone, serving as a freestanding, lightweight tarp; use this with a bivy sack for a good summer combination. A snow shelter is a haven from wind and storm, but building it is wet, hard work and time-consuming.

Curiously enough, shelter is often more necessary on a clear night than on a cloudy one. When two opposing surfaces differ in temperature, the warmer

45

radiates heat to the colder. Because the human body is usually warmer than the night sky, exposed portions of the body or sleeping bag radiate heat and grow cold. Any shelter at all serves as a baffle. Clouds often reflect heat back to earth and, thus, have the effect of a huge tarp between sleeper and sky. The clear nights are the cold ones.

# Tents

Your choice of a tent depends on what you like and what you plan to use it for. Will it be used only in the summer or for three or four seasons of the year? Above or below timberline? For you alone, or for two people, or three, or four? Are you after luxurious space or just the bare minimum? How much weight are you willing to carry? How much money are you able to spend? Manufacturers offer almost any combination of size, weight, and design. The choice is yours, after consulting catalogs, stores, your friends, and neighboring campers.

Tents are generally categorized as either three-season tents for general use or as four-season tents for all situations including snow camping. Three-season tents tend to be lighter in weight and construction. The side or top panels of many three-season tents are made with see-through netting, providing ventilation and light weight. Be aware that blowing snow can come in through the netting. A four-season tent, heavier and stronger, provides solid side and top panels. Combination tents incorporate netting but are sold with solid panels that can be zipped into place for converting the tent from three-season to four-season use.

A four-season tent is usually built tougher to withstand winter conditions, with a stronger frame and more durable reinforcing. The doors and vents have solid panels that can be zipped as near to closed as you wish (keeping ventilation requirements in mind), and the fly comes down close to ground level all the way around. A four-season tent commonly includes the small, protruding protected area known as a vestibule, provided by an extended rain fly. Some heavy-duty expedition rain flies come with their own poles for extending the vestibule area farther. You'll find great diversity in the price, quality, and features of four-season tents, but they all have the same mission: to provide secure shelter from the snow loads and high winds of winter camping. (For further information on using tents in the snow, see the section later in this chapter on snow and winter camping.)

## Water Resistance

Tents are built with either single or double walls, of either waterproof or breathable materials. A completely enclosed unit must be well ventilated and preferably should "breathe." If the tent is waterproof, the moisture you exhale condenses on the cold walls and runs down to collect in puddles on the floor. In a single night, you and your tentmate can expel enough water vapor to drench the sleeping bags. A few manufacturers offer single-walled tents made of material that is advertised as both waterproof and breathable, but ventilation must be increased except in very dry conditions. Watch out for the lightweight tents built of a single layer of nonbreathable waterproof material. They are only good for the mildest of conditions below timberline where the door and windows can be left open for ventilation; even then, you can expect some condensation. Some single-walled tents have a design that uses gravity to spread and remove condensation, but to be effective the tents must be well ventilated.

The dilemma of a waterproof yet breathable tent is usually solved by using double walls. The inner wall is breathable: it is not waterproof, so it allows your breath and perspiration to pass through to the outside. The outer layer is a waterproof rain fly, usually separate, that keeps the rain off the tent and also collects and disposes of the body moisture from inside the tent. The rain fly must not touch the inner walls, because where it touches, water will condense inside. The fly should come fairly close to the ground to cover the tent and entrance, discouraging wind-driven rain. Even in a double-walled tent, sleeping bags can get wet from condensation that forms on the waterproof side panels that extend a foot or so up from the floor in some models.

An important step in keeping a tent dry is to close up the needle holes by coating all seams with waterproof seam-sealer. Do this before the tent is ever used. Some tents come with factory-sealed seams; on others, it's up to you, but it's got to be done. When camping on forest floor or earth, put a plastic or coated-nylon ground cloth or space blanket under the tent to stop ground moisture from entering the floor of the tent and to keep the bottom clean and protected from abrasion. Tuck the edges of the ground cloth beneath the tent so that the cloth cannot channel rain under the tent, where it may seep up through the floor. On snow, the space blanket is usually put inside the tent to protect the floor from above and as added thermal protection.

## Strength

Many tents are rated by a "relative strength factor," the speed of wind a tent can withstand before the frame deforms. If you expect to run into wind and snow, this is an important consideration. The tent should stand up to high winds and snow loads without structural failure.

## Weight

It's usually a tradeoff: light weight, or more comfort and durability. Lightweight tents are available, but the question is whether they are big enough or tough enough for your particular uses. Simply look for the lightest tent that meets your requirements for number of occupants, headroom, floor space, gear storage, strength, climate, and weather conditions. A three-person, four-season expedition tent may weigh twice as much as a two-person, three-season tent and be two or three times as expensive.

## Shape

The trend in tent shapes has been to tunnels and domes (fig. 3-1). These designs make maximum use of space and minimize the number of stakes and guy lines. The freestanding dome needs no stakes to hold its shape and can be picked up and moved as a unit, but it still must be staked down and attached to guy lines so it won't blow away. The two- or three-hoop tunnel tent, usually not freestanding, offers efficient use of space and has wind-shedding characteristics. The traditional A-frame tent doesn't give as much usable space, but it's a simple, proven design. A freestanding tent is much easier to assemble and to move to the best location than a tent that must be staked down before it will hold its shape.

## Size

The two-person tent is probably the most popular size and offers the greatest flexibility in weight and choice of campsite. For versatility in a group, it's generally better to bring, for example, two two-person tents rather than one four-person tent. Many two-person tents handle three in a pinch yet are light enough to be used by one person. Some three- and four-person tents are light enough to be carried by two people who crave luxurious living. Larger tents, especially those high enough to stand in, are big morale boosters during an expedition or long storm. For carrying, you can distribute the weight among a group by dividing the tent into parts.

## Color

Warm tent colors such as yellow, orange, and red are cheerier if you're stuck inside, and they make it easier to spot camp on the way back from a summit. On the other hand, more subdued hues blend into the landscape. One's an eyesore; the other may be camouflaged only too well if you're having a little trouble finding camp.

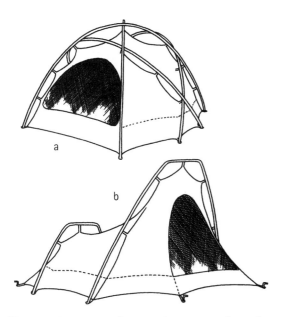

*Fig. 3-1. Two types of mountain tents: a, dome; b, tunnel (hoop).*

## Other Features

Entrance designs offer zip doors, tunnels, alcoves, vestibules, and hoods. Compare designs to find the one that looks like it will keep out the most rain and snow as you're coming and going. Vestibules can be nice as a way to shelter the entrance and provide more room for gear, boots, cooking, and dressing. There are a lot of options in the arrangement and type of ventilation holes and windows. Mosquito netting can help keep out rodents as well as flies and mosquitoes.

## Care and Cleaning

Your tent will give more years of good service if you are careful to air-dry it thoroughly before storing it away after each trip. To clean a tent, hose it off with water, or wash it with mild soap and water. Scrub stains with a sponge or brush. Don't put the tent in a washer or dryer. High temperatures or prolonged exposure to sun are damaging to tent material.

# Tarps

A tarp is light in weight and low in cost and may offer adequate shelter (fig. 3-2) from all but extreme weather in lowland forests and among subalpine trees. It gives less protection than a tent from heat loss and wind, none at all from insects or rodents, and demands ingenuity on your part and some cooperation from the landscape to set up.

Plastic tarps don't hold up very well but are cheap enough that you can replace them often. Coated-nylon tarps come with reinforced grommets on the sides and corners for easy rigging. If your tarp doesn't have grommets, sew on permanent loops of fabric, such as nylon or twill tape, before leaving home. Alternatively, you can just tie off each corner around a small cone or pebble from the campsite. Take along some lightweight cord to string the tarp and perhaps a few light stakes.

The most versatile tarp size is about 9 by 12 feet—luxurious space for two people and their gear and adequate for three or even four. A tarp measuring 11 by 14 feet will handle four campers comfortably. Because the outer margins of tarp-covered ground are usually only barely protected, usable space quickly approaches the vanishing point if your tarp is smaller than 9 by 12 feet. Put down a waterproof ground sheet, but if

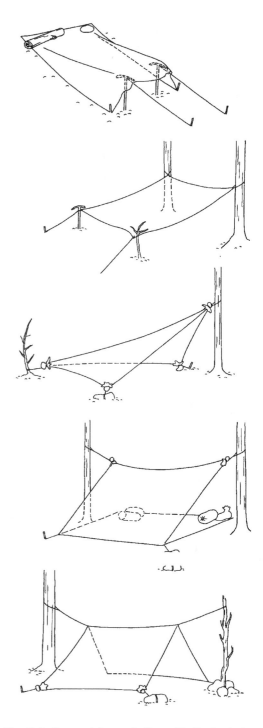

*Fig. 3-2. Improvising a shelter with the basic tarp*

rain results in a surprise flood, be ready to move camp. A tarp is not meant to be used as a blanket, because perspiration will condense inside the waterproof material and leave you damp.

## Bivouac Sacks

For super-lightweight alpine traveling, the bivy sack takes the place of a tent in providing shelter from wind and rain. The sack is a large envelope of tightly woven fabric with a zipper entrance at one end, sometimes with a zippered mosquito netting. The bottom side is usually made of waterproof coated nylon; the upper side is of a waterproof/breathable material such as Gore-Tex, which allows moisture to escape into the atmosphere. The bivy sack, laid on top of an insulated pad, is designed for one person, two in an emergency. It needs no poles or stakes but usually has strong loops for anchoring.

A variation of the bivy sack that is less claustrophobic and works like a minimum-sized one-person tent has one or two short arching poles in an enlarged end by the head and shoulders (fig. 3-3).

You can use a bivy sack in combination with a sleeping bag, slipping the bag inside the sack for extra warmth. This combination is sometimes used inside a tent in order to keep condensation off the sleeping bag. You can even slip your insulating pad inside the bivy sack, beneath your sleeping bag, as a way of keeping the pad, bivy sack, and sleeping bag all in comfortable alignment with your body.

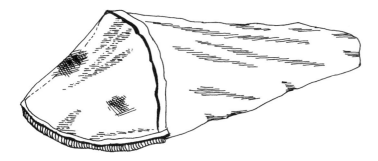

*Fig. 3-3. Bivy sack with enlarged end supported by short poles*

## Snow Shelters

Newcomers to snow camping are sometimes surprised at what a warm, comfortable, and beautiful experience it can be. To make it work, a good shelter and insulation are essential. At the very least, every snow traveler needs the skills and equipment to survive overnight in the snow. For information on snow shelters—including details on constructing snow caves, tree-pit shelters, snow trenches, and igloos—see the section on snow and winter camping later in this chapter.

## SLEEPING BAGS

Your sleeping bag should be lightweight, warm, comfortable, and easily compressible, have a hood or other way to keep your head covered, and generally suit the climate where you do your camping.

## Warmth

The warmth of a sleeping bag is provided by insulating material that traps dead air. How warm a particular bag is depends on the type and amount of this insulating fill, the thickness (loft) of the fill, and the bag's size (its fit to your body), style, and method of construction.

Sleeping bags are generally categorized as recommended for summer, three-season, or winter expedition use (this chapter's section on snow and winter camping has more details). Manufacturers give their bags comfort ratings, which are meant to indicate the lowest temperature at which the bag will be comfortably warm. Methods of rating the bags vary from manufacturer to manufacturer, so they can give only a general idea of how the bag will perform. Bags are usually rated to a minimum temperature of somewhere between 40 degrees and minus 20 degrees Fahrenheit (between about 5 degrees and minus 30 degrees Celsius).

How closely a rating matches you personally depends on whether or not you are also in a tent and/or bivy sack, the clothing you are wearing, the ground insulation, and your body size, metabolic rate, and caloric intake. Look for a rating that matches your use. For example, if you're mainly a summer backpa    a bag rated to minus 20 degrees Fahrenheit will b    warm.

The wa    st, lightest sleeping-bag design is the mummy bag,    pered toward the feet, hooded to fit over the head, a  d with a small face opening secured with drawstrings (  g. 3-4). The bag should be just your size: too small, and it will restrict loft and thus warmth; too large, and the increased radiation area will also result in less warmth. Special women's designs and sizes are available.

Whatever the design, your sleeping bag should have a form-fitting hood or a semicircular piece with drawstrings to keep your head warm and prevent heat loss. Some bags incorporate an insulated collar to provide extra warmth around the shoulders, and some include extra insulation at critical areas, such as chest or feet. Also available are sleeping bags that are baffled in a manner that permits you to redistribute insulation to meet your needs. You can buy a thin over-bag to put around the sleeping bag during colder weather to improve the bag's performance.

There are some basic procedures for sleeping warmer, regardless of the bag you are in. Dress and undress inside the bag. Wear a hat and dry socks to bed. Secure the bag closely around your face. Breathe through a sweater to reduce heat loss from exhalation. You can put your head inside the bag to help preserve heat, though you may feel too closed in and the water vapor from your breath will likely make it damper and thus colder inside.

The warmth of the bag offers not only comfort but also an opportunity to dry out some of your items, like mittens and socks. Don't try to dry larger items of clothing by wearing them to bed, because they will just keep you cold and make the bag wet. In very cold weather, you may want to bring boots inside, wrapped in plastic. You may also need to make room for a water bottle to keep it from freezing; for your comfort, be sure to warm the water first.

## Types of Insulation

The warmth, weight, and cost of a sleeping bag depend chiefly on the kind and quantity of insulation, which is either goose down or a synthetic material.

**Goose down** is still the most efficient insulation per unit of weight. Down bags are warm and very compressible, retain their loft well, and are longlasting. Down is rated by fill power in cubic inches

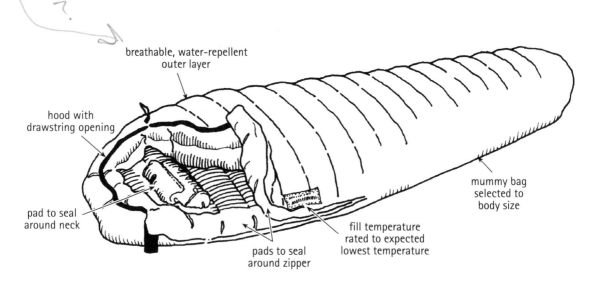

breathable, water-repellent
outer layer

hood with
drawstring opening

pad to seal
around neck

pads to seal
around zipper

fill temperature
rated to expected
lowest temperature

mummy bag
selected to
body size

*Fig. 3-4. Mummy bag*

per ounce, with 550 being standard and ratings going up to 800-plus. The higher the rating, the greater the loft and the greater the warmth from each ounce of down. In sleeping bags, higher fill power usually equates with lighter weight and more compressibility.

Disadvantages of down? High cost and water absorbency. A wet down bag loses most of its loft and insulating value, making it almost worthless until it can be dried out. A very wet down bag takes so long to dry—more than a day in good conditions—that it can't be dried during wet periods in the mountains. This characteristic makes down a questionable choice for more than one night in a wet climate, unless you take extra care to keep it dry (such as keeping it in a durable, sealed, watertight plastic bag).

**Synthetic insulation** is resistant to moisture, retains most of its loft when wet, and dries relatively quickly. Bags with synthetic insulation are less expensive than down-filled designs. These bags are still slightly heavier than comparable down styles and do not compress quite as easily, thus making a weightier, bulkier load. (You can bring this extra bulk under control by shoving the sleeping bag into a stuff sack equipped with a compression strap and then cranking on the strap.) Synthetic insulation is not as durable as down and loses much of its loft over time with long use. However, modern synthetics such as LiteLoft are beginning to challenge the performance of down, and at a lower price.

## Construction

Down bags are made with one of four basic construction methods to keep the fill uniformly distributed: sewn-through, slant-tube, trapezoidal-tube, or overlapping tube. In sewn-through construction, the inner cover is stitched directly to the outer, a simple and inexpensive method but one with substantial heat loss at the seams, making it unsuitable for mountaineering. Most down bags are of slant-tube construction, which eliminates cold spots at the seams. The most efficient design, overlapping tubes, is used only in the most expensive bags. In addition, many designs incorporate channel blocks, baffles that prevent down from shifting.

Synthetic bags are fabricated using a variety of methods. There are two basic types of synthetic fills. The first is a long, stable polyester fiber, manufactured in batts that stand up well to use and laundering. A widely used construction method is the shingle style, in which sections of batting are sewn in the bag, overlapping like roof shingles to cover cold spots. The second type of fill is a short, stable polyester fiber that is quilted or sewn into fine scrims to keep it from wadding up or moving around. To avoid cold spots, these must be shingled or quilted in double or triple layers with quilted lines offset.

Zippers are the almost universal means of closure even though they sometimes snag the fabric or go off the trolley. Some bags have a stiffener sewn in next to the zipper to prevent snagging. Zippers are backed up with a tube of insulating material to reduce heat loss through them. Long zippers make it easy to get in and out of the bag and are a big help in ventilating the lower portion. If you want to zip two bags together, be sure one zipper is right-sided and the other is left-sided and that they are the same size.

## Effects of Wetness

Do yourself a big favor and keep your sleeping bag dry, especially if it is filled with down. Compared with down bags, polyester-filled bags retain much of their warmth when wet and are easier to dry, but a wet polyester bag is still a wet bag and, thus, colder than a dry one. You can buy a sleeping bag that is made with a waterproof/breathable shell (usually of Gore-Tex shell fabric), or you can buy an add-on waterproof/breathable shell. These shells let body vapor escape from your bag while helping to protect the bag from condensation inside a tent or dripping water in a snow cave. Consider putting your stuffed sleeping bag inside a plastic bag before putting it on your pack, because most stuff sacks don't keep water out.

## Care and Cleaning

Dirt decreases insulating efficiency. You should spot-clean soiled areas, especially around the head of the bag. A removable, washable liner or an outer cover of breathable material can provide protection from dirt and abrasion.

Both down and polyester bags can be hand-washed with any mild soap or with one of the excellent down soaps that are available. Rinse thoroughly to remove all soap. Squeeze water out gently by hand, or put the bag carefully through the spin cycle of a front-loading washing machine (with no agitator). Down or polyester bags can also be machine-washed, again in a front-loading washing machine on the gentle cycle. The lack of an agitator is important, because an agitator will blow out the interior structural baffles in a down bag.

Hang bags to air dry; do not put a wet sleeping bag in a dryer. Allow more drying time for a down bag (several days), and shake and turn the bag frequently to break up lumps of wet down. Once line-dried, both polyester and down bags can be put in a dryer. Use the fluff setting (air only; no heat) to fluff up the bag. A clean tennis shoe put in with the down bag may help break up any clumps of down.

Do not dry-clean a down bag, because the process can remove the natural protective oils from the down. A polyester bag can be dry-cleaned, but only by a professional who knows how to handle the material and only if it is thoroughly aired afterward to remove all traces of toxic fumes, which can cause illness or death. For best results, follow the manufacturer's instructions.

## Ground Insulation

The foundation for a comfortable night in the outdoors is a good piece of insulation under your sleeping bag. Summer or winter, in a tent or outside, that pad makes for a softer, warmer bed. On wet ground or snow, it's essential.

A thin pad of closed-cell foam, such as ensolite (more durable) or polyethylene (lighter weight), provides good insulation. Improved designs in closed-cell pads (such as Ridge Rest) feature softer sleeping surfaces, lower weight, and an increased ability to trap air, resulting in greater thermal efficiency. Other pads use open-cell foam that offers an inch and a half of padding, but they make for a bulky roll and must be protected from absorbing water.

An air mattress by itself is soft but provides no insulation. In fact, the air in the mattress convects heat away from the body by internal air circulation. A pad, such as the Therm-a-Rest, that combines the insulation of open-cell foam with the softness of an air mattress is very popular and effective.

Insulation pads come in a variety of lengths, but one that's only 4 feet long is usually adequate because you can use your sit pad or items of gear to support or insulate feet and legs. If you're stuck without a pad, use extra clothing, the pack, rope, or boots for padding and insulation.

## BIVOUACS

A bivouac is a lightweight, no-frills overnight stay—sometimes planned, sometimes not. Climbers sometimes plan spartan bivouacs so they can travel fast and light and start high on the mountain. An unplanned bivouac comes as a not-so-pleasant surprise due to injury, bad weather, a route that is longer than anticipated, or getting off route. (Also see the section on bivouacs in Chapter 16, Alpine, Winter, and Expedition Climbing.)

Climbers at a planned bivouac camp make sure they have the essentials for a tolerable if not comfortable night, such as a bivy sack, perhaps a space blanket, some special food, ground insulation, and plenty of clothing.

Sensible climbers always carry everything necessary for survival—all the Ten Essentials and usually a good bit more in preparation for emergency bivouacs. You can prepare for your own eventual unplanned bivouac by carrying an emergency shelter in your day pack, in the form of a very light bivy bag or plastic tube tent or even a couple of very large plastic trash bags. Another alternative for shelter from wind and rain is your pack. When it's time to settle down for a bivouac night, put your feet inside the empty pack, and pull the pack's load extension collar (the "bivouac sleeve") up over your legs and hips. Wear a waterproof parka to take care of the rest of your body.

A low-altitude bivouac might be a fairly comfortable affair, where you can do fine by donning some extra clothing and sitting on a small insulating pad while you enjoy a hot drink. Most bivouacs are less pleasant. For a climbing bivouac, you may have to anchor yourselves and your gear to the mountain for safety during the night. Always conserve body heat by taking off wet boots, putting on dry socks and other dry clothes, keeping snow off your clothes, loosening belts and other items that can impede circulation, using ground insulation, and putting on all the warm clothing you need or have. Huddle together with your bivouac-mates for as much warmth as possible.

How much clothing and gear should you carry to

ensure that you survive a bivouac? The answer depends on a lot of factors, including your experience, physical condition, and mental attitude. A mountaineer in top shape, who climbs 150,000 feet a year and has a positive outlook, might handle several planned bivouacs and perhaps a couple of emergency overnighters each year with no difficulty. Experience has shown this climber what we all can eventually figure out: how to distinguish that fine line between carrying too much and carrying too little.

## SNOW AND WINTER CAMPING

Winter camping, more so than summer camping, demands well-developed rituals and habits. Efficiency and safety will improve if everyone is familiar with their assignments. For example, a tent goes up quickly and easily if two or three members of the party know exactly who does what: who holds the tent to keep it from blowing away, who threads poles through the sleeves, and who pushes the poles.

For overnight winter trips, you can stay in a tent or in a snow shelter. Tents are much easier to set up, but a good snow shelter is much sturdier. Tents are by far the fastest to erect, taking perhaps 15 minutes or so. Snow trenches are next in order of time to complete, followed by snow caves; igloos require the most time. Both tents and snow shelters have their virtues, depending on the situation, and you should be prepared for using either. Winter travelers should know how to build snow shelters in an emergency, such as being caught out overnight on a day trip without tents.

Following is a look at tents, snow shelters, and the principal techniques and equipment that go into successful winter camping.

### Snow Shovels

The snow shovel is a fundamental piece of equipment for the winter mountaineer, and every member of a winter party should carry one. The shovel is used to excavate climbers from avalanche debris, dig emergency shelters, prepare tent platforms, and clear climbing routes.

Members of a summer climbing party will want to research their route to determine how much is on snow and glacier and whether any campsites will be on snow before deciding how many snow shovels to take. A general summer rule is one shovel per rope team or tent, with a minimum of two shovels per party.

In choosing a shovel, a climber is torn between the heavy, bulky grain scoop, ideal for moving large amounts of loose snow quickly but less useful for avalanche debris or snow caves, and the compact folding or sectional shovel, convenient to carry and therefore less likely to be left at home. The best general-purpose mountaineering shovel is made of aluminum, with a blade about 1 foot square and a stout, medium-length (20 to 24 inches), removable D-shaped handle (fig. 3-5). This shovel is small enough to carry full time and to use inside a snow cave. It's strong, can hold a significant amount of snow, and is stable to grip and use. If you expect to cut any sort of snow blocks for snow walls or shelters, you will also need a snow saw (fig. 3-5).

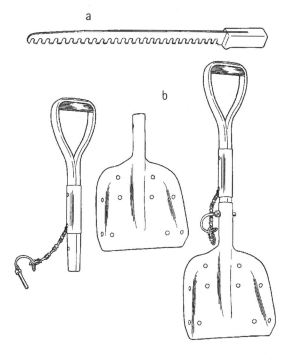

*Fig. 3-5. Snow construction tools: a, snow saw; b, snow shovel with removable handle.*

# Winter Tents

Tents are the first choice in shelters for the typical weekend winter outing. A quality winter (four-season) tent must be sturdy enough to withstand high winds and snow. Steep sidewalls aid in shedding snow and in clearing it off the tent, and an aerodynamic shape helps shed the wind. Freestanding dome-type tents work well, and so do the tunnel-style (hoop) tents, which require a few stakes (fig. 3-6). Every winter tent, freestanding or not, needs multiple lashing points for tying into anchors to keep it from taking off like a box kite in a strong gust. The considerations that go into selecting and using a good winter tent apply likewise to tents used for expeditions.

Certain conveniences simplify wintertime tent living. These include multiple entrances (in case one entrance bears the brunt of the weather), a vestibule for cooking or storage, gear pockets inside the tent for organizing small items, and inside loops for hanging clothes or a lantern.

For extreme routes, where flat real estate is rare and weight is a supreme consideration, consider the compact and lightweight "wedge" tent, a freestanding design with two poles that go from corner to corner and cross in the middle. On most winter trips, however, you will want a tent that is roomy, though heavy. The extra room is used to store packs and personal gear as well as reduce feelings of claustrophobia during 15-hour nights in the tent.

Although single-walled tents of waterproof/breathable fabric are lighter, double-walled tents (with an integral or separate rain fly) are somewhat warmer and less subject to icing on the inside wall. Aluminum tent poles are usually stronger than fiberglass poles.

## The Tent Site

You can't pitch a tent without giving some thought first to selecting and preparing a site. Use the terrain to your advantage. Select a spot that is as near to flat as possible to make site preparation easier. Watch out for hazards such as crevasses, avalanche paths, and cornices. Observe the local wind patterns: a rock-hard or sculpted snow surface indicates frequent wind, whereas a loose powdery area indicates a zone where wind-transported snow is deposited. Keep in mind that, although the powdery area may be protected from the direct wind, the tent may have to be cleared of snow frequently.

Compact a large-enough area for the tent and for movement around the tent to check tie lines or clear snow. Flatten and smooth the tent platform thoroughly to keep occupants from sliding toward one wall or the other during the night and to get rid of any uncomfortable lumps. This is especially important if you're staying for several nights, because the entire tent platform becomes rock hard with all features cast in ice after the first night. A square-ended shovel works well in flattening the tent site, and a ski does a great job of leveling it.

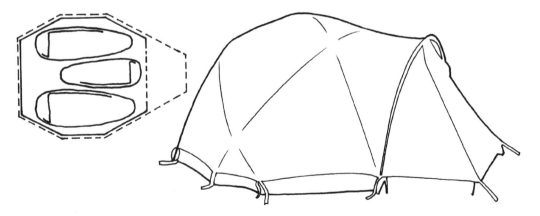

*Fig. 3-6. Hoop-style winter (four-season) tent*

If the site is slightly off level, heads should be to the high side.

After erecting the tent, dig a pit 1 foot or so deep in front of the tent door (fig. 3-7). The pit makes entering and leaving easier because you can sit comfortably in the doorway and place your feet in the pit. Put your cook stove on the snow directly across from the pit. In bad weather, the pit is a convenient wind-protected location for the stove, allowing you to wiggle forward in your sleeping bag and just reach out to do the cooking.

Build snow walls around the tent if the site is exposed to winds (fig. 3-7). The walls can be anywhere from about 3 to 6 feet high and will deflect some of the wind away from the tent. Keep the walls as far away from the tent as they are high (a 3-foot wall, for example, should be 3 feet away from the tent), because wind will deposit snow on the leeward side of the walls and fill this area quickly. Blocks cut by a snow saw or shovel make the easiest, quickest walls. You can also just shovel snow into a pile to serve as

a wall but, being rounded, the pile is less effective as a windbreak.

## Anchoring the Tent

There are a few tricks to anchoring a tent in snow, where driven stakes of wire, metal, or plastic can melt out during the day. Wide-profile stakes will sometimes work. Instead of driven stakes, you can use "deadman" anchors (fig. 3-8), such as a rock, a bag filled with rocks, or a nylon stuff sack filled with snow. Attach a cord or sling to the deadman, bury the deadman in the snow, stamp down the snow above it, and then connect a tent guy line to the cord or sling.

Tent stakes or snow pickets can be used as deadman anchors by burying them horizontally in a snow trench, perpendicular to the guy line. Even better, prepare the deadman in advance by drilling holes in a stake or metal plate and attaching a bridle, to which the guy line can be tied. You can also use a manufactured snow fluke, which usually comes with an attached wire bridle. Snowshoes, ice axes, skis, and ski

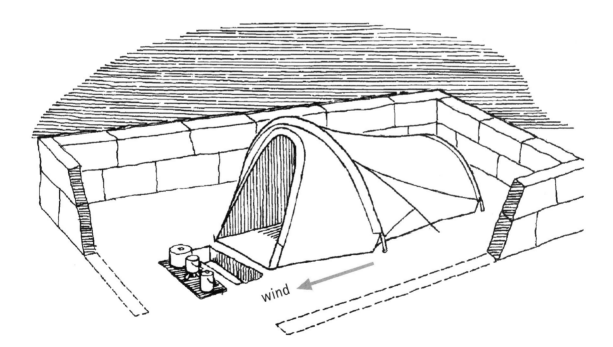

*Fig. 3-7. Typical winter camp: kitchen area, snow walls, and well-placed tent.*

poles also make solid anchors, but of course you can't use them for anything else while they're holding down the tent. Tie the tent to a tree if there is one nearby.

## Removing Snow

During a storm, you'll face the necessary chore of keeping snow cleared away from the tent. In most storms, it isn't the snow falling from the sky that creates the problem but, rather, the snow carried by the wind. Snow is deposited on the leeward side of tents and snow walls, and the tent begins to be muffled with snow, covering ventilation openings. Even a partially muffled tent poses the risk of asphyxiation, especially if you are cooking in the tent. Heavy, wet snow can pile up on the tent or fly with enough force to break rigging or tent poles and bring the whole structure down. A heavy snow load can even bury a tent and its occupants, asphyxiating them.

Shake the tent walls and shovel out around the tent regularly, taking care to remove snow from below the lower edge of the fly so that air can move in and out.

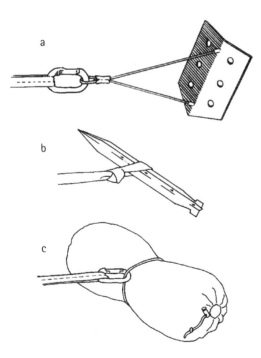

*Fig. 3-8. Deadman anchors: a, metal plate (snow fluke); b, tent stake; c, nylon stuff sack.*

Avoid cutting the tent with the shovel; nylon cuts easily when it is tensioned by a snow load. In a severe or prolonged storm, your tent may begin to disappear into the hole created by neighboring snowdrifts. You may need to move the tent up on top of the new snow surface.

## Tenting Hints

A number of special tent items are useful for winter camping. Each tent should have a small whisk broom to sweep snow from boots, packs, clothing, and the tent. Each tent also needs a sponge for cleaning up cooking or drinking-cup spills and removing condensation from the inside walls. A cheery addition to a tent, especially during the long nights near the winter solstice, is a candle lantern. For a larger community tent, you might even consider a gas lantern, which can repay its price in weight and bother by bringing tremendous brightening and warming to the tent.

To help make your winter tent-bound hours more pleasant, you need some house rules. They will depend on the weather, the size of the tent, and the experience of the occupants. For example, a small tent may require that packs be kept outside. Most four-season tents have vestibules where gear can be stored under cover. If the tent is large enough and packs are brought inside, they should be thoroughly brushed of snow first. It often helps to have one person enter the tent first to lay sleeping pads and organize gear before others enter.

House rules may dictate that boots be taken off outside, brushed of snow, and placed in a waterproof boot bag inside the tent. Boots can bring in snow, and they also can cut or tear holes in the tent floor. Plastic boots are best for winter camping, as the shells can be left covered outside or in the vestibule while the liners can be brought inside to keep them from freezing. Use stuff sacks or a large personal tent sack to help you organize and protect personal gear and keep it out of the way of your tentmates. Put your dry next day's clothing in a waterproof plastic sack so that it does not get wet from tent condensation.

## Cooking Inside the Tent

Cooking in the tent is risky and not recommended; it's also at times a necessity. The risks go from the relatively minor ones of spilling pots onto sleeping bags or increasing condensation inside the tent, to the deadly dangers of tent fires or carbon monoxide poisoning. Nevertheless, cooking inside may be required if it's so windy the stove will not operate outside or if it's so cold the cook risks frostbite. A tent vestibule is a big advantage because it provides the protection of cooking inside, with fewer risks.

Inside or out, your stove must be set on a stable platform to insulate the tent floor or snow from the heat of the stove and to keep it from tipping over. Also, some stoves work significantly better if the fuel is insulated from the snow. A piece of quarter-inch plywood wrapped in aluminum foil to provide a reflective surface is a good stove pad. A snow shovel or snow fluke also may be pressed into service as a platform.

Here are some additional tips on inside cooking:

- Light the stove outside (or near an opening so it can be tossed outside if it flares) and bring it inside only after it is running smoothly.
- Cook near the tent door or in the tent vestibule. This puts the stove near the best ventilation and lets you throw the stove outside quickly in an emergency.
- Provide plenty of ventilation. This is critical. Carbon monoxide is colorless and odorless, so you can't detect it. It is better to err on the conservative side by cooling off the tent with too large a ventilation hole rather than risk carbon monoxide poisoning with too small an opening.

# Snow Shelters

A well-made snow shelter is far more secure than a tent. In a storm, as the snow piles up, the snow shelter becomes even more secure while the tent must be continually cleared of snow to maintain ventilation, keep the tent from collapsing, and prevent asphyxiation of the occupants. Sometimes a snow shelter is the only possibility, such as on a narrow, windy ridge with no space for a tent. A snow shelter requires no special equipment other than a shovel and, sometimes, a snow saw.

Even if you use tents for sleeping, a snow shelter is a useful addition for an extended stay in one spot. It can be the communal hall where cooking and socializing take place without fear of spilling soup on a sleeping bag or tearing a hole in a tent wall. The extra shelter also serves as a warehouse for equipment and a place of refuge if a tent fails in extreme conditions.

Snow-shelter construction is a useful skill and it can be fun, but building one for a short winter trip is not usually practical because it commonly requires 2 or 3 hours. Building a snow shelter is hard work and may leave the construction crew wet from perspiration and from the snow. It is on longer trips, where the investment in the snow shelter can be amortized over several nights or where conditions are too extreme for a tent, that snow shelters are most valuable.

In some circumstances, a snow shelter is warmer than a tent. But if it's midday and the sun is out, the inside of a tent can be 40 or 50 degrees warmer than the outside air, making it a great place for drying sleeping bags and clothing. A snow shelter does not have this advantage.

## Snow Caves

Knowing how to build snow caves is an essential mountaineering skill. A snow cave (figs. 3-9 and 3-10) provides more protection, comfort, and insulation from a storm than a flapping, gale-swept tent. The temperature inside the tent may be, at best, 10 degrees Fahrenheit above the outside temperature—and if it's minus 10 degrees outside, that's a cold tent. The environment in a snow cave, meanwhile, will be a very still, quiet, 32 to 35 degrees Fahrenheit no matter what the wind and temperature outside.

You can dig an emergency cave with a cooking pot, a hard hat, or whatever gear might be handy, but a lightweight snow shovel is the best tool. Holes can be drilled in the shovel blade to make it lighter, without sacrificing its scooping power. Be prepared for the fact that it's a time-consuming job to build an optimum camping snow cave—perhaps 2 or 3 hours to dig a four-person shelter, using two shovels. With experience, though, a two-person minimum-sized emergency cave can be built in as little as 30 minutes.

### Building a Snow Cave

Snow caves require both adequate snow depth and the right topography. First look for obvious hazards. Are you on a potential avalanche slope? Could wind blow snow over the opening and seal you in? Try to find a short, steep slope to dig into, such as along a riverbank or on the side of a snowdrift—one that is angled at about 30 to 40 degrees. It's much easier to dig a cave into a steep slope than into a shallow one.

The snow must be deep enough–usually 5 or 6 feet–so you won't hit ground before you finish excavating the entire cave.

As you work, keep your clothing dry. Limit yourself to a moderate work pace in order to avoid excessive sweating.

The following are the step-by-step instructions for building a snow cave:

1. Dig an entryway into the slope. Make the entryway 1¹/₂ feet wide and about 5 feet high, and extend it 3 feet into the slope (fig. 3-9a).
2. Dig a waist-high platform that is centered on the entryway, forming a T; make the platform 4 feet wide and 1¹/₂ feet high. Develop this platform into a horizontal slot extending into the slope (fig. 3-9b). This slot provides a handy exitway for all the snow you'll be shoveling out as you excavate the interior of the cave. (When the cave is done, you'll close up the slot.) The bottom of this horizontal slot helps determine the floor level of your snow cave: the floor level should be about 6 inches higher than the bottom of the slot.
3. Continue to dig inward from the entryway and start creating the main room of the cave. Expand the room to the front, to the sides, and upward–in all directions except down. As you dig, simply shovel the snow out through the slot. A second person, working outside, can clear the snow away and shift off with the excavator working inside. Keep digging until you've excavated all the snow within easy reach.
4. Extend the original entryway another 2 feet into the slope, permitting you to get farther in to continue excavating the cave outward and upward. You should be approaching the point where you can almost stand inside (fig. 3-9c). Now nicely out of the wind, continue to excavate. When you've cleared enough snow to let you sit up on the main cave floor, a partner can enter and help you continue to expand the cave in all directions.
5. Excavate until the inside dimensions are about 5 feet front to back by 7 feet wide by 3¹/₂ feet high, a comfortable minimum for two people. Make the cave larger and more accommodating if you have the time and energy or if you'll have more occupants. You need at least 1 foot of firm snow on

the slope above the cave ceiling to provide enough strength to keep it from collapsing. Even then, you may notice some sagging in the ceiling overnight. Avoid building a flat ceiling; the more dome-shaped you make the ceiling, the stronger it will be and the less it will sag.

6. Begin filling in the temporary horizontal slot with snow blocks or snowballs (fig. 3-9d). One large block, or two smaller ones leaning against each other, is generally sufficient to close the horizontal slot area of the entrance tunnel. With snow, caulk any spaces around the blocks in the slot. The top of the finished tunnel entrance should be at least 6 inches lower than the cave floor, keeping warm air in the cave and cold drafts out.
7. Poke a pair of ski-pole-basket–sized ventilation holes through the ceiling of the cave to the outside–important for preventing asphyxiation. You can enlarge the holes if it gets too warm inside.
8. Make the domed ceiling smooth, without bumps or protrusions, so that melting water will flow down the walls instead of dripping on the occupants. Scratch a small trench at the base of the wall to help channel meltwater away. Put down a space blanket or ground sheet to keep things dry and prevent loss of equipment in the snow.
9. Keep the weather out by putting a small tarp or a pack (inside a plastic bag) over the entrance, but leave some opening for breathing air to flow in. To ensure that no uninvited guests drop in, mark the area around your cave with wands so that no one inadvertently walks onto the top of it.
10. Customize the cave to your heart's content. Adapting the interior to suit the tastes of the builders is limited only by the time and energy of those involved. Small alcoves can be dug into the walls for storing boots, stove, cooking utensils, and so forth. A small candle lantern can provide a warm glow. Entrance-area seats, a cooking platform, and whatever else your imagination comes up with add personal touches to your snow home. Figure 3-10 shows side and top views of a fully completed snow cave.

### Building a Cave in Shallow Snow

There is even a way to build an emergency snow cave in shallow powder snow (fig. 3-11). You need at

Fig. 3-9. Snow-cave construction

least 6 inches of snow, and it takes about 3 hours. Step by step, this is the way to do it.

Drive a 6-foot stick vertically into the snow. Take another stick and draw a circle 12 feet in diameter around the stake. Lay the second stick on the snow, one end touching the vertical stick. (The second stick becomes a "guide" to point you toward the vertical stick after you've buried it within the cave.)

Shovel snow into a big pile within the circle, packing it down until its center is about 1 foot above the

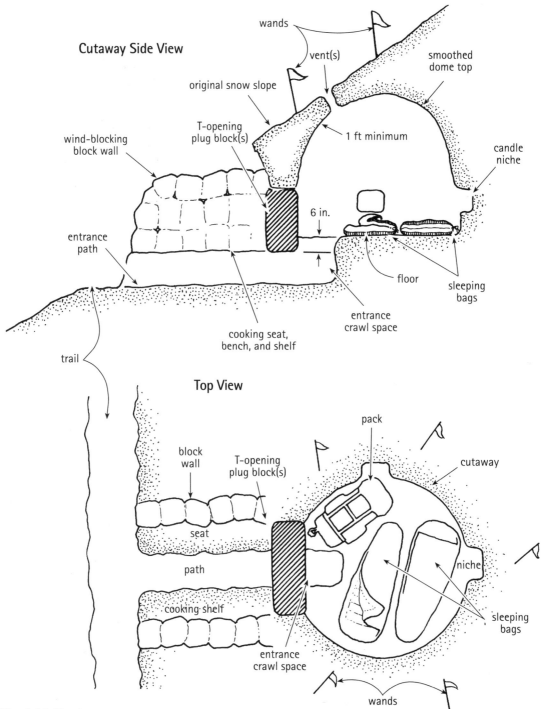

Cutaway Side View

wands

vent(s)

original snow slope

smoothed dome top

1 ft minimum

candle niche

T-opening plug block(s)

wind-blocking block wall

6 in.

entrance path

floor

sleeping bags

entrance crawl space

cooking seat, bench, and shelf

trail

Top View

pack

cutaway

block wall

T-opening plug block(s)

seat

path

niche

cooking shelf

sleeping bags

entrance crawl space

wands

*Fig. 3-10. T-entrance snow cave*

*Fig. 3-11. Snow cave built in shallow snow*

*Fig. 3-12. Tree-pit shelter*

top of the vertical stick. Let the pile sit for an hour or so, and then tunnel into the pile following the guide stick. Excavate enough snow to make a small room, large enough for two or three people, with 2-foot-thick walls. Remove the vertical stake.

## Tree-Pit Shelters

With a little improvisation, natural shelters can be converted into snow hideaways in an emergency. Such shelters occur under logs, along riverbanks, or in the pits formed when snow has been deflected away from large conifer trees by their limbs. For a tree-pit shelter (fig. 3-12), enlarge the natural hole around the trunk and roof it with any available covering, such as ice blocks, tree limbs, a space blanket, or a tarp. Boughs and bark can provide insulation and support (but don't cut live boughs unless it is a life-or-death emergency).

## Snow Trenches

When it is getting dark or the weather is especially bad, a snow-block shelter might be your answer. The trench igloo (fig. 3-13), built on either a slope or on the flat, is a quick emergency shelter for one or two people. Dig a narrow trench and then roof the trench, A-frame style, with snow blocks. The blocks can be created as part of the process of removing snow for the trench, or they can be quarried nearby. Then enlarge the interior down and out and provide a vent hole. Caulk any gaps between blocks and smooth out any irregularities in the ceiling so that condensation will run down the blocks and not drip on the occupants.

Cover most of the entrance with a pack that is protected with a plastic bag. This shelter is not as easy to build as it looks, so practice first in good weather.

A more basic emergency snow-trench shelter (fig. 3-14) can be built by digging a trench some 4 to 6 feet deep and large enough for the party and then stretching a tarp over the top and weighting its edges down

*Fig. 3-13. Trench igloo*

*Fig. 3-14. Basic snow-trench shelter*

with snow. In a flat area, give a slope to the tarp by building up the snow on one side of the trench before putting the tarp down. This snow trench works well in wind or rain, but a heavy snowfall can collapse a roof that is so nearly flat. The smaller the trench, the easier it is to keep warm. Again, be sure to provide for ventilation.

## Igloos

Igloos, constructed of snow blocks, aren't as dependent as snow caves or snow trenches on the depth of the snow. Therefore it's often possible to build a spacious igloo when snow conditions don't permit a large snow cave. Igloos are equal in protection to snow caves, but igloos can take twice as long to build. The traditional dome-shaped igloo (fig. 3-15) built of snow blocks that spiral upward and inward to the top requires proper snow consistency or preparation, plus a builder with a good bit of expertise.

If the snow isn't just right, and the snow blocks fall apart as you move them, forget about building an igloo. Moist, packed snow provides blocks that stick together and stay in place but makes them heavy and difficult to handle. Wind-packed snow is the easiest to work with. If the snow is soft, stomp it down and let it consolidate for a few minutes before starting to saw blocks with a snow saw or shovel. Each snow block should measure about $2\frac{1}{2}$ feet by $1\frac{1}{2}$ feet by $\frac{1}{2}$ foot. Use smaller blocks if the snow is poor or heavy, but

be aware that this will make igloo construction take longer.

To build the igloo, start with a compacted base area. Put the first three blocks into place. Then cut an angle down these three blocks to create a snow-block ramp that starts the spiral forcing subsequent layers to circle ever upward. Bevel the bottom and mating edge of each block in the igloo so the wall will tilt inward at the proper increasing angle, spiraling upward. Start this inward tilt immediately so that the igloo doesn't get so tall that you can't reach the top to cap it off. Set each block firmly and hold it in place while it is installed and until the next block in the spiral is set and held and the cracks caulked with snow.

One person works inside, shaping and setting blocks and caulking. Others work outside, cutting and carrying blocks and caulking the outside. After capping off the igloo, enlarge the interior by excavating into the floor. An outside worker digs down below the wall and inward to create an arched entrance. Like the snow cave, the igloo should have its floor above the top of its entrance. It also requires air vents.

You can also create hybrid snow shelters, combining igloo and snow-cave techniques. To make a typical hybrid shelter, dig into a snow slope through a relatively large opening; this makes it easy to excavate snow. When the space is big enough, close the opening over with snow blocks. Then dig a smaller entrance for access to the shelter.

## Winter Sleeping Systems

A comfortable sleeping system is critical for winter trips, as the climber may spend the greater part of each day in the sack. Obviously you need more insulation than in summer. This can come from a heavier sleeping bag or an overbag with additional insulation.

The type of insulation you want in your sleeping bag depends on the climate. In the mild damp cold of coastal areas, synthetic bags work well as they absorb little or no moisture. As the temperature drops, there is less moisture in the air and the high loft of down clearly excels.

An overbag must be large enough that it does not restrict the loft of the insulation in the inner bag. A

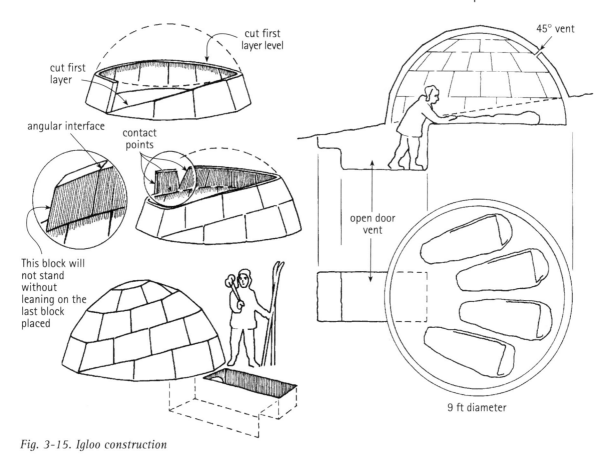

*Fig. 3-15. Igloo construction*

noninsulating overbag, such as a bivouac sack, provides some extra warmth and protects the main bag from spills, condensation, and snow. The bivy sack can also serve as emergency shelter when you're out climbing and away from base camp. If you don't use any kind of overbag, it may be helpful to have a sleeping bag with a cover made of material such as Gore-Tex shell fabric to help keep the bag dry and windproof.

Putting a vapor-barrier liner inside the sleeping bag will add to the sleeping system's warmth, increasing your bag's comfort range by 10 or 15 degrees Fahrenheit, especially in cold, dry environments. Liners are best used at below-freezing temperatures. The liner adds warmth by blocking evaporative heat loss from your body. Less evaporation means less water vapor condensing on the sleeping bag and, therefore, a drier bag. The liner reduces your perspiration during the night and the subsequent necessary drinking the next morning to replace the lost fluid.

The clothing you wear as you sleep inside a vapor-barrier liner will get damp from your body vapor. Wear a single layer of synthetic underwear, which retains very little moisture and dries quickly or can be changed in the morning. As an alternative to the liner, you can wear a vapor-barrier suit (shirt and bottom). The suit provides advantages similar to the liner, but it can also be worn when you're not in the sleeping bag.

An insulated pad is a critical component of the sleeping system, as the snow is virtually an infinite heat sink held at a constant 32 degrees on the surface beneath you. Inflatable foam pads such as the Therm-a-Rest are an excellent choice. You can add a closed-cell foam pad beneath the inflatable pad for added comfort, warmth, and reliability.

## Melting Snow for Water

In winter, snow melted by your stove provides the only reliable source of water. Winter stoves must be tougher than stoves relegated to summer use because, in addition to heating food, they have to melt many pots full of snow. The stove must have a high heat output in order to melt snow quickly, stability so that it supports a full pot of snow, and relative ease of repairing when this becomes necessary. It also must operate well at low temperatures (which pretty much rules out self-pressurizing white gas stoves, which do not have a pump).

The snow that you melt for drinking water should come from a "drinking snow" pit, well away from the designated toilet and cleaning areas. Be sure everyone understands the location of each. Collect the snow as small pot•size chunks rather than as loose snow in order to make stoking the melting pot simpler and neater. If you are cooking in the tent, the process also is easier and cleaner if you collect the snow in a sack and then just bring the sack into the tent.

As you melt snow in the evening for next day's water supply, melt an extra amount for drinking during the night to rehydrate your body. For a great feeling, put tightly sealed water bottles filled with hot water into heavy insulating socks and bring them inside your sleeping bag. Place one cozily at your feet and another at your middle. This will also keep the water from cooling too much, thus making it less likely to freeze on the next day's climb. On the climb, put one bottle in an insulated carrier within easy reach and the remainder deep in your pack to retain the heat.

## ——— WATER ———

Water is as vital to life as oxygen. You need it for energy metabolism, control of your core and body temperatures, and elimination of metabolic wastes. In mountaineering, the body's need for water becomes a simple matter of deposit and withdrawal. By exerting yourself in the mountains, you will sweat, heavily—making big withdrawals from your body's water supply. Without drinking—making "deposits" to replace this "withdrawal"—your water supply will become depleted and you will experience dehydration.

During the sedentary activities of everyday life, mild dehydration simply causes thirst. But combined with the sustained exertion of mountaineering, a lack of fluid intake may cause fatigue, disorientation, and headaches and contribute to carelessness as you try to continue climbing. Dehydration can become debilitating more quickly than you might expect. It is a factor in a number of mountain maladies, including acute mountain sickness. (See Chapter 19, First Aid, for more information on dehydration, acute mountain sickness, and other health hazards.)

One of the fundamental requirements of mountaineering health is drinking copious amounts of water. Often you have to force down more water than feels necessary. Your skin and lungs can release large amounts of moisture into cold, dry, high-altitude mountain air without your being aware of it. At high elevations, dehydration can contribute to nausea that, ironically, reduces the desire to gulp down fluids. Don't wait until you're thirsty to drink; thirst is a sign that dehydration is already in progress. A better indicator of proper hydration is lightly colored or colorless urine.

One method of maximizing your strength and endurance is to gulp down a generous quantity of water immediately before beginning your climb. Drinking large amounts of water during the 24-hour period prior to the climb also can boost performance.

The loss of body salts that accompanies heavy sweating is normally not a major problem, as most electrolytes are replaced naturally in a well-balanced diet. Replacing electrolytes becomes more important in hot weather or on extended trips, and sports drinks can be used for this purpose.

It's also wise to maintain a carbohydrate intake to fuel working muscles, beginning an hour or two into the climb. Your source of carbos can be food; the source may also be high-performance sports drinks, which provide an option for replacing water, carbohydrates, and electrolytes simultaneously. Before relying on sports drinks in the mountains, try them at home to verify that your system tolerates them. You may want to dilute sports drinks, or drink additional water, to make them easier to digest.

### Water Sources

Water is sometimes at a premium in the wilderness. High peaks are often bone dry or frozen solid, and your

only water will be whatever you brought with you from home or carried up from base camp. On multiday trips, the water sources will be lakes, streams, and snow. The importance of finding water is clear when you consider that during a tough three-day climb you might drink 6 quarts while hiking and climbing and an additional 5 quarts in camp.

You can often melt some snow for drinking by carrying it packed inside a water bottle. Start with a bit of water already in the bottle in order to hasten the melting time. When there is both sun and enough time, you can set out pots of snow to melt. Or find a tongue of snow that is slowly melting into a trickle, dredge a depression below, let the water clear, and channel the resulting puddle into a container. You can also try catching the drips from melting overhanging eaves of snow. The most convenient and reliable way to get water on a snow camping trip is to melt snow in a pot on the stove, though this obviously takes time and uses up cooking fuel.

On one-day climbs, your water source will normally be the water tap at home. A single quart of water may suffice for a very short day climb. For a grueling climb, you may need to pack 2 or 3 quarts of water.

## Purification Techniques

In the old days, there were few joys as supreme as drinking the pure, refreshing water of the high peaks. How the times have changed. Many water sources in the wilds are now tainted with microscopic pathogens. Climbers and backpackers themselves are to blame for much of the contamination, stemming from careless disposal of human waste. Nowadays it's unwise to trust water from even the most pristine-looking mountain spring.

There are three types of waterborne pathogens to guard against: viruses, bacteria, and large parasites (such as protozoa, amoebas, tapeworms, and flatworms).

Viruses are typically found only in tropical waters. Hepatitis A (infectious hepatitis) is an example of a virus-caused disease that can be contracted by drinking contaminated water. Although wildland waters in North America are usually free of viruses, it never hurts to treat your water against them. Viruses are easily killed with chemical treatment but are too tiny to be removed by filters. They are also killed by boiling.

Bacteria are present in mountain waters in a wide range of types and sizes. Examples of common waterborne bacteria to guard against include *Salmonella* and *Escherichia coli*. In undeveloped parts of the globe, bacteria that cause severe illnesses such as cholera, dysentery, and typhoid may lurk in the waters. Like viruses, bacteria can be effectively killed with chemicals or by boiling. Being larger than viruses, bacteria can also be filtered out with the proper filters.

Large parasites, most notably the protozoa *Giardia* and *Cryptosporidium* (or "crypto"), are major health concerns for alpine travelers. Both are commonly present in backcountry waters worldwide, including all of North America. The illnesses giardiasis and cryptosporidiosis take two to twenty days to manifest themselves, with symptoms that include intense nausea, diarrhea, stomach cramps, fever, headaches, flatulence, and belches that reek like rotten eggs. Large parasites are easy to filter out, but some have tough cell walls that are resistant to chemical treatments. Boiling kills them.

The principal methods of purification to rid your water of these critters are boiling, iodine treatment, and filtering. As with many aspects of mountaineering, no single method is the best for every situation, nor is any single method guaranteed. The purification methods are detailed in the following paragraphs and summarized in Figure 3-16.

**Boiling** your water is the most surefire method of water purification. Boiling will kill all waterborne pathogens. Simply bring the water to a boil. Sustaining the boil is unnecessary, even at elevations as high as the summit of Mount Everest. (For more information on water while camping in snow and in winter, see the preceding section on snow and winter camping.)

Fresh-fallen snow is as pure as pure can be and requires no purification. But there's a catch! Human waste can contaminate snow, and microscopic organisms can survive freezing. Tainted snow can subsequently melt, trickling and percolating its way to cross-contaminate other snow a long distance away. Thus it is wise to subject melted snow to treatment just as you would any other water. When you heat snow on a stove to melt it, boil it the same as if it were obtained from a lake or stream.

**Iodine treatment** is effective against bacteria and viruses but doesn't work against *Cryptosporidium*.

| METHOD | EFFECTIVENESS | ADVANTAGES | DISADVANTAGES |
|---|---|---|---|
| Boiling | Very effective against all pathogens. | Most effective method. | Very slow and inconvenient. Requires fuel, which may be too heavy for long trips. |
| Iodine | Very effective against bacteria and viruses. Effective against *Giardia*, but requires soak time. Not effective against *Cryptosporidium*. | Can be combined with filtering to protect against all pathogens. | Not to be used as the sole method of purification. Slow; extra slow for cold water; disagreeable taste. |
| Filtering | Very effective against large parasites. Effectiveness varies against bacteria, depending on filter. Not effective against viruses. | Relatively quick. | Expensive; may be bulky or heavy; may clog or break. |

*Fig. 3-16. Comparison of water purification methods*

Because of crypto, iodine should not be relied upon as your sole method of water purification. Iodine is effective against *Giardia,* although a soak time is required for penetrating the cyst walls. Backcountry iodine treatments include iodine tablets (tetraglycine hydroperiodide) or iodine crystals (saturated aqueous iodine solution). A drawback of iodine tablets is that they dissolve very slowly in cold water. You may have to wait up to an hour before you can safely drink iodine-treated water from a glacial stream.

The usual procedure is to drop iodine tablets or crystals into the water in a water bottle. But the bottle you drink from should not be dipped into a stream to obtain the water, as it is difficult to purify the water that collects on the threaded top. Iodine treatments impart a mildly disagreeable taste to the water. Powdered drink mixes can mask the iodine taste, but they should not be added until the soak time has lapsed and possible pathogens have been killed, because the drink mixes may contain vitamin C, which also removes the iodine itself.

**Water filters** work wonderfully well against protozoa, including *Giardia* and crypto, but aren't effective against viruses. Against bacteria, it depends on the filter's pore size and rating. Buy only filters that remove particles down to at least four-tenths of a micron; any larger, and you risk passage of bacteria that can make you ill.

Water filters, although expensive, are relatively quick to use compared with other purification methods. To guard against viruses, you can treat the water with iodine before pumping it through the filter. Some filters feature an integral iodine chamber designed to do this for you. Others come with an integral charcoal element that removes iodine (and its taste) after the iodine has completed its task. Whichever special features you seek, look for a filter that is compact, lightweight, and easy to use, clean, and maintain.

# FOOD

The art of camping includes the ability to set up a safe and comfortable camp and to provide food that's tasty and nutritious. Because mountaineering is such a strenuous and demanding activity, your body will need a variety of foods to provide sufficient carbohydrates, protein, and fats. With planning, it's not hard to choose foods that keep well, are lightweight, meet your nutritional needs, and are appropriately geared to your objective. For example, monotonous preprepared foods might work best for a short climb, whereas a week-long trip requires more variety and complexity. And don't forget the other requirement of camping food: it must taste good, or you simply won't eat it. If fueling your body quickly and simply is the first aim of alpine cuisine, the enjoyment of doing so is a worthy secondary goal.

## Composition of Foods

Each of the three major food components—carbohydrates, proteins, and fats—provides energy, and each must be supplied in approximately the right amount to maintain a healthy mind and body. For optimum performance in general mountaineering, try to consume total calories in roughly the following proportions: 50 to 70 percent carbohydrates, 20 to 30 percent proteins, and 20 to 30 percent fats.

Energy expenditure for mountaineers can go as high as 6,000 calories per day, possibly even higher for larger folks. You will have to determine what is best for you depending on how demanding a trip you are planning and your own size, weight, metabolic rate, and level of conditioning.

**Carbohydrates** are the easiest food for the body to convert into energy, so they should constitute most of the calories in your diet. Think of carbohydrates as the main "fuel food" to keep your body functioning most efficiently. Foods high in carbohydrates provide vitamins, minerals, proteins, fiber, water, and essential fats. Good sources of carbohydrates include whole grains, rice, potatoes, cereals, pasta, bread, crackers, and granola bars.

**Proteins** are important to include in your basic diet; the daily requirement is nearly constant regardless of activity. Your body cannot store proteins, so once the requirement is met, the excess is either converted to energy or stored as fat. High-protein foods include cheese, peanut butter, nuts, beef jerky, canned meats and fish, powdered milk and eggs, and foil-packaged meals with meat or cheese.

**Fats** are also an important energy source, as they pack over twice the calories per gram of proteins or carbohydrates. A characteristic especially notable to climbers is that fats are digested more slowly than carbohydrates or proteins, so they help keep you satisfied longer. Fats occur naturally in small amounts in vegetables, grains, and beans, and when these are combined with fish, red meat, or poultry, your requirements for fat are easily met. High-fat foods include butter, margarine, peanut butter, nuts, canned bacon, salami, beef jerky, sardines, oils, meat, eggs, seeds, and cheese.

Many people find foods high in fat more difficult to digest during the day while they are exercising strenuously. Eat mainly carbohydrates during the day; replenish calorie stores by adding fats and proteins to the evening meal.

### Eating for Endurance

How efficient your body is in using its energy fuels is closely related to physical condition, rest, and nutrition. The better your condition, the greater the efficiency with which food and water will provide energy during heavy exercise. A well-rested, well-fed climber is less likely to experience difficulties from exertion, heat, cold, and illness.

Affluent people who have rarely faced food deprivation may have little direct experience to show them just how food fuels the body. But the need for the body to have adequate fuel to function well becomes immediately apparent on a strenuous climb. Beginning climbers sometimes make the mistake of assuming that a climb is a good time to eat lightly and shed extra pounds. However, using stored body fat as fuel is usually not the most efficient way for the body to function. If you are not eating enough while climbing, you will find yourself tired and out of sorts, unable to enjoy yourself fully or to function at your peak.

## Food Planning

Put a reasonable amount of thought and effort into planning, and you should have no trouble ensuring the right combination of foods for optimum performance and enjoyment, whether your trip is for a day or for a week. As a rough general guideline, provide 2 pounds of food per person per day.

On very short trips, you can carry homemade sandwiches, fresh fruits and vegetables, and just about anything else you wish—even leftover pizza. For trips of two or three days—or longer if base camp is close to the road—any food from the grocery store is fair game. You can concoct a grocery-store stew from items selected almost at random or by intuition. Canned or

*Powerbar emergency food $, and/or not relished*

packaged items can be cooked together in one pot and then eaten with bread, a hot drink, and a dessert.

Cup-cooking works well for one-person meals. From one pot of hot water, eat each course in sequence from your cup, using instant foods such as soup, potatoes, rice, applesauce, or pudding.

For longer trips, planning becomes more complicated and weight more critical. Freeze-dried foods serve as an easy, compact, lightweight option. Outdoor stores carry a large array of these prepackaged meals and snacks. They're expensive, but very convenient. Some require little or no cooking; you just add hot water, soak for a while, and eat from the package. Others are less easily hydrated and require cooking in a pot. Freeze-dried meals include just about everything: main courses, potatoes, vegetables, soups, breakfasts, and desserts. Persons with access to a food dehydrator can make simple and nutritious mountaineering foods from fruits, vegetables, and meat at a substantial savings.

## Planning for a Group

Because meals are social events, small groups often plan all food together. A common, carefully planned menu reduces the overall weight carried by each person. Another typical arrangement is to leave breakfast and lunch to each individual, with only dinner, the most complicated meal of the day, as a group effort.

The ideal number of people in a cooking group is two to three per stove, with four as a maximum. Beyond that, group efficiency is outweighed by the complexities of large pots, small stoves, and increased cooking times. For longer trips, an extra stove is a good idea in case one breaks down.

### Selecting the Menu

A group can pack along just about whatever its members want on a short outing, but longer trips require precise food planning. It takes careful figuring to achieve nutrition, variety, and good taste while meeting the conflicting goals of minimizing weight and providing ample calories.

Meals can be planned by the group or by a chosen individual. In either case, the usual procedure is to write down a menu, discuss it with the group, compile an ingredients list, and then go shopping.

### Packaging

The elaborate packages of commercial foods are too bulky and heavy for most trips, so repack the food in plastic bags, sealable plastic packets, or other containers. Include a label or cooking instructions inside, or write on the outside with a felt pen. Smaller packages can be placed in larger ones that are labeled in broad categories, such as "breakfast," "dinner," or "drinks." For precise planning and packaging, a small kitchen scale is useful.

# Menu Suggestions

Try out various menu items and food combinations on day hikes or short outings before you rely on them to meet your needs for an extended trip in the mountains. Many products on the market advertise themselves as "complete meals" in a bar format (for example, PowerBars). These products can be a valuable part of your menu, but they don't agree with everyone.

## Breakfast

When you're in a hurry to get under way, breakfast is merely the first in a series of small meals and snacks. For a fast start, prepackage a standard meal before the trip, measuring a prepared cold cereal (such as granola), raisins or other fruit, and powdered milk into a breakfast bag. Stir in water—cold or hot—and breakfast is ready.

Other possibilities for breakfast are cooked grains such as oatmeal or rice, toaster pastries, bakery items, dried fruits, nuts, meat or fruit bars, and applesauce. If there's time, you can prepare a full-scale breakfast, with such items as potato slices, hash browns, omelets, scrambled eggs, bacon (canned or bars), and pancakes with syrup (made with brown sugar or syrup crystals).

A hot drink is a pleasant addition to a breakfast. Common choices are instant cocoa, coffee, malted milk, coffee-cocoa (mocha), tea, eggnog, and instant breakfast drinks. Fruit-flavored drinks include hot cider and flavored gelatin.

## Lunch and Snacks

During a climb, lunch begins shortly after breakfast and is eaten throughout the day. Eat small amounts and eat often. Plan at least half of your daily food allotment for lunch and snacks.

A good munching staple is gorp, a mixture of nuts, candy, raisins, and other dehydrated fruits. One handful makes a snack, several make a meal. Also good for munching is granola, with its mixture of grains, honey or sugar, and perhaps some bits of fruit and nuts. Gorp and granola are available premixed at many food stores, or you can make your own. Other snack items are fruit leather and fruit pemmican.

Your basic lunch can include any of the following:

**Proteins:** Canned meats and fish, beef jerky, precooked sausage, meat spreads, cheese, nuts, and seeds (sunflower and others). Because these foods also contain fats, they are more suited for extended lunch breaks rather than brief rest stops.

**Starches:** Whole-grain breads, bagels, granola and other cereals, crackers, brown-rice cakes, chips or pretzels, and granola bars.

**Sugars:** Cookies, chocolate, candy bars, hard candy, muffins, pastries, and honey.

**Fruits:** Fresh fruit, fruit bars, jam, and dried fruits such as raisins, peaches, and apples.

**Vegetables:** Fresh carrot or celery sticks, cucumbers, etc.

## Dinner

The evening meal should have it all. It should be both nourishing and delicious, yet easily and quickly prepared. To supplement your liquid intake, include some items that take a lot of water, such as soup. A cup of soup makes a quick and satisfying first course while the main course is being prepared.

One-pot meals with a carbohydrate base of noodles, macaroni, rice, beans, potatoes, or grains are easy and nutritious. To ensure adequate protein, fat, and flavor, you can add other ingredients such as canned or dried chicken, beef or fish, sausage, freeze-dried vegetables or fruits, butter or margarine, and a dehydrated soup or sauce mix.

Prepackaged meals from the grocery store—such as spaghetti, macaroni, rice mixes, ramen noodles, and instant salads—are relatively quick and easy to fix. There are also meals packaged in Styrofoam cups—just add boiling water, cover, and let sit for a few minutes, and your dinner is ready.

Freeze-dried meals offer a lot of dinner choices: almond chicken, chili, shrimp Newburg, turkey, beef Stroganoff, and many more. Theoretically, what they lack in flavor they make up for in convenience.

A hearty soup can serve as the main course for dinner. Good choices include minestrone, multibean, beef barley, or chicken. Add instant potatoes, rice, crackers, cheese, or bread, and the meal is complete. Bouillon is an old favorite that has minimal food value but weighs little and is helpful in replacing water and salt.

Side dishes of freeze-dried vegetables or beans add variety and substance. They can also be added to soup, along with instant rice or potatoes. Precooked beans or processed soy products (in powdered or textured forms) are excellent low-cost protein additions. People particularly interested in nutrition and health foods can find packaged supplements and organic items at stores that specialize in natural foods.

## Staples and Seasonings

Sugar is a matter of preference. Brown is one-third heavier than white because of moisture, but it's preferred by many for flavor. Instant powdered milk is a good protein supplement that can be added to many dishes. Margarine, which keeps better than butter on long trips, improves the flavor of many foods and is available in liquid form or in small tubs. Dried butter substitutes are available, but they don't have the fat content of the original. For seasonings, try salt, pepper, herbs, garlic, chili powder, bacon bits, dehydrated onions, Parmesan cheese, or a dash of soy sauce.

## Drinks and Desserts

Cold drinks during a hot day are necessary and can be especially satisfying. Lemonade, orange juice, grape juice, and sugar-free drinks are all available in powdered mixes. Just add water. Hot drinks such as cocoa, tea, or mocha taste good after the evening meal.

Occasional full-scale desserts are possible if you've planned the menus carefully. They can include cookies, candy, no-bake cheesecake, applesauce, cooked dried fruit, and instant pudding. Freeze-dried desserts include pies, ice cream, and berry cobblers.

# High Altitude

High-camp cooking is often difficult because cooking times are longer and conditions can be challenging.

*melt snow*
*prime @ water*

As you gain altitude and the atmospheric pressure decreases, water boils at lower and lower temperatures. Therefore, it takes longer to cook things. For every drop of about 10 degrees Fahrenheit (or 5 degrees Celsius) in boiling temperature, cooking time is approximately doubled (fig. 3-17). The most suitable foods are those that require only warming, such as canned chicken and instant rice. The weight of the fuel you have to pack is another argument for simple menus.

The rigors of rapid ascent to higher altitudes require special attention to food. An example is Mount Rainier in Washington state, where climbers typically spend Friday night near sea level, Saturday night at 10,000 feet (about 3,000 meters), and reach the 14,411-foot (4,392-meter) summit early Sunday, perhaps only 20 hours after leaving sea level. Many climbers fall victim to symptoms of mountain sickness, ranging from a slight malaise to vomiting and severe headaches. Under these conditions, food becomes more difficult to digest because the stomach and lungs are competing for the same blood supply.

To repeat, eat light and eat often, stressing carbohydrates, which are easiest to digest. Bring foods that have proven themselves appealing at high altitude, because climbers often lose their appetite up high. Trial and error will teach you what foods your body can tolerate at altitude. For example, spicy foods are sometimes unappetizing. Keeping yourself well hydrated is essential. You must continue to eat and drink, whatever the effort, for the loss of energy from a lack of food or water will only reinforce the debilitating effects of reduced oxygen.

| Elevation | | Temperature | | Cooking Time |
| ft | m | °C | °F | (sea level = 1) |
|---|---|---|---|---|
| sea level | | 100° | 212° | 1.0 |
| 5,000 | 1,525 | 95° | 203° | 1.9 |
| 10,000 | 3,050 | 90° | 194° | 3.8 |
| 15,000 | 4,575 | 85° | 185° | 7.2 |
| 20,000 | 7,000 | 80° | 176° | 13.0 |

*Fig. 3-17. Boiling point of water*

## Utensils for Cooking and Eating

The simplest eating utensils are a spoon and a single large insulated cup or small pot. Some people like to add a bowl; bowls are available in plastic, stainless steel, and light aluminum. Cook sets (fig. 3-18) should be durable and lightweight and nest for convenient carrying. You can purchase cook sets in aluminum, stainless steel, and Teflon-coated for easy cleaning. What you decide to buy and carry will depend on the needs of a particular trip. For example, if you are planning an overnight glacier trip, you might choose to take two pots: one for melting water and one for cooking your meal.

To minimize weight on an extended wilderness trip, you can get by with one pot if you use only freeze-dried dinners that are rehydrated in their own packaging or if you take foods that just require the addition of boiling water. Most mountaineers, however, use one pot for boiling water and another one for food. Be sure your pots have bails or handles for carrying and tight-fitting lids to conserve heat (and serve as makeshift fry pans).

## Stoves

Stoves are now a necessity for backcountry travelers because many camping areas no longer have enough firewood and others have banned natural-fuel fires. Stoves have a minimal impact on the wilderness and can be used in a variety of conditions.

In choosing a stove, consider a number of factors, including its weight, the altitude and temperature where it will be used, fuel availability, ease of operation, and its reputation for reliability. Some stoves run on more than one fuel, a valuable trait if availability of a particular fuel is limited. Whichever stove you select, it should be easy to start, operate, and maintain, even in cold, wet, or windy conditions.

Read the operating instructions for the stove before you buy it, and ask a salesperson to answer any questions you may have. Practice starting the new stove at home before a trip to be sure it's working and that you know how to operate it. You can prolong the stove's life and increase fuel efficiency with regular cleaning of dirt and carbon buildup. Stoves with pumps periodically need replacements for deteriorated pump leathers and gaskets. It helps to keep a

*Fig. 3-18. Cooking accessories: pots and lids; windscreen; utensils and cup.*

maintenance kit, spare pressure pump, and replacement parts on hand.

Mountaineering stoves typically weigh 1 to 1½ pounds and burn about an hour on approximately ½ pint (a quarter-liter or so) of fuel. You'll be rewarded with a more productive stove if you make sure it has a wind shield to screen the flame and prevent heat from being blown away. If you don't have a shield, improvise a way to block the wind. Most mountaineering stoves will boil about 1 quart (approximately 1 liter) of water at sea level in 4 to 8 minutes. Wind can increase the time to as much as 25 minutes or even prevent boiling.

Check the stability of the metal framework that supports the pot on the stove and see that the stove is solidly supported underneath, so that your dinner doesn't accidentally end up on the ground. A large flat rock can provide a sturdy base. In snow, a small square of Masonite or ensolite serves well as both a smooth base and insulation under the stove.

A direct flame under the pot is desirable for boiling water or melting snow. Use of a pot with a base that covers about the same area as the flame will bring a faster boil. For simmering, you might consider some means to diffuse the direct heat of the flame, such as a large metal lid. Simply place the lid on the burner and then sit the pot on the lid. Some stoves have an adjustment valve that permits you to further control the stove's output, which allows for simmering and prevents scorched food and wasted fuel.

Mountaineers have a range of choices in stoves (fig. 3-19) and in fuel, with white gas, kerosene, and butane being the most common (fig. 3-20). All stoves require a means of pressurization to force the fuel to flow to the burner. This is usually provided by a hand pump for white gas and kerosene stoves and by a pressurized cartridge for butane units. All stoves also need a way to vaporize the liquid fuel before it is burned. With white gas and kerosene stoves, a common method is to prime (preheat) the stove by burning a small amount of fuel in a priming cup to start the fuel vaporizing in the main supply line. With butane stoves, the fuel vaporizes inside the pressurized cartridge.

A pump on a stove lets you increase the pressure in the fuel tank; this causes the fuel to burn faster and hotter and brings water to a boil more quickly. Stoves that boil water fastest often do not simmer well, whereas those with a lower heat output give you more control at lower cooking temperatures.

## Stove Fuels

**White gas** is probably the most popular fuel in the United States for mountaineering stoves. It tends to burn hotter than butane and is excellent for melting large amounts of snow, boiling water, or heating food quickly. Unlike kerosene, white gas can be used as its own priming agent. Use only refined or white gasoline prepared for pressurized stoves; don't use automotive gasoline, including unleaded gas. The correct fuel is less likely to clog jets, build up excess pressure, or emit toxic fumes. Spilled white gas evaporates readily, with little odor, and is very flammable.

**Kerosene** is not as volatile as white gas and therefore is safer to transport and store. Kerosene stoves need to be pressurized in addition to being primed with either white gas, alcohol, or lighter fluid. (Liquid kerosene does not burn hot enough to preheat its own burner.) If the burner has not been heated sufficiently, the stove will burn with a sooty yellow flame, producing a lot of smoke and carbon. But when it burns efficiently, a kerosene stove has a high heat output, equal to or greater than white gas.

**Butane** or butane/propane cartridge stoves are

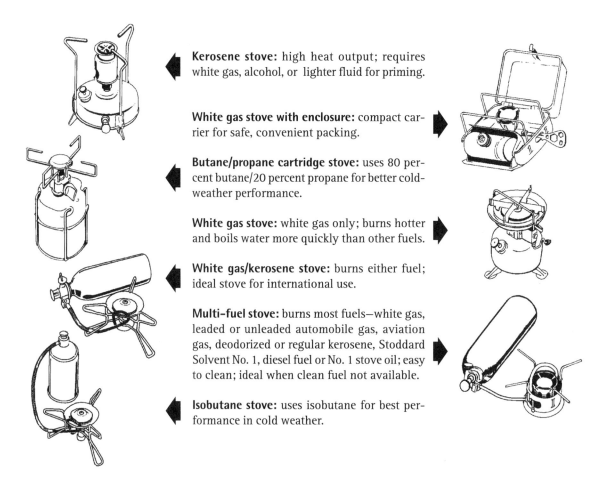

**Kerosene stove:** high heat output; requires white gas, alcohol, or lighter fluid for priming.

**White gas stove with enclosure:** compact carrier for safe, convenient packing.

**Butane/propane cartridge stove:** uses 80 percent butane/20 percent propane for better cold-weather performance.

**White gas stove:** white gas only; burns hotter and boils water more quickly than other fuels.

**White gas/kerosene stove:** burns either fuel; ideal stove for international use.

**Multi-fuel stove:** burns most fuels—white gas, leaded or unleaded automobile gas, aviation gas, deodorized or regular kerosene, Stoddard Solvent No. 1, diesel fuel or No. 1 stove oil; easy to clean; ideal when clean fuel not available.

**Isobutane stove:** uses isobutane for best performance in cold weather.

*Fig. 3-19. Types of outdoor stoves*

popular because of their convenience: easy to light, good flame control, immediate maximum heat output, and no chance of fuel spills. The pressure forces the fuel out as soon as the valve is opened, eliminating both pumping and priming. Most butane stoves are not recommended for temperatures below freezing unless the fuel is warmed. An exception is a stove that uses isobutane fuel, which has performed well at high altitude and in cold, wet conditions. With its windscreen/heat reflector, this stove has proven superior in the wind as well.

The disposable butane cartridges cannot be refilled. Therefore, you may end up leaving home with a cartridge that is only half full because it was already used

on an earlier trip. The cartridges are bulky, and all too frequently the spent canisters are found discarded in the wilderness. Pack them out. Another drawback is that as the butane is used up, the pressure in the cartridge is reduced, resulting in a drop-off in flame intensity. This problem is partly compensated for at higher elevations, where lower atmospheric pressure means the interior cartridge pressure is relatively higher. Some cartridges cannot be changed until they are empty. Always change cartridges outside your tent because residual fuel in spent canisters can be a fire hazard.

**Solid fuels** such as candles and canned heat serve primarily as fire starters. They are lightweight and cheap but provide only limited heat. Most are carried

| FUEL | ADVANTAGES | DISADVANTAGES |
|---|---|---|
| White gas | High heat output; spilled fuel evaporates quickly; readily available in U.S.; stove fuel for priming. | Priming sometimes required; spilled fuel very flammable; self-pressurizing stoves must be insulated from cold or snow. |
| Kerosene | High heat output; spilled fuel won't ignite readily; fuel available throughout world. | Requires priming; spilled fuel does not evaporate readily; does not burn clean. |
| Butane/propane | Immediate maximum output; no-spill fuel container; readily available in U.S. and other countries; no priming required. | Lower heat output; fuel canister disposal is a problem; fuel cartridges expensive; fuel must be kept above freezing for efficient burning. |

*Fig. 3-20   Fuel comparisons*

for emergency use only, along with a metal cup for heating small amounts of water.

## Foreign Travel

On foreign trips, fuel filters may be necessary because a high grade of fuel is often hard to find. Find out beforehand what fuels are available, and take an appropriate stove. Kerosene is generally available worldwide, whereas white gas is not. Check airline restrictions about carrying fuel on planes. Most do not allow it.

## Fuel Storage

Carry extra fuel in a tightly closed metal container that has a screw top backed up by a rubber gasket. Plastic containers aren't good because fuel gradually diffuses out through the material. Plainly mark the fuel container and stow it in a place where it can't possibly contaminate any food. Some stoves have their fuel bottles directly attached to them, whereas others require a pouring spout or funnel to transfer the fuel from a storage container to a stove fuel tank.

How much fuel should you take along? It will depend on the conditions of the trip and the food you plan to cook. For instance, you will use more fuel if you cook your dinners on the stove rather than simply heating water to pour into a food package. Practice and experience will eventually tell you how much fuel you need, but a good beginning would be to bring between $1\frac{1}{2}$ and 2 quarts for two people for one week (roughly $\frac{1}{4}$ pint, or 125 milliliters, per person per day). If you have to melt snow for water, expect fuel consumption to be greater than that.

## Fuel Safety

Tents have been blown up, equipment burned, and people injured by careless stove use. Apply rules of safety and common sense. Before lighting the stove, check fuel lines, valves, and connections for leaks. Don't use a stove inside a tent unless it is absolutely necessary. If you must cook in a tent, provide plenty of ventilation to minimize the danger of fuel escaping and igniting. Always change pressurized fuel cartridges, and fill and start liquid-fuel stoves, outside the tent and away from other open flames.

Leave an air space in the stove's fuel bottle, rather than filling it to the brim, to prevent excessive pressure buildup. And when you're finished mountaineering for the season, put the stove into storage and remember to empty the fuel bottle.

# 4 NAVIGATION

**W**here am I? How can I find my way from here to there? How far is it to the summit? These are three of the most frequently asked questions in mountaineering, and this chapter shows how to find the answers by using orientation and navigation.

By the time you finish this chapter, you will have a good handle on the tools of navigation and the proven techniques of top-notch navigators, acquired through years of roaming the hills. You will have the basic knowledge to eventually head into the wilds, work out the way to the mountain, and, most importantly, find your way home.

These tools and techniques are simple and straightforward—but exacting. Study them carefully to help make your mountain adventures successful and keep you safe within the ranks of surviving navigators. Before you immerse yourself in this chapter, remember two things: Navigation is easy. Navigation is fun (so much fun, in fact, that some people engage in the sport of *orienteering*, in which participants compete with one another over a structured course, getting to various destinations using map and compass).

First, a few definitions:

**Orientation** is the science of determining your exact position on the earth. It requires mastery of map and compass, plus the ability to use an altimeter and perhaps even a global positioning system (GPS) receiver. People who spend a reasonable amount of time and effort usually gain these skills, even when they have little background or interest in math or science.

**Navigation** is the science of determining the location of your objective and of keeping yourself pointed in the right direction all the way from your starting point to this destination. Like orientation, navigation requires map and compass and other instruments and techniques and is a required skill for all wilderness travelers.

**Routefinding** is the art of selecting and following the best path appropriate for the abilities and equipment of the climbing party. It takes a lot to be a good routefinder: an integrated sense of terrain and a combination of good judgment, experience, and instinct. Wilderness routefinding will be covered in more detail in the next chapter, but its understanding requires a solid foundation in the orientation and navigation skills described in the following sections.

## TRIP PREPARATION

Routefinding begins at home. Before heading out the door, you need to know not only the name of your wilderness destination but also a great deal about how to get there. The information is accessible to anyone who takes the trouble to seek it out, from guidebooks and maps and from people who have been there.

Prepare for each trip as if you were going to lead it. Each person in a climbing group needs to know wilderness navigation and must keep track of where the party has been, where it is, and where it's going. In case of emergency, each climber must be able to get back alone.

Guidebooks provide critical information such as a description of the route, the estimated time necessary to complete it, elevation gain, distance, and so forth. Climbers who have made the trip will tell you about landmarks, hazards, and routefinding hassles. Useful details are packed into maps of all sorts: Forest Service maps, road maps, aerial maps, sketch maps, and topographic maps. For a trip into an area that's especially unfamiliar, more preparation is needed. This might include scouting into the area, observations from vantage points, or study of aerial photos.

If the route comes from a guidebook or from a description provided by another climber, plot it out on the topographic map you'll be carrying along, noting junctions and other important points. It can help to highlight the route with a yellow felt-tip marking pen, which doesn't obliterate map features. Other maps or route descriptions should be taken along with the topo map, marked with notes on any more up-to-date information. In selecting the route, consider a host of factors, including the season, weather conditions, the abilities of the party members, and the equipment available.

Before you've even shouldered your pack, you should have a mental image of the route. From experience, and from all the sources of information about the climb, you'll know how to make the terrain work in your favor. To avoid brush, try not to follow watercourses or drainages; select ridges over hillsides and gullies. Clear-cuts are often full of slash or brushy second-growth trees, so stick to old-growth forest if possible.

A rock-slide area can be a feasible route—providing you watch carefully for new rockfall. One problem in planning the route, however, is that a rock-slide area may look the same on a map as an avalanche gully, which can be an avalanche hazard in winter and spring and choked with brush in summer and fall. If your sources aren't helpful, only a firsthand look will clear up this question.

The most straightforward return route is often the same as the route going in. If you plan to come back a different way, that route also needs careful advance preparation.

Don't let outdated information ruin your trip. Check beforehand with the appropriate agencies about roads and trails, especially closures, and about

climbing routes and regulations, permits, and camping requirements.

## THE MAP

A map is a symbolic picture of a place. In convenient shorthand, it conveys a phenomenal amount of information in a form that is easy to understand and easy to carry. No mountaineer should travel without a map or the skill to translate its shorthand into details on the route. Note the publication date of the map because roads, trails, and other features may have changed since that time. Try to use the latest information. A number of different types of maps are available:

**Relief maps** attempt to show terrain in three dimensions by using various shades of green, gray, and brown, terrain sketching, and raised surfaces. They help in visualizing the ups and downs of the landscape and have some value in trip planning.

**Land management and recreation maps** are updated frequently and thus are very useful for current details on roads, trails, ranger stations, and other marks of the human hand. They usually show only the horizontal relationship of natural features, without the contour lines that indicate the shape of the land. These maps, published by the U.S. Forest Service and other government agencies and by timber companies, are suitable for trip planning.

**Climbers' sketch maps** are generally crudely drawn but often make up in specialized route detail what they lack in draftsmanship. Such drawings can be effective supplements to other map and guidebook information.

**Guidebook maps** vary greatly in quality. Some are merely sketches, whereas others are accurate modifications of topographic maps. They generally contain useful details on roads, trails, and climbing routes.

**Topographic maps** are the best of all for climbers. They depict topography, the shape of the earth's surface, by showing contour lines that represent constant elevations above sea level. These maps, essential to off-trail travel, are produced in many countries. Some are produced by government agencies, whereas others are printed by private companies, with special emphasis on trails and other recreational features. As an example of topographic maps, we will look in detail at the maps produced by the U.S. Geological Survey (USGS).

# USGS Topographic Maps

It might be interesting to start this discussion of USGS maps with a refresher on how cartographers divide up the earth. The distance around our planet is divided into 360 units called *degrees*. A measurement east or west is called *longitude*. A measurement north or south is *latitude*. Longitude is measured 180 degrees, both east and west, starting at the Greenwich meridian in England. Latitude is measured 90 degrees, both north and south, from the equator. New York City, for example, is situated at 74 degrees west longitude and 41 degrees north latitude.

Each degree is divided into 60 units called *minutes,* and each minute is further subdivided into 60 *seconds*. On a map, a latitude of 47 degrees, 52 minutes, and 30 seconds north would probably be written like this: 47°52′30″N.

One type of USGS map commonly used by mountaineers covers an area of 7.5 minutes (that is, ⅛ degree) of latitude by 7.5 minutes of longitude. These maps are known as the *7.5-minute series*. An older type of USGS map covers an area of 15 minutes (that is, ¼ degree) of latitude by 15 minutes of longitude. These maps are part of what is called the *15-minute series*.

The *scale* of a map is a ratio between measurements on the map and measurements in the real world. A common way to state the scale is to compare a map measurement with a ground measurement (as in 1 inch equals 1 mile) or to give a specific mathematical ratio (as in 1:24,000, where any one unit of measure on the map equals 24,000 units of the same measure on the earth). The scale is usually shown graphically at the bottom of a map.

In the USGS 7.5-minute series, the scale is 1:24,000, or roughly 2½ inches to the mile, and each map covers an area of approximately 6 by 9 miles. In the 15-minute series, the scale is 1:62,500, or about 1 inch to the mile, and each map covers an area of about 12 by 18 miles. Mountaineers prefer the 7.5-minute maps because of the greater detail.

The 7.5-minute map is now the standard for the United States, except for Alaska. The 15-minute maps are no longer in production for the other 49 states. For Alaska only, the 15-minute map is still the standard, and the scale is somewhat different: 1:63,360, or exactly 1 inch to the mile. The east–west extent of each Alaska map is actually greater than 15 minutes because the lines of longitude are converging toward the North Pole.

In some areas, private companies produce maps based on USGS topographic maps, but they are updated with more recent trail and road details and sometimes combine sections of USGS maps. These maps are often useful supplements to standard topographic maps.

## How to Read a Topographic Map

Consider this a language lesson, but a map's language is quite easy to learn and pays immediate rewards to any wilderness traveler. Some of this language is in words, but most of it is in the form of symbols. The best way to follow the lesson is to study it along with an actual USGS topographic map. Any map will do.

Each map is referred to as a quadrangle (or quad) and covers an area bounded on the north and south by latitude lines that differ by an amount equal to the map series (7.5 minutes or 15 minutes) and on the east and west by longitude lines that differ by the same amount. Each quadrangle is given the name of a prominent topographic or human feature of the area.

### What the Colors Mean

Colors on a USGS topographic map have very specific meanings. This is what the different colors stand for:

**Red:** Major roads and survey information.

**Blue:** Rivers, lakes, springs, waterfalls, and other water-related features.

**Black:** Minor roads, trails, railroads, buildings, bench marks, latitude and longitude, UTM (Universal Transverse Mercator) coordinates and lines, and other features not part of the natural environment.

**Green:** Areas of heavy forest. Solid green marks a forested area, while mottled green indicates scrub vegetation. A lack of green doesn't mean an area is devoid of vegetation but simply that any growth is too small or scattered to show on the map. Don't be surprised if a small, narrow gully with no green color on the map turns out to be an avalanche gully, choked with impassable brush in the summer and fall and with significant avalanche hazard in the winter and spring.

**White:** The color of the paper on which the map is printed; it can have a variety of meanings, depending on the terrain.

*White with blue contour lines:* A glacier or permanent snowfield. The contour lines of glaciers and permanent snowfields are in solid blue, with their edges indicated by dashed blue lines.

*White with brown contour lines:* Any dry area without substantial forest, such as a high alpine area, a clearcut, a rock slide, an avalanche gully, or a meadow. Study the map for other clues.

**Brown:** Contour lines and elevations, everywhere except on glaciers and permanent snowfields.

**Purple:** Partial revision of an existing map.

### Translating Contour Lines

The heart of a topographic map is its overlay of contour lines, each line indicating a constant elevation as it follows the shape of the landscape. A map's contour interval is the difference in elevation between two adjacent contour lines (usually 40 feet on 7.5-minute maps and 80 feet on 15-minute maps). Every fifth contour line is printed darker than other lines and is labeled periodically with the elevation.

One of the most important bits of information a topographic map reveals is whether you will be traveling uphill or downhill. If the route crosses lines of increasingly higher elevation, you will be going uphill. If it crosses lines of decreasing elevation, the route is downhill. Flat or sidehill travel is indicated by a route that crosses no lines, remaining within a single contour interval.

This is only the start of the picture that contour lines paint of your actual wilderness route. They also show cliffs, passes, summits, and other features (fig. 4-1). You will get better and better at interpreting these lines by comparing actual terrain with its representation on the map (fig. 4-2). The goal is to someday glance at a topographic map and have a sharp mental image of just what the place will look like. The following listing gives the main features depicted by contour lines:

**Flat areas:** No contour lines at all.

**Gentle slopes:** Widely spaced contour lines.

**Steep slopes:** Closely spaced contour lines.

**Cliffs:** Contour lines extremely close together or touching.

**Valleys, ravines, gullies, and couloirs:** Contour lines in a pattern of U's for gentle, rounded valleys or gullies; V's for sharp valleys or gullies. The U's or V's point uphill, in the direction of higher elevation.

**Ridge or spur:** Contour lines in a pattern of U's for gentle, rounded ridges; V's for sharp ridges. The U's or V's point downhill, in the direction of lower elevation.

**Peak or summit:** A concentric pattern of contour lines, with the summit being the innermost and highest ring. Peaks often are also indicated by X's, elevations, bench marks (BM's), or a triangle symbol.

**Cirques or bowls:** Patterns of contour lines forming a semicircle (or as much as three-quarters of a circle), rising from a low spot in the center of the partial circle to form a natural amphitheater at the head of a valley.

**Saddle, pass, or col:** An hourglass shape, with higher contour lines on each side, indicating a low point on a ridge.

The margin of a USGS map holds important information, such as date of publication and revision, names of maps of adjacent areas, contour interval, and map scale. The margin also gives the area's magnetic declination, which is the difference between true north and magnetic north (declination will be discussed later in this chapter).

Keep a couple of cautionary thoughts in mind as you study a topographic map, because it does have certain limitations. The map won't show all the terrain features you actually see on the climb because there's a limit to what can be jammed onto the map without reducing it to an unreadable clutter. If a feature is not at least as high as the contour interval, it may not be shown, so a 30-foot cliff may come as a surprise when you are navigating with a map that has a 40-foot contour interval. Check the date of the map because topographic maps are not revised very often, and information on forests and on roads and other manufactured features could be out of date. A forest may have been logged or a road either extended or closed since the last updating. Although topographic maps are essential to wilderness travel, they must be supplemented with information from visitors to the area, guidebooks, and other maps. As you learn about changes, note them on your map.

Sometimes a trip runs through portions of two or more maps. Adjoining maps can be folded at the edges and brought together, or you can create your

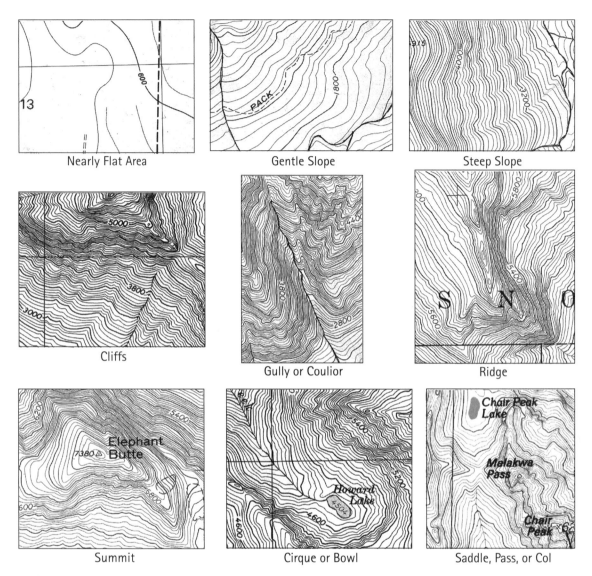

Fig. 4-1. Basic topographic features

own customized map by cutting out the pertinent areas and splicing them with tape. Include plenty of territory so that you have a good overview of the entire trip, including the surrounding area. Black-and-white photocopies are good for marking on, but because they don't show colors they should be used only in addition to the real thing.

As the precious objects they are, maps deserve tender care in the wilds. A map can be kept in a plastic bag or map case. You can also laminate the map with plastic film or coat it with waterproofing, though these coatings are difficult to mark on and make the map hard to work with. Some maps come already waterproofed. On the trip, carry the map in a jacket pocket or some other easily accessible place so you don't have to take off your pack to get at it.

# Routefinding with the Map

## Before the Trip

Most wilderness orientation, navigation, and routefinding is done by simply looking at your surroundings and comparing them with the map. This process is often aided by making some navigational preparations before the trip, like identifying *handrails, base lines,* and possible routefinding problems.

A handrail is a linear feature on the map that parallels the direction you are traveling. The handrail should be within frequent sight of the route, so it can serve as an aid to navigation. Features that can be used from time to time as handrails during a trip include roads, trails, powerlines, railroad tracks, fences, borders of fields and meadows, valleys, streams, cliff bands, ridges, lakeshores, and the edges of marshes.

A handrail helps in staying on route. Another map technique can help in finding the way home if you've gone off track. This is the base line, a long, unmistakable line that always lies in the same direction from you, no matter where you are during the trip. Pick out a base line on the map during trip planning. It does not have to be something you can see during the trip. You just have to know that it is there, in a consistent direction from you. A base line (sometimes called a catch line) can be a road, the shore of a large lake, a river, trail, powerline, or any other feature that's at least as long as your climbing area. If the shore of a distant lake always lies west of your climbing area, you can be sure that heading west at any time will get you to this identifiable landmark. Heading toward this base line may not be the fastest way to travel to your destination, but it may save you from being truly lost.

Also before the trip, anticipate specific routefinding problems. For example, if the route traverses a glacier or any large, featureless area, such as a snowfield, you may consider carrying route-marking wands, especially if the weather outlook is marginal. Make a note of any escape routes that can be used in case of sudden bad weather or other setbacks.

## During the Trip

Get off on the right foot by making sure that everyone understands the route. Gather the party around a map and take time to discuss the route and make contingency plans in case the party gets separated. Point out on the map where you are, and associate the surroundings with the piece of paper in front of you. This is a good time for everyone to make a mental note of the main features the party will see during the trip, such as forest, streams, or trails.

Along the way, everyone needs to keep associating the terrain with the map. Ignorance of the territory is definitely not bliss for any daydreaming climber who gets separated from the party. Whenever a new landmark appears, connect it with the map. At every chance—at a pass, at a clearing, or through a break in the clouds—update your fix on the group's exact position. Keeping track of progress this way makes it easy to plan each succeeding leg of the trip. It also may turn you into an expert map interpreter because you'll know what a specific valley or ridge looks like compared with its representation on the map.

### Look Ahead to the Return Trip

The route always looks amazingly different on the way back. Avoid surprises and confusion by glancing back over your shoulder from time to time on the way in to see what the route should look like on the return. If you can't keep track of it all, jot down times, elevations, landmarks, and so on in a notebook. A cryptic few words—"7,600, hit ridge"—can save a lot of grief on the descent. It will remind you that when the party has dropped to 7,600 feet, it's time to leave the ridge and start down the snow slope.

### Think

Your brain is your most valuable navigational tool. As the party heads upward, keep asking yourself questions. How will we recognize this important spot on our return? What will we do if the climb leader is injured? Would we be able to find our way out in a whiteout or if snow covered our tracks? Should we be using wands or other route-marking methods right now? Ask the questions as you go and act on the answers. It may be a matter of think now or pay later.

### Mark the Route If Necessary

There are times when it may be best to mark the route going in so you can find it again on the way out. This situation can come up when the route is over snowfields or glaciers during changeable weather, in

*Fig. 4-2. Photograph of a mountainous area; keyed features are represented on the accompanying topographic map.*

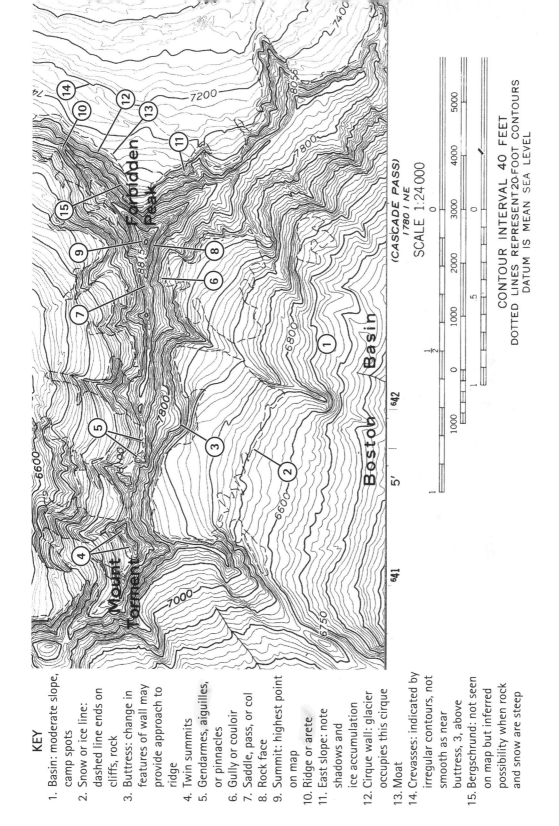

## KEY

1. Basin: moderate slope, camp spots
2. Snow or ice line: dashed line ends on cliffs, rock
3. Buttress: change in features of wall may provide approach to ridge
4. Twin summits
5. Gendarmes, aiguilles, or pinnacles
6. Gully or couloir
7. Saddle, pass, or col
8. Rock face
9. Summit: highest point on map
10. Ridge or arete
11. East slope: note shadows and ice accumulation
12. Cirque wall: glacier occupies this cirque
13. Moat
14. Crevasses: indicated by irregular contours, not smooth as near buttress, 3, above
15. Bergschrund: not seen on map but inferred possibility when rock and snow are steep

(CASCADE PASS)
1780 I NE
SCALE 1:24 000

CONTOUR INTERVAL 40 FEET
DOTTED LINES REPRESENT 20-FOOT CONTOURS
DATUM IS MEAN SEA LEVEL

heavy forest, or when fog or nightfall threatens to hide landmarks. On snow, climbers use thin bamboo wands with tiny flags on top to mark the path. (Chapter 13, Snow Travel and Climbing, explains the construction and use of wands.) In the forest, plastic surveyors' tape is sometimes tied to branches to show the route, but its use is discouraged due to its permanence. From an ecological standpoint, unbleached toilet paper is the best marker, because it will disintegrate during the next rainfall. Use the toilet paper if you are assured of good weather. If not, use brightly colored crepe paper in thin rolls. It will survive the next storm, but will disintegrate over the winter.

One commandment here: REMOVE YOUR MARKERS. Markers are litter, and mountaineers never, ever litter. If there's any chance you will not come back the same way and will not be able to remove the markers, be especially sure to use paper markers.

Rock cairns appear here and there as markers, sometimes dotting an entire route and at other times signaling the point where a route changes direction. These heaps of rock are another imposition on the landscape, and they can create confusion for any traveler but the one who put them together—so don't build them. If there comes a time you decide you must, then tear them down on the way out. The rule is different for existing cairns. Let them be, on the assumption someone may be depending on them.

### Keep Track

As the trip goes on, it may be helpful to mark your progress on the map. Keep yourself oriented so that at any time you can point out your actual position to within half a mile on the map.

Part of navigation is having a sense of your speed. Given all the variables, will it take your party 1 hour to travel 2 miles or will it take 2 hours to travel 1 mile? The answer is rather important if it's 3:00 P.M. and base camp is still 5 miles away. After enough trips into the wilds, you'll be good at estimating wilderness speeds. Here are some typical speeds for an average party, though there will be much variation:

- On a gentle trail, with a day pack: 2 to 3 miles per hour.
- Up a steep trail, with full overnight pack: 1 to 2 miles per hour.
- Traveling cross-country up a moderate slope, with a day pack: 1,000 feet of elevation gain per hour.
- Traveling cross-country up a moderate slope, with full overnight pack: 500 feet of elevation gain per hour.

In heavy brush, the rate of travel can drop to a third or even a quarter of what it would be on a good trail. At high altitudes (above 12,000 feet), your rate of travel will also greatly decrease, perhaps down to as little as a hundred feet of elevation gain per hour.

With a watch and a notebook (or a good memory), you can monitor your rate of progress on any outing. Always make sure to note the time of starting from the trailhead. And note the times you reach important streams, ridges, trail junctions, and other points along the route.

Experienced climbers regularly assess their party's progress and compare it with trip plans. Make estimates—and re-estimates—of the time it will be when you reach the summit or other destination and of the time you will get back to base camp or the trailhead. If it begins to look like your party could become trapped in tricky terrain during darkness, you may decide to change your plans and bivouac in a safe place or to call it a day and return home.

## On Technical Portions of the Climb

When the going gets tough, the tough forget about navigation and start worrying about the next foothold. But keep your map and other route information handy for occasional rests. On rock climbs, don't let the mechanics of technical climbing overwhelm the need to stay on route.

## On the Summit

Here is your golden opportunity to rest, relax, and enjoy—and to learn more about the area and about map reading by comparing the actual view with the way it looks on the map.

On the summit is the place to lay final plans for the descent, a journey often responsible for many more routefinding errors than the ascent. Repeat the trailhead get-together by discussing the route and emergency strategies with everyone. Stress the importance of keeping the party together on the descent, when some climbers will want to race ahead while others lag behind.

## During the Descent

The descent is a time for extra caution as you fight to keep fatigue and inattention at bay. As on the ascent, everyone needs to maintain a good sense of the route and how it relates to the map. Stay together, don't rush, and be even more careful if you're taking a different descent route.

Now imagine your team is almost back to the car after a tough 12-hour climb. You follow a compass bearing right back to the logging road, but you cannot see the car because you are off route by a few degrees. The car is either to the left or the right, so you may have to guess which way to go. It's a bad ending to a good day if the car is a half-mile to the right and you go left. It will be even worse if the car is parked at the end of the road and a routefinding error takes the party beyond that point and on and on through the woods (fig. 4-3a). The intentional offset (also called "aiming off") was invented for this situation (fig. 4-3b). If you fear you might get into this kind of trouble, just travel in a direction that is intentionally offset some amount (say, 20 to 30 degrees) to the right or the left of where you really want to be. When you hit the road (or the river or the ridge), there will be no doubt about which way to turn.

## After the Climb

Back home, write a description of the route and of any problems, mistakes, or unusual features, and do it while the details are fresh in your mind. Imagine what you would like to know if you were about to make the climb for the first time, so you'll be ready with the right answers when another climber asks about it. If the guidebook was confusing or wrong, take time to write to the publisher.

## THE COMPASS

The compass is a very simple device that can do a wondrous thing. It can reveal at any time and any place exactly what direction you are heading. On a simple climb in good weather, the compass may never leave your pack or pocket. But as the route becomes more complex or as the weather worsens, it comes into its own as a critical tool of mountaineering.

A compass is nothing more than a magnetized needle that responds to the earth's magnetic field. Compass-makers have added a few things to this basic unit in order to make it easier to use. But stripped to the core, there's just that needle, aligned with the earth's magnetism, and from that we can figure out any direction.

These are the basic features (fig. 4-4a) of a mountaineering compass:

- A freely rotating magnetic needle—one end is a different color from the other so you can remember which end is pointing north.
- A circular rotating housing for the needle—this is filled with a fluid that dampens (reduces) the vibrations of the needle, making readings more accurate.

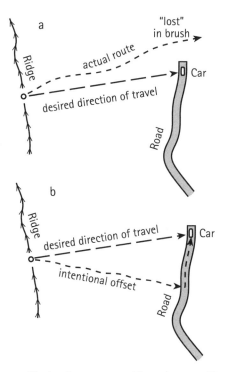

*Fig. 4-3. Navigating to a specific point on a line: a, inevitable minor errors can sometimes have disastrous consequences; b, to avoid such problems, follow a course with an intentional offset.*

- A dial around the circumference of the housing—the dial should be graduated clockwise in degrees from 0 to 360.
- An orienting arrow and a set of parallel meridian lines—these are located beneath the needle.
- An index line—read bearings here.
- A transparent, rectangular base plate for the entire unit—this includes a direction-of-travel line (sometimes with an arrow at one end) to point toward

your objective. The longer the base plate, the easier it is to get an accurate reading.

The following are optional features (fig. 4-4b) available on some mountaineering compasses:

- An adjustable declination arrow—it's well worth the added cost because it's such an easy, dependable way to correct for magnetic declination.
- A sighting mirror—this provides another way to improve accuracy.
- A ruler—this is calibrated in inches or millimeters. Use it for measuring distances on a map.
- A clinometer—use it to measure the angle of a slope. It can help resolve arguments over the steepness of slopes, and it can determine whether you are on the higher of two summits. If there is an upward angle between you and the top of another mountain, then the other summit is higher.
- A magnifying glass—use it to help read closely spaced contour lines.

Some compasses have an adjustable declination arrow but no mirror. Such compasses are midway in price between the basic compass of Figure 4-4a and the full-featured compass of Figure 4-4b. These compasses offer a good compromise for someone who prefers the adjustable declination feature but does not want to pay the added cost of the mirror.

Most compasses have a lanyard—a piece of string a foot or so long for attaching the compass to your belt, jacket, or pack. It's not a good idea to put the lanyard around your neck; this can be an unsafe practice, particularly when doing any technical climbing.

The small, round, cheap compasses without base plates are not precise enough for mountaineering, nor can they be used for precise work with a map. For routefinding, the compass must be accurate to within 1 or 2 degrees. A larger margin of error, say 5 degrees, would land a mountaineering party more than half a mile off target at the end of a 6-mile trip.

## Bearings

A bearing is the direction from one place to another, measured in degrees of angle with respect to an accepted reference line. This reference is the line to true north.

The round dial of a compass is divided just as

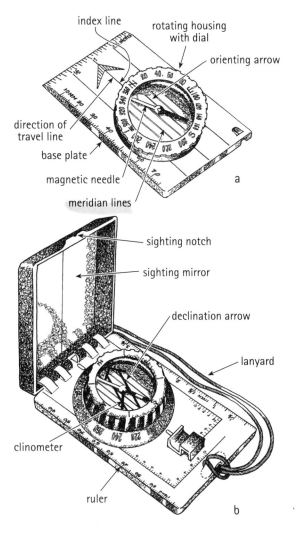

Fig. 4-4. Features of mountaineering compasses: a, essential features; b, useful optional features.

cartographers divide the earth, into 360 degrees. The direction in degrees to each of the cardinal directions, going clockwise around the dial starting from the top, is: north, 0 degrees (the same as 360 degrees); east, 90 degrees; south, 180 degrees; and west, 270 degrees.

The compass is used for two basic tasks regarding bearings:

1. The compass is used to *take* bearings. (You can also say that the compass is used to *measure* bearings.) To take a bearing means to measure the direction from one point to another, either on a map or on the ground.
2. The compass is used to *plot* bearings. (You can also say that the compass is used to *follow* bearings.) To plot a bearing means to set a specified bearing on the compass and then to plot out, or to follow, where that bearing points, either on a map or on the ground.

## Bearings on the Map

The compass is used as a protractor to both measure and plot bearings on a map. Magnetic north and magnetic declination have nothing to do with these calculations. Therefore, ignore the magnetic needle. Never make any use of the magnetic needle when taking or plotting bearings on a map. (The only time the magnetic needle is used on the map is whenever you choose to orient the map to true north, which will be explained later in this chapter. But there's no need to orient the map to measure or plot bearings.)

**To take (measure) a bearing on the map:** Place the compass on the map with one long edge of the base plate running directly between two points of interest. As you measure the bearing from Point A to Point B, see that the direction-of-travel line is pointing in the same direction as *from* A to B. Then turn the rotating housing until its set of meridian lines is parallel to the north–south lines on the map. (Be sure the orienting arrow that turns with the meridian lines is pointing to the top of the map, to north. If you point it toward the bottom, your reading will be 180 degrees off.)

Now read the number that is at the index line. This is the bearing from Point A to Point B.

In the example shown in Figure 4-5, the bearing from Point A, Panic Peak, to Point B, Deception Dome, is 35 degrees. (In this figure, the magnetic needle has

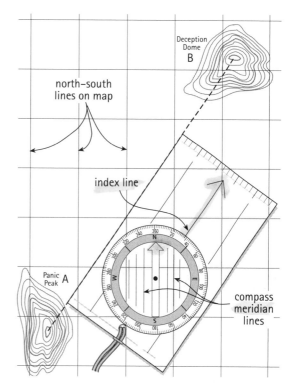

*Fig. 4-5. Taking a bearing on a map with the compass as a protractor (magnetic needle omitted for clarity)*

been omitted to provide a better view of the meridian lines.)

If your map doesn't happen to have north–south lines, just draw some in, parallel to the edge of the map and at intervals of an inch or two, or between the UTM (Universal Transverse Mercator) "tick marks" at the margins of the map. (UTM is a coordinate system, with grid lines at 1,000-meter intervals, that can be used instead of latitude and longitude.)

**To plot (follow) a bearing on the map:** In this case you are starting with a known bearing. And where does that bearing come from? From an actual landscape compass reading. Let's take a hypothetical example (fig. 4-6): A friend returns from a trip, disgusted at himself for leaving his camera somewhere along the trail. During a rest stop, he had taken some pictures of Mount Magnificent. At the same time, he had taken a

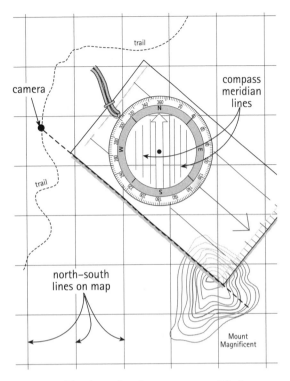

*Fig. 4-6. Plotting a bearing on a map with the compass as a protractor (magnetic needle omitted for clarity)*

bearing on Mount Magnificent and found it to be 130 degrees. That's all you need to know. You're heading into that same area next week, so get out the Magnificent quadrangle, and here is what you do.

First set the bearing of 130 degrees at the compass index line. Place the compass on the map, one long edge of the base plate touching the summit of Mount Magnificent. Rotate the entire compass (not just the housing) until the meridian lines are parallel with the map's north–south lines, and make sure the edge of the base plate is still touching the summit. Again, be sure the orienting arrow points to the top of the map, toward north. Follow the line made by the edge of the base plate, heading in the opposite direction from the direction-of-travel line because the original bearing was measured *toward* the mountain. Where the line crosses the trail is exactly where your friend's camera is (or was).

## Bearings in the Field

Now the magnetic needle gets to do its job. All bearings in the field are based on where the needle points. For the sake of simplicity in these first two examples, we will ignore the effects of magnetic declination, a subject that will be taken up in the next section. Let's imagine we are taking the bearings in Wisconsin along the line of zero declination.

**To take (measure) a bearing in the field:** Hold the compass in front of you and point the direction-of-travel line at the object whose bearing you want to find. Rotate the compass housing until the pointed end of the orienting arrow is aligned with the north-seeking end of the magnetic needle. Read the bearing at the index line (fig. 4-7). And that's all there is to it.

If the compass has no sighting mirror, hold it at or near arm's length and at or near waist level. With a sighting mirror, fold the mirror back at about a 45-degree angle and hold the compass at eye level with the sight pointing at the object. Observe the magnetic needle and the orienting arrow in the mirror as you rotate the housing to align the needle and the arrow. In either case, hold the compass level. Keep it away from ferrous metal objects, which can easily deflect the magnetic needle.

**To plot (follow) a bearing in the field:** Simply reverse the process used to take a bearing. Start by rotating the compass housing until you have set a desired bearing at the index line, say 270 degrees (due west). Hold the compass level in front of you and then turn

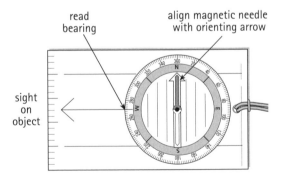

*Fig. 4-7. Taking a compass bearing in the field in an area with zero declination*

your entire body (including your feet) until the north-seeking end of the magnetic needle is aligned with the pointed end of the orienting arrow. The direction-of-travel line is now pointing due west. And that's all there is to that.

## Magnetic Declination

A compass needle is attracted to *magnetic* north, while most maps are oriented to a different point on the earth, the *geographic* north pole ("true north"). This difference between the direction to true north and the direction to magnetic north, measured in degrees, is called *magnetic declination*. A simple compass adjustment or modification is necessary to correct for magnetic declination.

In areas west of the line of zero declination, the magnetic needle points somewhere to the east (to the right) of true north (fig. 4-8), so these areas are said to have *east declination*. It works just the opposite on the other side of the line of zero declination. Here, the magnetic needle points somewhere to the west (left) of true north, so these areas have *west declination*.

Consider a mountain traveler in the state of Nevada, where the declination is 15 degrees east. The true bearing is a measurement of the angle between the line to true north and the line to the objective. The magnetic needle, however, is pulled toward magnetic north, not true north. So instead it measures the angle between the line to magnetic north and the line to the objective. This "magnetic bearing" is 15 degrees less than the true bearing. To get the true bearing, you must *add* 15 degrees to the magnetic bearing.

As in Nevada, climbers in all areas west of the zero declination line must add the declination to the magnetic bearing. In Colorado, for example, about 12 degrees must be added. In Washington State, it is about 19 degrees.

East of the zero-declination line, the declination is

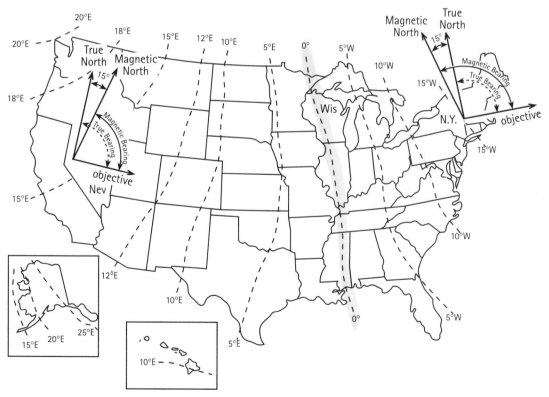

*Fig. 4-8. Magnetic declination in the United States in 1998*

*subtracted* from the magnetic bearing. In the state of New York, for example, the magnetic bearing is 15 degrees greater than the true bearing. Subtracting the declination of 15 degrees gives a wilderness traveler in New York the true bearing.

This is all very simple in theory but can be confusing in practice, and the wilderness is no place for mental arithmetic that can have potentially serious consequences. A more practical way to handle the minor complication of declination is to pay somewhat more for your compass and get one with an adjustable declination arrow instead of a fixed orienting arrow. The declination arrow can be easily set for any declination by following the instructions supplied with the compass. Then the bearing you read at the index line will automatically be the true bearing, and concern about a declination error is one worry you can leave at home.

On compasses without adjustable declination arrows, you can get the same effect by sticking a thin strip of tape to the top or (preferably) the bottom of the rotating housing to serve as a customized declination arrow. Trim the tape to a point, with the point aimed directly at the specific declination for the area where you will be climbing.

In Nevada, your taped declination arrow must point at 15 degrees east (clockwise) from the 360-degree point (marked N for north) on the rotating compass dial (fig. 4-9a). In New York, the declination arrow must point at 15 degrees west (counterclockwise) from the 360-degree point on the dial (fig. 4-9b). In Washington State, the declination arrow must point at 19 degrees east (clockwise) from 360 degrees.

To take or to follow a bearing in the field, follow exactly the same procedure used in the earlier examples from Wisconsin, where the declination is zero. The only difference is that, from now on, you will align the magnetic needle with the *declination arrow* instead of with the orienting arrow.

From here on in this chapter, it is assumed you are using a compass with a declination arrow—either an adjustable arrow or a taped arrow that you have added. For all bearings in the field, you will align the needle with this declination arrow. Unless otherwise stated, all bearings referred to are true bearings, not magnetic.

## Practicing with the Compass

Before you count on your compass skills in the wilderness, test them in the city. The best place to practice is a place where you already know all the answers, like a street intersection where the roads run north–south and east–west.

Take a bearing in a direction you know to be east. When you have pointed the direction-of-travel line or arrow at something that you know is due east of you, and have lined up the declination arrow with the magnetic needle, the number at the index line should be 90 degrees, or within a few degrees of 90. Repeat for the other cardinal directions: south, west, and north. Then do the reverse. Pretend you don't know which way is west. Set 270 degrees (west) at the index line and hold the compass in front of you as you turn your

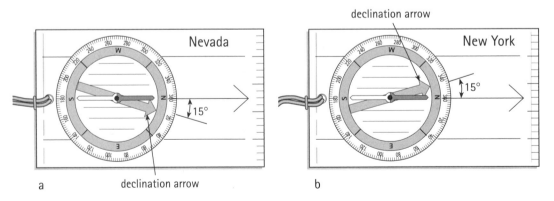

*Fig. 4-9. Compass declination corrections: a, for the area west of the zero-declination line; b, for the area east of the zero-declination line.*

entire body until the needle is again aligned with the declination arrow. The direction-of-travel line should now point west. Does it? Repeat for the other cardinal directions. This set of exercises will help develop skill and self-confidence at compass reading and also is a way to check the accuracy of the compass. And if you make a mistake or two, well, no harm done.

Look for chances to practice in the mountains. A good place is any known location—such as a summit or a lakeshore—from which you can see identifiable landmarks. Take bearings as time permits, plot them on the map, and see how close the result is to your actual location.

## Cautions about Compass Use

As you've gathered by now, there's a big difference between using a compass for working with a map and using a compass for field work. When measuring and plotting bearings on a map, the compass needle is ignored. Just align the meridian lines on the compass housing with the north–south lines on the map. In the field, however, you *must* use the magnetic needle.

You may have heard that metal can mess up a compass reading. It's true. Ferrous objects—iron, steel, and other materials with magnetic properties—will deflect the magnetic needle and produce false readings, as will a battery-powered watch that is within a few inches of a compass. Keep the compass away from belt buckles, ice axes, and other metal objects. If a compass reading doesn't seem to make sense, see if it's being sabotaged by nearby metal.

Keep your wits about you when pointing the declination arrow and the direction-of-travel line. If either is pointed backward—an easy thing to do—the reading will be 180 degrees off. If the bearing is north, the compass will say it's south. Remember that the north-seeking end of the magnetic needle must be aligned with the pointed end of the declination arrow and that the direction-of-travel line must point from you to the objective, not the reverse.

There's yet another way to introduce a 180-degree error in a compass reading. The way to do it is to align the compass meridian lines with the north–south lines on a map but have the declination arrow pointing backward. The way to avoid this is to check that your declination arrow is pointing more or less to north (rather than more or less to south). This check has

nothing to do with declination. It just happens that the arrow is placed in a convenient spot to serve as a reminder of which way to direct the meridian lines.

If in doubt, trust your compass. The compass, correctly used, is almost always right, while your contrary judgment may be clouded by fatigue, confusion, or hurry. If you get a nonsensical reading, check to see you aren't making one of those 180-degree errors. If not, and if there is no metal in sight, verify the reading with other members of the party. If they get the same answer, trust the compass over hunches, blind guesses, and intuition.

## The Map and Compass: A Checklist

Do you have the hang of it? Let's run through the whole procedure. Check off each step as you do it.

### To Take (Measure) a Bearing on a Map

1. Place compass on map, with edge of base plate joining two points of interest.
2. Rotate housing to align compass meridian lines with north–south lines on map.
3. Read bearing at index line.

### To Plot (Follow) a Bearing on a Map

1. Set desired bearing at index line.
2. Place compass on map, with edge of base plate on feature from which you wish to plot bearing.
3. Turn entire compass to align meridian lines with map's north–south lines. The edge of the base plate is the bearing line.

### To Take (Measure) a Bearing in the Field

1. Hold compass level, in front of you, and point direction-of-travel line at desired object.
2. Rotate housing to align declination arrow with magnetic needle.
3. Read bearing at index line.

### To Plot (Follow) a Bearing in the Field

1. Set desired bearing at index line.
2. Hold compass level, in front of you, and turn your entire body until magnetic needle is aligned with declination arrow.
3. Travel in the direction shown by direction-of-travel line.

### AND FOR THE LAST TIME

- Never use the magnetic needle or the declination arrow when measuring or plotting bearings on the map (except to check that the declination arrow is pointing more or less north on the map, not south, as a check that the compass meridian lines are not upside-down).
- When taking or following a bearing in the field, always align the pointed end of the declination arrow with the north-seeking end of the magnetic needle.

## THE ALTIMETER

An altimeter (fig. 4-10), like a compass, provides one simple piece of information that forms the basis for a tremendous amount of vital detail. The compass points the direction to magnetic north. The altimeter gives the elevation. By monitoring the elevation and checking it against the topographic map, mountaineers keep track of their progress, pinpoint their location, and find the way to critical junctions in the route. Every climbing party should have an altimeter.

An altimeter is basically a modified barometer. Both instruments measure air pressure (the weight of air). A barometer indicates air pressure on a scale calibrated in inches or millimeters of mercury, or in millibars. But an altimeter is scaled to read out in feet or meters above sea level—which is made possible because air pressure decreases at a uniform rate with increasing altitude.

The most popular mountaineering altimeter is the digital type (fig. 4-10a), usually combined with a watch and worn on the wrist. The digital wristwatch altimeter has a number of advantages over the analog type (fig. 4-10b). Some digital altimeters display additional information, such as the temperature and the rate of change in altitude gain or loss. Since most climbers wish to wear a watch anyway, this type of altimeter is helpful by combining two functions in one piece of equipment. The altimeter worn on the wrist is more convenient to use than one kept in a pocket or pack and therefore will be used more frequently.

A disadvantage of the digital type is that it requires a battery—which can die out, or become temporarily disconnected due to mechanical shock, causing all data

to be reset to zero. In addition, the liquid-crystal display (LCD) usually goes blank at temperatures below about 0 degrees Fahrenheit (minus 18 degrees Celsius), making it essential to keep the instrument relatively warm. When starting a technical rock-climbing pitch, it's a good idea to remove the altimeter watch from your wrist and attach it to your pack strap or put it into your pack to keep it from getting banged up on the rock.

The analog altimeter has the advantages of being a simpler instrument than a digital one, requiring no battery, and working at temperatures well below zero. To read an analog altimeter, begin by holding it level in the palm of one hand. Look directly down on the needle, your eyes at least a foot above it, to reduce errors due to viewing angle. Tap it lightly several times to overcome any slight friction in the mechanism, and then take an average of several readings.

The accuracy of an altimeter depends on the

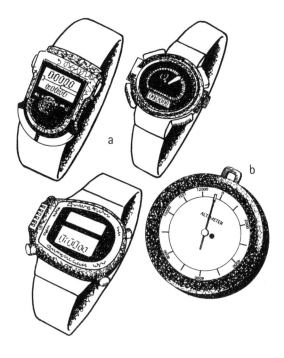

*Fig. 4-10. Typical altimeters: a, digital wristwatch type; b, analog type.*

weather, because a change in weather is generally accompanied by a change in air pressure, which can cause an error in the altimeter reading. A change in barometric pressure of 1 inch of mercury corresponds to a change in altitude reading of roughly 1,000 feet. If you're in camp during a day in which the air pressure increases by two-tenths of an inch (for example, from 30.00 to 30.20 inches), your altimeter will show a reading about 200 feet less than it was at the beginning of the day, even though you've remained at the same place. If you had gone out on a climb during that same day, your elevation readings would likewise be about 200 feet too low. During periods of unstable weather, your indicated elevation may change by as much as 500 feet in one day although your actual elevation has remained the same. Even during apparently stable conditions, an erroneous indicated change in elevation of 100 feet per day is not uncommon.

Because of the strong influence of weather on an altimeter's accuracy, you cannot trust the instrument until you first set it at a location of known elevation. Then it's important while you're traveling to check the reading whenever you reach another point of known elevation so you can reset it if necessary, or at least be aware of the error.

## How Altimeters Aid Mountaineers

The altimeter helps in deciding whether to continue a climb or to turn back, by letting you calculate your rate of ascent. Let's say you have been keeping an hourly check on time and elevation during a climb. It has taken the party 4 hours to climb 3,000 feet, an average of 750 feet per hour. But you know that the actual rate of ascent has been declining with each hour. In fact, the party gained only 500 feet in the past hour, compared with 1,000 feet the first hour. You know that the summit is at an elevation of 8,400 feet, and an altimeter reading shows you're now at 6,400. So you can predict that it will take roughly 4 more hours to reach the summit. Take that information, courtesy of the altimeter, combine it with a look at the weather, the time of day, and the condition of the party members, and you have the data on which to base a sound decision on whether to proceed with the climb or turn back.

An altimeter also can help determine exactly where you are. If you are climbing a ridge or hiking up a trail shown on the map, but don't know exactly where you are along the ridge or trail, check the altimeter for the elevation. Where the ridge or trail reaches that contour line on the map is your likely location.

Another way to ask the altimeter where you are is to start with a compass bearing to a summit or some other known feature. Find that peak on the map, and plot the bearing line from the mountain back toward the climbing party. You now know you must be somewhere along that line. But where? Take an altimeter reading and find out the elevation. Where the compass bearing line crosses a contour line at that elevation is your likely location. This could lead to an ambiguous answer, of course, because the line might cross that contour at several points. That's when you turn to further observations, common sense, and intuition.

Navigation gets easier with the aid of an altimeter. If you top a convenient couloir at 9,400 feet and gain the summit ridge, make a note of that elevation. On the way back, descend the ridge to that elevation and you will easily find the couloir again.

Guidebook descriptions sometimes specify a change in direction at a particular elevation. If it's on an open snowfield or a forested hillside, good luck in making the turn at the right place without an altimeter. The route you have worked out on a topographic map also may depend on course changes at certain elevations, and again the altimeter will keep the party on target. An altimeter obviously helps in mapping, providing elevations of key points along routes included on the map.

The altimeter can help in predicting weather. The readings on an altimeter and on a barometer operate in opposition to each other. When one goes up, the other goes down. An altimeter reading showing an increase in elevation when no actual elevation change has taken place (such as at camp overnight) means a falling barometer, which often predicts deteriorating weather. A decreasing altimeter reading, on the other hand, means increasing barometric pressure and improving weather. This is an oversimplification, of course, as weather forecasting is complicated by the wind, local weather peculiarities, and the rate of barometric pressure change. Stay observant on climbing trips if you want to figure out the relationship between weather and altimeter readings in your area. (See Chapter 23,

Mountain Weather, for more information on interpreting barometric change.)

Some digital wristwatch altimeters can be adjusted to read barometric pressure instead of altitude. But keep in mind that changes in barometric pressure are useful in assessing the weather only when the readings are taken at a single location (such as in camp). Using the altimeter as a barometer while you are climbing will give readings that are influenced not only by changes in the weather but also by changes in your elevation as you climb.

Last but not least, an altimeter will reveal if you're on the real summit when the visibility is too poor to be able to tell by looking around.

## Cautions About Altimeter Use

Try to keep the temperature of an altimeter as constant as possible. Body heat will usually accomplish this with a wristwatch altimeter, particularly if it's worn under a parka when the outside temperature is low. With an analog altimeter, you can keep its temperature relatively constant by carrying it in your pocket rather than in your pack. An altimeter expands and contracts due to variations in its temperature, causing changes in the indicated elevation. A bimetallic element in *temperature-compensated* altimeters adjusts for this effect of temperature when there is no actual change in elevation. The element counterbalances the effect on other parts of the instrument. When you are gaining or losing elevation, however, this adjustment sometimes is not enough, resulting in errors even in altimeters that are temperature-compensated.

Because even the most precise and costly altimeters are strongly affected by the weather, don't be misled into trusting them to accuracies greater than are possible. A typical high-quality altimeter may have a precision (smallest marked division of an analog instrument, or smallest indicated change of a digital altimeter) of 10 or 20 feet. This doesn't mean the altimeter will always be that close to the truth; changes in weather could easily throw the reading off by hundreds of feet. Get to know your own altimeter, use it often, check it at every opportunity, and note differences of opinion between it and the map. You'll soon know just what accuracy to expect, and your altimeter will then be a dependable aid to roving the wilds.

## THE GLOBAL POSITIONING SYSTEM

Global positioning system (GPS) receivers (fig. 4-11) have gained wide acceptance among sailors, arctic explorers, surveyors, and others. They have been available for many years, but it is only recently that they have become small and affordable enough to use in mountaineering. Most weigh less than a pound and are small enough to fit in a jacket pocket.

### How the GPS Works

The U.S. Department of Defense has placed twenty-four GPS satellites into orbit. These satellites continuously broadcast position and timing information to every point on the earth. A small, handheld, portable GPS receiver can acquire signals from these satellites and decode the signals to provide position and altitude. To obtain two-dimensional position information (latitude and longitude), the receiver must acquire signals from three satellites. If a fourth signal is acquired,

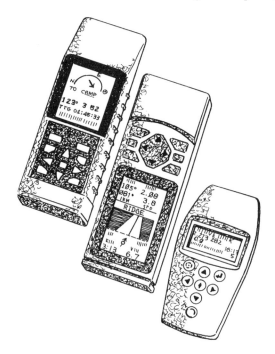

*Fig. 4-11. Different types of GPS receivers*

altitude can also be displayed. Prices and features vary considerably, and some receivers are easier to use than others.

GPS receivers have a basic accuracy capability of approximately 50 feet (15 meters). However, the Department of Defense can degrade this accuracy to prevent its use by perceived enemies. This degradation is called selective availability (SA). When SA is in effect, GPS accuracy is degraded to approximately 300 feet (100 meters). This degree of accuracy is often sufficient to find your way down from a mountaintop to a trailhead parking lot. However, it is generally not adequate for use in detailed routefinding on rock or ice climbs, where route changes may involve finding features only a few yards in size.

A refinement of the GPS called *differential GPS* can provide much more accurate position information. Differential GPS receivers are more complex and more expensive, because they require receiving signals from a ground station in addition to satellites. They can be used only within about 200 to 300 miles of a ground transmitter. Thus, they cannot be used everywhere, as conventional GPS receivers can.

## Using the GPS in Mountaineering

One function of the GPS is to determine your exact position. The GPS receiver is turned on, and within 3 minutes the satellite signals are acquired. The receiver displays your location in latitude and longitude or in UTM coordinates. You can then find this position on a map.

The GPS receiver also can guide you to an objective. If your intended destination is shown on the map but isn't visible in the field, simply enter the map coordinates into the GPS receiver. The receiver then tells you the distance and compass bearing to that objective. Once you are under way, the receiver can tell you the actual bearing that you are following, the distance to the objective, your speed, and other navigational information. If you are not heading directly toward your objective, the receiver will tell you to turn left or right until you are again on the required route.

The receivers also have a *waypoint* feature as an aid to routefinding. Waypoints are positions along the route that are entered into the receiver's memory. To store a waypoint location, simply turn the unit on, allow it to acquire the satellite signals, and push a sequence of buttons to establish the position as a waypoint. There is no need to determine your coordinates on a map. Imagine leaving high camp in good weather but reaching the summit just as thick clouds roll in. Luckily you have been setting waypoints all morning at crucial route junctures. With a few deliberate keystrokes from you, the GPS receiver leads you back to camp, waypoint by waypoint.

A GPS receiver has some obvious advantages over a magnetic compass. A compass can tell you your position only if you have two or more pieces of information, such as bearings from two visible landmarks. The GPS receiver, on the other hand, can tell you your position (to within a sphere of uncertainty with a diameter roughly the size of a football field) *without* any visible landmarks. This can be particularly helpful in fog, white-out, or featureless terrain.

In following a compass bearing, any errors from the desired direction of travel are cumulative. A GPS receiver, however, will always tell you the correct bearing to the objective, no matter how far you stray from the intended direction of travel. For example, if you are using a magnetic compass and are forced to go around an obstruction, you must estimate the distance and bearing you travel so that you can eventually get back on the desired bearing. Even then, it's partly guesswork. But with a GPS receiver, you can simply travel around the obstruction, ask the unit to tell you the *new* bearing to the objective, and follow it.

When planning a climb, you should determine the coordinates of important sites—such as the trailhead, the summit, and critical intermediate points—and enter these into the GPS receiver as waypoints. This is more convenient to do at home than on a climb.

Using the GPS is easiest if the map is overlaid with a grid of UTM coordinates (this applies to many 7.5-minute maps printed in 1989 or later). The distance between UTM coordinate grid lines is 1,000 meters. It is fairly easy to eyeball the position of any point to one-tenth of the UTM grid coordinates, even without a ruler. This will get you to within about 100 meters of the correct position. With the Defense Department's "selective availability" in effect, 100 meters is about as close to the correct position as the GPS receiver will get you anyway.

If your map does not have UTM coordinate lines, it should at least have tick marks on the map's borders that indicate locations of the UTM 1,000-meter coordinate lines. You can then draw in the UTM lines at home before your climb, using a pencil and a long ruler. This will greatly simplify the use of GPS navigation.

Carry at least one extra set of fresh batteries. On a winter trip, keep the receiver in a warm place, such as in an inside jacket pocket.

Some magazine articles and advertising have suggested that GPS receivers will soon make magnetic compasses obsolete. However, one of the most effective uses of the GPS is *in addition to* a compass. For example, you can establish your position and your destination as waypoints on the GPS receiver and have the instrument tell you the distance and compass bearing from your position to your destination. Then you can set this bearing on your magnetic compass, using the compass to travel at the correct bearing, with the GPS receiver turned off to save battery power. You can place the GPS receiver safely in your pack, protecting it from harm as you travel with the compass as a guide. For instance, this technique has been used by parties crossing Greenland. Position fixes are obtained two or three times each day, and the GPS receiver is turned off the rest of the time, saving considerably on battery use and weight.

## Cautions About the Use of GPS Receivers

As marvelous as they are, GPS receivers have a few drawbacks. A major problem is that the unit may not pick up adequate satellite signals while under heavy forest cover or in deep valleys or gullies. In this case, you must either move to an open area or switch to conventional compass techniques.

The GPS receiver is a delicate, complex, battery-powered electronic device that doesn't always prevail over the rigors of the wilderness. Most GPS receivers will not work at temperatures below about 10 degrees Fahrenheit (minus 12 degrees Celsius). They are easily damaged by being dropped or bumped on rock. They are more complicated to use, and more susceptible to human error, than magnetic compasses.

A GPS receiver is no substitute for a good altimeter, because the GPS altitude information is nowhere near as accurate as that provided by an altimeter. In addition, an altimeter can provide barometric pressure information not available from a GPS receiver.

A GPS receiver can be a useful addition to your navigational tools, but it should never replace the use of conventional map and compass techniques for wilderness navigation. Magnetic compasses work at temperatures well below zero, require no batteries, and are so simple that there is very little that can go wrong with them. In addition, they are so inexpensive that every party member can carry one. They are easier to operate and understand than GPS receivers and will operate even in the thickest of forests. The magnetic compass remains the cornerstone of wilderness navigation.

This chapter's discussion of GPS receivers is intended only as a brief introduction to these instruments. A thorough understanding of their use requires close study of the instruction manual provided with the instrument, along with considerable practice. An excellent reference is *GPS Made Easy: Using Global Positioning Systems in the Outdoors,* by Lawrence Letham (Seattle: The Mountaineers, 1995).

## — ORIENTATION BY INSTRUMENT —

Figuring out exactly where you are is usually a relatively simple affair, just looking around and comparing what you see with what is on the map. Sometimes this is not accurate enough, or there is just nothing much nearby to identify on the map. The usual solution then is to get out the compass and try for bearings to some faraway landscape features. This is orientation by instrument. (You can also use a GPS receiver to find your location; however, this section is concerned solely with traditional map-and-compass orientation.)

The goal of orientation is to determine that precise point on the earth where you now stand. Your position can then be represented by a mere dot on the map, which is known as your *point position.* There are two lower levels of orientation. One is called *line position:* the travelers know they are along a certain line on a map—such as a river, a trail, or a bearing or elevation line—but they do not know where they are along the line. The lowest level is *area position:* they know the general area they are in, but that's about it. The primary objective of orientation is to find out your exact point position.

## Point Position

With point position known, there is no question about where you are, and you can use that knowledge in identifying on the map any major feature visible on the landscape. You can also identify on the landscape any visible feature shown on the map.

For example, climbers on the summit of Forbidden Peak know their point position. It's at the top of Forbidden Peak. (You can refer back to the Forbidden topographic map in Figure 4-2.) They see an unknown mountain and want to know what it is. They take a bearing and get 275 degrees. They plot 275 degrees from Forbidden Peak on their topographic map, and it passes through Mount Torment. They conclude that the unknown peak is Mount Torment.

However, if you start by wanting to find Mount Torment, do the map work first. The climbers measure the bearing on the map from where they are, Forbidden, to Mount Torment, and come up with 275 degrees. Keeping 275 at the index line on the compass, the compass is turned until the magnetic needle is aligned with the declination arrow. The direction-of-travel line then points to Mount Torment.

## Line Position

With line position known, the goal is to determine point position. Knowing they are on a trail, ridge, or some other identifiable line, the climbers need only one more trustworthy piece of information. For example, they are on Unsavory Ridge (fig. 4-12)—but exactly where? Off in the distance is Mount Majestic. A bearing on Majestic indicates 220 degrees. Plot 220 degrees from Mount Majestic on the map. Run this line back toward Unsavory Ridge, and where it intersects the ridge is exactly where the climbers are.

## Area Position

The climbers know their area position: they are in the general area of Fantastic Crags (fig. 4-13). They want to determine line position and then, from that, point position. To move from knowing area position to knowing point position, two trustworthy pieces of information are needed.

The climbers may be able to use bearings on two

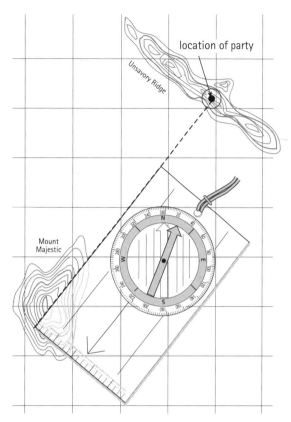

*Fig. 4-12. Orientation with line position known (magnetic needle omitted for clarity)*

visible features. They take a bearing on Fantastic Peak and get a reading of 40 degrees. They plot a line on the map, through Fantastic Peak, at 40 degrees. They know they must be somewhere on that bearing line, so they now have line position. They can also see Unsavory Spire. A bearing on the spire shows 130 degrees. They plot a line on the map, through Unsavory Spire, at 130 degrees. The two bearing lines intersect, and that's where they are.

When you know the area position and there is just one visible feature to take a bearing on, the compass can't provide anything more than line position. That can be a big help, though. Climbers in the general vicinity of Fantastic River then know they are near where the bearing line plotted from the one feature intersects the river. Perhaps from a study of the map they can

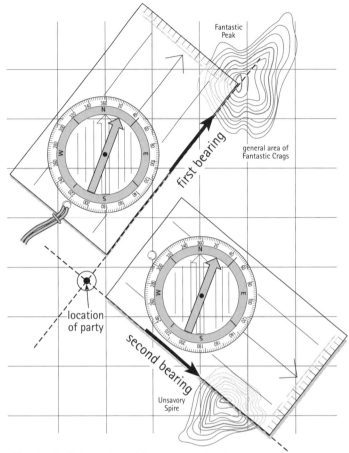

Fig. 4-13. Orientation with area position known (magnetic needle omitted for clarity)

rocks, or you may have an inaccurate map. And who knows? Maybe those peaks weren't really Fantastic and Unsavory in the first place.

## Orienting a Map

During a trip it sometimes helps to hold the map open so that north on the map is pointed in the actual direction of true north. This is known as orienting the map, a good way to gain a better feel of the relationship between the map and the countryside.

It's a simple process (fig. 4-14). Set zero or 360 degrees at the index line of the compass, and place your compass on the map, near its lower left corner. Put the edge of the base plate along the left edge of the map, with the direction of travel line or arrow pointing toward north on the map. Then turn the map and compass together until the north-seeking end of the compass needle is aligned with the pointed end of the declination arrow of the compass. The map is now oriented to the scene before you. (Map orientation can give you a general feel for the area but can't replace the precise methods of orientation that we covered in the preceding paragraphs.)

then figure out just where they are. They can also read the altimeter and see on the map where the bearing line intersects the contour line for that elevation. The closer an angle of intersection is to 90 degrees, the more accurate the point position will be.

Use every scrap of information at your disposal, but be sure your conclusions agree with common sense. If the climbers who took bearings on Fantastic Peak and Unsavory Spire find that the two lines on the map intersect in the river, but the climbers are on a high point of land, something is wrong. Try again. Try to take a bearing on another landmark, and plot it. If lines intersect at a map location with no similarity to the terrain, there might be some magnetic anomaly in the

## NAVIGATION BY INSTRUMENT

Getting from here to there is usually just a matter of keeping an eye on the landscape and watching where you're going, helped by an occasional glance at the map. However, if the current objective is out of sight, you can take compass in hand, set a bearing, and follow the direction-of-travel line as it guides you to the goal. This is navigation by instrument. (You can also use a GPS receiver to direct you to the objective; however, this section is concerned solely with traditional map-and-compass navigation.)

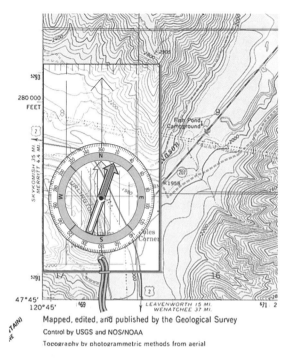

*Fig. 4-14. Using the compass to orient a map in western Washington state*

Navigation by instrument is sometimes the only practical method for finding the pass or base camp or whatever. It also serves as a supplement to other methods and a way of verifying that you're on the right track. Again, use common sense and challenge a compass bearing that defies reason. (Is your declination arrow pointing the wrong way, sending you 180 degrees off course?)

## Map and Compass

The most common situation requiring instrument navigation comes when the route is unclear because the topography is featureless or because landmarks are obscured by forest or fog. You do know exactly where you are and where you want to go and can identify both the current position and the destination on the map. Simply measure the bearing to your objective on the map and then follow that bearing. Let's say you get a bearing of 285 degrees (fig. 4-15a). Read this bearing at the index line and leave it set there as is

(fig. 4-15b). Then hold the compass out in front of you as you rotate your body until the north-seeking end of the magnetic needle is aligned with the pointed end of the declination arrow. The direction-of-travel line now points to the objective (fig. 4-15c). Start walking.

## Compass Alone

Navigators of air and ocean often travel by instrument alone; so can climbers. For example, if you are scrambling toward a pass and clouds begin to obscure it, take a quick compass bearing on the pass. Then

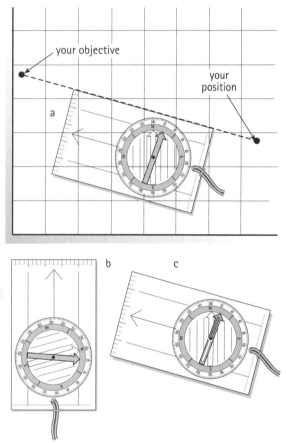

*Fig. 4-15. Navigation using the map and compass: a, measuring the bearing from your position to your destination on the map; b, bearing at index line; c, following the bearing (on a and b magnetic needle omitted for clarity).*

follow the bearing, compass in hand if you wish. You don't even have to note the numerical bearing; just align the magnetic needle with the declination arrow and keep it aligned. Likewise, if you are heading into a valley (fig. 4-16) where fog or forest will hide the mountain that is your goal, take a bearing on the peak before you drop into the valley. Then navigate by compass through the valley. This method becomes more reliable if several people travel together with compass in hand, checking each other's work.

## Using Intermediate Objectives

A handy technique is available for those frustrating times you try to stay exactly on a compass bearing but keep getting diverted by obstructions such as cliffs, dense brush, or crevasses. Try the technique of intermediate objectives. Sight past the obstruction to a tree or rock or other object that is exactly on the bearing line to the principal objective (fig. 4-17a). Then you're free to scramble over to the tree or rock by whatever route is easiest. When you get there, you can be confident that you are still on the correct route. The technique is useful even when there is no obstruction. Moving from intermediate objective to intermediate objective means you can put the compass away for those stretches, rather than having to check it every few steps.

Sometimes on snow, on glaciers, or in fog, there *are* no natural intermediate objectives, just a white, undifferentiated landscape. Then another member of the party can serve as the target (fig. 4-17b). Send that person out to near the limit of visibility or past the obstruction. Wave this person left or right, directly onto the bearing line. That person can then improve the accuracy of the route by taking a *back-bearing* on you. (For a back-bearing, keep the same bearing set at the index line, but for this purpose align the *south-seeking* end of the magnetic needle with the pointed end of the declination arrow.) The combination of a bearing and a back-bearing tends to counteract any compass error.

## LOST

Why do people get lost? For a lot of reasons. Some travel without a map because the route seems obvious. Others fail to check on recent changes in roads and trails. Some folks trust their own instincts over the compass. Others do not bother with the map homework that can start them off with a good mental picture of the area. Some don't pay enough attention to the route on the way in to be able to find it on the way out. Some rely on the skill of their climbing partner, who is just now in the process of getting them lost.

Why *do* people get lost? They don't take the time to think about where they are going, because they are in a hurry. They miss junctions or wander off on game trails. They charge mindlessly ahead despite deteriorating weather and visibility, fatigue, or flagging spirits.

Good navigators are never truly lost—but having learned humility through years of experience, they always carry enough food, clothing, and bivouac gear to get them through hours or even days of temporary confusion.

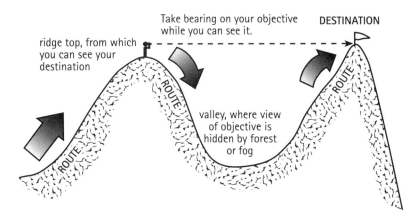

*Fig. 4-16. Following a compass bearing when the view of the objective is obscured by forest or fog*

## What if Your Party Is Lost?

The first rule is to STOP. Avoid the temptation to plunge hopefully on. Try to determine where you are. If that doesn't work, figure out the last time the group *did* know its exact location. If that spot is fairly close, within an hour or so, retrace your steps and get back on route. But if that spot is hours back and you can at least make an intelligent guess about the current position, continue forward, but cautiously and with a sharp eye out for landmarks. If the party tires or darkness falls before you find the route, bivouac for the night.

Groups of two or more rarely become dangerously lost, even if they have no wilderness experience. The real danger comes to an individual who is separated from the rest of the party. For this reason, always try to keep everyone together, and assign a rear guard to keep track of the stragglers.

## What if You Are Lost Alone?

Again, the first rule is to STOP. Look around for other members of the party, shout, and listen for answering shouts. If the only answer is silence, sit down, try to regain your calm, and combat terror with reason.

Once you've calmed down, start doing the right things. Look at your map in an attempt to determine your location, and plan a route home in case you don't connect with the other climbers. Mark your location with a cairn or other objects, and then scout in all directions, each time returning to the marked position. Well before dark, prepare for the night by finding water, firewood, and shelter. Staying busy will raise your spirits. Keep a fire going to give searchers something to see, and try singing so you will have something to do and they will have something to hear.

The odds are that you will be reunited with your group by morning. If not, fight panic. After a night alone, you may decide to hike out to a base-line feature you picked out before the trip—a ridge or stream or highway. If the terrain is too difficult to travel alone, it might be better to concentrate on letting yourself be found. It's easier for rescuers to find a lost climber who stays in one place in the open, builds a fire, and shouts periodically, than one who thrashes on in hysterical hope, one step ahead of the rescue party.

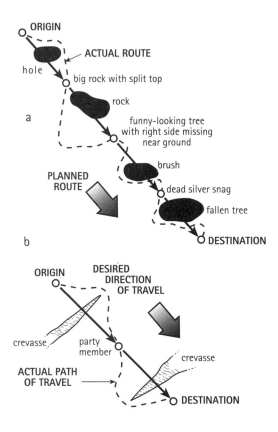

*Fig. 4-17. Use of intermediate objectives: a, in a forest; b, on a glacier.*

## ——— FREEDOM OF THE HILLS ———

The mountains await those who have learned the skills of routefinding and navigation. In large part, navigation is the subject of this entire book because it is so essential to all off-trail adventure.

In medieval times the greatest honor a visitor could receive was the rights of a citizen and the freedom of the city, sometimes even today symbolized by presenting a guest with the "keys to the city." For the modern alpine traveler, navigation is the key to wandering at will through valleys and meadows, up cliffs and over glaciers, earning the rights of a citizen in a magical land, a mountaineer with the freedom of the hills.

# 5
# WILDERNESS TRAVEL

Climbing the mountain is one thing. Getting from the trailhead to the mountain is another. Wilderness travel is the art of getting there—around brush, along trails, and over snow.

When climbers leave the trailhead deep in a valley of Washington State's Cascade Range or head inland from the beach of a British Columbia fjord, tough wilderness travel may lie ahead. The techniques of muddling through brush are not as glamorous as fifth-class rock climbing, but many a peak has been lost in thickets of slide alder. The biggest barriers on the way to a mountaintop often appear below snow line. Learn the skills of wilderness travel and you open the gateway to the summit.

## —— WILDERNESS ROUTEFINDING ——

Whereas navigation is the science of using a map and specialized instruments to determine the direction to an objective, routefinding is the art of working out an efficient route that is within the abilities of the climbing party. Navigation points the way from where you are to where you want to be, but it takes skill in routefinding to surmount the hazards and hurdles between here and there. Intuition and luck play a role in routefinding, but there also are skills that can be learned, and there is no substitute for firsthand experience. Climb with experienced mountaineers, watch their techniques, and ask questions. Routefinding is one of the most satisfying of mountain crafts to master.

Each mountain range has its own peculiarities of geology and climate that affect routefinding. Mountaineers familiar with the Canadian Rockies, accustomed to broad valleys and open forests, will need to learn new rules to contend with the heavily vegetated, narrow canyons of British Columbia's Coast Range. The Pacific Northwest mountaineer used to deep snow at 4,000 feet in June will discover drastically different June conditions in the Sierras of California. Prolonged mountaineering in a single range teaches the lore of routefinding in that area, but a climber entering a new range has to be ready to learn again.

Doing your homework makes for easier trips with fewer routefinding frustrations. Some of the most detailed advice on routes will come out of conversations with local experts. Talk to geologists, rangers, and fellow mountaineers. Ask about climbers' trails that don't appear on the maps and about the best place to ford streams. Take a look at books and other publications about the area you will be visiting. Even though the ascent of a particular peak may be your goal, publications that cover other aspects of the area—its skiing, hiking, geology, and history—also will have something to offer as you plan your trip. Call ahead to the ranger station in the area to get all the information you can—and then stop by in person on your way to the mountain and pick up the latest word on weather and route conditions. Chat with other climbers who have stopped at the station on their way to or from their own mountain adventures.

## APPROACH OBSERVATIONS

Keep an eye on the mountain during the climb approach, studying it for climbing routes. The distant view reveals gross patterns of ridges, cliffs, snowfields, and glaciers, as well as the average angle of inclination.

As you get closer, details of fault lines, bands of cliffs, and crevasse fields show up. Gross patterns seen from far away usually are repeated in finer detail when viewed closer. Ledges revealed by snow or shrubs from a distance often turn out to be "sidewalks" with smaller ledges between. The major fault lines, or weaknesses, visible at a distance are usually accompanied by finer, less obvious repetitions.

If the approach skirts the base of the mountain, it can be viewed from various perspectives. Even moderate slopes can appear to be steep when viewed head-on. A system of ledges indistinguishable against background cliffs may show clearly from another angle with the sky behind. The change of light as the sun traverses the sky often creates revealing shadows. A study of these lengthening or shortening shadows may disclose that apparently sheer cliffs are only moderately angled slopes.

The presence of snow often promises a modest angle and easy climbing, because it doesn't last long on slopes greater than 50 degrees. But beware of nature's illusions. Rime ice adhering to vertical or overhanging cliffs can at first appear to be snow. Deep, high-angle couloirs (gullies) often retain snow or ice year-round, especially when shaded. And what look like brilliantly shining snowfields high on the mountain may actually be ice.

As you near the peak, look for route clues: ridges with lower average incline than the faces they divide; cracks, ledges, and chimneys leading up or across the faces; snowfields or glaciers offering easier or predictable pitches.

Stay alert to climbing hazards. Study snowfields and icefalls for avalanche danger and cliffs for signs of possible rockfall. Snowfields reveal recent rockfall by the appearance of dirty snow or the presence of rock-filled "shell-craters." If the route goes through avalanche and rockfall territory, travel in the cold hours of night, or very early morning, before the sun melts the ice that bonds precariously perched boulders and ice towers. Avoid such areas in heavy rain, which can also loosen this mortar.

Throughout the approach, follow the old mountaineering dictum to "climb with your eyes." Keep evaluating hazards and looking for continuous routes. If the route you are taking begins to look questionable, search for alternatives—and make your decisions on alternatives as early as possible.

The approach is also a time for looking ahead to the end of the day. Think about where you have to be by dark, and consider whether you can travel safely by headlamp if necessary. While you're at it, keep an eye out for emergency campsites, water supplies, and anything else that might make your return trip easier and safer.

## WALKING

The basic skill for mountaineering is a simple act we all do every day: walking. But just as the ability to write doesn't mean you're a writer, the ability to walk doesn't mean you're a wilderness-ready walker. To walk efficiently in the mountains, you must take into account the varied terrain, the weight of your pack, and your physical condition.

### Pace

One of the most valuable techniques in wilderness walking is setting the right pace. Beginners often make one of two mistakes: they walk faster than they should, or they walk slower than they could.

The most common mistake is walking too fast, perhaps out of concern for the long miles ahead or from a desire to perform well in front of companions. But why wear yourself out on the first mile of a 10-mile approach if the whole day happens to be available for the walk? Take your time and enjoy it. A simple test will reveal whether your pace is too fast. If you cannot sustain it hour after hour, you're going too fast.

The other mistake is walking too slowly. Your body complains long before it is hurt. Your muscles may ache but still have 10 miles left in them; your lungs may gasp but be able to go on gasping another 3 hours. A degree of suffering is inevitable on the way to becoming a good long-distance walker. Walking too fast can be fatiguing, but so can walking slower than your body's natural pace.

The most desirable walking speed varies during a day. Get ready for a long trek by stretching your legs, hips, back, and shoulders. Walk slowly at the start, letting the body become aware of the demands to come. Then start striding out, using willpower to get through this period of increasing work until your body experiences its "second wind." Physiologically, this means your heart has stepped up its beat, your blood is circulating more rapidly, and your muscles have loosened. Psychologically, it likely means you are feeling strong and happy.

Vary your pace depending on the trail. Plod slowly and methodically up steep hills; as the grade lessens, pick up the tempo. Each walker has a "natural pace" that works best for the conditions of the moment: time of day, steepness of trail, weight of pack, and so forth. Find your own natural pace and stay with it. Going either faster or slower than your natural pace only creates additional fatigue. Your pace will slow late in the day as fatigue sets in. You may find that adrenaline fuels short bursts of exertion, but there is no "third wind."

## The Rest Step

On steep slopes, in snow, and at higher elevations, an important way of controlling your pace and limiting fatigue is the rest step (fig. 5-1), used whenever legs or lungs need a little time to recuperate between steps. Once you learn it, you'll use it often.

The pace is slow, because for every step there is a pause. The rest takes place after one foot is swung forward for the next step. Support the entire weight of your body on the rear leg while relaxing the muscles of the forward leg. Important: Keep your rear leg straight and locked at the knee so that bone, not muscle, supports the weight.

Synchronize breathing with the sequence. In a typical sequence, you may take a new breath with each step—but the number of breaths per step will be less or more depending on how hard the work is. With one breath per step, inhale as you bring your back foot up to the front; exhale as your front leg rests and your rear leg supports the body's weight. Keep repeating this sequence. Where the air is thin, the lungs need an extra pause—sometimes three or four breaths per step. Make a conscious effort to breathe deeply. Also at higher elevations, take your water in short swallows, because a long pull could leave you breathless.

Mental composure is important with the rest step. The monotony of the pace, especially on glaciers and snowfields, can undermine morale. This is particularly true if you are simply following another climber up the route, and you have no routefinding or step-kicking to

*Fig. 5-1. The rest step*

occupy your thoughts. But be patient. You must trust the technique to slowly but steadily chew up the miles, even when the summit seems to be getting no closer.

## Rests

Even the strongest and most experienced climbers need occasional full rests. During the first half-hour of a trek, stop for a shakedown rest. This lets trekkers loosen or tighten bootlaces, adjust pack straps, add or take off layers of clothing. If the trail starts out steeply, a shakedown rest could be needed after only 10 minutes.

In groups that include both men and women, remember to declare regular party separations (toilet stops), especially out of courtesy to the person who may be too shy to express the need. The day's first party separation should be before the climb begins, at a service station or outhouse near the trailhead.

During the early part of the day, while your body is fresh, take short, infrequent breathers, say once every 1 to 1½ hours. Rest in a standing or semi-reclining position, leaning against a tree or hillside to remove pack weight from the shoulders, take deep breaths, and have a bite to eat and something to drink.

Later in the day, fatigue may demand more complete relaxation, and the party can take a sackout rest every 2 hours or so. When it's about time for a stop, look for a place with special advantages, such as water, a view, flowers, and convenient slopes for unslinging packs. Put on additional clothing to avoid chilling. But don't prolong such lovely rests. It's agonizing to resume a march once muscles become cold and stiff.

A climbing party sprawled along the trail is not getting any closer to its objective. Take rests when necessary; otherwise keep moving, unless there's so much extra time in the day that you can afford a luxury rest.

## Downhill and Sidehill

Walking downhill is less tiring than walking uphill, but it's a mixed blessing. More accidents occur going down than going up. Going down a trail, body weight drops roughly and abruptly on legs and feet. Toes are jammed forward. Jolts travel up the spine to jar the entire body. The result can be blisters and knee cartilage damage, sore toes and blackened nails, headaches, and back pain.

Climbers use a few tricks to ease their way downhill.

Tighten laces to reduce movement inside the boot (and keep your toenails trimmed close). Try using adjustable cross-country ski poles to take some of the load off your knees and provide added stability. Maintain a measured pace that is slower than the one urged by gravity. Bend your knees to cushion the shock with each step, and place your feet lightly, as if they were already sore. This restraint will tire your upper leg muscles, and you'll learn that rests going down a trail are just as essential as on the way up.

The ups and downs of climbing are far preferable to the torments of sidehilling (traversing). Walking across a sidehill twists the ankles, contorts the hips, and destroys balance. If you can abandon a sidehill in order to drop down into a brush-free valley or go up onto a rounded ridge, do it. It's worth going the extra distance. If you're stuck with sidehilling, switchback now and then to shift the strain. Work into your route any flat spots of relief provided by rocks, animal trails, and the ground just above clumps of grass or heather.

## Hiking with the Group

Walking with others involves certain courtesies and considerations that help make travel more efficient and enjoyable.

- Avoid following too closely. Instead of shadowing your companion, give the person ahead of you some space by staying three to five paces back.
- Avoid following too far back, so you don't lose contact with the other hikers or make them continually wait for you.
- Take a look back before you release a branch that you've had to push aside. Call out "branch" so that the person behind you does not get swatted. It's preferable to just slide past a branch rather than to grab it, unless you need it for a "bush belay."
- Step aside when you stop to tie a shoelace, adjust your pack, take a photo, or just admire the view. Step above those passing by, if possible.
- Ask permission to pass, and pick a good spot to do so, instead of elbowing your way forward.
- Act courteously when you meet a party coming the other way. Traditionally the party heading downhill steps aside to let a group of uphill climbers continue upward without breaking pace. However, in

steep terrain or if the downhill party is much larger, it may be more appropriate for the climbers moving uphill to step aside for a few breaths.

- Set a pace that makes good time but does not burn out the slower climbers. If someone cannot keep up, adjust the party's pace so that he or she does not fall too far behind, based on trail and weather conditions. Do not allow anyone to travel alone, either last or first. Give the last person time to catch up with the party at rest stops—and time to rest after getting there.
- Consider having a party member who is moving at an unacceptably slow pace turn back in the company of another hiker or wait at a safe rendezvous point.
- Try putting your slowest person in front, setting the pace. This incentive can cause a slow hiker to set a faster pace than usual.
- Establish designated gathering points for the party during long approaches and descents where routefinding is not a concern. Ask the most experienced members to take front and rear (sweep) positions. This allows party members to move more closely to their own best pace in smaller groups.
- Be cheerful; be dependable. Be someone you would want to hike with.

# TRAILS

The simplest way into the wilderness is a trail. Trails vary widely. One will be spacious and well marked, while another will have a quality of magic about it: now you see it, now you don't.

## Trail Finding

For a wilderness traveler, a trail is any visible route, no matter how ragged, that efficiently gets you where you want to go without battling through brush. Even in popular areas with heavy foot traffic and a lot of signs, keep alert to find and stay on the trail. It's easy to miss a turnoff where a sign is missing or where logging has obliterated part of the trail.

Old blazes cut in tree trunks or ribbon tied to branches often mark the trail through a forest, and rock cairns may show the way above timberline. But these pointers don't last forever, and they aren't always reliable. A tiny cairn or a wisp of ribbon may reflect nothing more than the passage of a climber who was lost or was laying out a route to another destination.

As a trail-seeker, you become a detective who combines the clues (a bit of beaten path here, a tree blaze there) with the use of map, compass, and altimeter and with tips from guidebooks and the experts. On an established trail in the woods in deep snow, saw-cut log ends from maintaining the trail may be the most visible indicator of its location.

The trick is to stay on the trail until the inevitable moment it disappears or until it becomes necessary to head off-trail in order to keep going in the right direction. A trail might go for a long way in the right direction for you, but then head into the wrong valley. It's then time to create your own route, choosing a course that a trail would follow if there were one. Trail builders look for the easiest way to go. Do as they do.

## Sound Trail Practices

Finding the trail is only one half of trailcraft. Using it in a sensitive, caring way is the other. Following are some guidelines for trail use, and also for travel in trailless areas.

- Stay within the bounds of the existing trail, in order to protect trailside vegetation. This usually means walking in single file.
- Stay on the trail even if it's muddy or rutted. Travel on snow when you can.
- Step lightly. Take extra care when traveling through the fragile transition zone between dirt and snow where the soil is water-saturated, especially during spring and late fall.
- Help save vegetation and prevent erosion by not cutting switchbacks.
- Perform light trail maintenance and remove any litter.
- Select resilient areas instead of fragile vegetation for rest breaks.
- Look and photograph instead of picking or collecting.
- Avoid damaging stream banks, in order to help minimize erosion.
- Choose talus or scree instead of fragile meadows for cross-country travel.
- Spread the party out when it's necessary to travel

through trailless meadow, with each hiker taking a separate route to minimize damage to vegetation.

- Leave trailless areas free of cairns and flagging unless they're already there. Let others have the same adventure of routefinding that you experienced. If you need to mark your route, remove the markers on your way down.

## BRUSH

Brush can be a backcountry horror, making for difficult, dangerous travel. Down-slanting vine maple or alder is slippery; brush obscures the peril of cliffs, boulders, and ravines; brush snares ropes.

Brush grows readily in wet, low-altitude, subalpine areas that have few trees. A river that changes course frequently, preventing growth of large trees, permits brush to thrive. In gullies swept by winter avalanches, the shrubs that flourish in summer simply bend undamaged under the snow and quickly sprout again in spring.

Mountaineers prefer mature forests or open ridges. Mature forests help by blocking sunlight, stifling growth of the brush that makes for rough going. In young forests, however, brush thrives. The second-growth timber that springs up densely after a fire or windstorm or logging is at its worst for brush when about 20 feet high.

Blowdowns, avalanche fans, and logging trash are even tougher to get through. The chaotic jumble can slow progress to a crawl and justify a major change of route. Tough and twisted scrub cedar that clings to cliffs and bands of rock presents another hurdle.

When a skirmish with brush is inevitable, there are ways to minimize the hassle. Choose the shortest route across the brushy area. Use fallen trees with long straight trunks as elevated walkways. Push and pull the bushes apart, sometimes by stepping on lower limbs and lifting and clinging to higher ones to make a passageway. On steep terrain, use hardy shrubs as handholds.

The best policy is to avoid brush. Here are some tips:

- Use trails as much as possible. Five miles of trail may be less work than 1 mile through brush.
- Consider traveling when snow covers brush. Some

valleys are easy going in May when you can walk on snow but almost impossible in July when you must burrow through brush.

- Avoid avalanche tracks. The best route up a long valley may be on southern or western slopes, where avalanches hit less frequently. When climbing a valley wall, stay in the trees between avalanche tracks.
- Aim for the heaviest timber. Brush is thinnest under the big trees.
- Travel on talus or scree and remnants of snow, rather than in adjacent thickets.
- Look for game trails. Animals generally follow the path of least resistance.
- Consider traveling on ridges and ridge spurs. They may be dry and brushless, while creek bottoms and valley floors are choked with vegetation.
- If you are bush-bashing up one side of a stream, scout the other side for a better route.
- If your route parallels a stream, consider going right into the stream channel. The streambed could be a tunnel through the brush, though you may have to do some wading. Dry streambeds are sometimes ideal. In deep canyons, however, streams can be choked with fallen trees or interrupted by waterfalls.
- If your route parallels a valley, consider climbing directly to timberline or a ridge top to take a high route above the brush.
- If your valley route has side bluffs, go up to their base. There is often an open flattened corridor next to the rock.

## TALUS AND SCREE

Mountain peaks constantly crumble, dropping rock fragments that pile up below as talus and scree. Most of the rubble pours from gullies and spreads out in fan-shaped cones that often merge into one another, forming a broad band of broken rock between valley greenery and the peaks. These fans can also alternate in vertical strips with forest. Talus consists of the larger fragments, usually big enough to be stepped on individually. Scree is smaller—from the size of coarse sand up to a couple of inches across—and may flow a bit around your feet when you step on it.

These slopes of talus and scree can either help or hinder the climber. Most offer handy brush-free pathways to the mountains, but some are loose and dangerous, with sharp-edged rock that can cause serious injury if you fall.

Talus slopes build gradually over the ages. On the oldest slopes, soil fills the spaces between rocks, locking them together to create smooth pathways. But talus can be very loose on volcanoes and younger mountains, where vegetation hasn't filled in the spaces. Move nimbly on talus, ready to leap away if a rock shifts underfoot. Even large rocks can roll. Disturbing one key stone on a glacial moraine or a talus slope can set off a serious rock avalanche. Try for a route in which the rock is lichen-covered, indicating the rock hasn't moved for a long time. Careful, though: Wet lichen is slippery.

Climbers on talus slopes need to keep alert because it's easy to knock rocks loose. Put your weight onto each rock slowly, ready to change your step if the rock starts to move. Make it a point of personal pride—almost an art form—to not knock a single rock loose. Try to travel outside the fall line of climbers above and below. If you're in a narrow gully and this isn't possible, tread gently and be ready to shout "ROCK!" if a stone is dislodged. Keep close together so a rock set off by one climber can't gain dangerous momentum by the time it reaches other team members. Or permit only one climber to move at a time, while the rest stay in protected spots.

Loose scree can make the uphill going a slow-motion torment, with much of each step being lost as your foot settles in. Stepping on or just above a larger rock in scree can pry or wedge it out. But, happily, on the descent you may be able to move down the scree in a sliding stride something like cross-country skiing. Watch out, though, because scree can sometimes consist only of a thin "ball-bearing" cover over large rocks. If there is any vegetation on the slope, avoid setting off scree slides that can damage the plants.

## SNOW

Snow can be a blessing in wilderness travel. Many peaks are best climbed early in the season because talus, brush, and logging slash are covered by consolidated snow, and snow bridges provide an easy way over streams.

There are hazards, however. Streams will melt the underside of a snow bridge until it can no longer support your weight. You may break through, the result being wet feet, a turned ankle, or, much worse, being carried under the snow by a swift stream. To guard against a dunking, watch for depressions in the snow and variations in color or texture, and listen for sounds of running water. Water emerging at the foot of a snowfield gives a clue to the existence and perhaps the size of a cavity beneath the snow. Probe for thin spots with your ice ax.

The snow next to logs and boulders often covers holes and soft spots called moats, created when the snow melts partially away from the wood and the rock. A moat is common around smaller trees where lower limbs keep the snow from filling in. Probe or avoid likely trouble spots; step wide off logs and rocks and away from treetops poking above the snow. As spring

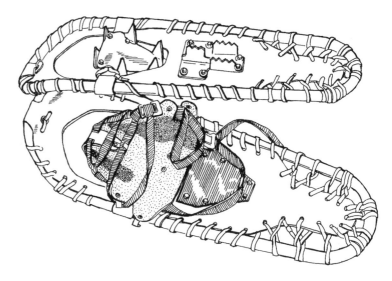

*Fig. 5-2. Modern snowshoes for winter mountaineering*

merges into summer, the best route along a valley floor may be somewhat erratic, taking advantage of each remaining snow patch for the few steps of easy walking it provides.

The techniques of snow travel are the same whether the snow lies high in the mountains or deep in the woods. On steep slopes, you may need safeguards such as an ice ax, a handline, or crampons. With experience, you'll recognize both the dangers and the advantages of snow and learn to use the medium to make wilderness travel easier and more enjoyable.

## STREAMS

In a wilderness without trails or bridges, streams can become a major impediment. In Alaska or the Canadian Coast Range, climbers may spend a great deal of time and energy crossing a perilous river—a crossing that could be the most dangerous part of the entire trip.

### Finding the Crossing

When the peak lies on the far side of a sizable river, the crossing is a major factor in route selection. Try to get a distant overall view of the river, perhaps from a ridge before dropping into the valley. This view can be more useful than a hundred close looks from the riverbank. When a distant view isn't possible or isn't helpful, you're stuck with either thrashing through the river-bottom brush looking for a way across or traversing the slopes high above the river in hopes of spotting a sure crossing.

In deep forest there's a good chance of finding easy passage on a large log or logjam over even the widest river. Higher in the mountains, foot logs are harder to come by, especially if the river changes course periodically and prevents growth of large trees near its channel. If a river is fed by snowmelt, it may be passable in early morning at the time of minimum flow, and a party may camp overnight to wait for this morning low water.

### Making the Crossing

Unfasten the waist and chest straps of your pack before trying any stream crossing that would require swimming if you fell. You must be able to shed the pack in a hurry.

A foot log is a great way across, with an ice ax, a stick, crampons, or a tightly stretched handline to help with balance, traction, and support if the log is thin, slippery, or steeply inclined. Sit down and scoot across if that helps.

Boulders offer another way. Move from boulder to boulder—but only after mentally rehearsing the entire sequence of leaps. Safety lies in smooth and steady progress over stones that may be too slippery and unsteady for you to stop for more than an instant. Use an ice ax or pole for added balance.

If you must wade across, use the widest part of the river. The narrows may be appealing as the shortest way, but they're also the deepest, swiftest, and most dangerous.

If the water is placid and the stones rounded, put your boots in the pack and keep them dry as you wade across. In tougher conditions, wear your boots, but put socks and insoles in the pack. You can drain the boots on the far side, replace the insoles, and put the dry socks back on. You may decide to remove your pants or other clothing in deeper crossings. Loose clothing increases the drag from the water, but it also reduces chilling and may permit a longer crossing before your legs go numb.

The power of swift water is easy to underestimate. It's a relentless force that can push you under and dash you against rocks and logs. A swift stream flowing only shin-deep boils up against the knees. Knee-deep water may boil above the waist and give a disconcerting sensation of buoyancy. Whenever water boils above the knee, it is dangerous, and one false step could have you bouncing in white water from boulder to boulder. Frothy water, containing a great deal of air, is wet enough to drown in but may not be dense enough to float the human body. Streams fed by glaciers present an added difficulty because the bottom is hidden by milky water from glacier-milled rock flour.

If you are trying to cross a stream in which the water is deep but not swift, you can cross with the least force against you by angling downstream at about the same speed as the current. But it's usually best to face upstream, lean into the current, and stab an ice ax or stout pole upstream for a third point of support. The leading foot probes for solid placement on the shifting bottom, the following foot advances, and the ax or pole is thrust into a new position.

Two or more travelers can cross together, taking turns securing each other as one person moves to a solid new stance. Team-crossing with a pole is another method. Team members enter the water, each grasping the pole, which is held parallel to the flow of the stream. The upstream member breaks the force of the current. Anyone who slips hangs onto the pole while the others keep the pole steady.

Using ropes for stream crossings is hazardous and not generally recommended. A taut handline can be helpful, but belaying someone across a river holds the danger that the person could be held by the belay and trapped under water.

If you're being swept downstream in a swift current, the safest position is on your back with feet pointed downstream, backstroking to steer. This position vastly improves your chances for survival with minimal injuries. But if you spot an approaching "strainer" (small dam or collection of debris), switch quickly to normal headfirst swimming; swim furiously to stay high in the water and on top of the debris as you are forced into it. Be alert; the strainer may be your route ashore.

If a member of your party is trapped by the water, you can try to reach out with a pole, ice ax, or branch. Or you may be able to throw a floating object to the person, such as an inflated water bag. Make a realistic evaluation of the danger to yourself before you decide to go into the stream to attempt a hands-on rescue.

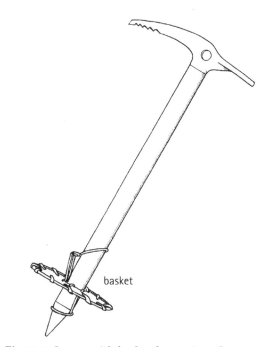

Fig. 5-3. Ice ax, with basket for use in soft snow

--------- THE ICE AX ---------

The tool is called an ice ax, but it's really an invaluable all-purpose item that often goes to work long before snow or ice is reached. Carrying an ax without the skill to use it, however, provides a false sense of security. All too often, climbers slip on hard snow and discover they don't know enough about self-arrest to stop their fall. This indispensable skill comes from practicing on slopes with safe run-outs. (See Chapter 13, Snow Travel and Climbing, for details on this technique and much more information on ice axes.)

The ice ax should be sized both to your body and to the ax's intended use. A simple test can help determine a good size for you. Grasp the head of an ice ax with one hand, fingers extending down the side of the shaft. Stand up straight as you point the ax straight down. For basic climbing or general use, the length of your ax should be the longest length that does not quite touch the floor. For intermediate climbing or higher-angle climbing, the ax should be 5 to 10 centimeters shorter than this; for snowshoeing, 5 to 10 centimeters longer.

The ice ax has a lot of unsuspected uses. It provides a "third leg" during stream fording. It gives a brief touch-and-go balance point while you hop across talus. It also helps with balance on steep trails, serving as a heavy-duty cane going uphill and a brake going down. The ax held diagonally across the body, spike touching the slope, will help you hold a stable, vertical stance on steep hillsides. The ice ax self-arrest is learned as a technique for snow, but many climbers are happy to use their "dirt ax" to stop themselves in steep meadow, forest, and heather.

On open trails, climbers generally strap the ax onto the pack. The straps should be cinched tightly so that the head of the ax lies flat against the pack and the spike points straight up, in order to minimize danger to the people around you. The ice ax comes off the pack and into your hands as the route gets rougher (and as the ax on the pack begins snagging on brush and tree limbs). Leather or rubber guards are available to cover sharp points and edges when the ax is not needed. Be aware that these guards often get knocked off by brush. Remove the guards when the terrain gets difficult. The adze (the broad end of the head), which is seldom used in lower-grade climbing, can be covered with duct tape for safety. If the adze is needed, a couple of blows into ice will quickly cut through the tape.

## ── READY FOR THE WILDERNESS ──

Wilderness travel can be a complicated business because of all the variables of season, terrain, weather, snow, water, and vegetation. By putting the information in this chapter into practice, you can learn to travel safely and efficiently through some of the most awe-inspiring landscapes on earth. Combine this information with the advice in earlier chapters on navigation, camping, food, clothing, and equipment, and you should be ready for the wilderness.

Overleaf: *Mount Rainier (Mount Adams in distance) ©Tom Kirkendall;* overleaf inset: *©Bill Hatcher/ Adventure Photo;*

# PART TWO

# CLIMBING FUNDAMENTALS

# 6
# ROPES, KNOTS, AND CARABINERS

The rope, more than any other piece of equipment, symbolizes climbing and the climber's dependence on another person. Most climbers remember that very first tie-in—and their sudden dependence on the rope and on their partner or partners who joined them on that length of lifesaving line.

The rope is a "safety net" to catch you when the difficulty of a pitch exceeds your abilities or when the unexpected happens—a foothold crumbles, a snow bridge collapses, or a falling rock knocks you off an exposed stance. It is also fundamental to climbing because, when anchored, it can be climbed or descended.

The rope does not work alone in protecting you but is one link in your chain of safety. Other links in that chain include the knots that allow you to use the rope for specialized tasks, the seat harness the rope is tied to, the loops of webbing, known as runners, that help connect the rope to rock or snow, and the carabiners that join parts of the climbing system. These links are the topics of this chapter.

## ROPES

During climbing's infancy, ropes made of natural fibers (manila and sisal) were used to protect climbers, but these ropes were not reliable for holding severe falls. The development of nylon ropes during World War II forever changed the sport. Climbers now had lightweight lines capable of bearing more than 2 tons. The nylon ropes also had a remarkable quality of elasticity. Rather than bringing a falling climber to an abrupt, jolting stop, these nylon ropes stretched and dynamically dissipated much of the energy and reduced the forces associated with the fall.

The first nylon ropes were of "laid" or "twisted" construction. They were composed of many tiny nylon filaments bunched into three or four major strands that were then twisted together to form the rope.

The early nylon ropes were light-years ahead of natural-fiber ropes, but they were stiff to handle and created substantial friction when run through the points of protection used by climbers. Also, they were so elastic that direct-aid climbing with them was inconvenient; they stretched too much when climbers ascended the rope.

Gradually, twisted nylon ropes were replaced by kernmantle ropes, synthetic ropes designed specifically for climbing. Today's kernmantle ropes (fig. 6-1) are composed of a core of braided or parallel nylon filaments

*Fig. 6-1. Construction of a kernmantle rope*

encased in a smooth, woven sheath of nylon. Kernmantle rope maintains the advantages of nylon but minimizes the problems associated with twisted ropes—stiffness, friction, and excessive elasticity. Kernmantle ropes are now the only climbing ropes approved by the Union Internationale des Associations d'Alpinisme (UIAA), the internationally recognized authority in setting standards for climbing equipment.

## Varieties of Climbing Rope

Climbing ropes are available today in a great variety of sizes, lengths, and characteristics. Any rope that you consider buying should have the manufacturer's label, the UIAA rating, and specifications such as length, diameter, and stretch percentage.

A longtime standard for all-around recreational climbing has been a rope that is 11 millimeters in diameter and 50 meters (165 feet) long, with stretch of 6 or 7 percent. However, ropes are also offered in many other diameters, and which one you choose will depend on your intended uses (fig. 6-2). Some ropes are also available in 55-meter or 60-meter lengths.

The smaller-diameter ropes (down to about 8.8 millimeters) are typically used in pairs as part of a double-rope system (see Chapter 11, Leading on Rock). Don't think you're saving weight by using just one of the ropes in the pair; they need to be used together.

You may also encounter no-stretch or very low-stretch ropes. These static ropes are often used for cave exploring or rescue work or as fixed line on expedition-style climbs. Although static ropes may be sold through climbing equipment sources, they are not for recreational climbing. Climbing ropes are dynamic; they stretch.

Specialty ropes are increasingly common. On one style, the last 10 or 15 feet of each end is softer than the rest of the rope for ease of tying and for a little more stretch to cushion short falls. Ropes with just the opposite construction—firmer ends and normal middles—are popular in rock gyms and top-roping situations because they don't "yo-yo" the climber as much when being used for support.

Ropes are also offered with different patterns and colors woven into the sheath. Some have a contrasting color at the midpoint to make it easy to find the middle of the rope; others have distinctively colored ends so it's easier to be aware that you're reaching the end of the rope while belaying—or rappelling.

## Water-Repellent Ropes

Wet ropes are more than unpleasant to handle and heavy to carry. They can freeze and become difficult to manage. Equally important, studies show that ropes hold fewer falls and have about 30 percent less strength when they are wet.

Rope manufacturers treat some of their ropes to

| Rope | Common Use |
|---|---|
| 8 mm static | Fixed lines on expedition-style climbs |
| 8.8 mm dynamic | As part of a double-rope system for rock and ice climbing |
| 9 mm dynamic | Lightweight single rope for simple glacier travel |
| 10 mm dynamic | Lightweight single rope for rock and ice climbing and glacier travel |
| 10.5 mm dynamic | Moderate-weight single rope for rock, ice, and glacier |
| 11 mm dynamic | Standard-weight single rope for rock, ice, and glacier |
| 12 mm static | Caving and rescue (not for climbing) |

*Fig. 6-2. Some typical ropes and their common uses*

make them more water-repellent and therefore stronger in wet conditions. The sheaths and cores of these "dry" ropes are treated with either a silicone-based or Teflon-based coating. The treatment improves the abrasion resistance of some ropes and also reduces friction of the rope as it runs through carabiners. The dry ropes usually cost about 15 percent more than untreated ropes.

## Performance Tests

The UIAA tests equipment to determine which gear meets its standards. In a sport where equipment failure can be fatal, it's wise to purchase equipment that has earned UIAA approval.

In its rope tests, the UIAA checks the strength of the single ropes used in most climbing—which generally measure 10, 10.5, or 11 millimeters in diameter—and also the thinner ropes used in double-rope climbing. The tests mimic real-life climbing falls. To receive UIAA approval, a rope must survive a required minimum number of falls. The tests also measure the impact force of the rope, which determines the stress of the fall on the climber's body and on the pieces of protection.

The UIAA also applies static tension tests to determine how much the ropes elongate under load. Approved ropes must not stretch by more than a specified percentage.

## Rope Care

When you consider what a climbing rope protects—your life—it's easy to understand why it deserves pampering. A new rope is extremely strong, but abusive treatment can soon destroy it.

Stepping on a rope is a common form of abuse that grinds sharp particles into and through the sheath. Over time, the particles act like tiny knives that slice the rope's nylon filaments. Stepping on the rope creates even more damage if it happens to be trapped between a sharp edge and your boot. Be doubly careful about keeping off the rope when you're wearing crampons. The havoc these metallic points can wreak is obvious, although it is not always visible. Crampons can damage the core of a rope without leaving any visible gash on the sheath.

Nonetheless, the sheath gives the best picture of the rope's overall condition. If a crampon wound, excessive abrasion, rockfall, or a sharp edge leaves the sheath looking tattered, the rope's integrity should be seriously questioned. Often the damaged portion of the sheath is near the end, and cutting off a small segment of the rope solves the problem. (Always seal and fuse any cut with a small flame.) But if the damaged section is closer to the center, retire the rope.

Get in the habit of inspecting your rope frequently. Is the sheath clean? If not, wash the rope. Are the ends of the rope fraying or unraveling? If so, fuse them with a flame.

If no obvious blemishes scar the sheath, it's harder to decide when to retire the rope. Its actual condition depends on many factors including frequency of use, the care it has received, the number of falls it has endured, and how old it is. Following are some general guidelines to help you decide when to retire your rope:

- A rope used daily should be retired within a year.
- A rope used during most weekends should give about two years of service.
- An occasionally used rope should be retired after four years (nylon deteriorates over time).
- After a severe fall, it may be wise to replace your rope. A *new* rope may be certified to take five falls, but if your rope is not new, consider all the other factors affecting its condition.

These guidelines assume proper cleaning and storage. Follow the manufacturer's recommendations for care. Generally, a rope should be washed frequently with tepid water and a gentle soap, although some manufacturers recommend against using detergents on water-repellent ropes ("dry ropes"). Wash the rope by hand or in a front-loading machine (ropes can get caught under the agitator in a top-loading machine). Rinse it several times in fresh water and then hang it to dry, out of direct sunlight. Proper cleaning is important for all ropes. Dirt can work its way into the weave, where the particles will grind against individual rope fibers, causing destruction on a microscopic level that could be avoided by washing.

Before storing any rope, be sure it is completely dry. Remove all knots, coil the rope loosely, and store it in a cool, dry area away from sunlight, heat, chemicals,

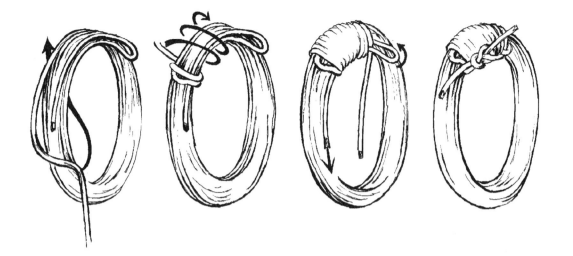

*Fig. 6-3. Mountaineer's coil*

and acids. Fuels and oils don't degrade nylon to any large degree but are best kept away from ropes because they spoil the "feel" and help dirt stick.

## Coiling the Rope

For carrying or storing, the rope is normally coiled, most commonly in the mountaineer's coil (fig. 6-3) or the butterfly coil (fig. 6-4). Most climbers prefer one or the other, but knowing both is useful. The mountaineer's coil is advantageous when the rope is carried over a pack. The butterfly coil is usually a little faster, doesn't kink the rope, and ties snugly to your body if you are not wearing a pack.

Whatever your method, uncoil the rope carefully before use. Untie the cinch knot and then uncoil the rope, one loop at a time, into a pile (a procedure known as "flaking the rope out"). If you just drop the coils and start pulling on one end, you'll probably create a tangled mess. With practice

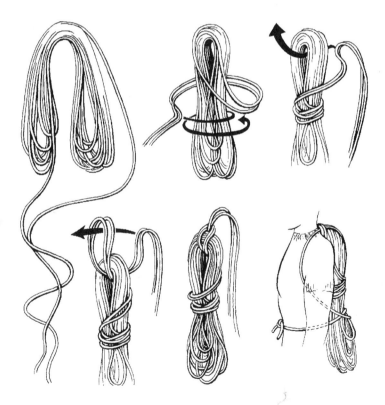

*Fig. 6-4. Butterfly coil*

115

and care, you may be able to get by without flaking the rope out by laying it down carefully so that the coils pay out cleanly. But if you have the least doubt, go ahead and flake it out. You can't take the chance of having a knot or tangle appear as you're belaying.

Rope bags and rope tarps are alternatives to coiling the rope. Both can protect a rope during transport. The tarp, unfolded, helps protect a rope from the ground. The bags and tarps add weight and cost, but for some climbers in some situations, they are worth it.

## KNOTS

Knots allow you to use the rope for many special purposes. They let you tie into the rope, anchor yourself to the mountain, tie two ropes together for long rappels, use slings to climb the rope itself, and much more.

Climbers rely most heavily on a dozen or so different knots and some hitches (figs. 6-6 through 6-27). Practice these until tying them is second nature. If you really want a test, try tying them in a cold, dark shower to give you an idea of the conditions you may someday encounter on a climb.

In some cases, more than one knot can perform a particular task, and the knot chosen is a matter of personal preference. Some knots may be preferred because

they have a higher breaking strength (fig. 6-5). Others may be chosen because they are easier to tie or are less likely to come apart in use.

Regardless of the knot, tie it neatly, keeping the separate strands of the knot parallel and free of twists. Cinch every knot tight, and tie off loose ends with an overhand knot.

Always tie knots in perfect form so that it becomes second nature to recognize a properly tied knot. Then, when it's getting dark or you're tired, and you or someone with you ties a knot that's less than perfect, it will stand out immediately and you'll know to check it closely. Get in the habit of inspecting your knots regularly.

### Overhand Knot

The overhand knot (fig. 6-6) is most often used to secure loose rope ends after another knot has been tied. For instance, it can be used to secure rope ends after tying a square knot (fig. 6-6b) or a rewoven figure-8 (fig. 6-6c).

| | |
|---|---|
| Without knot | 100% |
| Double fisherman's | 65–70% |
| Bowline | 70–75% |
| Water knot (ring bend) | 60–70% |
| Figure-8 | 75–80% |
| Clove hitch | 60–65% |
| Fisherman's | 60–65% |
| Overhand | 60–65% |

Fig. 6-5. Relative breaking strength of rope with knots for single kernmantle rope (courtesy the American Alpine Journal)

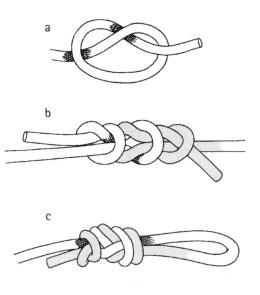

Fig. 6-6. Overhand knot: a, tying an overhand knot; b, overhand knots backing up both sides of a square knot; c, overhand knot backing up a rewoven figure-8.

## Overhand Loop

The overhand loop (fig. 6-7) is often used for leg loops in prusik slings or to make a loop in a doubled rope or a length of webbing.

Fig. 6-7. *Overhand loop*

## Water Knot

The water knot (fig. 6-8), also known as the ring bend, is used most often to tie a length of tubular webbing into a runner. This knot can work loose over time, so be sure the knot is cinched very tight and the tails of the knot are at least 2 inches long. Check the knot often in runners and retie any that have short tails.

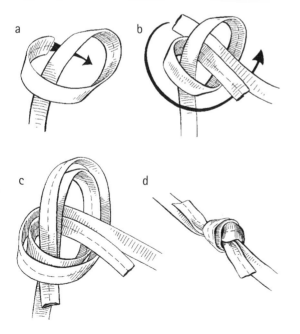

Fig. 6-8. *Water knot (also known as ring bend knot)*

## Square Knot

The general-purpose square knot (fig. 6-9) has many applications. It is often used to finish off a coil of rope.

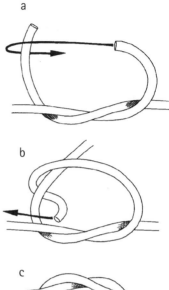

Fig. 6-9. *Square knot*

## Fisherman's Knot

The fisherman's knot (fig. 6-10) can be used to join two ropes together. It has been replaced to a large degree by the double fisherman's knot and is shown here primarily to provide a clearer understanding of the double fisherman's knot.

Fig. 6-10. *Fisherman's knot*

## Double Fisherman's Knot

The double fisherman's knot (fig. 6-11), also known as the grapevine knot, is the most secure and preferred knot for tying the ends of two ropes together for a rappel. It is preferred over two rewoven figure-8 knots because it is less bulky and tends to hang up less when the rope is being pulled down after a rappel.

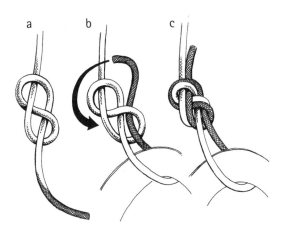

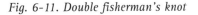

*Fig. 6-11. Double fisherman's knot*

*Fig. 6-13. Rewoven figure-8*

## Figure-8 Loop

The figure-8 loop (fig. 6-12) is a strong knot that can be readily untied after being under a load.

## Double Rewoven Figure-8

The double rewoven figure-8 (fig. 6-14) can be used by the middle person in a three-person rope team to tie the rope to the seat harness. Secure the resulting end loop with an overhand knot or a locking carabiner (the locking carabiner makes a cleaner finish and a smaller knot).

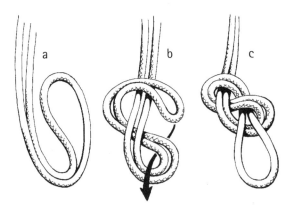

*Fig. 6-12. Figure-8 loop*

## Rewoven Figure-8

The rewoven figure-8 (fig. 6-13) is an excellent knot for tying into a seat harness at the end of the rope. Finish it off by tying an overhand knot in the loose end. This knot also can be used to connect a rope to an anchor.

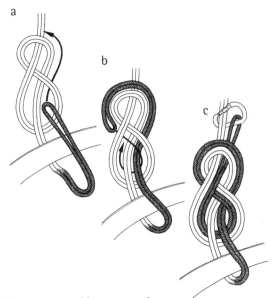

*Fig. 6-14. Double rewoven figure-8*

## Single Bowline

The single bowline (fig. 6-15) makes a loop at the end of the climbing rope that will not slip, and it can secure the rope around a tree or other anchor. The tail end of the rope should come out on the inside of the loop; the knot is much weaker if this end finishes on the outside of the loop. Tie off the tail with an overhand knot.

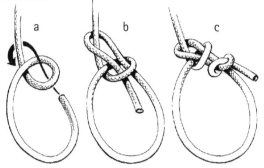

*Fig. 6-15. Single bowline: a, b, tying a single bowline knot; c, single bowline backed up with an overhand knot.*

## Double Bowline

The middle person on a three-person rope can tie the double bowline (fig. 6-16) to the seat harness. Secure the resulting end loop with an overhand knot or a locking carabiner (the locking carabiner makes a cleaner finish and a smaller knot).

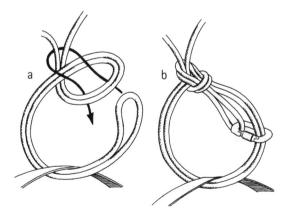

*Fig. 6-16. Double bowline*

## Rewoven Bowline

The rewoven bowline (fig. 6-17) is another excellent knot for tying into a seat harness at the end of the rope. It can be used in place of the rewoven figure-8. If the rewoven portion of the bowline comes untied, you are still tied in with a single bowline.

*Fig. 6-17. Rewoven bowline*

## Single Bowline with a Yosemite Finish

The single bowline with a Yosemite finish is the same as a single bowline, except that the tail retraces the rope until it is parallel with the standing end (fig. 6-18). This knot is easy to untie after it has been loaded, making it a good choice for a top-roping tie-in.

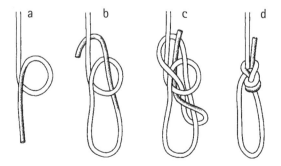

*Fig. 6-18. Single bowline with a Yosemite finish*

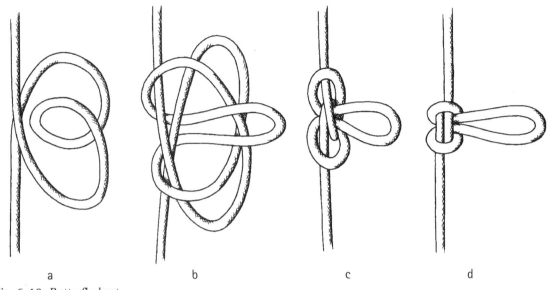

Fig. 6-19. Butterfly knot

## Butterfly Knot

The useful characteristic of the butterfly knot (fig. 6-19) is that it can sustain a pull on either strand of the rope or the loop and not come undone. A connection to this knot is made with a locking carabiner through the loop.

## Clove Hitch

The clove hitch (figs. 6-20 and 6-23) is a quick knot for clipping into a carabiner attached to an anchor. With the clove hitch, it is easy to adjust the length of the rope between the belayer and the anchor without unclipping.

## Girth Hitch, Overhand Slip Knot, and Clove Hitch

The girth hitch (fig. 6-21), the overhand slip knot (fig. 6-22), and the clove hitch (fig. 6-23) are simple knots that can be used to tie off partially driven pitons or ice screws.

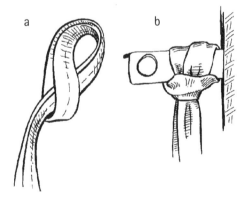

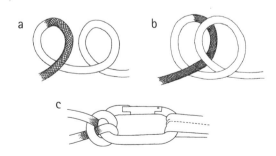

Fig. 6-20. Clove hitch

Fig. 6-21. Girth hitch

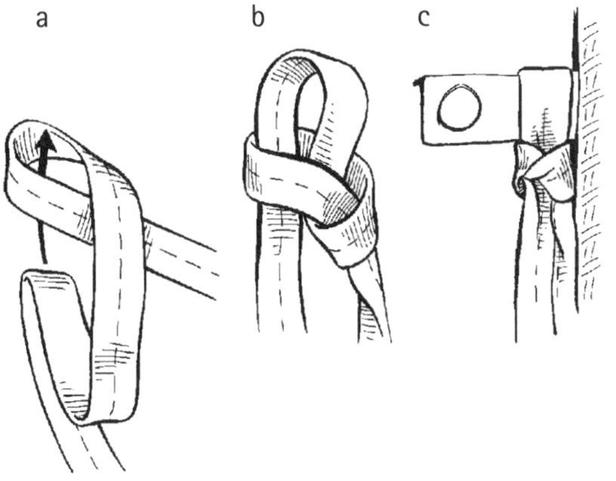

*Fig. 6-22. Overhand slip knot*

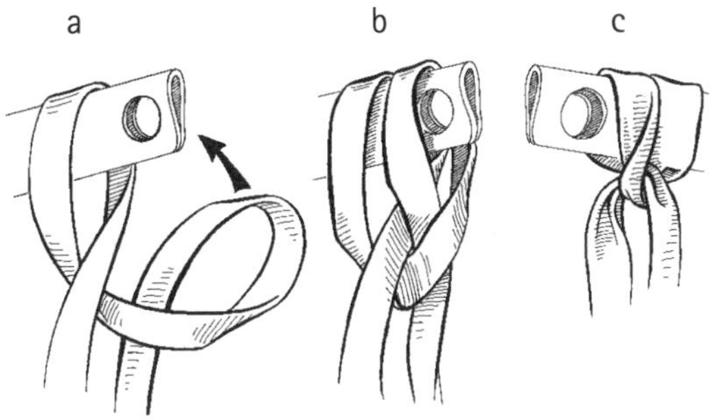

*Fig. 6-23. Clove hitch*

## Friction Knots

Friction knots provide a quick and simple way to set up a system for ascending or descending a climbing rope. The knots grip the climbing rope when weight is on them, but are free to move when the weight is released. The best known friction knot is the prusik, but others such as the Bachmann and the Klemheist are also useful.

### Prusik Knot

The prusik knot (fig. 6-24) requires a few wraps of an accessory cord around the climbing rope, and it's ready to go to work. The cord is usually a loop (sling)

of 5-millimeter to 7-millimeter perlon, wrapped two or three times around the rope. Icy ropes or heavy loads require more wraps than dry ropes or light loads.

The accessory cord must be smaller in diameter than the climbing rope, and the greater the difference in diameter, the better it grips. However, small-diameter cords make the prusik knot a little harder to manipulate than cords of larger diameter. Experiment to see which diameter of cord works best for you. Webbing isn't usually used for prusik knots because it may not hold.

By attaching two slings to a climbing rope with prusik knots, you can "climb" up the rope. Chapter 14, Glacier Travel and Crevasse Rescue, explains two methods of ascending the rope using prusiks.

The prusik knot is also used to help in raising and lowering people and equipment during rescues.

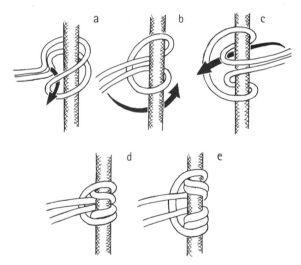

*Fig. 6-24. Prusik knot: a–c, tying sequence for the prusik knot; d, two-wrap prusik knot; e, three-wrap prusik knot.*

### Bachmann Knot

The Bachmann knot (fig. 6-25) is used for the same purposes as a prusik knot. The Bachmann is tied around a carabiner, making it much easier to loosen and slide than a prusik. It has the virtue of sometimes being "self-tending" when it is used to help hoist an injured climber.

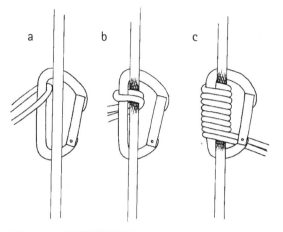

*Fig. 6-25. Bachmann knot*

## Klemheist Knot

The Klemheist knot (fig. 6-26) is another alternative to the prusik, with the advantage that it allows you to use a sling made from either accessory cord or webbing. This can be a big help to a climber caught with an ample supply of webbing but little cord.

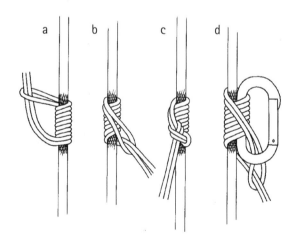

*Fig. 6-26. Klemheist knot: a and b, winding and threading the basic Klemheist; c, Klemheist tied off; d, Klemheist tied around a carabiner.*

The cord or webbing is wound around the main rope in a spiral and then threaded through the loop of the top wrap. The Klemheist tied off (fig. 6-26c) is less likely to jam and easier to loosen and slide than the basic Klemheist (fig. 6-26b). The Klemheist can also be tied around a carabiner (fig. 6-26d), providing a good handhold.

## Münter Hitch

The Münter is a simple hitch in the rope that is clipped into a carabiner to put friction on the line. It provides an excellent method of belaying a leader or lowering a climber because the hitch is reversible (you can feed rope out of the carabiner or pull rope back in through the carabiner) and because the hitch slides (yet is easy to stop if you hold the braking end of the rope). It can also provide the necessary rope friction for rappelling, though it puts more twist in the rope than other rappel methods.

The Münter hitch (fig. 6-27) is very easy to set up and use, and the only equipment needed is a large pear-shaped locking carabiner. Even if you prefer to use a specialized belay device, this hitch is worth knowing as a backup for the time you forget or lose your device.

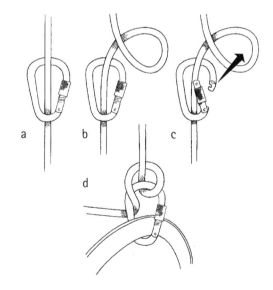

*Fig. 6-27. The Münter hitch*

*Butterfly knot*

## HARNESSES

In the old days, climbers looped the climbing rope around the waist several times and tied in with a bowline on a coil (fig 6-28). That practice is no longer encouraged because long falls onto waist loops can injure your back and ribs. Falls that leave you hanging, such as a fall into a crevasse or over the lip of an overhang, will cause the rope to ride up and constrict your diaphragm and could suffocate you.

Nowadays, climbers who value their health tie the rope into a harness designed to distribute the force of a fall over a larger percentage of the body. (The bowline on a coil is an option for emergency use if no harness or harness material is available.) A climber at the end of a rope ties into the harness with a knot such as

the rewoven figure-8 or the rewoven bowline. A climber in the middle of a rope usually ties into the harness with a double rewoven figure-8 or a double bowline.

Harnesses deteriorate with use, abuse, and disuse. Consider replacing them about as often as your climbing rope.

### Seat Harness

With properly fitted leg loops, a seat harness rides snugly above your hip bones yet transfers the force of a fall over the entire pelvis. It also provides a comfortable seat while rappelling.

Several features are particularly desirable in a mountaineering seat harness (fig. 6-29). Adjustable leg loops allow you to maintain a snug fit no matter how few or how many layers of clothing you wear. Loops

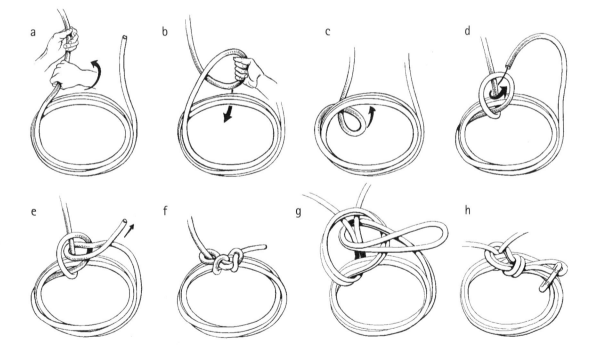

*Fig. 6-28. Bowline on a coil, to attach rope around the waist of a climber who does not have a harness: a–f, for climber at the end of a rope; g and h, for middle climber. It is not recommended that these knots be used around the body except in emergencies.*

*Fig. 6-29. Seat harness*

that can be unbuckled permit toilet calls without having to remove the harness or even untie from the rope. Having the waist buckle located toward one side helps avoid conflict with your rope tie-in or with the locking carabiner that you will attach to the harness for use in belaying and rappelling. Hardware loops are desirable for carrying carabiners and other pieces of climbing gear, while padded waist and leg loops give added comfort. Before buying a harness, try it on to be sure it fits properly over your climbing clothes.

With the profusion of harness styles on the market, you will need to consult the manufacturer's instructions to know how to safely wear and tie into a particular harness. Printed instructions accompany any new harness, and they also are usually sewn inside the

waist belt. For most harnesses, you will need to pass the waist strap back over and through the main buckle a second time for safety. Be sure at least 2 inches of strap extends beyond the buckle after reweaving it.

A variant on the seat harness is the waist band known as a swami belt combined with leg loops. Just like a full seat harness, commercial swami belts are secured with a buckle, and they usually include padding and hardware loops. Climbers normally combine the swami belt with separate leg loops to complete a full seat–harness system.

Swami belts have been used alone, without the addition of leg loops, but this use is not recommended. If you are left hanging, the belt can creep up and restrict your breathing. Leg loops keep the swami from creeping up, and it distributes the force of a fall to a larger area of the body.

## Homemade Seat Harness

A homemade seat harness is an option for linking yourself to the rope, and you can make a simple one from 22 feet of 1-inch tubular webbing (fig. 6-30). Starting about $4\frac{1}{2}$ feet from one end of the webbing, tie two leg loops just large enough to fit over your climbing clothing, and leave about a 6-inch bridge between the loops. Once they are tied and adjusted, leave the loops in place. That completes construction of the harness.

To wear it, step into the leg loops and wrap the webbing (fig. 6-30a–d). Use a square knot or water knot to tie off the harness, and then secure the ends with overhand knots.

To complete this system, wrap a separate piece of webbing (about 12 feet long) around your waist two times and tie it with a water knot. Connect this safety loop to the harness with a locking carabiner.

While this is a low-cost seat harness, it's not comfortable to hang in for long. The webbing is narrower than in commercial harnesses and tends to cut into your body.

## Body Harness

The only harnesses approved by the UIAA are full body harnesses (fig. 6-31). Body harnesses, which incorporate both a chest and a seat harness, have a higher tie-in point. This reduces the chance of flipping over

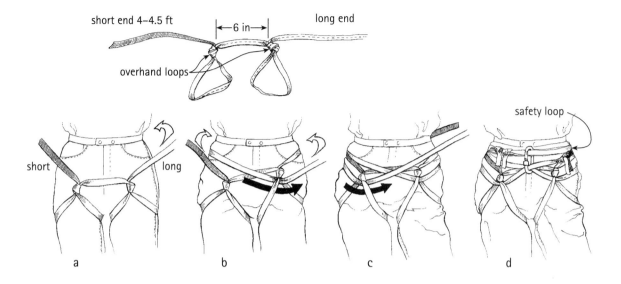

Fig. 6-30. Homemade seat harnesses

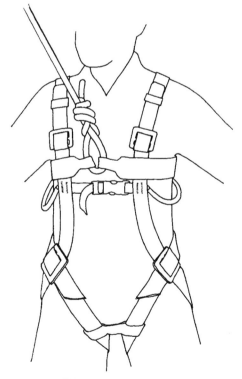

Fig. 6-31. Full body harness

backward during a fall, especially if a pack makes you top-heavy. Because a body harness distributes the force of a fall throughout the trunk of your body, there is less danger of lower-back injury.

Although they are unquestionably safer, body harnesses have not found popular favor in mountaineering. They are more expensive and restrictive and make it hard to add or remove clothing. Instead, most climbers use a seat harness and then improvise a chest harness when one is warranted, such as when climbing with a heavy pack, crossing glaciers, or aid climbing under large overhangs.

## Chest Harness

A chest harness can be readily improvised with a long loop of webbing (a long runner). One popular design depends on a carabiner to bring the ends of the harness together at your chest.

To make this carabiner chest harness (fig. 6-32), start with $9^{1}/_{2}$ feet of 1-inch tubular webbing. Tie it into a loop, with a water knot. Use a distinctive color for the webbing if you want to keep the chest harness identifiable; otherwise, it looks just like any other double-length runner (see the next section, on runners).

125

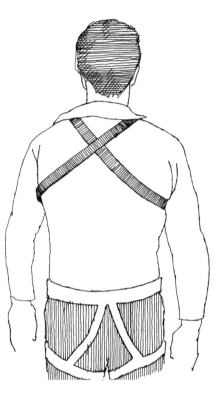

*Fig. 6-32. Carabiner chest harness*

Give the loop a half twist to create two temporary loops, and push one arm all the way through each loop. Lift the runner over your head and let it drop against your back; then pull the two sides together and clip with a carabiner at your chest.

A chest harness will help keep you upright after a fall or while ascending a rope using prusiks or mechanical ascenders. Following a fall, you simply clip the climbing rope through the carabiner of the chest harness, providing stability and helping you stay right side up. The rope isn't usually clipped into the chest harness during rock climbing or general mountaineering; it is sometimes clipped into the chest harness during glacier travel (see Chapter 14, Glacier Travel and Crevasse Rescue).

## RUNNERS

Loops of tubular webbing or cord, called runners, are among the simplest pieces of climbing equipment and among the most useful. You'll use them in endless ways as a critical link in climbing systems that involve you, your rope, safety anchors, and carabiners.

Runners are usually made by tying a loop with $9/16$-inch to 1-inch tubular webbing or with 8-millimeter to 9-millimeter perlon accessory cord. With webbing, a water knot is typically used to make the loop; with cord, a double fisherman's knot does the job. Melt the ends of any webbing or cord with a small flame to keep the ends from unraveling.

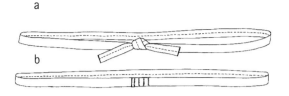

Fig. 6-33. *Runners made of webbing: a, tied runner;*
*b, sewn runner.*

The most common choice for making runners is
1-inch tubular webbing. Standard runners are made
from $5^1/_2$ feet of webbing. Double-length runners require $9^1/_2$ feet of webbing, and triple-length runners
need 15 feet. A beginning climber should own about
six single runners, two doubles, and a triple.

To help you quickly identify the different lengths,
make singles from one color of webbing, doubles from
another color, and triples from a third color. Write your
initials and the date you made a runner on the tails
that are left after you tie the water knot. Runners
should be retired regularly, using the same considerations as for retiring a rope.

Tied runners (fig. 6-33a) have
several advantages over commercially made sewn runners. They
are inexpensive to make, can be
untied and threaded around trees
and natural chockstones, and can
be untied and retied with another
runner to create extra-long runners. However, sewn runners (fig.
6-33b) also have some advantages. Sewn runners are generally
stronger, usually lighter, and less
bulky than knotted runners. They
also eliminate the possibility of
the knot untying, a continual
concern with homemade runners.

Sewn runners come in four normal lengths: 2-inch and 4-inch
("quick draws"), 12-inch (half-
lengths), and 24-inch (full-
lengths). They also come in a

variety of widths, with $9/_{16}$-inch, $11/_{16}$-inch, and 1-inch
being the most common. Runners made from Spec-
tra, a high-performance fiber that is stronger, more
durable, and less susceptible to ultraviolet deterioration, are usually made in $9/_{16}$-inch webbing.

Some sewn runners used in high-angle climbing
are designed so that part of the stitching rips apart in
a controlled manner during a fall, lessening the shock
on the anchor. Once this stitching is broken, the runner is retired.

## CARABINERS

Carabiners are another versatile and indispensable tool
of climbing. These ingenious metal snap-links are used
for belaying, rappelling, prusiking, clipping into safety
anchors, securing the rope to points of protection, and
numerous other tasks.

Carabiners come in many sizes and shapes (fig. 6-34).
Ovals (fig. 6-34a) are very popular because their symmetry makes them good for many purposes. D carabiners (fig. 6-34b) also offer a good general-purpose shape
and are stronger than ovals because more of the load
is transferred to the long axis and away from the gate,

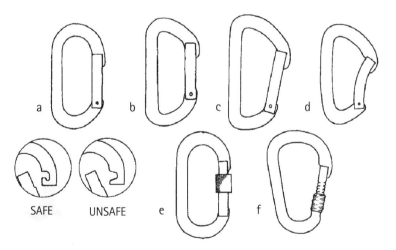

Fig. 6-34. *Carabiners: a, oval carabiner, with inset showing safe*
*(notched) and unsafe (unnotched) carabiner gates; b, standard D*
*carabiner; c, offset D carabiner; d, bent-gate carabiner; e, standard*
*locking carabiner; f, pear-shaped locking carabiner.*

the typical point of failure. Offset D's (fig. 6-34c) have the strength advantage of standard D's, but the gate on an offset D opens wider, making them easier to clip in awkward situations. Bent-gate carabiners (fig. 6-34d) are a specialty design most commonly used on difficult routes where it's important to quickly clip and unclip the carabiners from the feel of the gates alone. Bent-gate carabiners should always be used with a runner so that they are free to rotate.

Locking carabiners (fig. 6-34e–f), with a sleeve that screws over one end of the gate to prevent accidental opening, give a wider margin of safety for rappelling, belaying, or clipping into anchors. Some locking carabiners even have a spring that automatically positions the sleeve whenever the gate is closed. You must not forget to lock these carabiners, but you must always unlock them as well, which can be a nuisance.

Pear-shaped locking carabiners (fig. 6-34f) are much larger at the gate-opening end than at the hinge end and are ideal for belaying with the Münter hitch. They are also a good choice for your seat-harness carabiner. The extra cost and weight are more than justified by the increased ease of loading and managing all the ropes, knots, cords, runners, and such that accumulate there.

Two regular carabiners can be substituted for a locking carabiner when they are used together with their gates on opposite sides (fig. 6-35). This configu-

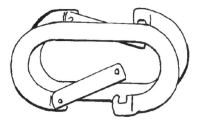

*Fig. 6-35. Proper positioning of gates on double carabiners. The gates are on opposite sides and form an X when both are opened.*

ration keeps them from being forced open and accidentally unclipping. Check to see you have them lined up correctly by opening both gates at the same time; the gates should cross, forming an X.

Some carabiners are made from bars with cross-sections that are oval, T-shaped, or cross-shaped—as opposed to round—in order to save weight (fig. 6-36). Be aware that the T-shaped and cross-shaped material will greatly increase friction if they are used in contact with a running rope.

A few basics apply to the use and care of all carabiners. First, always make sure the force on a carabiner falls on the long axis, and be especially careful

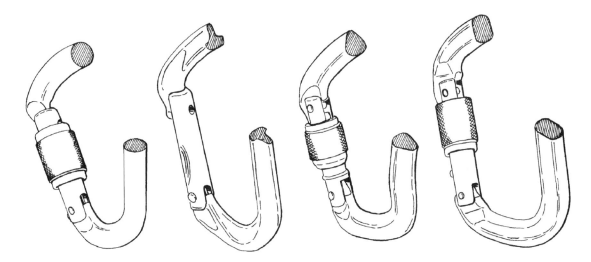

*Fig. 6-36. Carabiner cross-sections*

that the gate does not receive the load. Check the carabiner gates occasionally. A gate should open easily, even when the carabiner is loaded, and the gate should have good side-to-side rigidity when open.

A dirty gate can be cleaned by applying a solvent or lubricant to the hinge (the lightest-weight oil, citrus solvent, or products such as WD40), working the hinge until it operates smoothly again, and then dipping the carabiner in boiling water for about 20 seconds to remove the cleaning agent.

Finally, remember that a carabiner that has fallen off a cliff onto a hard surface has probably suffered hairline fractures and should be retired. Resist using such a "treasure" found at the base of a climb. In fact, you should resist using any critical climbing equipment if you don't know its history. Ropes, harnesses, runners, carabiners, protection pieces, and belay devices are all vital links in your chain of protection. Secondhand equipment, whether found or passed along without an account of its use, increases the possibility of a weak link in the chain you depend on for safe climbing.

# 7

# BELAYING

Belaying is a bedrock technique of climbing safety, a system of using a rope to stop a fall if one should occur. Belaying works like magic but, like any good magic trick, it takes a lot of practice to do well and requires a basic understanding of underlying principles.

In its simplest form, a belay consists of nothing more than a rope that runs from a climber to another person, the belayer, who is ready to stop a fall. Three things make the magic work: a skilled belayer, a stance or anchor to resist the pull of the fall, and a method of applying a stopping force to the rope. There are many ways to apply this force, a variety of stances, and many methods of setting up and tying into an anchor. This chapter introduces the principal techniques and major options of belaying.

## THE BASICS OF BELAYING

### A Simple Top-Rope Belay

Suppose you and I want to go climbing. We get our rope and other equipment and hike to the base of a local peak on a side with a steep cliff, broken by occasional ledges. We each tie into an end of the rope. Then you climb up the cliff, simply trailing the rope behind you, while I watch. When you are almost out of rope, you stop at a ledge with a tree a few feet away from the edge.

You were taking a risk as you climbed the cliff; if you had slipped, you would have fallen all the way

down to the start of the climb, and there would have been nothing I could do to minimize your fall. We'll see later what you could have done to reduce your risk, but for now we'll concentrate on your next job, which is to find a way to let me climb up to you with little danger of any serious fall.

To do this, you put a runner around the tree, clip a carabiner into it, and then attach the climbing rope to the carabiner with just enough rope between your harness tie-in knot and the carabiner so you can sit comfortably near the edge and perhaps brace your feet on something. The rope runs from your tie-in knot around your left side to the carabiner. You are now *anchored* to the mountain.

Now you pull up the slack rope. When the slack is all out and I feel a tug on my body, I yell "That's me!" or some other prearranged signal. Next, you put the rope around your back and grip the rope with your right hand with the palm up, making sure that none of the slack you pulled up is between your right hand and me: the rope runs from your right hand around your back or hips from right to left, running over the section of rope that attaches you to the anchor (fig. 7-1a). The right hand is now the *braking hand* and the left hand is the *feeling hand*.

Now you yell down "Belay on!" which tells me that I can start climbing. There may be a couple more voice signals, or I may just start climbing while you take in the rope, knowing that if I slip off the rock and yell "Falling!" you will stop me after a very short drop and I can then regain my footing.

And how will you be able to stop me? Simply by

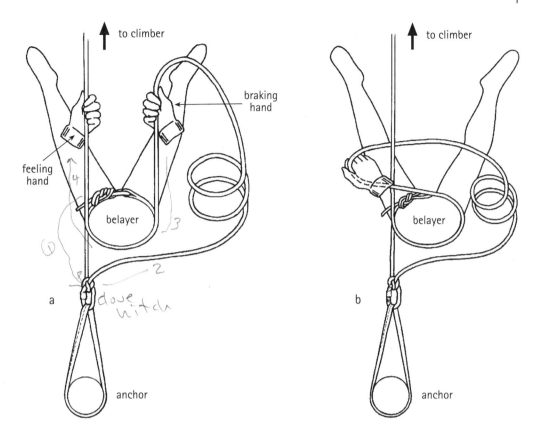

*Fig. 7-1. Belaying a follower: a, the belayer is anchored and ready to belay a follower—the rope goes from the belayer's braking hand, around the back (to produce friction), and down to the climber; b, the braking position, with the braking arm pulled across the stomach to create additional friction.*

gripping the rope tightly with your braking hand and assuming the *braking* (or *arrest*) position (fig. 7-1b) at the instant I shout "Falling!" The force you exert by gripping the rope is *amplified* by the *friction* of the rope running around your body so that the upward, or stopping, force the rope exerts on me is much greater than what you can exert with your hand alone. The purpose of the braking position—your right arm pulled across your stomach—is to increase the amount of friction between the rope and your body, thereby increasing the stopping force.

But what if I fall at a time when you have your braking hand momentarily off the rope? Simple: I'll fall farther, perhaps all the way to the bottom of the cliff.

However, a skilled belayer *never* removes the braking hand from the rope. There is a specific sequence of hand motions (fig. 7-2) you will use to take in the rope as I climb that eliminates this possibility: With both hands on the rope, starting with your braking hand close to you and the feeling hand extended, pull in the rope with both hands (fig. 7-2a-b). Then slide the feeling hand forward beyond the braking hand and grasp both strands of rope with the feeling hand (fig. 7-2c). Finally, slide the braking hand back toward you (fig. 7-2d); then let the feeling hand drop the braking-hand strand of the rope, and repeat the sequence of hand motions. You never need to take your braking hand off the rope.

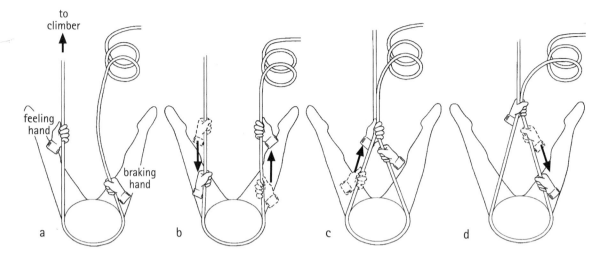

*Fig. 7-2. Hand motions for taking in rope; the braking hand never leaves the rope.*

Now let's look at some of the other features of this arrangement and see what they're for. What is the point of attaching yourself to an anchor? Consider that the upward–stopping–force you can exert on me through hand grip and friction is there only because you are resisting a downward force on you, a force that could pull you off. What normally enables you to resist that force is your weight and position, with your feet braced. But if I am much heavier than you, or the ledge is sloping downward and there is nothing for you to brace your feet on, you could be pulled completely off the mountain if not attached to an anchor.

Now consider your position. You are facing away from the anchor, roughly in line with the direction of force. This contributes to stability; if the force of a fall is fairly high, you won't be jerked one way or the other, possibly losing control of the belay. You also have a certain stance, a sitting one in this case, with your two legs and butt forming a tripod, with the rope running between your legs down to me. If you are able to brace your feet, this is a very strong stance, one you can hold against fairly large forces without being pulled off or out of position. It thus enables you to protect the anchor–that is, to prevent any force from going on it, so the anchor becomes a backup to your stance.

The specific method of belaying we have described–a

method of applying friction to the rope to stop a fall–is called the hip belay (or body belay). As we'll see, there are other and (mostly) better ways to apply friction to the rope. But here we have all the elements of belaying, as it has been done for decades: a means of applying friction to the rope to stop a fall, a way of taking in the rope without removing the braking hand, position and stance, an anchor and a means of attachment to it, and a system for communicating.

## Holding the Fall

Let's look in a little more detail at what happens when I slip off the rock as you are belaying me up. The notion of a force is familiar from everyday life. Try tying a 10-pound weight to a rope and then, grasping the rope a couple of feet from the weight, hold it up a few inches off the floor. The weight exerts a downward force on the rope while you exert an equal upward force to hold it up.

Is this what happens when I slip off the rock and you hold me by gripping the rope? Not quite, because it suggests that the forces are there instantaneously and I am instantly stopped, hanging from the rope. What happens is that at the instant I slip, the rope starts to stretch–but without at first exerting much stopping force on me. So for a fraction of a second I am falling and gaining speed. Then, as the rope stretches more and you hang on without letting any rope slip through your hand, the stopping force slows me down as it increases to some maximum—as much as double my weight if I am on vertical rock—and then goes back down to just my weight as I come to a stop and hang there motionless, held up by the rope. This all takes place in a second or less.

Suppose that by merely gripping the rope, you can resist a pull of about 40 pounds of force before the rope starts to slip through your grasp. But you've run the rope around your hips, adding the friction of the rope against your body. You will therefore be able to resist a pull of about 250 to 350 pounds of force. You may not actually exert that much force when I fall—only what's necessary to stop me without the rope slipping. But it's important to realize that you may have to exert a force significantly greater than my weight to stop even a simple fall.

Now go back to the little experiment of holding up a 10-pound weight on the end of the rope. Try this variation: While holding your arm still and gripping the rope tightly, have someone lift up the weight and drop it. When the weight hits the end of the rope, there will be a sudden, sharp force downward, greater than when you were just holding the weight up. Your arm will dip down, and perhaps a few inches of rope will slip through your hand.

Something similar might happen on our climb. Suppose I climb up faster than you can take in rope and neither of us notices the resulting slack. Now if I fall, I will gain more speed before the rope begins to stop me, and the peak force, assuming you don't let the rope slip, will be greater than before.

But what if the force becomes too great and the rope starts to slip through your hand? Does this mean I will fall to the bottom of the climb while you lose a lot of skin off your hand? No. A surprising but important fact is that, even as the rope runs through your hand, as long as the stopping force that you are exerting by continuing to grip the rope is greater than my weight, I will eventually slow to a stop and end up hanging motionless as before. Though not necessarily a disaster, this may not be an ideal result either. The farther I fall, the more risk there is of hitting something and being injured—and even if I'm not injured, I'll get more excitement than I wanted.

## Protecting the Leader

Now that we understand the elements of belaying, it might seem that we can continue up the rest of the climb, knowing that if either one of us falls the other's belay will catch us quickly. Stop right there. Think what happened on the first pitch (the first lead). You led up while I just watched. If you had fallen, I could not have done anything to stop you from falling all the way to the ground. Now that it's my turn to lead the next pitch (to the next belay spot), I don't much like this arrangement. You probably didn't like it much yourself on the first pitch, but now it's worse. Not only could I climb partway up the pitch and then fall, injuring myself as I land next to you on the belay ledge, but I could bounce off the ledge or miss it entirely and continue falling. I'm going to insist that we find some way to prevent this possibility.

Belaying is about to get more complicated. Of course, you could continue to belay me as before, perhaps after turning around and facing the mountain so you can watch me climb. This belay will not stop me from falling back to the ledge—but if I miss the ledge and then fall as far past the ledge as I was above it, your belay will take hold and stop the fall. Maybe. But this is an extreme fall, with many problems. If you've chosen the wrong hand as the braking hand, the rope could completely unwrap from around you, and you could end up with a broken arm as I fall to the bottom of the mountain. Or, because you are probably standing up, you may suddenly have a large force pulling you violently down onto the ledge. Even if you avoid these problems, when the force reaches, say, 350 pounds of force, the rope will start to run through your hand and across your back, resulting in severe burns.

The way to reduce, if not eliminate, the risk that you will have to try to stop such a horrible fall is for me to place *protection* as I climb (see Chapter 10, Rock Protection, and Chapter 11, Leading on Rock). I will be carrying a lot of climbing paraphernalia: carabiners and runners, plus the metal devices known as chocks, which can be secured into the rock as points of protection. After climbing up, say, 30 feet, I will place protection. The placement might make use of a tree or of a crack in the rock that I can slip a chock into. I'll attach a runner to the tree or to the chock and

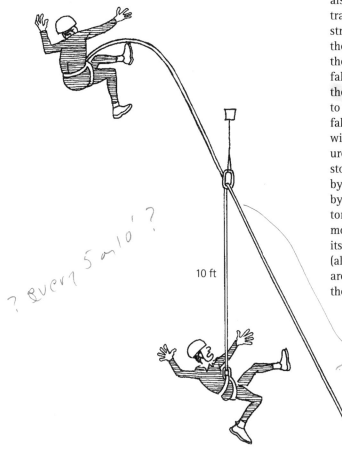

also on the amount of friction created as the rope travels through pieces of protection and around obstructions (the more friction, the easier it is to stop the fall) and on how much I bounce and slide down the rock rather than falling freely. The severity of the fall also depends significantly on something called the *fall factor.* This is the ratio of the length of the fall to the length of rope between belayer and climber. If I fall from 10 feet beyond my last piece of protection with 40 feet of rope between us, as in the fall in Figure 7-3, I will fall 20 feet before your belay begins to stop me. The fall factor is the length of the fall divided by the length of rope between you and me: 20 divided by 40, for a fall factor of 0.5. The higher the fall factor, the higher the force of the fall. Despite what common sense might tell you, the mere length of a fall by itself has no effect on the maximum force of the fall (although it does affect the length of time the forces are there). For further discussion, see the section on the fall factor in Chapter 11, Leading on Rock.

10 ft

30 ft

*Fig. 7-3. A falling climber will drop twice the distance that the climber was above the last point of protection; in this case, the climber falls 10 feet to the protection and then another 10 feet below it, for a total fall of 20 feet.*

then clip the climbing rope into a carabiner that is attached to the runner; then I'll continue climbing.

If I fall after climbing up another 10 feet, I will drop a total of only 20 feet before tension goes on the rope and your belay brings me to a stop (fig. 7-3). The rope will not unwrap from your body regardless of which hand you are belaying with, because the force on you will be upward. I may go on to establish a number of points of protection before I get to the next belay spot. In any fall that I take, I will drop twice the distance between me and where the rope is clipped into the latest protection before the stopping force of your belay begins to take hold.

The severity of a fall—and the difficulty you will have in stopping it—depends partly on my weight but

Many such protected leader falls are surprisingly easy to hold and can be held readily with the method we are using. So it seems that all I have to do is make sure I place a lot of protection and then we've solved our problems and we can be on our way. Sorry, not quite. Remember, we have reduced but not eliminated the risk of my falling as far past the belay ledge as I was above it: a *factor-2 fall,* the most severe possible. This risk has not been eliminated because the quality of the available protection may be poor and it could all rip out when I fall, or I could fall before I put in the first piece of protection, falling from a point perhaps 10 feet above you. And this 20-foot factor-2 fall would be as hard on both of us as a 100-foot factor-2 fall.

Therefore, we have to consider the possibility that, in the event of a fall, you as the belayer could get either an upward pull—and not all protected leader falls are easily held—or a very severe downward pull. For this reason, anchors, stances, and the choice of a belay method—a method for amplifying one's hand grip with friction—become extremely important. These are the principal topics we will study in the rest of this chapter.

## APPLYING FRICTION TO THE ROPE

In any belay method, the rope from the climber goes around or through some friction-producing element (the belayer's hips, a specialized device, or a Münter hitch knot on a carabiner) and then to the belayer's braking hand. Except for one device (the Grigri, discussed later), the braking hand produces the initial force by the friction of the belayer's hand gripping the rope. This force is amplified by the friction-producing element to stop the falling climber.

Because everything starts with the belayer's grip, we should consider what kind of force it can exert before looking at specific devices and methods. In fact, considering its importance, remarkably little is known about what kind of stopping force a belayer's hand can exert when in a braking position. From what little testing has been done, and from the common experience of climbers, a few tentative conclusions may be made. (Much of the following is drawn from a

1994 study conducted by Kirk and Katie Mauthner—see Appendix B, Supplementary References.)

- The average amount of force that can be exerted by a person's grip is probably something under 50 pounds, whether the rope is running through the hand or being held statically.
- The variation from one person to another is large and cannot be predicted from obvious physical characteristics (such as weight, size, and muscle mass); some adults can exert a force of only about 10 pounds of force, others as much as 90.
- The position of hand and arm relative to the direction of pull is significant: the strongest position is with the rope pulling from the little-finger side of the hand to the thumb-forefinger side with the forearm roughly parallel with the direction of pull (fig. 7-4).
- Bare hands can generally exert more force than gloved hands, though the texture and thickness of the glove probably make a difference (thinner and rougher is stronger).
- You can exert more force with larger-diameter ropes.
- Choice of hand appears to be insignificant.
- Common sense and common experience, but no hard information, suggest that a hand that has become tired and crampy after several pitches of hard rock climbing ("forearm burnout") is less able to exert a stopping force.

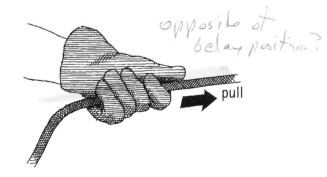

*opposite of belay position?*

*Fig. 7-4. The strongest hand position for gripping the rope*

Given the great variation among people, the beginner would do well to take part in some weight-drop tests, attempting to hold falls of a dead weight, using various belay methods. This can give you a rough idea of whether you are at least near average in your ability to stop a fall.

## Belay Devices

Most belay devices amplify the friction of the braking hand by passing the rope through an opening and wrapping it around a post. The opening guarantees a minimum of wrap, or bend, in the rope to produce enough friction on the post. The post is usually a locking carabiner or part of the device itself. The opening must be large enough to allow the device to touch the carabiner.

To stop a fall, the belayer pulls back on the free end of the rope to create a separation of at least 90 degrees between the rope entering the device and the rope leaving it. Nothing must be in the way of your braking hand or elbow carrying out this critical task, and it must not require an unnatural body twist or motion. The simplest way to learn to do this conveniently in all situations is to clip the device into a locking carabiner on your harness (currently the most popular belay method in the United States) rather than directly

to the anchor. In this section, we will describe the use of belay devices when attached to the harness.

Contrary to a popular misconception, there is no automatic clamping effect with most properly designed belay devices. Your hand is the initial, and critical, source of friction; without your braking hand on the rope, there is no belay. The total friction is determined by the strength of your grip, the total number of degrees in the bends or turns the rope makes, and the rope's internal resistance to bending and deforming against the sides of the device and carabiner.

The fact that most belay devices depend on the belayer pulling back on the rope to stop a fall can be a disadvantage, especially when belaying a follower. The belayer often is unable to see the follower—and tests have suggested that the normal reflex, when an unexpected fall occurs with the belayer unable to see the falling weight, is to grip the rope but not to pull back. Thus the two strands of the rope remain parallel, and the belay device produces very little friction, allowing the rope to run through. The result in tests is usually that the weight is dropped to the ground. In a real situation, the result would be a longer fall but not necessarily total failure of the belay. It's possible that through practice, using a weight-drop setup, a belayer would develop the proper reflex.

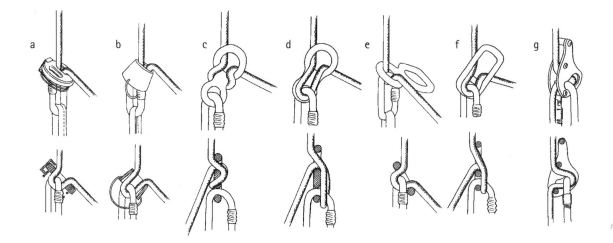

Fig. 7-5. Types of belay devices: a, slot or plate; b, tube; c, figure-8 in rappel configuration; d, figure-8 in "sport mode"; e, figure-8 in aperture configuration; f, Yates Belay Slave; g, Single Rope Controller.

## Types of Belay Devices

There are many popular belay devices (fig. 7-5). One general type may be referred to as an aperture device: it simply provides an aperture through which a bight (loop) of rope is pushed and then clipped to the locking carabiner on your harness. In one widely used version of this type, the aperture consists of a slot in a metal plate. (The original and best known of these is the Sticht plate, shown in Figure 7-5a.) In another version, the aperture is a cone-shaped or somewhat square tube (fig. 7-5b). The Lowe Tuber II, the Black Diamond Air Traffic Controller (ATC), and the Trango Pyramid are examples of such devices. Some have two modes: a higher-force mode and a lower-force mode.

Plates and tubes must be attached to some sort of tether to keep them from sliding down the rope and out of reach. Some of these devices include a hole for attaching the tether; others include a wire loop that is clipped into the locking carabiner on your harness. A tether to your harness must be long enough so it doesn't interfere with belaying in any direction.

Figure-8 devices (not to be confused with the figure-8 knot) were originally designed only for rappelling, not belaying, but some figure-8's can serve for both. Figure-8's are seen in three different configurations as belay devices. One is the standard rappel configuration (fig. 7-5c). Another (the "sport mode") is set up by putting the bight of rope through the large hole and then clipping the rope into the carabiner (fig 7-5d). If the hole in the small end of the figure-8 is the size of a typical aperture device hole, it can also be used similarly to a plate or tube (fig. 7-5e). Make certain that your figure-8 was intended for belaying use by the manufacturer; many are not.

The Yates Belay Slave (fig. 7-5f) is, in appearance, a sort of streamlined figure-8. The bight of rope goes up through the large hole and is then clipped into a locking carabiner or two nonlocking carabiners attached both to your harness and to the small hole in the device.

The Single Rope Controller (fig. 7-5g) and the Raptor are aperture devices (both made by Wild Country) whose design uses a camming action to increase the stopping force. The Variable Rope Controller (also by Wild Country) is essentially a plate device with two configurations, one with a higher stopping force than the other, though the difference is quite small.

The Petzl Grigri is a specialized belay device that has the extremely useful feature that it doesn't require any stopping force at all from the belayer's hand. It works on the same principle as the safety belts in your car. It has some tendency to lock up when the lead climber makes a sudden move up. It also works badly or not at all with icy or wet ropes; that, together with its weight and bulk, makes it largely unsuitable for mountaineering but quite useful in climbing gyms and in rock-climbing areas.

## Special Considerations in Using Belay Devices

When you are using a belay device and are facing away from the belay anchor, your tie-in to the anchor using the climbing rope should be on the braking-hand side. This way, your body rotation under the force of a fall will assist, rather than hinder, you in separating the ropes. This is not a consideration, however, when you are attached to the anchor by a runner clipped into your seat harness at the back (see "Tying into the Anchor," later in this chapter).

When facing toward the anchor (usually when belaying a leader), the braking hand should be opposite the side where the leader would likely drop in case of a fall before the first protection is put in place. For example, if the climber leads up and to the right, so that in an unprotected leader fall he would fall past you on your right, the braking hand should be your left hand.

The question of whether to wear gloves when using a belay device has no easy answer. As noted earlier, your gripping ability is greater bare-handed than with most gloves. With the use of any standard belay device, a bare-handed belayer who is near average in gripping ability can easily stop the routine leader and follower falls that are common in rock-climbing areas. Furthermore, gloves can make your hands damp and soft, undesirable when it's your turn to climb.

On the other side, you may be required at any time to hold an extreme fall, the force of which can pull the rope through your hand. Heat buildup is quick; the sliding rope can burn your bare hand, causing you to drop the rope. Of course, gloves may be necessary to keep your hands warm in cold weather.

137

Another choice you must make when using a belay device is between having the braking hand in the palm-up or palm-down position. With the palm-down position, the hand motions for taking in rope, which are the same as for the hip belay (fig. 7-2), are somewhat more awkward and put more strain on the upper arm. However, when braking with palm down, the grip on the rope in the braking position is more natural and grip strength is probably higher. But when suddenly going into the braking position with the palm down, the tendency is to slap your closed hand up against your hip, possibly hitting the thumb knuckles against any equipment carried on the hardware loops of your harness. This can be a problem even when wearing gloves.

When taking in or letting out slack with an aperture device (plate or tube), keep the ropes strictly parallel; otherwise, the rope will pull the device up against the carabiner, and braking begins. Eventually the practice becomes automatic.

Like any piece of critical equipment made of metal, a belay device that is dropped a significant distance should be retired because internal stresses could cause it to break when holding a big fall.

### Differences in Performance

Belay plates and tubes produce the least friction in routine rope handling, which allows you to take in rope faster when the climber is on easy ground and provides a slightly improved feel for small movements of the climber and elimination of slack. Figure-8 devices in rappel or sport configuration not only produce more friction in routine rope handling but also generate *less* friction than most other devices when holding a fall. This characteristic lends them to use on ice and snow, where stances and anchors are usually weaker and would benefit from a lower force, and where the consequences of a longer fall are often less important.

The Single Rope Controller (SRC) provides significantly greater stopping force than most other devices. However, it is not as easy to feed rope quickly through the SRC or the Raptor, and they have a tendency to lock up. Inattention can result in the rope being threaded through them incorrectly.

A belayer is called upon not only to stop falls but also to hold the climber stationary under tension or to lower the climber to a ledge. Devices vary significantly

in how easily they perform these tasks. Plate devices require the least force to hold the climber's weight but are the least smooth in lowering the climber. The Raptor and SRC are very smooth in lowering.

Hard-anodized devices tend to glaze the outermost surface of the rope when stopping a fall, but this effect is purely cosmetic and not harmful. (The metallurgic process of hard-anodizing produces a thin layer of aluminum oxide whose surface is hard and microscopically pitted and appears dull gray, black, or brown.)

Belay devices are also used for rappelling. Plates and tubes produce a jerky ride that puts unnecessarily high loads on the anchor; however, the plate design that has a spring is better. The figure-8's are the smoothest for rappelling, but figure-8's put twists in the rope, later producing snarls in the coils.

All belay devices come with manufacturer's instructions. Always read these carefully and follow them.

## The Münter Hitch

The Münter hitch is a very effective method of using only the rope and a carabiner to provide the friction necessary to stop a fall. This method requires a large pear-shaped locking carabiner in order to allow the knot to pass through the interior. It amplifies the

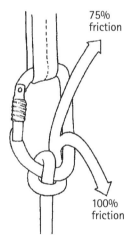

75%
friction

100%
friction

*Fig. 7-6. The Münter hitch provides sufficient friction for belaying regardless of the angle between the ropes entering and leaving it.*

effect of your braking hand with the friction both of rope on rope and of rope on carabiner. It is probably the strongest method, in the stopping force it can exert, except the Grigri. When attached to the front of a harness it works much like a belay device.

The Münter hitch is the only traditional belay method that provides sufficient friction regardless of the angle between the ropes entering and leaving it (fig. 7-6). This offers two advantages. First, no special braking position is required. The problem noted previously—that a belayer taken by surprise by a fall might not pull back on the rope—doesn't occur with the Münter hitch: it will hold if the belayer just grips the rope. Second, it works well in the special situation where all of the slack rope is hanging down a wall. With the slack hanging below, you may be unable to raise your braking hand high enough, as required by a standard belay device, to arrest a follower fall. The problem is caused by the weight of the rope, the extra force exerted by the falling climber, and the difficult arm position. But with a Münter hitch, it doesn't matter, whether belaying off the harness or directly off the anchor (fig. 7-7).

The friction of the Münter hitch is also unique in being less when the ropes are 180 degrees apart than when 0 degrees apart. This usually means its friction is relatively less for leader falls than for follower falls. But in absolute terms it often provides more friction than any other belay method except the Grigri, SRC, and Trango-8, regardless of the angle between the ropes. This high friction means a quicker stop to an extreme fall.

The Münter hitch has some drawbacks. It kinks the rope more than any other method, producing snarls in the last few feet of rope after several pitches, especially if the same person always leads. To unsnarl the rope, shake it out while it is hanging free. After a big fall, the outermost layer of the sheath is glazed (which, like the effect of hard-anodized devices, is only cosmetic). The Münter hitch isn't good for rappelling because it twists the rope once for every 5 feet of descent, and makes ropes very fuzzy if used regularly. Every time the direction of pull on the hitch reverses, the entire knot first flip-flops through the carabiner oval. This can get a bit awkward when the leader clips into protection above, moves up toward it, and then passes it, because it requires the belayer

*Fig. 7-7. The Münter hitch works when the slack rope must be hanging down a wall.*

to pay out, take in, and pay out rope in rapid succession, reversing the direction of pull on the Münter hitch each time. This reversal in the direction of pull also occurs when holding a fall, producing an additional drop of 6 inches as the knot pulls through the carabiner before braking begins.

You may run across the Münter hitch under a variety of names, such as the friction hitch, Italian hitch, half ring bend, carabiner hitch, running R, half-mast belay, and UIAA method. It was introduced in Europe in 1973 as the *halbmastwurf sicherung* ("half clove-hitch belay"), now abbreviated as HMS. (Chapter 6, Ropes, Knots, and Carabiners, gives details on tying the Münter hitch.)

## The Hip Belay (Body Belay)

The hip belay, described in some detail near the beginning of this chapter, is used by fewer and fewer climbers as their primary method of belaying because of its significant disadvantages:

- Where there is any possibility of having to hold a serious fall, you must wear heavy clothes because your back and sides provide most of the friction on the rope. Even a short leader fall can cut through a polypropylene jacket.
- If the climbing rope runs over the anchor attachment during a hard fall, the attachment may be burned. The outermost layer of the rope sheath may be glazed and covered with melted fabric from your clothes.
- Because more time is required to attain the braking position and because it has the least stopping force of any method, the hip belay more often results in rope slippage and a longer fall.
- If your stance fails, you will probably also lose control of the rope, which is less likely with other methods. There is usually no very good choice of stance and position when belaying the leader.

Despite its disadvantages as a general-purpose method, the hip belay has advantages that make it worth learning, if only for special purposes. It is probably most useful when bringing up a fast-moving partner, because you can take in rope much faster than with other methods and it can be set up quickly with a minimum of equipment. Assuming you and your partner don't let slack develop and there is no possibility of a pendulum fall (in which the climber pendulums toward the fall line, creating larger forces), there is little reason to worry about the rope burning you or the anchor attachment. A common and efficient practice is to use a simple hip belay to bring one's partner up a relatively easy pitch and then switch to another method when this climber leads the next pitch. The hip belay can also be useful for belaying on snow, where, because anchors are often suspect, it may be desirable to have a method that will cause the rope to run at a fairly low force. Also, if you have lost or forgotten your belay device and don't have the right kind of carabiner for a Münter hitch, you may have no choice but to use the hip belay.

There are a number of pitfalls to be aware of when learning the hip belay. To catch a fall with this method, your elbow should be straight before you begin to grip hard (fig. 7-8). (Your natural reaction will be to grip the rope first, but this may pull your arm into a helpless position, requiring you to let go and grasp the rope again.) Then bring your braking arm across in front of your body, to increase the amount of wrap for maximum friction. An optimal braking position can only be learned with practice, ideally with a weight-drop setup.

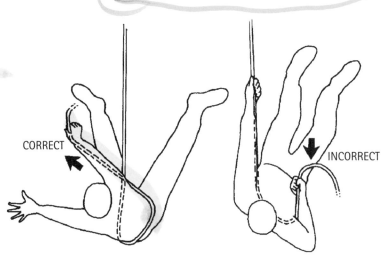

CORRECT

INCORRECT

*Fig. 7-8. The correct braking arm position for the hip belay must be achieved before braking begins (left) or the arm will be pulled into a helpless position (right).*

140

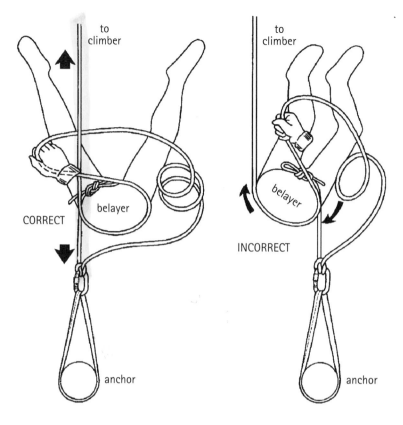

Fig. 7-9. *The correct anchor attachment for the hip belay is on the side opposite the braking hand (left). Having the anchor attachment on the same side as the braking hand (right) can allow the hip belay to unwrap.*

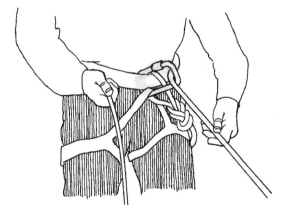

Fig. 7-10. *A control carabiner on the harness helps keep the hip belay from unwrapping.*

Remember that in the initial description of the hip belay, you were facing away from the anchor with the anchor rope (the part of the rope from your harness tie-in to the anchor) running around your left side to the anchor, and your braking hand was the opposite (right) hand. The reason for this setup is that if the braking hand and anchor rope are on the same side, the force of a fall can partly unwrap the rope from around your body, decreasing friction and stability (fig. 7-9).

Another precaution is to clip a control carabiner on your harness (fig. 7-10). The carabiner goes in front, or on the same side as the rope coming from the climber but well forward of the hip bone. Clipping the rope into this carabiner keeps the rope where you want it, at your hip, and also counteracts body rotation. If you don't use a control carabiner, take advantage of your anchor attachment to keep the climbing rope from being pulled over your head or under your seat. If the pull will come from below, put the rope above the anchor attachment. If the pull will come from above with no possibility of a downward pull, put the rope below the anchor line.

## Choosing a Method

It might seem that the choice of a general-purpose belay method, one that you would always use except for special situations, would be a straightforward matter of picking the one that enables you to exert the most stopping force, as long as it has no problems of inefficiency, locking up, likelihood of manufacturing defects, and so forth. Unfortunately, there is a significant trade-off in risks that must be considered.

If the rope starts to run during an attempt to hold

a fall, the climber will fall that much farther than if the fall were held with no run-through; the extra fall is generally undesirable and occasionally disastrous. However, an important fact in any protected leader fall (where at least one piece of protection holds) is that the maximum force on the top piece of protection is perhaps 1.5 times as high as the maximum force on the climber—and the latter can easily be 1,500 pounds of force for a high-factor fall on vertical rock. If the protection fails under this force, the climber will definitely fall farther. To reduce this force on the protection, some climbers choose a relatively weak method of belaying, one that will let the rope start to run at a lower force so there is less likelihood of the protection failing. Climbers may choose this method for general use or just for when the protection is expected to be fairly weak.

This choice of a general-purpose belay method is

| DEVICE | STRENGTH | ROPE FEEDING | LOWERING | RAPPELLING |
|---|---|---|---|---|
| Plates | 3 | B | C | C |
| Lowe Tuber II | 3 | A | C | B |
| Air Traffic Controller | 3 | A | B | B |
| Figure-8 | 2–5 | B | A | C |
| Grigri | 1 | B | B | N/A |
| Belay Slave | 4 | C | B | B |
| Raptor | 3 | C | A | C |
| Single Rope Controller | 2 | B | A | N/A |
| Variable Rope Controller | 3 | B | C | C |
| Münter hitch | 2 | B | B | C |
| Hip belay | 5 | A | C | N/A |

1 = strongest, 5 = weakest. A = very efficient, B = moderately efficient, C = inefficient, N/A = not applicable.

This table provides some broadly drawn information that may help in selecting a belay device. The table is at best a starting point in choosing your principal device; it does not substitute for getting the opinions of knowledgeable climbers and trying out as many devices as possible. Devices are graded on strength (weaker or stronger depending on whether the rope starts to run at a relatively low force or relatively high force), ease of taking in and paying out rope, ease of lowering a climber, and ease of rappelling. The hip belay and Münter hitch are included for convenience. Figure-8's are graded under their use for belaying in "sport mode" and rappel mode; they are otherwise grouped with plates. Plates and figure-8's are of different types and manufacture and are not all alike. The ratings in the last three columns are necessarily subjective, and some climbers will disagree with them. The ratings for rappel efficiency take into account the twisting effect of some devices. Devices that allow rappelling only on a single strand are not rated for rappelling.

*Fig. 7-11. Belay device comparison*

sometimes discussed in a confused and confusing way, as though the choice were between "static" and "dynamic" methods of belaying. However, it is not a method of belaying but an attempt to stop a fall that is either static or dynamic: static if there is no run-through, dynamic if there is. Even if two methods differ significantly in the maximum stopping force you can exert with them, there will be no practical difference at all between them for a very wide range of falls (almost all you will ever have to hold); the falls will be held statically because the force you need to exert will not reach the level at which the rope will start to run with either method. The situations where the difference between the two methods will mean the difference between the rope running and not running are high-factor falls on high-angle rock with little or nothing to produce friction other than the belay. Still, these are the critical falls, where things are most likely to go wrong.

To make a choice of a general-purpose method, it would be helpful to study comparative performance data on belay devices to see which are relatively strong (meaning that the rope will run through the device at a relatively high force), which allow for easy paying out and taking in of the rope, which are easy to lower a climber on, and which can most effectively double as rappel devices. Figure 7-11 provides some rough data on these factors. You may occasionally see published figures that purport to state at what forces the rope will start to run for given devices or methods. All such figures should be viewed skeptically. Even if they are roughly accurate as averages (and many undoubtedly are not), given the great variation in grip strength among individuals and the fact that the actual stopping force of a given device for a given rope in a given condition is related to this grip strength, the average is of little interest.

## ANCHORS

The normal result of the failure of the belay anchor in an unprotected leader fall is the death of both members of the rope team. And the failure of any belay anchor under the force of a fall under any circumstances is likely to produce at least injuries. You might therefore believe, given the critical importance of the security of the anchor, that well-trained, experienced climbers would always make sure their belay anchors are secure against the force of any possible fall. If so, you would be wrong. There are undoubtedly thousands of pitches led every year on essentially worthless anchors. Then surely there must be scores of tragedies every year from belay anchor failure? Wrong again. Such catastrophic events do happen but are quite rare. The reason they are rare is that extreme falls that put large forces on belay anchors are likewise quite rare. And that is also the reason for the large number of climbs done on bad anchors, for this rarity can induce an insidious and deadly complacency. You go out year after year, holding an occasional routine, protected leader fall or follower fall without incident and with never more than a small force going on the anchor; gradually you can become more and more careless about setting up anchors that never seem to have made any difference in the past.

Don't fall into this trap. Secure anchors are vital. Remind yourself, as you acquire more experience, that the moment you will have to stop an extreme leader fall cannot be anticipated. And the anchor had better hold when it happens.

### Selecting an Anchor

You'll get a few tips here on selecting good anchors for belays, but for full details on finding and using natural features, and on setting artificial anchors on rock, snow, and ice, study Chapter 10, Rock Protection; Chapter 11, Leading on Rock; Chapter 13, Snow Travel and Climbing; and Chapter 15, Ice Climbing.

A large natural feature, such as a live, well-rooted tree or pillar of sound rock, makes an ideal anchor. However, it's easy to overestimate the stability of large boulders, which may be more lethal than stable. As important as size is the shape of the boulder's bottom, the shape of the socket it is sitting in or the angle of the slope it is on, and the ratio of height to width. Imagine the hidden undersurface and the block's center of gravity: Will it pull over under a big load? Test it, gently at first so you don't send it over the edge. Occasionally, one has to set up a belay at a jumble of large boulders, with some resting on others. A boulder underneath other large boulders might be quite solid but can be difficult to assess even with careful checking.

Any rock feature used as an anchor should be

checked for fracture lines, which may be subtle and difficult to judge, such as at the base of a rock horn or near the edge of a crack. When using chocks for anchors, check to see whether one side of the crack may actually be a detachable block or movable flake; a crack has to widen only a fraction of an inch under the force of a fall for the chock to pull out. Bolts and fixed pitons are commonly used for anchors and are solid more often than not, but they are notoriously difficult to assess (see "Bolts and Pitons," in Chapter 10, Rock Protection).

Beware of making strong assumptions about what you can know about the security of an anchor based on textbook knowledge and local observation and testing. Virtually any manufactured object used to establish an anchor can have hidden defects, and the usual inspection and testing of natural features will rarely establish their soundness conclusively. For these reasons, the normal practice of most climbers is to set two or more belay anchors for a downward pull.

Do not accept the first anchors that look good enough, but search widely for simple and obviously solid placements. To save time, don't immediately pull out earlier placements that seem less than optimal, as you may find nothing better.

## Tying into the Anchor

The most common way for the belayer to tie in to the anchor is with the climbing rope itself, using the first few feet of rope as it comes from its tie-in at the belayer's harness. The rest of the rope is available for use by the climber. Another way to attach oneself to an anchor is with a runner from the anchor to the seat harness. Although this is often slower and less efficient and uses up more equipment—especially when attaching to multiple anchors—it is a good idea when the length of the next pitch is not known and running out of rope could be a problem.

We will concentrate here on attaching to an anchor with the rope. The belayer faces quite an array of choices when it comes to knots and methods for tying in to the anchor. Let's take a look at them to identify some of the more useful ones.

One method of dealing with a large natural anchor is the simple technique of looping the rope around it and clipping the loop back on itself with a carabiner (in a quasi-girth hitch). Tie an overhand knot in the

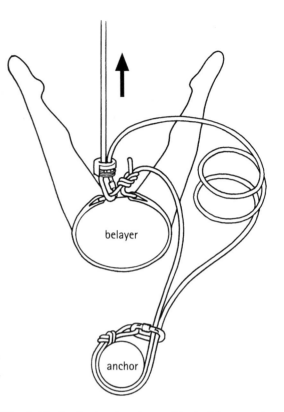

*Fig. 7-12. Anchoring to a large object with a quasi-girth hitch*

end of the loop and clip the carabiner through that (fig. 7-12).

More commonly, a runner is put around or over the natural anchor, and a carabiner is clipped to the runner. Then the climber uses a knot in the climbing rope to clip into the carabiner. The figure-8 knot and the clove hitch are the preferred knots. The figure-8 is strong, stable, and easy to untie. The clove hitch has the advantage of being adjustable after it is tied and is the easiest way to back up a stance with a taut line from you to the anchor. When using the clove hitch on a nonlocking carabiner, make sure it is tight, or normal rope play will make it expand and possibly open the carabiner's gate. Beware of any pull on a clove hitch that makes it slide away from the end of the carabiner, which could also make it expand and open the gate.

When the belay depends on a single anchor, use one locking carabiner or two regular carabiners with the gates reversed and opposed (see Chapter 6, Ropes, Knots, and Carabiners, for a drawing of the correct configuration for double carabiners). Avoid chaining carabiners in succession, as a twisting motion relative to each other weakens them and can open a gate.

It is normal to attach to multiple anchors for belaying—commonly two or three that will hold a downward pull and one that will hold an upward pull. The upward-pull and downward-pull anchors are not necessarily separate: a multidirectional anchor (such as a bolt or a tree) may serve as one of the downward-pull anchors and also as the upward-pull anchor. When using chocks, a common arrangement is to create a multidirectional placement with at least one pair of opposing chocks (see the section on opposing chocks in Chapter 10, Rock Protection).

There are several different ways to attach yourself to multiple anchors, and a number of considerations affect the choice. A quick and easy way is to tie separately, with the climbing rope, into a series of anchors, using clove hitches because of their adjustability (fig. 7-13a). This method can cause problems. If a serious fall occurs, all the impact goes first to a single anchor. The other anchors come into play only if the first one fails. Although the force that goes on the second anchor may be less than on the first (because some of the energy of the fall has been absorbed), it also may *not* be less. And as each anchor fails, the belayer

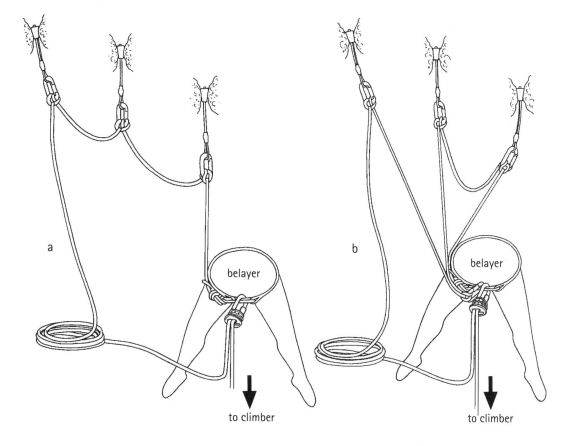

*Fig. 7-13. Tying into several anchors with a series of clove hitches: a, only one anchor holds weight at any given time; b, all anchors hold weight simultaneously.*

may suddenly drop a short distance, perhaps losing some control of the belay.

If you use this method, be careful about the assumptions you are making. You might check each of the three anchors and conclude, for each one, that it is highly probable that it is free of defects and could hold the worst possible fall by itself. It would then be reasonable to conclude that the probability that all three anchors would fail in succession is negligible. But now consider a situation in which one or more of your anchors is a fairly small chock that can't be expected to hold more than a few hundred pounds. Even if the anchor is free of defects and the chock is perfectly placed in solid rock, you can't expect this chock—on its own—to hold the worst possible fall.

In this situation, you should look for some way of *equalizing* the load among two or more anchors. One way to do this is to tie a clove hitch to each anchor carabiner, as before, but to run the rope back to a locking carabiner at the harness and tie in (with a clove hitch) after every other clove hitch at an anchor (fig. 7-13b). This results in a section of rope tied between your seat harness and each anchor carabiner. You can then adjust the clove hitches to snug up the strand to each carabiner. Then if the anchor takes the force of a fall, the impact will be shared by the multiple placements and, if one fails, no drop results before the others come into play. However, this method uses a lot of rope (perhaps too much given the length of the pitches) and is somewhat cumbersome to set up; therefore, it is not often used. Preferred methods of equalizing the load among multiple anchors are discussed in the following section.

## Static Equalization Versus Self-Equalization

Most ways of equalizing the load on multiple anchors make use of runners or other loops and can be roughly divided into two types: static equalization and self-equalization.

Self-equalization under some circumstances automatically distributes any force among all the anchors. Two-point equalizing, using two anchors, is the simplest method of self-equalization (fig. 7-14). Clip a runner into the anchor carabiners; then grasp the top part of the runner, between the two anchors, and put a half twist in it, forming a loop (fig. 7-14a).

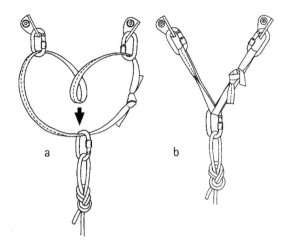

*Fig. 7-14. Two-point self-equalization: a, clip a single runner to the anchor carabiners and form a loop at top; b, then clip into the loop and the bottom part of the runner.*

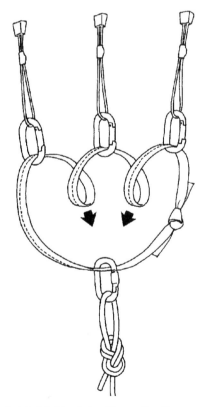

*Fig. 7-15. Multipoint self-equalization*

146

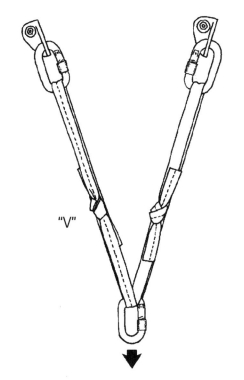

*Fig. 7-16. Simple static equalization*

Then clip the loop and the bottom part of the runner together with a carabiner into which the rope is tied (fig. 7-14b). The point of putting the loop in the runner is that if one anchor fails, the carabiner providing the point of attachment will not simply slide off but will be caught by the runner and the other anchor.

Multipoint self-equalization, using any number of anchors, works essentially the same way but generally requires a longer runner (fig. 7-15).

A very simple kind of static equalization uses two separate runners attached to two separate anchors, with the two ends clipped together at the bottom with a carabiner (fig. 7-16). This can distribute the load fairly well if the runners are of the right length, which often means untying and retying them, but you will probably never get close to perfect equalization.

Another kind of static equalization, gaining in popularity, uses a *cordelette,* a high-strength, long (about 16-foot) runner, usually made of Spectra cord and tied with a triple fisherman's knot. With three anchors, clip the cordelette into all three anchors, pull the top segments between the anchors down, and join them with the bottom part of the cordelette. Then tie all three segments together into an overhand or figure-8 knot and clip a carabiner into them (fig. 7-17).

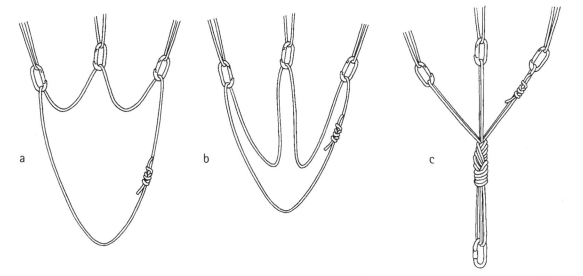

*Fig. 7-17. Static equalization with cordelette: a, clip cordelette into three anchors; b, then pull the segments between the anchors down; c, then grasp all three segments together, tie an overhand or figure-8 knot, and clip a carabiner into the loops.*

Of course, you could also use the cordelette on just two anchors.

There is a common factor, affecting both static equalization and self-equalization, that must be clearly understood. How well an equalization setup reduces the pull on each individual anchor depends on the angle at the bottom where the parts of the runner or runners come together. The smaller the angle, the less force each anchor will be subject to. As the angle increases, each anchor faces an increasing force. For example, when the angle is 60 degrees in a two-anchor setup, each anchor will take 60 percent of the force downward at the point of attachment (fig. 7-18). Above 120 degrees, each of the two anchors will actually be subject to a greater force than if equalization wasn't even used.

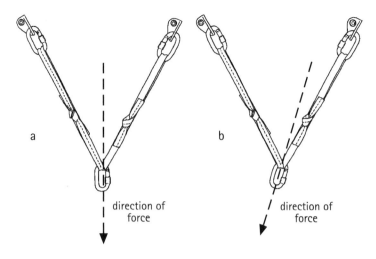

Fig. 7-19. Static equalization: a, line representing direction of force bisects angle, thus load on the two anchors is equal; b, direction of force is to one side, thus load on right-hand anchor is greater than on left-hand anchor.

The pros and cons of self-equalization versus static equalization are a subject of controversy. The big advantage of self-equalization is that you don't have to estimate the direction the force will come from; the point of attachment moves with the direction of force, automatically equalizing the load. (To see how this

| Angle (in degrees) | Force on Each Anchor |
|---|---|
| 0 | 50% |
| 60 | 60% |
| 90 | 70% |
| 120 | 100% |
| 150 | 190% |
| 170 | 580% |

Fig. 7-18. The force on each of two equalized anchors (see figs. 7-14 and 7-16) increases as the angle at the bottom of their connecting sling (or slings) increases.

works, set up a self-equalizing system at home, attach yourself to it, and then move side to side as you lean back and put force on it.)

The advantage is mainly found when setting up to belay off your seat harness. You can easily move back and forth to "aim" yourself in the direction of expected force and can adjust the aim quickly if the direction of expected force changes. However, a self-equalized anchor will lock up when under a significant load. Once it locks up, it is equivalent to a static arrangement. So there is little or no advantage when, for example, trying to stop a pendulum fall while belaying directly off the anchor.

Now consider a simple two-point static equalized anchor, as we saw in Figure 7-16. If the line representing the direction of force bisects the angle at the V, the load will be equalized (fig. 7-19a). If not, more of the load will be on the anchor that is closer to being parallel to the direction of force (fig. 7-19b), because the point of attachment does not move. This means that to get approximate equalization, you have to do two things right. First, you must guess fairly closely what the direction of force will be. Second, you must express that guess correctly by sizing the two runners just right for an equal distribution of force (or, for the cordelette, by grabbing the loops in the proper place and holding your hand just so as you tie the knot).

Furthermore, the desire to equalize the load and the desire to have a relatively small angle at the V work against each other: the smaller the angle, the more any wrong guess about the direction of force will load the anchors differently. Whether anyone can consistently get any better than a 65–35 distribution of forces for a given angle (say, 45 degrees) with this kind of two-point static equalization is unknown. And there is scant reason to believe that one becomes better at getting approximate equalization with experience. A further difficulty is that the direction of force may not be known at all. For instance, if a climber is leading out on a traverse and falls before placing any protection, the fall may be downward, or it may be to the side if the rope runs over a block near the point of fall. When a belayer's guess on direction of force is so wrong that all the force of a fall initially goes onto one anchor, static "equalization" is no equalization at all; it's no different than simply tying separately into two anchors.

A disadvantage of self-equalization is that if one anchor fails in a self-equalized system, there is a sudden drop, which could cause the belayer to lose control and which results in some "shock-load" effect on the remaining anchor or anchors. Another disadvantage is that if the runner itself fails—if the knot comes loose or the runner is cut on the rock—the whole system fails. Of course, you can use two runners of the same length, treating them as one, or use two additional runners as non-load–bearing backups, each clipped into the carabiner and one of the anchors. But all this requires more equipment and more fussiness.

A general disadvantage that applies to both types of equalization is that they depend on finding places for anchors that are close enough together to make equalization feasible without an unacceptably large angle at the V. This could lead a person who follows rules blindly—"One must *always* equalize anchors!"—to equalize a good anchor with a nearby inferior anchor, while ignoring a much better anchor 6 feet away.

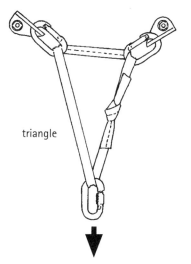

*Fig. 7-20. The triangle method of attaching to two anchors*

Some climbers use the "triangle" method, instead of equalization, to spread the weight between two separate anchors (fig. 7-20). In a triangle, the runner simply goes through each carabiner in turn, without returning to the main carabiner between each anchor. Just as in equalization, the angle at the bottom where the two sides of the runner come together is critical. But with triangles, a significantly greater force hits each anchor for any given angle, compared with equalization. With triangles, the maximum angle can only be 60 degrees; beyond that, each anchor faces a greater force than if the method wasn't used at all. And for any given length of runner, the triangle puts more force on the anchors than equalization. The triangle is falling into disuse among climbers.

Sometimes the length of the tie-in from you to the anchor is critical to the stability of your stance. Until now we have mainly discussed the situation in which the knots are located at the anchor. But if the anchor is out of reach, you can't adjust the knots while in your stance, so precise adjustment is tedious or impossible. A solution is to tie in with a knot only on your harness. Take the rope—after it has run from the harness and simply been clipped through the anchor carabiner—and tie it to your seat harness. Use a clove

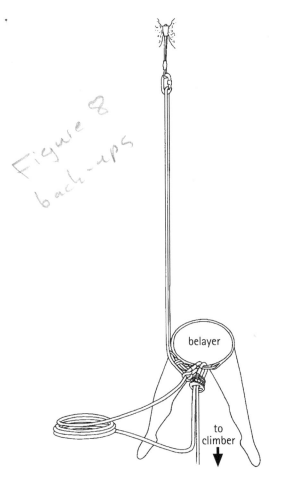

*Figure 8 back-ups*

*Fig. 7-21. Tying the belay rope to the climber's harness to allow convenient adjustment of tension on the anchor rope*

hitch, so you can easily adjust the tension on the rope between you and the anchor. In this option, the rope runs freely around a natural anchor or through a main anchor carabiner (fig. 7-21).

## POSITION AND STANCE

In the United States, most climbers belay by having their belay device or hitch attached to a carabiner on their harness. The alternative, more popular in Europe, is to belay from the anchor by attaching the device or hitch directly to the anchor. To use this method, you must be in a position to put your hand and arm in the correct braking position the instant a fall occurs, and you must be close to the anchor in a position to comfortably take in and pay out rope. An advantage of belaying from the anchor is that the belayer's body is not subject to the sometimes violent forces created by a serious fall, so the belayer is less likely to be injured or lose control of the belay. The issues of stance and position that are discussed in this section are hardly issues at all when belaying from the anchor.

A small advantage of belaying from the body is that the movement of the belayer's body under the force of a fall introduces a dynamic element that may somewhat reduce the forces on the protection and on the climber's body. What is often believed to be a significant advantage of belaying from the body is that the belayer may be able to adopt a stance so strong that little or no force goes on the anchor—and the anchor essentially becomes a backup. When you are belaying a follower with little possibility of a serious pendulum fall or of significant slack in the rope, this belief often makes sense; with a good stance, you can usually prevent any force from going on the anchor. Sparing the anchor can be a definite advantage, given the fact that even the most solid-looking anchor may have critical hidden defects. And belaying directly from the anchor certainly would reveal any such defects in a devastating way if a fall occurred. But in a situation where an extreme leader fall or a serious pendulum fall is a possibility, it's probably an illusion to think that the belayer can protect the anchor by maintaining a stance; whatever force goes on the belayer is likely to go, undiminished, onto the anchor.

### Facing In/Facing Out

When belaying a follower, it's normal to face out, usually with the anchor at your back as you look down to watch for your partner coming up. There is usually no reason to consider any other position.

When belaying a leader, however, the choices are more complex. Most belayers prefer to face in to the mountain most of the time. Facing in often allows you to watch your partner climb, enabling you to anticipate movements and to pay out or take in rope more efficiently. You may also be able to figure out how to get past some of the difficult sections when it's your turn to climb by seeing where your partner had difficulty or found a good solution to a problem. You are better able to protect yourself from rockfall. And you are in the best position to see a leader fall start, brace yourself, and go into the braking position. Being able to see a leader fall start is a particular advantage when the first piece of protection is low and the force of the fall would tend to pull you into the rock.

These advantages of facing in are lost in the event you are belaying in an alcove with a small roof or bulge overhead that prevents you from watching your partner and the first piece of protection is directly above you. Facing out in this situation, you are no worse off when it comes to holding a protected leader fall, and you are probably in a much better position to hold an unprotected leader fall because you're not in danger of being spun around.

## Position and Anchor

Your position relative to the anchor or anchors when belaying off your harness is a relatively straightforward matter: just make sure you are tied in as close as feasible to the anchors, with no slack, so that you won't be jerked about by a severe fall. When you are belaying a follower, this tie-in only needs to hold a downward pull. But remember that in the event of a leader fall you cannot be sure whether the force will be upward (most likely) or downward (unlikely but potentially deadly).

Consider an upward pull first. In a severe fall, you as the belayer may be jerked sharply upward for a few feet, especially if you are much lighter than your partner. This can cause you to lose control and can result in injury if you are yanked up against an obstruction. It can even result in the downward-pull anchors pulling out if they are not multidirectional, leaving you and your partner hanging from the top piece of protection. Your sudden upward movement actually can reduce the force that is put on the top piece of protection—but it's still probably best to avoid such a surprising jolt by maintaining a fairly tight tie-in to an upward-pull anchor somewhat below your waist. A standing, rather than a sitting, position is best for this tie-in.

Now consider an unprotected leader fall where the force is downward. It's very common to see someone in a standing belay of a leader, with a fairly long attachment to an anchor at about waist height or lower. Is this belayer prepared to stop an unprotected leader fall? Think about it. You are standing on a belay ledge, your partner falls past you, you try to brace yourself and go into the braking position, and the force downward on your waist builds quickly toward the point where the rope will start to run. Do you think you can stand there and stop the fall? Given the rarity of such events, and the lack of significant published reports of relevant accidents, it is not possible to predict exactly what would happen, but it probably would not be pretty. You would be pulled violently off the ledge or driven sharply down onto it, with almost certain loss of control of the belay and probable injuries. To prevent this possibility, you need to be tightly attached to anchors above your waist so that you cannot be pulled down more than a few inches. (You might also develop a preference for a sitting stance or for belaying directly off the anchor.)

In settling on your position in relation to the belay anchors, think through the possibilities of what could go wrong given this or that position and this or that kind of fall. Then draw your best conclusion about the optimum arrangement.

## The Stance

Consider the strength of the stance alone, apart from any attachment to an anchor, since in most cases it is primarily the stance that prevents you from being jerked around by a fall or reduces the consequences of being tossed about. The following findings on the comparative value of different stances are based in part on studies conducted many years ago by the Sierra Club. Although the studies used the hip belay, the results apply to stances with modern belay devices (fig. 7-22).

**Located behind a solid object:** In unusually fortunate situations, you can assume the strongest stance of all, directly behind an immovable object, such as a rock protrusion. Don't count on this luck often.

**Sitting stances:** The most common and versatile is the sitting stance, in which your feet and seat make three solid contacts with the mountain. It is most stable if the rope passes between your feet or legs, for it then resembles a tripod. The tripod's apex is the attachment of the belay to the front of your harness; one leg is your pelvic bones and seat, the other two your own

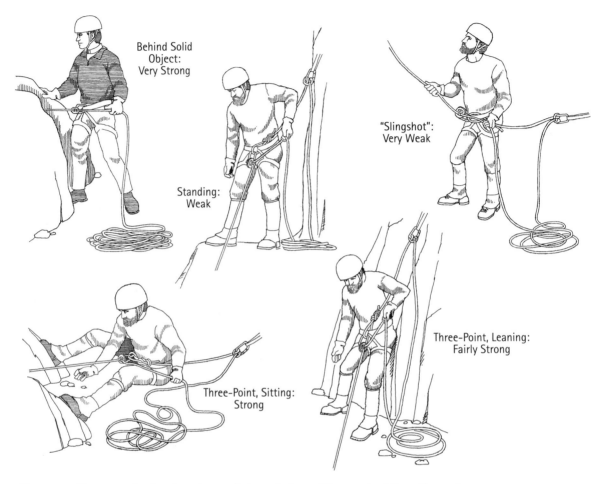

*Fig. 7-22. The strength of various types of stance before adding support from the anchor*

legs. In that configuration, the tests indicated that the average person can hold 350 pounds of tension on the rope for several seconds, or an impact about twice as great. Knees are strongest when the angle at the joint is nearly straight (180 to 140 degrees). The stance is only about half as strong if the knees are bent at an angle below 100 degrees or if the rope runs over the foot support (directed slightly outside the tripod). The stance is suitable for rock, snow, or brush.

**Standing stances:** In the standing position there are only two points of contact with the rock. With one foot well forward, the average belayer can hold 200 pounds from below but less than half as much with a pull to the side or with the feet together. Belaying a leader from a standing position ("slingshot" belay) is extremely weak if the pull is forward. It should be done only with a short, tight rope to the anchor, which will take most of the force, or when standing just below the first protection, so that you cannot be pulled over.

## ROPE HANDLING

When belaying the leader, never let the rope get taut, because that would impede the climber's next move. An alert belayer keeps just a hint of slack and responds immediately to the leader's advance by paying out more rope.

As the leader climbs, it is common for some friction to develop along the rope. This rope drag can greatly increase the difficulty of the climb or make the leader stop, creating time-consuming extra belays, often in uncomfortable spots. The problem can be caused by the terrain the climber passed, such as blocks of rock or rope-sized notches, or by protection that forces the rope over convexities or into an angle (see Chapter 11, Leading on Rock, for further discussion). Any friction applied by the belayer is multiplied by these, so if the leader tells you that rope drag is a problem, keep a few feet of slack in the rope and do everything possible to eliminate any pull. If the climber falls when there is a lot of friction in the system, the belayer may actually be unsure whether a fall took place. If it is impossible to communicate with the climber, you can find out by letting out a few inches of rope. If the same tension remains, then you are probably holding the climber's weight.

Ideally, when you are belaying a follower, there is no slack in the rope. At the same time, the rope should not be taut, which would hamper the climber's movement and balance.

An especially acute problem with slack can occur when belaying someone who is leading out on a traverse with a significant distance between the belayer and the first piece of protection. Because of the weight of the rope, any attempt to keep only a little slack will exert a potentially dangerous pull on the climber. So it's natural to allow quite a lot of slack. This extra slack can't always be avoided, but it's important for both belayer and climber to realize that it can greatly increase the length of a fall. Only a few feet beyond the last protection, the leader could be facing a fall of, say, 15 feet because of the slack.

When belaying a follower up to you, pile the rope where it won't be disturbed later. Don't let loops hang down if there are projections that could snag a loop. If the entire pile must be moved, picking it up is tempting but will produce snarls later. It is best to repile the entire rope twice, so that the leader's end is on top. If the follower is climbing rapidly, you can take in more rope with each pull by leaning forward or bending over.

Occasionally when belaying a follower, rope drag is so great that it is almost impossible to pull the rope in with your hands in the usual way. Here is a technique that works when belaying in a sitting position, though it is extremely slow: Bend forward and simultaneously pull the rope through the device (this is easy, because you are not actually pulling the rope up yet). Then, gripping the rope tightly, in the braking position if necessary, lean back. This pulls the rope up a few inches; you are using your upper body, not your arms, to pull the rope. Then repeat the process. Once the climber is past the first few bends or obstructions, rope drag decreases and you can revert to normal rope handling.

To minimize falling distance, leaders preparing to make difficult moves often place protection well above their harness tie-in and clip in before moving up. This means the direction of rope movement will reverse twice. As you are belaying the leader and letting out rope, you will suddenly find yourself taking in slack as the climber moves up to the protection and then letting it out again as the climber moves past the protection and puts renewed pull on the rope. These switches call for extra attention, especially as this tends to happen at the most difficult spots.

## COMMUNICATION

As climber and belayer get farther apart and hearing each other begins to be difficult, stick exclusively to a set of short commands designed to express essential climbing communications (fig. 7-23). Prefacing them with explanations or justifications makes them harder to recognize and defeats their purpose. Use the commands alone. They have been chosen to produce a distinctive pattern. When you are a long way from your partner, shout as loudly as possible and space out each syllable, using very big spaces if there are echoes. In a crowded area, preface commands with your partner's name. Don't expect an audible response; just do your best the first time.

Three problems are common at or near the end of each pitch, when hearing is most difficult. First, when calling out to your leader the length of rope remaining in the coils, the first syllable is often lost, and if normal word order is used the leader hears only "--ty feet." Instead, invert the word order and pronounce

| | | |
|---|---|---|
| **Follower:** | "That's me" | You have pulled up all the slack in the rope and are now tugging on my body; don't pull any more. |
| **Belayer:** | "Belay on" | I am belaying you. |
| **Climber:** | "Climbing" | I am, or will resume, moving up. |
| **Belayer:** | "Climb" | Response to "Climbing." |
| **Climber:** | "Slack" | Give me some slack in the rope and leave it out until I call "Climbing." (If you want to indicate how much slack you need, the command would be "Slack *X* feet," with *X* being the amount of slack.) |
| **Climber:** | "Up rope" (Usually to upper belayer.) | There is slack in the rope; pull it in. |
| **Climber:** | "Tension" (Usually to upper belayer.) | Take up all slack and hold my weight. (Should be used sparingly by beginners, to avoid overdependence on rope. Say "Watch me" instead.) |
| **Climber:** | "Falling!" | Assume your braking position and brace for a pull on the rope. |
| **Belayer:** | "Halfway" | About half of the rope remains. |
| **Leader:** | "How much rope?" | What length of rope remains? |
| **Belayer:** | "Feet . . . four . . . zero" | Forty feet of rope remains; find a belay soon (best used when 50 to 20 feet remain). |
| **Leader:** | "Off belay" | I am secure and no longer need your belay. Take it apart and prepare to follow the pitch. |
| **Anyone:** | "OK" | I heard you. |
| **Follower:** | "Belay off" (After taking apart the belay.) | You may pull in all the slack and remaining coils when you are ready. |
| **Anyone:** | "Rock! Ice!" (Very loudly, immediately, and repeatedly until falling object stops; mandatory.) | Falling objects. Look up or take cover. |
| **Anyone:** | "Rope" | A rappel rope is about to be thrown down by another party. Look up or take cover. |

Climbers also use some discretionary voice commands, depending on local custom or prior agreement with a climbing partner. These are examples; many variations are used:

| | | |
|---|---|---|
| **Leader:** | "Pro in" or "Clipped in" | I have just clipped into the first protection. Or I have clipped into protection located above my harness tie-in, so the direction of rope movement will reverse twice as I move up through a difficult spot. |
| **Climber:** | "Protection" or "Cleaning" | I am placing or cleaning protection and will not move up for a while. |
| **Climber:** | "Good belay" or "Watch me" | I anticipate a fall or difficult move. |
| **Climber:** | "On top" | I have passed the difficulty. |

*Fig. 7-23. Basic voice commands used by climbers*

each digit separately: "Feet: . . . three . . . zero," for 30 feet. The climber will pause upon the first word and have a better chance of understanding the remainder. Second, when the leader completes a pitch and calls "Off belay," do not respond with "Belay off" to indicate you heard him. "Belay off" means you have taken apart your belay and the rope coils are ready to be pulled up, and you won't be ready to shout that command truthfully for a while yet. Third, avoid the impatient question "On belay?" unless an inordinate amount of time has passed. Often the leader, at work setting up anchors, is out of earshot anyway.

Commands are sometimes transmitted by rope pulls, but there is no universal system. Because of rope stretch at the end of long leads, it's necessary to greatly exaggerate the pulls. A simple tug will seldom be felt at the other end. Take in all slack, and for each signal reach way down and pull the rope as high as possible, holding it tight for a while before releasing the tension. If there is much friction, pulls may not be distinguishable from normal rope movements. The most common commands correspond to the number of syllables in their verbal equivalents: one pull from the follower means "Slack," two means "Up rope," and three from the belayer above means "Belay on."

## OTHER TECHNIQUES

### Tying off the Belay

There's at least one aspect of belaying you hope you'll never have to use: tying off the belay in order to help an injured partner. If your climbing partner is seriously injured and other climbers are nearby, it is usually best to let them help while you continue to belay. By staying there you could also help in raising or lowering the victim, if necessary. But if the two of you are alone, it is unlikely but conceivable that you may have to tie off the climbing rope to remove yourself from the belay system, so you can investigate, help your partner, or go for help.

If you are belaying directly off the anchor using a belay device or Münter hitch, you need only prevent rope from sliding through the belay. Simply form a knot such as the clove hitch in the braking rope and clip it to another carabiner on the anchor. You can now

take your hand off the braking rope and it will be held by the knot.

If you are using a stance, with a belay device or Münter hitch attached to your harness, it is possible to tie off using one hand. However, it is easier and safer to wrap the rope a few times around one foot or leg. Then, while the leg wrap is doing the job of holding the belay rope, attach a prusik loop or runner to the climbing rope with a friction knot (prusik or Klemheist). Clip the sling into the anchor, chaining slings if necessary to make the connection long enough (fig 7-24a). (If you can't reach the anchor, you can create a new anchor, extended from the existing anchor, by tying a figure-8 knot in the slack part of the rope as close to the anchor as possible.) Transfer tension from the belay to the anchor by undoing the leg wrap and letting rope slip through the belay, after first telling the climber to expect to be lowered a few inches. Once tension is on the anchor, get out of the belay and back up the arrangement by tying the climbing rope itself directly to the anchor, with a figure-8 knot on a separate carabiner (fig. 7-24b).

### Self-Belayed Solo Climbing

Self-belay devices, which allow roped solo climbing, have been available for several years. They are worn by the climber and work like a ratchet, sliding up the rope during the climb but not down it in a fall. To lead a pitch, the rope is first anchored at the bottom, and the climber protects as he ascends. Then the rope is anchored at the top, and the climber rappels. Finally, the climber removes the bottom anchor and climbs the pitch a second time, retrieving the protection as he goes.

This is not just another belaying alternative to be chosen on occasion. It is a different form of climbing, requiring a commitment to relearn many fundamentals. Shortcomings compared to a belay by a live partner are inevitable. Read the manufacturer's literature critically, and practice in a safe situation. In evaluating the device, ask yourself some questions: Is the belay static? Does it work if you fall in a horizontal or head-down position? When climbing, does the rope feed automatically, without producing extra slack or drag, especially at the top of a pitch, or on a traverse? Can you clip into protection above your waist without trouble?

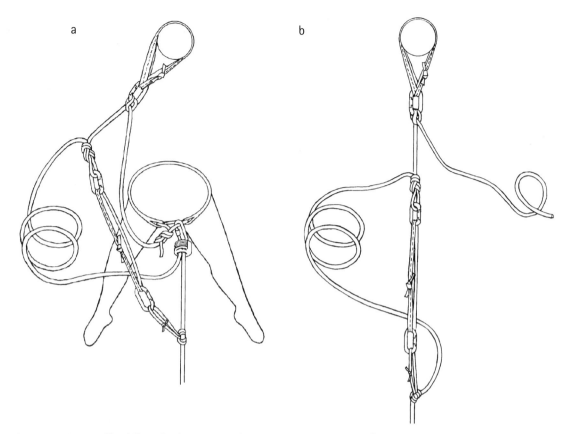

*Fig. 7-24. Tying off a fallen climber: a, attach a runner or prusik loop/runner chain to the anchor; b, belayer out of system, anchor tied off.*

## Belaying in Sport Climbing

Much climbing today takes place on artificial rock and manufactured climbing walls, in gyms or outdoors, and on short routes in rock-climbing areas. Most such "sport climbing" is top-roped; when led, it is usually protected by clipping into bolts. Although the general principles of belaying are the same as in other climbing environments, there are some characteristic features and pitfalls that make sport climbing worth separate treatment.

Many sport climbers get into this activity as a kind of rock gymnastics, and they often have little interest in the equipment-handling techniques that climbers must master. This can be a deadly kind of ignorance, because falls are extremely common in sport climbing where climbers are continually trying to push their physical limits. And the sport-climbing environment, which usually seems less threatening than that of longer, multipitch climbs, can induce a serious complacency.

Typically, when a sport pitch is being top-roped, the belayer will stand at the bottom, with the rope running up through a preplaced anchor and back down to the climber, who then ascends while the belayer takes in rope. The belayer will generally not be anchored; there is often nothing to anchor to, and even when there is anchoring seems too fussy and time-consuming.

Belaying without an anchor can cause problems. If you are belaying and standing well away from the rock or off to one side, the force of a fall—even a top-roped fall—can pull you sharply into or along the wall. You may not be injured or lose control of the belay, but the

*but ock fill*

fall will certainly be lengthened—perhaps enough to make it a ground fall. When considering what kind of force could have this effect, remember that the peak impact force, even with a top rope, is significantly greater than your partner's weight; remember also that pendulum falls create even greater forces. If you're belaying without an anchor, it's usually best to position yourself as nearly as possible directly beneath the anchor. Even then, if you are considerably lighter than your partner, you could be lifted upward by the force of a fall. This movement isn't always serious, but it does provide a reason to use a belay device that is very unlikely to result in loss of control of the belay (such as a Grigri).

The problems of unanchored belaying can be even more serious when the pitch is being led instead of being top-roped, with the climber using preplaced bolts for protection. If the bolts are in a straight line and a fall is taken low on the pitch—after the first or second bolt—the force on the belayer can be considerable. As the belayer, you should stand as close as possible under the first bolt. And if your partner is much heavier than you are, you might insist on being tightly anchored. Or tell your partner to find another belayer.

A common practice in top-roping areas is to run the rope through a runner on the anchor, rather than through carabiners, and then have several people take turns climbing the pitch. This is extremely dangerous because the runner can weaken quickly with this kind of treatment, creating a risk of anchor failure. Don't even consider climbing this way.

Remind yourself that even in seemingly benign climbing environments—with everyone having fun, pushing their limits, taking a lot of falls without getting a scratch—all the basic climbing hazards remain, requiring constant attention to safety.

# 8

# RAPPELLING

Rappelling can be so easy and exhilarating that you forget what a serious undertaking it really is. It's an indispensable activity in climbing, but it's also one of the more dangerous. If you learn it carefully from the start, you should have no trouble using this technique for sliding down a rope, controlling your speed with friction on the line. You will be able to descend almost any climbing pitch on rappel and, in fact, rappelling will be the only way to get down some faces of rock or ice.

You can get a sense of the danger by considering that as you rappel down a high cliff, full body weight on the rope, your life depends all the way on the anchor to hold the rope and on you to use the correct technique. If you fail or the anchor fails, you fall. Unlike belaying, where a force comes on the system only if the climber falls, the force on the rappel system is always there. Despite the danger, it's easy to become cocky and careless after one learns how simple rappelling can be, and the exhilaration can encourage hazardous technique.

Coming down from a climb, there's often a choice between rappelling and downclimbing. Sometimes rappelling is the fastest and safest way to descend a particular pitch, but many times it is not. Think it through, considering the terrain, the weather, how much time is available, and the strength and experience of the party. If you decide to rappel, do it safely and efficiently. One of the hidden dangers of rappelling is that it can waste considerable time in the hands of inexperienced rappellers.

## THE RAPPEL SYSTEM

A rappel system has four basic elements: an anchor, a rope, a means of applying friction to the rope, and someone to rappel. Each element is equally important. Without all four working together, each securely attached to the next, the system could fail, possibly with disastrous results. It's always important to remember all four of the rappel components—even when you're cold, tired, and hungry, and racing to beat the darkness—and to check and double-check that every element is in place, functioning properly and connected together to make up the system.

The most fundamental element of the system is the anchor, which is the point on the mountain to which the rest of the system is attached. The anchor must be carefully selected for strength and reliability. Once the rappel has begun, not only is the climber's life entirely dependent on the anchor, but returning to the anchor to make adjustments can be problematic, if not impossible.

The second element of the rappel system is the rope. The midpoint of the rope is looped through the anchor, with the two ends hanging down the descent route. The rappeller slides down this doubled rope and retrieves it from below by pulling on one end. Short rappels can be handled with just one rope, but longer rappels need the extra length of two ropes tied together, usually with a double fisherman's knot. The ropes are joined next to the anchor, with the two ends hanging down. With a two-rope rappel, you can even join ropes of different diameters, mating, for example, an 11-millimeter line with a 9-millimeter. On rare occasions, climbers use a single-strand rappel, in which the rope is simply tied at one end to the anchor.

The third element is the means of applying friction to the rope while at the same time remaining firmly attached to it. There are two methods for applying this friction as you proceed downward. In mechanical rappel systems, the doubled rope passes through a friction device attached to your seat harness. In nonmechanical systems, friction is provided by wrapping the rope around your body. In either case, your braking hand grasps the rope to control the amount of friction. Gloves are usually worn to prevent rope burns.

The most variable element in the rappel system is the climber—the point where such factors as personal attitude, fatigue and anxiety, poor weather and impending darkness, and varying levels of skill and training all come together to affect the outcome.

If you learn to treat the four elements of rappelling as an integrated system—a system of which you are a critical part—rappelling becomes easier to understand and, therefore, safer.

## Mechanical Rappel Devices

Most climbers use a mechanical system (fig. 8-1) as their principal rappelling method, and all operate essentially the same. The two strands of rope are run through a rappel device attached to your harness. As you begin the rappel and gravity pulls you downward, the rope slides through the device. Your braking hand controls this natural pull by adjusting the amount of friction on the rope as it runs through the device. It does this through a combination of variations in grip and hand position. With some setups, you get additional friction by wrapping the rope partly around your back. You control the speed of descent, and you can come to a stop anytime you wish.

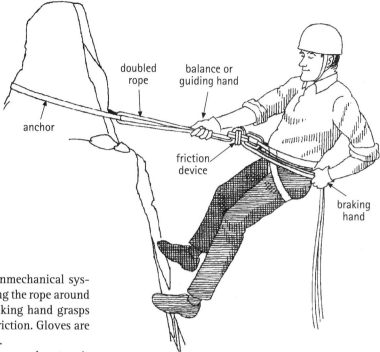

*Fig. 8-1. Mechanical rappel system*

It takes less effort to produce friction at the top of a rappel than at the bottom, because the weight of the rope hanging below you puts added friction on the rappel device. This is especially so on very steep or overhanging rappels where most of the rope hangs free. But no matter how little grip strength may be required to control your descent, your braking hand must never leave the rope. Your other hand—the guiding, or uphill, hand—slides freely along the rope to help maintain balance.

To rappel with a mechanical system, you need to wear some sort of a seat harness. In an emergency, you can put together an improvised diaper sling or a figure-8 rappel seat (figs. 8-2 and 8-3). Neither of these would ordinarily be used for climbing. (More general-purpose homemade and commercial harnesses are discussed in Chapter 6, Ropes, Knots, and Carabiners.) Never rappel with just a waist loop—a simple loop of webbing tied around your waist—because it can

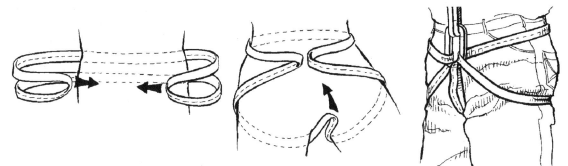

*Fig. 8-2. Diaper sling*

constrict your diaphragm enough to make you lose consciousness.

**The diaper sling** (fig. 8-2) takes about 10 feet of webbing tied into a large loop. With the loop behind your back, pull an end around to your stomach from each side. Bring a piece of the webbing from behind your back, between your legs, and up to your stomach to meet the other two parts. Clip them together in front with doubled carabiners or a locking carabiner. The diaper may also be clipped to a waist loop.

**The figure-8 seat** (fig. 8-3) is improvised from a standard-length runner. It must be clipped to a waist loop for stability.

## Carabiner Brake Method

A very widely used mechanical system, the carabiner brake, is somewhat complex to set up but has the virtue of not requiring any special equipment—just carabiners (fig. 8-4). All climbers should know how to use the carabiner brake method, even if they normally use a specialized rappel device. It's a great backup if the device is lost or forgotten, and it's the safest method of rappelling without a special device.

The carabiner brake system works best with oval carabiners and can also be managed with standard D-shaped carabiners; the system will not work correctly with so-called "bent-gate" carabiners (see Chapter 6, Ropes, Knots, and Carabiners).

To create the carabiner brake setup, start by attaching one locking or two regular carabiners to your seat harness. Any time a regular carabiner could be subjected to a twisting or side load, two carabiners or a

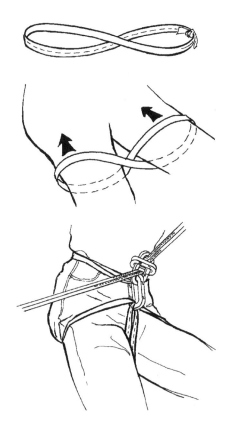

*Fig. 8-3. Figure-8 seat*

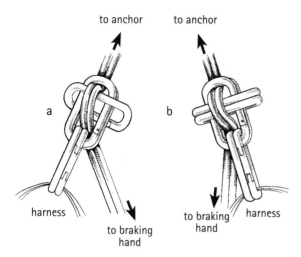

*Fig. 8-4. Carabiner brake system with: a, one carabiner clipped across the outer carabiner pair and b, two carabiners clipped across the outer carabiner pair in order to give greater friction.*

locking carabiner are needed, and this is one of those cases. If you use two regular carabiners, position the gates to keep them from being forced open and accidentally unclipping (fig. 8-5). The correct position is with the gates on opposing sides and reversed from each other, forming an X when they are opened at the same time.

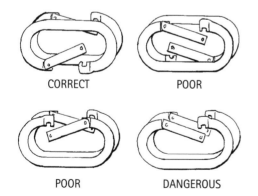

*Fig. 8-5. When substituting doubled carabiners for a locking carabiner, the correct position of the gates is opposed and reversed.*

After attaching the harness carabiners (or locking carabiner), clip another pair of carabiners to that, with the gates opposed and reversed. Then face the anchor, if you can. Lift a loop of the rappel ropes through the outer carabiner pair, from the bottom. Take yet another carabiner and clip it across the outer carabiner pair, beneath the rope loop. The rope then runs across an outer edge (not the gate!) of this final carabiner, known as the braking carabiner.

One braking carabiner (fig. 8-4a) provides enough friction for most rappels on ropes that are 10 to 11 millimeters in diameter. You might need a second or even a third braking carabiner (fig. 8-4b) for thinner ropes, heavy climbers, heavy packs, or steep or overhanging rappels. The ropes must always run over the solid side of the braking carabiners, never across the gate.

There are a couple of things to watch for as you're setting up the carabiner brake system. First, it's sometimes not possible to face the anchor as you pull the loop of rappel rope into the carabiner brake, and this can get confusing. A common beginner's mistake is to pull the rope into the system backward, as if preparing to rappel uphill toward the anchor.

Second, the weight of the rope hanging down the cliff may make it very difficult to pull the loop of rope up through the outer pair of carabiners and hold it while you clip in the braking carabiner. It helps to get that weight off the system. You can do that before pulling the loop of rope through by pulling up some slack rope and throwing a couple of wraps around a leg to take the weight. Or you can do it by pulling the loop through first, but making it extra large so you can lay it over your shoulder while you clip in the braking carabiner. Then drop the downhill strands back through the system so the brake remains close to the anchor.

If you are near the edge while setting up the carabiner brake or any other rappel method, you should be attached to an anchor for safety. This can be done by girth-hitching a long sling (runner) through your harness and securing it to the anchor, preferably with a locking carabiner.

## Figure–8 Rappel Device

The figure-8 is probably the most popular special device for rappelling (fig. 8-6). It is simpler to set up

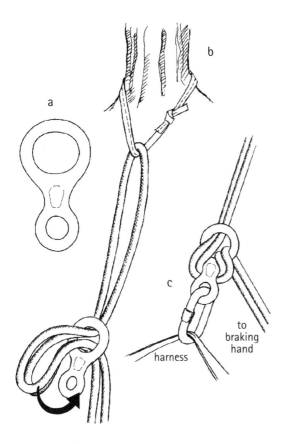

## Other Rappel Devices

Many other devices are used for rappelling. Most are primarily belay devices that can also be used for rappelling, such as belay plates (slots) and tubes. (See Chapter 7, Belaying, for an illustration of the various types of belay devices.) Some of these devices have disadvantages for rappelling, such as being difficult to feed rope through or heating up easily. Before buying any new device, check climbing literature for evaluation and test data, and read and follow the manufacturer's instructions closely.

## Other Mechanical Systems

Several mechanical rappel systems require no special device, just a locking carabiner. It can be worthwhile insurance to learn at least one of them.

To set up the carabiner wrap system (fig. 8-7), clip a locking carabiner into the locking carabiner or doubled carabiners that are clipped to your seat harness. Run the rappel rope through the outer end of the outside carabiner and wrap it around the carabiner's solid back, giving it more turns if you want more friction. Two turns are usually just about right. Position the outer carabiner so that the locked gate opening is at the far end. A potential disadvantage of the carabiner wrap system is that the carabiner could flip

*Fig. 8-6. Attaching a figure-8 device for use in rappelling: a, figure-8 rappel device; b, attaching rope to the figure-8 device; c, figure-8 rappel device in use.*

and requires less force to control than the carabiner brake method.

Keep in mind the disadvantages. It means carrying an extra piece of equipment, and most figure-8's are relatively heavy. If you lose or forget it, you must be prepared to use another rappel method. Most figure-8's require use of a locking carabiner for attaching to the harness (fig. 8-6c) and don't give you the option of using doubled carabiners. And the figure-8 puts some twists in the rope. The figure-8 was designed for rappelling, though some climbers use the device in one of several possible configurations for belaying.

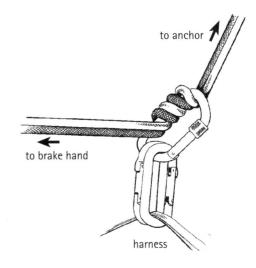

*Fig. 8-7. The carabiner wrap system*

around, and the movement of the wrapped rope might then unlock it.

The Münter hitch that is used for belaying can also be used for rappelling (see Chapter 7 for details on using the Münter hitch for belaying). It's very easy to set up but is the worst method for twisting the rope.

A method common in Europe merely runs the rappel rope through a locking carabiner at the harness, up over the climber's shoulder, and then down across the back to the opposite hand for braking. A danger is that, like nonmechanical systems, it is easy to fall out of.

## Nonmechanical Methods

Two traditional rappel methods use no hardware whatsoever to create friction on the rope. It's just the rope and your body.

**The arm rappel** (fig. 8-8) isn't used much, but it's occasionally helpful for quick descent of a low-angle slope. Lay the rappel rope behind your back, under your armpits, then wrap it once around each arm. Be sure the rope doesn't run over any exposed flesh; it will get surprisingly hot. Control your rate of descent by hand grip. For an arm rappel with a pack, be sure the rope goes outside and behind the pack rather than on top or underneath.

**The dulfersitz** (fig. 8-9) is a simple, all-purpose method that should be mastered by every climber for emergency use if you have no carabiners or seat harness. Face the anchor and step into the dulfersitz by straddling the rope. Bring it from behind around one hip, up across your chest, over the opposite shoulder, and then down your back to be held by the braking hand (the downhill hand) on the same side as the wrapped hip. The other hand is your guiding hand to hold the rope above you to help stay upright.

The dulfersitz has a number of drawbacks compared with mechanical rappel systems. It can unwrap from your leg, especially on high-angle rappels, though it helps to keep the wrapped leg slightly lower than the other. Stay under careful control and try to pad your body, because rope friction around your hip and across the shoulder will be painful, especially on steep rappels. Turn your collar up to protect your neck. If you're wearing a pack, the dulfersitz is even more awkward.

*Fig. 8-8. The arm rappel*

(providing you can get a solid anchor). This affords the longest possible rappel. It also makes it easier to pull the rope down from below after the rappel and often reduces the danger of rockfall as you do so.

Think about possible effects on the rope as you are looking for an anchor. Locate the anchor so as to minimize chances of the rope being pulled into a constricting slot or otherwise hanging up when you try to pull it down from below. Check the position of the rope over the edge of the rappel route as the person before you finishes rappelling. If the rope moves near or into a slot in the surface that could restrict its movement, consider relocating the anchor. In winter conditions, be cautious of the rope cutting into snow or ice and freezing in place.

You can use natural anchors or artificial (manufactured) anchors, just as you do for belaying or for placing points of protection during a climb. This section principally discusses anchors for climbing on rock. For information on anchors for use in snow and ice, see the sections on anchors in Chapter 13, Snow Travel and Climbing, and Chapter 15, Ice Climbing.

## Natural Anchors

The best natural anchor is a living, good-sized, well-rooted tree. The rappel rope usually goes through a runner that is attached to the anchor. If you can attach this runner to an unquestionably stout tree branch rather than low on the trunk, it helps limit the rope's contact with the ground, making it easier to retrieve the rope and reducing rope abrasion and the risk of rockfall. But note that connecting to a branch rather than the trunk puts more leverage on the tree, increasing the danger that it could be pulled out.

Be cautious in using bushes as an anchor, and if you do use one you'll probably want an additional anchor or two for safety. Also be careful using trees and bushes in very cold weather, when they can become brittle. Rock features—horns, columns, chockstones, large boulders—are commonly used as anchors. On snow or ice, you can make bollards.

*Fig. 8-9. The dulfersitz*

The dulfersitz is used in modern climbing only when there is no reasonable alternative or for short and easy low-angle rappels to save the trouble of putting a seat harness back on.

## RAPPEL ANCHORS

You will often be hanging your full weight on the rappel anchor, which is simply some point of attachment to the rock, snow, or ice. Set up the anchor as close as possible to the edge of the rappel route

Test a natural anchor if there's any question about whether it can support the weight of the heaviest climber and provide a large safety margin in case a rappeller puts extra force on the anchor by stopping quickly. You can test rock horns and smaller trees by pushing against them with your foot. Test the anchor before rappel gear is attached, and never after the rope or the rappeller is hooked in.

If you run the rappel rope through a runner looped around a rock horn (fig. 8-10a), be rigorous in determining the angle of force on the horn. You must eliminate the deadly possibility the runner could ride up and off the horn during a rappel (fig. 8-10b). Most climbers use only a single anchor if it's a solid, dependable natural anchor but add another anchor or two if there are any doubts.

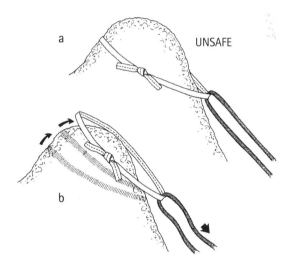

Fig. 8-10. Runner looped around a rock horn: a, a dangerous rappel anchor; b, runner rides up and off rock horn.

## Artificial Anchors

As a rule of thumb, if you are using artificial (manufactured) anchors, use at least two and try to equalize the load between them.

In unknown alpine terrain, some climbers carry pitons and a hammer to set anchors. The most common artificial rappel anchors are bolts or pitons that have

been left in place by previous climbers and which must be evaluated for safety just as if you were using them for belaying or for protection while climbing.

The climbers' hardware known as chocks—nuts, hexes, and so forth—are usually used only if no good alternative is available, but better a couple of good chocks than a shaky rock horn. It's not a good idea to trust chocks that you find already in place, left behind by climbers who weren't able to work them loose from their crack in the rock. However, sometimes you can take advantage of an abandoned chock by using it like a natural chockstone—looping a runner directly around it and making no use whatsoever of the sling attached to the old chock.

## THE ROPE

Before setting up the rappel, it's a good idea to run through the entire length of the rope to be sure it hasn't been cut or frayed during the climb. Then to get the rope ready for rappelling, you attach it to an anchor. In the simplest case, you untie a runner and retie it around a tree as a rappel sling. Then the midpoint of the rope is suspended from the sling (fig. 8-11a).

If you're using just one rope, put one end of the rope through the sling and pull it until you reach the midpoint. Or you can put the sling around the midpoint before you retie it around the tree. If you're

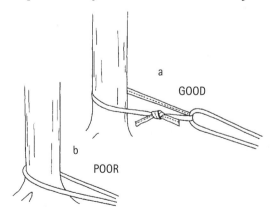

Fig. 8-11. Rappel rope attached to tree: a, rappel rope through a sling around a tree; b, rappel rope directly around tree.

joining two ropes together for the rappel, put one end of a rope through the sling and tie it to the other rope with a double fisherman's knot, backed up with overhand knots.

You could put the rope directly around the tree (fig. 8-11b), without use of a rappel sling–but this causes rope abrasion, soils the rope with tree resins, makes it harder to retrieve the rope, and if done enough times can kill the tree.

If your anchor is a rock feature or bolts or pitons, always attach a sling to the anchor, then run the rappel rope through the sling. Never put the rope directly around the rock or through the eye of the bolt hanger or piton, because the friction may make it impossible to pull the rope back down from below. Some climbers prefer to use two slings instead of one for added security. If you normally carry only sewn runners (which cannot be untied), you may want to bring along some $^9/_{16}$-inch webbing to cut and tie as needed for rappel slings.

On popular climbs, you'll find established rappel anchors encircled with the slings that must be left behind when a rappel rope is retrieved. Some of the older slings will feel dry and less supple. It's a good idea to

cut out a couple of the oldest slings and add a new one before running your rappel rope around them. If you are using more than one sling, try to use the same length to help distribute the load. (And don't forget to pack out the old slings you've removed.)

When using two anchors to support the rappel, the most common method is to run a separate sling from each anchor, with the slings meeting at the rappel rope. Generally try to adjust the slings so the force is the same on each anchor. For the strongest setup, keep a narrow angle between the two slings (fig. 8-12a). (You can also use just a single sling run through the two anchors, employing either self-equalization or the triangle method; both are described in Chapter 7, Belaying.)

You can help to avoid binding and abrasion of the rappel rope by making sure the point of connection

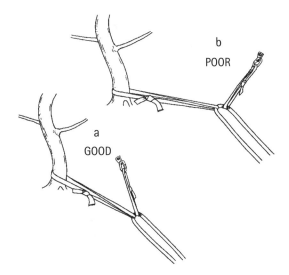

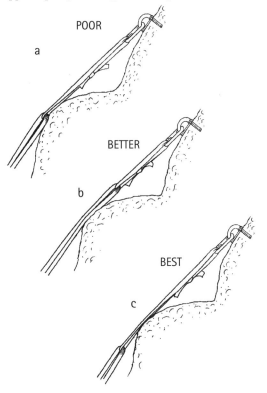

Fig. 8-12. The most common method of attaching the rappel rope to multiple anchors, with a separate sling attached to each of two anchors and meeting at the rappel rope: a, a narrow angle between slings is best; b, the angle between slings is too wide.

Fig. 8-13. The point of connection between the rappel sling and the rappel rope: a, rope binds and abrades against rock; b, rope doesn't bind but will still abrade; c, rope free to move and clear of rock.

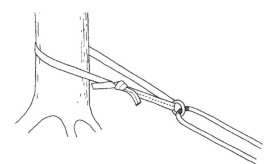

*Fig. 8-14. Rappel rope through descending ring*

between the rappel sling and the rope is away from the rock (fig. 8-13).

You can use a small piece of rappel hardware known as a descending ring to help reduce rope wear and make retrieval easier. It's simply a metal ring, 1¹/₂ inches or so in diameter. Thread the rappel sling through the ring before tying the sling. Then thread the rappel rope through the ring until you reach the rope's midpoint (fig. 8-14). When you pull the rope down later, it slides more easily through the descending ring than it would directly over the sling, which also can be weakened by rope friction.

The descending ring, however, does add another possible point of failure. Newer rings are continuous, nonwelded designs, much better than the welded type, which cannot be trusted. Some climbers insist on two rings, even if both are nonwelded. An alternative is a single ring, backed up by a non-weight–bearing sling from the anchor through the rope, ready to hold the rope in case the ring fails.

## Throwing Down the Rope

After the rappel rope is looped at its midpoint through an anchor, it's time to get the rope ready to toss down the rappel route.

Beginning from the rappel sling, coil each half of the rope separately into two butterfly coils. You'll end up with four butterfly coils, two on each side of the anchor. Throw the coils out and down the route, one at a time. Start on one side of the anchor by tossing the coil nearest the anchor, then the rope-end coil. Repeat for the other half of the rope (fig. 8-15). This sequence reduces rope snags and tangling. Before tossing, anchor one end of the rope or have another climber hold onto the rope near the anchor to make sure your tosses won't cause the rope to pull through the anchor. (Commercial rope bags make it easier to carry ropes and to keep them clean and tangle-free, and rope-tossing is usually easier if you are using a rope bag.)

You won't always end up with a perfect toss, with the rope hanging straight down the rappel route. If you end up with tangles, hang-ups, or bunching, it's usually best to pull it back up, recoil, and toss again. But sometimes it's just as well to work with what you've got. For instance, in a high wind, you're not likely to get a perfect toss. So one of the more experienced climbers in the party can rappel down to just above the first problem, stop, recoil the strands below that point, toss again, and continue the rappel. (The following section on rappel technique explains how to stop in midrappel.)

Shout "Rope!" before you throw the rope down a rappel route. Some climbers shout the word two times,

*Fig. 8-15. Throwing down the rope. Climber is tied in to an anchor for safety while working near the edge.*

to give anyone below a little time to respond or to watch out for the rope. Others shout just once, but wait for a moment for any response. Be sure you're attached to an anchor as you stand at the edge of the route to toss the rope.

## RAPPEL TECHNIQUE

When a climbing party reaches a rappel point, typically the first person down is one of the more experienced members of the group. This first rappeller will usually fix any tangles or problems with the rope and clear the anchor area and route of any debris that might be dislodged onto subsequent rappellers or other climbers.

Many climbers use the four elements of the rappel system—anchor, rope, rappel method, and climber—as a kind of checklist each time they rappel. Start with the anchor and assure yourself that it is as solid as it can be.

You've already inspected the rappel rope or ropes to be sure they haven't been cut or frayed during climbing. Now that the rappel is set up, check the rope to be sure it is properly threaded through the anchor and that it's not tangled or knotted or arranged in such a way that it will fray dangerously against the rock. If you're using two ropes, check the knot joining them.

Then check your attachment to the rope, through your rappelling device or setup. If your harness is involved (as it usually will be), be sure it is fastened properly. Have one of your climbing partners check your setup again. Pay special attention to the brake system: it's not set up backward, is it, as if you were rappelling uphill? Are the gates of carabiner pairs correctly opposed and reversed? Are locking carabiners securely closed? (If another climber rappels before you, don't let the rappel begin until you've thoroughly checked out the entire setup and the climber's attachment to it.)

Lastly, prepare yourself mentally and physically. Concentrate on a mental review, thinking through the entire rappel and making a mind's-eye check of the complete setup and the process you're using to get down the route.

In preparing to rappel, you've now gone through a sequence of establishing the anchor, attaching the rope to the anchor, throwing the rope down, attaching yourself into the rappel system, and finally unhooking from whatever belay or tie-in you've had while doing all this work at the edge of the route.

At this point, you are facing the anchor, your back to the descent route, ready to head down the rope.

## Getting Started

Just before you begin the rappel, shout "On Rappel!" to warn other climbers you're on the way down.

Now comes the most nerve-wracking part of most rappels. To gain stability, your legs must be nearly perpendicular to the slope. Therefore, at the very brink of a precipice, you're required to lean backward, out over the edge (fig. 8-16). In some cases you may be able to ease the transition by climbing down several feet before leaning out and putting your full weight on the rope to start the rappel (fig. 8-17).

With the carabiner brake or other mechanical systems, you may be able to sit on the edge of the rappel ledge and wiggle gently off, simultaneously turning inward to face the slope. This technique is particularly useful when starting the rappel above an overhang (fig. 8-18).

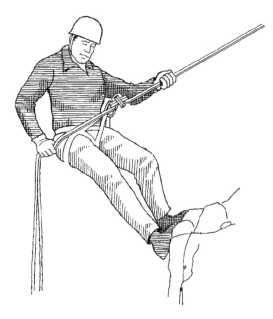

*Fig. 8-16. Starting rappel from a high anchor*

*Fig. 8-17. Climbing below a low anchor before starting rappel*

## Position, Speed, and Movement

As you move downward, your position should be something like this: feet shoulder-width apart, knees flexed, body at a comfortable angle to the slope, and facing a little toward the braking hand for a view of the route. The most common beginners' mistakes are keeping the feet too close together and failing to lean back far enough. (Some go to the other extreme and lean too far back, increasing the chance of tipping over.) If anything should happen, such as tipping over or losing your footing, remember the most important thing: Hang onto the rope with your braking hand. Once the situation has stabilized, work on getting your feet back against the rock, in the basic position shown in the final panel of Figure 8-18.

Move slowly and steadily, with no bounces or leaps. Feed the rope slowly and steadily into the rappel system, avoiding stops and jerks. Higher rappel speeds put more heat and stress on the rappel system, and it's especially important to go slowly on any questionable anchor. If you have to stop quickly while moving fast down the rope, the anchor is subjected to a great deal of additional force. Use extreme caution rappelling a face with loose or rotten rock. The danger here

*Fig. 8-18. Sitting down on ledge and squirming off to get started*

is that rock can be knocked loose and hit you or damage the rope.

Overhangs on the route can be a problem. It's easy to end up swinging into the face below the overhang and banging your hands and feet. There also is the danger of getting the brake system jammed on the lip of the overhang. One way to help get past that difficult transition from moving down against the rock wall to hanging below the overhang is to bend your knees sharply while your feet are at the edge of the overhang, then quickly drop three or four feet. This stresses the rappel system, of course, but it helps reduce both the chance of swinging into the face below and of jamming the brake on the lip. Another method is to put your feet on the edge of the overhang and then lower your butt down below your feet. Then walk your feet in on the roof of the overhang until the rope makes contact with the rock face.

Below an overhang, you will be dangling free on the rope. Assume a sitting position, hold yourself upright with the guiding hand on the rope above, and continue steadily downward. Don't be surprised if you spin as twists in the rope unwind.

Sometimes, in order to reach the next rappel spot, you'll have to move at an angle to the fall line, walking yourself to one side instead of moving straight down. Be careful you don't lose your footing here. If you do, you will swing on the rappel rope back toward the fall line in what could be a nasty pendulum fall. And it could leave you in a position you can't recover from without climbing back up the rope with prusik slings or ascender devices.

## Potential Problems

Shirttails, hair, chin straps from a hard hat, and just about anything else have the potential to get pulled into the braking system. Keep a knife handy in case you have to cut foreign material out of the system, but be extremely careful with a sharp knife around ropes under tension. It may not take much of a nick to part the rope.

If you run across a tangled or jammed rope on the way down, fix it while you're still above the problem. Stop at the last convenient ledge above the area, or stop with a leg wrap (explained in the next section). Pull the rope up, correct the problem, then throw it down again. Sometimes there's a simple solution. For instance, rappelling down blank slabs, you can often just shake out tangles as they are encountered.

## Stopping in Midrappel

If it's ever necessary to stop partway down a rappel, you have a couple of good methods for securing the rope and stopping the rappel. The first is to wrap the rope two or three times around one leg (fig. 8-19a). The friction around your leg, increased by the weight of the hanging rope, is usually enough to hold you and to free your hands. Keep a braking hand on the rope until the wraps are completed and tested with your weight. Make the wraps tight, or you could end up a foot or two lower than you intended as you put weight on the wraps and they tighten.

A second method is to pass the rope around your waist and tie two or three half-hitches around the rappel rope above the brake system (fig. 8-19b). This can be released easily when you're ready to continue the rappel.

Some rappel or belay devices have other ways to secure the rope in the device. Consult the manufacturer's instructions or obtain reliable instruction on their use.

## Finishing the Rappel

Near the end of the rappel, you will notice that it is much easier to feed rope through the rappel device than when you started. This is because the extra friction caused by the weight of the rope below you is now considerably less.

You will also notice a surprising amount of rope stretch, particularly on a two-rope rappel. You need to be aware of this stretch factor as you clear the rope from your device after completing the rappel. If you let go of the rope, it could spring back to its normal length and suddenly be up out of your reach. Better to end the rappel near the end of the rope rather than at the very end.

As you near the end of the rope, be sure to find a good place to stop the rappel. Clear the rope from your device only after you are in a good stance, and tied in if necessary. Be sure you are in as secure a spot as possible, safe from rockfall and out of the way of the next person coming down. Then shout "Off Rappel!" to let your party know you're done and safe and that the next person can begin the rappel.

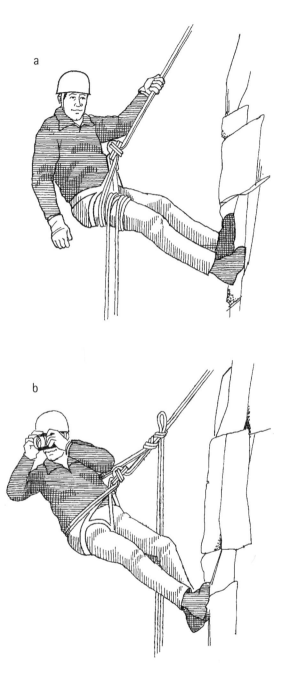

## MULTIPLE RAPPELS

A descent route often involves a series of rappels. These multiple rappels, especially in alpine terrain, present special problems and require maximum efficiency to keep the party on the move.

The trickiest is a rappel into the unknown, down a route you're not familiar with. Avoid this kind of multiple rappel. If you cannot, take the time to check out the possible rappel lines as carefully as time and the terrain permit. Sometimes you can find a photo of the route before you leave on the climb and bring it with you. Keep in mind that the first couple of rappels down an unfamiliar route may commit you to it all the way, for better or for worse.

If you can't see to the bottom of an unfamiliar rappel pitch, the first person down has got to be prepared to climb back up in case the rappel leads nowhere. This rappeller should carry prusik slings or mechanical ascenders for going up the rope.

Rappelling down unfamiliar terrain brings an increased risk of getting the rope hung up. You can minimize the problem by downclimbing as much of the route as possible, instead of rappelling. You might also consider doing rappels using just one rope, even if two ropes are available, because one rope is easier to retrieve and less likely to hang up than two.

Even though it's nice to gain the maximum distance from each rappel, don't bypass a good rappel spot even 40 feet or so from the end of the rope if there are doubts about finding a good place farther down.

As a party moves through a series of rappels, the first person down each pitch usually carries gear to use in setting up the next rappel (after tying into an anchor at the bottom and trying to find shelter from rockfall). The more experienced climbers in a party can take turns being first and last, while it's best for beginners to be somewhere in the middle.

## SAFETY BACKUPS

Climbers have several options to increase the safety of a rappel. The options are occasionally useful in specific situations or for helping a beginner gain confidence in rappelling.

*Fig. 8-19. Stopping in midrappel: a, with rope wrapped around leg; b, with two half-hitches tied above the rappel device.*

**Knots in the end of the rope:** It's possible to rappel off the end of the rope if you're not paying attention. Some climbers put a knot in the end of each rope, or tie the ends together, to eliminate this danger. If you add knots, don't rely blindly on them to tell when you've reached the end of the rope. The knots might come untied, of course, and in any case you want to keep an eye on the end of the rope so you can plan where to stop. The knots themselves can cause a problem by jamming in the rock if you ever find it necessary to pull the rope back up to work on it. They can also jam in the rappel device if you get too near the end of the rope.

**Pulling on the rappel ropes:** A person standing below a rappeller can easily control the rappeller's movement or stop it altogether—thus providing an effective belay—by pulling down on the rappel ropes, putting friction on the brake system. To safeguard the rappeller with this method, the person at the bottom simply holds the rope strands loosely, ready to pull them tight the instant the rappeller has difficulty (fig. 8-20).

**Top belay:** The rappeller can also be protected by a belay from above with a separate rope. If the belayer uses a separate anchor, the rappeller is safe from even a total failure of the rappel anchor. A top belay is recommended for all beginners, for climbers with minor injuries, and for the first person down on a suspect anchor. The belays are too time-consuming for routine use because they drastically increase a party's descent time.

**Prusik backup:** Some climbers like the security of a prusik or Bachmann knot while rappelling, sliding the knot along the rappel ropes as they descend. The knot is in place above the brake system, and the prusik loop is clipped to a carabiner linked to your seat harness. If the brake system fails and you start to drop, the pull causes the prusik knot to automatically grip the ropes and stop the fall (fig. 8-21).

*Fig. 8-20. Rappel halted by climber below, who is pulling down on the ends of the rope*

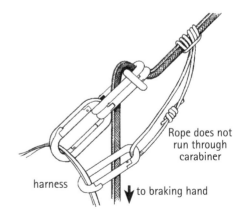

Rope does not run through carabiner

harness

to braking hand

*Fig. 8-21. Prusik backup for a carabiner brake rappel system*

Backing up your rappel with a prusik knot has its dangers. Be careful it doesn't lock up unexpectedly—once it's under tension it can be tough to get loose—and keep the loop short so you can reach it if it locks. There's also the opposite danger: that the prusik knot will fail to lock when it should, particularly if you forget to release your hold on the knot. The prusik knot also can generate a lot of heat during a sudden stop from a high-speed rappel, possibly weakening the knot or sling material. Remember that controlling the prusik requires the full-time use of your guiding hand, which then isn't available for balance or protection.

## — RETRIEVING THE RAPPEL ROPE —

Successful rope retrieval after a rappel depends on some important steps even before the last rappeller starts down the rope. It takes just one frightening experience with a stuck rappel rope to guarantee that you'll always take these precautions.

If you're using two ropes for the rappel, they will be tied together near the anchor. It's critical that you know which rope to pull on from below. Pull the wrong one, and you'll be attempting the impossible task of pulling the knot through the rappel sling. In some parties, the last two rappellers say out loud which rope is to be pulled, as an aid to remembering which is which.

The last rappeller should take a good final look at the rope and the rappel sling to see that everything is in order and that the rope isn't about to catch on the rock or the sling. Before the last person starts down, a climber at the bottom should test the rope by pulling to check that it can be moved and to see that the connecting knot in a two-rope rappel can be pulled free of the edge.

With such a two-rope rappel, the last person who starts down may want to stop at the first convenient ledge and pull enough of the rope down so that the connecting knot is clear of the edge. This helps take

some of the uncertainty out of the difficult business of recovering a long rappel rope. However, it also shortens one rope end, so be sure the rappeller still has enough rope to reach the bottom.

The last rappeller has the main responsibility for spotting any retrieval problems. This last person can get twists out of the rope by keeping one finger of the braking hand between the ropes throughout the descent. (The same purpose is served by splitting the two ropes through a carabiner on your harness, just uphill of the braking hand.)

With the last rappeller down, it's time to retrieve the rope. First take out any visible twists and remove any safety knots in the end of the rope. Then give the rope a slow, steady pull. Other climbers should take shelter to stay out of the way of falling rope or rockfall. If you've taken all the right steps and luck is on your side, the rope will pull free.

A jammed rappel rope is among a climber's worst nightmares. If it hangs up, either before or after the end clears the anchor, try flipping the rope with whipping motions before trying to get it down with extreme pulling. If you can, move both left and right and try more flipping or pulling. If the other end is still in reach, try pulling on it to see if you can dislodge the stuck portion above.

If all else fails, it may be necessary to climb up and free the rope. Belay the climber if enough rope is available. As a final resort if the party can't proceed without the rope, a climber might decide to attempt the desperate and very dangerous tactic of ascending the stuck rope with prusik slings or mechanical ascenders. The extreme danger of climbing an unsecured rope should be weighed very carefully against the option of staying where you are until another rope is available.

After you've studied rappelling and tried it a few times, it will be easy to see why climbers approach the technique with a fair degree of caution. But it's one of the activities central to climbing, and if you know what you're doing, it works well.

Overleaf; *Grand Canyon, Arizona ©Bill Hatcher/ Adventure Photo;* overleaf inset: *©Greg Epperson/ Adventure Photo;*

# PART THREE

# ROCK CLIMBING

# ROCK-CLIMBING TECHNIQUE

Climbing is a joyous, instinctive activity. As children, we scurry up trees, garden walls, building facades, and anything else steep and enticing. Then we grow up. For some of us, however, the adult urge to climb finds a beautiful outlet in rock climbing.

It's an exciting activity you can go at in many different styles and many different settings. For many climbers, the ultimate pleasure is scaling steep solid granite in an isolated alpine setting far from the city. For them, the crags close to home are only a practice ground to hone skills in preparation for an escape to the mountains. For others, the primary pleasure is the kinesthetic joy of moving on rock, or even climbing on artificial holds in a climbing gym, executing the most difficult and gymnastic of moves. Mastering the physical challenge of climbing may be more important than the setting, and a long alpine approach a nuisance rather than a pleasure. And there are those who treasure the whole range of rock-climbing experiences, from working out a single move in a difficult bouldering problem or training on an artificial climbing wall, to completing sustained challenging pitches on a towering rock wall or climbing short sections of rock during an alpine climb on a glaciated peak.

The joys of rock climbing are found in all these ways, and despite their differences, the skills and techniques are essentially the same. This chapter, in keeping with the focus of this book, discusses basic and intermediate-level rock-climbing skills needed in an alpine setting. With the growing popularity of rock climbing, several excellent texts on more advanced techniques are widely available (see Appendix B, Supplementary References).

## GEAR

### Footwear

Mountaineering boots are commonly used on alpine climbs of modest technical difficulty or where weather or conditions (such as presence of snow or ice) favor their use. Boots generally hold on larger edges quite well, but they are less useful on tiny edges or for "smearing" on holds.

For more difficult rock climbs, there are shoes made specifically for rock climbing (fig. 9-1). For many routes, rock shoes are essential. They are generally superior for smearing, edge quite well, and are well-suited for crack climbing.

Most rock shoes consist of a flexible upper, usually made of soft leather that is sometimes lined with canvas or nylon, and a smooth, flexible rubber sole. The rubber sole is made from a compound developed to create "stickier" soles that provide greater friction between rock and sole, important on increasingly difficult routes. Rock shoes should fit very snugly to allow maximum control and feel of the rock. Specialized rock shoes are available that are especially well suited for certain types of climbing. A high-top shoe (fig. 9-1a) is excellent for crack climbing because it protects the ankles. Shoes with

used for more gymnastic climbing, as you may need to wear them for many hours at a time. Although rock shoes are generally worn without socks, some individuals prefer adding a lightweight pair of socks, particularly for lengthier climbs.

Shoes resembling running shoes but with soles and rands made from sticky rubber, and with more durable uppers, have gained popularity in recent years (fig. 9-1d). These shoes offer a compromise between a cumbersome mountaineering boot and a rock-climbing shoe (which works well for climbing but makes for uncomfortable walking). Such shoes are useful when the approach to a climb involves moderate terrain with no snow or ice and the climb itself does not require the superior edging, crack-climbing, and smearing capabilities of a rock shoe.

## Helmets

Climbing helmets (fig. 9-2) protect your head from rockfall and from gear dropped by climbers above you. Helmets also protect from the many possibilities of

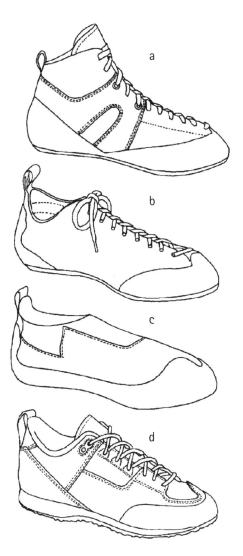

*Fig. 9-1. Rock shoes: a, all-around shoe; b, more specialized edging shoe; c, slipper; d, combined approach/climbing shoe.*

a stiff midsole are excellent for edging (fig. 9-1b). The extra-light, flexible slipper (fig. 9-1c) works well on overhanging routes.

For most alpine climbs, a rock shoe that covers the ankle provides better protection from cuts and scrapes (fig. 9-1a). Rock shoes selected for lengthy but moderate alpine climbs should not fit as snugly as shoes

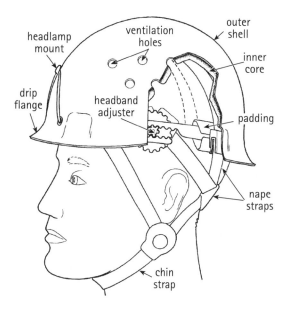

*Fig. 9-2. Climbing helmet features. (Generally, no individual helmet will come with all these features.)*

sudden impact against the rock: a fall to the ground, a leader fall that swings the climber into the rock, or a quick move upward against a sharp rock outcropping.

It's necessary to evaluate the risks in reaching your decision on when to wear a helmet. You'll see helmets most commonly on alpine climbs, where cliffs are often prone to loose rock and consequent rockfall hazard. There's less rockfall danger at popular sport-climbing crags because the routes are kept relatively clean by frequent ascents, but climbers still aren't immune to head injury from dropped gear or from falls.

Helmets can be bulky and heavy, although newer models are more comfortable than their predecessors, with no sacrifice in safety. But comfortable or not, a helmet can mean the difference between life and death, or between a minor scrape and serious injury. Wear the helmet properly so that it also helps protect your forehead (fig. 9-3).

Climbing helmets must be strictly that: helmets for climbing. Don't even think of getting by with a bicycle or football helmet. In buying a helmet, check for the mark of approval by the UIAA (Union Internationale des Associations d'Alpinisme). Helmets are available in plastic, fiberglass, and/or graphite materials, providing some choice in helmet weight.

Comfort and ease of adjustability are two major factors to consider when shopping for a helmet. You will probably have to wear the helmet for long periods of time, greatly magnifying any discomfort you can detect while donning it in the store. Think about the temperature extremes you will encounter while climbing. Will you need ventilation holes? Will a hat fit underneath the helmet? Can the helmet be adjusted while you are wearing it, or does adjustment require removing the helmet? How convenient is it to strap a headlamp onto the helmet?

UIAA approval by no means signifies that all helmets provide equal protection. For instance, some climbing helmets feature nape straps that help to maintain a secure fit in the event of a frontal hit, much in the same way that many bicycle helmets do. Other climbing helmets are constructed with a polystyrene core inside the shell, designed to shatter upon severe impact, thereby absorbing energy and providing more protection. Such a core is also likely to come with the drawback of poorer ventilation.

## Clothing

Clothing for rock climbing should be chosen for appropriateness to weather conditions and for freedom of movement. Some climbers prefer loose-fitting pants; others choose body-hugging tights made of stretchy spandex fabric, such as Lycra. You can wear shorts, but of course they leave your legs more susceptible to abrasion and sunburn. Remove jewelry and watches that can get caught in equipment or abraded on holds or in cracks. (For general information on clothing, see Chapter 2.)

## Tape

Athletic tape can protect hands from abrasion against rock, especially when climbing difficult cracks. There are a number of different taping methods, but no matter what the method the tape must stay securely in place and not begin to peel off partway up a pitch. The tape also must protect vulnerable areas, especially wrists and the back of the hand, while allowing maximum

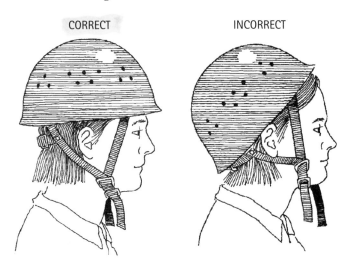

CORRECT          INCORRECT

*Fig. 9-3. Proper versus improper way of wearing a helmet. Many climbers wear their helmet tipped back on their head, leaving their forehead exposed to rockfall. Very jaunty but dangerous!*

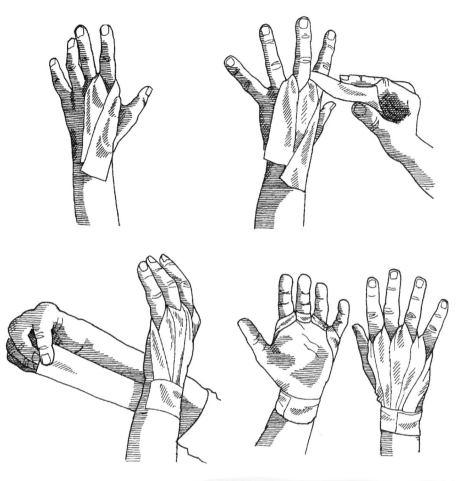

*Fig. 9-4. Hand taped for climbing: back of hand and knuckles are protected; palm is mostly left open.*

freedom of hand movement. A common mistake is to wrap the tape too tightly.

One taping method leaves most of the palm untaped to increase gripping sensitivity on the rock (fig. 9-4). Tape can also be used to provide support and/or protection for finger joints that are easily overstressed by difficult rock climbing or vigorous training.

## Chalk

Many climbers use gymnastic chalk to improve their grip, especially in hot weather. The chalk is usually carried in a chalk bag worn on the back of the harness or attached to a separate runner tied around the waist, so you can dip a hand in the chalk whenever you need it.

Chalk is available as loose powder, as small blocks that can be crushed in your chalk bag, and as fist-size balls of loose chalk covered with a porous cloth that allows some chalk to get on the hands when the cloth is manipulated. The latter method prevents spillage, although climbers who prefer climbing with very chalky hands may find loose chalk more to their liking.

Some climbers feel that chalk detracts from the rock by leaving white smudges. They also argue that the chalk identifies the holds, robbing other climbers of the experience of finding the holds and figuring out the climbing sequence for themselves. A compromise solution used by some is colored chalk that blends in with the rock, although the consistency of such chalk is generally not as desirable as that of gymnastic chalk.

On frequently climbed pitches, sweat and chalk can leave holds slimy and difficult to use. Some climbers carry a small brush, such as a toothbrush, to clean the holds.

## Other Gear

A stiff wire brush for "refreshing" the rubber on rock shoes may improve the shoes' stickiness. Knee pads are often used on rock climbs that involve considerable chimney technique, such as many of the great routes in Yosemite Valley. These items can be found in hardware stores.

Additional gear is covered in other chapters. This includes equipment that is less specific to rock climbing, such as ropes and harnesses and the varieties of hardware specific to the skills of leading and placing protection.

## CONSERVING ENERGY

To the beginner, rock climbing appears to require great arm strength. Not surprisingly, beginning climbers tire quickly, and as the terrain steepens they resort to flailing about for handholds and footholds. This saps energy. Several proven techniques help conserve energy instead.

### Climb with Your Feet

Pay attention to footwork and balance and you'll reduce the need to rely on arm and hand strength. Stand erect over your feet and fight the tendency to lean in and hug the rock. On very steep rock, however, pressing the hips close to the rock can help push body weight directly down onto small footholds.

When possible, keep arms outstretched to avoid hanging on bent arms, which is very tiring. As you raise a foot to the next foothold, try to keep your arms straight, avoiding the tendency to use them to haul yourself from one hold to the next. Once you begin to step up on a foothold, transfer all your weight and complete the move. Shift your hips over your foot and stand up by using leg muscles, not by pulling yourself up with your arms. Legs are much stronger than arms. Let the legs lift the body.

If you must hang on handholds, the least tiring way is to hang on straight arms rather than bent arms (fig. 9-5). Do this either by lowering your center of gravity (bend knees, even squat) or by leaning out, away from the rock. Always maximize the proportion of weight being supported by the feet rather than the arms. It also helps to hang your arms down and shake them out, allowing a brief rest and return of circulation to stressed muscles.

Fig. 9-5. "Resting" an outstretched arm

## Climb with Your Eyes

Look carefully at the rock. Remember to look down to spot footholds as well as up to find handholds. Plan a move and sequence before trying to execute it. Move smoothly and deliberately, without wasted motion. Strive for fluidity to conserve both time and energy. Don't flail aimlessly in an attempt to find handholds and footholds.

Look for natural resting places such as ledges or secure footholds. If a no-hands rest isn't possible, try for a stance that uses as natural a body position as possible and that requires the least amount of upper body strength.

Look for footholds that are comfortably spaced whenever possible. High steps are strenuous and make balance awkward, whereas steps close together waste energy without providing much upward progress.

Look for handholds that are at about head height, because these provide a good stance and often are not as fatiguing as handholds above the head. They also let you lean away from the rock to view other potential handholds and footholds. Often, however, you won't have much choice in the matter, because the nature and difficulty of the rock will dictate where the holds are.

## Use Three-Point Suspension

Three-point suspension is an elementary approach to rock climbing in which you move one hand or foot at a time while the other three limbs remain stationary (fig. 9-6). Be sure you're in balance over your feet before releasing a handhold to reach for the next one. This is an especially useful approach when the rock may be unsound, because it allows you to balance securely on three holds while testing the next one.

Know where your center of gravity is. The optimal position will vary, but it's often useful to keep a low center of gravity, with weight directly over the feet. Move your center of gravity over a new foothold before committing weight to it. Only when your body is in balance over the new hold should you transfer weight onto it.

As you try more difficult climbs, you'll learn moves that don't adhere to the principle of three-point suspension. There may be only one or two sound holds,

*Fig. 9-6. Three-point suspension: hands and right foot provide secure stance; left foot is moved to a higher hold.*

and body position will be used to maintain a delicate balance over those holds. For example, a hand or foot may be positioned over a nonexistent hold, or hips may be thrust in one direction to counterbalance other parts of the body.

## Avoid Loose Rock

In general, select holds based on solidness, convenience, and size. A visual inspection will often tell you all you need to know. But if you doubt the soundness of a hold, test it with a gentle kick or with a blow from the heel of the hand. When a section of loose rock is struck by the heel of the hand, it will often sound hollow. You can also push or pull on rocks to test for looseness. Keep alert to the consequences if the hold fails during testing. Be sure it won't fall on people below, and be sure your stance is secure so you yourself won't fall.

Remember that the hold must be useful in the context of the route. A large firm hold is useless if it leads away from the planned route and puts you into a position where you can't move to the next hold. A smaller but more conveniently placed hold may be a better choice.

When circumstances force you to climb rock that is loose, move carefully and deliberately. Often, a somewhat loose handhold or foothold can be used if you are careful to push down on it without dislodging it.

## FACE CLIMBING

Face climbing is just what the name says: climbing rock faces, as distinct from the crack climbing that will be covered later in this chapter. Face climbing generally involves using the hands to grasp irregularities on the rock and then utilizing these same holds for the feet. Face climbing also involves the ascent of seemingly featureless slabs, using friction and balance. In some ways, face climbing is the most natural type of climbing (fig. 9-7). You move up a series of handholds and footholds, somewhat like climbing a ladder.

The important thing to remember in face climbing is that a single hold may be used in a variety of ways, by feet and hands. What initially appears to be a good cling hold may also allow use of one of the other techniques that will be discussed in the following sections, such as a lieback, a mantel, or a stemming move. Be creative.

Fig. 9-7. Face climbing

## Handholds

You can use handholds for balance, to help raise yourself by pulling up on the hold, or to provide various forms of counterpressure.

Handholds (fig. 9-8) offer maximum security when all fingers are used. Ways to use fingers aren't always obvious on small holds. For example, with fingers holding onto a tiny ledge, you may be able to use the thumb in opposition on a minor rugosity (fig. 9-8a). On a very narrow hold or a small pocket in the rock, you can stack fingers on top of each other to increase pressure on the hold (fig. 9-8b).

The most common handhold is the cling hold (fig. 9-8c). Large cling holds allow the entire hand to be cupped over the hold, while smaller variations

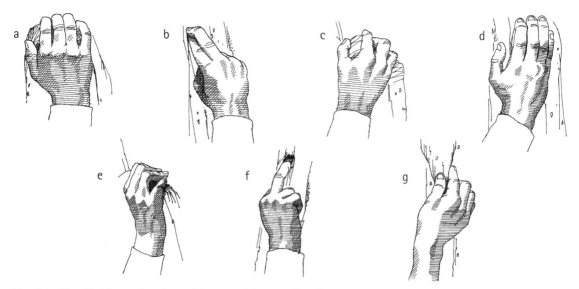

*Fig. 9-8. Handholds: a, thumb used in opposition to other fingers; b, stacking fingers to apply greater pressure on a small hold; c, large cling hold; d, open grip–keeping distal finger joints flexed puts less stress on joints and tendons; e, cling grip on small hold–extension of distal finger joints is more stressful and is more likely to cause injury than the open grip; f, pocket grip, useful for small pockets only large enough to admit a single digit–keeping other fingers curled helps get the most force out of the muscle/tendon system, but stresses the finger and may cause injury; g, pinch grip.*

(fig. 9-8d) may allow room for only the fingertips. Keeping fingers close together provides a stronger grip on the hold. If the hold is not large enough for all fingers to be placed on it, at least curl the other ones, which permits the fingers in use to get the most force from the muscle/tendon system (fig. 9-8f). When using cling holds, be aware that certain hand configurations put extreme stress on the fingers and may lead to injury (fig. 9-8e).

Because you will depend mainly on your legs for upward progress, handholds are sometimes used only for balance. The pinch grip (fig. 9-8g) is a handhold that may allow you to maintain a balanced stance on good footholds long enough to shake out your free arm and to reach for a higher, more secure handhold or place protection.

## Footholds

Climbers use most footholds by employing one of two techniques, edging or smearing. On many holds,

either technique will work, and the one to use depends on your own preference and type of footwear. We'll take up a third technique, called the foot jam, in a later section.

In edging, the edge of the sole is placed over the hold (fig. 9-9a). You can use either the inside or outside edge, but the inside is usually preferred for greater ease and security. The ideal point of contact may vary, but generally it's between the ball of the foot and the end of the big toe. Keeping the heel higher than the toes provides greater precision, but lowering the heel is a more restful position. Using the actual toe of the boot or rock shoe ("toeing in") may be very tiring. With practice, you will become proficient using progressively smaller footholds.

In smearing, the foot points more uphill, with the sole "smeared" over the hold (fig. 9-9b). The technique of smearing works best with rock shoes or flexible boots. On lower-angle rock, you may not need an actual hold, but will only have to achieve enough friction between

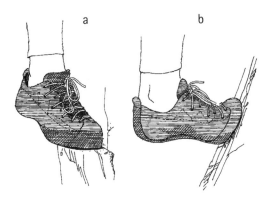

*Fig. 9-9. Footholds: a, edging; b, smearing.*

sole and rock. On steeper terrain, smear the front of the foot over a hold, and see how even tiny irregularities in the rock can provide significant friction and security.

Fatigue, often aggravated by anxiety, can lead to troublesome spastic contractions of the muscles of the leg, known as "sewing-machine leg." The best way to stop it is to try to relax your mind and to change leg position, either by moving on to the next hold, lowering the heel, or straightening the leg.

In using footholds, optimize the direction of force on the hold. Flexing the ankle may increase the surface area of contact between sole and rock, giving maximum holding power. Leaning away from the rock creates inward as well as downward force on the hold, increasing security.

Decide the best way to use a hold before you put your foot on it. Then maintain your position on the hold. Although it's sometimes necessary to reposition the foot into a better relationship to the hold, avoid thrashing and repeated repositioning to try to find something better. This wastes time and energy and may cause you to slip off altogether. On marginal footholds, it may be mandatory to maintain the position exactly, as any movement or rotation could cause the foot to slip off. Keeping your foot in position can take a lot of concentration and skill as you move up on the hold and step above with the other foot.

With the large footholds called buckets, place only as much of your foot as necessary on the hold (fig. 9-10). Putting your foot too far into the bucket can sometimes force the lower leg outward, making for an out-of-balance stance.

Generally avoid using your knees, which are susceptible to injury and offer little stability. Nevertheless, even experienced climbers occasionally use a knee to avoid an especially high or awkward step. The main considerations are to avoid injury from pebbles and sharp crystals and to avoid becoming trapped on your knees, unable to rise to your feet. This can be a big problem if you find yourself beneath an overhanging bulge with insufficient space to easily stand up.

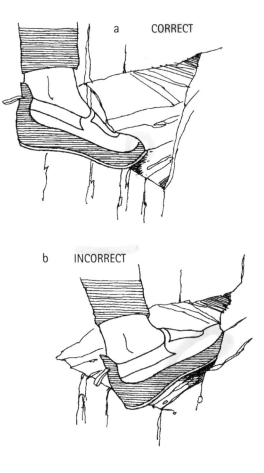

*Fig. 9-10. Bucket hold: a, correct; b, incorrect.*

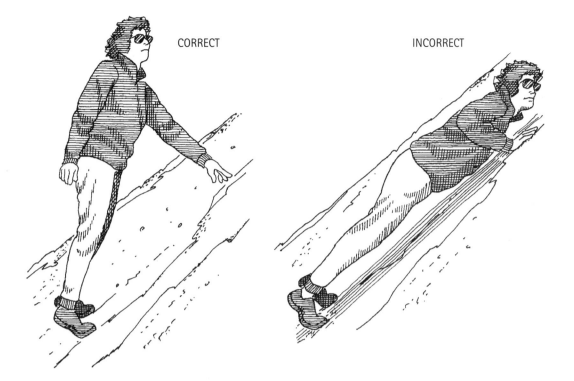

CORRECT                    INCORRECT

*Fig. 9-11. Slab (friction) climbing*

Slab climbing (fig. 9-11), also referred to as friction climbing, requires liberal use of smearing moves. Balance and footwork are the keys to success, and smearing with the feet is the primary technique.

Remember to flex the ankle (lowering the heel) and keep weight directly over the ball of the foot for maximum friction between rock and sole. Avoid leaning into the slope with your body, which pushes your feet away from the rock. Instead, keep weight over the feet, bending at the waist to allow your hands to touch the rock and pushing hips and buttocks away.

Take short steps to maintain balance with weight over the feet. Look for the small edges, rough spots, or changes in angle that provide the best foot placements. On the toughest slabs, footholds may be so subtle you'll have to feel with your hand or foot to find the roughest surface.

Other techniques can also be useful on slabs. Face holds may be intermittently available, as well as cracks. You can use downpressure on small edges or irregularities, with the fingertips, thumb, or heel of your hand. A lieback with one hand might be possible using tiny edges. Look for an opportunity for stemming, which could mean a chance to rest. These techniques are described in the section that follows.

## Face-Climbing Techniques

### Downpressure

For the downpressure technique, place the fingertips, palm, side, or heel of your hand on the hold and press down (fig. 9-12a). Pressing down with a thumb can be useful on very small holds.

Holds are often used as cling holds from below and then as downpressure holds as you move above them. Downpressure holds may be used by themselves or in combination with other holds (fig. 9-12b), such as in counterforce with a lieback hold or as part of a stemming move. With your arm extended and elbow locked, you can balance one-handed on a downpressure hold as you move the other hand to the next hold.

## Mantel

The mantel is a very specific use of the downpressure technique. It lets you use hand downpressure to permit your feet to get up onto the same hold as your hands when no useful handholds are available higher.

For the classic mantel (fig. 9-13), place both hands flat on a ledge at about chest height, palms down, with the fingers of each hand pointing toward the other hand. Then raise your body up onto stiffened arms. This will be easier if you can first walk your feet a ways up the rock or if you can spring up from a foothold. Then lift one foot up onto the ledge and stand up.

This basic mantel, however, isn't always possible, because a ledge will often be higher or smaller or

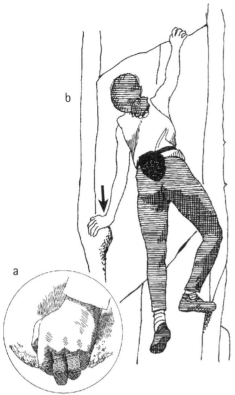

*Fig. 9-12. Downpressure: a, using heel and palm of hand; b, used in combination with other holds.*

*Fig. 9-13. Mantel: the climber turns his hand with the fingers pointed down to make use of the natural shape of the ledge, then reaches up to use a face hold.*

steeper than you might wish. If the ledge is narrow, you may be able to use the heel of your hand, with the fingers pointed down. If the ledge is over your head, you'll use it first as a cling hold and then convert to a downpressure hold as you move upward. If the ledge isn't big enough for both hands, you'll mantel on just one arm while the other hand makes use of any available hold, or perhaps just balances against the rock. Don't forget to leave room for your foot.

Avoid using knees on a mantel because it may be difficult to get off your knees and back on your feet, especially if the rock above is steep or overhanging. Sometimes in midmantel you'll be able to reach up to a handhold to help as you begin standing up.

## Counterforce

Counterforce plays a part in many of the climbing maneuvers described in this chapter. Counterforce is the use of pressure in opposing directions to help keep you in place. For instance, with both hands in a vertical crack, you can create outward pressure by pulling in opposite directions on the sides of the crack—a pulling-apart action (fig. 9-14a). Or you can create inward pressure by pulling in on widely spaced holds—a pulling-together action (fig. 9-14b) or by

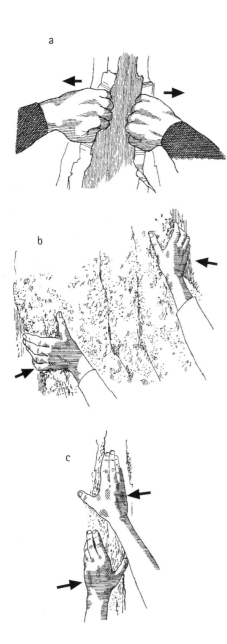

pressing in on both sides of a sharp ridge (9-14c). You can also use the hands in counterforce to the feet, as in the undercling.

## Undercling

In the undercling, the hands (palms up) pull outward beneath a flake or lip of rock while the body leans out and the feet push against rock (fig. 9-15). The arms pull while the feet push, creating a counterforce. Try to keep your arms extended. Both hands can undercling at the same time, or one hand can undercling while the other uses a different type of hold.

An undercling hold may have multiple uses. For example, you can hold the bottom edge of a rock flake in a pinch grip from below and then convert to an undercling as you move up to the flake.

*Fig. 9-14. Counterforce: a, outward pressure; b, inward pressure, pulling together; c, inward pressure, pressing in on a sharp ridge.*

*Fig. 9-15. Undercling; arrows show direction of pressure.*

*Fig. 9-16. Stemming: a, across a chimney; b, on a steep face.*

## Stemming

Stemming is a valuable counterforce technique that lets you support yourself between two spots on the rock that might be of little or no use alone. It often provides a method of climbing steep rock where no holds are apparent, simply by pressing in opposing directions with the feet or with a hand and a foot.

The classic use of stemming (also called bridging) is in climbing a rock chimney. It also comes into play in climbing a dihedral (also called an "open book"), where two walls meet in approximately a right-angled inside corner. One foot presses against one wall of the chimney or dihedral, while the other foot or an opposing hand pushes against the other wall (fig. 9-16a).

Stemming may also open an avenue of ascent on a steep face, where you can press one foot against a slight protrusion while the other foot or a hand gives opposing pressure against another wrinkle in the rock (fig. 9-16b).

## Lieback

The classic lieback technique, another form of counterforce, uses hands pulling and feet pushing in opposition as the climber moves upward in shuffling movements (fig. 9-17). It's used to climb a crack in a corner, or a crack with one edge offset beyond the other, or along the edge of a flake. Grasp one edge of the crack with both hands and lean back and to the side on straightened arms. Push your feet against the opposite wall of the crack. Then get a move on. It's a strenuous technique, and it's best to move as quickly and efficiently as possible.

Keep arms extended to minimize stress on tensed

189

a                                                    b

*Fig. 9-17. Lieback: a, a classic lieback; b, combining a lieback (right hand and foot) with face holds (left hand and foot).*

muscles. The right relationship of hands and feet will vary, but it becomes easier to determine with practice. In general, keep your feet high enough to maintain friction on the rock, unless a foothold is available. But the higher you bring your feet, the more strenuous the lieback becomes.

The lieback has variations. You can lieback on a single handhold in combination with other holds, or use one hand and foot in a lieback while utilizing face holds for the opposite hand and foot (fig. 9-17b).

When using the lieback technique, your body will sometimes have a tendency to swing out of position, or "barn-door" (fig. 9-18). To avoid the barn-door effect, don't apply too much pressure with the leg closest to the rock.

## Counterbalance

Counterbalance, or flagging, is not a specific type of move but, rather, is a principle that can be used in all kinds of climbing. It's the principle of distributing your body weight in a way that maintains your balance.

This means selecting holds that do the best job of keeping your body in balance. But it also sometimes means putting a hand or foot in a particular location, even if no hold is available, in order to provide counterbalance to the rest of the body. The hips and shoulders also come into play as you move them to provide counterbalance. Flagging is useful because it enables you to extend your reach (fig. 9-19).

*Fig. 9-18. Beware of the "barn-door" effect during a lieback.*

*Fig. 9-19. Two examples of counterbalance: a, the left foot is extended to the side to provide counterbalance; b, the left foot is flagged behind the right for counterbalance.*

191

## Long Reaches

What do you do when the next available handhold is a long reach away or even out of reach?

The climber has several techniques available. First, make the most of available holds, by using one or more of these tips: stand up on your toes; pull your body into the rock to achieve maximum extension of the body; use a foot for counterbalance to help in standing up completely on the other foot; move your foot higher on a sloped hold; move your foot more to the side that the next handhold is on. Additional tips include: move your foot to the edge of a foothold for a traversing move; lean your body and hips out or to the side to allow a longer sideways reach; use a handhold for downpressure to allow maximum upward reach with the opposite hand. Sometimes a longer reach is possible by standing on the outside edge of your boot, which tends to turn your body somewhat sideways to the rock. And remember that the longest reach is possible with the hand that is opposite of the foot you're standing on.

Another option is to consider quick intermediate moves, using holds that are marginal but will be used just long enough to scamper up to the next good hold.

The last resort may be a dynamic move that could involve a lunge or simply a quick move before you lose your balance or grip. The time to grab the next higher handhold while making a dynamic move is at the "dead point"—at the apex of your arc of movement when the body is weightless for a fraction of a second before it begins to fall. Movement is most efficient at that point.

There's a built-in danger if a dynamic move fails: you're no longer in complete control and a fall is likely. Make a dynamic move only after calculating and accepting the consequences of failure. You should know beforehand that the protection is secure and that a fall onto the protection won't result in hitting a ledge or the ground or otherwise risking injury. Keep in mind that dynamic moves are for accomplished climbers, not for desperate novices.

## Exchanging Placements on a Small Hold

Sometimes you need to move one foot onto a small hold already occupied by the other foot, or one hand onto a hold being used by the other hand. Either move can be made several different ways.

To exchange a foot placement, you can make an intermediate move, using a poorer, even marginal, hold to get the one foot off the good hold long enough for the other one to take it over. And there's the hop, in which you hop off the hold as you replace one foot with the other.

You can also try sharing the hold by matching feet, moving one foot to the very edge of the hold to make enough room for the other. Another technique is the crossover, in which you cross one foot in back of the other to occupy the far side of the hold (fig. 9-20).

To trade hands, you can make an intermediate move, much as you might in exchanging feet. You

*Fig. 9-20. Foot crossing to change feet on a small hold*

have the option to match hands, placing both hands on the same hold. If space is limited, you can also try picking up the fingers of one hand, one finger at a time, and replacing them with the fingers of the other hand. The crossover technique also is occasionally useful.

## CRACK CLIMBING

Many climbing routes follow the natural lines of vertical cracks in the rock. For the lead climber, cracks are often easy to protect (see Chapter 10, Rock Protection). However, the techniques for climbing cracks of varying sizes are not as intuitively obvious as are the techniques involved in face climbing. Despite this, once basic crack-climbing technique is mastered, it provides one of the most secure feelings that a climber can have on rock.

## Jamming

The basic technique of crack climbing is jamming. Jamming consists of wedging parts of the body, such as hands or feet, securely enough into a crack to bear weight. Jamming isn't as instinctive or natural-feeling as many other climbing techniques, but it works. It's the principal technique for working your way up the cracks that constitute a big part of rock climbing.

The basic procedure is to insert part of a hand or foot, usually just above a narrower part of the crack. Jams are usually locked by twisting (torquing) or flexing, so the hand or foot is wedged against both sides of the crack.

Cracks may be climbed with a pure jamming technique, with both feet and hands utilizing jams, or in combination with other types of holds. For example, as you move up on a jam handhold, you can maintain the jammed position but use it almost like a downpressure hold. A very potent approach is to combine jamming with the use of face holds (fig. 9-21).

Cracks vary a great deal in size and configuration. The descriptions of jams that follow are just some basic techniques, with a lot of room remaining for creativity and ingenuity.

### Hand-Size Cracks

The easiest crack to master is the hand-size crack (fig. 9-22). As the name implies, you insert your entire hand, cupping it as needed and pressing downward with the thumb to provide adequate expansion against the walls of the crack (fig. 9-23a). To increase pressure against the walls, you'll sometimes tuck your thumb across the palm, especially in wider cracks (fig. 9-23b). You can often improve the hold by bending your wrist so the hand points into the crack rather than straight up and down.

The hand jam is done either thumbs up or thumbs down. Thumbs up often is easiest and most comfortable for a vertical crack, and it works especially well when the hand is relatively low. The thumbs-up configuration is most secure when the body leans to the same side as the hand that is jammed.

*Fig. 9-21. Combining jamming with face climbing*

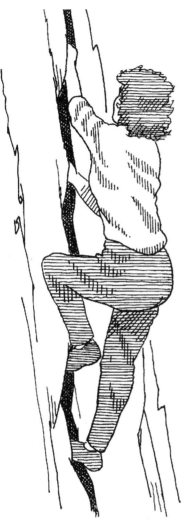

*Fig. 9-22. A hand-size crack*

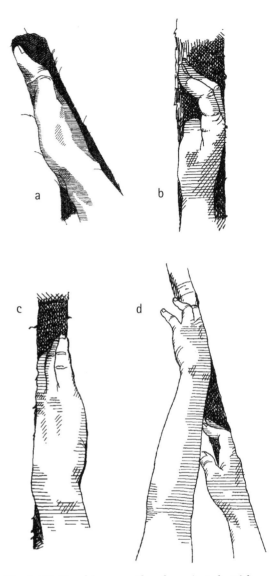

*Fig. 9-23. Hand jams: a, thumb-up jam; b, with thumb tucked across palm; c, thumb-down jam; d, combining thumb-down and thumb-up jams in a diagonal crack.*

The thumbs-down technique may allow a more secure reach to a jam high above your head, because the hand can be twisted for better adhesion and you can lean in any direction off this jam (fig. 9-23c). Climbers use a combination of thumbs up and thumbs down, especially in diagonal cracks, where it's often useful to jam the upper hand thumb down and the lower hand thumb up (fig. 9-23d).

With hand jams, keep alert to the effect of your elbow and body position on the security of the hold. As you move up, you may have to rotate your shoulder or trunk to keep sufficient torque and downward pressure to maintain the jam. Direction of force should be pulling down, not out of the crack. In general, keep your forearm parallel to the crack as you climb.

In dealing with hand jams, you'll run across

194

variants at both ends of the size scale: thinner cracks that won't admit the entire hand but are larger than finger cracks, and wider cracks that aren't quite large enough for a fist jam but require extra hand-twisting to create enough expansion for a secure jam. The size of your hand is a major factor in determining the appropriate technique and the degree of difficulty for any particular crack.

Hand-size cracks are good for foot jamming, and it's generally possible to wedge a shoe in as far as the ball of the foot. Insert the foot sideways, with the sole facing the side of the crack, and then twist to jam (fig. 9-24a). Avoid the common beginner's mistake of twisting your foot so securely that it gets stuck, leaving you open to serious injury in case of a fall. A foot jam that's

twisted too tightly can be painful, and you can waste a lot of time getting it loose.

## Fist-Size Cracks

In a crack that's too wide for a hand jam, you can insert your fist (fig. 9-25). The thumb may be inside or outside the fist, depending on which provides the best fit. Your palm may face the back of the crack, the front, or either side. Flexing the muscles in the fist can expand the fist slightly to help fit the crack. Fist jams are often painful, but they can be very useful. For the most secure hold, try to find a constriction in the crack that you can jam your fist above.

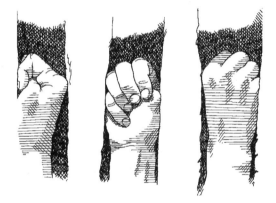

*Fig. 9-25. Fist jam: three different positions*

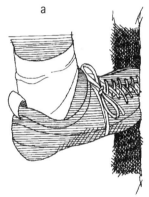

Foot jams in fist-size cracks can generally accept the entire foot. As with hand-size cracks, insert the foot sideways, sole facing the crack, and rotate the foot to jam it securely in place. In even wider cracks, you can jam the foot diagonally or heel to toe (fig. 9-24b).

## Finger-Size Cracks

Finger jams make it possible to climb some of the narrowest cracks, where you may be able to insert only one or more fingers or perhaps just the fingertips. Finger jams are commonly done with the thumbs down. Slip fingers into the crack and twist the hand to lock the fingers in place (fig. 9-26a). You get added strength by stacking fingers and also by pressing the thumb against the index finger in a ring jam (fig. 9-26b).

In slightly wider cracks, you can try a thumb lock. Place the up-pointing thumb in the crack, the pad

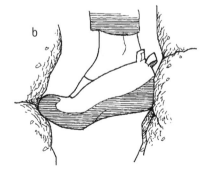

*Fig. 9-24. Foot jams: a, foot jam in a crack; b, heel and toe jam.*

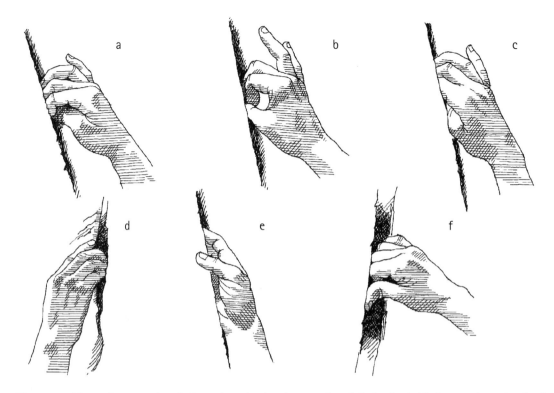

*Fig. 9-26. Finger jams: a, thumb-down jam; b, ring jam; c, thumb lock; d, pinkie jam; e, jamming heel of hand as well as finger; f, using counterpressure with thumb.*

against one side of the crack and the knuckle against the other. Slide the tip of the index finger tightly down over the first joint of the thumb to create the lock (fig. 9-26c).

Here are two other variations on the finger jam, done with the thumbs up (fig. 9-26d–e). You can put the little finger in a crack and stack the other fingers on top (fingertips down, nails up) for a "pinkie jam." In slightly larger cracks, you may be able to wedge the heel of the hand and the smaller fingers into a crack that isn't quite wide enough for a full hand jam. The weight here is borne by the heel of the hand.

For another variation, you can use counterpressure of thumb pushing against one side of the crack, fingers pushing against the other (fig. 9-26f).

Finger-size cracks aren't big enough to accept your foot, but there's often room for toes. You can wedge your toes into a crack by turning your foot sideways—usually with the inside ankle up—and inserting the

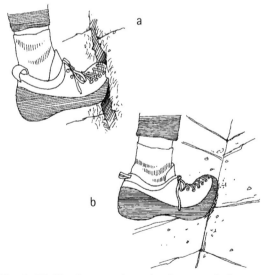

*Fig. 9-27. Toe jams: a, jamming in a crack; b, smearing in a corner.*

196

toes in the crack and then twisting the foot to jam it (fig. 9-27a). You can also wedge the toes into a steep inside corner with a smearing technique, keeping the heel lower than the toe and putting pressure down and in to keep the toes in place (fig. 9-27b). Using smearing and friction for the feet also works well when climbing a finger-size crack.

## Chimneys

A chimney is any crack big enough to climb inside, ranging in size from those that will barely admit the body (squeeze chimneys) to those the climber's body can barely span.

The basic principle is to span the chimney with the body, using counterforce to keep from falling. Depending on the width of the crack, you will either face one side of the chimney or face directly into or out of the chimney. The best body position and technique to use depend on the situation, the size of the climber, and whether a pack is worn. Which direction you face may depend on what holds are available outside the chimney and on how you plan to climb out of it.

In squeeze chimneys, wedge your body in whatever way works best and squirm upward (fig. 9-28). Look for handholds on the outside edge or inside the chimney. Arm bars and arm locks may be useful. It's helpful, sometimes, to press the left foot and knee, for example, against opposite sides of the chimney. You might try stacking your feet in a T configuration, with one foot placed parallel to one side of the rock while the other is placed perpendicular to it, jammed between the first foot and the opposite wall. Squeeze chimneys can be very strenuous, and the best approach here may be to look for an alternative way to climb that section.

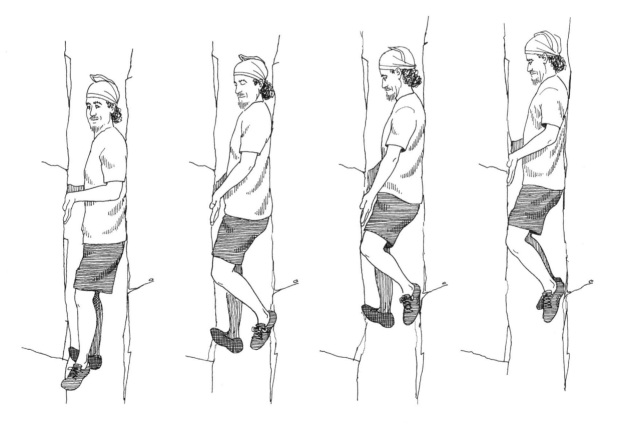

*Fig. 9-28. Chimney technique in a squeeze chimney*

In a crack that's somewhat wider than a squeeze chimney, you begin to have some room to maneuver (fig. 9-29a). You can then press your back and feet against one side of the chimney as your knees and hands push against the other side. You can move upward by squirming your way. Or try a sequence of wedging the upper body while raising the feet and knees and then wedging them and raising the upper body.

A wide chimney calls for stemming technique, with the climber facing directly into or out of the chimney (fig. 9-29b). Counterforce is between the right hand and foot on one side and the left hand and foot on the other. Press down as well as against the sides, especially if there are holds on the sides of the chimney.

Ascend either by alternately moving arms and legs or by moving each leg and then each arm.

In a standard moderate-width chimney, perhaps 3 feet wide, you'll again face one wall of the chimney, your back to the other. For the upper body, your hands may push against one wall in counterforce to your back pressed against the other. Or the counterforce may be between hands on opposing walls. For the lower body, your feet may push against one wall in counterforce to your buttocks against the other. Or the counterforce may be between your two feet.

To climb this moderate-width chimney, use the following sequence (fig. 9-30): Start with your back toward one wall. Press one foot against each wall and

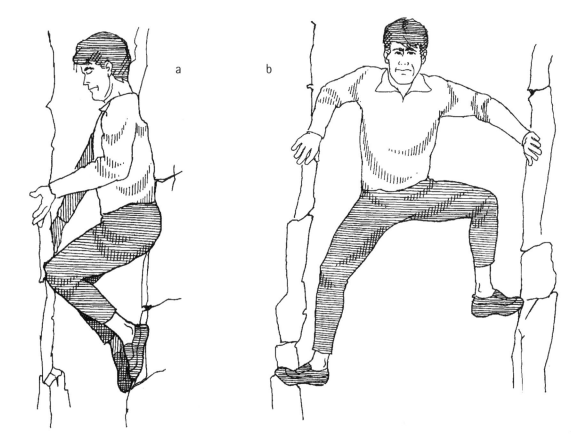

*Fig. 9-29. Chimney techniques: a, in a narrow chimney; b, in a wide chimney.*

*Fig. 9-30. Chimney techniques in a moderate-width chimney*

one hand against each wall. Move upward by straightening your legs and then reestablishing hand positions. Immediately bring your back leg across to the same side as the forward leg. Then swing the forward leg across to the back position. You're now again in position to move upward by straightening your legs.

Beware of getting too far inside a chimney. Although psychologically it may feel more secure, you can get lodged deep inside and find it difficult to move back out. You have a better chance of finding useful handholds and footholds if you stay near the outside of the chimney.

Climbing deep inside the chimney also can make it harder to exit at the top. The transition from the top of the chimney to other types of climbing is often challenging and may require extra thought and creativity.

Chimney technique may be useful in places that don't look like classic chimneys. It can be used to climb dihedrals (fig. 9-31) or short, wide sections of otherwise narrower cracks.

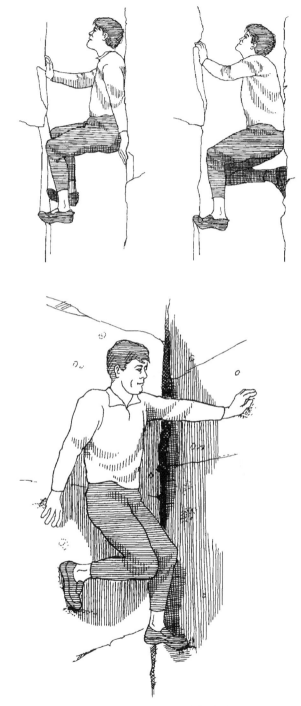

*Fig. 9-31. Chimney techniques in a dihedral*

199

## Off-Width Cracks

Climbers have figured out ways to jam arms, shoulders, hips, knees, and just about anything else into the difficult and awkward features known as off-width cracks. They are "off-width" because they are too wide (too large) for hand or fist jams but too narrow (too small) to admit the entire body for chimneying.

The basic off-width technique calls for standing sideways to the crack and inserting one full side of your body into it. When confronted by an off-width, first decide which side of your body to put inside the crack. This depends on several things, such as holds in the crack or on the face, and the lean, flare, and offset of the crack.

After you've settled on which side to use, the inside leg goes inside the crack and forms a leg bar, usually with counterpressure between foot and knee or foot and hip. This foot is often placed in a heel-toe jam.

The outside foot also is inside the crack in a heel-toe jam. Try to keep the heel above the toe (for better friction) and turned into the crack (to allow the knee to turn out).

As for the arms, a primary body-jam technique is the arm bar (fig. 9-32a). With the body sideways to the crack, insert the arm fully into the crack, with the elbow and the back of the upper arm on one side of the crack giving counterpressure to the heel of the hand on the other side. Get the shoulder in as far as possible, and have the arm lock extend diagonally down from the shoulder.

In a variation, the arm lock, fold the arm back at the elbow and press the palm against the opposite side in counterforce to the shoulder (fig. 9-32b).

The outside arm is used to give downpressure to help hold you in the crack or is brought across the front of the chest and pushed against the opposite side of the crack, elbow out.

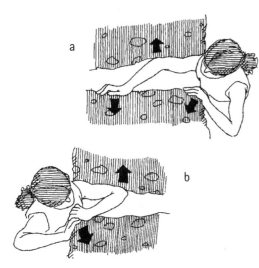

Fig. 9-32. Off-width technique: a, arm bar; b, arm lock.

Fig. 9-33. Climbing an off-width crack

You're now wedged securely in the crack. To climb, move the outside leg upward to establish a higher heel-toe jam. When this jam is set, stand up on it. Then reestablish the inside leg bar and arm bar (or arm lock), and reposition the outside arm. This again wedges your body in the crack. You're now ready to move the outside leg upward again to establish a yet higher heel-toe jam. Continue repeating this procedure (fig. 9-33).

You may use your outside foot occasionally on face holds, but watch out for the tendency for these outside footholds to pull you out of the crack.

## Combining Crack and Face Climbing

Cracks also may be climbed with a pure lieback technique or by liebacking with one arm in combination with face holds for the other hand (fig. 9-34). This may result in a kind of stemming action.

Dihedrals (inside corners) may be climbed by pure stemming. You can also use various combinations, such as hands jammed in a crack splitting the dihedral combined with feet stemming on opposite sides of the dihedral (fig. 9-35).

Useful edges or other holds may be found hidden

*Fig. 9-34. Liebacking combined with face holds*

*Fig. 9-35. Climbing a dihedral using stemming and hand jams*

within cracks—on the sides or even at the back of wide cracks. Remember that horizontal cracks can also be used as cling holds.

# — OTHER CLIMBING TECHNIQUES —

## Negotiating Overhangs and Roofs

Depending on the situation, overhangs and roofs require a variety of techniques such as manteling, face climbing, and crack climbing.

There are two important points to remember: maintain balance and conserve strength.

To maintain balance on overhangs, look for good footholds and make the most of them. This often means keeping feet high and hips low to help press weight against footholds (fig. 9-36). In some situations, it means pressing your hips into the rock, with back arched, to keep weight over the feet while poised

*Fig. 9-36. Climbing an overhanging route*

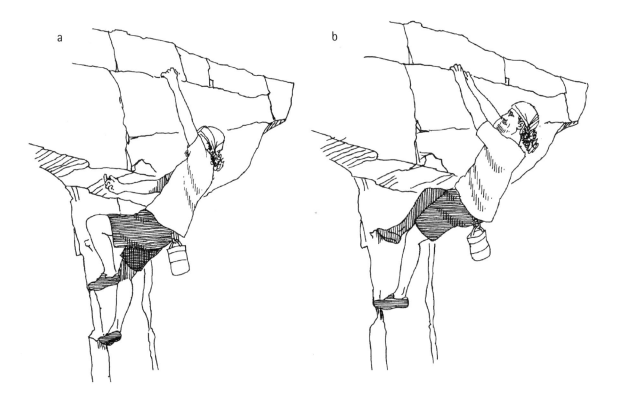

under an overhang. While balanced over your feet beneath the overhang, locate the handholds you will use to move up and over the bulge. A cling hold, a jam, a lieback, or a combination of these may be the key.

To conserve strength, weight your feet as much as possible, even when negotiating a roof (fig. 9-37). Keep arms straight while raising the feet. When the feet are as high as possible, lift the body with your legs rather than pulling up on your arms. Avoid hanging on bent arms, as this will quickly exhaust arm strength. Move quickly through crux (most difficult) sections of the pitch to minimize the time spent in strenuous positions.

Occasionally you may need to raise up on your feet while making a dynamic reach (a lunge or "dyno") to a handhold. Another trick is to throw one foot up onto a ledge, perhaps hooking the heel on it while pushing with your other foot and pulling with your arms to swing up onto the top foot.

## Traversing

Traversing—going sideways across a section of rock instead of up or down—again calls for a wide variety of climbing techniques (fig. 9-38). The main ones are side clings, liebacks, and stemming. And counterbalance is important when making a long sideways reach.

The climber usually faces into the rock, feet pointed away from each other. Hands and feet are commonly shuffled sideways, although exchanging one hand for the other, or one foot for the other, on a single hold can be very useful. You may occasionally cross one foot behind the other to reach the next hold, or cross one hand over the other.

On a steep pitch, it's very tiring to hold yourself

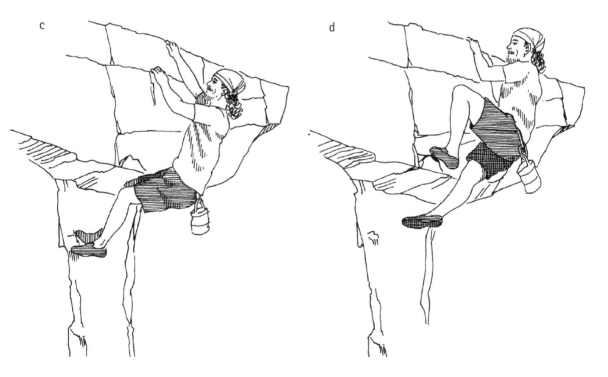

*Fig. 9-37. Climbing over a roof: a, the climber leans out on an outstretched arm to locate a hold above the roof, keeping his hips close to the rock; b, he has both hands above the roof; c, feet are high, pushing against the rock; d, finally, he brings one foot up and begins to pull over the roof.*

Fig. 9-38. Traversing a steep face: a, lieback with one hand, leaning out to reach another hold with the other hand; b, climber twists body to take long sideways reach—an advanced technique; c, climber moves to a new position.

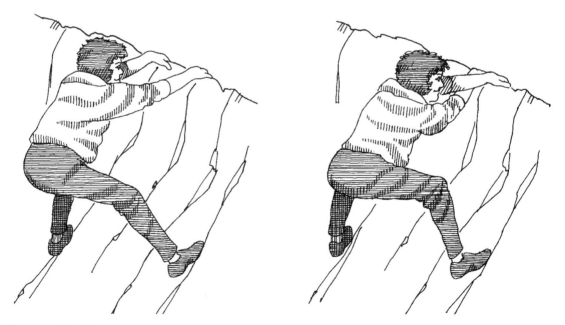

Fig. 9-39. Hand traverse

c

into the rock on bent arms. When possible, lean out from the rock on straight arms. This conserves arm strength, and it gives a better view of where you're going.

A specialized type of traverse is the hand traverse, used when footholds are marginal or nonexistent (fig. 9-39). The hands grip a series of holds or shuffle along an edge, while the feet provide a counterforce by pushing against the rock, as in a lieback or undercling. Keep the feet high and the center of gravity low so the feet are pushed into the rock. And once again, keep the arms straight to conserve arm strength and to let the legs do as much of the work as possible.

## Exiting onto Ledges

As you approach a ledge, avoid the temptation to reach forward and pull yourself onto it. This may throw you off balance and also make it impossible to keep an eye on your footholds (fig. 9-40b).

Instead, continue to walk your feet up the rock, and then use downpressure with the hands near the edge of the ledge. You might do a classic mantel (fig. 9-40a).

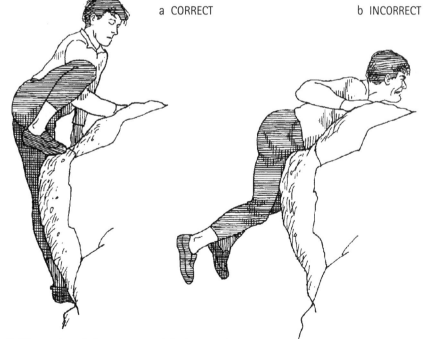

a CORRECT

b INCORRECT

*Fig. 9-40. Exiting onto a ledge: a, correct; b, incorrect.*

## Putting It All Together

Once you've learned the basic climbing techniques, you are ready to begin combining them in ways that make different types of climbs possible.

You'll soon discover the value of planning before you start up a new pitch. Always plan several moves ahead to help you conserve energy and stay on route. Identify and examine difficult sections before you get to them, make a plan, and then move through them quickly. Look ahead for good rest spots.

Many climbs require a variety of techniques, rather than pure jamming, or pure stemming, or pure anything. You'll often use one technique with one hand, or one side of the body, and another technique with the other. You can be jamming with one side of the body as you use face holds with the other. A single pitch may require different techniques in sequence: a jam followed by a lieback, then face climbing followed by a mantel onto what had been a cling hold.

Basic techniques are combined in various ways for climbing faces, slabs, cracks, dihedrals, chimneys, and overhangs.

## SPECIAL DEMANDS OF ALPINE ROCK CLIMBING

When you take the rock-climbing skills you've learned during pleasant days on small nearby crags out into the mountains, some of the conditions of the game change. There are new things to keep in mind when it comes to alpine climbing, which involves a mix of hiking, scrambling, routefinding, snow and ice climbing, and rock climbing.

First of all, you'll probably be climbing with a pack, a significant impediment to speed and performance. With a pack, it can be a challenge to climb rock several levels easier than what you lead comfortably on the crags. For a real test, try climbing a chimney or an off-width crack. Sometimes it's necessary to haul the pack up separately with a rope, and this again slows the climb.

Decisions about how much gear to take become extremely important, as each extra pound cuts into speed and performance and, ironically, adds to the possibility that the extra gear may be needed to survive an unplanned bivouac or accident.

On the crags, you use light, flexible shoes specially designed for rock climbing. But on alpine climbs, heavy mountaineering boots are the usual footwear for approaches, for snow travel and often for much or all of the climbing. As with carrying a pack, climbing in mountaineering boots adds to the challenge of otherwise moderate rock. If you decide to change to rock shoes for the more technical portions of a climb, you're stuck with packing the mountaineering boots. If you're wearing boots and crampons for hard snow or ice and encounter a short section of rock, you may have to ascend the rock in crampons, adding yet another dimension to the climb.

Use special care in testing holds on alpine climbs, where loose rocks may not have been discovered and discarded by previous climbers, the way they are at popular crags. Unsound rock is common on alpine climbs because of the many different types and the constant weathering it receives. You may want to place protection even on rock that appears easy to climb. However, occasionally on low-angle loose rock, using the rope may be more hazardous than climbing unroped, because the rope can dislodge rocks onto climbers below.

Unpredictable weather, arduous approaches, high altitude, and routefinding problems all add to the commitment and challenge of alpine rock climbing.

### Downclimbing

While you're learning a lot of ways to climb upward, also allow some time to learn the valuable technique of downclimbing (fig. 9-41). Confident downclimbing skills are critical to the success of many alpine climbs. Downclimbing at times is faster, safer, or easier than rappelling, such as when rappel anchors aren't readily available. In all styles of climbing, downclimbing provides a way to retreat when you find yourself off route or on a pitch where the route above is more difficult than you care to attempt.

Downclimbing has its special difficulties, however, which helps explain why some climbers resist learning the skill. Holds are harder to see than when you're climbing upward, and holds on the steepest, most difficult sections are the most difficult to see, especially

*Fig. 9-41. Downclimbing: a, facing out; b, facing sideways; c, facing in; d, going down a friction slab.*

if the rock is undercut below a bulge or small roof. It's hard to test holds without committing to them, an unpleasant fact if you doubt the soundness of the rock. And unless you climbed up the same way, the terrain below is unknown, and you may not be able to anticipate the consequences of a fall.

For downclimbing on low-angle rock, face outward for the best visibility. Keep hands low and use downpressure holds whenever possible. Going down friction slabs, keep weight over your feet to maximize friction. It may help to keep your center of gravity low, with knees well bent. As the rock steepens, turn sideways, leaning away from the rock for better visibility. If the cliff gets even steeper, face into the rock. Keep hands low, and lean away from the rock to look for holds below.

## Speed and Safety

A speedy ascent is sometimes an important part of safety on an alpine climb. On long routes, speed minimizes the risk of being caught by darkness. It provides extra time to deal with equipment breakdown,

routefinding problems, injury, or illness. It lessens the length of exposure to rockfall, storms, or lightning.

Speed doesn't mean careless rushing. It means developing efficiency in such activities as testing holds, belaying, exchanging gear, and rope management. It means looking ahead at the route, formulating a plan, and moving smoothly ahead without thrashing over routefinding dilemmas.

As a team, climbing efficiently requires planning and practice, as well as development of a systematic approach to all basic activities. Moving efficiently over the rock saves a lot of time, promotes safety, and conserves energy for each member of a climbing team.

A light pack helps in completing a route quickly. Safety lies in having enough gear to do the climb and survive unexpected situations—not in carrying every piece of gear and shelter that might possibly come in handy.

The size of the climbing party and of the rope teams has an important bearing on speed. The more rope teams there are, the slower the party generally will move. However, rope teams of two are considerably more efficient than teams of three on an alpine route. Other things being equal, two rope teams of two can move much more quickly than a single team of three.

# TRAINING FOR ROCK CLIMBING

Climbing is physically demanding and, if you don't have the needed strength, some climbs will be too difficult. However, many climbs are possible without an abundance of strength. To some extent, technique can compensate for a lack of strength, whereas extra strength can sometimes compensate for a deficiency of technique. Some climbs, especially at the higher end of the rating scale, demand a high degree of both strength and technique.

Rock climbers need a fitness program tailored to their needs. Overall fitness is helpful, but general conditioning programs don't usually promote the forearm and finger strength needed by climbers.

## Training Goals and Regimens

A training program should be designed to develop and maintain strength, endurance, balance, and flexibility. Added benefits will be greater confidence and fluidity on the rock.

The energy required for muscular contraction is derived from three energy-producing systems (each of which produces adenosine triphosphate, the final common source of chemical energy for muscle).

The primary source of energy for sustained or repeated muscular contraction requires oxygen and is referred to as the aerobic system.

The other two systems do not utilize oxygen and are referred to as anaerobic. They are important when the demand for energy temporarily exceeds the capacity of the aerobic system or during sudden muscular contractions demanding energy before the aerobic system can supply it.

Training should include use of all three of these energy-producing systems.

Be careful you don't hurt yourself while you train. Common causes of injury are overtraining, trying to increase strength and endurance too quickly, and failing to pay attention to early signs of overuse or acute

injury, especially to tendons of the elbows and of the fingers. Stretching is useful in avoiding injury.

## Strength

Strength refers to the maximum force that can be exerted against a resistance. A practical example might be the heaviest weight you could lift a single time.

Developing strength is useful for individual moves or short sequences when maximum strength is required for a brief time. Maximum muscular effort requires use of the anaerobic energy systems. These can be trained using routines that alternate periods of intense muscular work, from seconds to less than 2 minutes, with periods of rest.

The best approach is progressive muscular overload exercises. This includes weight training with heavy loads and few repetitions or other short-duration, near-maximal efforts, such as hanging from small holds for brief periods. Remember that strength training is important for the legs as well as the upper body. A description of training regimens is beyond the scope of this chapter, but climbers can consult books and magazine articles devoted to strength training.

## Endurance

Endurance is the ability to sustain muscular effort over time. Although crux sections of a pitch may require considerable absolute strength, climbing a full pitch, or more particularly a multipitch route or long alpine climb, requires muscular endurance.

The primary energy system involved is aerobic, and the best training approach is lower-resistance, higher-repetition exercises than the ones used for strength training. You can adapt this approach to weight training, fingerboard routines, or sustained bouldering.

## Cardiovascular Fitness

Aerobic activities such as jogging, bicycling, swimming, or rowing help develop cardiovascular fitness, which aids in any sustained rock-climbing effort. This is particularly true for alpine climbs, where the approach may be strenuous and where rapid progress up a long route can be essential.

## Balance

Perhaps the best way to improve your balance is simply to climb. Try climbing exercises, such as moving up a slab without the use of hands, or working on difficult boulder problems that require balance. You can also devise other exercises, such as walking across a tightly stretched rope suspended above the ground.

### Flexibility

Flexibility is essential for all rock climbing beyond an elementary level. Many books are available that describe stretching exercises to improve flexibility. They should be done regularly, like any training exercise. Take care to avoid injury.

### Weight Loss

You can increase your relative strength and endurance by losing excess weight, thereby decreasing the number of extra pounds you have to lift with your arms and legs. A lower body weight may enhance balance and flexibility as well. Aerobic training, such as running, biking, and swimming, not only builds cardiovascular fitness but also aids in weight loss.

## Training Resources

The growing popularity of climbing gyms has enabled many people to obtain frequent climbing-specific training to build strength and endurance and to develop technique. Climbers can also take advantage of natural resources to train specifically for the required strength, endurance, and technique.

Look for opportunities to climb on boulders at local crags or at developed climbing areas. Bouldering lets you practice close to the ground without needing a belay. Work on low-level traverses and on short but difficult problems. Traversing boulders for lengthy periods (at least 20 minutes) is an excellent way to build endurance specific to climbing.

Top-roped climbing is another training tool. In top roping, you are belayed so that any fall will result in only a short drop—just the distance the rope stretches when it takes your weight. Because you're safe, you can practice techniques and push the limits of your ability, increasing strength and confidence. You can try moves you wouldn't be willing to go for if you were leading a climb, belayed only from below and risking a leader fall.

Top roping can also be used to build endurance. Climb the route several times in rapid succession, without resting. Add small Velcro-fastened weights to your harness to approximate the weight of a big rack or a heavy backpack.

## Specialized Equipment

A growing catalog of manufactured climbing aids lets you train whenever you want and tailor a fitness program to your own needs.

Artificial climbing walls are available both indoors and out, where you can boulder or top rope in the absence of readily available natural areas. The walls help develop both strength and technique, and they allow creation of specific problems to work on. These problems can even simulate a difficult sequence on an established natural route. Although artificial walls principally feature face climbing, many walls also offer cracks of varying widths. Of course, indoor walls are especially welcome during bad weather.

Modular climbing holds used on many indoor artificial walls are now sold through stores that handle climbing equipment. Small, personal climbing walls can be constructed in a basement or garage.

Manufactured fingerboards (fig. 9-42a) have a selection of handholds and finger holds to hang from or pull up on. Using a fingerboard improves upper body

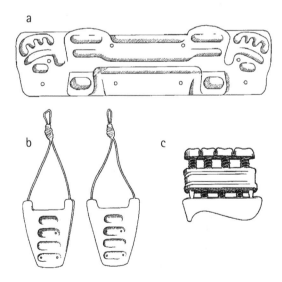

*Fig. 9-42. Specialized training devices: a, fingerboard (Metolius Simulator); b, Metolius rock rings; c, Gripmaster to develop grip strength.*

strength and also lets you concentrate on developing the finger strength needed to take advantage of small holds.

Other training tools have been developed and more are on the way (fig. 9-42b). There are rope ladders and peg boards for improving upper body strength. A number of small devices for improving grip strength are also widely available (fig. 9-42c).

## Attitude

To climb rock well, you must have the desire. Rock climbing calls for a commitment of both mind and body, and making the necessary moves requires total concentration and complete confidence. This confidence can come by practicing with a top rope, which minimizes possible injury and allows you to safely attempt harder and harder moves.

Confidence goes hand in hand with physical conditioning. If hand, arm, or leg strength is not sufficient, it doesn't matter that the mind is willing. Conversely, physical ability alone won't move you if your mind says no.

An equally important component of attitude is an awareness of safety. This includes knowing your limits and knowing when and how to back off when you don't have the strength or technique for a given route on a given day. A constant analysis of conditions, both external and internal, will enhance safety.

## STYLE AND ETHICS

Climbing generates endless debate over which styles are fair and which are less than sporting, over which practices are harmful and which are "none of your damn business." The terms "style" and "ethics" are sometimes used interchangeably by climbers, but style usually refers to a person's mode of climbing, which is principally a personal decision. Ethics usually refers to issues where preservation of the rock itself, and thus the experience of other climbers, is at stake.

Climbers soon discover that getting to the end of the pitch or the top of the peak isn't the only goal—that it's also getting there in a way that feels right, that respects the rock, and that tests a person's skill and resolve as a climber. These are questions of style and ethics.

## Diversity of Styles

Styles change and attitudes evolve, but the core of the debate on climbing styles is about how to maintain the challenge of climber against rock and how to play the game in a way that fairly tests the climber.

Climbers adhering to traditional style prefer to climb each route strictly from the ground up, with no help from such aids as top ropes or preplaced protection. New routes are explored and protected only on lead. This type of climbing characterizes rock climbing in the alpine setting, but it's also found at many popular crags.

Climbers following the European-influenced sport-climbing style are more likely to find other techniques acceptable as well. This can include inspecting the route on rappel before trying to lead it from below. It can also mean cleaning the route and perhaps placing protection on rappel. Routes may be climbed with multiple falls, by resting on the rope while checking out the next move ("hang-dogging"), or by rehearsing moves with the help of a top rope.

These sport-climbing techniques have made it possible to climb harder and harder routes. A particular climbing area may lend itself more to one style than another because of the type of rock, the difficulty of the routes, or the conventional style of the local climbers. In the world of climbing, there's room for a diversity of styles, and most climbers will experience a variety of them.

## Ethics and the Rock

The subject of ethics has to do with respecting the rock and every person's chance to use it. Unlike climbing style, ethics involves personal decisions that do affect the experience and the enjoyment of others. This includes the sticky question of the manner in which bolts are placed on a route. Are bolts placed on rappel different—less "ethical"—than bolts placed on the lead? Traditional climbers may argue that bolts placed while on rappel rob others of the chance to try the route from the ground up. But other climbers may say that placing the bolts gives a chance at a route that otherwise would be unclimbable.

Each area has its own tradition of what styles and ethics are acceptable, and visiting climbers should observe the local standards. It's not hard to find out what they are. The guidebook will say, the locals can tell you, and you can always just look around at what the other climbers are doing.

This book won't try to resolve issues of style and ethics, but there is general agreement on a couple of principles.

First of all, preservation of the rock is paramount. Chipping the rock to create new holds is almost universally condemned. And while bolt-protected routes are common in many areas, bolting should not be indiscriminate. In the mountains or other wilderness areas, away from concentrated centers of rock climbing, it's particularly important to preserve the environment for those who follow. If possible, stick to clean climbing, using only removable gear for protection.

Second, it's almost never justifiable to add a bolt to an existing route. If you feel you can't safely climb the route as it is, don't try it. Exceptions may occur when a consensus of local climbers, usually including the person who first climbed the route, agree that another bolt should be placed to promote safety and enjoyment. If you have the necessary skills and experience, there's rarely any objection if you replace an old bolt with a newer, stronger one or add a bolt at an established belay or rappel point.

## Courtesy

Keep other climbers in mind when you're out climbing. If your party is moving up a multipitch route much slower than the people behind you, let them pass at a safe spot, such as a belay ledge.

Beware of tackling climbs that are beyond your abilities. You may prevent more capable climbers from enjoying the route. If your inexperience gets you in trouble, you may involve other climbers in a time-consuming and dangerous rescue of your party.

## Climbing Access

Access to many climbing areas is threatened, and two issues are usually at stake. The people who own or manage the land are worried about liability for accidents and are concerned that climbers are defiling the environment.

As climbers, we can help by taking responsibility for our own actions. It's up to us to put in dependable anchors and otherwise promote safety—and to provide rescue services when they're needed, rather than expecting others to do it for us.

It's also up to us to leave areas in as natural a state as possible. Chalk, rappel runners, fixed protection, and litter can be eyesores. We can help by establishing rappel anchors that don't require leaving slings (or by using slings that blend in with the color of the rock, if they must be left), keeping bolt placements to a minimum, and removing all litter. These efforts can promote public acceptance of the sport and help maintain access to climbing areas. Future access to climbing areas is the responsibility of today's climbers.

# ROCK PROTECTION

A party setting out on an alpine climb involving a few hundred feet of rock scrambling may need no specialized climbing equipment. But if the rock is too difficult or too exposed for unroped travel, the climbers will rope up and belay. The basic procedure of belayed climbing is simple: one climber, belayed by a second, leads up a pitch, establishes a belay, and belays the second climber up. This procedure is repeated up the next pitch, and the next, until the objective is reached or the protection of the rope is no longer needed.

If the lead climber falls, the length of the fall will be about twice the distance between the climber and the belayer (fig. 10-1a). But if intermediate points of protection have been placed, the length of the fall will be reduced to only twice the length of the rope between the climber and the *last point of protection* (fig. 10-1b). These critically important points of protection—how to create them and what equipment and techniques to use—are the subject of this chapter.

Climbers use both *natural protection* and *artificial protection*. Natural protection includes trees and rocks that provide places of attachment for the rope. Artificial protection consists of manufactured metal devices that are joined in various ways to the rock. But whether you're taking advantage of natural protection or of artificial protection, your most basic tools will be carabiners and runners (slings).

Carabiners—"biners" for short—are used to connect almost anything and everything in the climber's world. As part of your climbing safety system, biners are used to attach pieces of protection to the rope, often with one or more intervening runners (fig. 10-2a). The biner should almost always be used in the down-and-out position, meaning that the gate of the biner points down and away from the rock surface (fig. 10-3). This position lessens the chance of accidental (and potentially disastrous) opening of the carabiner gate during a fall and also makes it easier to clip the rope. The rope itself should be clipped in so that it runs freely through the carabiner in the direction of travel without twisting the biner around.

Runners serve to lengthen the distance between the point of protection and the rope, helping to keep the rope running in a straight line—which reduces stress on the protection and friction on the rope as the climber continues upward. Runners are also used to connect directly to a point of protection, most often natural protection (fig. 10-2b).

## NATURAL PROTECTION

Trees and rock features can make excellent points of protection, and they are generally preferred over artificial protection. However, natural protection must be carefully evaluated for stability and strength. "Test before you trust" is a good rule. Be wary of brittle rock, poorly rooted vegetation, and other suggestions of weakness. An error in judgment could result not only in failed protection but also in a rock or tree pulling loose and crashing down on you, your belayer, or other parties on the route.

In evaluating a rock feature, consider its relative

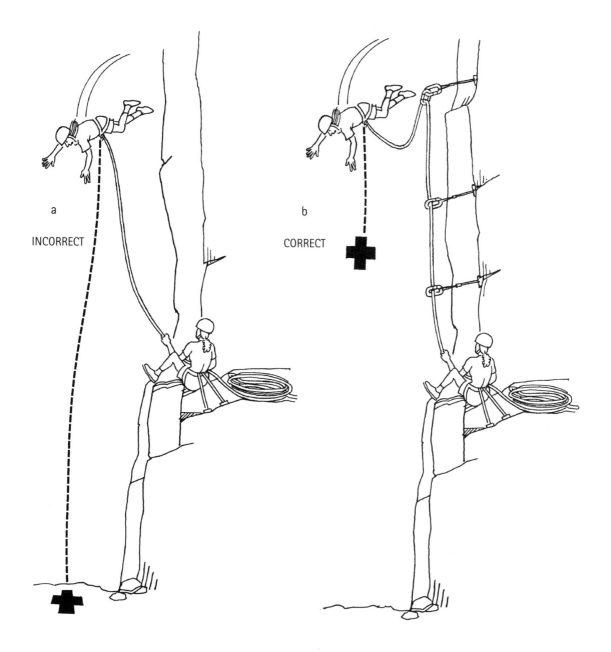

*Fig. 10-1. Leader fall: a, with no intermediate points of protection; b, with intermediate points of protection in place.*

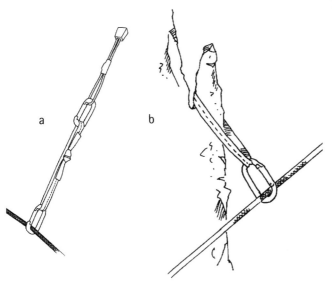

*Fig. 10-2. Attaching the protection to the rope: a, using two carabiners and one runner to link a piece of artificial protection with the rope; b, using one runner and one carabiner to link a point of natural protection with the rope.*

hardness, how friable (crumbly) or broken up it is, and whether it is firmly attached to the rock around it. Attempt to move the rock, being careful not to pull it loose. Whack it a few times with your hand or fist. If it seems loose or sounds hollow, beware. With trees or bushes, look for a healthy trunk at least 4 inches thick, with live branches and a solid root system. If the tree or shrub is loose or appears weak or brittle, don't trust it.

Trees and large bushes provide the most obvious points of attachment. A common method of attaching a runner to a tree is to loop the runner around the trunk and clip the ends together with a carabiner (fig. 10-4a). You can also untie a runner and then retie it around the trunk (fig. 10-4b). A third method is to use a girth hitch (fig. 10-4c), though this attachment magnifies stress on the runner in a fall. The runner usually should be as close to the roots as possible, although with a strong tree it may be placed higher if necessary.

Horns are the most common type of natural rock protection. They are also called spikes,

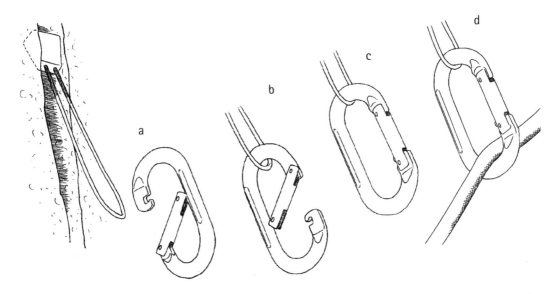

*Fig. 10-3. Correct down-and-out positioning of a carabiner: a, clip the carabiner in a downward direction; b, then rotate it out and away from the rock; c, gate opening is now down and facing out from rock; d, rope clipped through biner in direction of travel.*

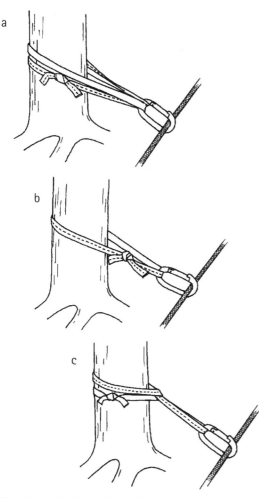

Fig. 10-5. Securing a runner to a rock horn with a clove hitch

formed by the contact point between two boulders), and natural chockstones (rocks firmly lodged in a crack). To attach a runner, first thread it around the column or chockstone or through the tunnel. Then connect the ends with a carabiner (fig. 10-6a) or secure the runner to the rock feature with a girth hitch (fig. 10-6b). Another method is to untie a runner and retie it after threading it through the point of protection.

*Fig. 10-4. Methods of attaching a runner to a tree trunk: a, looped around the trunk, the ends clipped together with a carabiner; b, retied around trunk; c, girth-hitched around trunk.*

knobs, or chicken heads, depending on their shape and size. A runner can often be simply looped over the horn and clipped into the rope—but it's urgent that you first carefully evaluate the risk of the sling being pulled off by rope drag. Use of a girth hitch or clove hitch to tighten the runner around the horn will help prevent it from slipping off (fig. 10-5).

Other features that can provide excellent natural protection are rock columns, rock tunnels (such as those

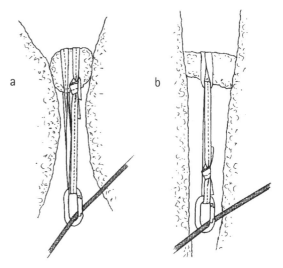

*Fig. 10-6. Attaching a runner to a chockstone: a, looped around a chockstone; b, using a girth hitch around a chockstone.*

215

## BOLTS AND PITONS

Bolts are permanent pieces of artificial protection, driven into a hole that has been drilled into the rock; pitons are metal spikes pounded into cracks. Bolts and pitons are used to provide protection where there is no place to lodge a removable metal chock. In your climbing, you are likely to encounter bolts and pitons placed by previous climbers. You will also run across other fixed pieces, usually metal chocks that have been abandoned after efforts to free them failed. The focus of this section is on how to use these forms of fixed protection and how to recognize potential failures. (Chapter 12, Aid Climbing, includes information on how to place pitons. Placement of bolts is beyond the scope of this book.)

### Bolts

Bolts are most commonly used on aid-climbing routes and in sport-climbing areas, but they may also be seen as fixed protection on otherwise unprotectable climbing routes. A bolt hanger provides attachment for a carabiner (fig. 10-7). A threaded nut is sometimes needed to attach the hanger to the bolt.

A well-placed bolt will last for years, but weather will eventually take its toll. Be especially wary of quarter-inch bolts, which were placed primarily in the 1960s and 1970s. Bolts measuring three-eighths

of an inch in thickness have been used since the mid-1980s and are now the standard.

Every bolt should be visually checked for signs of weakness, especially for cracks, excessive corrosion, or brittleness. A rust streak below the bolt indicates metal wear. You can test whether the bolt is securely anchored into the rock by clipping into the bolt hanger with a carabiner and trying to pull the bolt around or out. If the bolt can be moved in any direction, however slight, it is probably not trustworthy. Avoid banging on the bolt, as this will weaken it. Also check that the rock surrounding the bolt is solid. If the rock is deteriorating or cracked around the bolt, look for another option. Back up any suspect bolt with another point of protection if possible.

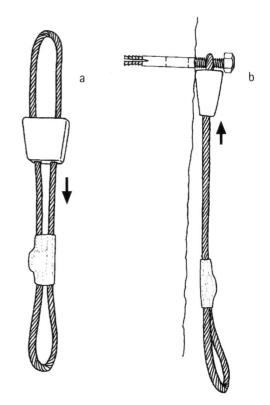

Fig. 10-8. Placing a wired chock on a hangerless bolt: a, create a loop by sliding the chock down the chock sling; b, slide the chock up the sling to form a noose around the hangerless bolt.

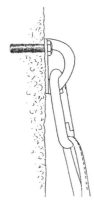

Fig. 10-7. Bolt and bolt hanger, with a carabiner clipped into the hanger

If the bolt and its placement seem solid, use a carabiner to clip a runner to the bolt hanger. If the hanger is missing, a small wired chock may be substituted (fig. 10-8). Simply slide the chock down the cable to expose a short loop that can be placed over the bolt; then slide the chock back up the sling to create a snug noose around the head of the bolt. You can then clip into the chock sling with a carabiner, preferably with a long runner attached to minimize the risk of pulling the chock off the bolt by rope movement. In climbing areas where threaded bolts are commonly left without hangers attached, it may be useful to carry a few bolt hangers, a small wrench, and threaded machine nuts in quarter-inch and three-eighths-inch sizes.

## Pitons

Pitons were commonly used in North American mountaineering until the 1960s, but they have largely been replaced by the removable metal chocks that make "clean climbing" possible, with no damage to the rock. Many pitons remain, however, as fixed placements on various routes. The blade of the piton is the part driven into the crack; the eye is the point of attachment for the carabiner.

Pitons, even more so than bolts, are vulnerable to weathering. Years of melt–freeze cycles widen cracks and loosen pitons. Examine the piton closely for signs of corrosion or weakness; examine the crack for deterioration around the piton.

Ideally, the piton will have been driven in all the way, with the eye close to the rock and the piton perpendicular to the likely direction of pull (fig. 10-9). If the piton seems to be strong, secure, and in good condition, clip a carabiner (with runner attached) through the eye of the piton. Try to place the biner where it will not bind against the rock under load, which could cause the carabiner to break or the gate to open.

If a piton is only partially driven in but otherwise seems secure, you can use a runner to tie it off next to the rock, using a girth hitch or a clove hitch (fig. 10-10). This tie-off reduces the leverage on the piton under the impact of a fall.

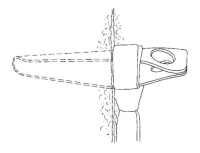

*Fig. 10-10. Partially driven piton, with a tie-off next to the rock to reduce leverage*

## Other Fixed Pieces

You will occasionally find metal chocks that became lodged so tightly in the rock that previous climbers were unable to remove them. These fixed pieces can be valuable as protection, but they require at least as much careful scrutiny as old bolts or pitons.

Note whether the sling attached to the chock appears to be worn or perhaps damaged by rodents. Be suspicious of possible failure of the sling, especially if it is made of accessory cord or webbing rather than wire cable. Study the condition of the rock, and test whether the chock remains securely lodged. Check whether it is oriented properly to hold a fall. It's usually wise to use these chocks only as backup protection because it is so difficult to evaluate their strength.

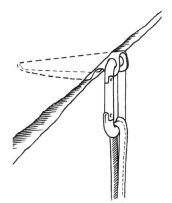

*Fig. 10-9. Piton driven into rock*

## CHOCKS

"Chocks," "nuts," and "pro" are generic terms, used somewhat interchangeably, for the various types of artificial protection other than bolts and pitons. These generally consist of a metal device that can be secured into the rock, with a sling for use in linking the metal piece to the rope (fig. 10-11).

Chockcraft—the art of placing and removing chocks—is the preferred technique for protecting climbs when natural protection is not available. Chocks are relatively easy to place and to remove and, unlike bolts and pitons, leave no scars on the rock.

### Chock Slings

Most chocks are slung with wire cable (fig. 10-11a), which is much stronger than cord or webbing of the same size. The stiffness of the wire cable also makes the chock easier to place.

Some larger chocks come with holes drilled for accessory cord, which may be added either by the manufacturer or, more commonly, by the climber (fig. 10-11b). Some chocks come preslung with webbing (fig. 10-11c). There are times you may need to sling your own chocks. When you do, here are a few things to keep in mind.

**Material:** Most larger nuts are designed to accept 5.5-millimeter Spectra cord or Gemini (Spectra/Kevlar) cord. These materials are stronger and less bulky than the previously common 8-millimeter perlon cord. If you are reslinging an old piece, plastic inserts or tubing may be used with the 5.5-millimeter cord to prevent abrasion of the cord against the metal and to secure a snug fit of cord to chock.

**Connections:** Spectra and Gemini cord do not hold a knot as well as perlon due to their greater stiffness. A triple fisherman's knot is recommended for tying a Spectra or Gemini sling (fig. 10-11b). (The triple is the same as the double fisherman's knot shown in Chapter 6, but with the addition of a third loop.) A double fisherman's knot is adequate for tying a perlon sling.

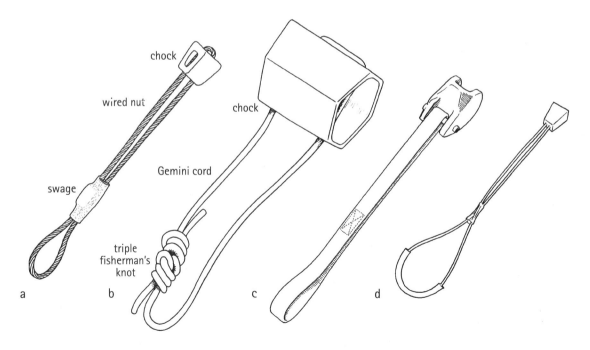

*Fig. 10-11. Chock slings: a, wire cable on a wedge-shaped chock (a "wired nut"); b, Gemini cord tied through a Hexentric chock; c, preattached webbing on a Lowe Tri-Cam; d, molded-in sling on a micronut.*

Leave at least a 1-inch tail on each side of the fisher-man's knot. Tighten the knot under body weight, and check it frequently.

**Length:** A chock sling is usually 8 to 10 inches long when tied. The cord you use for making a sling should be twice as long as the desired sling length, plus another 12 inches or so for the knot.

**Chock preparation:** Inspect the holes that are drilled in the chock for the cord. They should have smooth, rounded edges to avoid damaging the sling. Some manufacturers provide plastic inserts for these holes, through which the cord is threaded.

## Types of Chocks

Chock designs generally fall into two categories, wedges or cams. A wedge holds by jamming, or wedg-ing, into a constriction in a crack. Cams hold by rotating slightly within a crack or pocket, creating a camming action that jams the chock against the rock. Some chocks, such as the Lowe Tri-Cam or the Black Diamond Hexentric, may be used either as wedges or cams.

Wedges and cams are either passive or spring-loaded. The passive devices are single pieces of metal with no moving parts. Spring-loaded devices have moving parts that can be retracted in order to fit them into a spot in the rock and then released so they can grip the rock. Spring-loaded wedges and cams are gen-erally easier to place and more versatile than passive protection.

### Passive Wedges

Passive wedging chocks come in a wide variety of shapes and sizes, but most have a generally wedge-shaped appearance (fig. 10-12). They are called by a lot of names, from brand names such as Stoppers to simply "wired nuts."

These chocks are narrower at the base than at the top, which lets them slip down into a constriction, and they widen toward the top on all sides. Variations on the theme include chocks with one or more curved sides, or with nonparallel end faces, or with central notches to accommodate irregularities in the rock. A curved side on one or both of the wide faces of the chock provides more placement options and frequently greater contact with the rock than a straight-sided de-sign. Viewed from the top, many of these chocks are trapezoidal in shape.

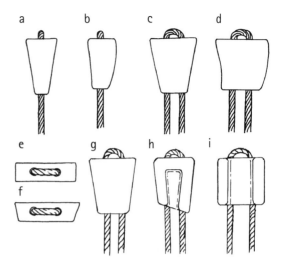

*Fig. 10-12. Design variations in passive wedging chocks: a, wide face, straight sided, symmetrical; b, wide face curved, non-symmetrical; c, end sides sraight, symmetrical; d, end sides curved, non-symmetrical; e, end sides parallel; f, end sides with transverse taper; g, wide face smooth; h, side face cut-out; i, wide face grooved.*

Some of the smallest wedging-type chocks, referred to as micronuts, are designed for very thin cracks and for aid climbing. Manufacturers construct the nuts with softer metals that bite into the rock better than stan-dard aluminum chocks—but this also makes them less durable. These nuts have less holding power than larger chocks because of their smaller surface area and small-diameter cables (fig. 10-11d). The thinness of the micronut's cable makes it more prone to damage from rough handling, such as repeated flexing and jerking during placement and removal. The micronut and cable should be inspected often for nicks and other signs of wear, and retired if any cable damage is seen.

### Spring-Loaded Wedges

Spring-loaded wedges use a small sliding piece to expand the profile of the chock after it is placed in a crack (fig. 10-13). To operate the device, first retract the smaller piece by pulling back on the spring-loaded trigger, thereby narrowing the profile of the chock so it can be inserted into a thin crack. Then release the trigger, permitting the smaller piece to press up between the larger piece and the rock, filling in the gap and increasing the area of the chock in contact with the rock.

Spring-loaded wedges work particularly well in small, parallel-sided cracks where larger chocks or camming devices may be difficult to place. But like micronuts, these chocks have less holding power than larger wedges because of the smaller surface area gripping the rock and because the spring may allow some movement—or "walking"—within the crack after placement.

## Passive Cams

A passive camming device is designed to cam, or rotate, slightly when under load. This serves to lock the piece more firmly in place. The most commonly used passive cams are Black Diamond Hexentrics, often just called hexes (fig. 10-11b), and Lowe Tri-Cams (fig. 10-11c).

Each pair of opposing sides on a Hexentric is a different distance apart, which permits the climber to choose among four different placement options per piece (two cam positions and two wedge positions). The chock sling is placed off-center to create the camming action (fig. 10-14a).

Tri-Cams are curved along one side, with side rails

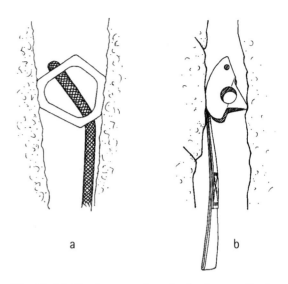

*Fig. 10-14. Passive camming chocks, in a vertical crack: a, Hexentric; b, Tri-Cam.*

on the curved side opposing a point, or "stinger," on the other side. Cam action is gained by running the sling between the curved side rails and positioning the piece so that the stinger is set in a small depression or irregularity in the crack (fig. 10-14b).

Another device that acts as a passive cam is the

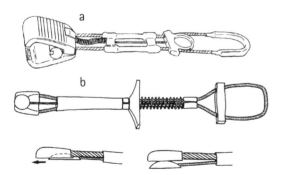

*Fig. 10-13. Examples of spring-loaded wedging devices: a, Perrin; b, Lowe Ball, contracted and expanded.*

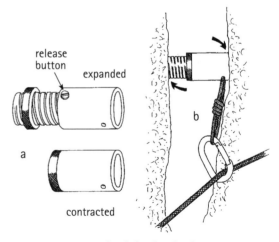

*Fig. 10-15. Spring-loaded tube chock: a, Sidewinder Big Bro, contracted and expanded; b, Big Bro correctly placed in a vertical crack, where it acts as a passive cam.*

telescoping tube chock called the Big Bro (fig. 10-15). This chock has a spring-loaded inner sleeve that pops out to bridge a crack when a release button is pressed. The extended sleeve is then locked into place by spinning the collar down snugly against the outer tube. The sling attachment at one side creates a camming action when the chock comes under load.

## Spring-Loaded Cams

Spring-loaded camming devices were first introduced in the mid-1970s. They quickly expanded the limits of free climbing by providing protection that could be placed easily and quickly with one hand and that could adapt to a variety of cracks.

The basic design has three or four cams mounted on one axis or two, connected to a trigger mechanism on a stem (fig. 10-16). When the trigger is pulled, the cams retract, narrowing the profile of the device for placement in a crack or pocket (fig. 10-17a). When the trigger is released, the cams open up against the sides of the rock (fig. 10-17b).

The cams move independently of each other, permitting each to rotate to the point needed for maximum contact with the rock. This movement sets the device in place. If the climber falls, the stem is pulled downward or outward, increasing the camming action and causing the cams to grip the rock even harder.

## Placements

Placing protection in the rock is both art and science. Developing an eye for good placement sites, and then being able to slip just the right piece into the right place safely and efficiently, takes many hours of practice.

First consider the rock. Look for constrictions in a crack, irregularities in crack surfaces, and prominences behind a flake. A good site for chock placements

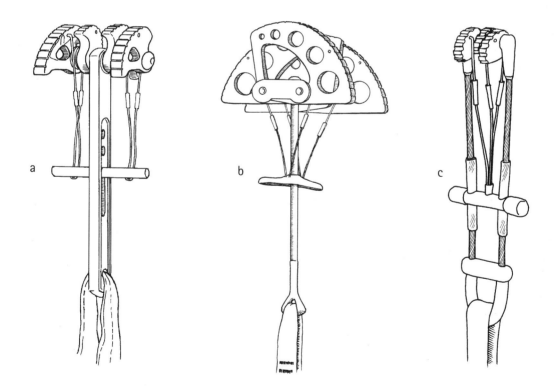

*Fig. 10-16. Examples of spring-loaded camming devices: a, Friend (Wild Country); b, Camalot (Black Diamond); c, TCU 3-Cam (Metolius).*

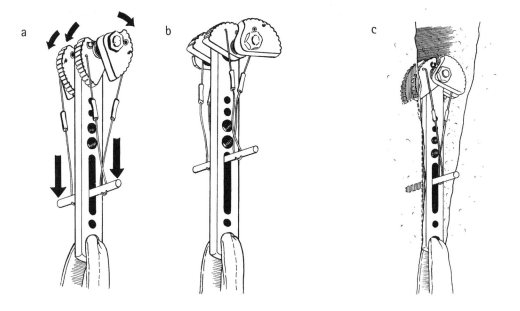

*Fig. 10-17. Spring-loaded camming device: a, retracted; b, expanded; c, correctly placed in a vertically oriented crack*

will have solid rock sides—free of vegetation, dirt, or deteriorating rock. Check for loose blocks or flakes by hitting the rock with your fist or shaking it; if the rock moves or sounds hollow, look for a better spot.

The next consideration is what type of chock to use. Passive wedges and cams—Stoppers, Hexentrics, Tri-Cams—work best when placed behind constrictions in a vertically oriented crack. Passive camming devices take more time to place than wedges, but they also work very well in horizontal cracks and behind small irregularities in cracks or flakes where it may be difficult or impossible to position wedges. Tri-Cams are often the only device that will work in old piton scars and shallow flaring pockets.

Spring-loaded devices, both wedges and cams, are easiest to place, but they are heavier, more expensive, and somewhat less reliable than passive chocks. However, they often work in parallel-sided and flaring cracks where it is difficult or impossible to get anything else to hold.

Often more than one type of chock will work in a given spot; the decision is then based on which type is easiest to place and, more importantly, on what you are likely to need farther up the pitch. Ration the chocks you expect to need higher up.

Some other general considerations in placing chocks follow:

- Learn to estimate the right chock size and shape for a particular placement. The better the estimate, the faster the placement—and the less chance you will tire and possibly fall.
- Choose the best chock, not necessarily the largest or the most easily placed. A larger chock usually will hold a harder fall, but first decide whether it actually provides the soundest protection or if a smaller or differently shaped piece would be more secure.
- Decide whether a particular chock is likely to be adequate, based on the characteristics of the rock and the magnitude of a possible fall. Some things to consider include the relative hardness of the rock, the direction of the fall, and the inherent strength of the piece. If in doubt, you should probably reinforce the piece with another chock, or use a load-limiting runner to decrease forces on the piece, or find a better placement.

- Check out every chock after it's in place. Look to see that it's placed correctly, in good contact with the rock. Tug on it to help determine the reliability and security of the placement, especially in the likely direction of pull.
- Guard against the chock being dislodged by rope movement. A runner is usually attached, with carabiners, between the chock and the rope to minimize the effect of rope movement on the piece. Wired chocks and spring-loaded cams are especially vulnerable to rope movement and have a tendency to rotate out of place.
- Guard against the chock being dislodged by an outward or upward pull in a fall. Many chock placements are one-directional—they will take a load in only one direction. If a one-directional placement could come under load from multiple directions, make it multidirectional by placing opposing chocks (explained later in this chapter) or by using a different placement—perhaps a sling around a tree.
- Remember the climber who will be following behind you and removing the protection. Make your placements secure, but also try to make them reasonably easy to remove.

## Placing Passive Wedges

The basic procedure in placing wedging-type chocks is quite simple: find a crack with a constriction at some point, place an appropriate-size chock above the constriction, slide it into place, and pull

*Fig. 10-18. Placing a passive wedge: a, placing wedge into crack above constriction; b, sliding it into place; c, tugging on chock sling to set it.*

223

down on the sling to set the chock firmly in position (fig. 10-18). Slot the chock completely into the crack, with as much of the chock surface as possible contacting the rock.

Because the strength and holding power of the chocks depend on good rock contact, the best choice for any given placement will be whichever size and shape offers the best fit. As a general rule, greater contact between chock and rock means a stronger placement. Therefore, larger chocks will generally be stronger than smaller ones, and wide-side placements will be stronger than end-side placements (fig. 10-19).

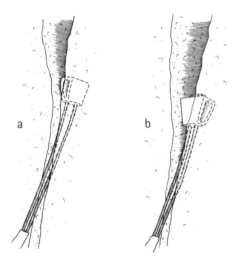

Fig. 10-19. Wide-side and end-side placement of passive wedging chocks: a, wide sides are in contact with the rock, a stronger placement; b, ends are in contact with the rock, a weaker placement.

Carefully evaluate the potential effects of rope drag and of the direction of loading in the event of a fall. In vertical cracks, gravity will usually keep your chock in place, as long as the rope isn't pulling it sideways or upward. In horizontal cracks, it may be more difficult to keep the chock in position. Setting the chock in place tightly enough to avoid being pulled out of place by rope drag will help. You can also place opposing chocks, with a second chock to help hold the first one in place (a technique that will be discussed near the end of this chapter).

If you must use one of the small wedging chocks called micronuts for climbing protection, place it especially carefully and make sure it has excellent contact with the rock. Use of a load-limiting runner such as the Yates Screamer will improve the odds that the micronut will hold a leader fall. This type of runner has a series of bar tacks designed to rip out as they absorb some of the load in a fall.

## Placing Spring-Loaded Wedges

Spring-loaded wedging chocks (fig. 10-13) can be used almost anywhere you would use a passive wedge. But they really come into their own in thin cracks, including parallel-sided cracks (fig. 10-20), where passive wedges may not fit well or won't hold safely.

In placing spring-loaded wedges, it's important to

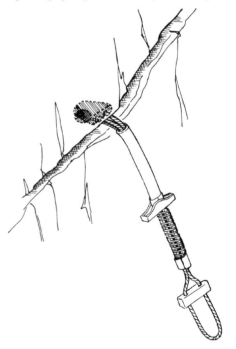

Fig. 10-20. Placement of spring-loaded wedging chock

select just the right size for the crack because the placement size range for any one of these devices is quite narrow. They are susceptible to being pulled out of place by rope movement, so a long runner is advisable. As with any piece of rock protection, it is extremely important to calculate the direction of force on the device. A miscalculation will likely result in the spring-loaded wedge rotating out of its placement. Consider using a load-limiting runner to increase protection in case of a fall.

## Placing Passive Cams

Camming chocks are designed to rotate slightly under load in order to cause the chock to grip the rock more tightly. Therefore, these chocks should be placed so that they fit tightly enough in a crack for good contact with the rock, yet still have sufficient room for camming to occur. They also need to be set firmly enough to keep them from being pulled out of place by rope movement.

In vertically oriented cracks, the piece will be more secure if it is placed just above a constriction or irregularity in the crack and if it is oriented so that the camming action pulls it more tightly against any irregularity (figs. 10-21a and 10-22a).

In horizontally oriented cracks, the piece must

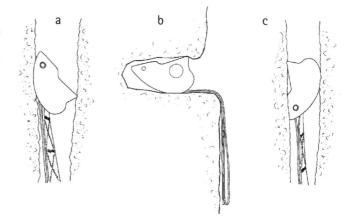

*Fig. 10-22. Placements of the Lowe Tri-Cam: a, in a vertical crack, as a passive cam; b, in a horizontal crack, as a passive cam—stinger is up for better stability; c, in a vertical crack, as a passive wedging chock.*

be placed so that the downward pull of a potential fall will create the maximum camming action. Hexes should be positioned so that the sling leaves the crack closer to the roof than to the floor (fig. 10-21b). Tri-Cams, however, are more stable if the sling is on the floor of the crack, with the "stinger" pointing up (fig. 10-22b). These passive camming chocks must be set well to keep them from being pulled out of place by rope movement.

Hexes and Tri-Cams also can be used as passive wedges (figs. 10-21c and 10-22c). The principles of placement are the same as for other wedges: maximize contact with the rock, and make sure the chock will hold in the expected direction of a fall and of potential rope drag. Hexes are placed sideways as wedges and lengthwise as cams or wedges. Tri-Cams are designed for lengthwise placement only.

## Placing Spring-Loaded Cams

Spring-loaded camming devices are terrific for making a quick placement in a desperate situation, and they are highly valued for this purpose. They are the device of choice for parallel-sided cracks that lack the constrictions or irregularities needed for more traditional chocks (fig. 10-23a). They are also used in flaring cracks, in parallel-sided spaces behind flakes, and

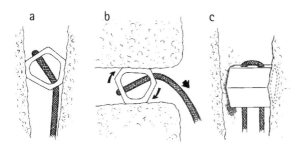

*Fig. 10-21. Placements of the Hexentric chock: a, in a vertical crack, as a passive cam—good contact with the rock results in greater holding power; b, in a horizontal crack, as a passive cam—sling exits near the roof of the crack for proper camming action; c, sideways in a crack, as a passive cam.*

CORRECT AVOID AVOID

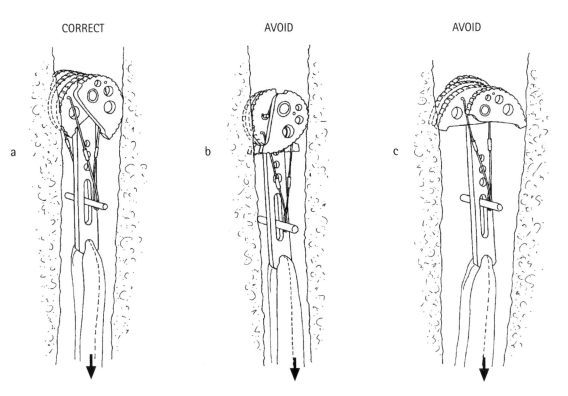

a                                  b                                  c

*Fig. 10-23. Placement of spring-loaded camming devices: a, correct—cams expanded to midpoint, stem in likely direction of pull; b, cams are overretracted; c, cams are overexpanded—failure likely.*

in cracks under roofs where other chocks may be difficult if not impossible to place.

Within their given range, the three or four individual cams in the device will adjust to the width and irregularities of the crack as the trigger is released. The stem of the device must be pointed in the likely direction of pull during a fall to provide maximum strength and to help keep it from being pulled out of position. Spring-loaded cams work best in harder rock—for instance, granite rather than sandstone—and in cracks with relatively even sides.

If the device you are using has a solid stem rather than a flexible one, be careful that the stem won't be forced against the edge of the crack during a fall, which could cause the stem to bend or break. This consideration is especially important in horizontal or near-horizontal cracks, where the stem hangs out over the edge of the crack (fig. 10-24). You can add a tie-off loop through one of the holes in the stem so that the weight of a fall is taken closer to the cams and farther from the end of the solid stem (fig. 10-24b). A flexible-stem device is more reliable in this situation (fig. 10-24a).

Despite the ease of placing spring-loaded camming devices, there are a few things you should be aware of:

- If the cams are fully retracted in the placement, camming action may not occur (fig. 10-23b). The device may become jammed in the crack, making it impossible to remove.
- If the cams are overexpanded, with only the tips touching the rock, no camming action will occur, and the device is likely to pull loose during a fall (fig. 10-23c).

- In softer rock, such as sandstone or limestone, spring-loaded camming devices can be pulled out by a hard fall (even when they are placed properly).
- All cams must contact the rock or else the placement will be unstable. The cams also should be somewhat balanced in placement, with each pair of cams expanded about the same amount, to permit proper camming action.
- Rope drag can cause the entire piece to move, "walking" it deeper into the crack or sometimes making it fall out. Use a runner that is long enough to minimize the effects of rope movement.
- When using a three-cam device, the side with two cams should be more downward for best stability.

## Opposition Placement

There are several situations in which a second chock must be placed in order to keep the first one in position. Single placements can sometimes be dislodged by sideways or upward pulls on the rope as the lead climber advances, because of changes in the direction of the route. In horizontal cracks, or when there is a change in the angle of the rope, the chock must sometimes be pulled into the crack constriction by another piece to be effective in holding a fall.

To form an opposition placement, place two pieces that will pull toward each other when linked (fig. 10-25). Depending on how far apart the pieces are, you can use either carabiners or slings to link the chocks, with slings being the preferred option because they can be tensioned. Ideally the chocks

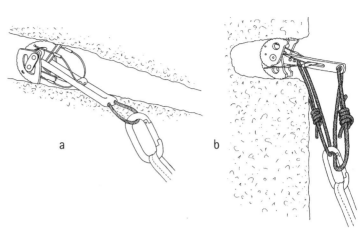

*Fig. 10-24. Spring-loaded camming device placement in a horizontal crack: a, flexible cable stem can bend and adjust to the direction of pull; b, a tie-off loop can reduce the danger of solid-stem breakage.*

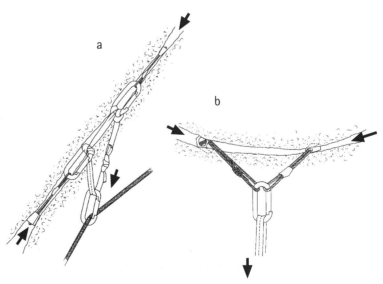

*Fig. 10-25. Opposing chocks: a, in a vertically oriented crack, connected by a runner secured with clove hitches; b, in a horizontal crack, connected by a carabiner.*

should be held together under a slight tension, which may be accomplished by using clove hitches to tie a runner between the carabiners on the chock sling and cinching up one side of the runner (fig. 10-25a). The climbing rope may then be clipped into the *slack* side of the runner.

## Equalizing Chocks

Faced with a hard move or questionable protection, a leader may decide to place two pieces of protection close together. If one piece fails, the other is there as a backup.

Another option is to equalize the load over two protection points, subjecting each to only a portion of the

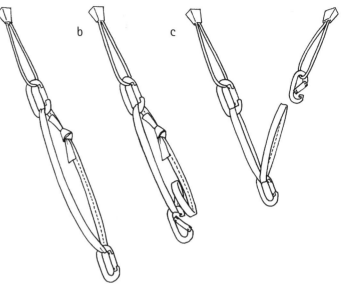

*Fig. 10-27. Alternative method for constructing two-point equalizing protection: a, clip biner into runner; b, wrap one side of runner around biner; c, pull runner up from biner and clip it to the second chock.*

total force. (A more complicated version of equalizing protection, with three or more protection points, can be used at belay points to establish an anchor; see Chapter 7, Belaying.)

Equalizing the forces between two points of protection can be accomplished with one hand and requires only one runner (fig. 10-26a). First clip the runner into one chock. Twist the runner in the middle, and then clip it into the second chock. Then simply clip an extra carabiner through the twist in the runner, with the rope attached to this carabiner. If one chock later pulls out, the twist in the runner will slide down and catch around the carabiner so that the rope remains connected to the remaining chock. Avoid clipping the carabiner across, rather than through, the twisted runner (fig. 10-26b), because the entire setup will then fail if one chock comes loose.

Another way to achieve this setup is to clip the runner into the first chock and then clip a carabiner into

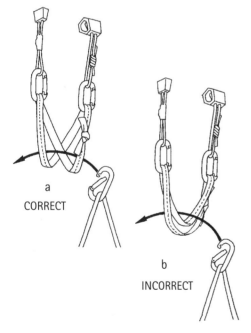

*Fig. 10-26. Constructing two-point equalizing protection: a, correct—the carabiner is clipped from one loop of the twisted runner to the other; b, incorrect—the carabiner is clipped across the twisted runner and will fail if one of the chocks pulls out.*

the other end of the runner (fig. 10-27). Open the carabiner gate long enough to give one side of the runner a 360-degree wrap around the biner wall. Grab the center of the wrap and pull it up from the biner and clip in into the second chock. (Chapter 7, Belaying, also outlines and illustrates a somewhat different but effective way to achieve this protection setup.)

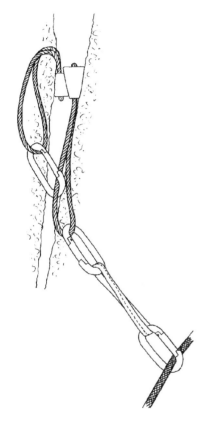

*Fig. 10-28. Stacking chocks*

## Stacking

There are times when nothing on your rack will accommodate the crack you need to protect. If it's a parallel-sided crack and you're out of spring-loaded cams, the advanced technique called stacking can sometimes do the job. You'll need two passive wedges. Place the wedges in opposition to each other in the crack, with the larger one on top (fig. 10-28). A downward pull on the larger chock causes it to wedge between one side of the crack and one side of the other chock. Seat the larger chock with a firm tug before use. Connect the two chocks with a carabiner to avoid having one become a flying missile should the placement fail. Use only straight-sided wedges; the curved-sided wedges prevalent now will not seat well against each other.

## Building Your Skills

The main technique for becoming proficient at placing protection is very basic: practice, practice, practice. One good way to practice is to place as many pieces of protection as possible while standing on the ground, free of concerns about climbing itself. When you're on a climb, following as a second on the rope, observe closely how the leader places protection. Practice placing pieces while climbing with the safety of a top rope.

When you believe you've learned enough to try some leading on your own, take on an easy pitch that you have already climbed as a second or while top-roped. Place as many pieces as possible, just for the practice. Don't be discouraged if the first time turns out to be harder than it looks. Bring along a knowledgeable, experienced climber as your second. It's a great way to get valuable feedback. Just keep at it, and soon *you* may be the one giving the advice.

# 11

# LEADING ON ROCK

A climber who has learned to follow a lead climber up a variety of routes and who has practiced the basics of placing protection is ready for the next step: leading a climb. Leading is the skill of climbing first up a pitch, placing pieces of protection as you go. You are now on the sharp end of the rope, in charge of navigating the way up the route. Because the success of the climb is largely in your hands, leading can be the most satisfying of climbing experiences.

The techniques described in this chapter are aimed primarily at leading on fifth-class rock routes that require belayed climbing and chock placements. But as a leader, you will discover that the strategies you use can depend considerably on the nature of the route and on your skill level.

A climb will usually be categorized as either nontechnical or technical (fig. 11-1). It can be a nontechnical *scramble,* in which you climb unroped. Or it can be technical: a *free climb,* in which you climb roped and belayed, placing protection but never putting weight on the rope or the protection except in case of a fall; or an *aid climb,* in which you use the protection for direct support (see Chapter 12, Aid Climbing).

Depending on your ability and confidence, you will have a certain amount of latitude in categorizing your climb and thus in choosing your method of leading it. A newcomer to leading may tend to be conservative, perhaps categorizing an exposed third-class scramble as a technical climb and placing protection while being belayed up the

| Nontechnical Scrambling | Fifth-Class Free Climbing | Aid Climbing |

*Fig. 11-1. Categories of rock climbing*

route. A master climber, on the other hand, might choose to scramble a moderate fifth-class route where other mountaineers would call for a rope. And this same expert climber might attempt to free-climb a route that others have aided. In fact, one of the favorite pursuits of today's best rock climbers is to "free" routes that previously have been climbed only with direct aid.

Other factors also come into play in plotting your approach to leading. On a vertical sport-climbing face route, for instance, you'll probably find bolts in place, and your job as leader will be to clip your rope into this existing protection as you climb. On most high-angle alpine rock, you will place your own protection. On mixed alpine climbs, all-around mountaineering skills become as important as the ability to place protection (see details on alpine climbing in Chapter 16).

## LEADING ON NONTECHNICAL TERRAIN

A climbing party will often travel unroped or unbelayed over third-class and fourth-class rock, each person climbing in balance and maintaining three points of contact with the rock. If the risks of the climb escalate beyond the party's comfort level, a leader has several options short of full belayed climbing for using the rope to help minimize danger. These include the hand line, the running belay, and the hip belay.

**Hand line:** One option is to set up a fixed hand line for members of an unroped party (fig. 11-2). The leader anchors a rope at the bottom of a difficult section and then scrambles up this section, bringing along the loose

*Fig. 11-2. A hand line as limited protection for an unroped party*

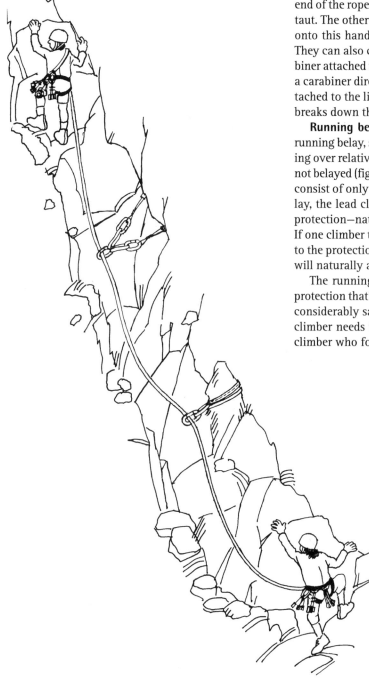

end of the rope. At the top, the leader anchors the rope taut. The other climbers then move up, either holding onto this hand line or prepared to grab it if needed. They can also choose to clip into the line with a carabiner attached to a runner from their harness or to clip a carabiner directly from their harness into a sling attached to the line with a prusik knot. The last climber breaks down the hand line while ascending.

**Running belay:** Another protection option is the running belay, sometimes useful when a team is climbing over relatively easy terrain, still roped together but not belayed (fig. 11-3). Roped climbing teams normally consist of only two people. To establish a running belay, the lead climber simply clips the rope into some protection—natural or artificial—every 50 feet or so. If one climber takes a fall, the rope will remain linked to the protection—and the weight of the other climber will naturally arrest the fall at some point.

The running belay is a rough-and-ready form of protection that's less secure than belayed climbing but considerably safer than no protection at all. The lead climber needs to be sensitive to the skill level of the climber who follows and be ready to set up a regular anchored belay if the follower needs that degree of security.

**Hip belay:** The hip belay (see Chapter 7, Belaying) can be a fast

*Fig. 11-3. A running belay as limited protection for a two-member climbing team*

and efficient technique for providing a secure belay for the leader of a climbing team that is moving together on relatively low-angle rock. If the difficulty or exposure becomes great enough, the leader may call for a belay for security over a worrisome section. The second climber sets up a belay anchor and clips into it and then can simply use the classic hip belay to protect the leader. Of course, the belayer also has the option of using a belay device, but the hip belay is a practical way to protect the leader on a lower-angle, lower-grade route. It should not be used for belaying on continuous difficulties because of the danger of rope burns, compromising the belay, if a long hard fall occurs.

## — LEADING TECHNICAL CLIMBS —

Technical climbing is generally climbing that utilizes ropes, belaying techniques, and intermediate points of protection along the route. The leader of a technical climb accepts more risk than the second climber, who has the luxury of a belay from above and does not have to worry about dropping more than a very short distance before the belayer stops the fall. Because the risk is greater, a leader needs a higher level of skill in climbing and protection placement than is required of the climber who follows.

The leader also needs a full understanding of the belay system, rope management, fall forces, gear selection, and routefinding—some of the subjects that will be explored in this chapter. Confidence in your knowledge of these subjects will help quiet any fears as you learn to lead technical climbs.

An aspiring leader should learn the mechanics of leading while climbing well below his or her actual climbing ability. The person who can follow on a rock route that is rated 5.9 may find leading 5.6 a terrifying experience. Gain experience by learning the basics of leading on simpler routes; then you can begin pushing the limits of your ability. It may sound obvious, but always be sure your climbing ability is consistent with the route you decide to lead. You may be good at face climbing but have trouble with cracks; if the route requires crack climbing, you may want to make sure it's rated lower than what you're accustomed to handling on a face climb.

Steep sport-climbing routes, with bolts already in place as protection, can be relatively safe places to attempt hard moves as a leader. And if you fall, you'll probably only "catch air." It's said that leading a bolted, overhanging 5.11 route can be safer than leading a slabby 5.7 because the risk of hitting rock during a fall is considerably less.

In contrast to sport climbing, alpine rock climbing and mountaineering often take you into remote areas with long climbs, where the consequences of a fall can be great. You'll be carrying a pack and probably wearing mountain boots instead of rock-climbing shoes. With all these additional challenges, it's a good idea to be more conservative in choosing the level of climbing difficulty to attempt in the mountains than in crags just a few minutes from the parking lot.

## — GEARING UP TO LEAD A CLIMB —

You're planning a climb. And the question before you is: What should I carry along for protection? Just as important is how you carry that gear.

### What to Carry

If the climb you've selected is in an established climbing area, a guidebook will often tell you what you need to know: the type of rock, width of cracks, amount of fixed or natural protection, length and direction of each pitch, difficulty rating, even the precise sizes of chocks needed.

It's a different matter if you decide to attempt a first ascent or plan to do any climbing in a remote area. The leader then has much less information to use in estimating what to take along. Take too much, and the extra weight and equipment make the climbing awkward and harder than necessary. Take too little, and you may be forced to "run it out"—to climb higher above the protection than is safe.

For protection, a leader always packs a selection of chocks, carabiners, and runners. But how many and what kind? These questions cannot be answered until you consider some specifics of the climb at hand. Is it a bolted face climb where the only protection you need to carry are the very short runners known as quick draws, with carabiners already attached? Or is the route along an unbolted thin crack where passive wedging chocks might work best? Or is it a very wide crack where spring-loaded camming devices or the Big Bro tube chock will fit comfortably?

In most cases, each protection placement requires two carabiners. Nonlocking carabiners are the norm, though locking carabiners can be used in cases where the gate might be forced open during a fall. For instance, a load-limiting runner such as the Screamer can produce carabiner vibration during a fall, and this could cause the gate to open. The lead climber should carry extra carabiners as insurance against running short.

The leader usually carries a selection of short, medium-length, and long runners. Each point of protection commonly requires one runner. The proper runner at any point is the one that helps the rope stay in as straight a line as possible. Additional runners are needed for belay anchors, unanticipated protection placements, and rappel slings.

Sometimes chocks are difficult to remove from the rock. That is why each climbing team needs a chock pick—the thin metal tool that helps a climber extract pieces of protection (fig. 11-4). The climber who follows on a pitch can use the tool to help loosen a chock that refuses to come out easily.

In addition to chocks, carabiners, runners, and a chock pick, a rock climber will usually carry a belay device, plus a tie-off loop (a short loop of accessory cord) for emergency prusiking or for tying off a climber after a fall. A chalk bag also is often included to carry chalk for keeping hands dry.

## How to Carry the Gear

Once you have decided what gear to take, it must be organized for carrying. The technique of organizing the gear is called racking. The collection of gear used for protection is the rack (fig. 11-5).

Typically, pieces of protection are carried on a gear sling, which is slung over one shoulder and under the opposite arm. The gear sling should be carried in such a way that the hardware is away from the rock, making it more readily available. If you're climbing an inside corner, for instance, and your right side is farthest away from the rock, the gear should hang from that side, with the sling riding on your left shoulder. You can buy a padded gear sling from a climbing shop or

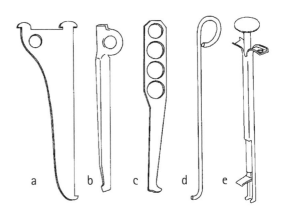

Fig. 11-4. Chock picks: a, shelf bracket; b, piton type; c, Leeper; d, skewer type or tent stake; e, Friend of a Friend.

use a single-length runner for the job.

The ideal racking method would permit the leader to place protection efficiently and climb without awkwardness despite carrying the gear. No racking method is perfect, but several are commonly used.

One method of racking is for each chock to have its own carabiner (fig. 11-5b). This method can be very efficient for placing protection. The leader simply places the chock in the rock, clips the chock's carabiner to a runner, and clips the runner's carabiner to the rope. However, this method has the major disadvantages of bulkiness and poor weight distribution. The rack tends to be relatively wide and cumbersome, and there are few free carabiners. If the chock you choose for protection is the wrong size, time and energy are wasted in returning to the rack to find the right one.

Another method of racking is to combine several similar-size pieces of protection on one carabiner (fig. 11-5c). Grouping the protection by size reduces the number of carabiners needed to carry your chocks. This method can make climbing easier because it results in a less bulky rack with better weight distribution. But it can make it more difficult to place protection. First of all, you have to decide whether to remove a single piece from the group of chocks on a carabiner and hope that it fits or to unclip the carabiner and hold the whole

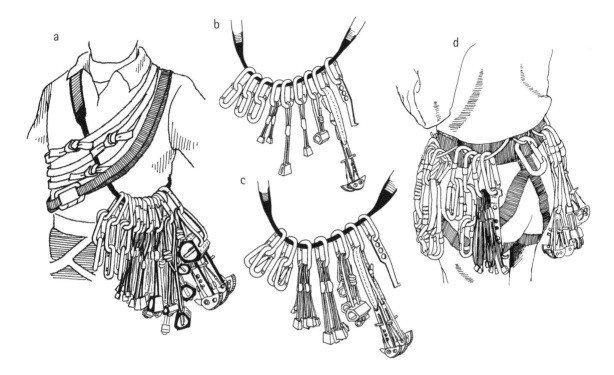

*Fig. 11-5. Examples of racking methods: a, climber carrying runners and a typical rack; b, racking method where most pieces of protection get their own carabiner; c, racking method where most pieces of protection are grouped together, each group held by a single carabiner; d, racking method where the protection is attached to the gear loops on the climbing harness.*

batch of chocks up to the placement. If you opt for the latter, you can easily try out each chock and place the one that fits. Then unclip the carabiner from the chock and return the carabiner and unused chocks to the gear sling.

This method of racking gear with several chocks per carabiner usually means slower placements and more equipment handling. Even after placing a chock, the leader must handle one quick draw (carabiners already attached) or two free carabiners and a runner to create the proper extension to the rope. All this increases the danger that the leader will drop gear or become exhausted. But many climbers feel the increased ease of climbing offered by this racking method is worth the extra work.

Another method is to rack gear on the gear loops of your climbing harness (fig. 11-5d). This helps distribute the weight of the rack, but be sure the gear doesn't hang down far enough to interfere with footwork. Rack the chocks on one side of your harness and the runners, quick draws, and carabiners on the other side.

Whatever your method, rack the protection in a systematic order that never varies, so you can find a particular piece in a hurry. The usual order is to start at the front with your smallest wired chocks and to work back with larger-size pieces. Each carabiner clipped to the gear sling should have the gate up and toward your body, making it easier to unclip.

A final point about runners: It's a good idea to carry a couple of runners readily accessible on the harness gear loops in case you cannot get to the ones slung

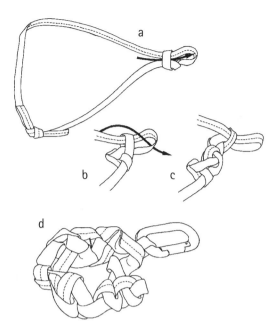

Fig. 11-6. Chaining a long runner: a, form a slip knot; b, pull runner through the loop formed by the slip knot; c, repeat this process until the runner is chained; d, the final loop can be attached to a carabiner for carrying and to ensure it does not unravel.

under one arm. To shorten a longer runner so it will not trip you up, you can double it. You can also chain the runner (fig. 11-6) before attaching it to the harness. When needed, just shake out the chained runner to remove the knots.

## LEADING ON ROCK, STEP BY STEP

Now that you know the tools for protection, and how to carry and place them, it is time for the next move, literally.

It is one thing to recognize a Stopper, hex, or Friend and be able to use them in individual placements. You probably learned all this while standing at the base of a rock face or while safely top-roped. It is another thing to get up on the rock and take the lead. You now need to learn the protection techniques that let you use these tools and skills safely in mapping out a strategy for an entire pitch.

You will learn to think of the entire pitch as you make each placement. How will this placement affect the total climbing system? Learn these techniques and you should not have any nasty surprises in a fall. That beautifully placed chock will not pop out, because you used the right tricks to make it do its job in the context of protecting the entire pitch.

Leading is a complex business. Beginners usually need an apprenticeship, moving behind seasoned climbers before they can safely take the sharp end of the rope. Never take the lead if you don't feel ready, and do not pressure others into leading. Keep the art of leading what it ought to be: exciting, challenging, satisfying, and safe.

## Planning the Route

The matter of finding your way to the top of a route that you are leading depends somewhat on where the climb is. If you're sport climbing in a popular spot, just follow the line of fixed pitons, bolts, and chalked holds, or look up the climb in the guidebook. Finding the way in alpine rock climbing is not as simple. The route is likely to be longer and less clearly defined. Even with a guidebook, the description may be sketchy: "Ascend NE buttress for several hundred feet of moderate climbing." Routefinding may be more important to success than other skills.

Start working out the route as soon as you can see the buttress, face, ridge, or whatever you plan to climb. Look for major features that the line of ascent might follow: crack systems, dihedrals, chimneys, areas of broken rock. Note areas of small trees or bushes that could indicate belay ledges. Identify landmarks that will help you determine your position on the route when you reach them. For this kind of small-detail planning, your eyes will be able to tell you what your topographical map cannot.

Keep a watch out for deceptively tempting lines that lead to broad roofs or blank walls. These may not be visible from near the start of the ascent, and if climbers don't pay attention on the approach, they could climb four or five pitches only to hit a dead end.

Develop a flexible plan for the line of ascent, keeping in mind likely alternatives. Continue planning the routefinding as the actual climb begins, looking for more local features and landmarks. Seek out natural lines to follow as you lead the route. Form a tentative plan for the pitch, perhaps including a place for the first piece of protection and a spot for the next belay station. And always be prepared to look around the corner for easier route alternatives not visible from below.

Faced with a choice between pitches of varying difficulty, look at the next pitch before deciding. It is better to climb two moderate pitches than to go for an easy pitch and then be faced with one that exceeds the party's ability.

On the way up, keep track of retreat possibilities in case the climb is aborted, as well as good descent routes from the summit if you don't know of any established route.

## Planning the Belay

If you're leading a route that is only one pitch long, your belay setup at the top of the pitch needs to be directed only against a downward pull from the second climber. But if it's a multipitch climb, the belay station will also be used to belay the next lead. You will need to set up this dual-purpose station with anchors that will handle a downward pull from the second climber and then, with minimal change, the upward pull of the lead climber on the next pitch. An efficient belay setup is faster and safer and leaves more time for climbing.

## Deciding How Often to Place Protection

The universal fear of falling leads some climbers to place protection before almost every move. They deplete their hardware and waste valuable time. They also miss one of the great attractions of rock climbing, the exhilaration of moving smoothly and continuously up the rock.

Other climbers underprotect, sometimes to show off their strength and daring. They get a psychological lift that doesn't do a thing to counteract the laws of gravity. A better choice is to base decisions about protection on a careful assessment of your personal abilities, the character of the rock, and the time and equipment available.

The closest thing to a general rule is to place protection where you feel uncomfortable without it, usually protecting before the hard moves. In coming to your own decision on when to place another piece of protection, keep in mind the quality of the placements you have already made. If they are tending to be poor or questionable, it's a good idea to put in more to increase the likelihood that at least one will hold. Knowing the fall factor, discussed next, also helps in deciding the next placement.

## Determining the Fall Factor

The relative forces generated by a leader fall are measured by the fall factor, determined by dividing the length of fall by the length of rope run out from the belay. The higher the fall factor, the greater the force. The maximum fall factor is 2—which would occur if a climber took an unobstructed leader fall with no protection in place (as shown in Figure 10-1a, in Chapter 10, Rock Protection).

The fall factor is lower when the length of rope runout from the belay is relatively great, because a long length of rope stretches more and absorbs more energy than a short length. The practical effect of this fact is that when the length of rope between belayer and climber is great, a fall will usually result in a smaller force than the same fall on a short length. Therefore, it is possible to place protection less frequently toward the end of a pitch without increasing the fall factor.

The fall factor is an important concept for the lead climber to understand because it provides an estimate of the relative forces that will be generated in a fall. The lead climber, not the belayer, determines the fall factor by deciding when to place protection. Therefore, the leader should keep the fall factor in mind and take steps to minimize it. To eliminate chances of a fall with the maximum fall factor of 2, you can place your first piece of protection even before leaving the belay station or as soon as possible after you begin climbing. Then place intermediate protection as the need and the opportunity arise.

You can roughly estimate the potential fall factor at different points during the lead, to help in deciding when to place more protection. Just remember that a fall near the start of a pitch puts more force on the belayer and protection, so it generally promotes safety to place more protection near the beginning.

## Selecting a Placement

As you lead a pitch, moving up from the belay station, you will reach a point where you want to put in a piece of protection. Find a stance for yourself that is as secure and comfortable as possible. It can take some time to put in a good placement, so you need a stance where you will not slip off or become dangerously tired.

If there is no good stance, you are stuck with some unpleasant options: downclimb and ask the belayer to lead the pitch, hang on desperately and hope to get a placement before arms and legs give out, or charge on to the next available stance. This unhappy situation usually can be avoided by planning ahead and placing protection before it is urgently needed. But when such a situation does develop, don't panic. Make a decision and stick with it. Surprisingly often, the correct decision is to continue without protection to the next available stance.

When you find a good stance, go ahead with the protection placement. Sometimes you will be faced with a choice between two or more possible placements. It's tempting to always place the largest possible chock, but the decision on which one to use

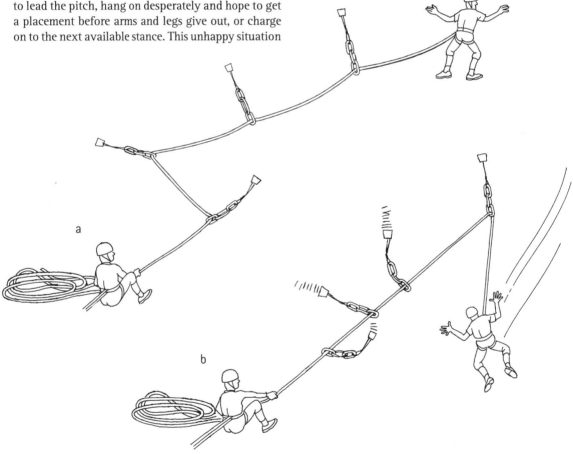

*Fig. 11-7. Judging the direction of fall forces: a, a zigzagging rope can bring unanticipated fall forces to bear on the protection; b, as the rope tries to straighten, it can pull up or outward on the protection, causing it to fail, especially if it was placed only for a downward pull.*

should depend on a consideration of several factors. Which placement will be strongest? What size chocks should be conserved for use higher on the pitch? Which placement will be easiest for the second climber to remove? Which placement will avoid conflict with the footholds and handholds you need as you move upward? Select your placement after thinking through all the consequences of your choice.

At spots where you are especially concerned about falling or where placements are questionable, you can ease your fear and make the climb safer by placing two separate pieces of protection near each other or by equalizing the load over two placements linked with a runner (see "Equalizing Chocks," near the end of Chapter 10).

## Judging the Direction of Fall Forces

In placing protection, the leader also must anticipate the direction of forces that will be created by a fall and how they could affect each placement. It's easy to get so wrapped up in placing the next piece of protection that you fail to analyze the effect it will have on the entire climbing system. This can create a false sense of security. A protection point may seem solid and secure, but it may not withstand a fall that generates forces in directions you haven't anticipated.

A zigzagging climbing rope can set up some especially worrisome fall forces. The zigzag not only puts a dangerous amount of drag on the rope, but also can bring unanticipated forces to bear on the protection. The chocks may have been placed only with the thought of holding a downward pull. Now they are in danger of taking sharp pulls from a number of directions during a fall (fig. 11-7a).

When a climber falls, the rope becomes taut in an attempt to form a straight line from the belayer up to the highest protection point and then back down to the falling climber. The zigzag rope tries to go straight, tugging sideways or up or outward on every piece of protection as it does so. If the placements are designed to take a pull in only one direction, they may come loose (fig. 11-7b). If the highest piece of protection fails, the whole system fails.

During a fall, the top piece of protection is loaded with the sum of two forces: the impact of the falling climber and the force exerted by the belay in arresting the fall (fig. 11-8). If a fall is taken by a weak piece

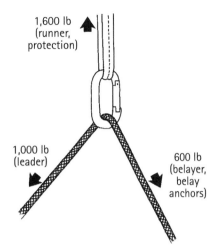

*Fig. 11-8. The combined force on the top protection placement during a fall*

of protection, it could fail. In this situation, it would be nice to know the protection below could be counted on to stay in place. But with the rope zigzagging all over the route, this might not be the case.

Keeping the rope in a straight line will prevent most of the problems caused by fall forces acting in multiple directions. A straight rope will also solve the problem of excessive rope drag. Try to make all the protection placements form a straight line back to the belayer, or extend the protection with runners to permit the rope to run straight.

It also helps to work for multidirectional placements—using natural protection or opposing chocks—so they can withstand forces in several directions. ("Opposition Placement," in Chapter 10, Rock Protection, explains how to set up opposing chocks.)

### The Zipper Effect

The full-scale zipper effect is a dramatic demonstration of the importance of anticipating force directions. The zipper effect occurs most readily where the belay is established away from the base of the pitch or, as in the last example, where the rope runs in a zigzag up the route. As the rope goes taut during a leader fall and strains to run in a straight line from belayer to top chock, there can be tremendous outward pressure on the bottom chock. If it pulls out, the line of chocks could be yanked out one by one as the zipper opens from the bottom up (fig. 11-9). Danger points also are found on overhanging and traversing routes.

The zipper effect can be prevented by making the suspect placements multidirectional (fig. 11-10). At the bottom of a pitch, another method of prevention is to move the belay to the very base of the route so that the rope begins its run upward in a straight line.

Fig. 11-9. The zipper effect in action: force on the bottom chock is up and out.

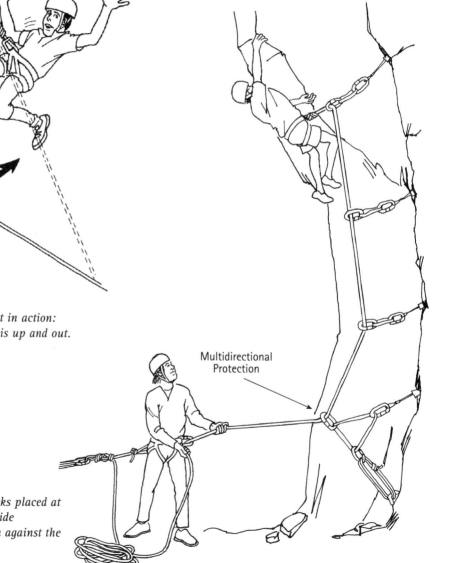

Multidirectional Protection

Fig. 11-10. Opposing chocks placed at the bottom of a pitch provide multidirectional protection against the zipper effect.

## Protecting Special Situations

### Overhangs

Keep the rope running as free of an overhang as possible. Extend the rope with runners in order to reduce rope drag, prevent dangerous fall forces such as the zipper effect, and keep the rope from being cut by the edge of the overhang (fig. 11-11). On small overhangs, it may be possible to lean out and place protection above it.

### Traverses

On a traverse, the lead climber should place protection both before and after a hard move. This guards not only the leader but also the climber who follows from the possibility of a long pendulum fall (fig. 11-12). In addition to the danger of injury, that kind of

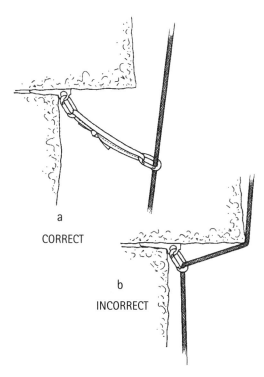

a

CORRECT

b

INCORRECT

*Fig. 11-11. Placements under overhangs: a, correct—rope runs free of the overhang; b, incorrect—bends cause rope drag and rope could be cut by rock edge during a fall.*

fall could leave the second in a tough spot, off route and with no easy way back.

As you lead a diagonal or traversing section, keep in mind the effect each placement could have on the second climber. Put yourself in the second's shoes and ask: Would I like some protection here? If so, place it.

It's possible to belay the second with an extra rope, which may help protect against a long pendulum fall, providing better protection than using the leader's rope. If you happen to be using double-rope technique (described later in this chapter), do not clip in both ropes during the traverse so that the follower can receive a belay from above on the free rope.

## Cleaning a Pitch

The climber who follows the leader should climb as quickly and efficiently as possible after being put on belay. While ascending, this second climber cleans the pitch, removing the protection from the rock in a neat and orderly way. A second who is slow and sloppy can drop chocks, allow dangling protection to interfere with the next move, and hold up the climb while the gear is untangled at the belay station.

Following are some suggestions for the second, aimed at saving time and energy.

- Start preparing to climb as soon as the leader is off belay. Begin breaking down your belay station (but always stay clipped into at least one anchor until the leader has you on belay).
- Put your pack on before anything else. If you're already carrying climbing hardware on a gear sling, that sling goes on next. Then put a second gear sling or runner over one shoulder and under the opposite arm for use in racking the protection as you clean the pitch.
- Give the area a last look to make sure nothing is left. Then, once you are on belay, yell "Climbing!" and start out.
- Remove each chock in reverse order of the way it was placed. If it was slotted down and behind a constriction, remove it by pushing it back and up.
- Be persistent. Use your chock pick to tap on a stubborn chock to loosen it; then lift the chock out gently. Prying, poking, and tugging may also do the job, but more often than not this will only tighten or wedge the chock more. Some chock picks also

241

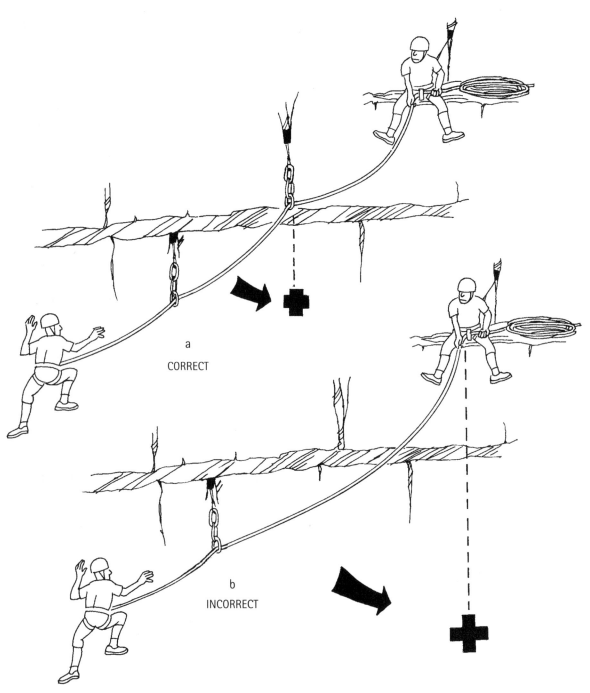

*Fig. 11-12. Protecting a traverse: a, correct—placing protection after a hard move on a traverse can reduce the potential for a long pendulum fall; b, incorrect—if the second climber falls on a traverse with inadequate protection, he faces a long pendulum fall.*

can be used to pull the retraction trigger on spring-loaded camming devices that have "walked" back into a crack.

- If the chock refuses to budge, consider asking your belayer for tension so you can put your weight on the rope, freeing your hands to work on removing the piece.
- As a final option, you can simply abandon the chock. Too much time and effort can be wasted on a chock that isn't going to come out.

The second can minimize the risk of dropping gear by using a careful cleaning procedure, which may depend on how you prefer to rack the hardware. In general, cleaning from rock to the rope is best.

Consider a typical placement consisting of chock–carabiner–runner–carabiner–rope. If your rack features one carabiner on each chock and on each runner, the following cleaning procedure is very efficient. First, remove the chock from the crack. Hold the carabiner that is clipped to the chock, and clip the carabiner-chock combination directly to your gear sling; then unclip it from the runner. Then loop the runner over your head, unclip the carabiner from the rope, slip the carabiner–runner combination under one arm, and continue climbing. This procedure will have the pieces clipped to something at all times, and there is little possibility of dropping any gear.

If your rack features several chocks per carabiner, the following cleaning procedure will work well. First, remove the chock from the crack, unclip it, and rack it. Then remove the carabiner from the runner and rack it, then the runner, and finally the carabiner on the rope. This method requires more care in guarding against dropped gear.

## Transferring Equipment at the Top of a Pitch

The first thing the second climber needs to do when arriving at a belay station—before being taken off belay—is to clip into the belay anchors. If the second was neat, organized, and efficient in cleaning the pitch, the transfer of gear at the belay station will probably go quickly and the fun can resume.

First, reconstruct the original leader's rack. The second clips the removed pieces to the leader's rack or

hands them to the leader, who can rack them. Be careful not to drop any gear. The second then passes over the removed runners. If the original leader plans to lead the next pitch, the rope needs to be restacked and the climbers then carefully switch places in the belay setup. Both climbers always stay anchored to the rock.

If the second is also a competent leader, it's a lot more efficient to swing leads, with the second now taking the lead. To swing leads, the second usually takes over the leader's rack and runners. The original leader hands the runners to the second. The rack is passed to the second, who places it over the head and under one arm. The runners then go over the head and under the other arm. The new leader checks and adjusts the rack to ensure that everything is ready for the new lead. Again, both climbers remain anchored—and the new leader, as a backup, can remain on belay.

## Climbing with a Party of Three

Most rock climbing is done in teams of two, but occasionally a party will end up with three climbers. This works, though it is usually more awkward than climbing with just two people.

A three-person team climbing on one rope is limited to pitches of only 70 to 80 feet, just half of the rope length. Because many climbs have pitches much longer than this, a three-person team should carry two ropes.

Here is one method of climbing with a three-person team, using two ropes: The leader climbs while the second belays and the third remains anchored at the belay station. At the top of the pitch, the leader sets up a belay and brings up the second. If the pitch follows a straight line up, the second can clean the pitch. If the line includes some traversing, the protection should stay in for the third climber, to help prevent a pendulum fall. In this situation, the second climber unclips each piece of protection from the first rope and clips it to the second rope, which is tied to the back of the second climber's harness. At the top of the pitch, the belay is reset to bring up the third climber. The climbers then may decide to swing leads, with the third climber leading the next pitch. The second climber generally does not do any leading in a party of three.

Another way to climb with three is to use the twin-rope technique (described in the next section of this chapter). The leader ties into one end of each rope, the second climber ties into the other end of one of the ropes, and the third climber ties into the remaining end. The leader then climbs the pitch, belayed on both ropes by one of the other climbers, and sets up a belay station. Then the leader can either belay one follower at a time or bring both up together, one just ahead of the other.

This technique takes great belay concentration from the leader and much rope management—but it's a way for three climbers to ascend nearly as fast as two. The original leader remains on lead throughout the climb.

With all the anchors, ropes, and climbers involved in a three-person team, it can get messy and confusing at the belay stations. A lot of time can be taken up setting and resetting belays. Throughout the commotion, it's critical that each of the three climbers be securely anchored.

There are occasional advantages to a three-person team, such as added help in hauling packs and the availability of an extra rope for full-length rappels. But the disadvantages usually outweigh the advantages.

## Special Rope Techniques

Most of this book describes climbing situations in which a single rope, with a diameter between 10 and 11 millimeters, is usually used. However, climbers can also opt for one of the methods that use two smaller-diameter ropes: double-rope technique or twin-rope technique.

### Double-Rope Technique

The double-rope technique uses two ropes that serve as independent belay lines (fig. 11-13). The leader clips each rope into its own protection on the way up, and the belayer manages the ropes separately.

Yes, it's complicated, but the double-rope technique offers some important rewards, such as reducing rope drag. The technique is widely

used by British climbers and by an increasing number of climbers everywhere to protect highly technical routes.

The double-rope technique usually employs ropes of about 9 millimeters in diameter, with one rope a different color than the other. The leader may call for slack on the green rope, for instance, in order to clip into a piece of protection, while asking for tension on the yellow rope.

The technique offers great advantages when the route meanders. The leader clips one rope into one series of protection placements and the other rope into another series, the goal being to keep each rope in as straight a line as possible so that rope drag is at a minimum. The drag is usually less than what it would be on a single rope on the same pitch because the single

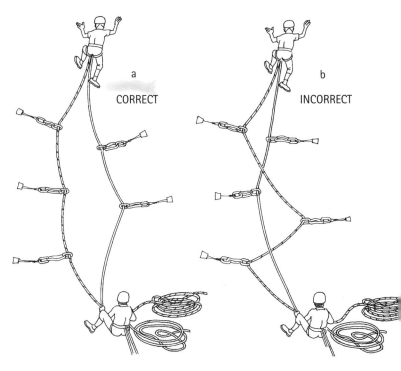

Fig. 11-13. Double-rope technique: a, correct—the two ropes do not cross but run reasonably straight to reduce rope drag; b, incorrect—the two ropes cross and run in a zigzag, increasing rope drag and sideways stress on the protection.

244

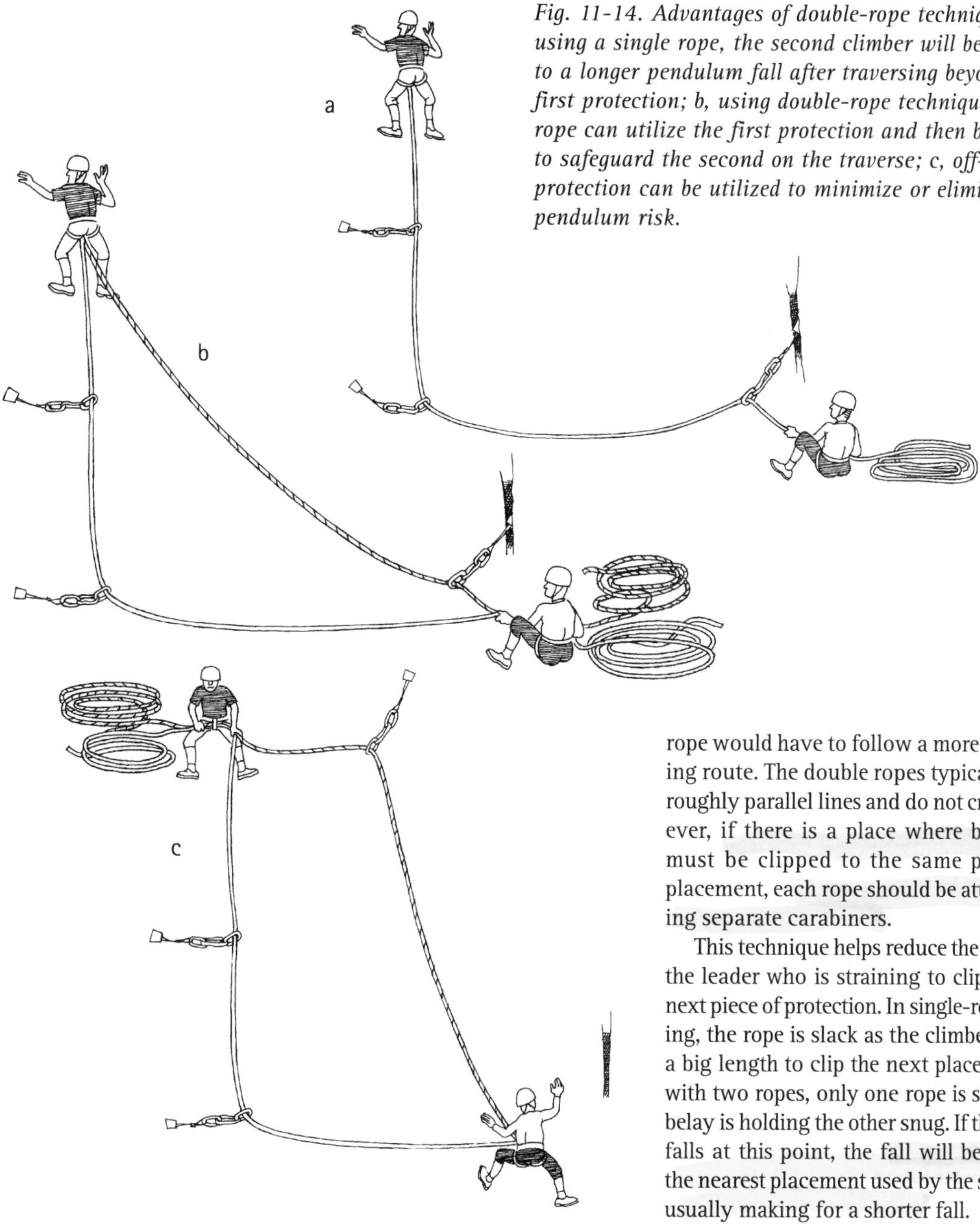

Fig. 11-14. Advantages of double-rope technique: a, using a single rope, the second climber will be exposed to a longer pendulum fall after traversing beyond the first protection; b, using double-rope technique, one rope can utilize the first protection and then be left free to safeguard the second on the traverse; c, off-line protection can be utilized to minimize or eliminate the pendulum risk.

rope would have to follow a more meandering route. The double ropes typically run in roughly parallel lines and do not cross. However, if there is a place where both ropes must be clipped to the same protection placement, each rope should be attached using separate carabiners.

This technique helps reduce the worries of the leader who is straining to clip in to the next piece of protection. In single-rope climbing, the rope is slack as the climber pulls up a big length to clip the next placement. But with two ropes, only one rope is slack if the belay is holding the other snug. If the climber falls at this point, the fall will be taken on the nearest placement used by the snug rope, usually making for a shorter fall.

This method also has the advantage that both ropes are unlikely to be cut by sharp rock edges or rockfall, or to otherwise fail, at the same time. It also provides two ropes for making long rappels.

Double ropes can be very helpful in protecting a traverse, especially one that is at the start of a pitch that then heads straight upward after the traverse. The leader can use one rope for protection on the traverse and leave the other free to belay the second climber from above. If the climbers were using only a single rope, the second climber could risk a long pendulum fall (fig. 11-14a). But with double ropes, the belay on the free rope can minimize or prevent a long pendulum (fig. 11-14b–c).

The double-rope technique has certain disadvantages. The belayer's job is complex, handling the movements of two ropes at the same time—often letting out slack on one rope while taking it in on the other. The ropes must be constantly monitored to avoid tangling and knots. Also, the two ropes weigh more and cost more than a single rope.

For this technique, a double-slotted belay device—such as the classic Sticht-type plate or the Black Diamond Air Traffic Controller—is particularly useful. With practice, the difficulties of the double-rope technique can be mastered. Many climbers find that on long and complex rock pitches, the advantages greatly outweigh the disadvantages.

## Twin-Rope Technique

The twin-rope technique uses two ropes as one (fig. 11-15). Both ropes—which usually are between 8 and 9 millimeters in diameter—are clipped into each piece of protection, just as in the single-rope technique.

The twin ropes absorb more energy and thus can withstand more falls than a single rope. Two ropes also are safer running over a sharp edge, as it's unlikely that both ropes would be cut through at the same time. The smaller-diameter ropes can be easier for the lead climber to

handle than a fatter single rope. This system also gives the climbers two ropes, making long rappels possible.

As with double-rope technique, the belayer has to deal with two ropes, so rope management is critical. Both the belayer and leader need a good bit of practice before taking this technique out on the cliffs.

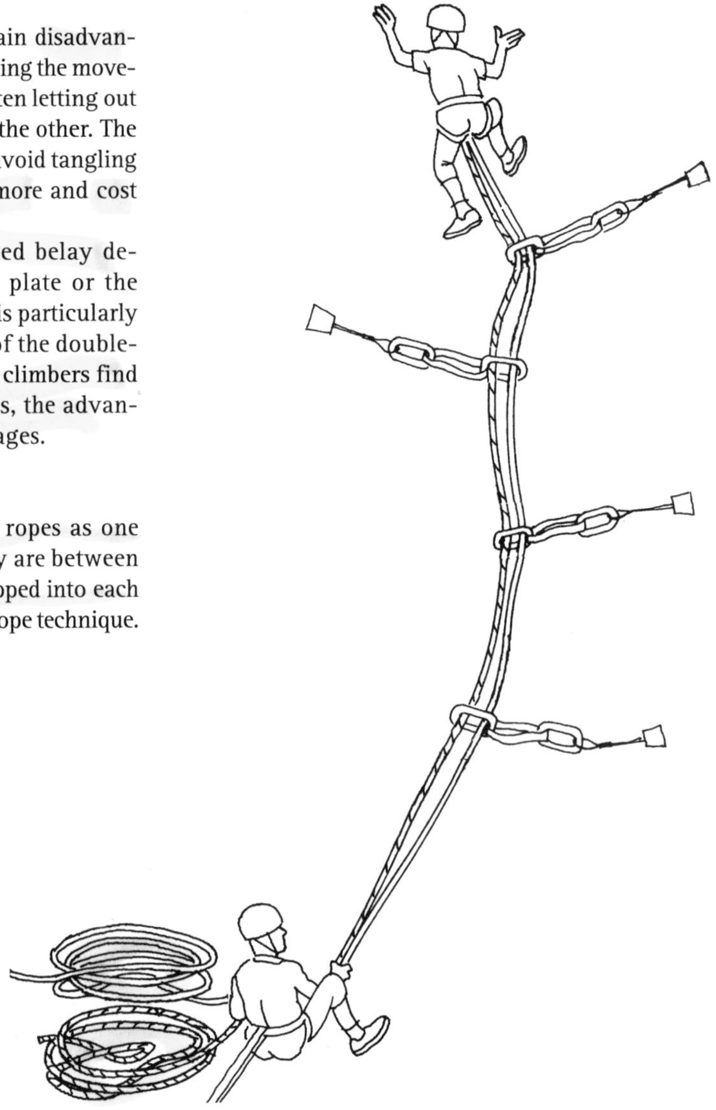

*Fig. 11-15. Twin-rope technique: two small-diameter ropes are used as one, with both attached to each protection placement.*

## —— PERSONAL RESPONSIBILITY ——

Local climbers at each area have usually settled on some basic rules to climb by, including standards for placing protection. Some climbing areas are more traditional, encouraging leading and placing protection "from the ground up." Other areas have embraced newer techniques, such as inspecting a route on rappel before climbing it or placing bolts on rappel. You will have your own opinions regarding protection, of course, but be sensitive to the climbing ethics and styles developed and demonstrated by local climbers.

Everything about mountaineering, including rock climbing, is linked to affection and respect for the environment and consideration for the travelers who come after you. The general rule is the same whether you are hiking, backpacking, alpine mountaineering, or rock climbing: leave the world the way you found it. Specifically on a rock pitch, this means avoiding permanent scarring of rock, trees, and vegetation. If possible, stick to clean climbing, using only chocks for protection.

You know by now that climbing is a balancing act in more ways than one. There is not always one "correct" technique for doing something, and you often need to balance different factors in deciding on a course of action.

Likewise there are no simple commandments to memorize and mechanically follow to ensure safety. You may be called on to make life-and-death decisions despite incomplete knowledge, with no clear rule to follow, and without the luxury of being able to consult your favorite expert, even if that expert is on the other end of the rope. Controlling the risks of climbing is a matter of understanding the reasons that underlie the techniques you have learned, being aware of everything that affects a safe choice, and being able to gauge all the consequences of your actions.

The important thing is that you will be acting on knowledge, not ignorance; on solid understanding, not superficial rules. A climber who uses techniques without understanding them or who mechanically follows a set of safety rules is not thinking and is a danger to himself and fellow climbers. Learn the principles, make them yours, and you'll be free to climb hard, high, and safe.

Remember that leading on rock is serious business. Keep your head cool and calm—and always wear your helmet.

## —— SOME PRACTICAL TIPS FOR —— LEADING ON ROCK

Here are additional recommendations for safe and effective leading on rock. These tips supplement the information given throughout this chapter.

### Questions to Ask Yourself before You Lead a Pitch

- What is the length of the pitch?
- What is the rated difficulty of the pitch (5.6? 5.9?) or of its principal moves?
- Where are the crux moves on the pitch? What are they like?
- What sizes of chocks will I need? Small? Medium? Large?
- What types of chocks will I need? Nuts? Hexes? Spring-loaded cams?
- How much protection will I need to carry, including runners and carabiners, considering my leading ability?
- What climbing techniques will I be using? Liebacks? Foot jams? Hand jams? Stemming?
- Does my partner know to shout out how much rope is left at various points as I climb (calling out "Halfway," "25 feet," "15 feet," "10 feet")?
- Will I be able to verbally communicate with my belayer throughout the climb? Have we established rope signals to use if we can't hear each other well?
- Have I and my belayer agreed on a good location for the belay station at the bottom of this pitch?
- Is the belay station on a steep part of the route where I could drop past my belayer in a fall? If so, where can I put a "bombproof" placement before I start climbing, to ensure that the pull on my belayer in case I fall will be "up and in"—not "down and backward."

- What's the best way to place my first piece of protection so that it minimizes chances of setting off the zipper effect?
- Where is my first stop on the pitch to place protection? What will I stand on? What pro will I use there?

## Placing Protection during the Lead

- Transfer your weight to your feet while placing protection. If you cannot comfortably release one hand to place pro, you haven't completely transferred your weight; adjust your stance or try to find a better place.
- Take advantage of natural protection—trees, bushes, rock tunnels, horns—when possible because it can be easy to use, it saves on chocks, and it's often multidirectional. But remember that a runner tends to slip off a rock horn as you climb above it.
- Protect the hard moves. Place protection above you if possible so that, in effect, you are top-roping these moves.
- Keep rope drag to a minimum: generally use single or double runners rather than the shorter quick draws in order to keep the rope in a relatively straight line between you and your belayer.
- Be alert to the zipper effect and to the direction of fall forces when making a placement: keep the rope reasonably straight, or make the placement multidirectional.
- Constantly monitor your position so that you know when you're in danger of hitting a ledge or the ground in case of a fall, and try to place protection to guard against this possibility.
- Pick out the next likely spot for placing protection

before leaving your current one. Plan the techniques needed to reach this next "rest spot" and the pro you will place there. Climb from stop to stop.
- Remember that a poorly placed piece may be better than nothing if you need to protect a move.

## Setting up the Belay for Your Second after Leading the Pitch

- At the top of the pitch, tie into a "bomber" anchor to the mountain before you signal "Off belay." It's a good idea to also set up an additional independent anchor so that you have two solid, multidirectional anchors at the belay station. (See Chapter 7, Belaying, for complete information on establishing belay anchors.)
- Never be the high point in the belay system when you are belaying a climber ascending from below you. Have at least one of your anchor attachments to an anchor that is above you.
- Try to set the anchors 5 to 10 feet away from the climbing route and your belay site in order to give you room to maneuver and to settle in for the belay.
- Keep your belay system simple. Strive for straight, easily traceable lines from the anchors to you.
- Never lay belay devices, gloves, carabiners, or other items on the ground. If you aren't using an item, keep it attached to yourself or to an anchor.
- Have only one item—such as the rope, a chock, a carabiner—in your hands at a time. The moment you no longer need this item for whatever you are doing, reattach it to yourself or an anchor.
- Take off your pack and your rack and attach them to an anchor, but keep them within easy reach. You'll be more comfortable as you belay your second.

# 12
# AID CLIMBING

Aid climbing is the technique of using gear to support your weight as you climb. It can be as simple as using a bolt as a single handhold or as complex as climbing an entire route with your full weight on pieces of specialized gear you have placed. Aid climbing is an intricate and personal art, and everyone who participates does it somewhat differently.

Aid climbing is clearly a sharp departure from free climbing, where weighting the rope or the protective hardware is poor style. Free ascents are one of the goals of the sport of climbing, while aid climbing is a valuable skill for ascending currently "unfreeable" routes and for use in emergencies.

As standards of difficulty continue to rise, top climbers are freeing many of the routes originally climbed with aid. But despite the rise in free-climbing standards, there will always be tempting routes that are more difficult still—and so devoid of natural features that a climber will need some artificial assistance.

Skills in aid climbing and pitoncraft can also help overcome unexpected difficulties during normal free climbing. They can provide a way to move safely up or down when weather or accident puts your party in jeopardy. Knowing how to use pitons for aid also helps you in evaluating the soundness of fixed pitons you encounter while free climbing. In winter mountaineering, pitons may be the only protection that will hold in ice-filled cracks.

Any advice to use pitons or bolts always comes with a stern caveat: they permanently damage the rock. Don't use them unless you must. And don't use them at all on established free routes.

Aid climbing and pitoncraft require skill, judgment, and a lot of practice. To learn both the basics and the many "tricks" of the techniques, try to work with an experienced partner, and climb often.

## CLEAN AID CLIMBING

Aid climbing takes a lot of gear, but it needn't be damaging to the rock. With all the chocks and camming devices on the market, you now have a better chance to climb routes clean, without putting in a single piton or bolt. The chocks and other devices can be removed without defacing the rock, and the next climber won't even be able to tell you were there.

Aid climbing may still require bolts and pitons, but keep them to a minimum. Pitons (also called pins) chip the rock, especially when you remove them. On popular routes, tiny cracks sometimes evolve into finger or hand cracks after generations of climbers force them to accept pitons.

When climbers make the first ascent of a major wall, they often carry bolts and pins to make it go. Once placed, the best approach is to leave them so future parties can use them without marring the rock further. In general, make clean climbing your goal.

## —— TYPES OF AID CLIMBING ——

We can roughly categorize aid climbing based on the extent of its use on a particular climb.

**Mountaineering alpine aid climbing** uses a minimal amount of aid techniques and equipment to overcome short, blank (or extremely difficult) sections of a route that otherwise goes free. This type of climbing requires little or no specialized aid equipment. Usually you'll just use the free-climbing gear you have along.

**General aid climbing** often uses aid for extended distances, although artificial and free-climbing techniques may be interspersed. Long one-day climbs may involve "fixing" the initial pitches—putting up ropes and leaving them in place so they can be climbed quickly with mechanical ascenders the following morning to reach the previous high point.

**Big-wall aid climbing** involves ascents that take longer than one day to complete, even if the initial pitches are fixed. These climbs include either a hanging bivouac or ledge bivouac and require sack-hauling techniques.

(See Appendix A, Rating Systems, for information on the various grades of difficulty in aid climbing.)

## —— AID-CLIMBING EQUIPMENT ——

Probably more so than in any other type of climbing, you're now in for the true "nuts and bolts" of the sport. This section details the range of equipment used in aid climbing and builds on all the gear and techniques described in Chapter 10, Rock Protection, and Chapter 11, Leading on Rock. If you're not interested in aid climbing, this section may hold all the drama of a hardware catalog. But if you've become intrigued with the subject, you'll find this material both thorough and fascinating.

### Basic Equipment for Clean Aid Climbing

Clean aid relies heavily on standard free-climbing equipment. You'll simply need more of it.

**Chocks and camming devices:** Because you'll be setting placements every several feet, a long pitch can require more than fifty assorted chocks and camming devices. The sling attached to each piece should be as short as possible to help you get the maximum elevation gain out of each placement.

**Carabiners:** While a minimum of 40 free carabiners are needed on an aid rack, it's not unusual to use 80 on a long pitch and more than 100 on a particularly difficult pitch. Many aid climbers prefer oval carabiners rather than D carabiners because ovals minimize the unnerving shifting that occurs when a D takes your weight. Regardless of the shape, you should be able to open the carabiner gate whenever you wish, even while it is holding your weight.

**Small nuts:** Aid racks include specialty small nuts, beyond those on free-climbing racks. These tapered nuts are often used instead of thin pitons, but they are not as strong. They are designed to support body weight, and may fail if fallen upon.

Two general styles of nuts are available. The first is a smaller version of a normal tapered Stopper. The second style has both horizontal and vertical taper and is more secure in flaring cracks and old pin scars (piton scars).

The heads of small nuts are made from aluminum, brass, or stainless steel. Aluminum and brass bite into the rock and hold better in marginal placements, but steel nuts are less likely to deform and fail if you take a fall on one of them.

**Ropes:** The tough duty of aid climbing usually requires an 11-millimeter or 12-millimeter kernmantle rope, 50 meters (165 feet) long. The haul line is typically an 11-millimeter or 9-millimeter static line that doubles as a backup rope and a second rope for long rappels. If your route entails pendulums or other unusual problems, you may need a third rope—either another kernmantle rope or another static line.

**Hero loops:** Very short slings are useful for aid climbing. These tie-off (hero) loops—4 to 6 inches long—are threaded through fixed protection in place of a carabiner. Climbers usually tie their own out of $1/2$-inch or $5/16$-inch webbing. You'll use many of them if the route has a lot of fixed bolts or pitons. They are also used to prevent the loss of stacked pieces (described later) and to tie off partially driven pins. Also carry at least six regular-length slings for establishing anchors, extending placements to reduce rope drag, and other normal rock-climbing uses.

**Chock picks:** Picks used for aid climbing should be sturdy, because you'll often hammer on the pick to tap out lodged nuts.

**Gloves:** Over and above their value for belaying and rappelling, gloves protect your hands while "jugging" (ascending the climbing rope with mechanical ascenders) and removing protection placements.

**Rock shoes:** If the route involves only a small amount of aid, normal free-climbing rock shoes perform best. If sustained aid is anticipated, boots with greater sole rigidity provide a better working platform and more comfort. Some boots on the market provide a rigid arch support and good torsional rigidity for aid climbing, yet have a flexible toe and a sole of soft friction rubber for good free-climbing capabilities.

**Energy-absorbing slings:** These slings increase security when climbing above placements of questionable strength. In a fall, the slings limit the shock delivered to the protection. Their use, however, limits the amount of elevation gained from the placements to which they are attached.

## Universal Aid–Climbing Equipment

In addition to equipment normally used in free climbing, you will need a selection of gear that is used for both clean aid climbing and for aid that involves placing pins.

**Etriers:** These ladder-like slings (fig. 12-1) allow climbers to step up from one placement to the next when they are clipped to a chock, piton, or other aid piece. Consider the intended use when making or buying etriers. For alpine climbs, minimize weight by using a single pair of etriers made of $^9/_{16}$-inch or $^{11}/_{16}$-inch webbing. For most aid climbing, four-step or five-step etriers made of 1-inch webbing are standard. Etriers should be long enough to let you step smoothly from the top step of one to the bottom step of another that has been clipped into a piece at arm's reach above.

Tying your own etriers lets you tailor their size to your own. However, commercially made or home-sewn etriers are preferred for routes with extensive aid because they remain open for foot placement when weighted.

Some climbers use two pairs of etriers while aid climbing—of equal length but different colors—whereas others use a single pair; it depends on the nature of the route and on how much you want to weight your

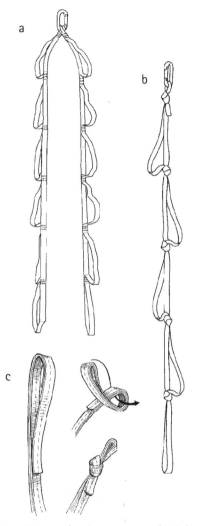

*Fig. 12-1. Types of etriers: a, sewn; b, tied; c, the frost knot. Tied etriers require twice their finished length plus 10 inches for each step (overhand knot) and the frost knot. A 60-inch etrier with five steps (four overhand knots) takes 170 inches of runner.*

protection. Likewise, some climbers prefer to attach a short grab sling to the carabiner loop of their etriers.

**Daisy chains:** Daisy chains are tied or sewn slings with a loop—formed by a knot or stitching—every 3 to 6 inches (fig. 12-2). The proper length for you is a daisy chain that, when attached to your harness, reaches as

Fig. 12-2. Tied daisy chain

far as your raised hand. Attach a carabiner to every loop (or every other loop) in the chain so you can quickly clip into an aid placement and rest on your harness.

Carry a second daisy chain, without carabiners in each loop, for other purposes, such as attaching yourself to your ascenders while jugging or for preventing loss of etriers if a hook placement fails.

**Fifi hooks:** Fifi hooks function somewhat like daisy chains but are attached to your harness with a sling only 2 to 6 inches long (fig. 12-3). You can quickly clip the hook into an aid piece, allowing you to rest on your harness. Be careful. If you release the tension or change the angle, it could come unhooked. Aid climbers usually carry one fifi hook for use on bolt ladders and fixed pitches.

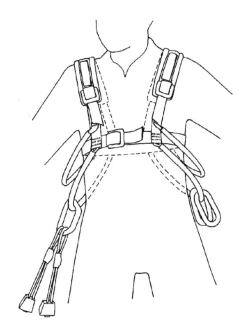

Fig. 12-4. Double rack

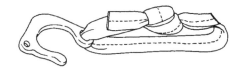

Fig. 12-3. Fifi hook with sling

**A double rack:** With equipment slings on both sides of the body, a double rack distributes the weight of the hardware (fig. 12-4). It improves your balance and comfort and reduces the neck strain caused by a single rack. If it's built right, a double rack can also serve as a chest harness as you jug up a rope with mechanical ascenders. Some climbers carry a single rack in addition, for their free carabiners or as a supplemental free-climbing rack.

**A belay seat:** A great creature-comfort during hanging belays is a belay seat with a two- or three-point attachment (fig. 12-5). One urgent warning: Never let the belay seat be your sole means of attaching to an anchor. Clip in from your harness to the anchor with

the climbing rope as usual—and then set up the belay seat for comfort.

**Mechanical ascenders:** Serving the same function as prusik knots, mechanical ascenders (fig. 12-6) are stronger, safer, faster, and less tiring. The devices are a requirement for sack hauling on big walls.

All ascenders employ a cam, allowing the ascender to slide freely in one direction on a rope but to grip tight when pulled in the opposite direction. They also have a trigger or locking mechanism to keep them from accidentally coming off the rope. Some triggers are difficult to release, decreasing the chance of accidental removal but making it harder to get them off when you want to. If your ascenders are made of cast aluminum, back up their frames with webbing to reduce the danger created should they break.

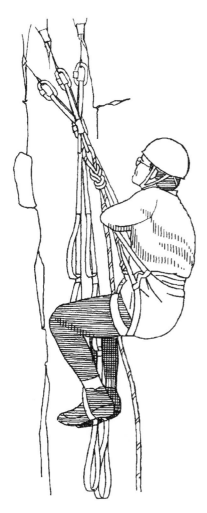

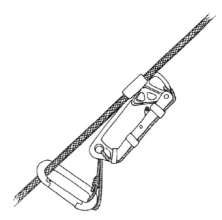

*Fig. 12-6. Mechanical ascender with backup sling; ascender is attached in preparation for diagonal ascent.*

should be long enough to forcefully drive pins and short enough to fit comfortably in a belt holster. The shafts should also be sturdy and taped for protection. A carabiner hole in the head is useful for cleaning pins and malleable pieces.

Attach a sling to your hammer that allows full arm extension when the hammer is in use (fig. 12-8). If you

*Fig. 12-5. Two-point belay seat; note the anchored climbing rope.*

If you plan to use ascenders for cold-weather climbing, look for a pair with openings large enough to accommodate heavily gloved hands. Carabiner holes at the top and the bottom of the ascender come in handy for a number of purposes, such as sack hauling. If the ascender doesn't have these holes, you'll have to attach slings for clip-in points.

**Piton hammers:** These tools have a flat striking surface for cleaning and driving pitons and a blunt pick for prying out protection, cleaning dirty cracks, and placing malleable pieces (fig. 12-7). Hammer shafts

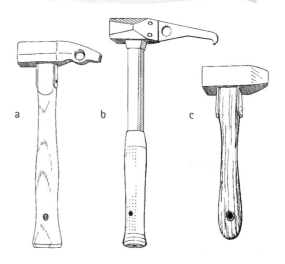

*Fig. 12-7. Piton hammer styles: a, Mjollnir; b, Chouinard; c, less adequate.*

Fig. 12-8. Hammer sling properly used

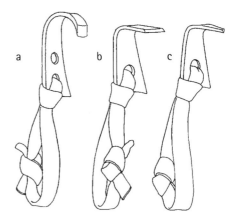

Fig. 12-9. Hook types: a, sky hook; b, Logan hook; c, bat hook.

happen to drop the hammer, it will just hang below your feet on the sling. Be sure to check the sling regularly for wear.

**Hooks:** In many shapes and forms, hooks are most commonly used to grip ledges or small holes (fig. 12-9). With etriers attached to a hook, you have a rather delicate placement for moving upward. Hooks should be made of chrome-moly steel (for strength), and the nonhook end should be wider and curved (for stability). Attach slings to the bottom of your hooks with a girth hitch, positioned so that when the sling is weighted the "legs" (lower end) of the hook are pulled into the rock. To accomplish this, the sling should hang from the rock side of the hook.

Sky hooks look almost like giant fishhooks and are useful for small flakes and ledges. Greater stability is achieved on some routes if the tip of the hook is filed to a point, which can be set into small holes drilled at the back of tiny ledges. Fishhooks, or ring claws, are like large sky hooks and are used to grip larger flakes

and ledges. Logan hooks are L-shaped: the wide style is stable on tiny ledges and flakes, and the narrow style can be used in shallow pockets. Bat hooks are basically a narrow-style Logan hook with a pointed blade, allowing their use in shallow 1/4-inch holes drilled for their use.

**Wire hangers:** Wire hangers (fig. 12-10a–b) are loops of wire 1/8 inch or 3/32 inch in diameter, with a slider to cinch the wire tight over bolt studs and

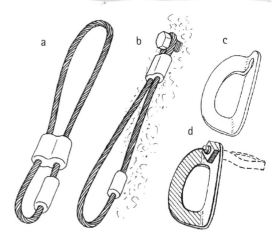

Fig. 12-10. Hangers: a, wire; b, wire hanger on a bolt; c, keyhole; d, regular hanger on a bolt.

rivets (basically, bolts with a wide head). Small tapered chocks (Stoppers) with wire slings can also be used for this purpose, with the chock itself acting as the slider to tighten the wire against the bolt stud. However, because the chocks have a longer wire loop than the wire hangers, you won't get as much elevation gain from them.

**Regular hangers and keyhole hangers:** Serving a similar function to wire hangers, regular and keyhole hangers are shaped pieces of metal rather than wire loops (fig. 12-10c–d). They are useful especially at belay anchors and for fixed bolts that have no hangers. Keyhole hangers have the metal between the bolt hole and carabiner hole filed out to allow placement over rivets and buttonhead bolts.

## Ironmongery for Full Aid Climbing

To master the full range of aid-climbing techniques, climbers must have a knowledge of pitons and bolts.

### Pitons

Modern pitons—or pins—are made of chrome-moly (hard) steel. Rather than molding to cracks like the malleable pitons of old, they mold the crack to their form. Because of the damage that pitons cause and because of improvements in clean-climbing hardware, piton use has declined greatly. They are still important, however, on overhanging rock and very thin cracks. For winter mountaineering, when cracks are filled with ice, they may offer the only viable means of protection. To fit the diverse cracks encountered on rock walls, pitons vary tremendously in size and shape (fig. 12-11).

**The Realized Ultimate Reality Piton** (RURP) is the smallest piton, a postage-stamp–size, hatchet-shaped pin used in incipient cracks. It will usually support only body weight and derives what little strength it has by minimizing the leverage between the piton and carabiner supporting your etriers. Some styles come with offset sides for use in corners.

**Birdbeaks** are similar to RURPs but have a longer arm for attaching a carabiner or sling. They are generally easier to place and remove.

**Knifeblades** are long thin pitons that have two eyes—one at the end of the blade and a second in the offset portion of the pin. They come in different lengths and in thicknesses between $1/8$ inch and $3/16$ inch, and

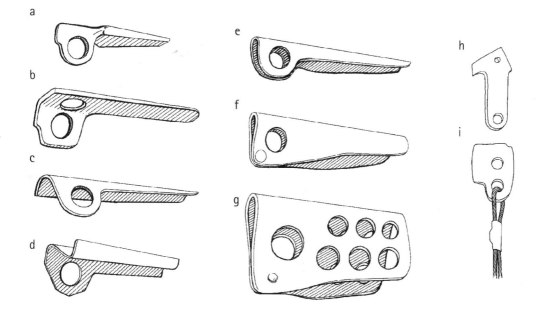

*Fig. 12-11. Piton (pin) types: a, lost arrow; b, knifeblade; c, shallow angle; d, Leeper Z; e, angle; f, large angle; g, bong; h, birdbeak; i, RURP.*

they are commonly used to fit many cracks that are too thin for tiny nuts.

**Lost arrows** are similar to knifeblades but have a single eye that is centered and set perpendicular to the end of the blade. These too are commonly used pitons that come in several lengths and thicknesses ($5/32$ to $3/8$ inch). They are very good in horizontal cracks.

**Angles** are pitons formed into a V. The V varies in height from $1/4$ inch to $1^1/2$ inches (smaller ones are most popular). Their strength is derived from the metal's resistance to bending and spreading. Angles and other large pitons have largely been replaced by modern free-climbing hardware.

**Leeper Z pitons** obtain their thickness through their Z profile as opposed to the V profile of an angle. These pitons are very solid and work well for stacking because of their short length, useful in bottoming cracks.

**Bongs** are large angle pitons that vary from 2 to 6 inches in width. In addition to their use as pitons, they can double as large chocks. Spring-loaded camming devices have largely replaced bongs.

**Sawed-off pins** are handy on routes that have been heavily climbed using pitons, leaving shallow pin scars. Several $3/4$-inch and 1-inch angles with a few inches cut off the end are useful for shallow placements.

## Malleable Hardware (Bashies)

Malleable hardware (fig. 12-12) is designed to hold weight by melding the soft head of the placement to the irregularities of the rock. The security of these bashies varies greatly, and it is difficult to gauge their strength, making them last-resort equipment.

**Copperheads** (fig. 12-12a) have a swage of copper attached to one end of a short cable that has a loop at the other end. They are placed by pounding the copper head into an irregularity in the rock. They tend to form well and are more durable than similar pieces with aluminum heads (aluma-heads).

**Aluma-heads** (fig. 12-12b) are not as tough as copperheads but are more malleable, so they tend to be used for the larger sizes, while the smaller heads are usually copper.

**Circleheads** (fig. 12-12c) consist of a wire loop with an extra copper swage on the loop, which is pounded into the rock like a copperhead. They are used in horizontal cracks.

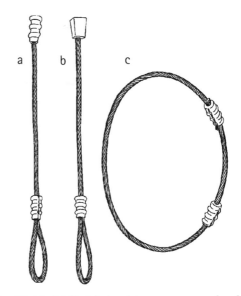

*Fig. 12-12. Malleable head types: a, copperhead; b, aluma-head; c, circlehead.*

## Bolts

Chapter 10, Rock Protection, includes a section on the use of existing bolts found on climbing routes. Bolts permanently scar the rock and alter the style of a climb, and very serious consideration should be given before placing one. Proper bolt placement is a special skill, beyond the scope of this book. Bolt placement is best left to the skill and judgment of very experienced climbers.

# Big-Wall Equipment

Climbers undertaking a big wall have other specialized equipment to consider.

**Pulleys** are required to ease the chore of sack hauling. They receive much abuse, so they must be durable. Pulleys with bearings and larger wheels operate more smoothly.

**Haul bags** carry your clothing, water, food, sleeping bag, and other nonclimbing paraphernalia. A good haul bag should have adequate cargo capacity, a solid haul suspension, durable fabric, an absence of snag points, and a removable backpacking harness system. Duffels can be converted into haul sacks by reinforcing the wear areas. A top cap to the haul bag is a good idea to protect the knot connecting the sack to the haul line and help reduce snagging problems while hauling.

**Cheater sticks** allow you to clip a carabiner into a piece of hardware beyond your reach. Although rarely needed, they are often used to avoid "top stepping" in etriers. Cheater sticks should have a means of holding a carabiner solidly while you clip in with your arm fully extended.

**Knee pads** protect your knees, which are regularly in contact with the rock during aid climbing. Pads should be comfortable and allow good circulation.

**Portaledges or hammocks:** Portaledges, which are lightweight cots, offer greater comfort from a single point of suspension than hammocks. Unfortunately, they are much heavier and bulkier. As with belay seats, climbers must always be anchored to the rock when using this equipment.

If you take on a big wall, safeguard important equipment with tie-in loops to attach anything you might drop. Bring gear that will get you through the worst possible weather, because there's not likely to be any easy way to retreat. Be sure your equipment is durable, and beef up any item that could fail, such as water containers. Select only the sturdiest, and reinforce them with duct tape.

## A𝖨𝖣 P𝖫𝖠𝖢𝖤𝖬𝖤𝖭𝖳𝖲

The main rule for aid climbing is to place each aid piece as high as possible. If you make placements at 5-foot rather than 4-foot intervals, over the course of a 160-foot pitch you'll save eight placements, many more carabiners, and much time.

Most of the techniques for placing free-climbing protection apply to aid climbing. For aid climbing, if possible, you'll shorten the slings to your pieces and often use hero loops on fixed protection rather than clipping in directly with a carabiner.

Placing small nuts during an aid climb is similar to placing larger ones on a free climb. But because aid nuts take the weight of the lead climber and because they may be smaller than the chock pick, they can be difficult to remove. If you place small nuts near the outside of the crack, they will be easier to remove and there will be less danger of damaging them in the process. Test small nuts gently before committing your weight to them.

Fixed pins, bolts, or rivets must be evaluated before use (see Chapter 10, Rock Protection). If you decide to use a fixed piece, thread a hero loop through its eye and clip a single carabiner into the two ends of the loop. This saves a carabiner. *Note:* Use a direct carabiner clip-in every three or four pieces as a backup. The hero-looped pieces are not as safe for stopping a fall because of the danger the loop could be cut by the edge of the metal eye. It's also wise to carry a few bolt hangers and nuts (in both $1/4$-inch and $3/8$-inch sizes) for bolts with missing or damaged hangers.

## Piton Placement

Here are some basic guidelines for the sound placement of pitons (pins) (fig. 12-13):

- Horizontal placement of pins is generally more secure than vertical placement because rotation is reduced or eliminated.
- Ideally, the eye should point downward.
- As with chocks, place pins in locally wider portions of a crack. If the crack is thinner below and above the pin, the pin will be supported when it has to take a climber's weight.
- A properly sized pin can be placed one-half to two-thirds of the way by hand. The remainder of the pin is hammered in place. Select the correct pin to fit the crack. Don't try to make the crack fit the pin; this practice causes needless destruction of the rock.
- A sound piton rings with a higher-pitched "ping" with each strike of the hammer. After the pin is driven, tap it to test for rotation. Rotation indicates the pin is not biting the rock. Replace such pins with a larger size.
- Knowing just how much to hammer a piton is a matter of touch and experience. Excessive hammering wastes energy, makes it harder for the second to remove the piton, and needlessly damages the rock. Underdriving a piton, however, increases the risk of it pulling out. If several pins are underdriven, the failure of one could result in a long fall as the series of pins zippers out.
- When possible, avoid placing a pin in a three-way corner. Such placements are often impossible to clean because the pin cannot be tapped back and forth for removal. Just leave it as a fixed pin.

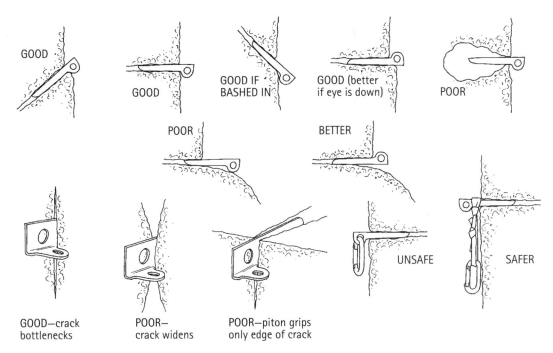

Fig. 12-13. Piton placements and problems

- If the position of the piton causes the connecting carabiner to extend over an edge, add a hero loop to the piece (fig. 12-14). This prevents loading the carabiner across its sides.
- On overhangs, place pins with some horizontal orientation when possible (fig. 12-15). This reduces the odds of total failure should the pin shift when weighted.
- Place knifeblades in vertical cracks with the offset eye down.
- When placing angles, keep the three points of the V in contact with the rock (fig. 12-16). The back (point of the V) *always* must contact one wall, while the edges (two tips of the V) contact the opposing wall. In a horizontal crack, put the back of the angle up and the edges down.
- Bongs (fig. 12-17), being made of aluminum, are quite fragile, so pound them as little as possible. Bongs are often placed as chockstones, and you can add a sling to a bong before using it that way.
- Expanding cracks present problems for pins because, as subsequent pins are placed, lower ones loosen. When possible, use chocks in such situations, because they minimize flake expansion. If pins must be used, try to work with long minimum-taper pins placed lightly in natural slots, to minimize expansion of the rock flake.
- In shallow cracks and flutings, a piton may be driven over a chock. The chock creates a second "wall" against which the pin wedges. Because the

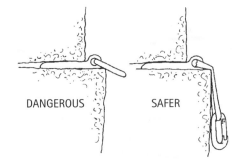

Fig. 12-14. Safely extending a piton; right figure eliminates side loading the carabiner.

258

chock would fall and be lost if the pin failed, attach a "keeper" sling to the chock and clip it into the sling or carabiner of the load-bearing pin. The keeper sling must not bear any weight (fig. 12-18).

• When a pin "bottoms out" in a crack (that is, cannot be driven in all the way), stop hammering, to avoid loosening it. The piton must be tied off around the shaft at the point where it emerges from

the rock. A hero loop tied to the piton with a girth hitch or clove hitch supports your weight and reduces the levering action on the pin (fig. 12-19). Bongs can be tied off through their lightning holes. Loop a longer keeper sling (or a second carabiner) through the eye of the pin and clip it into the hero loop or hero-loop carabiner. The keeper sling doesn't bear weight but will catch your pin if it pops.

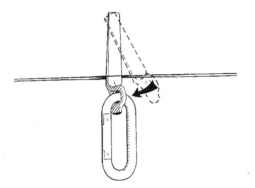

*Fig. 12-15. Overhang piton placement*

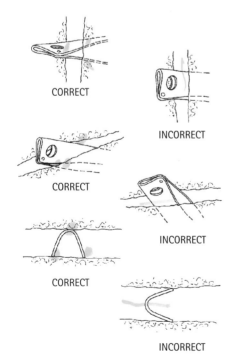

*Fig. 12-16. Proper placements for angle pitons*

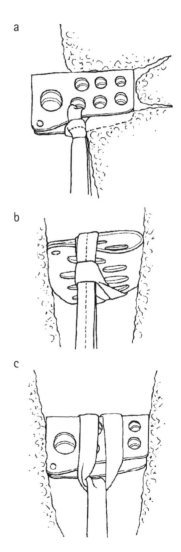

*Fig. 12-17. Bong placements: a, driven and tied off through lightning holes; b and c, girth-hitched for use as a large chock.*

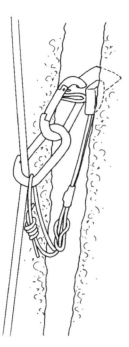

*Fig. 12-18. Sawed-off piton driven over a Stopper; note the non-load-bearing keeper sling on the Stopper.*

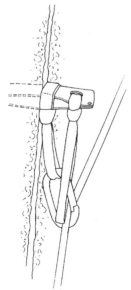

*Fig. 12-19. Tied-off piton; note the use of a keeper sling through the piton eye.*

## Stacking and Nesting

When no single pin or chock fits the crack at hand, aid climbing gets very creative. Whether you've run out of the proper-size pieces or are facing a shallow flaring crack, it's time to improvise by stacking or nesting your hardware in whatever combination works (fig. 12-20).

Blades are nested back to back and are usually driven together. If a third blade is necessary, the first two are inserted by hand, and then the third is driven in between.

Some disagreement exists about the best way to stack angles. Most climbers stack them by keeping the backs of both angles against the rock, but any combination will work. Try to avoid stacking angles by simply placing one over the other, as these may be very hard to separate once removed. Leeper Z pitons are especially useful in stacking.

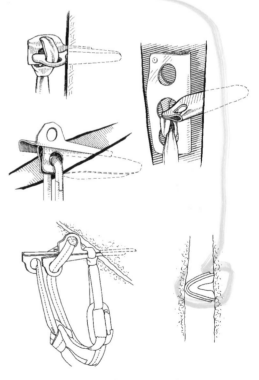

*Fig. 12-20. Examples of pitons stacked and nested and of angles stacked (some keeper slings omitted for clarity).*

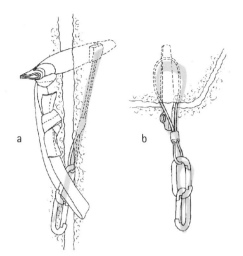

*Fig. 12-21. Camming combinations: a, piton and chock; b, piton and wire hanger (keeper sling omitted for clarity).*

It may be possible to use a camming combination of a pin and a chock—or a pin and a wire hanger—in very difficult situations (fig. 12-21). The concept relies on the camming force exerted by the chock or wire on the back of the pin. The chock or wire loop is partially inserted into the crack. Then, the pin is inserted to anchor the chock or wire and to create an artificial wall against which the chock or wire can cam. You can often achieve a solid aid placement this way with minimal use of the hammer. Note, however, that wires used this way wear quickly.

These special combinations present another situation that requires non-load-bearing keeper slings to catch any pitons should the placement fail.

## Hook Placement and Use

Before placing a hook, clip an etrier to it. Also make sure to connect a sling (or daisy chain) between the etrier's carabiner and your harness. The sling will prevent the loss of your gear if the hook pops off its purchase.

Now set the hook on the ledge, flake, or hole where it will be used. Test it gently before applying full body weight (or gently "ooze" onto the hook). Avoid standing with your face directly in front of the hook because it could pop out with a good deal of force.

If the hook is used in a shallow bolt hole, a very slight tap to set the point is sometimes useful. However, this practice increases the possibility the hook will pop out. It also erodes the existing hole, and eventually a bolt will need to be placed.

## Malleable Placements

Because you often can't tell how secure they are, do not use malleable heads unless you're dealing with a pocket or flare where other protection just won't work.

Copperheads, aluma-heads, and circleheads take more practice to place than other types of aid and require some specialized tools. The hammer pick works for setting large heads, but small heads require a striking tool like a blunt chisel or, in a pinch, a lost arrow.

Figure 12-22 illustrates the following procedure for placing a head:

1. Place it. Insert a head as you would a chock—in a narrowing portion of a flare or seam.
2. "X" it. Pound it in using angled strokes that form an X pattern on the head.
3. Paste it. Now pound the right and left sides to "pin" the head.

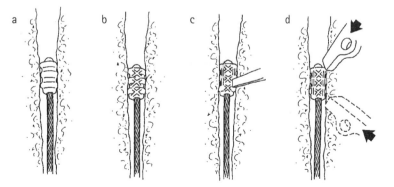

*Fig. 12-22. Placing a malleable piece: a, place it; b, "X" it; c, paste it; d, rotate test it.*

4. Rotate it. Hit the bottom and top to see whether the head rotates. If so, X it and paste it again.

5. Sniff it. If the head emits a metallic odor, it is underdriven or overdriven; do not use it. The smell arises from the cutting or cracking of the head rather than its molding to the rock.

6. Use it. Heads are used like any other aid piece—but remember their inescapable weakness. Inspection cannot guarantee the molding of the head to the rock. Some heads may hold a short fall, others will just support body weight, and others might fail. All malleable head placements are suspect, and an acceptance of this fact is inherent in their use.

_Remove?_
_Reuse?_

## BASIC AID TECHNIQUES

Before starting up any aid pitch, study the terrain and make a plan. Determine the best rest spots, figure how to minimize rope drag, plan what gear you'll need and what you can leave for the second to carry, spot any obstructions that might plague sack hauling, and decide whether to save certain sizes of aid pieces for the end of the pitch.

Then gear up for the pitch. Place pitons (between three and six to a carabiner) on one side with the larger pieces to the rear. Place chocks and other gear for clean aid climbing on the other side, again with the larger pieces to the rear. Balance the weight with free carabiners racked in groups of four (two pairs). Short

slings are best racked (several to a carabiner) and clipped to an easily accessible part of your harness. Finally, check that the hammer is accessible, with its sling untangled.

## The Basic Sequence

The basic aid sequence (fig. 12-23) is the same whether you are starting from the ground, a comfortable free stance, or the top step of your etriers:

1. Look and feel the terrain above and select an aid piece to place at the highest spot within reach (fig. 12-23a).

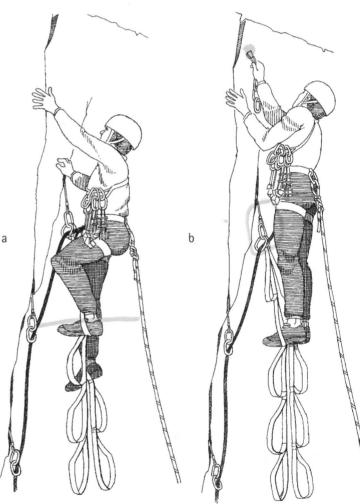

a      b

_Fig. 12-23. The basic sequence (some equipment omitted for clarity): a, climb high; b, place piece; c, clip etrier to carabiner on higher piece; d, test, move onto new placement, remove lower etriers; e, clip rope into lower carabiner on new piece and clip in daisy chain if desired._

2. Place the piece (fig. 12-23b).
3. Clip in a free carabiner. Some climbers prefer to clip in a two-carabiner chain (fig. 12-23c); the second carabiner will later take the climbing rope. Other climbers feel two carabiners get in the way at this point. If you are moving onto a pin, first attach a hero loop to the pin, and then clip a carabiner to the loop.
4. If the aid piece you are currently weighting is questionable, you may want to clip the rope to the second carabiner of the higher piece if you are positive the higher placement is solid. Otherwise, the rope is not clipped into the higher piece yet.
5. Clip your free etrier(s) to the carabiner on the higher piece (the higher of the two carabiners if you used two) (fig. 12-23c). If moving onto a pin, clip the etrier(s) directly into the hero loop.
6. Test the new piece with a gentle, one-footed hop (the other foot is kept in an etrier on the lower piece). If the new piece is questionable, you may decide to avoid the test and simply "ooze" onto the new placement, applying your weight as gradually and smoothly as possible. Warn your belayer when you are about to test or move onto a dubious placement.

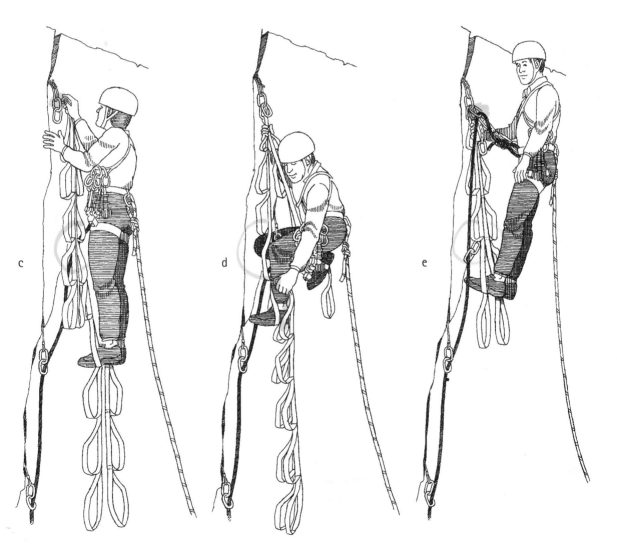

c          d          e

263

7. Move onto the higher etrier(s) (fig. 12-23d). Clip the daisy chain into the new piece while in the lower step, if you wish.

8. Remove the lower etrier(s) (fig. 12-23d). For extended aid climbing, you will normally carry two pairs of etriers, so now you will remove the lower pair and clip it to your harness. (If you are climbing with just a single pair of etriers, remove the lower etrier and clip it to the highest aid piece.) Climb up the etriers until the daisy chain (or fifi hook) can be clipped in close to the new piece, if you wish.

9. Add a second carabiner (in chain fashion) to the new piece and clip in the rope. If you initially clipped two carabiners to the piece, clip the rope into the lower carabiner (fig. 12-23d).

10. Study the area immediately above to determine likely spots for the next placement. Then climb as high as possible, reclip the daisy if desired, and begin the process anew. Note that how high you climb in your etriers depends on the terrain, but ideally you want to place the new piece from the top step.

## Top Stepping

Moving onto the top step of your etriers can be unnerving, but the ability to do so greatly improves the efficiency of aid climbing. The process is simple on low-angle rock, where the top steps are used like any other foothold and the hands provide balance.

Vertical and overhanging rock makes top stepping difficult because your center of gravity moves away from the rock and above the point where the etriers are clipped to the aid placement. If the rock offers any features, your hands may provide the balance. If the rock is blank, keep your weight on your feet while leaning back and applying tension to the daisy chain between your harness and your aid placement. That tension provides the means of balancing yourself (fig. 12-24).

## Special Considerations

Problems encountered while aid climbing may cause you to add variations to the basic sequence. As in free climbing, rope drag can become a problem. Use long slings to keep the rope running straight. Add the slings after you have moved to the next higher piece so that you obtain the maximum gain out of each placement.

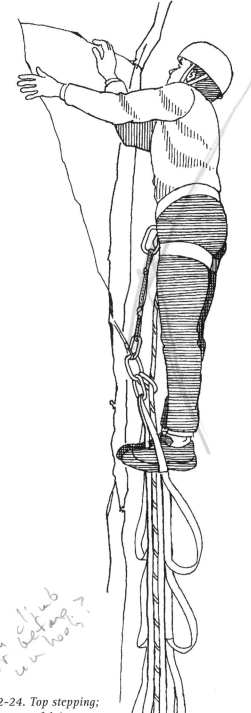

*Fig. 12-24. Top stepping; note the use of daisy-chain tension.*

You may also realize that you're short on pieces of a certain size and that you will need to reuse these sizes. As you move onto a higher placement, you may opt to pull the piece you were just using and save it for future use. As a general rule, however, leave at least every other piece as your protection against a fall.

## Resting

Don't wear yourself out. Climb in a relaxed fashion and take rests as often as necessary to conserve your strength or plot the next series of moves.

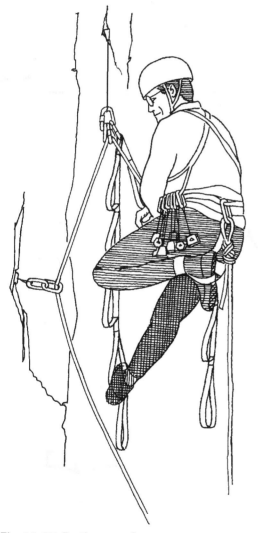

*Fig. 12-25. Resting on a foot*

Here's a quick and easy rest: with each foot in separate etriers and one foot one step below the other, bend the knee of the higher leg and bring that foot under you. Most of your weight rests over the bent leg. The outstretched leg takes minimal weight but maintains balance (fig. 12-25).

You can also clip your daisy chain or fifi hook into the piece supporting you and rest in your harness.

Once the climbing rope is clipped into the supporting piece, you can also ask the belayer for tension and rest on the climbing rope. This is not an efficient method, however, due to stretch in the rope. It also places unnecessary strain on the belay system.

Finally, you can often find relaxing stances in your etriers. Generally, the greatest stability is obtained with the heels together and the toes spread apart against the rock.

## Switching between Aid and Free Climbing

Timing is the key problem in switching between the techniques of aid and free climbing.

**From free to aid:** Free climbers must remember that the switch to aid requires some preparation. Begin the aid sequence before stretching yourself to the limit of your ability. This is easy if you know you will be changing to aid, but problems arise if you are not expecting to use aid but suddenly need it. Finding yourself in this bind, you can improvise etriers by interconnecting several slings and aid your way over the blank area. Such creativity is particularly important when climbing in a remote alpine environment. The climb's style may be damaged, but your body will be spared.

**From aid to free:** To free-climb a few moves during an aid pitch, simply clip the etriers to the back of your harness, and then make the moves. It is best to continue climbing on aid until you can comfortably switch to free techniques. If the change is made too early, you may have trouble retrieving your etriers from the last aid placement.

When beginning a longer section of free climbing, clip etriers, daisies, and so forth to your harness and be sure they will not hinder your movement. This may entail removing most of your aid implements and hanging them behind you.

265

## Tension Traverses and Pendulums

Tension traverses and pendulums allow you to move horizontally across blank sections of a wall that would normally require placement of bolts.

**Tension traverses** are the simpler technique, useful for short traverses. The leader takes tension from the belayer and then leans to the side and uses friction on small holds to work sideways.

**Pendulums** let you cross wider blank sections without bolts but often require more ropes and pose special problems for the second climber. Start by placing a bombproof anchor at the top of the planned pendulum. The equipment used for this anchor cannot be retrieved unless it is possible to come back to it from above.

Next, you'll be lowered by the belayer (or rappel while on belay) until you have enough rope to run back and forth across the rock and swing into a new crack system. If a rappel is used for the pendulum, an extra rope will be required. When being lowered by the belayer, it is better to be lowered too little than too much, because if you're too low it may be very difficult to correct the error.

Once in the new crack system, climb as high as safety allows before clipping your belayed climbing rope into aid pieces for protection. The higher you get, the easier and safer it will be for your belayer, who will second the pendulum.

See the section later in this chapter on seconding pendulums for more details and an illustration of pendulum technique.

## Overhangs

Before leading an overhang, check that you have enough equipment for the job. It may be impossible to obtain more gear later from the second climber. Keep your ascenders handy, because if a piece pulls and you end up hanging, you'll need ascenders to climb back up to your last secure piece. Also, check that your belayer is securely anchored, or you could both end up hanging free in the event of a fall.

Balance will be difficult as you scale an overhang because you can't effectively place your feet against the rock. Use of a daisy chain or fifi hook, however, allows you to hang from the harness and achieve a stable position. As an overhang approaches the horizontal, you can achieve greater balance still by clipping a sling from a chest harness to the supporting aid piece (fig. 12-26).

Despite the difference in balance, the basic sequence for aiding over a roof is the same as described earlier, but you may find it more comfortable to sit with your legs through the middle step of the etriers rather than standing in the bottom steps. Expect to experience some swinging. Finally, because your belayer will probably aid over the overhang rather than use ascenders, consider the length of your partner's reach when making your placements.

*Fig. 12-26. Aiding under a roof; note the use of a chest harness for support and the availability of ascenders.*

Rope drag is a common side effect of overhangs, but liberal use of longer slings will help. You may also want to pull along a second belay rope and start climbing on it after clearing the lip of the overhang.

Finally, try to relax when working out over a big roof. Have confidence in your pieces. Clutching at them won't keep them in place but will drain your strength.

## Hanging Belays

Upon reaching the end of the pitch, the leader establishes an anchor as a new belay station (fig. 12-27). Place this anchor, when possible, to the side of the route (especially if you are sack hauling) so that your second can easily climb through. Also try to place at least one aid piece at the start of the next pitch to give the second a stance while changing leads.

When establishing your anchor, make sure *all* anchor points (including the haul anchor) are connected to *all* other anchor points. If an existing anchor system is in place, do not simply place a sling over the system. This is an easy mistake to make and experienced climbers have paid for this error with their lives. Clip in, instead, in such a way that, should any portion of the anchor fail, your attachment won't slide off the failed end.

Similarly, complete anchor systems have failed when a separate haul anchor, which was not interconnected with the main anchor, failed. In these cases, the force generated by the falling haul sack overloaded the main anchor.

Once you are clipped in, anchor the climbing rope so that the second can ascend it as a fixed line. Now prepare the hauling system, if you are hauling. Remove the aid rack and use it as the counterweight for the hauling system. Inform the second to free the haul sack so that you can hoist it while the second ascends the fixed climbing rope.

After the hauling is completed (or after the climbing rope was fixed if you are not hauling), establish your belay seat, get comfortable, and prepare for the exchange of leads. Sort the rack, organize the ropes, prepare your belay system, and so forth.

## Tyrolean Traverses

Tyrolean traverses are most often used to return to a main wall after ascending a detached pillar. Ropes are strung between the main wall and the top of the pillar, allowing you to traverse through the air, attached to the rope.

You can establish a Tyrolean traverse like this:

1. After setting up a bombproof anchor on the main wall—one that can take both a horizontal and vertical pull—rappel on two ropes to the saddle between the main wall and the pinnacle. (You can use just one rope for the rappel if the traverse will be short enough.) Do not pull down the rappel ropes. If it takes more than one rappel to reach the saddle, you'll have to tie a light line to the two ends of the main rappel rope to give you a way to retrieve the ends once you're on top of the pinnacle.

2. Climb the pinnacle using an additional climbing rope. The second climber brings up the free ends of the rappel ropes.

3. Once atop the pinnacle, the free ends of the rappel ropes (now the traverse ropes) are stretched tight and anchored to the pinnacle. After the traverse, you will not be able to recover the equipment used for the pinnacle anchor.

4. While belayed, one climber now "jugs" across the open area on *one* of the ropes, using the Texas prusik (which is explained in Chapter 14, in the section on crevasse rescue). The forward ascender is attached to the harness with a daisy chain. An etrier is attached to the rear ascender, and a daisy chain is attached to the climber's harness. Finally, the climber connects an additional safety sling between the traverse rope and the harness. This sling rides on a carabiner between the two ascenders. What would normally be the lower ends of the ascenders must be clipped to the rope with a safety carabiner (as shown in Figure 12-6, earlier in this chapter).

5. After the first climber has jugged across, the second climber unties the ropes at the pinnacle anchor, threads the end of one rope through the anchor, and ties the ropes together as if preparing a rappel. This climber notes which rope will be pulled when it comes time to retrieve the ropes. (If it's a short traverse and you are using just a single rope, the climbers on each side of the traverse need to pull the rope around so that its center moves to the pinnacle anchor and the two ends are back on the main wall; otherwise, you will have problems retrieving the rope later.)

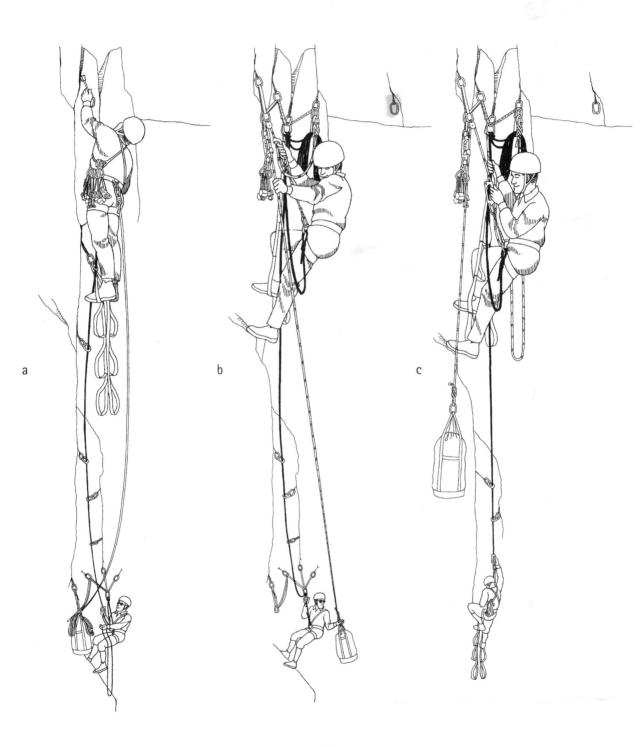

a

b

c

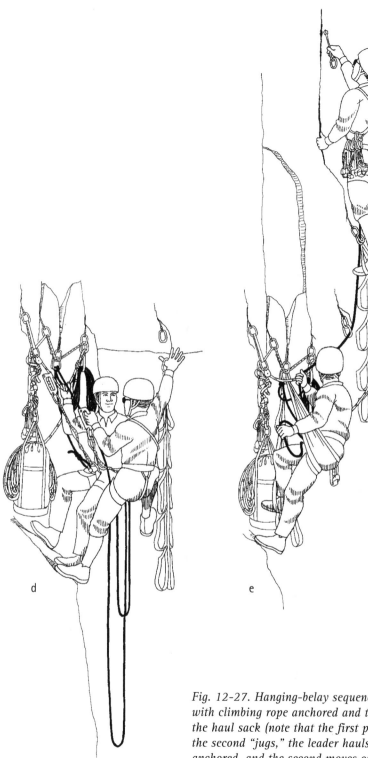

*Fig. 12-27. Hanging-belay sequence: a, leader establishes anchor; b, with climbing rope anchored and the haul system set, the second frees the haul sack (note that the first piece of the next pitch is set); c, while the second "jugs," the leader hauls the sack; d, the haul sack is anchored, and the second moves onto the first piece of the next pitch; e, after reracking, the new leader begins to lead.*

6. The first climber then tightens and anchors the rope ends on the main wall and belays the second, who will traverse in the same manner as the first.

7. Once both climbers are reunited, the ropes are untied at the main wall and retrieved by pulling on the appropriate rope.

## SECONDING

As the second climber on short sections of aid, you will usually follow the same sequence as the leader, while belayed from above. You will, however, unclip the rope from a placement before clipping on the etriers and clean the placement below you after stepping up higher. If you cannot reach a lower piece after moving up, lengthen your etriers with another sling, and then step down to clean the piece.

When climbing long sections of aid, a different strategy is called for. You will use mechanical ascenders to jug the fixed climbing rope and clean the route as you go. Before heading up, free the haul bag so the leader can start hauling it up the route. If it hangs up along the way, you will be the one to free it.

### Using Ascenders

Although you could ascend fixed climbing ropes on slings attached with prusik knots, mechanical ascenders are both safer and more efficient (fig. 12-28). Attach an etrier and a daisy chain to each ascender. The etriers give you a platform to stand on, and the daisy chains positively connect the ascenders to your harness. Use a carabiner—not a fifi hook—to clip each daisy chain to an ascender. To expedite the process of preparing your ascenders, mark the loops in both the daisies and etriers where the gear is properly adjusted for length while jugging.

You do *not* untie from the end of the climbing rope while ascending. Remaining tied in serves as a backup in case both ascenders fail. To further decrease the likelihood of a long fall, you should periodically "tie in short."

Tying in short is an easy precaution that has saved lives. As the second ascends, an ever-lengthening loop of climbing rope forms below her, making for a long fall if the ascenders fail. To avoid this danger, stop periodically and, using the climbing rope just below the

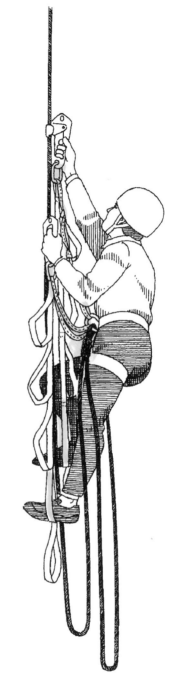

*Fig. 12-28. Use of ascenders; note daisy chains from each ascender to harness, and climber tied in short.*

ascenders, tie a figure-8 loop and clip the loop into your harness with a locking carabiner. This guarantees a much shorter fall. Repeat this procedure about every 20 feet. Each time, unclip and untie the last figure-8 loop *after* the new figure-8 loop is clipped into your harness. Even when tying in short, *do not untie from the end of the rope.*

Often while jugging, it is necessary to remove the upper ascender from the rope and place it above a piece from which the rope cannot be unclipped while weighted from below. This same situation arises when the rope runs over an edge. Before removing the ascender, tie in short; this is a convenient time to do so.

After reattaching the upper ascender above the piece, check that the cam trigger is fully locked or the ascender could pop off the rope. This is especially true if you are jugging on a diagonal rope, because the ascender has a tendency to twist to a vertical position once weighted. This twisting can be minimized by clipping a carabiner between the ascender and the rope as well (fig. 12-6). Once the upper ascender is reattached and your weight is on it, you will be able to unclip the rope from the problem piece of aid.

Other precautions should also be taken while ascending. First, carry a spare prusik sling just in case an ascender fails. And, as in all climbing, beware of sharp edges. Jugging places the rope under tension and sharp edges can damage it. Ascend as smoothly as possible to minimize the sawing motion of the rope running over an edge.

## Cleaning

Efficiency in aid climbing is very much related to organization. While ascending and cleaning a pitch, rack the equipment as it will be placed on the lead rack. This greatly facilitates the lead changes.

Clean protection and aid placements that are lightly set often pop out if you jug right through them. Lift up on the placement as you slide your ascender up the rope. If clean aid has been used, you can often ascend from one tying-off–short spot to the next without stopping. After tying in short again, rack the pieces that have accumulated on the rope above your ascender.

This general system works even if a placement does not pop out as you move the ascenders upward. Keep the piece clipped into the climbing rope and use a chock pick and hammer to dislodge it. Once it pops free, continue ascending without reracking until you

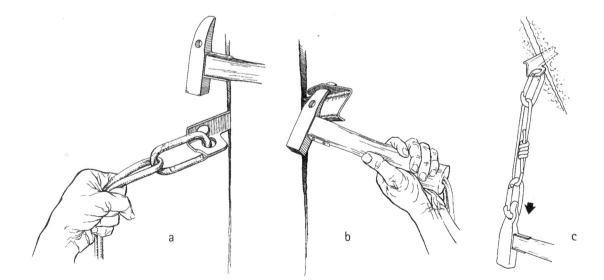

*Fig. 12-29. Piton removal: a, use of "cleaner biner"; b, hammer used to pry; c, hammer swing.*

tie in short again. If, however, you must remove the upper ascender frequently, you should rack the pieces as they are removed.

Fixed pins found on the route should be left in place unless they are obviously unsafe or interfere with a chock placement. Take care not to break the eyes off these old pins, leaving a useless pin.

When cleaning one of your own pins, pound it back and forth along the axis of the crack, as far as it will go in each direction. Once the pin is loose enough to move easily back and forth, you can remove it by any of several means (fig. 12-29):

1. Attach a "cleaner biner"—a carabiner no longer used for climbing—and a sling to the pin. Pull out on the sling while tapping the pin back and forth until it pops out (fig. 12-29a).
2. Pry out on the loose pin with the pick of the hammer, taking care not to break the hammer (fig. 12-29b).
3. Attach a "cleaner biner" and sling to the loose pin, and then attach the sling to the hammer with another carabiner. Starting with slack in the sling, swing the hammer in the direction the pin should come out (fig. 12-29c).

Because the heads of malleable placements can only be reused a limited number of times, it is often best to leave them fixed. This is especially true if you think the wire will pull off the head as you remove the piece. If you decide to remove a malleable piece, attach a cleaner biner and sling between the head and your hammer. Then, as with pins, give the hammer a quick swing outward. It may take several swings before the head pops out. Inspect the head closely before reusing it because they deteriorate quickly. But if your attempt to remove the head merely strips the wire away, take the time to clean the head out of the rock. It is easier for you to do so on a fixed rope than for another climber on lead.

## Seconding Traverses and Overhangs

When traversing a long distance, it is generally more efficient if you aid across the traverse as if leading. Aiding in this fashion, you can receive a belay from above or self-belay by attaching ascenders to your harness with slings and sliding the ascenders along the climbing rope as you aid. When using the latter method, tie in short from time to time.

Short traverses, and those that are more diagonal than horizontal, can be crossed using normal jugging (mechanical ascender) techniques. The nearer the traverse is to horizontal, the less efficient this technique becomes, for at each piece you are faced with a small pendulum.

When jugging, remove the upper ascender at each placement and move it as far as possible above the currently weighted piece. This practice minimizes the pendulum that will result when you transfer your weight onto the upper ascender. Before doing this, however, allow some distance between the lower ascender and the placement so that the lower ascender does not jam into the piece as you transfer your weight to the upper ascender. Also, be sure to still tie in short at regular intervals.

The same basic methods just described for traverses also apply to seconding overhangs.

## Seconding Pendulums

The best method to second a pendulum depends on the length of the pendulum and the ropes available. The placements, slinging, and carabiner for the pendulum anchor usually will all need to be left behind, unless they can be reached from above after completing the pendulum.

### Seconding Long Pendulums

All long pendulums require at least one rope in addition to the climbing and haul ropes. There are a number of ways to second a long pendulum, but the method shown in Figure 12-30 will handle all such cases.

In Figure 12-30a, all pendulums begin with a leader, of course, who rappels off a bombproof pendulum point using either one rope or two ropes tied together, depending on the width of the pendulum. The rappel rope should be clipped into the anchor so there's no danger of losing it. While on the pendulum, the leader is belayed on the climbing rope, which is not clipped into the pendulum anchor. At the bottom of the rappel, the leader runs back and forth across the rock to gain enough momentum to swing into the new crack system. On a very long pendulum, the leader may haul along an extra belay rope. The belayer keeps one end of this rope as the leader drags the other end.

In Figure 12-30b, the leader ascends the new crack system and sets up an anchor. The leader attaches the

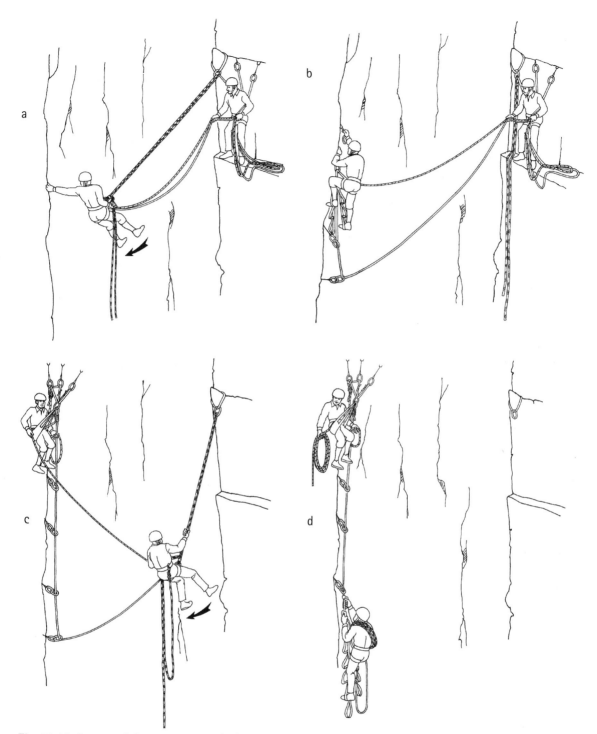

*Fig. 12-30. Long pendulum sequence: a, leader rappels on two ropes while belayed on two; b, leader begins climbing, clipping in one of the belay ropes; c, with anchor set, leader belays with rope not clipped to aid pieces (the second rappels across the pendulum—note that the end of one rappel rope is attached to the second climber to prevent its loss); d, the second pulls the rappel ropes, ties in short, and "jugs" anchored climbing rope.*

climbing rope and the extra belay rope to the new anchor, the latter to serve as a belay rope for the second climber. With the first climber now set to belay, the second climber frees or lowers the haul bag. The follower also unclips the rappel rope tie-in from the pendulum anchor so the rope can be retrieved later. (The follower can clip one end of the rappel rope to an out-of-the-way place on the seat harness to again ensure the rope can't be dropped.)

In Figure 12-30c, the follower rappels the pendulum, with the first climber belaying and helping to pull the follower toward the new crack system at the end of the pendulum. (There's an alternative if the leader didn't drag an extra pendulum rope across. The second can pull across the pendulum on the lead climbing rope by hand or with the help of mechanical ascenders.)

In Figure 12-30d, safely across, the second attaches ascenders to the climbing rope, ties off short, retrieves the rappel rope, and is ready to climb up the new crack system.

## Seconding Short Pendulums

Climbers also have a variety of ways to handle the challenge of seconding a short pendulum. One clever and useful method is shown in Figure 12-31. For this method to work, the slack rope from the pendulum anchor to the follower's harness must be at least double

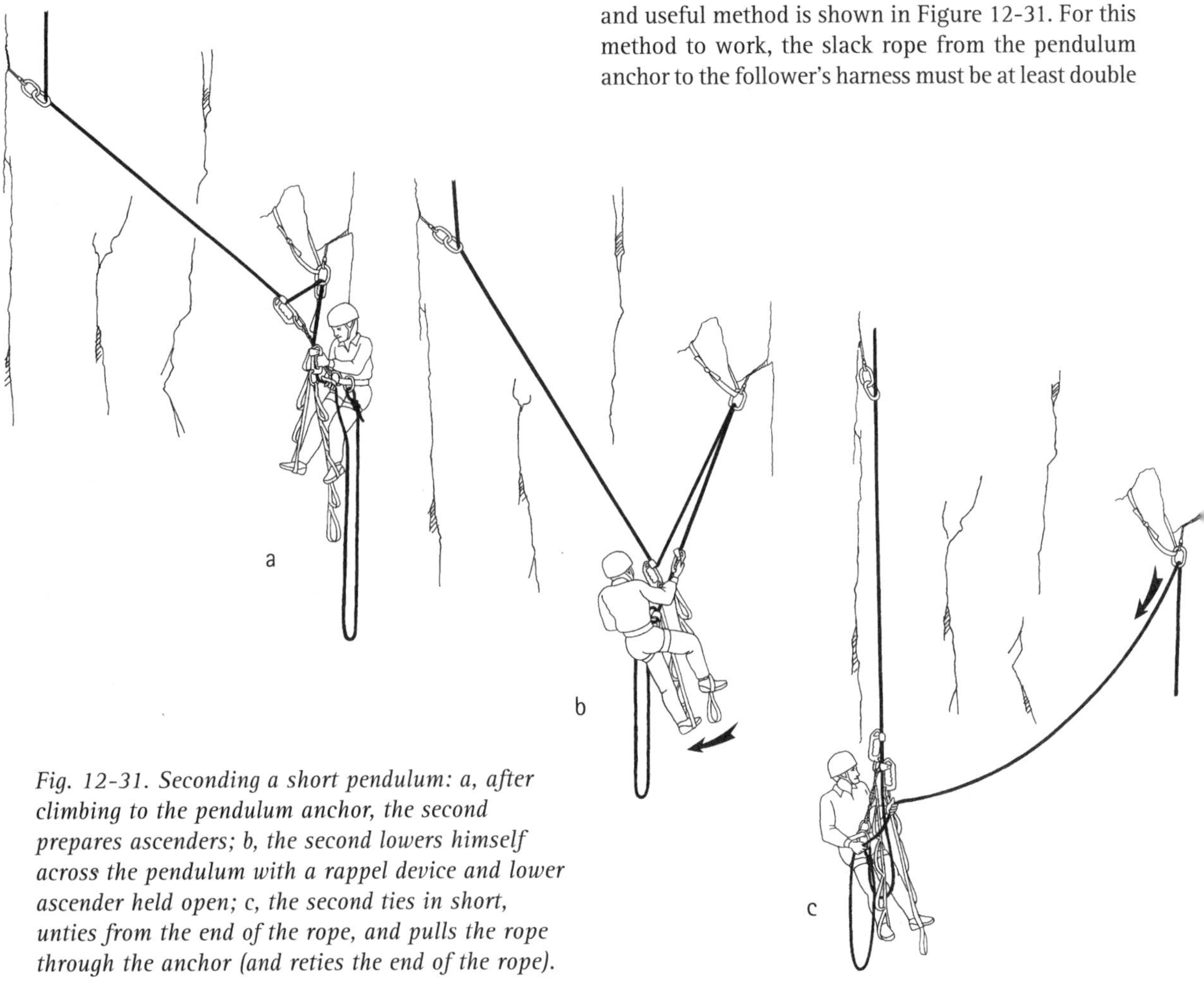

*Fig. 12-31. Seconding a short pendulum: a, after climbing to the pendulum anchor, the second prepares ascenders; b, the second lowers himself across the pendulum with a rappel device and lower ascender held open; c, the second ties in short, unties from the end of the rope, and pulls the rope through the anchor (and reties the end of the rope).*

the arc of the pendulum. The follower stays tied in to the climbing rope during the sequence.

As shown in Figure 12-31, here's how you as the follower could second a short pendulum.

In Figure 12-31a, connect the upper ascender with its attached etrier to the climbing rope beyond the pendulum anchor, facing across the pendulum. Clip a daisy chain from your harness to the ascender. Connect the lower ascender and etrier to the section of rope between the pendulum anchor and yourself. Clip it in with another daisy chain. Place your weight on the upper ascender. Next, attach a rappel device to the rope, below the lower ascender, and grasp the rope where it exits the device. Then, while keeping the safety trigger locked, release the cam of the lower ascender by pulling on the rope below it (this will take some effort). You're now ready to move.

In Figure 12-31b, with one hand grasping the climbing rope as it leaves the rappel device and the other hand sliding the lower ascender, lower yourself across the pendulum. To put the brakes on at any time, simply let go of the lower ascender and the cam will again lock. (In fact, if a rappel device is not used, this ascender will often lock onto the rope by itself, requiring you to repeat the previous tactic of pulling hard on the rope below it.)

In Figure 12-31c, once across the pendulum, tie in short and move the lower ascender above that point. Now untie yourself from the end of the rope so you can pull it through the pendulum anchor. Once you've retied into the end of the climbing rope, you're set to ascend the climbing rope again.

The rappel device makes it easier to hold the rope while lowering yourself across the pendulum; however, you can also second a short pendulum this way without the device.

## Changing Leads

Unorganized belay stations can become a rat's nest of tangled ropes, twisted slings, and assorted hardware. Basic organization keeps the belay station manageable and the team functioning efficiently. Following are several methods to improve organization:

- All ropes should be different colors.
- After hauling the sack, the leader stacks the haul

line and organizes the other ropes and hardware at the anchor.

- Once the second arrives at the anchor and begins consolidating the lead rack, the old leader (now the belayer) makes butterfly coils in the climbing rope and stacks these coils at the anchor with a sling. This prevents the climbing rope from getting snagged below and from tangling and helps it pay out smoothly.
- If the second was carrying a rucksack, it can be packed with gear that won't be utilized on the next pitch and clipped into the anchor.
- Finally, the second (now the new leader) clips the free end of the haul rope to his or her harness, is placed on belay, and starts climbing.

## BIG-WALL MULTIDAY TECHNIQUES

"Big walls," the saying goes, "are 90 percent work and 10 percent fun." Not everyone agrees with those percentages, but few climbers will say big walls are easy. There's no question that proper conditioning is essential for the hauling of heavy loads and the scaling of multiple aid pitches.

Big walls also call for a high degree of mental composure. Inexperienced wall climbers easily find themselves the victim of heightened fears brought on by prolonged and severe exposure. If you're new to the game, perhaps you can soothe your fears by realizing that techniques for dealing with major walls are much the same as those needed for smaller climbs. Concentrate on the problem at hand and work away at the objective one move at a time.

In preparing for a big wall, guidebooks and other climbers are often helpful sources of information. Beware, however, of overdependence on climbers' topographic maps and equipment lists. Routes do change over time, especially if pins are used regularly.

Solid, efficient aid technique is a prerequisite if a major wall is to be completed within the time constraints dictated by reasonable food and water supplies. For success on the big walls, you must develop competency in hoisting heavy sacks up the route, and

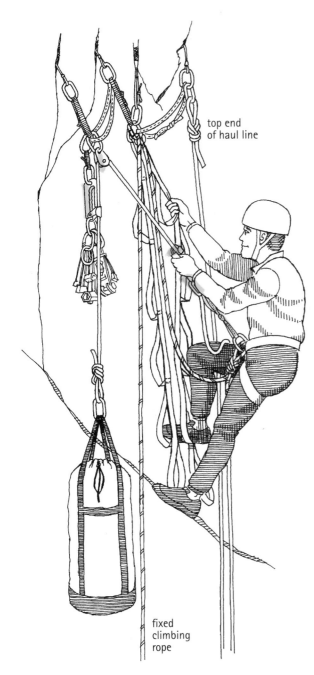

top end
of haul line

fixed
climbing
rope

*Fig. 12-32. Sack-hauling system; hauler is preparing to move ascender up haul line and ascend etriers for next power haul.*

you should be able to live comfortably in a vertical world for days at a time.

## Hauling

After anchoring yourself and fixing the climbing rope for the second, it's your job as the leader to begin hauling (fig. 12-32):

1. Attach a pulley, through which the haul line passes, to the anchor.
2. Attach an upside-down ascender to the haul line on the haul-sack side of the pulley. The end of the ascender closest to the pulley (normally the bottom) is clipped into the anchor, while the end pointing toward the haul sack is counterweighted with the remains of the rack (or another weight).
3. Attach a second ascender, in the normal direction, to the haul line on the opposite side of the pulley (between yourself and the pulley). Use a daisy chain to connect this ascender to your harness.
4. Push back from the wall using your legs and palms; your body weight will raise the haul sack. When you stop pushing, the upside-down ascender acts as a brake to prevent backward slippage of the haul bag. You'll need a little slack in the climbing rope between yourself and the anchor to allow your hauling movement.

You can also haul by allowing slack of 6 to 8 feet between you and the anchor. Then, with the daisy chain connected between your harness and the haul line ascender, walk down the wall 6 to 8 feet until the anchor rope tightens. Climb back to your original position by stepping upward in etriers attached to the anchor, pulling the ascender with you. Repeat the process.

This method is also used if two people are needed to lift a very heavy bag. Both of you clip to the ascender on the haul rope, give yourself 6 to 8 feet of slack, and walk down the wall together. Regardless of the method used, always connect yourself to the anchor with the climbing rope.

## Fixing Pitches

On multiday climbs, you will often fix two or three pitches beyond the bivouac site and leave gear not needed for the bivouac at the high point. The lower end of each fixed rope is attached to the anchor of the previous pitch.

The next morning the pitches are jugged—one climber on a rope at a time. This gives a head start on the day and lets you warm up before new climbing begins.

## Retreating

Before a major climb, plan retreat lines in case of bad weather, accident, or other emergency. Locate other routes that are easy to reach to speed the ascent or that have fixed retreat lines.

If no retreat route exists, consider carrying a bolt kit for emergencies, allowing you to place rappel anchors. Also, as you climb each pitch, consider how you would descend it. On major walls rescues may be slow and difficult, if possible at all. It may be up to you to get back down in an emergency.

## Living in the Vertical World

Living for days on a vertical wall of rock brings some intriguing problems. Dropped gear, for instance, is gone. All vital items must have clip-in loops. Learn your gear so you can work it confidently. Get acquainted with unfamiliar items, such as portaledges or hammocks, beforehand.

It's usually necessary to carry all your water with you. Each climber generally needs 2 quarts per day. For hot weather, especially if the route gets a lot of sun, you will need to carry even more.

Waste disposal poses another challenge. Tossing garbage down the wall is not acceptable, so you'll have to haul it up and off the climb. Keep all bivouac sites clean and sanitary, with no sign of your passing. (Chapter 24, Minimum Impact, has information on disposal of human waste during big-wall climbs.)

After completing a major wall, you need to get your gear back down. In the past, common practice was to toss the haul bag loaded with gear off the wall. Today, sack tossing is illegal at popular climbing areas like Yosemite; it endangers climbers below. Furthermore, many climbers have had their gear stolen by the time they got down to it. Carry down what you hauled up.

## — THE FUTURE OF AID CLIMBING —

Free-climbers may feel that aid climbing isolates the climber from the rock. But anyone who has struggled to place a piece of aid while standing above a series of marginal placements understands that aid is not only climbing but a test of technical abilities and nerves.

To ensure that these routes will continue to be a test of skill and nerves, aid climbers are asked to respect certain ethics. If you are climbing an established route, adhere to the ethics of the first-ascent climbers. If they did not need a piton or bolt, *don't place one*. Use creativity and boldness to overcome the difficulty. A party following you on a route should find it in the condition you found it.

If you're putting up a new route, you are establishing the style for those who follow. Remember that routes once considered difficult using pitons are now free-climbed and that old bolt ladders are often viewed with disdain. Make it your goal to climb cleanly and in a style that climbers can respect. As time goes on, more of today's aid routes will be free-climbed, while aid climbers will push their limits on ever thinner and more remote climbs.

Overleaf: *Icy, British Columbia ©Cliff Leight;* overleaf inset: *©Andy Selters*

# PART FOUR

# SNOW, ICE, AND ALPINE CLIMBING

# 13
# SNOW TRAVEL AND CLIMBING

Climbing in snow is fundamental to mountaineering. Snow is magical stuff, cloaking the landscape in a sparkling mantle. Gently falling snowflakes can be a balm to the human spirit, an aesthetic delight. But technically, snow is defined rather dryly as a "consolidated mass of water crystals." It is the degree of consolidation that is significant to the climber.

Snow falls in a variety of forms: tiny crystals to coarse pellets. In its initial phase, the snowpack can consist of 90 percent air by volume. Even though you're literally walking on air, climbing in snow is not to be taken lightly. Once the snow is on the ground, a cyclic process of melting and freezing begins. The snow becomes increasingly dense as the air is displaced. Ultimately, the density of glacial ice can be the same as the density of ice formed directly from water.

Snow displays a broad spectrum of physical characteristics, and the distinction between hard snow and ice is rather arbitrary. Snow climbing is described in this chapter, while ice climbing is discussed in Chapter 15, but techniques overlap with no distinct separation.

Climbers operate in a world that is affected by snow on two very different scales. On a rather grand scale, snow—in the form of glaciers—sculpts the terrain. On a more human scale, snow is often the climbers' landscape, largely determining how and where we travel.

Snow travel is trickier than trail hiking or rock climbing. A rock face stays basically the same, whereas the snowpack undergoes many changes. Depending on the degree of consolidation, snow presents a widely variable surface: seemingly insubstantial unconsolidated powder, consistently firm surface, or the rock hardness of alpine ice. The snowpack can appear to be firm, yet under certain conditions it will suddenly flow in an avalanche and then quickly set to icy hardness. Safe snow travel requires judgment based on experience.

During one season, a snowfield may start as a dusting of snow over a brushy slope, progress to a powder bowl waiting to avalanche, then to a solid surface offering rapid ascent to a ridge top, and finally back to scattered snow patches. In the course of a day, snow can change from firm surface in the morning to slush in the afternoon.

Snow can be helpful, making climbs easier by providing a pathway over brush and other obstacles on the approach hike and reducing the danger of loose rock on the ascent. But the changeable nature of snow requires mountaineers to be flexible in choosing their mode of travel, ready to use snowshoes, skis, or crampons. Snow conditions also affect decisions on route-finding and climbing technique. Should you hike up the comfortable snow-covered valley bottom or on the ridge crest away from avalanche hazard? Should you go for the easy stepkicking of the sunny slope or the firmer, more stable snow of the shaded hill? Is it safer to travel roped or unroped?

In this chapter we'll take a look at the equipment you need to travel in snow and the techniques for traveling quickly and safely.

## EQUIPMENT

At the top of the list of basic snow-climbing equipment are ice axes and crampons. Snowshoes, skis, and ski poles are other important snow-travel aids. Climbers also use equipment for snow anchors, which will be taken up later in this chapter in the section on roped climbing.

### Ice Ax

The ice ax (fig. 13-1) is one of the most versatile and important pieces of mountaineering equipment. Without it, safe alpine travel is restricted to easy scrambles. An ax, and skill in its use, allows you to venture onto all forms of snow and ice, enjoying a greater variety of mountain landscapes during more seasons of the year.

The modern ice ax is an inherently simple tool with many uses. Below the snow line, it's used as a walking cane and to help brake going downhill. But its main role is in snow and ice travel, where it provides balance or a point of security to prevent a fall and serves as a means to stop a fall.

The design of an ice ax often is a trade-off between features that make the tool better for particular uses. A long ax may be suitable for cross-country travel and scrambling, where it's used as a cane and to provide security in low-angle climbing. However, you'll probably want a shorter ax for the steeper slopes encoun-

tered in alpine climbing. Axes designed for ice climbing are characterized by even shorter shafts and by specialized design of such elements as the shape of pick and adze and the placement of teeth. (Ice-climbing tools are discussed in Chapter 15.)

Weight is another consideration. The adage says "Light is right"–but don't take this too far. Some very light axes are not designed to withstand the demands of general mountaineering. For example, the Cassin Dragon Fly weighs only about 11 ounces, but it's designed for ski mountaineering or trekking. General mountaineering axes tend to be lighter and less expensive than technical ice tools.

### Parts of the Ice Ax

**The head** of an ice ax–which includes the pick and the adze–is usually made of steel alloy, a material strong enough for snow and ice climbing. Although the hole in the head of the ax is commonly called a carabiner hole, most climbers attach their wrist leash through it.

**The pick** on most ice axes (fig. 13-2) is curved or drooped, a design that provides better hooking action

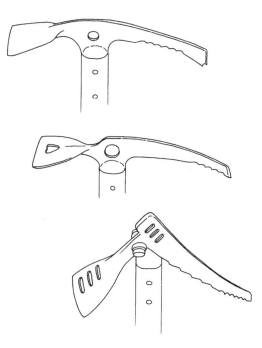

*Fig. 13-2. Ice-ax picks: shapes and teeth patterns*

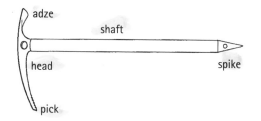

*Fig. 13-1. Parts of the ice ax*

in snow or ice, enabling the ax to dig in when you're trying to stop yourself (self-arrest) after a fall. A moderate hooking angle of 65 to 70 degrees from the shaft is right for general mountaineering uses. A sharper angle of 55 to 60 degrees is better for technical ice climbing, as it coincides with the arc followed by the ax head as you swing it to plant it into steep ice. Teeth on the pick provide grip for ice and hard snow. Ice axes designed for general mountaineering typically have only a few teeth, placed at the end of the pick. Ice tools designed for technical climbing have teeth along the entire length of the pick.

The pick may have positive, neutral, or negative clearance (fig. 13-3). The clearance is determined by comparison of the angle of the pick tip relative to the axis of the shaft. If the angle of the pick tip is parallel with the shaft, the pick has neutral clearance. If the angle points toward the shaft, it has negative clearance. If the angle points away from the shaft, it has positive clearance. In theory, the degree of clearance affects the performance of the ax in self-arrest. A pick with positive clearance should penetrate more readily; a pick with negative clearance would tend to skate on ice or hard snow. However, the type of clearance actually makes little difference: self-arrest is almost impossible on ice, and in softer snow the pick will dig in regardless of clearance. In any case, you can always modify clearance with a hand file.

The adze of the ax is used mainly to cut steps in hard snow or ice. The flat top of the adze also provides a firm, comfortable platform for the palm of your hand while holding the ax in the self-belay grasp. Adzes for general mountaineering may be flat or

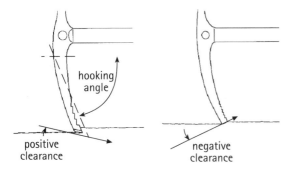

*Fig. 13-3. Ice-ax clearance*

curved, straight-edged or scalloped, straight-out or drooped. A flat, straight-edged, nondrooped adze with sharp corners is probably the best all-around tool for cutting steps.

The shaft of the ax will be made of aluminum or a composite material (fiberglass, Kevlar, or carbon filament), or a combination. The wooden shafts of yesterday—often dense, straight-grained hickory—have been replaced by these stronger and more reliable materials.

Some shafts are covered at least partly by a rubber material, which helps give surer command of the ax during self-arrest and also dampens vibrations and increases control in planting the pick. You can improve your hold on a shaft that doesn't have a rubber grip by adding athletic grip tape or using gloves with rubberized palms. However, the friction of the shaft covering may keep the ax from readily penetrating the snow when you're using it for a boot-ax belay, probing, or self-belay.

The spike, the metal tip of the ax, must be kept sharp so that it penetrates readily into snow and ice. The ax does come in handy on rocky trails and talus slopes by helping with balance, but this use will dull the spike.

## Ice-Ax Length

Ice axes range in length from 40 centimeters (about 16 inches) to 90 centimeters (about 3 feet)—still much shorter than the 5-foot alpenstocks of the alpine pioneers. The shortest axes are for technical ice climbing; the longest ones are for tall mountaineers using the ax as a cane on easy terrain.

The optimal length for an ice ax may depend more on what you plan to do with it than on how tall you are. Axes less than 60 centimeters long are ice-climbing tools, excellent for placements on steep slopes. However, these ice tools are not so good for self-arrest; the shorter shafts offer less leverage than a longer ax, and many of the technical pick designs do not lend themselves to the self-arrest technique. An ax of 70 centimeters is the longest that is generally useful for ice climbing. A length of 60 to 70 centimeters works well in most alpine situations, where you are climbing moderately steep snow slopes and using the ax for self-belay and self-arrest. Longer axes are better for cross-country travel and scrambling and also are good as snow anchors and for probing for cornices and crevasses.

## Ice-Ax Leash

The leash provides a way to attach the ice ax to your wrist or your harness when you want to ensure it won't be dropped. Although the length of a leash can vary, it usually consists of a piece of accessory cord or webbing attached through the carabiner hole in the head of the ice ax (fig. 13-4).

The leash is valuable insurance on crevassed glaciers or long steep slopes where losing an ax would leave you without a principal safety tool and put climbers below in danger from the runaway ax. The leash also lets the ice ax hang freely while you make a move or two on the occasional rock encountered during a snow climb.

Short wrist leashes are favored by those who find them adequate for basic snow and glacier travel. The short leash is easy to use and is an aid to quicker control of the ice ax during a fall. During an uncontrolled fall in which you lose your grip on the ax, an ax on a short leash will not flail around as much as one on a longer leash.

Most climbers prefer a longer leash. With a long leash, you no longer have to switch the leash from wrist to wrist as you move the ax to the other hand for a change in direction up a snow slope. The long leash also makes the ax more versatile for climbing steep snow or ice.

A long wrist leash is usually about as long as the ax itself and, if adjusted to the right length, it can help reduce arm fatigue during step-cutting and ice climbing. With your hand through the wrist loop, the leash should be just long enough to let you grasp the end of the shaft near the spike. This way, the wrist can share the work of the arm, and the head of the ax will be more stable. A long leash can be chained to a runner attached to your seat harness, so that the ax can be used as a personal anchor.

Many different designs of commercially manufactured leashes are available. You can easily make a leash yourself from a length of 5-millimeter or 6-millimeter accessory cord or $1/2$-inch to 1-inch flat webbing. Tie the ends of the material together with a suitable knot to create a sling, girth-hitch the sling through the carabiner hole, then tie an overhand knot to form a wrist loop.

### Ice-Ax Maintenance

Modern ice axes require very little special care. Inspect the shaft before each use for deep dents that might weaken it to the point of failure under load (but don't worry about minor nicks and scratches). Clean mud and dirt off the ax after each climb, and remove any rust.

Check the pick, adze, and spike regularly. To sharpen, use a hand file, not a power-driven grinding wheel. High-speed grinding can overheat the metal and change the temper, diminishing the strength of the metal.

## Crampons

Mountaineering is unthinkable without crampons, but when the first 10-point crampons came on the scene in Europe in the early 1900s, many alpinists thought the gadgets took unsporting advantage of the peaks. However, crampons proved to be the one aid that could relieve climbers of the tremendous burden of step-cutting and open up a vast array of new snow and ice faces. They have since evolved into the 12-point crampons of today.

As with ice axes, the different crampon designs involve a trade-off between what's good for general alpine

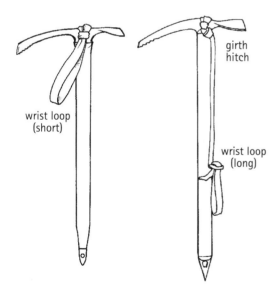

*Fig. 13-4. Ice-ax leashes (wrist loops), attached through carabiner hole in head of ax*

use and what's good for technical ice climbing. Most crampons are made from chrome-molybdenum steel, an extremely strong, lightweight alloy.

When should you wear crampons? There is no steadfast rule. The decision should be based on your assessment of conditions. Crampons are designed to penetrate a hard surface; you should wear them when traveling on snow or ice that is too hard and slick for your boot soles to gain sufficient traction or penetration. Climbers make this decision based on their skill and experience. If you feel that you need to wear crampons, put them on.

Climbers face a number of questions in shopping for crampons. What type of crampons should I buy? How will I know when the crampons fit my boots? Which attachment system should I use? This section provides information to help answer these questions and offers tips on crampon maintenance.

## Crampon Points

The early 10-point crampon has long-since been eclipsed in the 1930s by the addition of two forward-slanting points to create the 12-point crampon. The 12-point models eliminated step-cutting and permitted "front-pointing" up steep snow and ice. Because 10-point crampons usually don't have front points, they're no good for very steep ice and are no longer available except as used equipment.

The angles of the first two rows of points determine the best use for a set of crampons. When the first row (front points) is drooped and the second row is angled toward the toe of the boot (fig. 13-5), the crampons are better suited for front-pointing than for general mountaineering. This configuration allows the boot

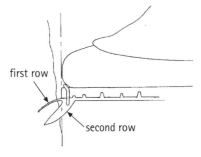

*Fig. 13-5. Angle of first two rows of points, best suited for front-pointing*

heel to be lower without additional calf strain. Straight points are better for flat-footing and general use.

Small instep crampons with 4 or 6 points are sold for use by backpackers who need to cross an occasional short snowfield. Because there are no points at the heel or toe, they're unsuitable for mountaineering and can be dangerous on steep snow or ice.

Some manufacturers produce 8-point crampons. They lack front points, but provide more traction than instep crampons while being lighter and smaller than 12-point crampons. The 8-point crampon, like the instep crampon, is no substitute for 12-point crampons.

## Hinged Versus Rigid Crampons

Mountaineers have a choice of either hinged or rigid crampons (fig. 13-6a-b). Rigid crampons are designed for technical ice climbing. For general mountaineering, the hinged 12-point crampon is the standard today.

A hinged crampon flexes at the instep and is meant to bend with the natural rocking action of walking. It can be attached to any mountaineering boot—full shank, half shank, or plastic. Attached to a stiff boot, hinged crampons perform nearly as well for ice climbing as rigid crampons because the boot provides the stable platform. If you buy only one set of crampons, buy a hinged model. If your goal is steep technical ice, then you should consider a rigid crampon. Some models (for example, the Grivel 2F) are convertible; they can be changed from flexible mode to rigid mode by the addition of a nut and bolt.

A rigid crampon is inflexible. Most rigid crampons require a stiff boot, because use with a flexible boot will eventually lead to crampon failure due to metal fatigue. Rigid crampons generally don't perform as well in mixed terrain, where some flexibility is desired, and they are typically heavier than hinged crampons. Rigid crampons are best suited for front-pointing up technical ice. They vibrate less than hinged crampons when you kick them into the ice, and their stiffness provides more support that makes for less tiring front-pointing.

## Crampon Attachment

Climbers can choose from a variety of traditional strapping methods or the newer step-in/clamp-on bindings. The various systems are available on either hinged or rigid crampons. Be sure to choose a fastening system that is compatible with your boots.

### Straps

Buckled straps do a good job of attaching crampons to boots. Neoprene-coated nylon is the best strap material because it is strong, doesn't absorb water, won't stretch, and can be easily transferred from one pair of crampons to another. Leather straps are less expensive but stretch when wet and will eventually rot or break. Nylon or fabric webbing is least desirable, because it readily accumulates snow and may freeze to the buckle.

Three strap-on designs are in general use:

- **Four independent straps per crampon:** Two short straps, with buckles, are attached to one side of the crampon and two longer straps are attached to the other side. One of the long straps wraps over the instep, connecting the front four attachment posts of the boot, while the other long strap wraps around the ankle, connecting the two rear posts (fig. 13-6c).
- **Two independent straps per crampon:** One strap wraps over the instep, connecting the front four attachment posts, and the other wraps around the ankle, connecting the two rear posts (fig. 13-6d).
- **The "Scottish" system:** A strap with a ring in the middle is permanently attached to the two front attachment posts. Another strap then runs from one side post through this ring to the other side post. The rear strap is the same as that in the four-strap system (fig. 13-6e). This method is quicker to use than the other two and is gaining popularity.

When attaching straps to crampons, place the buckles on the outer side of each crampon (so that the buckles are on the outside of your boots), to minimize chances of catching a crampon point on a buckle. To reduce the danger of the front straps loosening on the

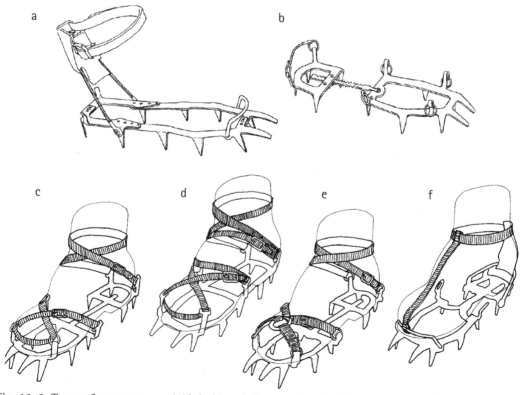

*Fig. 13-6. Types of crampons: a, rigid; b, hinged. Systems for attaching crampons to boots: c, four-strap; d, two-strap; e, Scottish; f, step-in/clamp-on.*

two-strap and four-strap systems, thread the strap through the hole at each front attachment post from the outside in, and then give the strap an extra twist.

An important word of advice: Practice strapping on your crampons in the comfort of home. You'll have plenty of chances later to put them on under less ideal conditions: in the dark, by feel, or in the illumination of your headlamp, with cold, numbed fingers. Lay the crampons on the floor with all straps started through the hole at an attachment post, put on your boots, place each boot in turn on its crampon, and attach the straps. Do the crampons fit? Do the straps have holes punched in them at the right places for a snug fit? Do the straps need to be longer to accommodate insulated gaiters or overboots? Are they tight enough to keep the crampons on through thick and thin, but not so tight that they restrict blood flow? As best you can, work out all the wrinkles before you get out on that steep slope of hard snow in the cold, dark morning.

### Step-in/Clamp-on Bindings

The agony of fumbling with crampon straps and buckles is largely eliminated by the step-in/clamp-on bindings (fig. 13-6f). The crampons attach to the boot with a wire toe bail and a heel lever/bail. They're fast and easy to put on, and each crampon has a safety strap so you won't lose it if it ever comes off. In addition, many models include a metal strap that is attached to the toe bail. Some crampons feature hybrid bindings that include a strap harness combined with a heel lever/bail.

There are a couple of considerations to keep in mind before you decide to use step in/clamp-on bindings. The fit to the boot is more critical than with crampons that are strapped on. The boot must have a pronounced welt or groove at both the heel and toe (the step-in/clamp-ons fit especially well on plastic boots). Crampons with straps often work better on leather boots, particularly those without a decided heel welt. And some climbers, nervous about the possibility of the clamp-ons accidentally releasing, continue to use strap systems for technical ice.

## Crampon Fit

To ensure that crampons stay attached and perform well, they must fit. When buying crampons, you must try them on with the boots you'll be wearing. If you plan to use them on more than one pair of boots, check the fit on all pairs.

Here are some tips to help in fitting crampons, either the kind that attach with straps or the step-in/clamp on type:

- If you'll be wearing gaiters with a rubber rand that fits around the welt and instep of the boot, be sure to wear the gaiters when you fit the crampons.
- The front crampon points should protrude about 3/4 inch to 1 inch beyond the toe of the boot.
- Many crampons are adjustable to one degree or another. This can include adjustments for length and for the width of instep, heel, and toe. Being able to adjust the heel and toe widths can be especially important if you're using telemark boots (for a climbing/skiing trip) or overboots.
- The attachment posts at the sides and rear of strap-on crampons should hug the boot snugly without significant bending to fit. Test the fit by lifting the boot with the crampon. The posts should hold to the boot without the use of straps (fig. 13-7).
- The heel wire found on some strap-on crampons helps keep the boot heel in place by preventing it from slipping through the rear post, especially when using plastic boots.

*Fig. 13-7. Testing crampon fit*

- The welt on a boot is especially important with step-in/clamp-on bindings, which grip the boot at toe and heel. Most desirable are Norwegian-style double-stitched welts on heavy leather boots and the grooved toe and heel on plastic boots and modern leather mountaineering boots.
- Some climbers place a flat piece of foam, shaped like the bottom of the boot, between the boot and crampon to help insulate the foot from the snow. If you want to do this, take it into account when you fit your crampons.

## Crampon Maintenance and Safety

Regular simple maintenance is required for safe, dependable crampons. Keep the points sharp, clean the crampons after every climb, and inspect them before the next outing.

Snow and ice routes often include short sections of rock that you'll climb wearing crampons. The crampons should be able to take the punishment, but too much of this will dull the points. As with ice axes, sharpen crampon points with a hand file, not a grinding wheel (fig. 13-8).

After you return home from each climb, wipe dirt and water from crampons to prevent rust. Check the points before each climb. They should be clean and reasonably sharp, though very sharp points are needed only for technical ice climbing. Also check alignment of the points, because splayed points make the crampons less efficient at gripping the snow and more effective as a weapon that can slash pants and legs. It's probably best to retire a pair of crampons with badly bent points. Check the tightness of nuts and bolts on adjustable crampons. And while you're looking over the crampons, don't forget to inspect the straps. Look for rotting, abrasion, cracks, or cuts.

In the mountains, following a few easy rules can protect you, your gear, and your companions from sharp crampon points. Walk deliberately. Avoid snagging your pants, gashing your leg, or stepping on the rope. When you're carrying the crampons, use a set of rubber protectors to cover the points, or keep the crampons in a special pouch. Rubber point protectors and crampon pouches are available commercially.

One little trick makes crampons safer and more effective in soft, sticky snow. Just wrap the bottom of the crampon with duct tape to minimize the amount of snow that balls up under the crampon. This balling of snow can be dangerous, particularly where slushy snow overlays an icy base. You can buy manufactured "anti-balling plates," which basically are fitted rubber or vinyl sheets. While wearing crampons in soft snow, ask yourself whether you need to wear them. You may be able to simply take them off.

## Wands

To enable them to retrace their path, mountaineers often mark their route with wands. The wands are available commercially, but climbers usually make their own, using green-stained bamboo garden stakes. Convert these stakes to wands by attaching to one end a piece of bright, durable, water-repellent material, such as plastic surveyor's tape, coated nylon, or colored duct tape.

A common method is to slit the first couple of inches at one end of a wand, slip the surveyor's tape or coated nylon into the slit, tie the material, and then tape the slit closed (fig. 13-9). Duct tape is easier to attach and, being stiffer, will be more visible at a distance. Be sure the flag is secure enough to withstand the high winds of open snow slopes and glaciers. Wands usually vary in length from 30 to 48 inches. If the wand is less than 30 inches, the flag may not be easily seen; if longer than 4 feet, the wands are awkward to carry.

Mark your wands with your initials and the date on the flag; you want to be certain that you're retracing your own path, not someone else's. Insert the wands firmly into the snow, planting them deeply enough to compensate for melting. If the wands fall over, they will not be visible. It's helpful to place them

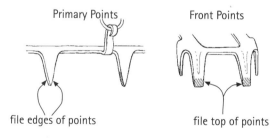

Primary Points      Front Points

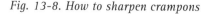

file edges of points      file top of points

*Fig. 13-8. How to sharpen crampons*

*Fig. 13-9. Wand construction*

so that they indicate the direction of travel. Use your longest wands in winter, when they have to be inserted deeper because of soft snow and when new snowfall can bury them. Be diligent about retrieving your wands on the way down.

## Ski Poles

Ski poles aren't only for use with skis. They are better than an ice ax for balance when you're trudging with a heavy pack over level or low-angle snow, slippery ground, or scree or when you're trying to cross a stream or boulder field. They also can take some of the weight off your lower body. And the basket at the bottom keeps the poles from penetrating deep into soft snow, a favorite trick of ice axes unless they're fitted with a special snow basket.

A variety of ski poles have features helpful to the trekker or mountaineer. Adjustable poles enable you to set the length to suit the conditions or the terrain; on a traverse, the uphill pole can be set to a length shorter than the downhill pole. You can fully compress these poles for ease of packing. Adjustable poles require more maintenance, and after each trip they should be disassembled, cleaned, and dried. Poles with removable baskets can serve as probes for crevasses. Some poles fasten together to form a serviceable avalanche probe (fig. 13-10), though this type of pole should not be considered a substitute for a commercial avalanche probe. For some ski poles, you can

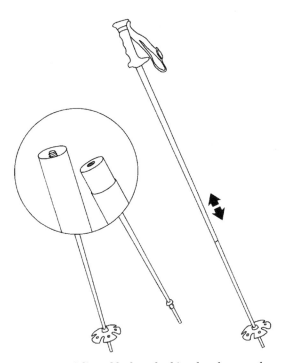

*Fig. 13-10. Adjustable-length ski poles that can be fastened together to create an avalanche probe*

buy a special self-arrest grip that has a plastic or metal-tipped pick protruding forward from the top, but this definitely is not a substitute for an ice ax on technical terrain. Ski poles can be used whether you're traveling by foot, snowshoes, or skis.

## Skis

Mountaineering has become a popular four-season pursuit with the widespread use of Nordic and mountaineering skis fitted with climbing skins. The Nordic ski is worn with a special boot held by a binding that leaves the heel free (fig. 13-11a). Depending on the design and purpose of the ski, it may be referred to as a cross-country, touring, or telemark ski. Because the heel is not attached, Nordic skiers can use the telemark turn for downhill travel.

Ski mountaineering employs a wider, heavier ski (sometimes called a randonée ski) that is closer to a traditional alpine (downhill) ski (fig. 13-11b). The randonée binding leaves the heel free for uphill travel but can secure the heel for standard alpine downhill

*Fig. 13-11. Ski equipment for mountaineering: a, Nordic skis; b, mountaineering skis, boots, and bindings; c, climbing skins for skis.*

technique. Special randonée boots are designed for use with mountaineering skis, though plastic mountaineering boots can be used as a poor substitute.

Either type of ski will get you into the backcountry. Climbing skins that are fixed to the bottom of the skis provide uphill traction (fig. 13-11c).

If you're accustomed to using only boots or snowshoes for backcountry snow travel, you may find certain disadvantages to skis. During the times that you have to carry them, they're awkward and heavy. Wearing skis complicates self-arrest. Skis are awkward on rocky or forested slopes, skiing can be difficult when you're carrying a heavy pack, and every party member must have similar skiing ability for the group to keep a steady pace (especially for roped glacier travel).

Skis can be faster for basic snow travel, and they can provide mountaineers a way to reach areas that are otherwise not accessible. Skis also offer a safety bonus for crevasse crossings: they distribute your weight over a wider area and may decrease the danger of breaking through. They can also come in handy for rescue work, as they can be converted into a makeshift stretcher or sled.

Backcountry ski travel is a complex activity, with special techniques and equipment. For detailed information, refer to articles and books devoted to the subject.

## Snowshoes

Snowshoes (fig. 13-12) are a traditional aid to snow travel that have been updated into the smaller and lighter designs of today. Modern designs feature tubular metal frames and lightweight, durable decking materials. The bindings are easier to use, are more stable, and include crampon-like toothed metal plates designed to improve traction on hard snow. Many models also include serrated heel plates that decrease side slippage.

Snowshoes permit efficient travel in soft snow, where hikers laboriously posthole. Snowshoes can be

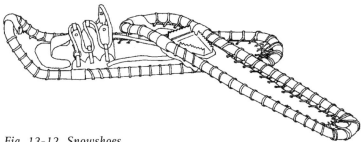

*Fig. 13-12. Snowshoes*

awkward for stepkicking uphill. Although snowshoe travel may be slower than travel on skis, snowshoes can be used in brushy or rocky terrain where skis would be awkward, and they're often more practical than skis when you have a heavy pack. If your climbing party includes some people who aren't very good on skis, it's much less frustrating and more efficient for the group to travel on snowshoes. Snowshoe bindings can be used with a variety of footwear, whereas most ski bindings require specialized boots.

### Shovel

A broad-bladed shovel is a utility and safety tool for snow travel (fig. 13-13). It's the only practical tool for uncovering an avalanche victim. Shovels are also used for digging snow shelters and constructing tent platforms and have even been used as a climbing tool to excavate a pathway up a particularly snowy route. Keep your shovel readily available for emergency use.

A good shovel has a blade large enough to move snow efficiently and a handle long enough for good leverage but short enough for use in a confined area.

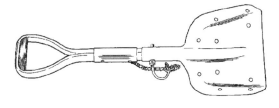

*Fig. 13-13. Snow shovel*

Some shovels feature extendable and/or detachable handles. Another desirable feature is a blade that locks perpendicular to the handle so that the shovel can be used as a trenching tool. A D-shaped grip can make shoveling more comfortable.

For projects such as building snow caves, mountaineers sometimes carry a modified grain scoop, a broad-bladed shovel that can move a lot of snow. In dry, powdery snow, a plastic-bladed shovel provides a good compromise of weight to strength. However, metal-bladed shovels are much stiffer and, therefore, better for chopping hard snow. The edge of a shovel blade (either metal or plastic) can be sharpened with a file.

## TECHNIQUES OF SNOW CLIMBING

### Using the Ice Ax

#### How to Carry an Ice Ax

The first rule is to carry your ice ax carefully. Keep in mind what its sharp points and edges could do to you or your partners. Whenever the ax is not in your hands, be sure it's secure against slipping down a snow slope or cliff.

When you're on the move and don't need the ax, the best bet is to slip it through the ice-ax loop on your pack and strap it down (fig. 13-14a). It's a good idea to keep rubber or leather guards on the pick, adze, and spike, particularly on an ax that's as sharp as it should be. If you're simply carrying the ax in one hand, grasp the shaft at the balance point (shaft parallel to the ground), the spike forward and the pick down (fig. 13-14b).

During travel on snow that alternates with rocks or steep brush where you need both hands free, you can get the ax out of the way by sliding it diagonally between your back and the pack (fig. 13-14c). The spike is down and the pick, between the two shoulder straps, is well seated, clear of your neck and pointing in the same general direction as the angle of the shaft. The

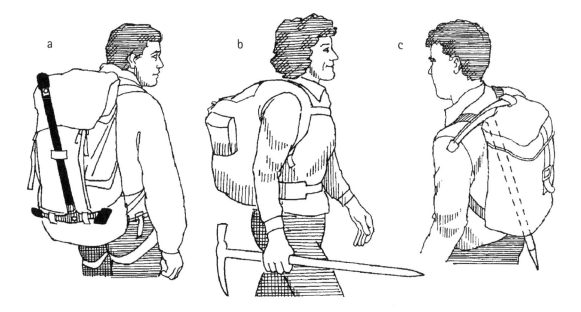

*Fig. 13-14. Carrying an ice ax: a, attached to a pack by an ice-ax loop, with guards on the pick, adze, and spike; b, in the hand while walking; c, temporarily between back and pack.*

ax can be stowed and retrieved quickly, and this works fine for short stretches. Don't forget to retrieve it before taking off the pack or you may lose it.

## How to Grasp an Ice Ax

How you hold the head of the ax when climbing in snow depends on your preference and on the climbing situation. There are two principal ways to grasp the ax.

**Self-arrest grasp:** The thumb goes under the adze and the palm and fingers go over the pick, near the shaft (fig. 13-15a). As you climb, the adze points forward.

**Self-belay grasp:** The palm sits on top of the adze and the thumb and index finger drop under the pick (fig. 13-15b). As you climb, the pick points forward.

Mountaineers differ on which grasp to use, and ultimately it's your decision. The self-arrest grasp puts you in position to use the ax to brake a fall down a steep slope. However, you're not going to fall very often, and in the meantime all the pressure of planting the ax as you climb is concentrated where the narrow

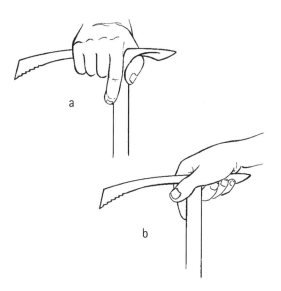

*Fig. 13-15. Grasping an ice ax: a, self-arrest grip; b, self-belay grip.*

top edge of the pick meets your palm. That hurts after a while, and you may not plant the ax as securely as you might otherwise. This compromises the safety of your self-belays.

The self-belay grasp is much more comfortable because the pressure of placing the ax is spread over the wide, flat top of the adze, where your palm now rests. Adequate self-belay should reduce the probability of a fall to almost zero. But if you fall, you'll have to immediately flip to a self-arrest grip. You should practice this move during self-arrest drills.

## How to Self-Belay

The technique of planting the ice-ax shaft to help guard yourself against falls while snow climbing is called self-belay. We'll learn later in this chapter about what to do in the event you or a ropemate start sliding down a steep snow slope. Then self-arrest and other techniques should be applied. But knowing how to avoid the slide in the first place with a self-belay is as important as knowing what to do if it occurs.

Self-belay (fig. 13-16) is a way to lessen the likelihood that a simple slip or misstep on a snow slope will turn into a long fall. It is used to safeguard the ascent or descent of a steep snow slope when the potential for a fall is the highest: when you are moving or when you are in an out-of-balance position. You can create the belay with either a self-belay grasp or a self-arrest grasp on the ax, though you'll probably find more power and ease with the self-belay grasp.

Here's how to do the self-belay: Be sure both feet are secure (in the position of balance described in the next section). Then jam the spike and shaft of the ax into the snow and continue to grip the head of the ax with one hand as you move a step forward with each foot. When both feet are again secure, pull the ax out and replant it farther along (fig. 13-16a). Continue this procedure until you feel it's safe to proceed without it.

Used like this, the ice ax is ready as a safety post as you are moving your feet. To be reliable, the shaft must be placed deep enough, in snow that's firm enough, to hold your full weight. If you slip, keep one hand on the head of the ax as you grab hold of the shaft

*Fig. 13-16. The self-belay: a, climbing; b, falling; c, recovering.*

at the surface of the snow and trust your weight to it (fig. 13-16b). The key to a successful self-belay recovery is the grabbing of the shaft right where it emerges from the snow, so that your pull is against the buried shaft while the hand on the head of the ax minimizes the risk of it levering out.

Practice this technique on a slope of hard snow with a safe run-out to develop the confidence to know when a self-belay will hold while you replant your feet after a slip. If you're on a climb and begin to doubt your self-belays, it's time to make a critical decision: whether to back off, to rope up, or to climb on, recognizing the risk you're taking.

## Ascending Snow

Climbing up and down snow slopes takes a set of special skills. Different techniques come into play depending on how hard or steep the slope is. (The related skills of cramponing and step-cutting are covered in Chapter 15, Ice Climbing.)

## Climbing in Balance

As with rock climbing, staying in balance while moving on snow is less tiring, more efficient, and safer than struggling to keep from falling only by clinging to something—in this case, the ice ax or the snow. Snow climbers move from one balanced position to another, avoiding any prolonged stance in an unbalanced position.

On a diagonal uphill route, the most balanced position is with the inside (uphill) foot in front of and above the trailing outside (downhill) leg, which is fully extended to make use of the skeleton and minimize muscular effort. In that position, let the trailing leg bear most of your weight. Always grip the ice ax with your uphill hand.

The diagonal ascent is a two-step sequence: from a position of balance through an out-of-balance position and back to a position of balance (fig. 13-17). From the in-balance position, place the ax above and ahead into the snow. Move up two steps before repositioning the ice ax. The first step brings the outside (downhill) foot in front of the inside (uphill foot), putting the climber out of balance. The second step brings

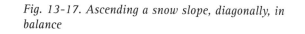

*Fig. 13-17. Ascending a snow slope, diagonally, in balance*

the inside foot up from behind and places it beyond the outside foot, putting the climber back in the balance position. Keep your weight over your feet and avoid leaning into the slope.

If you're heading straight up the fall line instead of moving diagonally, there's no longer an uphill or downhill leg or an uphill or downhill hand. So carry the ax in the hand that feels most comfortable and climb in a steady, controlled manner. Regardless of the direction of travel, placing the ax firmly before each move will provide self-belay protection.

## The Rest Step

Climbing a long featureless snow slope can give you the frustrating sensation that you're getting nowhere. Few landmarks help measure your progress, so distances are deceiving. Novice climbers try a dash-and-gasp pace in an attempt to rush the objective. But the only way to the top of the slope is to find a pace you can maintain—and then maintain it.

The solution is the rest step, a technique that conserves energy as it moves you methodically forward. (The rest step is illustrated in Chapter 5, Wilderness Travel.) Use the rest step whenever legs or lungs need a bit of recuperation between steps. At lower elevations, it's usually the leg muscles that require a break. At higher elevations, the lungs need the pause.

Here's a review of the rest step: the rest takes place after one foot is swung forward for the next step. Support all body weight on the rear leg while the unweighted forward leg muscles relax. During each rest phase, the weighted rear leg must be straight (locked at the knee) so that the bony structure, not muscle, carries the load. The climbing pace is slow, because for every step there is a pause. Synchronize breathing with the sequence. At higher elevations, make a conscious effort to breathe forcefully and deeply.

## Stepkicking

The technique of stepkicking is basic to snow climbing. It's a way to create a path of upward steps that provide the best possible footing with the least expenditure of energy. It is all that's needed for footing when the snow is yielding enough to permit security without the help of crampons or chopped steps.

The most efficient kick to create snow steps is a swing of the leg that lets its own weight and momentum provide the needed impact, with little muscular effort. This works fine in soft snow. On harder snow, you'll end up putting in more effort, and the steps will usually be smaller and less secure.

The definition of a secure step varies with the climber's skill and strength and with the effects of such factors as wind, altitude, and the weight of the pack. An average climber probably needs steps deep enough to take the ball of the foot when going straight up and at least half of the boot on a diagonal ascent. Steps that are kicked level or tilted slightly into the slope are more secure. The less space there is on a step, the more important it is that the step slope inward.

When you're kicking steps, keep the other climbers in mind. They can follow up your staircase in good balance if your steps are spaced evenly and somewhat close together. Make allowance for climbers whose legs aren't as long as yours.

Followers use the same leg swing as the leader, improving the steps as they climb. The follower must kick into the step, because simply walking onto the existing platform will not set the boot securely in position. In compact snow the kick should be somewhat low, the toe driving in and deepening the step. However, in very soft snow it is usually easier to bring the boot down from above, shearing off an edge of snow, which helps build a stronger step.

A basic principle of snow travel is that parties move in single file when ascending. If you're in the lead, you will be doing by far the hardest work. You also have to think harder in order to avoid potential hazards to the group and to choose the best route. Take turns leading so that no climber is worked to exhaustion. To switch, the leader should step aside and then fall in at the end of the line.

## Direction of Ascent

You can either go directly up a snow slope or ascend it diagonally. If you're in a hurry, a direct ascent is usually the way to go. Speed is a primary consideration on a long snow climb, and a fast, direct ascent is the order of the day if you face bad weather, avalanche or rockfall danger, poor bivouac conditions, or a difficult descent.

When time permits, most climbers prefer a diagonal ascent, switchbacking up moderately angled slopes.

They reason that the lower angle of ascent requires less energy for each step while it ends up gaining the same elevation as the fewer but steeper steps of a direct ascent. The strength of this argument probably depends on snow conditions. In good stepkicking snow, the energy you save at each step on a diagonal ascent can be used to kick the additional steps required by that angle. But in marginal conditions, many climbers figure that a diagonal route is more difficult because of the work of kicking edged, traversing steps in hard snow.

### Ice-Ax Technique: Direct Ascent

In a straight shot up a snowfield, stepkicking is the basic technique for your feet. Ice-ax technique, however, will vary depending on snow conditions and steepness.

**Cane position:** On a slope that is at a low or moderate angle (roughly up to 30 or 35 degrees), climb with the ax in the cane position, holding it in one hand by

*Fig. 13-19. Direct ascent, with ice ax in stake position*

the head and using it for balance (fig. 13-18). You can continue in the cane position as the snow gets even steeper, as long as you feel secure with it. Setting the ax firmly before each move will provide a self-belay.

**Stake position:** At some point as the snow steepens, a climber may choose to switch to the two-handed stake position, a more secure stance often used for angles over 45 degrees (fig. 13-19). Before moving upward, plant the ax, with both hands, as far as it will go into the snow. Then continue to grasp it with both hands on the head or with one hand on the head and one on the shaft. This position is particularly useful on steeper soft snow.

**Horizontal position:** This is a technique effective on steeper, harder snow that is covered with a soft layer. Hold the ax with both hands, one in the self-arrest grasp on the head and the other near the end of the shaft. Jab the ax horizontally into the snow above you, the pick down and the shaft at right angles to your

*Fig. 13-18. Direct ascent, with ice ax in cane position*

body (fig. 13-20). This jabs the pick into the harder base while the shaft gets some purchase in the softer surface snow. (Don't forget to take advantage of the rest step as you head up the hill, regardless of the ice-ax technique being used.)

### Ice-Ax Technique: Diagonal Ascent

On a diagonal route, remember to climb in balance as you kick steps up the slope. (Figure 13-17 shows the sequence of moves in a diagonal ascent.) For slopes angled less than about 40 or 45 degrees, the ax usually works fine in the cane position. As the slope steepens, the cane position becomes awkward and it's time to switch to the cross-body position.

**Cross-body position:** Hold the ax perpendicular to the angle of the slope, one hand grasping the head and the other holding the shaft, which is jabbed into the snow (fig. 13-21). The ax will cross diagonally in front of you. (Be sure the pick does not point toward your body.) Most of the weight placed on the ax should bear on the shaft, while the hand on the head merely stabilizes the ax. Move your feet upward in the same manner as with the cane position.

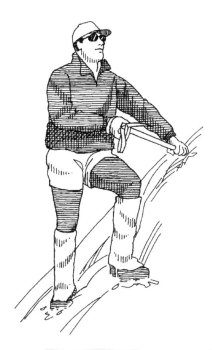

*Fig. 13-21. Diagonal ascent, with ice ax in cross-body position*

*Fig. 13-20. Direct ascent, with ice ax in horizontal position*

Diagonal ascents often mean switchbacks, which mean changes in direction. There's a specific sequence of steps for a safe change in direction on a diagonal route, whether you have the ax in the cane position or the cross-body position (fig. 13-22).

Start from a position of balance, the inside (uphill) foot in front of and above the outside (downhill) foot. Jab the ax shaft straight down into the snow at a spot as directly above your location as possible. Grasp the head of the ax with both hands as you move your outside foot forward, bringing you into the out-of-balance position. Continue holding onto the head with both hands as you move into a stance facing uphill, moving your inside foot toward the new direction of travel and ending with splayed feet. (If your splayed feet feel unstable on a steep slope, kick steps more directly into the slope.) Finally, a turn in the new direction of travel returns you to a position of balance, with the new uphill foot now in front and above. With the cane position, the new uphill hand now grasps the ax

*Fig. 13-22. Changing direction on a diagonal ascent: a, jab ax shaft straight down; b, face uphill with feet splayed; c, turn in new direction of travel.*

head. With the cross-body position, the hands holding the head and the shaft are now reversed.

## Traversing

Long horizontal traverses, which neither gain nor lose elevation, are rarely any fun. This "sidehill gouging" works okay on soft snow at low and moderate angles, though it's still not as comfortable or efficient as a diagonal route. On horizontal traverses over harder or steeper snow, you can face into the slope and kick straight forward for more secure steps. But try to avoid horizontal traverses in the first place.

## Descending Snow

One mark of a skillful snow climber is the ability to go downhill efficiently and confidently. Many otherwise competent and aggressive climbers blanch at the prospect of going forward down a steep snow gully. Why? Because there's a superb view of the exposure. And because on steep snow the ax must be placed very low to move down, leaving the climber without the comforting stance and handhold that was there on the way up. You can minimize those downhill jitters by mastering a few descent techniques.

## Plunge-Stepping

When going down, just like going up, technique is determined mainly by the hardness and angle of the snow. In soft snow on a moderate slope, simply face outward and walk down. With harder snow or a steeper angle, use the plunge step (fig. 13-23).

The plunge step is a confident, aggressive move. Face outward, step assertively away from the slope, and land solidly on your heel with your leg vertical, transferring weight solidly to the new position. No timid steps allowed. Avoid leaning back into the slope, which could result in a glancing blow, less secure steps, and perhaps an unplanned glissade. Plunge-stepping can be secure with steps that hold only the heel of the boot, but most climbers do not trust steps more shallow than that.

When plunge-stepping, keep the knees bent a bit, not locked, to maintain control of balance. The degree of bending depends on the angle of the slope (the steeper the slope, the greater the bend) and the firmness of the surface (the harder the snow, the greater the bend). With bent knees, a forward lean is also needed to help with balance. An aggressive stride creates a deep step, so be careful in very soft snow that a

plunging leg isn't injured by being buried so deep it can't be yanked back out as you take the next step.

The plunge-stepping climber holds the ice ax in one hand in either the self-arrest or self-belay grasp, with the spike close to the surface, well forward and ready to plant in the snow. You can spread and move the other arm for balance. Some climbers hold the ax in both hands in the full self-arrest position—one hand on the head, the other near the end of the shaft—but this allows less movement of the arms to maintain balance.

At some point, on harder or steeper snow, this style of plunge-stepping will not feel secure. Then it's necessary to plant the ax as low as possible in a self-belay before each move and advance the feet in a sort of crouched, modified plunge step (fig. 13-24).

*Fig. 13-23. Plunge-stepping, on moderate slope*

*Fig. 13-24. Plunge-stepping with self-belay*

## Glissading

Glissading is one of the joyous bonuses of mountain climbing, offering the fastest, easiest, and most exhilarating way down many snow slopes for a climber on foot. It's an alternative to walking or plunge-stepping, for use on slopes where you can keep your speed under control. There are three principal methods of glissading. Which one you use will depend on how hard and steep the slope is, how safe the run-out is at the bottom of the hill, and how good you are at glissading.

Before glissading, decide whether to use your ice ax leash. If you choose to wear the leash, you risk injury from a flailing ax in the event it's knocked loose from your hands. If you choose not to use the leash, you risk losing your ax. Whether you use the leash or not, the essential thing is to maintain control of your ice ax.

**The sitting glissade** (fig. 13-25a) is the easiest to learn and works on soft snow where you would bog down if you tried a standing glissade. Remove crampons before glissading; crampon points can catch in the snow and send you tumbling. You'll get the slickest and driest ride by wearing coated nylon rain pants. For the sitting glissade, simply sit in the snow and slide, holding the ax in self-arrest position as you go downhill. The standard posture is to sit fairly erect, knees bent and boot soles planing along the surface. However, to get started and maintain momentum in snow that is quite soft, it helps to stretch out your legs, spreading body weight over a greater area.

Run the spike of the ax, like a rudder, along the snow on one side of you. Keep both hands on the ax. Maintain control! Putting pressure on the spike helps reduce speed and thwarts any tendency of your body to pivot head-downward. The standard posture, with knees bent and feet flat, also reduces speed. This posture is the most helpful in uncomfortable conditions: when the snow is crusted or firmly consolidated, pitted with icy ruts or small sun cups, or dotted with rocks or shrubs. It provides more stability and control than with your legs straight out in front, and it helps minimize wear and tear on your bottom.

To stop, use the spike to slow down, then dig in your heels—but not at high speed or a somersault may be the result. For an emergency stop, simply self-arrest by rolling into position toward the side opposite the

*Fig. 13-25. Glissades: a, sitting; b, standing; c, crouching.*

spike. (Self-arrest technique is discussed in the next section of this chapter.)

Turns are almost impossible in a sitting glissade. The spike, dragged as a rudder and assisted by body contortions, can exert a change in direction of a few degrees at most. The best way to get around an obstruction is to stop, walk sideways to a point that is not directly above the obstacle, and take off again.

**The standing glissade** (fig. 13-25b) is the best one, if you know how to do it and conditions are right. This position offers the earliest look at hazards of the route, is the most maneuverable, and saves your clothes from wetness and abrasion. The standing glissade is most effective on a firm base with a softer layer on top. The softer the snow, the steeper the slope needed to maintain speed. You can do a standing glissade down slopes of harder snow, but these will usually be at lower angles and with a safe run-out. Slopes at very low angles can be skated, if the snow is firm.

Correct standing glissade technique is very similar to downhill skiing. The position is a semicrouch over the feet with bent knees and outspread arms. The feet can be together or spread, as needed for stability, with one foot advanced slightly to further improve stability and prevent nosedives. Increase speed by bringing the feet closer together and leaning farther forward over the feet. Slow down and stop any number of ways: stand up and dig in the heels; turn the feet sideways and edge; crouch and drag the ice-ax spike as in the crouching glissade (described next), or perform a turn similar to skiing in which you rotate the shoulders, upper body, and knees in the direction of the turn and roll the knees and ankles in the same direction to rock the feet onto boot edges.

Transition areas, where the snow texture changes, are tricky. If you hit softer, slower snow, your head and torso will suddenly be outpacing your legs, so move one boot forward for stability. If you hit harder, faster snow or ice below the surface, lean well forward to prevent a slip. Keep speed under control by regular braking and traversing.

**The crouching glissade** (fig. 13-25c) is done much like the standing glissade, except the climber holds the ax in the self-arrest position to one side of the body, sits back, and drags the spike in the snow. It's slower than a standing glissade and easier to learn. With three points of contact, it is also more stable. However, turning is more difficult, as is controlling speed with edging.

As in much of mountaineering, efficiency in glissading takes a smooth blend of several techniques. In particular, climbers who lack finesse in the standing glissade often use a combination: breaking into a plunge step to control speed, stepping off in a new direction rather than making a ski-style turn, and skating to maintain momentum as the slope angle lessens.

Glissading can be hazardous. Don't glissade in crevassed terrain. Glissade only when there is a safe run-out, close enough that if you slide out of control you won't be injured before reaching it. Unless there is a view of the entire run, the first person down must use extreme caution and stop frequently to look ahead. The biggest risk is losing control at such high speed that self-arrest is not possible. This is most likely to happen on the best glissading slope, one with firm snow. Maintain control of speed and of your ice ax.

Adjust equipment before beginning the descent, and stow crampons and other hardware in the pack. Wear mittens, even on a warm day; snow is so cold and abrasive it can chill and flay the hands until they lose control of the ax.

Sometimes in soft snow, a glissader accidentally sets off a mass of surface snow, which slides down the slope with the glissader aboard. These are really small avalanches, known as avalanche cushions. The trick is to decide whether it's a cushion safe to ride or it's about to become a serious avalanche. If the moving snow is more than a few inches deep, self-arrest won't work because the ice-ax pick can't penetrate to the layer below. Sometimes the spike can be driven deep enough to slow, though probably not to stop, the glissader. Unless you're sure the cushion is safe and your speed is under control, get off. Roll sideways out of the path of the moving snow and then self-arrest.

## Downclimbing

On steep snow where you may not feel secure glissading or plunge-stepping, you can face into the slope and climb down backward, kicking steps straight into the slope. Use the ax in the stake position as a self-belay.

## Self-Arrest

True to most aspects of safe climbing, the first priority of snow travel is to learn the fundamental skills that will prevent a slip or fall from occurring in the first place. But in the event of a slip on snow, you must know how to regain control as quickly as possible. Self-belay is the primary skill to prevent a slip in snow from becoming an uncontrolled slide; self-arrest is the primary recovery measure from a slide.

Some climbers learn self-arrest as the primary technique for security on snow and deemphasize the use of self-belay. But the purposes of the two techniques are different, and climbers need them both. Where the ax can be planted securely, self-belay is usually sufficient to stop a fall immediately. But if self-belay fails and you begin an uncontrolled high-speed slide down the snow slope, you've got to quickly go into self-arrest.

When the consequences of a fall can be serious injury or death, climbers must use sound judgment before entrusting their safety solely to the use of self-arrest. Here are some safety considerations to keep in mind:

- Don't fall. Stay in balance using proper snow-travel techniques, including the rest step and stepkicking with coordinated ax placements, as described earlier in this chapter. Practice these techniques and develop confidence in different snow conditions.
- Always be aware of the run-out. Are there cliffs at the bottom of the slope or short run-outs that end in rocks? If you cannot tell, assume the worst.
- If there is dangerous run-out, do not rely on self-arrest. If you are not completely comfortable with your safety as you ascend using the self-belay, arrange for an anchored belay or turn back and find another route. Carry and use appropriate gear for protection on snow climbs, such as pickets and flukes.
- Be aware of the snow conditions and steepness of the slope. If snow is turning hard or icy, use crampons and chop steps if necessary. Always consider whether protection is needed; the likelihood of an effective self-arrest in hard, steep snow is not good.
- Be alert to the party's overall condition and climbing ability. If it's late in the day, the effects of exhaustion may greatly diminish a climber's reaction time in the event of a fall.
- If you have to stop to adjust equipment such as crampons on an exposed slope, create a secure anchor first by planting your ice ax firmly in the snow and tying in.
- Wear gloves when crossing a steep slope. In the event of a fall, gloves prevent abrasion and improve your chances of holding onto your ice ax to successfully execute self-arrest.
- Use extra caution when carrying an overnight pack. Heavy packs can contribute to loss of balance and to falls that are very difficult to stop.

- If self-arrest is required, be very aggressive and act fast before you have accelerated to an unstoppable speed. Good form may be aesthetically satisfying, but fast is better than pretty when instantaneous action is critical.

Self-arrest technique also serves to brace you solidly in the snow if you have to hold the fall of a ropemate. An important use of this technique for roped teams is on glacier travel, where self-arrest is used to stop the rest of the team from sliding into a crevasse (as discussed in Chapter 14, Glacier Travel and Crevasse Rescue).

Because a climber's own life and the lives of fellow climbers could hinge on self-arrest skills, every climber must be proficient in the technique. Learn self-arrest by practicing on increasingly steeper slopes and hard snow above a safe run-out. During practice, leave the ice ax leash off your wrist so that there's less chance of the ax striking you in case you lose control of it. Also during practice, cover or pad the adze and spike to minimize chances of injury.

Strength obviously helps in self-arrest, but knowing the correct methods is more important than simple muscle power. An important consideration is the grasp you've chosen for holding the ax, that is, whether you are using the self-belay grasp or the self-arrest grasp (refer to Figure 13-15). If you are using the self-belay grasp and slip into a fall, you must be able to instantly flip the ice ax to a self-arrest grasp. To do this, grab the shaft of the ax just above the spike and then change the hand to the self-arrest grasp and arrest. This takes practice. If you don't have the skill or confidence to do it, then it will be safer to do your self-belays holding the ax head in the self-arrest grasp. Some climbers simply prefer to use the self-arrest grasp.

### The Completed Self-Arrest

The goal of self-arrest is to stop safely, ending up in a secure and stable position on the snow. The last panel of Figure 13-26 illustrates what you should look like as you complete a successful self-arrest, lying face down in the snow with the ice ax beneath you.

- The hands hold the ax in a solid grip, one hand in the self-arrest grasp with the thumb under the adze and fingers over the pick and the other hand on the shaft just above the spike.

- The pick is pressed into the snow just above your shoulder so that the adze is near the angle formed by the neck and shoulder. This is crucial. Sufficient force cannot be exerted on the pick if the adze is not in the proper position.
- The shaft crosses your chest diagonally and is held close to the opposite hip. Gripping the shaft near the end prevents that hand from acting as a pivot around which the spike can swing to jab the thigh. (A short ax is held the same way, although the spike will not reach the opposite hip.)
- The chest and shoulder are pressed strongly down on the ice-ax shaft. It is your body weight falling and pressing on the ax, rather than just arm strength driving the ax into the snow, that results in successful self-arrest.
- The head is face down, not looking up the slope, so that the brim of the helmet or hat is in contact with the slope. This head positioning prevents the shoulders and chest from lifting up and keeps the weight over the adze.
- The spine is arched slightly away from the snow. This arch is critical because it places the bulk of your weight on the ax head and on your toes or knees, which are the points that dig into the snow to force a stop. Also pull up on the end of the shaft, which starts the arch and rolls weight toward the shoulder by the ax head. (*Note:* the arch can be carried to excess by those unwilling to get their chest and face down into the snow.)
- The knees are against the surface, helping slow the fall in soft snow. On harder surfaces, where they have little stopping power, they help stabilize your body position.
- The legs are stiff and spread apart, toes digging in. But if you have crampons on, keep them above the snow until you've nearly come to a halt. A crampon point could catch on hard snow or ice and flip you over backward.

## Self-Arrest from Different Positions

The position you find yourself thrown into when you fall determines how you self-arrest. You'll likely be sliding in one of four positions: head uphill or head downhill and, in either case, face down or on your back.

The immediate goal is to get your body into the only

CORRECT

*Fig. 13-26. Correct self-arrest technique, head uphill, on your back*

effective self-arrest position: with your head uphill and your face down. And the first move toward that goal is to grasp the ax in both hands, one hand on the ax head in the self-arrest grasp and the other at the base of the shaft. From that point, here is how to handle each of the four situations.

**Head uphill, face down:** You're already in the desired self-arrest position. All you have to do is get your body over the ax shaft, ending in the secure final position described in the previous section, on the completed self-arrest.

**Head uphill, on your back:** This isn't much more difficult than the first version. Roll toward the head of the ax and aggressively plant the pick into the snow at your side as you roll over onto your stomach (fig. 13-26). If the ax head is on the right, roll to the right. If it's on the left, roll to the left. Beware of rolling the other way, toward the spike, which could jam the spike in the snow before the pick and wrench the ax from your hands (fig. 13-27).

**Head downhill, face down:** Self-arrest from headfirst falls is more difficult because the feet have to first be swung downhill. In this face-down predicament, reach downhill and off to the ax-head side and get the pick into the snow to serve as a pivot to swing the body around (fig. 13-28). Work to help swing the legs around so they are pointing downhill. Never jab the spike into the snow and pivot on that end of the ax. That would bring the pick and adze of the ax across your slide path and on a collision course with your chest and face.

**Head downhill, on your back:** Hold the ax across your torso and aggressively jab the pick into the snow; then twist and roll toward it (fig. 13-29). Once again, the pick placed to the side serves as a pivot point. But merely planting the pick won't bring you around to the final self-arrest position. You must work at rolling your chest toward the ax head at the same time as you work your legs to swing around and point downhill. A sitting-up motion helps the roll.

**Variations:** In the loose snow of winter and early spring, the pick may not be able to reach compact snow, making the usual self-arrest useless. The best brakes in this case are feet and knees and elbows, widely spaced and deeply pressed into the snow. The greatest drag potential of the ax then lies not in the

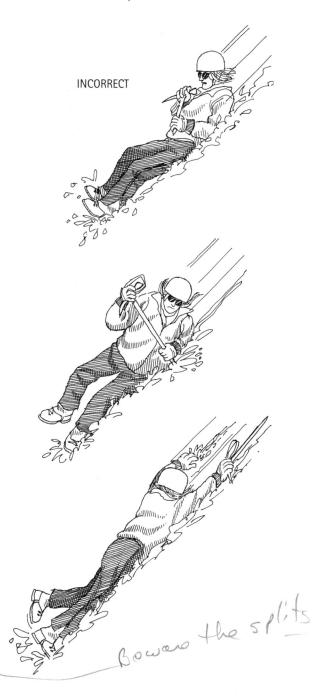

INCORRECT

*Fig. 13-27. Incorrect self-arrest technique; do not roll toward spike.*

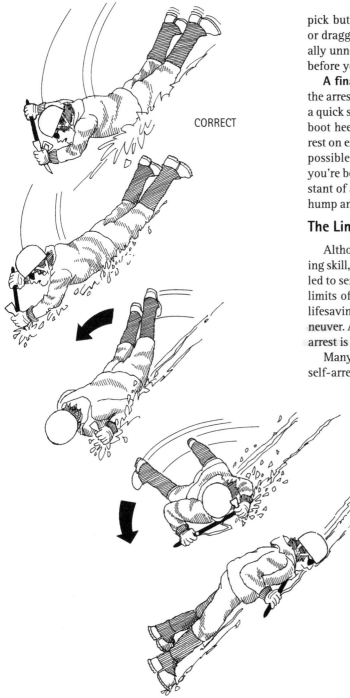

CORRECT

*Fig. 13-28. Self-arrest technique, head downhill, face down*

pick but in the shaft, thrust vertically into the slope or dragged in the self-arrest position. Pivoting is usually unnecessary on a headfirst fall because you stop before you can get turned around.

**A final reminder:** Act fast! How fast you get into the arrest position is the key to success. On hard snow, a quick stab at the slope with the pick or spike, or even boot heels, may stop a fall before it gets started. Arrest on extremely hard snow is very difficult if not impossible, but always give it an intense try, even if you're belayed on a rope. Occasionally, in the first instant of a fall, the pick lodges in a crevice or behind a hump and stops the action even on a very steep slope.

## The Limits of Self-Arrest

Although self-arrest is an important snow climbing skill, it is often a misunderstood technique that has led to serious accidents. It is critical to understand the limits of self-arrest and to not regard it as a reliable lifesaving technique but, rather, as a last-resort maneuver. A 50 percent success rate in executing the self-arrest is probably realistic.

Many climbers have a false sense of security in their self-arrest skills. Self-arrest is meant to stop a fall by friction of ax and body against snow. But when the slope is too steep or slippery, even the most skillful technique won't stop the slide. Acceleration, even on a relatively modest snow slope, can be so rapid on hard snow that the first instant of fall is the whole story. The climber rockets into the air and crashes back to the unyielding surface with stunning impact, completely losing uphill–downhill orientation. If you do not stop your fall in the first few seconds, the chances of stopping by self-arrest at all are poor.

Even successful arrests require at least a little time, during which the climber slides some distance. Therefore, the effectiveness of the self-arrest is limited by the climber's speed of reaction and the steepness and length of the slope. If all initial efforts at self-arrest are unsuccessful, don't give up. Keep fighting. Self-arrest

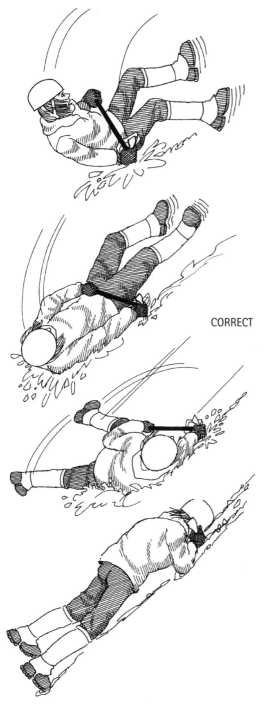

might work in softer snow or at a lower angle farther down the slope. Even if you don't stop, the attempt may slow you down and help prevent rolling, tumbling, and bouncing. It may also help keep you sliding feet first, the best position if you end up hitting rocks or trees. And if you are roped to other climbers, anything you can do to slow your fall increases the chance that their self-arrests or belays will hold.

If you lose your ax in a fall, use your hands, elbows, knees, and boots to dig into the snow slope, using positioning similar to what you would use if you still had the ax. It may help to clasp your hands together against the slope so that you accumulate snow in them and create more friction. On harder snow, you can try to push out from the slope with your arms, placing your weight on your toes to create friction (fig. 13-30).

Keep alert at all times to the limits of self-arrest. If

CORRECT

*Fig. 13-29. Self-arrest technique, head downhill, on your back*

*Fig 13-30. If you fall on fairly hard snow and lose your ax, try to push out from the slope and put weight on your toes.*

a slope seems too fast or too short, or members of a climbing party doubt their strength or skill, use one of the techniques of roped protection outlined later in this chapter.

# ROPED CLIMBING TECHNIQUES

When is it time to rope up on a snow climb? On a glacier, the risk of unroped climbers falling into a crevasse clearly exceeds the risks involved in roping up, so teams rope up. On a nonglaciated snow climb, the decision is not so clear-cut, and the climbers have to weigh several options. They can continue unroped, relying on each individual to stop a personal fall, or they may decide to travel roped together but unbelayed in order to offer some security for a weaker climber or in anticipation of needing the rope at a later point where no convenient rope-up place exists. They may also decide to travel roped together and to use belays because difficult route conditions or climber concerns dictate this level of safety. Any decision to place protection is a judgment based on many factors, including snow conditions, individual and party skill and experience, and the need for rapid progress.

The team risks of roping up are not trivial. They include the danger of one person's fall pulling the entire rope team off the mountain, increased risk of avalanche and rockfall exposure, and the possibility of an unplanned bivouac due to the slower pace of roped travel. It often becomes a delicate decision involving an evaluation of each climber's skill and the variety of alternatives for roped team protection.

## Options for Roped Team Protection

If your party decides it would be safer overall to rope up, there are several different ways to match the type of rope protection to the conditions of the climb and the strengths of the climbers.

### Team Arrest (Roped but Unbelayed)

Team arrest depends on each climber to stop a personal fall and on the rest of the rope team to provide backup in case the attempt fails. Everyone involved uses self-belay or self-arrest. Relying on team arrest as the ultimate team security makes sense only in selected situations, such as on a low- or moderate-angle glacier or on a moderate snow slope where a less skilled climber could be saved from a dangerous slide by the more proficient members of the rope team. On steeper, harder slopes you face that appraisal of risks, trying to decide which is safer: continuing to rely on team arrest, or unroping and letting each climber go it alone, or switching to a more secure mode of roped travel.

You may be able to increase the odds that team arrest will work on a snow slope by trying the following procedures:

- Carry a few feet of rope coiled in your hand if there are any climbers below you. If a climber falls, drop the loose rope and it will give you an extra instant to get the ax into self-belay position and to brace yourself.
- Put the weakest climber on the downhill end of the rope. As a rule, the least skilled climber should be last on the rope while ascending and first on the rope while descending. This puts the climber most likely to fall in a position where a fall will be of the least serious kind: below the other climbers and being quickly felt along the rope. Unfortunately, it also means the weakest climber will be the team's last hope if the climbers above fall.
- Climb on a shortened rope (fig. 13-31). This technique is most applicable to a two-person rope team. If a climbing pair uses only a portion of the rope, say 60 to 75 feet instead of the full length, they will reduce the sliding distance and the tug from the fall if one partner falls while above the other. To shorten the rope, wind as many coils as necessary until the desired length remains. Then tie an overhand knot through the coils with a loop of the climbing rope, and clip the loop into your harness with a locking carabiner. You can carry the coils over one shoulder and under the opposite arm. If more than two climbers are on the rope, the middle climber or climbers should take coils in the direction of the leader. (See the section on two-person teams on glaciers, in "Special Rescue Situations," in Chapter 14, Glacier Travel and Crevasse Rescue, for a description and illustration of a similar

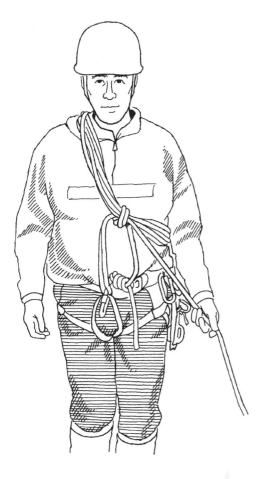

*Fig. 13-31. Climbing on a shortened rope*

technique, called the adapted Kiwi coil.) Climbing on a shortened rope can also be useful in rock climbing for moving on nontechnical scrambling terrain and in places where a longer rope might increase the danger of knocking rocks loose.

• Climb in separate parallel tracks. This is also most applicable to a two-person rope team. The climbers will be abreast of each other, separated by the rope. A falling climber will pendulum down, putting force on the rope to the side of and below the partner. The tug on the rope will be less than if the climber fell from high above. Also, the friction of the rope as it pendulums across the snow will absorb

some of the force. Traveling in separate tracks may be impractical on ascents where kicking two sets of steps would be a waste of time and energy. However, it might be used on ascents of harder snow and should be considered for any descent.

The proper techniques of handling the rope contribute to safe and efficient snow travel for a rope team. Keep the rope on the downhill side of the team so there's less chance of stepping on it. Hold the rope in your downhill hand, in a short loop. You can then take more rope into the loop or let the rope out, as a means of adjusting to the pace of the person ahead of you or the person behind, rather than getting into a tug-of-war with your fellow climbers.

Be attentive to when the rope goes taut between you and a ropemate. It's important to know whether the taut rope is being caused by your fellow climber or by the rope being hung up on the snow. Remain alert to that climber's pace and position, being especially sensitive to times that your ropemate may be in a delicate situation, such as moving on an icy slope, when any additional tug on the rope could yank him off his feet.

## Running Belays

Roped climbers can move together on snow with the help of running belays. This technique saves time over regular belayed climbing but still allows for protection to be placed to reduce the risk of a catastrophic fall. (Running belays are also useful in rock climbing, ice climbing, and alpine climbing and are discussed in the relevant sections of Chapters 11, 15, and 16.)

The running belay (fig. 13-32) offers a middle level of protection, somewhere between team arrest and fixed belays. It can help in situations where a successful team arrest is improbable but where fixed belays aren't practical because they would take too much time. For example, running protection may do the job on long snow faces and couloirs.

To place running belays, the leader puts in pieces of snow protection as needed and uses a carabiner to clip the rope into each one. (Types of snow protection are discussed in the next section of this chapter, on snow anchors.) The climbers continue to make good progress because all members of the rope team climb at the same time, just as in unbelayed travel, except that now there's protection in the snow that, if securely placed, will be likely to stop a fall. Traveling this way, the last climber on the rope removes each piece. Of course the use of running protection means the team must pack the extra weight of the gear and must take the time to place it.

## Fixed Belays

The ultimate in safety comes from having climbers belay each other up snow pitches, in the same manner as in rock climbing. The catch is that this procedure may be so time-consuming it becomes impractical on the snow faces of major alpine routes. However, there is a wide variety of snow belays, varying in security and in the amount of time they take to set up. They are described later in this chapter.

## Combination Protection Techniques

The reality of most serious snow climbs is that success calls for a combination of protection techniques. It's not likely a party will take on an entire climb

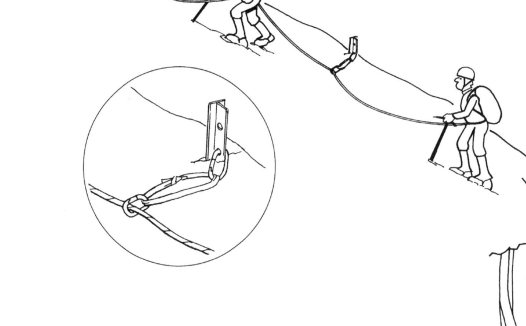

*Fig. 13-32. A running belay setup*

unroped. It's just as unlikely that the party will use fixed belays all the way.

In deciding when to rope up, a climbing team is actually asking itself a series of questions. The team always ropes up on glaciers, but on snow or mixed terrain the team asks the following:

1. Is each member of the party able to use self-belay or self-arrest to save himself or herself in case of a fall? If the answer is yes, the party can continue unroped. If the answer is no, the team asks question 2.
2. Can we stop all falls by roping up and depending on team arrest? If so, rope up and continue climbing, unbelayed. If not, then ask question 3.
3. Is it feasible to use some form of belay (a running belay or a fixed belay), and will this belay provide adequate protection? If so, begin belaying. If it's not feasible, because of poor terrain or lack of time, then the party must ask itself question 4.
4. Shall we turn around, or shall we proceed unroped and assume the risks?

Long snow routes often demand fast travel to reach the summit. Therefore, these routes are often climbed with a combination of roped and unroped travel and mostly unbelayed. Belays of some kind are typically used on steeper, harder snow or when climbers are tired or hurt. Most of the reliance is on team arrest or running protection, though some sections may lend themselves to unroped travel. The option of turning around is always worth considering. If things aren't going well, select a new route, another destination, or just head home.

## Snow Anchors

Anchors are needed in snow for the same reasons they are needed on rock. The equipment is different but the purposes are the same: to anchor belays and rappels and to provide intermediate points of protection. But rock anchors are usually easy to inspect and predictable in performance—snow anchors are not. They vary widely in strength depending on snow conditions and placement, and their strength changes during the day with changes in the snow. The medium of snow is more variable than rock and requires placement of different types of anchors depending on conditions. This uncertainty makes it even more imperative

than on rock to check and recheck any belay or rappel anchor. Snow anchors can also require a lot of time to put in place. They include deadman anchors (such as snow flukes), pickets, and bollards.

**A deadman anchor** is any object you bury in the snow as a point of attachment for the rope. The most common is the snow fluke, a specially shaped aluminum plate with a metal cable attached (fig. 13-33a). Snow flukes are available in various sizes, their holding ability generally increasing with size. For maximum strength and reliability, a buried fluke should be angled back about 40 degrees from the direction of pull (fig. 13-33b). Dig a slot in the snow to permit the cable to be pulled in as direct a line as possible.

In theory, the fluke serves as a dynamic anchor, burrowing deeper into the snow when it takes a load, such as the weight of a climber on rappel. In practice, it may behave in more complicated ways, even coming out if it is tipped too far forward or backward or if the load is to the side rather than straight out. If the plate or the cable travels down into the snow and hits a harder layer, the fluke could be deflected and pull out. Flukes are available with bent faces, flanged sides, or fixed cables—features intended to make them maintain the correct orientation and to make them self-correct if deflected.

Flukes are most reliable but also more difficult to place in the hard homogeneous snow of summer. They are generally used in a softer but dense pack, snow that is moist and heavy. They are least reliable under typical winter conditions, with snow layers of varying density where they may deflect off harder layers. Neither do they do well in dry, unconsolidated snow.

Ice axes, ice tools, and snow pickets can serve as deadman anchors (fig. 13-34a). Bury the implement horizontally in the snow, with a runner attached at the midpoint. Cut a slot in the snow to let the runner lie in the direction of pull, and then clip into the runner. In a variation of the buried-ax anchor, a second ax is placed vertically behind the horizontal ax (fig. 13-34b). In this variation, called the T-ax anchor, the runner is clove-hitched to the vertical ax and run over the horizontal ax.

**A picket** is a stake driven into the snow as an anchor (fig. 13-35). Aluminum pickets are available in lengths from 18 to 36 inches and are found in different

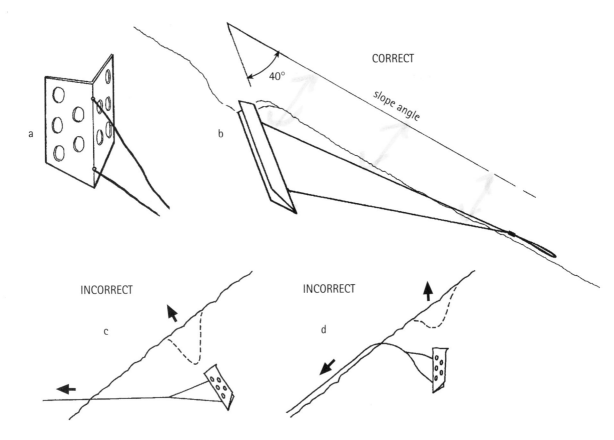

*Fig. 13-33. Placing snow flukes: a, typical snow fluke; b, correct angle for fluke placement; c, incorrect, not angled back sufficiently; d, incorrect, no slot for cable.*

styles, including round or oval tubes and angled or T-section stakes.

Pickets work well in snow too firm for flukes but too soft for ice screws. As with flukes, angle them back about 40 degrees from the direction of pull. Attach a carabiner or runner to the picket at the snowline—not higher on the picket, or a pull may lever it out. You can drive a picket into the snow with a rock or the side of an ice ax, but a North Wall hammer or other ice hammer works best and reduces the chance of equipment damage. An ice ax or ice tool can serve as a makeshift picket.

**A bollard** is a mound of snow that serves as an anchor when rope or webbing is positioned around it (fig. 13-36). Snow bollards provide highly reliable anchors for belaying or rappelling in hard snow and are possibly the most reliable in all snow conditions. There is a significant trade-off, however. It takes a long time to build one.

Create the mound by making a horseshoe-shaped trench in the snow, the open end of the horseshoe pointing downhill. In hard snow, chop out the trench using the adze of your ax; in soft snow, you can stamp out a trench or dig one. The trench should be to 6 to 8 inches wide and 1 to 1½ feet deep. The diameter of the bollard will depend on snow conditions: in hard snow, at least 3 feet; in soft snow, up to 10 feet. (Note that the bollard should not be in an oval teardrop shape in which the

310

legs of the trench come together, because this configuration results in a weaker anchor that stands apart from the strength of the main snow slope.)

During construction, assess the snow in the trench for changes in consistency or weak layers that could allow the rope or webbing to cut through. Try to use webbing instead of rope because it's less likely to saw into the mound. For the same reason, avoid pulling on the rope or webbing after placing it. Especially in softer snow, add security by padding the back and shoulders of the trench with packs, clothing, or ensolite pads. Ice axes planted vertically at the shoulders of the trench also prevent rope or webbing from cutting

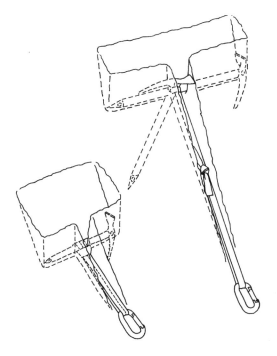

Fig. 13-34. Ice axes as deadman anchors: a, with one ax, buried horizontally; b, with two axes, one horizontal and one vertical (the T-ax anchor).

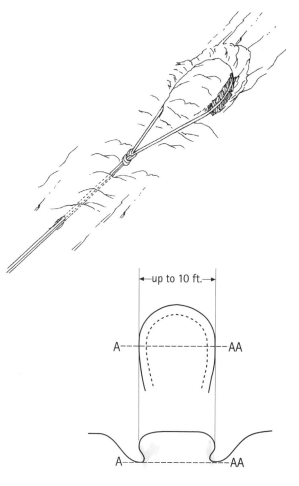

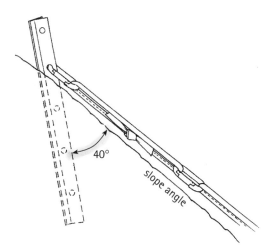

Fig. 13-35. Picket placement

Fig. 13-36. Snow bollard

in. You can also back up the bollard with a picket or fluke (which the last person on a rappel removes before rappelling). Inspect the bollard for damage after each use.

**Multiple anchors** are the best insurance because of the inherent weakness and unpredictability of snow anchors. As with questionable anchors in rock, multiple anchors are safest. Two anchors can be chained sequentially so that the first takes the hit but has a backup to absorb any remaining force. Or they can be connected in a way that will permit them to share any load (fig. 13-37). (More details and illustrations on joining multiple anchors are in Chapter 7, Belaying, and Chapter 10, Rock Protection.) In general, place multiple snow anchors one behind the other to reduce the angle of pull and the potential load on the surviving anchor if the other one fails. Keep the anchors several feet apart so they don't end up sharing any localized weakness in the snow.

## Belaying on Snow

Snow climbers choose from a range of techniques that provide belay protection to their ropemates. They sometimes give belays using established snow anchors, and sometimes they give quicker and less formal belays using the ice ax. The changeable nature of snow and the difficulty of inspecting snow protection usually result in anchors that can't be considered bombproof like a good anchor in rock. But they are still effective because most mishaps on snow do not generate the high loads of rock-climbing falls. Snow falls are usually slides on relatively moderate (30- to 60-degree) slopes, with help from the friction of rope against snow and with no direct vertical pull.

No matter what the belaying technique, every snow belay should be as dynamic as possible to help limit the force on the anchor. The dynamic, shock-absorbing quality of climbing rope helps to minimize chances

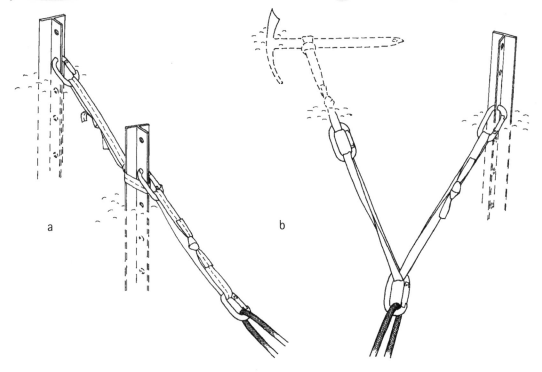

a

b

*Fig. 13-37. Two methods of connecting snow anchors: a, two pickets linked serially, where top anchor supports lower anchor; b, two independent anchors with equalized connecting runner.*

of an abrupt, static stop to a fall. As a belayer, plan your stance so the force is taken on your body and dissipated as much as possible by the belay and the dynamic quality of the rope. The standard hip belay provides a more gradual, dynamic belay than mechanical belay devices. Think of the consequences if a heavy hit on a questionable snow belay yanks you and any anchor off your perch.

Set up a belay close to the climbing difficulties. If you're belaying the lead climber, get out of the line of fire by setting up the belay stance to one side of the fall line—not within it. If the leader is heading up on a diagonal, get outside any point where the climber's route could cross directly above you. On a ridge crest, it is not always possible to predict a fall line and plan a belay in advance. If a ropemate slips off one side of the ridge, the best reaction may actually be to jump off the opposite side, with the rope running over the ridge saving you both.

## Quick Belays

Snow climbers have a couple of quick belays for times the consequences of a fall would not be great, as in a sliding pendulum across a snow face. They are useful for belaying a climber who is probing a cornice or crevasse edge or for providing a top belay to a weaker climber.

**The boot-ax belay** (also called the New Zealand foot brake) is a fast and easy way to provide protection as a rope team moves up together (fig. 13-38). Despite some naysayers, it has proven to be useful, provided its principal limitation is understood: it can't be expected to hold a high fall force. It is primarily a dynamic form of belay. With thorough practice, you should be able to set up this belay in a couple of seconds with a jab of the ice ax and a quick sweep of the rope.

Step by step, here is how to do it (and after trying it a few times, you'll realize it is not as complicated as it sounds):

1. Stamp a firm platform in the snow, big enough for the ax and uphill boot.
2. Jam the ice-ax shaft as deeply as possible into the snow at the rear of the platform, the shaft tilted slightly uphill against a possible fall. Have the pick perpendicular to the fall line, thus applying the broadest side of the shaft against the force of a fall.

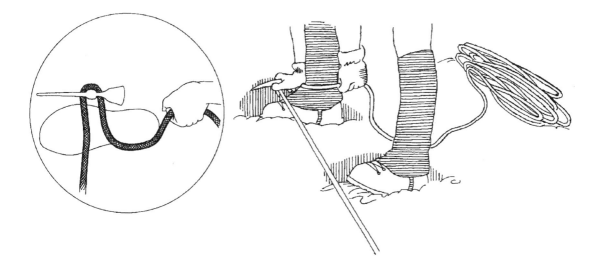

*Fig. 13-38. Boot-ax belay*

3. Stand below the ax, at approximately a right angle to the fall line and facing the side on which the climber's route lies.

4. Plant your uphill boot into the snow against the downhill side of the shaft, bracing it against a downward pull.

5. Plant the downhill boot in a firmly compacted step far enough below the other boot so that the downhill leg is straight, providing a stiff brace.

6. Flip the rope around the ax. The final configuration will have the rope running from the direction of potential load, across the toe of the uphill boot, around the uphill side of the ax, and then back across the boot above the instep.

7. Hold the rope with the downhill (braking) hand, applying extra friction by bringing the rope uphill behind the heel, forming an S bend. The braking hand must never leave the rope.

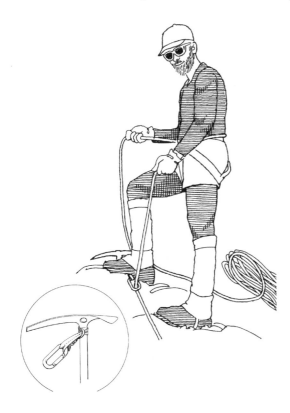

*Fig. 13-39. Carabiner/ice-ax belay*

8. Use the uphill hand for two jobs: to grasp the head of the ax to further brace the shaft and then, as the belayed climber moves upward, to take in rope.

Some climbers find the following alternate method for setting up the boot-ax belay to be quicker and easier. Stamp out the platform in the snow and then position your feet. Holding your ice ax by its head, sweep up a short length of the climbing rope with the shaft, and jam the ax into position in the snow, with the rope now in place.

Climbers must be equally adept at setting up the boot-ax belay with either foot uphill, because it is essential that the belayer face the climber's fall line. If a lead climber falls behind the belay, the rope unwraps from the ax and there is no belay.

**The carabiner/ice-ax belay** (also called the stomper belay) provides the same level of security as a boot-ax belay, with easier rope handling (fig. 13-39). To set it up, plant the ax as deeply as possible, the pick perpendicular to the fall line. Attach a very short sling with a girth hitch to the ax shaft at snowline and clip on a carabiner. Stand at right angles to the fall line, facing the same side as the climber's route. Brace the ax with your uphill boot, standing atop the sling but leaving the carabiner exposed. (Keep crampons off the sling.) The rope runs from the potential direction of pull up through the carabiner and then around the back of your waist and into your uphill (braking) hand. One nice thing about the carabiner/ice-ax belay is that the force of a fall pulls the belayer more firmly into the stance.

## Anchored Belays

Other snow belays usually are used with formal anchors, such as flukes, pickets, or bollards.

**The sitting hip belay,** with an anchor, is inherently dynamic and very secure on hard snow or deep, heavy, wet snow (fig. 13-40). The sitting belayer may face the prospect of a cold, wet assignment, and the belay can be difficult to work if the rope is frozen.

To set up the belay, stamp or chop a seat in the snow plus a platform to brace each boot against. Put down a pack, ensolite pad, or other material as insulation from the snow, and then settle into a standard hip belay, with outstretched, stiffened legs.

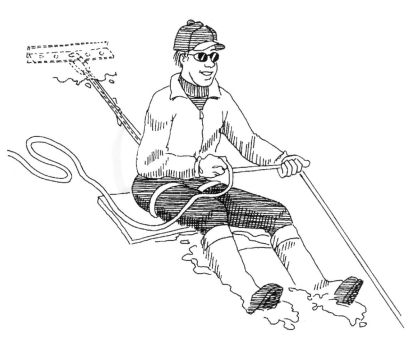

*Fig. 13-40. Sitting hip belay*

(fig. 13-41). The downhill leg is straight, locked at the knee, and braced in a snow slot. The uphill leg is on a line with the downhill leg and the direction of a potential fall. The downhill hand should be the braking hand to allow best control for a gradual dynamic belay.

**Mechanical belay devices** can be used in snow belaying. They are easy to set up and operate even with wet or icy ropes. With a device, you can belay directly from the anchor rather than from your seat harness, permitting you to get into

*[handwritten notes: ↑ control to make more dynamic slip more]*

**The standing hip belay** is easier to set up than a sitting hip belay, as it needs only deep, secure slots for each boot. However, it is far less secure because the belayer tends to be toppled under the force of a fall. Standing hip belays must be backed up with an anchor.

These belays can be arranged so the climber faces into the slope, out from the slope, or sideways. Facing into the slope is the poorest choice because the belayer will be completely wrapped by the rope if the climber falls below the belay stance. And it is difficult to pay out rope for a smooth belay. Facing out is an improvement because it gives a less complete wrap around the belayer and also permits a view of a fall below, important in timing a dynamic belay. But it shares a major weakness with the face-in stance: no way to brace the legs against toppling downhill. In both stances, the belayer should lean into the slope, against a downhill pull.

For the most reliable standing hip belay, stand sideways, facing the same side as the climber's route

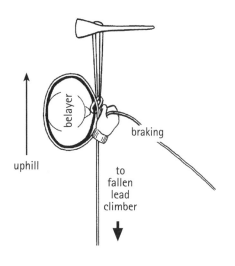

*Fig. 13-41. Standing hip belay*

315

a drier, more comfortable position. Be aware that belay devices provide a less dynamic belay than a hip belay, increasing the peak force of a fall on questionable snow anchors.

# ROUTEFINDING ON SNOW

Snow gives us passage over some frustrating obstacles, such as tundra, talus, brush, streams, and logging debris. At its best, it provides a smooth, uniform surface and a straight shot up the mountain. But because its very nature means it constantly changes, we always have to study typical seasonal weather patterns as well as current reports for an idea of what conditions to expect on any climb.

Snow can be too soft to support our weight, or it can be hard and slick. It covers obstacles in our path, but it also obscures trails, cairns, and other guideposts to the route, especially above tree line. Dangers often lie beneath the surface: moats, creeks, or glacier crevasses hidden by a thin snow cover. Unstable slopes avalanche.

You can minimize the frustrations and dangers of snow by studying the medium. (See Chapter 22, The Cycle of Snow, for information on snow formation, types of snow, and the creation of glaciers.) Mountaineers let the snow work for them. They read the snow surface and terrain features to determine a safe, efficient route.

## Surface Considerations

Evaluating the snow surface begins before you even leave home, by considering the effects of both the current weather and of conditions over the last several months.

If you are climbing during a cold, snowy spring following a prolonged late-winter thaw, the thaw's thick crust could hold a heavy load of spring snow ready to avalanche. If spring is cold but sunny, and follows a winter with little snow, a gully that usually offers good stepkicking in May could be filled with rock-hard consolidated snow. However, much of the change in the snow surface takes place rather quickly, so the weather just before and during a climb is the most important.

The best snow, from a mountaineer's point of view, is snow that is safe from avalanche and that will comfortably support a climber's weight for easy stepkicking. Such snow exists, but you have to seek it out. Location of the best snow varies from day to day, even from hour to hour. If the snow is slushy in one spot, or too hard or too crusty or too something, look around: there may be better snow a few feet away.

Here are some tips for making the best use of the snow surface:

- Find patches of firmer snow on a slushy slope by walking in shade or using sun cups as stairs.
- Try to find patches of softer snow on a slope that is too firm for good stepkicking.
- When the going is difficult, detour toward any surface with a different appearance and possibly more comfortable support.
- Use a different descent route if necessary to find the best snow.
- If you want a firmer surface, look for dirty snow, which absorbs more heat and therefore consolidates more quickly than clean snow.
- Remember that south and west slopes in the Northern Hemisphere, bearing the heat of afternoon sun, consolidate earlier in the season and quicker after storms. They offer hard surfaces when east and north slopes are still soft and unstable.
- Get an early start after a clear, cold night that follows a hot day, in order to take advantage of strong crusts on open slopes before they melt.
- Beware of the hidden holes next to logs, trees, and rocks, where the snow has melted away from these warmer surfaces.
- If you don't like the snow conditions on one side of a ridge, gully, clump of trees, or large boulder, try the other side. The difference may be just what you need.

## Terrain Considerations

Major terrain features present both obstacles and opportunities (fig. 13-42). Some you use, some you avoid, but they all have to be reckoned with.

### Couloirs

A main avenue for all mountain climbing is provided by angled gullies (couloirs). They can hold the key to upward progress because their overall angle is often less than that of the cliffs they breach, offering less technical climbing.

Deeply shaded couloirs are more often lined with ice than snow, especially in late season. Even in spring, however, when open slopes are deep in slush, the couloirs are likely to hold hard snow or ice caused by freezing or avalanche scouring.

Safe passage through a couloir usually depends on the time of day. They can be safe in early morning when the snow is solid and rocks and ice are frozen in place. It's often a different story later in the day, when they can turn deadly. Gullies are the garbage chutes of mountains, and with the arrival of the sun they begin to carry down such rubbish as avalanching snow, rocks loosened by frost-wedging, and ice blocks weakened by melting. Most of the debris comes down the center. But even if you keep to the sides, listen for suspicious sounds from above and keep an eye out for quiet slides and silent falling rock.

Avalanches erode deep ruts in many steep couloirs. Climbers usually avoid these ruts or cross them rapidly. However, early in the year the floors of the ruts offer the soundest snow available, and in cold weather they may be quite safe, particularly for a fast descent. Try to be out of a couloir before the sun hits. This means an early start for a round trip or else a bivouac or an alternative descent route.

Couloirs can become increasingly nasty the higher they are ascended, presenting the climber with extreme steepness, moats, rubble strewn loosely over smooth rock slabs, thin layers of ice over rock, and cornices. These difficulties need to be eyed carefully by climbers in judging whether a couloir will provide efficient passage or a hazardous barrier.

Finding the correct couloir on a particular route can be a challenge because they often look alike, and there may be many different couloirs in the area. The climber must choose carefully based on route information and knowledge of the terrain in order to find the couloir that gives access to the summit, rather than to a dead end.

## Ridges

Routes along a ridge crest are free of rockfall and avalanche hazard, so they can be the best choice for a long ascent in a region of moderate to heavy snowfall.

Routefinding on a ridge top is generally easier than other places on the mountain, and you can usually find a safe way to retreat. Ridge routes take the full brunt of wind and bad weather, but the most significant hazard of ridge routes is presented by cornices.

## Cornices

The shape of a ridge crest helps determine the extent of cornice-building (fig. 13-43). A ridge that slopes on one side and breaks into an abrupt cliff on the other is a good candidate for a gigantic cornice. A knife-edge ridge or one gentle on both sides will typically have only a small cornice, if any at all—although exceptions certainly exist on major alpine peaks with extreme conditions.

When the physical features are right for building cornices, wind direction decides their exact location. Because storm winds have definite patterns in each mountain range, most cornices in the same area face the same way. In the Pacific Northwest region of the United States, for example, most storms blow from the southwest so the wind-drifted snow of the cornices mostly overhangs on the north and east. These same northern and eastern exposures were steepened by past glaciation, making the ridges ideally shaped for cornice formation.

Temporary or local wind deflection can contradict the general pattern. In rare instances, cornices are even built one atop the other, facing in opposite directions, the lower one partially destroyed and hidden by later formations.

**Approaching from windward:** A cornice gives little sign of its presence as you approach from windward. It simply appears to be a smooth snow slope that runs out to meet the sky. Look at nearby ridges for an idea of the frequency, size, and location of cornices in the area.

Not every snowy ridge conceals a cornice—but be sure to find out whether the ridge you are on does. Try to view the lee side of the ridge from a safe vantage point, such as a rock or tree jutting through the crest. If you can't, have a belayed climber approach the ridge at right angles while probing with an ice ax or reversed ski pole to see whether the snow is solid. Look for a crack or indentation in the snow, which could indicate a cornice that has partially collapsed.

1. Horn or aiguille
2. Ridge
3. Rock arête
4. Cornice
5. Glacier basin
6. Seracs
7. Fallen seracs
8. Erratic blocks
9. Icefall
10. Glacier
11. Crevasses
12. Lateral moraine
13. Snout
14. Moraine lake
15. Terminal moraine
16. Glacial runoff
17. Rock band
18. Shoulder
19. Col
20. Couloir or gully
21. Hanging glacier
22. Bergschrund
23. Buttress
24. Cirque or bowl
25. Headwall
26. Flutings
27. Ice wall
28. Summit
29. Ice arête
30. Towers or gendarmes
31. Avalanche chute
32. Avalanche debris
33. Snowfield

*Fig. 13-42. Alpine terrain features*

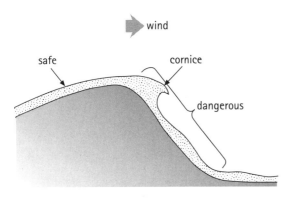

*Fig. 13-43. Cornice-building*

It's hard to judge the extent of a cornice overhang and the danger it presents. Don't be misled by appearances. For a mature cornice, the probable line of fracture could be 30 feet or more back from the lip—no doubt farther back than an examination would lead you to expect. And although rocks and trees projecting from the snow suggest safety, they could be on the tops of buttresses with a connecting ridge that curves far back into bays supporting wide cornices. A lot of climbers have had the enlightening experience of looking back along a ridge and discovering their tracks on snow poised above a chasm. The safe course along a corniced crest is well behind the probable fracture line.

**Approaching from leeward:** You can't miss a cornice from the leeward side. Resembling a wave frozen in the act of breaking, a large cornice close above you is an awesome sight. If you doubt the stability of the cornice, stay among trees or on spur crests as you travel below it. At times, it's quite safe to climb under a cornice. The colder the weather, the more secure the cornice. A late-season cornice, almost completely broken down, is not a problem.

Climbers sometimes even push directly through a cornice to force their way to a ridge crest or pass. It's easiest to penetrate an overhang at a rock spur or where the cornice already has partially collapsed. The leader cuts straight uphill at the point of least overhang, undermining as little of the mass as possible. Generally, though, the safest bet with cornices is to avoid traveling on them, under them, or through them.

## Bergschrunds

A bergschrund is the giant crevasse found at the upper limit of glacier movement, formed where the moving glacier breaks away from the ice cap. The downhill lip of the bergschrund can be considerably lower than the uphill edge, which may be overhanging. Sometimes the bergschrund is the final problem of the ascent. (See Chapter 14 for more information on glacier travel and crevasses.)

## Moats

The gap that separates a snowfield from its rock borders is a moat, formed when the snow melts and settles away from the warmer rock. Crossing a moat at the top of a snowfield can be as tough as getting past a bergschrund, with the main difference being that the far wall of a moat is rock instead of snow.

## Rockfall

Snowfields and glaciers are prime targets for rockfall from bordering walls and ridges—especially on volcanic peaks, where the rock is often rotten and unstable. Climbers can reduce rockfall danger by wearing hard hats in hazardous areas and by timing climbs for less dangerous periods.

Early-season outings usually face less rockfall than summer climbs because snow still helps cement loose rock in place. Whatever the season, the general rule for glacier climbs is "early on and early off." Nighttime cold often freezes rock in place and prevents most rockfall, but direct sun melts the bonds. The greatest hazard comes in the morning, when sun melts the ice, and in the evening, when meltwater expands as it refreezes, breaking rocks loose.

In the Northern Hemisphere, southern and eastern slopes get the sun first, and therefore should be climbed very early. The shadier northern exposures usually offer less rockfall danger.

# Routefinding Aids

Crossing a snowfield or glacier, especially at night or in a white-out, can feel like being at sea, without landmarks. However, mountaineers have a couple of navigational opportunities denied to mariners. Mountaineers have a solid surface for planting their own landmarks (wands), and they experience changes in elevation that can be measured by an altimeter as a way to show progress.

The thin bamboo wands topped with tiny flags are left to mark the return route. The wands can also be used to mark points of danger (such as moats and crevasses), changes in direction, the boundaries of safe areas for unroped walking in camp, and the location of buried supplies (caches).

An altimeter helps determine your progress and location when you use it along with a topographic map and compass, especially above timberline on a large snowfield with few natural features. You may know that an established camp is located at 11,000 feet, 5 miles due east of the trailhead. By determining the elevation periodically with an altimeter and then finding that elevation on the map along the route, you can find just where you are and how far you have to go. Also relate the altimeter's findings to natural features whenever possible. If you know you are supposed to cross a ridge at an elevation of 9,500 feet in order to keep on the right track to the camp, check the altimeter when you hit the crest. You'll get a good indication of whether you have topped the ridge at the right spot. Climbers who carry a global positioning system (GPS) receiver can use this device to determine their location. (Chapter 4, Navigation, has full details on use of GPS receivers, altimeters, compasses, and topographic maps.)

A good routefinder uses a variety of tools to stay on route or reach a destination, including a compass, a map, an altimeter, wands, cairns, the sun, and visual landmarks. The creative use of several methods becomes especially important when visibility is poor.

--------- AVALANCHE SAFETY ---------

Avalanches do not need to be a mysterious phenomenon to the backcountry traveler. Natural avalanches occur when snow deposited by systems of storms places too great a load on the snowpack for it to hold onto the slope. The stress on the snow exceeds the strength of the snowpack, and an avalanche is the result. A skier or climber may add sufficient stress to set off a slide.

This chapter introduces the subject of avalanches, reviews some of the ways that snow travelers can evaluate hazards and minimize risk, and explains methods of searching for avalanche victims. This material is not meant to be comprehensive. For a more complete understanding of the subject, mountaineers should consult specialized publications and take advantage of courses in avalanche awareness. (This chapter relies heavily on *Snow Sense* by Fredston and Fesler; for this title and other sources, see Appendix B, Supplementary References. See also Chapter 22, The Cycle of Snow, for an explanation of the formation of avalanches and an assessment of dangers associated with various forms of snow.) Climbers, backcountry skiers, and snowshoers are prime victims of avalanches, but avalanche education can make a difference. Informed backcountry users are safer.

### "Go" or "No Go"

Snow travelers facing possible avalanche hazard want the answer to one basic question: Is it "go" or "no go"? That is, can we proceed, or must we turn back or find another route?

Figure 13-44 is a checklist of critical data that snow travelers can use in evaluating avalanche hazard to reach a go/no go decision. The checklist can guide you in responding to four principal questions:

1. Is the terrain capable of producing an avalanche?
2. Could the snow fail?
3. Is the weather contributing to instability?
4. What are your alternatives and their possible consequences?

To respond effectively to these overall questions, you'll need to come up with answers to a series of secondary queries about the terrain, snowpack, weather, and your climbing party. You'll answer each one with an assessment of relative hazard, expressed as a green light (okay), a yellow light (caution), or a red light (danger). Keep in mind that most avalanche incidents occur on days when yellow signals are noted. A review of the completed checklist should give you enough input to reach a final go/no go decision.

The sections that follow discuss the elements to consider in your decision-making process.

*Ask Questions of Leaders*

## Avalanche Hazard Evaluation Checklist

| Critical Data | | Hazard Rating* | | |
|---|---|:---:|:---:|:---:|
| **PARAMETERS:** KEY INFORMATION | | G | Y | R |

**TERRAIN:** *Is the terrain capable of producing an avalanche?*
- Slope Angle (steep enough to slide? prime time?)    ❑ ❑ ❑
- Slope Aspect (leeward, shadowed, or extremely sunny?)    ❑ ❑ ❑
- Slope Configuration (anchoring? shape?)    ❑ ❑ ❑
  - *Overall Terrain Rating:*    ❑ ❑ ❑

**SNOWPACK:** *Could the snow fail?*
- Slab Configuration (slab? depth and distribution?)    ❑ ❑ ❑
- Bonding Ability (weak layer? tenter spots?)    ❑ ❑ ❑
- Sensitivity (how much force to fail? shear tests? clues?)    ❑ ❑ ❑
  - *Overall Snowpack Rating:*    ❑ ❑ ❑

**WEATHER:** *Is the weather contributing to instability?*
- Precipitation (type, amount, intensity? added weight?)    ❑ ❑ ❑
- Wind (snow transport? amount and rate of deposition?)    ❑ ❑ ❑
- Temperature (storm trends? effects on snowpack?)    ❑ ❑ ❑
  - *Overall Weather Rating:*    ❑ ❑ ❑

**HUMAN FACTORS:** *What are your alternatives and their possible consequences?*
- Attitude (toward life? risk? goals? assumptions?)    ❑ ❑ ❑
- Technical Skill Level (traveling? evaluating avalanche hazard?)    ❑ ❑ ❑
- Strength/Equipment (strength? prepared for the worst?)    ❑ ❑ ❑
  - *Overall Human Factors Rating:*    ❑ ❑ ❑

• *Alternatives + Consequences*

**DECISION/ACTION:**
  - *Overall Hazard Rating/Go or No Go?*    GO ❑ or NO GO ❑

* HAZARD LEVEL SYMBOLS: R = Red light (stop/dangerous), G = Green light (go/OK),
     Y = Yellow light (caution/potentially dangerous).

*Fig. 13-44. Avalanche hazard evaluation checklist. (©Alaska Mountain Safety Center, Inc., reproduced by permission.)*

## Terrain

### Slope Angle

Slopes between 25 and 60 degrees can produce avalanches. Most activity occurs on slopes of 30 to 45 degrees, but higher-angled slopes also may pose a special hazard for climbers in some climates (fig. 13-45).

The slope you are on is not the only concern, because an avalanche could propagate from an adjacent slope. It's difficult to estimate the angle of a slope just by looking at it; use an inclinometer, which is built into many compasses.

### Slope Aspect

Slope aspect—the direction in which a slope faces—determines how much sun and wind the slope gets, and this indicates a great deal about its avalanche potential. Here's how it works in the Northern Hemisphere, and of course it's just the opposite on mountains south of the equator.

South-facing slopes receive more sun; therefore, snow settles and stabilizes faster than on northern slopes. In general (with plenty of local exceptions), this may make south-facing slopes somewhat safer in winter. They tend to release avalanches sooner after a

storm, so if they are avalanching it's an indication that slopes facing in other directions may soon follow their lead. As warmer spring and summer days arrive, south slopes become prone to wet-snow avalanches and north-facing slopes may be safer.

North-facing slopes receive little or no sun in the winter, so consolidation of the snowpack takes longer. Colder temperatures within the snowpack create weak layers. Therefore, in general (again with local exceptions), north slopes are more likely to slide in midwinter. In spring and summer, as south slopes become dangerously wet, look to the north side for firmer, safer snow.

Windward slopes—those that face into the wind—tend to be safer than leeward slopes. Windward slopes may be blown clear of snow, or the remaining snow may be compacted by the force of the wind.

Leeward slopes—those that face away from the wind—are particularly dangerous because of wind-loading. These slopes collect snow rapidly when high winds move snow from windward slopes onto the leeward side. The result is cornices on the lee side of ridges, snow that is deeper and less consolidated, and the formation of wind slabs ready to avalanche.

### Slope Configuration

Smooth slopes—those that are covered beneath the snow with grass or smooth rock slabs—generally have a poor bond with the snow and provide a slick surface for a slide.

Trees and rocks may serve as anchors that tend to stabilize the snow—at least until the snow covers them. But in general, the trees and rocks need to be so close together to act as effective anchors that it can be difficult or impossible for a climbing party to move through them. After these trees and rocks are buried by snowfall, they can actually become a source of weakness in the snowpack.

Slides aren't likely to originate in a dense forest, but they can run through from above. Look around as you travel. Do you spot shattered trees in avalanche fans and wide swaths cut through old timber? This is evidence of large avalanches penetrating even thick forest. Does a slope grow only brush and small trees, all downslanting? This is probably a slope that avalanches so often that timber has no chance to grow. Are tree

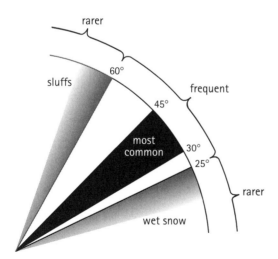

*Fig. 13-45. The frequency of avalanches on slopes of various angles*

limbs missing from the uphill side in open timber? It might be the result of avalanches. There's little or no avalanche protection in open timber, such as you can easily ski through.

The shape of a slope affects the hazard level. Snow on a slope that is straight, open, and moderately steep presents the most obvious danger. Snow on a convex slope, under tension as it stretches tightly over the curve of the hill, is more prone to avalanche than snow on a concave slope (fig. 13-46). Fracture lines frequently occur just below a convex area.

## Snowpack

The snowpack develops from a series of storms and intervening periods of weather and temperature changes that may help to consolidate the snow or lead to formation of both strong and weak layers. New snow may be able to adhere to the existing snow to create a homogeneous pack. But it may also form a slab—a cohesive layer of snow—with a thinner, weaker failure layer beneath it. Mountaineers trying to move safely through avalanche country need information on ability of the snow to bond and sensitivity of the snowpack to forces that might cause it to avalanche.

### Studying Snow Stability

You can get a lot of information on possible avalanche danger simply by paying close attention to the obvious signs of instability outlined later in this section. You can also test for snow stability. The Rutschblock test, described next, has shown a high degree of reliability.

### Rutschblock (Glide Block) Test

This test is considered a particularly good indicator of the likelihood that a slope will slide. As with the shovel shear test (described later), the Rutschblock test puts stress on a block, or column, of snow (fig. 13-47). But the block of snow is much larger, providing better results than the shovel shear test. Instead of a shovel that is pulled against the block, the Rutschblock uses a person on skis who stands atop the block.

Follow these steps in conducting the Rutschblock test:

1. Find a spot that is representative of the slope aspect and incline that you expect to encounter. The best information is usually garnered from an area that is not near trees or a ridge.
2. Using a shovel, a snow saw, or a ski, excavate to create three sides of a rectangular snow block. Dig down at least 3 feet, or deeper if necessary to reach suspected weak layers. The width of the block in the cross-slope direction should be about the same as the length of a ski; the width of the block in the downslope direction should be about the same as the length of a ski pole. Make clean, vertical sides on the snow block; don't disturb the snow on top.
3. Cut the back wall of the block free of the slope, using saw, ski, or rope. It may be difficult to cut through hard or icy layers without a snow saw.
4. Have a person on skis step onto the center of the block from the slope above. If the block supports the skier, that person then stresses the block with a series of jumps, leaping up with both skis. The amount of stress required to cause the block to shear (fail) at a weak layer is an indication of the relative stability of the slope.

The following list provides criteria for interpreting the Rutschblock test results.

#### EXTREMELY UNSTABLE

1 Fails while excavating the site.
2 Fails while approaching the test site.
3 Fails while standing on the block.

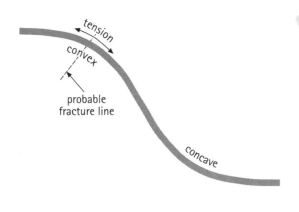

*Fig. 13-46. Convex and concave slopes*

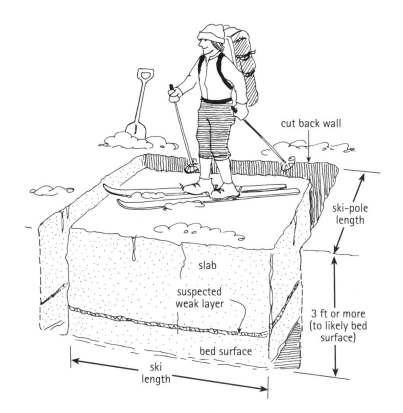

*Fig. 13-47. In the Rutschblock test for snow stability, a person on skis puts stress on top of a block of snow.*

### UNSTABLE

4  Fails while flexing for a jump.
5  (Questionable) Fails with a jump.

### RELATIVELY STABLE

6  Fails after repeated hard jumps.

### STABLE

7  Doesn't fail with repeated jumps. Try jumping with skis off.

Keep in mind that your result from the Rutschblock test is just one piece of information among many that you need to collect in assessing avalanche danger. After conducting the test, fill in the hole so that it's not a hazard for other travelers.

### Other Snow-Stability Indicators

Following are brief descriptions of several other methods of securing information on snow stability. These descriptions briefly introduce the methods, but you must look to specialized publications and expert instruction to learn how to carry them out and evaluate them correctly.

**Shovel shear test:** The purpose of this test is to discover snow layers most likely to slide. The procedure involves digging into the snow to create a column of snow that is freestanding on the front and sides and has a cut at the back that is deep enough to allow insertion of a shovel. The tester stands in front of the column, inserts the shovel in the cut at the back, and pulls forward on the shovel handle with both hands. If the snow has a pronounced sliding layer, the column will shear off evenly at that point. This test has been criticized for not providing reliable information on the amount of force needed to cause shearing. Although the shovel shear test may provide information about layering and stability, multiple test sites may be required. The Rutschblock test has proven to be a much more reliable indicator of snow stability.

**Snow-pit observation:** You can observe the pattern of layering in a snow pit (perhaps the same one you've dug for the Rutschblock test). The snow pit should be in a safe location that has an angle, aspect, and elevation similar to the nearby slopes that you plan to cross. It should be in a spot away from trees. It is not difficult to identify the various snow layers and determine their relative hardness or softness and strength by pushing against each one with a fist or jabbing them with a finger, pencil, or knife. Very hard layers or very soft layers may not bond well with other layers. Snow pits may not give you as much useful information as the Rutschblock test or the obvious signs of instability discussed later in this section.

**Ski-pole probe:** You can use a ski pole to puncture the snow surface and get an indication of what's below. If the snow is very soft, push the basket end of the pole smoothly into the snow; then pull it slowly out, trying to feel any hard or soft layers. You may be able to reach down into the ski-pole hole and feel the snow layers with your fingers. In most other snow, use the handle end of the ski pole or remove the basket to penetrate. Regularly making these observations and discussing them with party members reinforce an awareness of avalanche hazard and preparedness. This informal test won't give information on the bonding of snow layers and it will miss thin shear planes, but it can reveal gross discontinuities in the snowpack structure that suggest instability.

### Obvious Signs of Instability

Many valuable indicators of avalanche hazard are obvious to the eye or the ear. These indicators provide quick information that may point to danger even more clearly than actual stability testing. Stay alert to these danger signs, and discuss them with members of your party so that everyone remains aware of the potential for avalanches.

Among the questions you might ask as you seek signs of instability are the following:

- Do you see evidence of recent avalanche activity on the slopes you are traveling or on similar slopes?
- Do you see shooting cracks in the snow, indicating you are on an unstable slab?
- Does the snow have a "hollow" feel as you walk or ski across it, possibly indicating a cavity that has left the surface slab unsupported and ready to slide?
- Have you heard the "whumping" sound of a layer settling in the snow, warning of a slab that could release nearby?
- Does scouring of the snow indicate recent high winds that have transported snow to another area, where it may have settled as a dangerous wind slab? Try to spot the most likely area where this wind-transported snow would be deposited.
- Do you see rain runnels? By the time runnels are apparent, most rain-caused avalanches have already occurred and the snow is usually relatively stable.
- Do you see sun balls, those softball-size balls of snow that run down a sunny slope? They are a sign of new surface warming.

## Weather

Before and during any backcountry trip, study the weather closely. Heavy precipitation, high winds, or extreme temperatures mean changes in the snowpack. Be prepared to look critically at the snow to see how the snowpack has been affected by recent weather. The snowpack adapts poorly to sudden changes, so rapid turns in the weather contribute to instability. The snowpack can bend and adapt when forces are applied slowly, but sudden stress can cause it to break. (Also see the section on formation of snow avalanches, in Chapter 22, The Cycle of Snow.)

### Precipitation

Precipitation in the form of rain or snow adds to stress on the snowpack. Avalanche danger increases rapidly with snowfall of an inch or more per hour. If a heavy load of new snow accumulates too quickly for the strength of the existing snowpack, an avalanche can be the result.

Rain can percolate into the snow, weakening bonds between layers. This rain tends to lubricate the layers, making it easier for a slide to start. Rain adds significant weight, and it may also rapidly warm the snowpack. Rain can trigger avalanches very quickly after the rainfall begins.

With rain or new snow, the questions to consider are how well it bonds with the snowpack and how big a load it represents. The weight of the water in the snow is the primary contributor of stress on the snowpack.

### Wind

The high winds that transport snow from windward slopes and deposit it on leeward slopes break the interlocking bonds between snow crystals. These particles, now smaller, pack closely together, forming cohesive slabs that propagate fractures efficiently, resulting in avalanches.

High winds also shape the cornices that overhang lee slopes. Cornices can break and fall, sometimes triggering an avalanche.

### Temperature

Significant differences in temperature between the ground and the snow surface promote growth of highly faceted snow crystals (depth hoar, or "sugar snow") that can't support much load. This temperature differential and the resulting sugar snow especially appear early in the season, notably in interior snowy climates like the Rocky Mountains. Less severe temperatures and a deeper snowpack act as insulation that may allow this snow to stabilize. But highly faceted snow can persist as a dangerous underlying layer well into the snow season or until avalanches release it.

Another type of weak crystal growth, similar to dew, is surface hoar. It's common in all areas. The conditions that encourage its growth are cool, cloudless nights that are calm or nearly calm at the snow surface. When the thin, feathered crystals of surface hoar are covered by subsequent snowfall, they can form weak layers that—like sugar snow—increase avalanche hazard.

Temperature affects snow stability, especially that of new snow, in complicated ways. Warm temperatures accelerate the process of settlement, causing the snowpack to become denser and stronger, and thus, over the long term, more stable. But initially rapid, prolonged warming weakens the snow cover, particularly after a cold spell, making it less stable and more susceptible to human-triggered failure. The snowpack remains un-

stable until temperatures cool down. Cold temperatures make dense snow layers stronger but are unlikely to strengthen weak layers of new, low density snow.

## Human Factors

A prime component of avalanche hazard evaluation is the human factor. The judgments that you and your fellow mountaineers make will result in an increase or a decrease in the level of risk.

The hazard evaluation checklist asks each member of a mountaineering party to take a good look at himself or herself and to reach a judgment on several points.

**Attitude:** What is the general attitude of the party toward its goals, toward risk, and toward the hazard data each member has been collecting? Consider the tolerance for risk within the party and the degree of commitment to a climbing objective even in the face of hazard. Decide how willing the group is to look objectively at information on terrain, weather, and the snowpack. Many parties allow their desire to cloud the hard facts. Most avalanche victims were aware of the hazard but chose to interpret the information in a manner that allowed an accident to occur. An unsafe attitude can kill.

**Technical skill:** How skilled are members of the party at snow travel and at evaluating avalanche hazard? Are the overall mountaineering skills of the party high? Or just average? Or low? A balanced party of able, experienced mountaineers can be expected to do well at avoiding avalanches and at responding efficiently if one strikes. A relatively untested party, or one with a great difference in experience and skill levels among its members, may need to be more conservative in its decisions.

**Party strength and equipment:** What shape is the party in? Decide whether members of the group are strong and healthy enough to keep going on a demanding and possibly hazardous trip. How well equipped is the party to deal with an avalanche? Determine whether the party is actually prepared for the worst, with shovels, rescue beacons, first-aid supplies, and other gear that would be needed.

## The Decision

After all the avalanche hazard information has been collected and evaluated, it's time for the climbing party to reach its go/no go decision. Every member of the party needs to contribute freely. Groups that take each person's thinking into account usually make better decisions than individuals. Every climber has an obligation to express his or her concerns clearly, even in the face of differing opinions. Prudent reservations, based on sound information, are essential when the risk is loss of life.

Each person must understand the possible consequences of the decision and any alternatives to it. And everyone should understand any assumptions underlying the decision, such as the thinking that went into assessments of the party's risk tolerance or its ability to deal with an avalanche.

As you move toward a decision, the process you will be using proceeds something like this:

1. Identify potential hazards.
2. Continuously collect, evaluate, and integrate information.
3. Consciously explore your assumptions, the consequences of a decision, and alternatives to it.
4. Make a decision—but be willing to reevaluate based on new information.

The material in this chapter can help simplify your decision-making process. Using the avalanche hazard evaluation checklist, you will be able to assign a green go-ahead light or a yellow caution light or a red stop signal to each step of the process. The completed checklist points the way to a sound decision.

## Minimizing the Risk

Climbers have many ways to minimize the risk of avalanches and to increase their chances of survival if one hits. The preceding material in this section covered strategies for evaluating avalanche hazard during a trip. Climbers can also minimize avalanche risk by the things they do before heading into the mountains.

It's obvious advice, but check the weather and avalanche forecasts before the trip. Detailed avalanche reports are available from agencies in many mountain areas by telephone and through the Internet. Talk to people with local knowledge of your route, including any snow ranger who may be responsible for that area. Don't be afraid to rethink your well-laid plans, based on the pretrip information you uncover.

Be sure the people in your party have adequate training and equipment to head into areas of possible avalanche. You can also improve your safety margin by taking some of the normal precautions of any climbing trip, such as studying maps and photos of the area, researching alternative routes, preparing for an emergency bivouac, and identifying possible retreat routes.

### Safe Route Selection

You can improve your ability to travel safely in the backcountry by seeking routes that limit exposure to danger. The following guidelines summarize some of the important considerations introduced earlier in this chapter.

- Favor windward slopes, which tend to be more stable.
- Avoid leeward slopes where winds have deposited snow slabs.
- Choose the least-steep slopes that will get you where you want to go.
- Favor the edges of slopes; avalanches are less likely, and safety is closer in case one occurs.
- Be suspicious of the convex rollover at the top of a slope—a point of stress that can trigger an avalanche.
- Be careful of shaded slopes in winter and the very warm sunny slopes of spring.
- Be particularly cautious of slopes of 35 to 45 degrees; use an inclinometer to identify them.
- Avoid gullies, which can be chutes for large quantities of snow that can deeply bury you or sweep you away.
- Keep aware of the run-out below snow slopes and gullies, especially avoiding areas with cliffs below.
- Avoid camp locations in valleys that can be exposed to avalanche danger from above.
- Develop "avalanche eyeballs" by continually evaluating avalanche danger and its potential consequences.

### How to Cross a Questionable Slope

Nobody likes it, but sometimes there's no way to avoid questionable avalanche terrain. The problem then is to make the passage with the least danger of disturbing the slope and to minimize the consequences if climbers or skiers set off an avalanche or one sweeps down from above.

Before heading out onto the slope, put on hat, mittens, and warm clothing, and zip up. Decide whether you will abandon your pack if an avalanche hits. A light pack may protect your back and offer some buoyancy, but a heavy pack could drag you down. Some people sling their pack over one shoulder, ready to toss it away in an avalanche—but before you try this approach, be sure you can still cross the slope reliably, especially if you're on skis. Practice this ahead of the time you need to do it. Undo ski-pole straps. Use releasable bindings, and remove the straps that connect the boots to the bindings. (Consider that skis and snowshoes spread your weight over a relatively large area, putting less strain on the slope than boots do.)

When the route lies up a slope (and you're walking, not skiing), head straight up the fall line instead of switchbacking, which can undercut the snow.

On a traverse, only one person moves at a time, and everyone else watches from safe places, ready to shout if a slide starts. Cross with long, smooth strides, being careful not to cut a trench across the slope. Each climber follows in turn, stepping in the leader's footprints. Everyone listens and watches for an avalanche. The route should follow a line as high on the slope as practical. You may be able to hug cliff bands at the top of the slope.

Move from one position of safety to another, minimizing the period of exposure. Don't fall. Falling puts a sudden load on the snowpack; on an avalanche-ready slope, the impact of your body is like a little bomb going off.

If the climber is on belay, don't tie the rope directly to the belayer, who would risk being pulled in if it proved impossible to stop a climber hit by a wet, heavy avalanche. Use a mechanical belay device, not a body belay.

### How to Survive an Avalanche

Think ahead about what you would do in the event of an avalanche, because you won't have time after it starts. As you travel, keep an eye out for escape paths. But if you're caught in an avalanche, don't give up; fight to survive. Yell to your partners. Jettison any gear you want to get rid of.

At the start, grab a rock or tree, or dig your ax or ski pole into the snow, and hold on. Try to stop yourself before you're swept away. If that doesn't work, swim. Stay on the surface by using swimming motions, flailing arms and legs, or by rolling. Try to move to the side of the slide.

Close your mouth if your head goes below the surface. As the snow slows, thrust upward. If you are buried, try to make a breathing space by putting your elbow or hand in front of your face. Inhale deeply before the snow stops, in order to expand your ribs. As the snow closes around you, it will become impossible to move. Don't shout or struggle. Conserve oxygen and energy. Your partners should know what to do, and they will begin immediate rescue efforts.

## Rescue

The rescue effort starts even before the avalanche has stopped. The first step in a successful rescue is a tough one in the shock of the moment: someone must pay attention to the point where a victim is last seen. Identify the area to be searched based on the last-seen point.

Do NOT go for help. This is a critical principle of avalanche rescue. Do not send anyone for help. STAY and SEARCH. Survival depends almost certainly on locating the victim quickly. A person located in the first 15 minutes has roughly a 90 percent chance of survival. Survival probability drops off rapidly after that time. You can send someone for help after the victim is unburied or after search efforts turn out to be futile.

Select a search leader to direct a thorough and methodical rescue effort. Consider the safety of the search party. Evaluate the potential for other slides in the area, choose a safe approach to the search area, and designate an escape path in case of another avalanche.

### Searching with Avalanche Rescue Beacons

The electronic device known as an avalanche rescue beacon is the principal tool for finding buried victims. A rescue beacon can be switched to either transmit or receive signals. Rescue depends on each member of a climbing party carrying a beacon, which during the climb is left switched on to the transmit mode. If you're staying overnight in a snow cave or in an avalanche-prone area, consider leaving the beacon on to transmit even at night. All members of a party must know how to use the beacons correctly, a skill that requires regular practice.

The group should verify at the trailhead and at the beginning of each day that all beacons can transmit and receive properly. Fresh batteries usually last for about 300 hours, but it's a good idea to carry extras in case the signal from any beacon weakens.

Searchers switch their beacons to the receive mode to locate the transmission from a victim. It's critically important that every searcher switch to receive; if anyone leaves a beacon in the transmit mode, other searchers will waste valuable time trying to interpret this misleading signal.

A rescuer should be able to locate the spot where a victim lies beneath the snow in less than 5 minutes. Practice in the use of rescue beacons, also known as avalanche transceivers, is essential to ensure that searchers have the best chance of locating victims before they suffocate.

The international standard frequency for avalanche beacons is now 457 kilohertz. Beacons that work at 2,275 hertz are obsolete and should not be used. Dual-frequency beacons may be used by some rescue groups, but the recommended beacons for backcountry travelers and climbers operate exclusively at 457 kilohertz. The new standard beacons have a greater range.

A climber typically straps the beacon around the neck and carries it under the shirt to keep from losing it in an avalanche. Don't carry it in your pack. The device comes out for rescue work, and the searcher listens for beeps through an earphone. Some beacons use speakers and provide an optical display to help direct searchers.

## The Three Phases of a Beacon Search

A beacon search for an avalanche victim proceeds through three phases: coarse, fine, and pinpoint. The coarse phase and the pinpoint phase rely on a traditional technique called the bracket or grid method. But for the fine-search phase, a newer method—the tangential or induction method—has been shown to offer time reductions of up to 50 percent when used by trained individuals. It is essential that the bracket method be mastered. However, climbers should also learn the tangential method because of the critical time it can save during the fine-search phase.

### Coarse Search

The coarse search starts with an initial rapid "scuff search" of the snow surface, with rescuers looking for someone partially buried, any castoff equipment, or any logical spot the victim might have come to a stop against a tree or rock. Mark the location of any clues as an aid to further search, and probe the likely catchment areas. The missing climber could turn up in this fast and immediate search.

Then move quickly into the beacon search. Put the volume control all the way up on every beacon. Searchers, spaced no more than 50 or 60 feet apart, should move in a clearly defined pattern over the search area. It's usually easier to move downhill as you search. Work rapidly but efficiently. You may need to consciously control your feelings of shock and anxiety in order to be the most effective in trying to find the missing person.

Because the beacons employ a wire wrap antenna with directional characteristics, signals may be stronger or weaker depending on the position that a search beacon is held in, relative to the victim's transmitting beacon. For this reason, it's important for a searcher to rotate the beacon left and right, forward and back, trying to find the strongest signal position. When a signal is picked up, one or two persons start to track down the sound with a fine beacon search while other rescuers get ready to dig out the victim. (If there is more than one victim, the rest of the rescuers continue the coarse search. As each victim is found, turn off his or her beacon so searchers won't continue to pick up those signals.)

### Fine Search

#### Bracket Method for Fine Search

Using a single rescue beacon, searchers employing the bracket method follow a series of steps to find their way to a spot very near the buried victim (fig. 13-48).

1. Orient the beacon for maximum signal strength, moving the unit vertically and horizontally to find the best position. The beacon is now oriented toward the strongest sound. This orientation must be

maintained throughout the search. (Some beacons provide a visual display to show the strongest signal.)

2. Reduce volume as low as possible while still hearing the signal. (The ear is better able to distinguish changes in volume for low-volume sounds.)

3. Keep the beacon in the same orientation as you walk in any straight line. As soon as the signal reaches a peak and begins to drop, again reduce the volume as low as possible.

4. Still holding the beacon in the same orientation, continue on the same path. When the signal fades out, mark the spot.

5. Without changing orientation of the beacon, turn

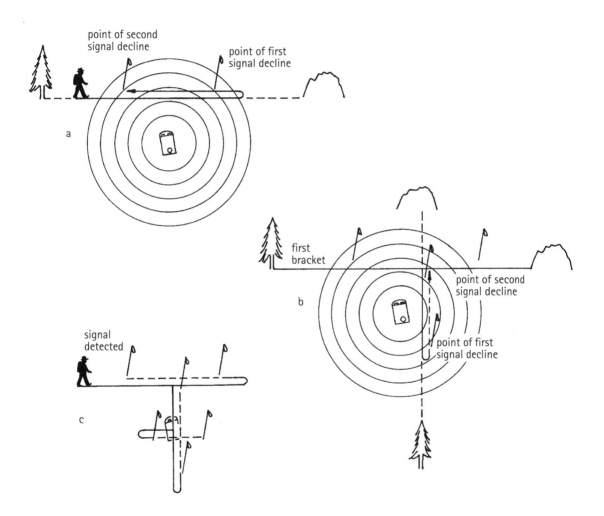

*Fig. 13-48. Fine search, using the bracket method: a, first bracket; b, second bracket; c, summary of beacon search bracketing. (Illustration by Ray Smutek, reprinted by permission, from "Avalanche Beacons,"* Summit, *March–April [1984].)*

yourself around and retrace the same pathway. When the signal fades out again, mark that spot. You now have a straight line bracketed at the end by points where the signal disappears.

6. Return to the center of this bracketed line and make a 90-degree turn. Now repeat the process: Reduce volume to the minimum, and walk in a straight line until the signal fades out. Mark the spot, turn around without disturbing orientation of the beacon, and retrace your steps until the signal again fades. You now have another straight line bracketed by two fade-out points.

7. Return to the center of this new line and again make a 90-degree turn in the direction of the signal. Work fast and efficiently, without worrying too much about precision. Continue this process of making bracketed lines until the distance between fade-out points on a line is less than 6 feet. You can usually reach this stage within the first three brackets. You are now very close to the victim and ready to move into a pinpoint search.

### Tangential Method for Fine Search

The tangential method (fig. 13-49) is an alternative to the bracket method for the fine search. The tangential method is faster when performed by a trained rescuer, but it takes more effort to learn and is not always successful. Be prepared to switch back to the bracket method if the tangential method isn't giving the results you need.

Following are the steps to follow for the fine search using the tangential method. (The first two steps are identical to the bracket method.)

1. Orient the beacon for maximum signal strength, moving the unit vertically and horizontally to find the best position. The beacon is now oriented toward the strongest sound.

2. Reduce volume as low as possible while still hearing the signal.

3. Head off in the direction of the strongest sound. If the volume drops before you have traveled about 15 feet (or about 5 meters) on this first leg of the fine search, turn and walk in the opposite direction.

4. After walking about 15 feet, again adjust the orientation of the beacon for maximum signal, reduce signal volume to the minimum, and start off in the direction of the strongest signal.

5. After walking another 15 feet, again adjust orientation and signal volume. Continue with a series of these 15-foot walks and signal adjustments, each time setting off again toward the strongest signal. On each leg, signal volume should increase as you walk.

These repeated procedures are designed to lead you progressively closer to an area very near the victim. Because transmissions from the victim's beacon follow a curved path, you will be following a curved arc to the buried person. You will know you are near the person when signal volume fades rather than increasing as you walk. You are now very close to the victim and ready to move into a pinpoint search.

### Pinpoint Search

With the searcher's beacon close to the snow surface, begin to pinpoint the victim by moving the beacon from side to side and front to back in a small crisscross. A loud signal when the volume control is reduced means you are very close. If the beacon can only identify a fairly large space—perhaps several feet across—mark the four corners of this area of maximum signal.

Use an avalanche probe or a ski pole to probe, very carefully, to determine the exact location of the person. Probe gently to avoid injury to the victim. As soon as you locate the person, begin digging. Leave the pole in place to guide your digging.

Take care to avoid injuring the victim with shovels or probes or otherwise endangering the person you are trying to save. Some people report that the most terrifying part of their avalanche experience was having their air space trampled on as they were being rescued.

### Recovery

As you uncover the victim, check to see that the person's mouth is not filled with snow and that there are no other obvious obstructions to breathing. Clear snow away from the victim's chest to allow room for it to expand and take in air. Be prepared to start cardiopulmonary resuscitation; the person need not

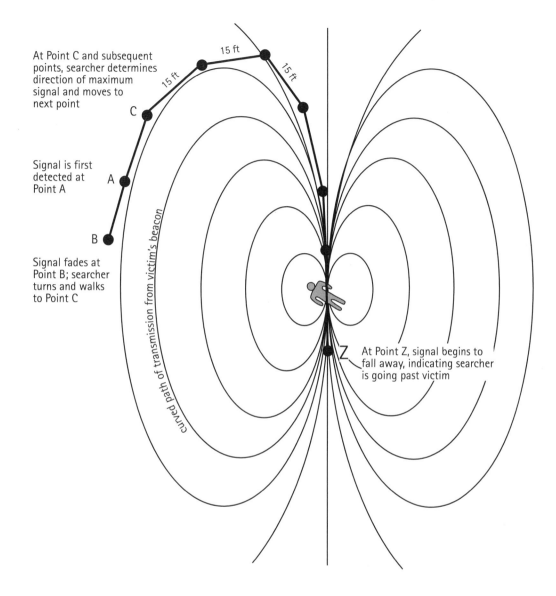

At Point C and subsequent points, searcher determines direction of maximum signal and moves to next point

15 ft

15 ft

15 ft

15 ft

C

Signal is first detected at Point A

A

B

Signal fades at Point B; searcher turns and walks to Point C

curved path of transmission from victim's beacon

Z

At Point Z, signal begins to fall away, indicating searcher is going past victim

*Fig. 13-49. Fine search, using the tangential method (also known as the induction method)*

be fully extracted from the snow before CPR begins. Be aware that a burial victim may be at risk for cardiac failure caused by sudden movement. Make the person as warm and comfortable as possible, and be prepared to treat for hypothermia and injuries. (See Chapter 19, First Aid, for related information.)

If the avalanche buried more than one person, switch off the beacon carried by the rescued individual so that its transmissions won't interfere with the ongoing search for other survivors.

## Probing

Formal probe searches for avalanche victims are not very effective because they take so much time, even for small areas. However, spot-probing is necessary for checking likely burial spots, especially the area identified by the pinpoint search with the rescue beacon.

Probing is a slow and uncertain mechanical process, but it may be the only alternative if rescue beacons fail to locate a victim or if the party is traveling without beacons. Probe first at likely areas: near pieces of the victim's equipment, at the points of disappearance, and around trees and rocks. Probing in a group is a skill that must be practiced before you need it. It's hard work involving discipline and concentration. In the backcountry, you may not have enough people to carry out formal probe procedures.

A probe tool may be anything you can use to poke into the snow in an attempt to feel the victim's body, such as wands, ski poles, ice axes, or commercial snow-probe poles. Commercial poles work far better than other probes.

Some suppliers advertise ski poles with the capability to be joined together to create an avalanche probe. If you have such poles, test them to verify whether they really work. You may conclude they do not. You may find you have difficulty removing the baskets or screwing in the adapter piece. Even then, the poles may not be strong enough to probe hard avalanche debris. Convertible ski poles are a poor substitute for commercial probes.

## The Well-Prepared Party

The level of preparedness of a climbing party is an important factor in minimizing avalanche hazard. The well-prepared party has the training, conditioning, equipment, and critical judgment to evaluate hazard and to respond effectively to an avalanche. Members of this party carry the beacons, shovels, snow saw, and probe tools they may need in an emergency, and they have practiced to gain the skill to use them. They know that seconds do count in the safety of their party.

The primary emphasis of the mountaineer should be on avalanche evaluation and safe travel. Every party needs rescue skills and equipment, but they are no substitute for the ability to make sound judgments that promote safe travel in avalanche country.

# 14

# GLACIER TRAVEL AND CREVASSE RESCUE

Glacier travel is a very specialized mountaineering skill, for one principal reason: the mountaineer must contend with crevasses, the chasms that split a glacier as its great mass of frozen snow slowly flows downhill. To travel safely on a glacier, you first need all the basic snow travel skills outlined in the preceding chapter. To that must be added the ability to detect and avoid crevasses and other glacier hazards and to get out of a crevasse if you fall in. The purpose of this chapter is to help in developing this ability so that you can step onto a glacier with a clear appreciation of the dangers and confidence in dealing with them.

## ── GLACIERS AND CREVASSES ──

Glaciers constantly change as snow supply and temperature influence their advance and their retreat. In their picture-book form, glaciers look like a frozen river creeping down the mountain (fig. 14-1), yet they differ in many ways from a river. Some glaciers are small, relatively stagnant pockets of frozen snow. Others are icefields of immense proportions, full of teetering forms and dramatic releases of ice. (See Chapter 22,

The Cycle of Snow, for information on the formation of glaciers.)

Glacial flow patterns can be very complex, but a typical mountain glacier may flow between 150 and 1,300 feet (roughly 45 to 400 meters) per year. Most glaciers flow faster in the warmth of summer than in winter because of the lubrication of increased meltwater. Glacial flow breaks the surface of the ice into those elemental obstacles of mountaineering known as crevasses.

Crevasses often form where the angle of the slope increases significantly, putting tension on the snow that causes it to split open (fig. 14-2). Crevasses also commonly form where a glacier makes a turn (with the outside edge usually crevassing more), where the distance between valley walls either narrows or expands, or where two glaciers meet. Crevasses often develop around a bedrock feature that obstructs the glacial flow, such as a rock formation protruding through the ice (a nunatak). At the point where a moving glacier breaks away from the permanent snow above, the large crevasse called a bergschrund is formed. The middle of a glacier tends to have fewer crevasses than the sides, and a gently sloping glacier usually has fewer crevasses than a steep, fast-moving one.

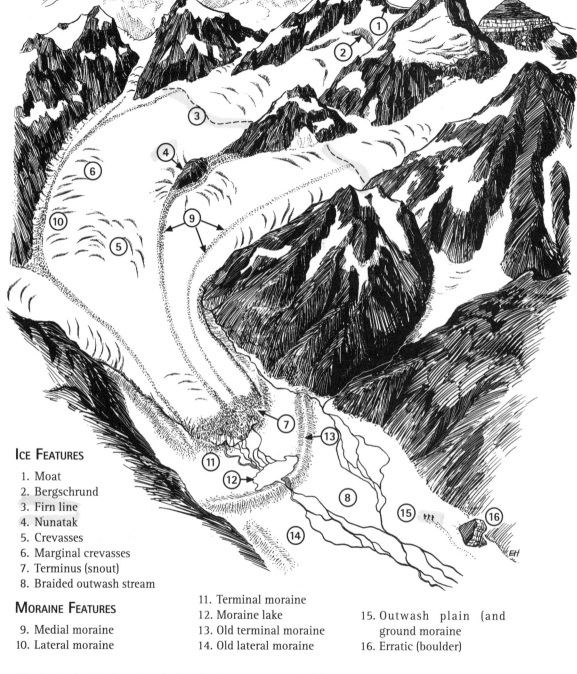

## ICE FEATURES

1. Moat
2. Bergschrund
3. Firn line
4. Nunatak
5. Crevasses
6. Marginal crevasses
7. Terminus (snout)
8. Braided outwash stream

## MORAINE FEATURES

9. Medial moraine
10. Lateral moraine
11. Terminal moraine
12. Moraine lake
13. Old terminal moraine
14. Old lateral moraine
15. Outwash plain (and ground moraine
16. Erratic (boulder)

*Fig. 14-1. Aerial view of a glacier showing some principal features*

Crevasses are most dangerous in the accumulation zone, that portion of a glacier high enough to receive more snow every year than it loses to melting. Here, crevasses are frequently covered with snow bridges that may be too weak to support a climber. Below the accu-mulation zone is the area of the glacier where annual melting matches or exceeds the yearly snowfall. Between the two zones is the firn line (also known as the névé line), named for the words that designate old snow.

The deeper layers of a glacier, denser and more

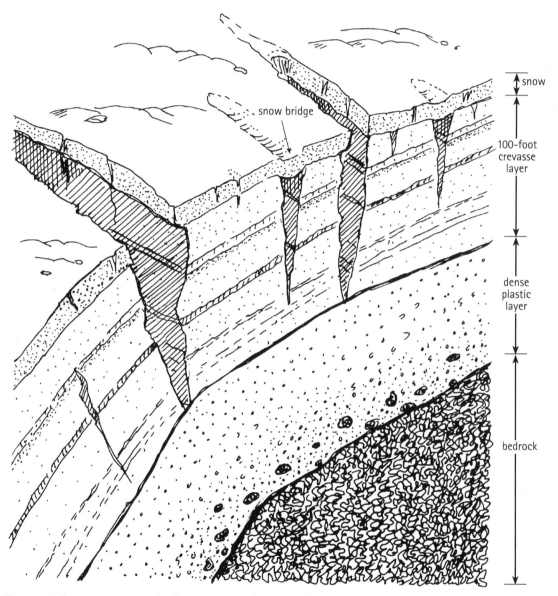

*Fig. 14-2. Crevasses open up in the upper snow layers as glacier angle increases. The denser lower area moves without splitting.*

337

plastic than the upper section, can move and deform without cracking (fig. 14-2). If this deeper, older ice becomes exposed, the glacier takes on a folded, seamless appearance, often without any true open crevasses. Travel on such a glacier can be relatively simple and safe. They are usually fairly flat, with narrow, shallow crevasses that are not difficult to cross.

## Other Common Glacier Hazards

**Ice avalanches** can pour from the steep, jumbled glacial sections known as icefalls when towers of ice (seracs) come crashing down (see Figure 13-42 in Chapter 13). The inexorable movement of a glacier means that ice avalanches can occur anytime; their activity is only partly related to season, temperature, or snowfall.

**Moats** pose another hazard. These big gaps that appear when winter snows melt back from a rock face can present major barriers to glacier travelers who need to regain the rock in order to stay on route. Belayed mountaineers may be able to cross a snow bridge over the moat or climb into the moat and back up onto the rock on the other side.

**Glacial moraines** also can stand in the way of efficient movement by a climbing party. These mounds of rocky debris that were carried and then deposited by the glacier make rugged venues indeed for mountain travel. The moraines are typically steep-sided, narrow ridges with partly buried boulders ready to dislodge at the slightest touch. You will often find the surface hard as cement. As you approach the fringe where the glacier begins, you may find a soupy mix of ice and moraine gravel.

**Meltwaters** flowing from a glacier can be a chilling challenge to cross. During warm weather, consider waiting to cross until the cooler hours of the next morning, when flow should be at its lowest. (See the section on streams in Chapter 5, Wilderness Travel, for more advice on crossing rivers.)

**White-outs** on a glacier can tax your routefinding skills to the utmost. In a white-out, sky and snow merge into a seamless blend of white, with no apparent up or down, east or west. You can defend against a white-out, taking such precautions as placing route-marking wands and noting compass bearings and altimeter readings during the ascent—even when it looks like clear weather will prevail. If snow or clouds close

in and leave your party in a white-out, your simple precautions will pay off on the way down.

## EQUIPMENT FOR GLACIER TRAVEL

Take a look at your gear with glaciers and crevasses in mind. Here are some considerations in getting ready for glacier travel.

### The Rope

The type of rope you need depends on the glacier. For "easy" glaciers, a single 8.5- to 9-millimeter rope will handle crevasse falls and save some weight in your pack on the approach. A 9-millimeter rope that is 50 meters (165 feet) long weighs only two-thirds as much as a standard 11-millimeter rope—about 6 pounds compared to about 9 pounds. The lighter, thinner rope is more than adequate for general glacier use, because crevasse falls are usually not free falls. The crevasse fall puts a relatively gradual impact on the rope because of rope friction on the snow and over the lip of the crevasse. Steep technical climbing, however, with the danger of severe leader falls, requires a standard 10- to 11-millimeter climbing rope or two smaller ropes used in the double-rope or twin-rope technique.

### Harnesses

For glacier travel, be sure the waist belt and leg loops of your seat harness can adjust to fit over several layers of cold-weather clothing. Glacier travelers also wear a chest harness, which is easily made from a piece of 1-inch webbing (see the section on harnesses in Chapter 6, Ropes, Knots, and Carabiners). Commercial full-body harnesses, more expensive and cumbersome, are not commonly used.

### Ice Ax and Crampons

An ice ax and crampons are as important for safe glacier travel as they are for travel on any firm, sloped surface of snow or ice. Crampons give you footing. The ice ax does its usual job of aiding with balance and providing a tool for self-belay and self-arrest. And if a ropemate drops into a crevasse, the ice ax helps you stop the fall when you go into self-arrest position.

## Prusik Slings

For personal safety, one of the most important pieces of gear a glacier traveler can carry is a set of prusik slings for ascending the rope after a crevasse fall. The slings are as simple as two loops of 5- to 7-millimeter perlon accessory cord attached to the climbing rope with friction knots. When you put your weight on a sling, the knot grips the rope firmly; when you remove your weight, the knot can be loosened and moved up or down the rope. (Details on making prusik slings with leg loops are found in "Prusiking Methods for Self-Rescue," later in this chapter.)

The two slings are commonly attached to the rope with simple prusik knots. Some climbers prefer the Bachmann friction knot because it incorporates a carabiner, which makes a good handle for loosening and sliding the slings and can be gripped easily with a gloved hand. If you don't have accessory cord and must improvise with webbing, the Klemheist is the best friction knot to use. (Chapter 6 shows how to make these knots.)

Some climbers attach etriers rather than conventional slings. The steps in these ladderlike slings can help you climb up and over a crevasse lip if the rope is entrenched in the snow. (Etriers are described more fully in Chapter 12, Aid Climbing.)

Some glacier travelers carry mechanical ascenders (such as Jumars or Petzls), which attach to the rope more easily than friction knots. The ascenders work better on icy ropes and can be operated more readily with gloved hands. On the debit side, ascenders are heavy and expensive. They are more prone to failure than knots and have popped off the rope under certain circumstances. On an expedition that fixes some of its ropes in place, most climbers will carry one or two ascenders for self-belay on the fixed lines. These climbers usually use the ascenders for glacier travel as well.

## Other Standard Glacier Gear

Each party member should also carry the following gear:

- **Rescue pulley:** If no pulley is available, a carabiner can be used in the rescue hauling system, but it adds considerable friction.

- **Anchor:** If conditions warrant, carry a snow or ice anchor, such as a snow picket, a fluke, or an ice screw.
- **Runners:** Bring at least two single-length and one double-length runner for attaching to anchors.
- **Belay device.**
- **Carabiners:** Carry one locking carabiner and at least four regular carabiners.

## Clothing

To be ready for a fall into a crevasse, you need to dress for the frigid insides of the glacier even when it's a hot day on top. Priorities collide here, because at the same time that you're preparing for the cold, you will also be trying to minimize sweating and keep well-hydrated.

Select outer garments that can be ventilated easily, such as pants with side zippers and a wind parka with underarm zippers. You can zip these closed if you end up in a crevasse. Use reflective colors, such as white, for your insulating layer. On a warm day, the insulating layer will be your outer layer, and light-colored garments will reflect the heat of the sun but still provide warmth inside a crevasse. To thwart the cold dampness in the hole, wear a synthetic-fiber shirt and long underpants for optimal comfort over a wide range of temperatures. Consider strapping a jacket to the outside of your pack, where you can reach it easily. Stash a cap and gloves in the pockets.

## Skis and Snowshoes

Skis or snowshoes are essential for winter or arctic mountaineering because they keep you from sinking too deeply into the snow by distributing your weight over a larger area. This same feature makes them helpful on some glacier climbs by reducing the danger of breaking through the snow bridges over hidden crevasses. Snowshoes are usually more practical than skis for roped glacier travel unless all members of the rope team have a high level of skiing skill.

## Wands

Bamboo wands are valuable aids in marking the location of crevasses, identifying turns, and showing the climbing route for a return that may occur in a white-out. Even on climbs where you intend to descend a different route, consider marking the ascent with these flag-topped sticks in case you're forced to retreat. (Chapter 13, Snow Travel and Climbing, explains how to make your own wands.)

The safest spacing for wands is a distance equal to the total length of your party (when roped and moving in single file). A party of nine (three rope teams) will use ten to twelve wands for each mile of glacier walking; smaller teams will need more.

# FUNDAMENTALS OF GLACIER TRAVEL

Mountaineers feel ambivalent at best about the virtues of the early alpine start for glacier travel. They want to be moving well before the sun rises and begins loosening snow bridges and avalanche slopes—but it means getting up in the cold and dark, often after a short, restless night. The climbers fiddle with headlamps, adjust crampons, and squirm into seat harnesses, too busy to think much about the adventure that lies ahead. But from training and experience, they know just what to do to get ready for a long day on a big glacier. It's one of those days when all the training and preparation for staying out of trouble around crevasses will pay off.

## Using the Rope

The first rule of safe glacier travel is very simple: rope up. This rule holds whether or not you're familiar with the glacier and whether or not you believe you can see and avoid all of its crevasses. Roping up is especially critical in areas above the firn line, where the glacier gets more snow every year than it loses to melting, making it likely that snow covers some crevasses.

It's tempting to walk unroped onto a glacier that looks like a benign snowfield, especially if you've gone up similar routes time after time without mishap. Avoid the temptation. The extra time and trouble of dealing with the rope, like wearing a seat belt in a car, greatly increases your chances of surviving the most likely accident on a glacier, falling into a crevasse.

Some climbers travel unroped on certain glaciers in the area below the firn line if crevasses are stable and easily seen. But this kind of unroped travel is best left to people with a great deal of glacier travel experience.

### Rope Teams

Rope teams of three climbers each are ideal for travel on glaciers where no technical climbing will be encountered. With a rope team of three, two people are available to arrest a ropemate's fall into a crevasse. A minimum party size of two rope teams is recommended so that a team involved in an accident will have backup help.

Glacier travelers usually put three people on a 120-foot rope and three or four on a 150- or 165-foot rope. These configurations space the climbers far enough apart so that only one is at risk at a time as the rope team crosses a typical crevasse. Where truly humongous crevasses exist—the Himalayas or Alaska—greater spacing may be necessary.

On technical glacier terrain (with slopes steeper than 40 degrees or severe crevassing), belaying may be necessary, making it more efficient to travel with two-person rope teams. In this situation, having a second rope team as rescue backup becomes even more important. While the person who is on the same rope as the fallen climber holds the rope fast, the second team can set up a snow anchor and initiate the rescue.

### Tying In

It's best to tie the rope directly into the tie-in loops on your seat harness—rather than simply clipping a figure-8 loop into a locking carabiner at the harness—because the carabiner adds an unnecessary link between climber and rope. Of course, a clip-in connection makes it easy to disconnect and reconnect to the rope, but you don't normally do this repeatedly over the course of a day.

Following are some general glacier tie-in procedures, depending on the size of the rope team.

**Three-person rope:** This is the standard size for a rope team on a nontechnical glacier. Two of the climbers tie in at the very ends of the rope, usually with a rewoven figure-8 through the tie-in loops of the seat harness (fig. 14-3). The middle climber ties into the very center of the rope, most commonly with a double bowline (fig. 14-4). The small loop that remains at the end of the bowline should be clipped with a locking

*Fig. 14-3. Rigged and ready end climber on three-person rope*

carabiner to the harness to ensure the knot can't come loose. The butterfly knot is also good for the middle-person tie-in.

**Four-person rope:** Divide the rope into thirds. Two climbers tie in at the ends, while the other two tie in at the one-third points.

**Two-person rope:** Although a three-person rope is the standard for glacier travel, ropes will sometimes have only two climbers. The most convenient procedure is to have only a portion of the rope stretched between the climbers because a full rope length can result in too much slack as they weave through a maze of crevasses. Using only part of the rope also leaves some rope free for rescue use. The adapted Kiwi coil system is the preferred method for tying into a

shortened rope. The adapted Kiwi coil is illustrated and explained in "Special Rescue Situations," at the end of this chapter.

## Chest Harness

Put your chest harness on before heading out onto the glacier. Some climbers then clip the rope through the carabiner on the chest harness, leaving it clipped in at all times so that the harness will automatically help them stay upright in case of a fall. Others prefer to wait until after a fall to clip into the chest harness, on grounds that the chest-harness attachment could hamper the self-arrest position they must assume to help stop a ropemate's fall. There's a good compromise approach to this question: clip the climbing rope into your chest harness anytime you cross a snow bridge or otherwise face obvious immediate danger

*Fig. 14-4. Middle climber, ready and rigged with one prusik on each rope leading from the waist*

of a crevasse fall; otherwise, travel with the rope unclipped (fig. 14-3).

## Prusik Slings

The usual practice is to attach your slings to the climbing rope just as soon as you have roped up to begin glacier travel, so that they are ready for immediate use in an emergency (fig. 14-3). Stuff the ends of both slings into your pockets, ready to be pulled out and slipped onto your feet when needed.

If you're a middle person on the rope, you won't know which end you might have to climb after a fall. Therefore, attach one prusik to the section of rope that goes to the climber in front of you and the other prusik to the section that goes to the climber behind you (fig. 14-4). After any fall, you'll have to move one of the prusik slings to the side that you'll be climbing.

If you are using mechanical ascenders, do not attach them to the rope until after a crevasse fall.

## Rope Management

The first rule of rope management on a glacier is to keep the rope extended—not taut, but without undue slack. A rope that is fully extended between climbers is insurance against a long plunge into a hidden crevasse. With a slack rope, a climber's initial breakthrough into a crevasse can't be immediately resisted by the climber who follows. The falling climber therefore drops farther, increasing chances of hitting something or becoming wedged if the crevasse narrows. For the climbers holding the fall, a slack rope can mean a much greater hit on the rope from the falling climber, along with the danger of being dragged into the hole themselves.

The second important rule of rope management on a glacier is to run the rope at right angles to a crevasse whenever possible. A rope team that travels more or less parallel to a crevasse is taking the risk that a climber who falls into the crevasse could take a lengthy pendulum fall (fig. 14-5). Although it's not always possible to keep the rope at right angles to a crevasse, constant awareness of the situation will help you choose the best possible route (fig. 14-6).

To help keep slack out of the rope, a rope leader needs to set a pace the others can follow for a long time. For their part, the second and third climbers must try to closely match the pace of the leader so the rope stays extended. Be alert going downhill, when it becomes easy to walk too fast. At sharp turns, there is a tendency for the rope to go slack as the climber in front of you heads in a new direction and then to tighten as you near the turn yourself. Throughout the turn, adjust

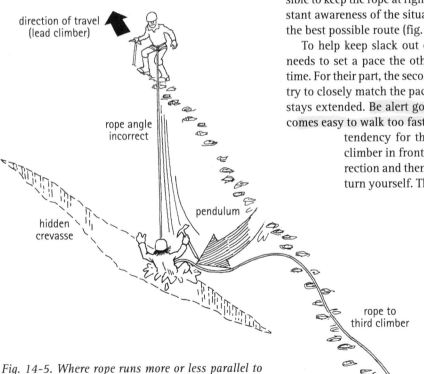

direction of travel (lead climber)

rope angle incorrect

hidden crevasse

pendulum

rope to third climber

*Fig. 14-5. Where rope runs more or less parallel to crevasse, fall is worsened by pendulum.*

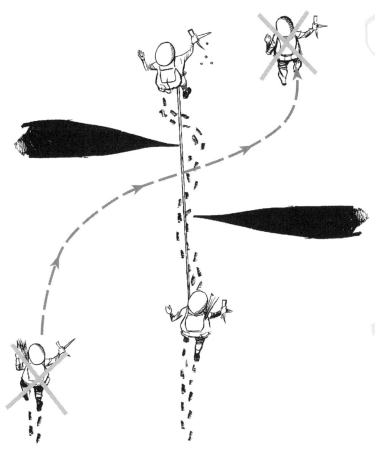

*Fig. 14-6. Be aware of rope partner's position to maintain perpendicular angle of rope to crevasse as much as possible.*

until the area has been thoroughly probed for crevasses. If you must camp on the glacier, mark the boundaries of the safe area with wands. Always belay climbers into and out of all rest and camp areas.

## Detecting Crevasses

The first step in safe glacier travel is figuring out where the crevasses are and picking a route through them. Routefinding on many glaciers is part planning, part experience, and part luck. You can sometimes get a head start on the planning by studying photos of the glacier before the trip, because some crevasse patterns remain fairly constant from year to year. Seek out recent reports from parties who have visited the area.

On the approach hike, try for a good up-valley or cross-valley look at the glacier before reaching it. You may see an obvious route that would be impossible to discover once you're there. Consider making notes or sketches to help in remembering major crevasses, landmarks, and routes.

Guidebook photos and distant views are useful, but prepare to be surprised. What appeared to be small cracks may be gaping chasms, and major crevasses may have been hidden from the angle of your view. Plan alternative routes from a distance if you can.

Once you're on the glacier, it's a continuous game of Find the Crevasse. Just because you can't see them doesn't mean there aren't any.

Here are some important tips for detecting crevasses:

your pace to keep out the slack. It's usually necessary to make new tracks, outside the leader's footsteps, in order to keep the rope fully extended (although at other times you will normally follow the leader's path for safety and ease of travel).

To keep the right amount of tension in the rope, it helps to travel with a small loop of rope (6 to 12 inches across) held in your downhill hand. The grip makes it easier to feel the progress of your ropemates so you can adjust your pace as needed, and it lets you keep the rope out from under your feet.

Don't forget safety when you reach a rest stop or campsite. The rope must stay extended and slack-free

• Keep an eye out for sagging trenches in the snow that mark where gravity has pulled down on snow over a crevasse. A sagging trench on the surface of the snow is a prime characteristic of a hidden crevasse. The sags will be visible by their slight difference in sheen, texture, or color. The low-angle light of early morning and late afternoon tend to accentuate this feature. (The sags may be impossible to detect in the flat light of a fog or in the glare of a midafternoon sun, and it takes additional information to distinguish them from certain wind forms.)

- Be wary after storms. New snow can fill a sagging trench and make it blend it into the surrounding surface. (At other times, however, the new snow can actually make the sagging trench more apparent by creating a hollow of new snow that contrasts with surrounding areas of old snow.)
- Be especially alert in areas where you know crevasses form, such as where a glacier makes an outside turn and where slope angle increases.
- Sweep your eyes to the sides of the route regularly, checking for open cracks to the left or right. Cracks could hint at the presence of crevasses extending beneath your path.
- Remember that where there is one crevasse there are often many.

## Snow Probing

Snow probing is the technique to use if you have found a suspicious-looking area and want to search it for crevasses. If your probe locates a crevasse, continue probing to find its true lip.

Probe with your ice ax, thrusting the shaft into the snow a couple of feet ahead of the snow you are standing on. Keep the ax perpendicular to the slope and thrust it in with a smooth motion. You need an ax with a uniform taper from the spike to the shaft, because a blunt spike or jutting ferrule makes it hard to feel the snow.

If resistance to the thrust is uniform, you have established that the snow is consistent to at least the depth of your ax. If resistance lessens abruptly, you've probably found a hole. If your route must continue in the direction of this hole, use further ax thrusts to establish its extent. The leader should open up the hole and mark it with wands.

The value of probing depends on your skill and experience at interpreting the changes felt in the snow layers. An inexperienced prober may think the shaft broke through into a hole when all it really did was hit a softer layer of snow. The length of the ice ax becomes a limiting factor in probing. The lead climber can also carry an avalanche probe ski pole, which is lighter, longer, and thinner than the ax for easier, deeper probes.

# Crossing a Crevasse Field

Climbers have a number of ways to get safely across a field of crevasses. The techniques described here are typical, but you'll have to adapt them as needed in the field. Routefinding on a glacier involves finding a path around or over all the crevasses that you see, guarding all the time against hidden crevasses. The crossing is seldom without its detours as you carefully pick your way over the glacier.

## The End Run

Crossing directly over a crevasse is seldom a preferred choice. Where a crevasse pinches down in width,

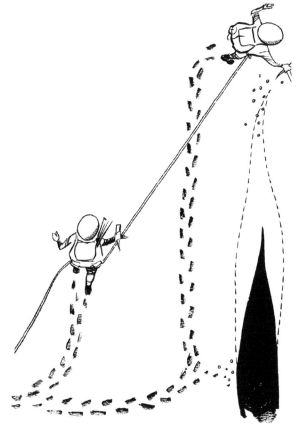

*Fig. 14-7. End run around a crevasse, keeping the rope extended fully by not following in the leader's footsteps*

often near its end, the safest and most dependable technique is to go around it, in an end run (fig. 14-7). A quarter-mile walk may gain you only 20 or 30 feet of forward progress, but it often beats a direct confrontation with the crevasse.

In late summer when the winter snow has melted down to the ice, you may be able to see the true end of the crevasse. But if seasonal snows still blanket the glacier, the visible end of the crack may not be its true end. Make a wide swing around the corner, probing carefully. Look closely at adjacent crevasses to judge whether one of them could be an extension of your crevasse; you could actually be crossing a snow bridge.

## Snow Bridges

If an end run is impractical, the next choice is to cross a snow bridge. Deep winter snow hardened by wind can develop into a crevasse bridge that lasts into the summer climbing season. Other, sturdier bridges are really thin isthmuses between two crevasses, with foundations that extend deep into the body of the glacier.

Study a bridge carefully—try for a side view—before putting any faith in it. If you're in doubt, the leader can go in to probe and get a close-up look while the second climber stays braced against the taut rope to help guard against a possible breakthrough (fig. 14-8). After the leader gets across, the rest of the party follows exactly in the leader's steps, also receiving a degree of protection from a taut rope held by a braced climber.

The strength of a snow bridge varies tremendously with temperature. An arch that might support a truck in the cold of winter or early morning may collapse under its own weight during an afternoon thaw. Cross every bridge with caution every time. Don't assume that because it held in the morning during the ascent that it's safe as you head down in the afternoon.

*Fig. 14-8. Crossing a snow bridge with caution*

## Jumping

Jumping is one of the least common tactics for crossing a crevasse (fig. 14-9). Most jumps across crevasses are short, simple leaps. If you're planning a desperate lunge, be sure you've ruled out all the alternatives and see that you are well belayed.

While being well supported by a taut rope or belayed, probe to find the true edge of the crevasse. If you need a running start for the jump, tramp down the snow for better footing. As final preparation, put on parka, mittens, and hat, check prusiks and harness, and spool out the amount of rope slack needed from the belayer. Then jump—with your ice ax in the self-arrest position, ready to help you claw over the edge if you're shy of a clean landing.

With the rope now linked to the landing side, the other climbers have a less dangerous jump ahead. The belay rope can help pull up on any jumper who falls just short of the target.

Use caution and common sense if the leap is from the high lip of a crevasse over to a lower side. (Bergschrunds, for example, often have a high overhanging wall on the uphill side.) You can be injured in a long, hard leap. If you go for it, keep your feet slightly apart for balance, knees bent to absorb shock, and ice ax held ready for a quick self-arrest. Beware of catching crampons on your gaiters.

Fig. 14-9. Jumping a crevasse (belay not shown)

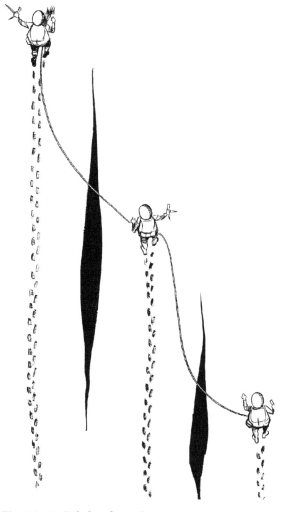

Fig. 14-10. Echelon formation

## Into the Crevasse

On rare occasions, it may be practical to get to the other side of a shallow crevasse by climbing into the crevasse, crossing it at the bottom, and climbing out the other side. This tactic should be attempted only by a strong, highly trained, and well-equipped party that is ready to provide a good belay, plus assistance in case the crevasse bottom collapses and leaves the climber hanging. One further caution: often, what appears to be a solid bottom isn't.

## Echelon Formation

Certain crevasse patterns preclude the rule of keeping the rope at right angles to the crevasses. If the route demands travel that is parallel to crevasses, the echelon formation can sometimes help (fig. 14-10). This formation is safest on stable, heavily crevassed glaciers where location of the crevasses is known and the risk of hidden holes is small. The formation offers an alternative to following in the leader's footsteps through a maze of crevasses where single-file travel is impractical. Avoid moving in echelon where hidden crevasses are likely.

# CREVASSE RESCUE

The depths of a great crevasse exhibit an awful beauty, both enticing and repellent. On a fine day, the walls are a sheen of soft blue ice in the filtered light from high above, and the cavern is cool and still as a church, or a tomb. It's a place every climber should visit once in a lifetime—for crevasse rescue practice. But if there's a second time, we hope it will be in the company of climbers who know the rescue techniques spelled out in the rest of this chapter.

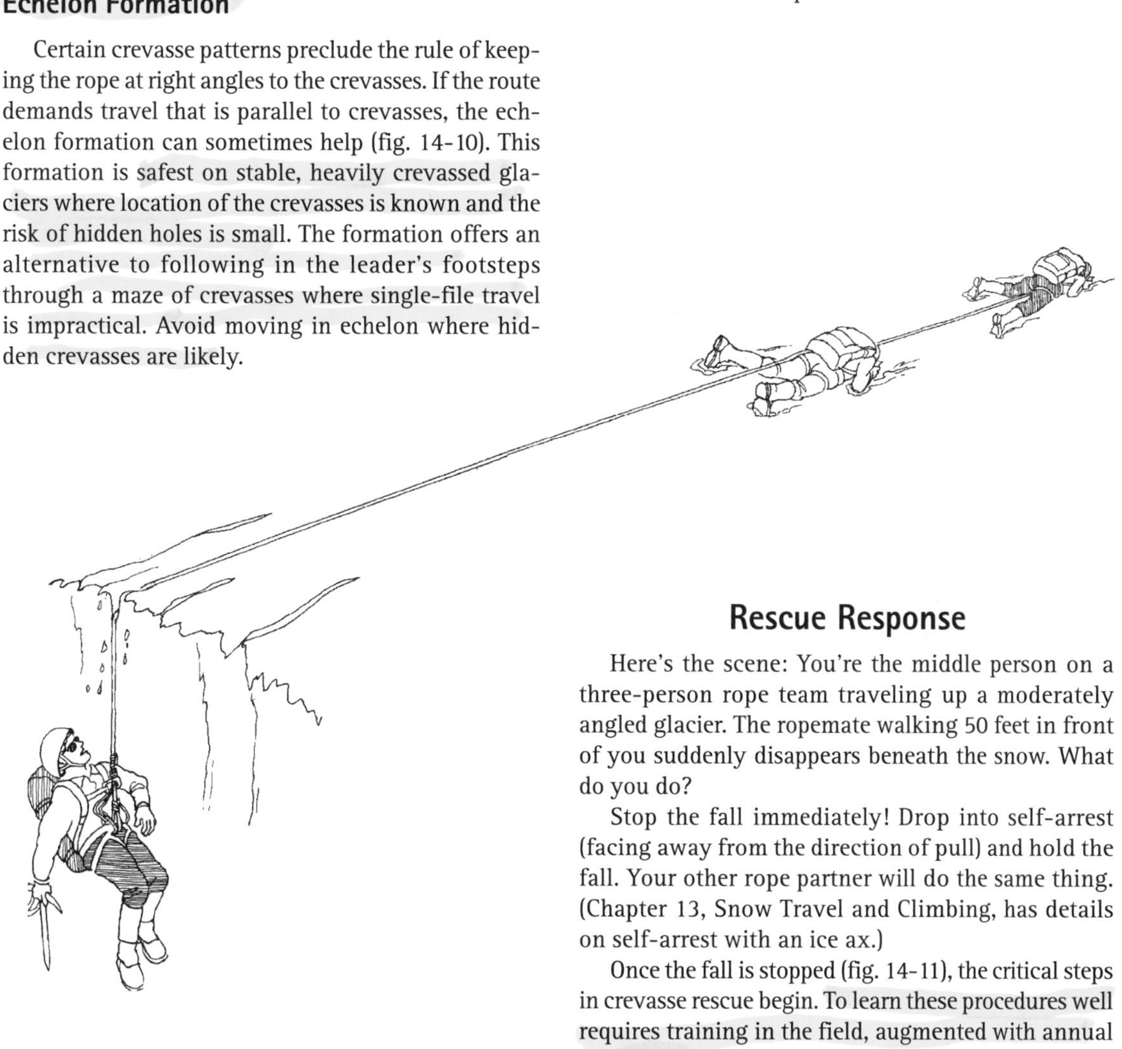

## Rescue Response

Here's the scene: You're the middle person on a three-person rope team traveling up a moderately angled glacier. The ropemate walking 50 feet in front of you suddenly disappears beneath the snow. What do you do?

Stop the fall immediately! Drop into self-arrest (facing away from the direction of pull) and hold the fall. Your other rope partner will do the same thing. (Chapter 13, Snow Travel and Climbing, has details on self-arrest with an ice ax.)

Once the fall is stopped (fig. 14-11), the critical steps in crevasse rescue begin. To learn these procedures well requires training in the field, augmented with annual practice.

*Fig. 14-11. Stop and hold the fall.*

The principal steps in a successful rescue, beginning the instant the fall is stopped, are the following:

1. Set up a secure anchor system.
2. Communicate with the fallen climber.
3. Devise a rescue plan. You have two basic choices:
   • Self-rescue—the fallen climber ascends the rope with prusik slings.
   • Team rescue—team members use a hauling system to pull the climber out.
4. Carry out the plan:
   • For a self-rescue, assist the fallen climber as needed.
   • For a team rescue, set up the chosen hauling system; then haul the climber out.

As you work to save the fallen climber, observe these primary safety considerations:

• All anchor systems must be absolutely reliable, with backup anchors to guard against failure.
• All rescuers must be connected to anchors at all times.
• The rescue must proceed as quickly as is consistent with efficient, thorough execution of every essential step.

(One brief note before moving on to the details of crevasse rescue: If the ropemate ahead of you had simply punched partially through into a crevasse without actually falling in, you wouldn't necessarily have to drop into self-arrest. You could provide adequate help by simply bracing yourself as you stand, one foot planted ahead in the direction of your ropemate, with your weight pulling back against the taut rope. As with self-arrest, your response must be immediate and decisive. This braced position is illustrated by the climber on the left in Figure 14-8.)

## Step 1: Set up a Secure Anchor System

The goal of Step 1 is to anchor the climber who is in the crevasse and allow the rescuers safe access to communicate with their fallen comrade.

### The Initial Anchor

It's the job of the end climber to set up the initial secure anchor. To free up the end climber, the middle climber on the three-person rope stays in self-arrest to support the weight of the fallen climber, usually an easy task because friction of the rope across the snow does much of the work.

The end climber slowly gets out of self-arrest, making sure the middle climber can hold the weight alone, and then sets to work establishing an anchor (fig. 14-12). Of course, if another rope team is on hand and trained, it is all right for both climbers to stay in self-arrest while the other team sets up the initial anchor.

A solitary ice ax driven vertically into the snow is not a good candidate for an anchor. For a solid anchor, consider a picket or a deadman for snow or an ice screw in ice. A picket is often a good choice for quick placement as the initial anchor in snow. Refer to the section on snow anchors in Chapter 13 for details on the various types of anchors and the best conditions for using each type.

The anchor is placed 5 to 10 feet down-rope from the middle climber, toward the lip of the crevasse. (If the anchor is placed instead on the other side of the middle climber, eventual tension on the rope could make it impossible for that person to untie.)

### Attaching the Rope to the Anchor

The person who has set up the anchor now attaches a short sling to the climbing rope with a prusik knot (a Bachmann knot may also be used). This person then attaches a runner to the sling with a carabiner, and clips the other end of the runner to the anchor with a locking carabiner.

The next move is to slide the friction knot down the rope, toward the crevasse, until the sling assembly is tight, ready to take a load. Now anyone who is still in self-arrest can ease the load off him- or herself and onto the anchor. Confirm that the anchor is solid and that the knot is gripping the climbing rope tightly. (Keep in mind that, if you choose to use a prusik knot, one rescuer will have to tend the knot later to keep it open any time the fallen climber is being pulled up. The Bachmann knot, on the other hand, usually requires less tending.)

Just as soon as the load is transferred to the anchor, back up the friction knot by tying a figure-8 loop in the climbing rope, a foot or so up-rope from the knot (fig. 14-13). At the same time, use a locking carabiner to clip a rescue pulley to the carabiner already on the sling, with the climbing rope through the pul-

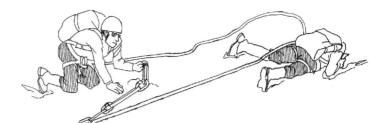

*Fig. 14-12. End man sets up initial anchor*

in place for the fallen climber, it's time to set up a second anchor. Meanwhile, the middle climber remains in self-arrest position as a temporary backup to guard the existing anchor.

The second anchor serves to make the anchor system as fail-safe as possible. This anchor needs to be good, so take the time to do it right. As with the initial anchor, you can use a picket or a deadman for snow or an ice screw in ice. A good combination in snow is a picket for the first anchor and a deadman (such as a buried fluke) for the second anchor (fig. 14-14).

ley. Clip the figure-8 loop into this new carabiner. With the pulley in place, you now have the beginnings of a Z-pulley hauling system, saving you time later if you end up needing to set up such a system to haul the climber from the crevasse.

## The Second Anchor

Never trust a single anchor that you know will be fully weighted. Back it up. With a single anchor now

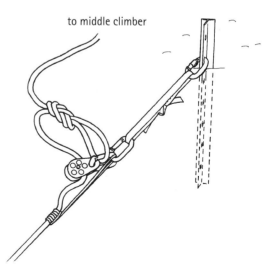

to middle climber

*Fig. 14-13. Pulley and back-up knot installed*

349

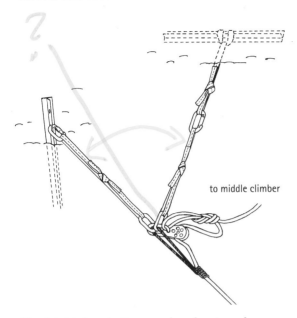

*Fig. 14-14. Locate the second anchor to make a tight and aligned connection.*

to middle climber

Link the second anchor to the sling on the climbing rope just as you linked the initial anchor to the sling: attach a runner to the sling with a carabiner (clipping through the pulley carabiner while you're at it), and then clip the other end of the runner to the anchor with a carabiner. Try to make a taut connection from anchor to sling.

## Step 2: Communicate with the Fallen Climber

The goal of Step 2 is to develop a complete understanding of the fallen climber's situation in order to be able to devise the rescue plan.

Someone now needs to check the fallen climber's situation closely (fig. 14-15). A rescuer can be belayed from the anchor by a teammate, or better yet a rescuer can move to the lip of the crevasse with a self-belay. This self-belay is not the one you've learned using an ice ax. For this self-belay at the crevasse, use a prusik knot to connect a sling to the free end of a rope that is attached to the anchor. Then clip the sling to your harness with a locking carabiner. By sliding this prusik knot along the rope, you can move toward the crevasse edge on an anchored self-belay.

Probe with your ice ax as you approach the crevasse lip to help discover any areas where the snow surface may be undercut by the crevasse. Approach the lip somewhat to the side of where the fall occurred so you won't knock snow onto the climber below.

Try to talk with the fallen climber. If you hear no answer, the climber may simply be out of earshot or a noisy wind on the glacier may be masking the response. If further effort still brings no response, a rescuer can rappel or be lowered on belay into the crevasse to help the climber. (See the information on dealing with an unconscious climber in "Special Rescue Situations," near the end of this chapter.)

However, if the fallen climber responds to your voice, ask questions to find out the full situation. Is the climber wedged in? Injured? In need of more clothing? Is the climber now standing in prusik slings? Most importantly, assure the climber that things are progressing topside but that you need help in deciding the best way to carry out the rescue.

The person who fell in should be able to tell you whether self-rescue is a good possibility—by climbing up the side of the crevasse or by prusiking out—or whether a hoist from above will be needed. You may even have the option of lowering the climber farther down, to a ramp or ledge where self-rescue or hauling might be easier. The rescuer perched at the lip of the crevasse will gain the most complete picture of the situation above and below, so will have the most important input in the decision on a rescue method.

## Step 3: Devise a Rescue Plan

The goal of Step 3 is to choose the method for getting the fallen climber safely out of the crevasse. Will the climber attempt self-rescue? Or will the team members topside set up a hauling system to pull the climber out?

With all the groundwork laid, it's time to devise a rescue plan. The first major decision is to choose between the options of self-rescue and team rescue; then comes the choice among the various methods of self-rescue or team rescue. Factors in these decisions are the condition of the climber, the number of rescuers, the equipment available (ice-climbing tools, additional ropes, pulleys, and so forth), weather conditions, topography of the crevasse area, and any other variables that will affect the safety of victim and rescuers.

*Fig. 14-15. Anchor system complete. Communicate with fallen climber.*

Regardless of the rescue method chosen, the lip of the crevasse must be prepared by padding it to minimize further entrenching of the rope. An entrenched rope will sabotage the rescuers' efforts to hoist the climber up over the lip and will confound a fallen climber's own attempts to prusik over it. It may take some excavation to properly prepare the lip. In fact, entrenching just from the climber's fall may force you to consider setting up a different rope from the one the climber is on.

For padding, slide an ice-ax shaft, a ski (watch the sharp edges), an ensolite pad, or even a pack under the rescue rope as close to the edge of the crevasse as you dare go. Anchor the padding so it can't fall into the crevasse.

### Option 1: Self-Rescue

Self-rescue is often the easiest and fastest form of crevasse rescue, regardless of party size. It has the added advantage of keeping the fallen climber active and warm. Of course, it requires that the climber be basically uninjured and able to maneuver in the crevasse.

For small parties without the muscle power to hoist the fallen climber or pinned down holding the rope, self-rescue may be the only practical option. This is especially true for a two-person party traveling alone.

Two good self-rescue methods for ascending the

rope are the Texas prusik and the stair-step prusik (described and illustrated later in this chapter).

### Option 2: Team Rescue

Climbers have several choices among team-rescue methods, each with its own particular advantages. (The single-pulley and Z-pulley methods are illustrated later in this chapter.)

**Brute force:** For a large party and a rope free of entrenchment, direct pull using brute force is an excellent method. It's fast and uncomplicated, uses minimal equipment, and requires little or no help from the fallen climber. It works best when perhaps half a dozen strong rescuers can haul on the rope and when the working platform for the pullers is flat or downhill.

**Single-pulley method:** For a badly entrenched rope or when the number of haulers is few, the single-pulley method may be best. An entrenched rope won't matter because this method requires a separate length of rope—either the unused end of the accident rope or another rope entirely. The rope must be at least twice as long as the distance from the anchor to the fallen climber. The mechanical advantage of the pulley makes hoisting a lot easier than with brute force alone, though it still usually takes a minimum of three or four people to do the pulling. The climber must be able to contribute to the rescue, with at least one good hand for clipping in to the rescue pulley and for balance.

**Z-pulley method:** For a fallen climber who is unable to help in the rescue or when few haulers are available, the Z-pulley is likely to be the best method. The pull force is on the accident rope, which may be partially entrenched in the snow, but the high mechanical advantage of the system gives haulers the power to overcome some entrenchment. You can gain even more power by piggybacking two systems together, such as a single-pulley setup coming from a Z-pulley system.

### Alternatives

A climber who falls into a crevasse does not necessarily have to come back out at the same spot. Check the possibility of lowering or swinging the fallen climber to a ledge. It might be a good spot to rest and perhaps a gateway to a different part of the crevasse where rescue will be easier. Consider whether the bottom of the crevasse looks solid. This could offer another resting spot and a possible path to a climbing route or a snow ramp back to the surface.

### Step 4: Carry out the Plan

The goal of Step 4 is to see the fallen climber safely out of the crevasse.

If self-rescue is the chosen plan, climbers topside will assist as needed. If it will be a team rescue, the climbers will set up the selected hauling system and pull the climber out.

A party with enough people should assign one climber to the lip of the crevasse as the communicator throughout the rescue. Good communication is especially important as the climber approaches the lip.

Upcoming sections provide detailed information on the principal prusiking methods for self-rescue and hauling methods for team rescue.

## Inside the Crevasse

While the climbers on top are busy going through the various steps leading toward final rescue, the fallen climber has work to do down below, beginning with the moment of recovery from the fall. Here are the immediate actions to take if you are the fallen climber:

1. Attain an upright position, if you haven't done so instinctively. Normally this is done by clipping the climbing rope through the carabiner at your chest harness.
2. Get into your prusik slings on the climbing rope, permitting you to alternate between standing and sitting as you dangle. You will be a lot more comfortable and will be ready to climb up the rope using the slings.
3. Get your pack and ice ax out of the way. You may be able to send them up on a rope from the rescuers. You can also clip the ax to your seat harness, letting it hang so it doesn't interfere with your movement. For the pack, you can also choose to girth-hitch a short sling through its haul loop and one shoulder strap and then clip the sling into the climbing rope with a carabiner. Clip into the climbing rope between your seat harness and prusik attachments. The pack will then hang below you; as you prusik up the rope, the hanging pack will slide freely along the bottom of the loop of

*mechanical advantage*

Parka of choice unde lid + @ hat/gloves mitts

climbing rope and weight the rope, making it easier to climb (fig. 14-21).

4. Keep warm. Close your parka, put on the hat and gloves you had stuffed in your pockets, and try to put on additional layers of clothing.

## Prusiking Methods for Self-Rescue

If you're just dangling free in the crevasse, it's usually okay to begin prusiking partway to the top as soon as you've gotten yourself upright, clipped into your chest harness, moved your pack and ice ax out of the way, and caught your breath. Let your ropemates on top know what you're doing if you can. Move carefully and deliberately so that you don't put sharp or sudden tugs on the rope that could interfere with their work in holding your weight and setting up an anchor. Normally, though, there is enough friction helping to hold the rope in the snow, especially at the lip, that your prusiking will not hamper your rescuers.

This preliminary prusiking serves to get you closer to the glacier surface, where it will be easier to communicate with rescuers. You and the other climbers can then decide together on the best rescue plan. If the final plan is to use a hauling system, your initial prusiking will have helped by making the haul shorter. Even if the final plan is self-rescue by prusiking, you will probably need their help in getting over the crevasse lip.

You'll take a different approach to prusiking if your fall did not leave you dangling free but, instead, dropped you onto a ledge, where most of your weight is off the rope. In this case, go ahead and get into your prusik slings, but wait to begin prusiking until you've talked it over with your rescuers. If you were to start prusiking without an okay

from topside, your full weight coming suddenly on the rope could unbalance and endanger them.

### The Texas Prusik

This method of ascending the rope, developed by spelunkers, is easy to learn and execute. It is the recommended method.

The Texas prusik uses one sling for the feet and a separate sling for the seat (clipped with a locking carabiner to the seat harness). The foot sling has a loop

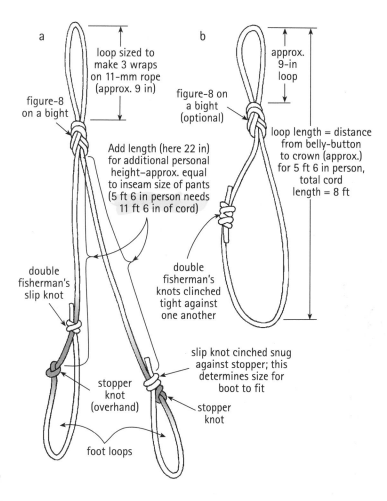

a
loop sized to make 3 wraps on 11-mm rope (approx. 9 in)

figure-8 on a bight

Add length (here 22 in) for additional personal height–approx. equal to inseam size of pants (5 ft 6 in person needs 11 ft 6 in of cord)

double fisherman's slip knot

stopper knot (overhand)

foot loops

b
approx. 9-in loop

figure-8 on a bight (optional)

loop length = distance from belly-button to crown (approx.) for 5 ft 6 in person, total cord length = 8 ft

double fisherman's knots clinched tight against one another

slip knot cinched snug against stopper; this determines size for boot to fit

stopper knot

*Fig. 14-16. How to make Texas prusik slings: a, the foot sling, with two foot loops; b, the seat-harness sling. Use 6-millimeter accessory cord.*

353

Fig. 14-17. Texas prusik dimensions

Fig. 14-18. Ascending a rope using the Texas prusik: a, leg-raise position; b, stand-up position.

for each foot, tied so that they will adjust and cinch down on your boots. See Figure 14-16 for details on how to make slings for the Texas prusik, using 6-millimeter accessory cord.

As with all prusik systems, correct sizing of the slings to your height is critical. Figure 14-17 shows a way to approximately gauge the correct sizing. When you are standing in the sling (fig. 14-18b), the top of the foot sling should be at about waist level and the top of the seat-harness sling should be at about eye

level. The distance between the two knots is the distance you will move up for each cycle of the inchworm motion you will make.

Before taking your slings out onto a glacier, check the sizing at home. Dangle yourself in the slings from a rope thrown over a garage rafter or a tree limb to find out what adjustments you need to make in the sling lengths.

Unlike the stair-step prusik, the Texas prusik will keep you upright without being connected to a chest harness. In fact, you must be unclipped from the chest harness to move the upper prusik.

This is how to use the Texas prusik after you've recovered from a fall into a crevasse (fig. 14-18):

1. Remove the foot loops from your pocket and slip one of the two adjustable loops over each boot. If you're wearing crampons, it won't be easy. Cinch up on the slip-knot loops to tighten them around the boots.
2. Stand up in the foot loops. You're now ready to move upward.
3. Unclip from your chest harness.
4. Loosen the friction knot attached to the seat-harness sling and slide it up the rope until it is taut.
5. Sit down in the seat harness, putting all your weight on the seat-harness sling, which releases your weight from the foot sling.
6. Loosen the friction knot attached to the foot sling and slide it up the rope (18 to 24 inches, if the sling is properly adjusted). Raise your legs with it.
7. Stand up again in the foot loops.
8. Keep repeating the process from Step 4.

The Texas prusik is a simple system that permits more progress per cycle and more comfortable rests (fig. 14-19) than the stair-step prusik. A climber with an injured leg can still ascend the rope with the Texas prusik by using just one of the foot loops. A slight disadvantage of the Texas prusik is that it is harder to use in a narrow crevasse.

## The Stair-Step Prusik

This is an alternative system that is a little more awkward and slightly harder to learn than the Texas prusik. This system lets you ascend the rope in a fashion that's a little like walking up a set of stairs. It uses a separate sling for each foot. Unlike the Texas prusik, it is necessary to be clipped into a chest harness to keep upright.

Figure 14-20 shows the details on how to make slings for the stair-step prusik, using 6-millimeter accessory cord. One sling is made shorter than the other. Each of the two slings consists basically of a single strand of cord, with equal-sized loops (1 foot long when stretched flat) tied at each end. The loop at one end, made to be nonadjustable, will be used in con-

*Fig. 14-19. Texas prusik system for a rest*

necting the sling to the climbing rope. The loop at the other end is the foot loop and is made to be adjustable.

In the longer sling, leave a 5-foot tail after you tie the loop that will be connected to the climbing rope. At the end of this tail, tie a small overhand loop that can be clipped into your seat harness as a safety strap to catch you in case your feet slip out of the two foot loops.

Twenty-five feet of 6-millimeter accessory cord is plenty of material to make both slings. Getting the size right requires some experimentation. When all the work is done, you should end up with one sling that is as long as the distance from the bottom of your feet to your eyes, and a shorter sling that is as long as from feet to elbows (or stomach). When you're standing in the slings, the tops of the slings should reach these same points: to gut level for the shorter sling, to eye

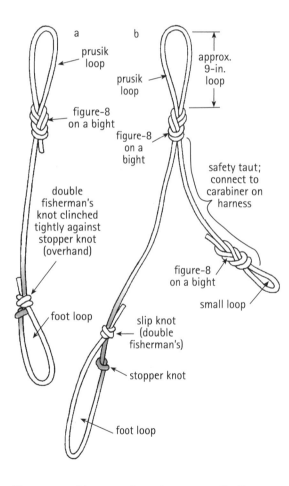

*Fig. 14-20. How to make stair-step prusik slings: a, the shorter foot sling; b, the longer foot sling. Use 6-millimeter accessory cord.*

level for the longer one. The distance between the two friction knots is the distance you will move up for each cycle of the stepping motion you will make.

This is how to use stair-step prusiks to climb the rope (fig. 14-21):

1. Take the foot loops from your pockets and slip them over your boots, cinching up on the slip knots. Keep your chest harness connected to the rope.
2. Stand up in the shorter prusik sling, putting all your weight onto it.
3. Unweight the leg attached to the longer prusik sling, and loosen the friction knot attached to that sling. Slide it up the rope (about 18 inches), lifting that leg with it.
4. Stand up in the longer sling, shifting all your weight to it.
5. Unweight the leg attached to the shorter sling; then loosen the friction knot attached to that sling. Slide it up the rope (about 18 inches), lifting that leg with it.
6. Keep repeating the process from Step 2.

## Hauling Methods for Team Rescue

All rescues are team rescues to some degree, because the fallen climber usually needs some help getting over the crevasse lip even in a self-rescue. A full team rescue usually involves hauling the climber to safety. The principal hauling methods—brute force, single pulley, Z-pulley, and piggyback systems—are described in the sections that follow. In any rescue system calling for pulleys, you can substitute carabiners if necessary. However, carabiners create far more friction and make the rope harder to pull, and the load on the anchor system is correspondingly increased. (The rescue method known as the Bilgeri is no longer considered to have much useful application in crevasse rescue and is not described here.)

### Brute Force

Here's a technique we can all understand. Just grab the rope and pull. A half dozen or so strong haulers line up along the accident rope and grasp it. They position themselves beyond the point where the anchor is attached to the climbing rope (with a prusik knot or Bachmann knot). The knot is then in the right place to hold the rope if the haulers slip or need a rest. Before the hauling begins, unclip the backup figure-8 loop from the anchor system. Then the haulers can go to work, pulling hand over hand on the rope or by moving step by step away from the crevasse.

One rescuer tends the knot to make sure the rope moves smoothly through it and also keeps an eye on the anchor system. If there are enough people, another person can be stationed at the lip of the crevasse to stay in communication with the fallen climber.

The haulers should pull the rope at a slow, steady pace, especially when the climber reaches the crevasse lip. If the rope has cut into the lip, the climber could be hurt by being pulled into the wall. At this point, rescuers may ask the climber to scramble over the lip (with the help of an ice ax) while they hoist.

## Single Pulley

The single-pulley method theoretically doubles the amount of weight that each hauler can raise compared with using no pulley, though friction lowers this ratio somewhat. Because the method uses a length of rope that is separate from the rope going to the climber, it's the hauling method to use if the accident rope is entrenched into the edge of the crevasse.

To carry out a single-pulley rescue (fig. 14-22), follow these steps:

1. Find a rescue rope (the unused end of the accident rope or a separate rope altogether). This rope must be at least twice as long as the distance from the anchor down to the fallen climber. You can use the existing anchor system or a new rescue anchor.
2. At the point where the rescue rope will go over the lip of the crevasse, prepare the lip with padding, such as an ice ax or pack, to keep the rope from entrenching itself in the snow.
3. Double the rescue rope into a big loop. Affix a rescue pulley to the loop and attach a locking carabiner to the pulley. Leave the carabiner unlocked.
4. Lower the pulley and carabiner dangling from the loop down to the fallen climber. Have the climber clip and lock the carabiner into the seat harness. Confirm that this has been done. Check that all the climber's equipment is secure and ready for hauling to begin. Have the climber clip the pulling side of the rescue rope into the chest harness, to help stay upright.
5. Assign a rescuer to attend to the slack that will

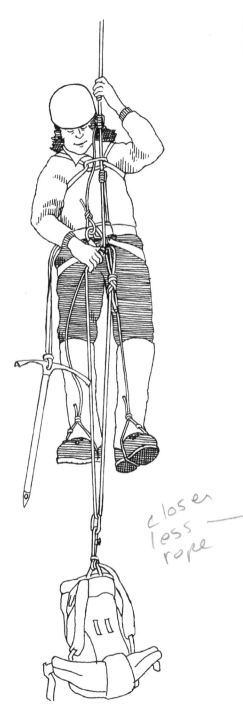

*closer*
*less*
*rope*

*Fig. 14-21. Self-rescue using the stair-step prusik*

*Fig. 14-22. Setting up and raising a climber with the single pulley (rescuer's personal anchors omitted for clarity)*

develop in the original accident rope as the climber is raised. It's critically important that this person pull slack through the friction knot so that the rope is always ready to accept the climber's weight, in case the pullers slip or need a rest. If the fallen climber has removed his or her pack and clipped it to the accident rope, there will be considerable weight on the rope, and it may even require two people to take in the slack. The existing figure-8 backup knot to the anchor remains in the system while the slack is taken in; do not remove it.

6. With everything ready, the haulers start pulling on the unanchored end of the rescue rope. To somewhat ease their task, the climber can pull up on the anchored half of the same rope while the hauling proceeds.

## Z-Pulley

The Z-pulley (fig. 14-23) magnifies the muscle power of small climbing parties by offering a 3-to-1 theoretical mechanical advantage through the use of two pulleys. It can be set up and operated with no help from the fallen climber, making it valuable in rescuing an unconscious person. The Z-pulley system normally uses the accident rope. It requires more equipment and is more complicated than the other hauling methods.

First confirm the solidness of your anchor system, because the Z-pulley will put considerable stress on it. Then take the loose end of the fallen climber's rope and lay out a long loop on the snow. This loop and the rope going from the anchor to the climber should form a giant flat S in the snow (somewhat like a Z or a backward Z, with the sharp edges worn off).

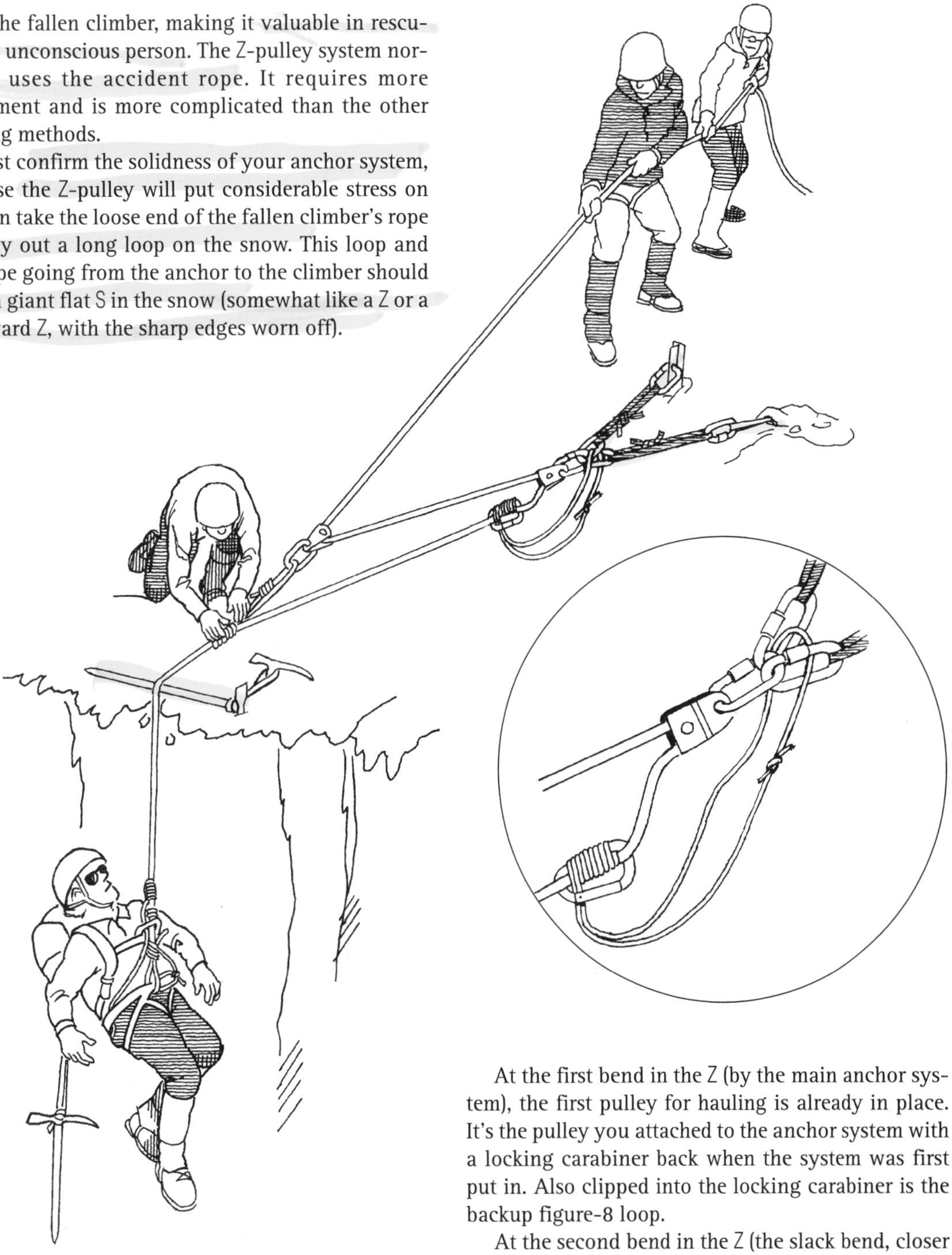

*Fig. 14-23. Raising a climber with the Z-pulley (Bachmann friction knot shown)*

At the first bend in the Z (by the main anchor system), the first pulley for hauling is already in place. It's the pulley you attached to the anchor system with a locking carabiner back when the system was first put in. Also clipped into the locking carabiner is the backup figure-8 loop.

At the second bend in the Z (the slack bend, closer to the crevasse lip), install a second pulley on the rope. Use a friction knot to attach a short sling to the taut rope going to the climber, and clip this sling with a carabiner into the second pulley. Drag the friction knot and pulley as far down the taut rope as you can toward the crevasse. You may have to see it to believe it, but you now have a Z-pulley setup, ready for use.

Here's how you haul with the Z-pulley system:

1. Unclip the backup figure-8 loop from the anchor system and untie the knot as soon as haulers and fallen climber are ready for pulling.
2. If a prusik knot was used to attach the accident rope to the anchor system, assign a rescuer to tend the knot so that the rope slips freely through it as the rope is pulled in. If a Bachmann friction knot was used instead, the attachment should tend itself, and the front hauler can simply keep an eye on it to see that all is well.
3. Start pulling at a steady rate, either hand over hand or by holding tight and walking backward.
4. The hauling will soon bring the second pulley in close to the stationary pulley at the anchor. Stop hauling while the pulleys are still a couple of feet apart. If you pull them too close, the figure Z is collapsed and its mechanical advantage is lost.
5. Now that you've stopped hauling, relax your pull on the rope enough to transfer the climber's weight back onto the friction knot at the anchor.
6. Reset the Z-pulley by loosening the friction knot that is linked to the second pulley and sliding it back down the taut line toward the crevasse lip once again.
7. Keep repeating the process from Step 2.

As the fallen climber nears the lip of the crevasse, beware of the pulling power of the Z-pulley. If you're not careful, the climber can be injured by being pulled sharply up into the lip.

## Piggyback Pulleys

To get even more mechanical advantage out of a rescue hauling setup, you can combine, or "piggyback," two systems. For example, you can establish a separate single-pulley setup to haul on the rope coming from a Z-pulley system. This now gives you a 6-to-1 theoretical mechanical advantage. Or set up a single pulley to haul on another single-pulley system for a 4-to-1 advantage.

To piggyback two systems, first create your initial hauling system, either a single pulley or a Z-pulley. Now establish a second anchor some distance behind the main one, to handle the second hauling system. Attach the second hoist, again either a single pulley or a Z-pulley, to the accident rope at the point where the rescuers would normally pull.

As you might guess, piggyback systems require an ample supply of slings, pulleys, carabiners, anchor material, and rope.

# Special Rescue Situations

A crevasse rescue can be complicated by any number of unusual twists. The following are some special situations you could encounter, and ideas on how to deal with them. The situations can become complicated, and you'll have to adapt your response to the conditions of the moment. Anything that works safely is fine.

## When the Middle Person Falls In

It's usually the first person on the rope who takes the fall when a rope team crosses a hidden crevasse. It's awkward at best when the middle person on a three-person rope team falls in, especially if there are no other climbers around to set up the rescue anchor. With no second team, the only two people who can help are separated by a crevasse, each in self-arrest. Here's a general procedure for getting out of this fix.

The climbers begin by deciding which side of the crevasse will be the rescue side; that is, which side should the fallen climber come out on? Usually, one of the two rescuers in self-arrest is holding more weight than the other. The one holding the least weight usually has the best chance to get up and establish an anchor while the rescuer on the other side stays in self-arrest to hold the fall.

After the climber on the rescue side sets up the rescue anchor (as described in Step 1 earlier in this chapter), the climber in self-arrest on the other side of the crevasse can slowly release tension on the climbing rope and ease the fallen climber's weight onto the anchor.

The climber on the rescue side now tries to belay the climber on the wrong side over to the rescue side, assuming that the second person is needed to help in the operation. The rope on the rescue side can be used for belaying, if it is long enough. Or a lightweight 100-foot accessory line (a precaution for a rope team traveling alone) can provide the belay. However, the climber on the wrong side could be stuck if no belay or safe route is available. This climber would then set up an anchor and stay put.

The most advantageous rescue plan now is for the fallen climber to ascend the rope on prusik slings, coming out on the rescue side, where the anchor has been placed. If a self-rescue by prusiking is not possible, then a Z-pulley or a piggyback system could be tried. This all takes plenty of time, competence, equipment, and resourcefulness. Learn to use the Bachmann knot for times when you might have to haul alone, because the knot requires less tending than a standard prusik knot in a hauling system.

In the case of a four-person rope team, the situation is a little simpler in the event that one of the two middle members falls into a crevasse. Conduct the rescue in a routine manner from the side that has two climbers topside.

## A Two-Person Team Alone

Glacier travel for a party of two people with no other rope team nearby is risky indeed. Both climbers absolutely need to know their rescue techniques. Period. The climber who stops a fall must set up an anchor alone while in self-arrest and then create a hauling system if one is needed. Therefore each climber needs to carry at least two pieces of snow or ice protection for an anchor appropriate to the conditions, plus the equipment (pulleys, carabiners, slings) to set up a hauling system. And all of this must be readily at hand, clanking from seat harness or pack straps.

Rope teams of two should use the tie-in method known as the adapted Kiwi coil (described in the following section), which automatically makes available an extra length of rope for rescue use. Packing along a 100-foot accessory line is a good optional precaution. And with only two people, it's even more important than usual to travel with your personal prusiking system ready for use.

Let's say you end up as the sole rescuer in a two-person rope team, holding your partner's fall with your self-arrest. Begin your rescue efforts by augmenting

the security of your arrest position by digging in your feet and pressing the ice ax more firmly into the snow. Imagine that you are establishing a belay stance while lying down.

Try to free one hand by rotating the upper half of your body—but keep leaning on the ax and bracing yourself with at least one stiff leg. Don't have the rope clipped into your chest harness.

When you get one hand free, place a fluke, picket, ice screw, second ice tool—anything secure enough to hold and allow you to get up and create a main anchor. At this point, you'll see the value of keeping the appropriate anchors easily accessible.

Now you'll go through the steps of rescue response described earlier in this chapter, though probably under more duress than a larger rope team or group of teams. Set up a secure main anchor. Communicate with your fallen partner, settle on a rescue plan, and carry it out. Ideally, your partner will be able to handle self-rescue, prusiking out. If not, you would probably try a Z-pulley or piggyback hauling system. Of course, if you're unable to set up an anchor in the first place, the climber in the crevasse has no choice but to try self-rescue while you remain in self-arrest.

### The Adapted Kiwi Coil

An adaptation of the Kiwi coil that was developed by alpine glacier guides in New Zealand is the preferred tie-in method for two-person glacier travel teams. The technique results in closer spacing between rope partners for more efficient, comfortable travel, and provides free rope for a hauling system or other rescue use.

The adapted coil also is valuable in providing a means of quick transition between the closer spacing of roped glacier travel and the full rope-length requirements of belayed climbing. This transition is important on an alpine climb where a glacier approach is followed by belayed rock or ice climbing.

To create an adapted Kiwi coil (fig. 14-24):

1. Tie in to the rope at your seat harness, as you would normally.
2. Take a series of coils of rope into your hand (usually five, but no more than nine) until you have the desired spacing between you and your rope partner.

*Fig. 14-24. Tying an adapted Kiwi coil*

Secure the coils together by tying an overhand knot around them, using a loop of the rope.

3. Get the coils out of the way for travel, stowing them securely anywhere you choose, such as in the top of your pack or over one shoulder, but easily accessible.

4. Tie the shortened length of climbing rope to your seat harness, with a double bowline. The rope is now tied twice to the seat harness, and any force coming onto the rope will be taken by this second knot.

## An Unconscious Fallen Climber

To help an unconscious climber, send a rescuer down by rappelling or being lowered on belay. This rescuer can administer first aid and also get the climber right-side up if necessary. Any of the standard hauling methods can then be considered for use. To help get the climber over the lip of the crevasse, a rescuer may have to work right at the edge or from inside the crevasse. Keep alert to the condition of the unconscious person, taking care to cause no further injury.

## More Than One Victim

In a case where more than one person has fallen into a crevasse, assess each person's condition and the best method for getting each one out, and then decide the order of rescue. Be sure each fallen climber is given warm clothing, if needed, and keep them informed of rescue plans as they develop.

## Cramped Working Space

The climber who drops into self-arrest position to stop a ropemate's fall could be lying so close to the lip of the crevasse that there's very little room for an anchor or pulley system. A solution to this situation is to set up the main anchor where there is enough room—on the up-rope side of the rescuer in self-arrest (instead of the usual place between the rescuer and the crevasse). Leave a couple of feet of slack between the main anchor and this rescuer, so that he or she isn't trapped in the system by tension on the rope.

Then set up a temporary anchor, between the rescuer and the crevasse, that will take the weight of the fallen climber, enabling the rescuer to get up from self-arrest position and untie. Once hauling begins, the prusik attached to the temporary anchor should be untied.

## Between Two Crevasses

Rescuers trying to work in a very narrow area between two crevasses can consider moving the operation. The rescue might proceed better if it is run from the opposite side of the crevasse that holds the fallen climber.

Another option is to change the direction of pull on a Z-pulley system. Hook another pulley to the anchor and run the hauling end of the rope through it. Now the rescuers can pull in a direction more parallel to the crevasses.

## Entrenched Ropes

The upward progress of a person climbing out or being pulled out of a crevasse can be stopped cold by a rope that has dug itself into the lip. The situation calls for some improvisation. For instance, a rescuer can attach prusik slings or etriers above the entrenched portion of the rope and drop them down for the climber to step into.

Another option is to switch to a new rescue rope. A rescuer can lower a new rope to the climber. Or the fallen climber can, in effect, provide a new rope by tossing the loose end of the climbing rope up to the rescuers. This is done by prusiking up to the lip, untying from the end of the climbing rope (after first tying in higher up), and throwing the loose end up to the rescuers.

A new rescue rope, carefully padded at the lip of the crevasse so it doesn't also get entrenched, opens up several rescue possibilities. The climber can switch prusik slings from the original climbing rope to the new free rope. Or the rescuers can haul the climber up and out on the new rope. Or the climber can merely transfer all weight to the new rope to give rescuers a much better chance of freeing the entrenched line.

## Roofed Crevasses

Wide roofed crevasses present special problems. The fallen climber may be hanging free, without a stabilizing wall for support, and the accident rope typically entrenches itself deeply into the snow of the crevasse roof. The climber may be bombarded by snow and ice dislodged by the rescuers above, who will be working in an area of proven instability.

Sometimes it's necessary for a well-belayed rescuer to take a shovel or ax and enlarge the hole the climber fell through. Do your best to keep snow and ice from hitting the climber.

Knowledge and preparation will minimize the hazards of roofed crevasses and the other problems of traveling near crevasses. Glacier travelers who learn about crevasses and regard them with a healthy respect may never fall in. If they do, they will know the techniques that give them the best chance to get back out.

# 15

# ICE CLIMBING

Ice appears in a variety of forms. The effects of pressure, heat, and time transform snow and other frozen precipitation into the alpine ice of glaciers, icefields, and couloirs. There is no clear distinction between alpine ice and hard snow. Alpine ice is sometimes seen as *blue ice,* a hue that tells you the ice is relatively pure. *Black ice* is another alpine variation—old, hard ice, mixed with dirt, pebbles, or other debris.

When water freezes, the result is *water ice.* It can be as dramatic as a frozen waterfall or as common as *verglas,* the thin, clear coating that forms when rainfall or melting snow freezes on rock. Verglas is difficult to climb because the thin layer provides scant purchase for crampons and ice tools. Water ice is usually harder, steeper, and more brittle than alpine ice, but at high altitudes and low temperatures the two may be indistinguishable.

Ice is as changeable and ephemeral as snow. In rock climbing, yesterday's crack and slab problem will likely be there next year, but this morning's ice route may be nothing but wet rock by afternoon. The ice climber learns to anticipate the ever-changing nature of the climbing medium.

Ice-climbing techniques vary depending on steepness of the slope. On flat ice, you can usually walk without crampons fairly easily, especially if there are rocks and dirt embedded in the surface. On short slopes, you can use an ice ax to chop steps, but longer sections call for crampons. French technique—"flat-footing"— works well on steepening ice, up to a limit. The steepest routes require front-pointing. This chapter will use some descriptive terms in referring to the approximate steepness of ice slopes. Here's roughly what they mean, in degrees of angle:

| | |
|---|---|
| Gentle | Up to 30 degrees |
| Moderate | 30 to 45 degrees |
| Steep | 45 to 60 degrees |
| Extremely steep | 60 to 80 degrees |
| Vertical | 80 to 90 degrees |
| Overhanging | Over 90 degrees |

## EQUIPMENT

Refinements in equipment have helped ice climbers improve and expand their techniques and use them on greater climbing challenges. Manufacturers are producing a steady stream of specialized clothing, boots, crampons, ice tools, and ice anchors. Review Chapter 13 for a general description of gear such as crampons and ice axes. This chapter will outline equipment features that are especially important for ice climbing.

### Clothing

Clothes for ice climbing should offer a combination of comfort and function. You will want to employ a layered system. In choosing a jacket or anorak, check to see that you can reach high and not have the anorak or jacket bottom rise above your waist. You don't want your torso exposed to the elements as you're reaching up to make a high tool placement.

Some climbers wear bibs or a one-piece suit as an alternative to the conventional outfit of jacket (or anorak) and pants. A one-piece suit of windproof, waterproof synthetic material retains warmth and repels debris. The suit should provide a convenient means of ventilation—for example, one zipper that opens from elbow to ankle and a second zipper that opens from stomach to back via the crotch. (The one-piece suit should not be confused with the expedition suit, essentially an insulated one-piece suit. Expedition suits are designed for use in the extreme conditions of high altitude or arctic environments.)

Your hands need protection from cold and abrasion. Climbing alpine ice on a summer day may require nothing more than a pair of light gloves. Water ice climbing will usually require much more elaborate layered systems. There are many glove and mitten systems available. Features to look for include waterproof shells (sealed Gore-Tex shells are good), articulated designs, removable liners, and retainer loops. Mittens are warmer than gloves but more cumbersome; several manufacturers offer "trigger-finger" mittens as a compromise.

Consider ease of use as you choose gloves and mittens. For instance, you should be able to adjust straps using your teeth. The components of layered systems must be compatible and should be easy to remove and replace. You will often have to remove a glove or mitten to manipulate ice protection. Note that Velcro straps may interfere with your tool leashes. Gloves or mittens should have rubberized palms to help in gripping an ice tool shaft; fabrics, especially nylons, tend to be rather slippery. One rather esoteric feature of high-density, boiled wool mittens (such as Dachsteins) is that you can temporarily freeze a mittened hand to the ice for help through a move.

## Boots

Winter ice climbers use plastic boots more commonly than leather footwear. Plastic boots are warmer and drier than double leather boots, and they also provide a rigid platform for crampons, especially important for front-pointing. Plastic boots have molded toe and heel grooves that help keep step-in/clamp-on crampon bindings securely attached.

For alpine ice climbing in more moderate conditions, modern leather mountaineering boots (for example, the Scarpa Eiger and LaSportiva K2) may be a better choice. Most models have molded toe and heel grooves, so they are compatible with hinged step-in crampons. Leather boots are lighter than plastic boots, generally more comfortable for hiking, and better for rock climbing. However, if you intend to use leather boots for extensive front-pointing, they need a stiff, full shank.

Because ankle rotation is so important in French technique (flat-footing), you need a boot that permits good range of motion. Leather boots are usually better in this regard. When fitting your boots, remember that you want ice-climbing footwear to fit well: snug in the heel and instep but with room for toes to wiggle. Be sure to fit your boots to accommodate the stockings you expect to wear.

Make sure your gaiters fit your boots. You'll need full-length gaiters that extend from your foot to just beneath the knee. If you choose to wear insulated supergaiters for added warmth, check the fit of your crampons.

## Crampons

Properly fitted hinged 12-point crampons are adequate for most alpine ice climbing. They work well with most types of climbing boots and are less expensive than rigid-frame designs.

Climbers who do a lot of front-pointing (especially waterfall ice climbers) prefer rigid-frame crampons, which vibrate less than hinged crampons when kicked into the more dense water ice. Rigid crampons should be worn with stiff, full-shank or plastic boots to prevent overstressing the crampon frame. Although some rigid crampons (for example, the Lowe Footfang) are strong enough to be worn with boots having less than full, stiff shanks, a soft boot could twist out of a step-in crampon binding. (See Chapter 13 for a full discussion of crampons.)

Crampon points must be sharp, and the harder the ice, the sharper the points need to be. Check the points before each climb and sharpen them if necessary. The angle of the front points and of the first row of downward points is critical in determining the best penetration. For regular ice, the front points are shaped straight but bent slightly downward, and the first row

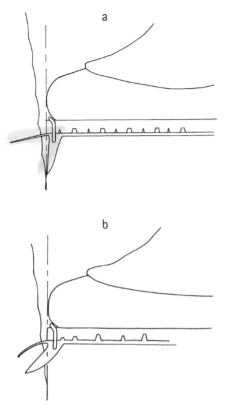

*Fig. 15-1. Angle of front points: a, for regular ice; b, for waterfall ice.*

is angled slightly forward (fig. 15-1a). For waterfall ice, the front points are curved downward, and the ends of the first row are angled more forward than those used for regular ice (fig. 15-1b). Some waterfall climbers prefer crampons with just a single front point (monopoint), which makes for easy placement (fig. 15-2). However, a monopoint has more tendency to rotate than double front points.

## Ice Tools

The perfect ice tool does not exist. However, most ice tools now being manufactured work quite well. Your selection of ice tools should be based on answers to a number of questions: Do the tools fit you? Can you comfortably handle the tools? Are they designed for the kind of climbing you intend to do?

Part of the fun of ice climbing is experimenting with the large variety of tools and learning how to use them. You can borrow, rent, or buy ice tools in order to discover which ones work best in your own climbing. Ice tools have shorter shafts than the standard axes used in snow climbing. The short shaft, commonly 45 to 55 centimeters, is easier to control, increasing the accuracy of placement of the pick and reducing the shaft vibration that can fatigue arm muscles. Ice hammers (fig. 15-3) often have an even shorter shaft length (as short as 35 centimeters). Ice tools generally weigh 24 to 32 ounces, and some feature removable head

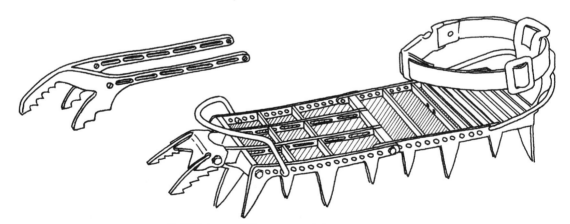

*Fig. 15-2. Rigid crampon with interchangeable single front point*

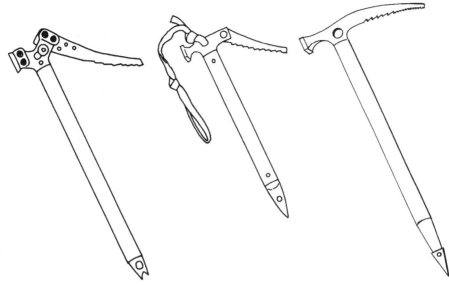

*Fig. 15-3. Typical ice hammers*

weights that allow you to fine-tune the tool's "swing weight."

On alpine ice, some climbers use a full-length ice ax paired with a shorter ice tool. On more technical routes, many climbers use two short ice tools. A versatile combination is an ax and a hammer. The adze of the ax is used to chop and scrape ice for steps, belay positions, ice protection, and ice bollards; the hammer is used to drive in pieces of protection. Some climbers prefer to hold the hammer in their dominant hand, making it easier to start ice screws or place ice and rock pitons. Practice using either hand to place protection.

Many tools feature modular designs. In some models, only the pick is interchangeable. Fully modular tools provide the option of interchangeable picks and adze/hammerheads. Picks, adzes, and hammerheads can be replaced as the need arises. This adds complexity to the tool and additional parts that can fail or be lost, but it also provides an added degree of flexibility. The tool can be assembled to accommodate prevailing conditions. A broken pick can be replaced in the field, even in midpitch if the fastening system is not too complex.

Note that there is no standard fastening system for parts. Components of one manufacturer's system will not be compatible with those from another company, and some systems are easier to use than others. The trend has been to design systems that require a minimum of tools. The components of some tools can be changed by using the pick or spike of your second ice tool.

Many climbers carry a third tool, which can be used as an anchor at belay points, as a protection placement, or to replace a lost or broken tool. The third tool can be short (35 to 40 centimeters) and light (16 ounces). The spike of a holstered tool is a potential hazard, so you may decide to carry a tool that does not have a spike. Try to select a model that is compatible with your other tools so that components are interchangeable. For example, the Stubai Eiger Hammer is compatible with Stubai FKW components.

To help in gripping the ice tools, you can wear gloves or mittens with rubberized palms. Most ice tools have a shaft covering that improves the grip. Inspect your tools before each outing, checking for cracks and other signs of wear or damage. Be sure that adzes, picks, and spikes are as sharp as possible. Keep these sharp edges covered with guards when they're not in use. If your tools are a modular design, also check to see that all fastening systems are secure. Consider using an industrial cement (such as Loctite) to ensure that parts will not work loose in the middle of a climb.

There is great variety in the styles of ice tools. Following are the principal design variations, categorized by the parts of the tool: pick, adze, shaft, and spike.

## Picks

The job of the pick is to penetrate the ice, hold against a downward pull, and release easily when its grip is no longer needed. The holding and releasing characteristics of a pick are determined by its weight, shape, and teeth. Modular ice tools typically include a variety of pick designs, but not all manufacturers offer all types. Tubular picks are rather limited in application (they're best suited for use in cold, dry ice); not surprisingly, they are made by only a few manufacturers.

A tool with a relatively heavy head cuts and penetrates most readily, but it may be difficult to extract because of its greater penetration. Some tool models have removable weights that can be added to the head to aid penetration.

The steeper the droop of a pick and the sharper,

deeper, and more numerous the teeth, the better the pick will hold; the smoother the pick, the easier it is to remove. The teeth should be shaped to bite into the ice as you pull on the end of the shaft. Although thin picks penetrate and hold best, they are more vulnerable to damage from hitting rock or from the twisting that often occurs when a climber tries to extract the tool. A thick-bladed pick, on the other hand, requires more force to place and is more likely to shatter the ice, but it is less prone to break.

With the conflicting demands on an ice tool, it's no wonder there is wide variation in pick design (fig. 15-4). Modular tools provide the option of several types of interchangeable picks, so you can choose the right one for a particular climb or replace a broken pick instead of discarding the tool. Talk to experienced ice climbers for help in choosing pick designs that will be suitable for you. Here are the principal pick designs you will encounter.

**Technically curved:** The pick on a standard ice ax used in snow climbing curves slightly downward. Most ice tools feature a pick that curves down more sharply and holds better in ice. This technically curved pick (fig. 15-4a) is most often used on alpine and glacial

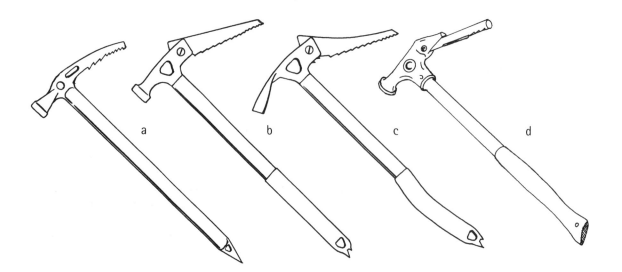

*Fig. 15-4. Ice tools with various pick designs: a, technically curved; b, straight drooped; c, reverse curved; d, tubular.*

ice. A good choice is an ice tool with a pick whose curvature matches your natural swing.

**Straight drooped:** An ice tool with a straight but sharply down-angled pick penetrates well in soft to hard ice (fig. 15-4b).

**Reverse curved:** The reverse-curved pick (also known as a banana pick or elephant pick) offers the security of a drooped pick but can be placed with a more natural swing (fig. 15-4c). The ease of removal of a drooped pick that has some reverse curve (upward curve) makes it a frequent choice for waterfall and other steep ice routes.

**Tubular:** Tubular-nosed picks—thin and sharp—are popular for hard water ice because the tube shatters the ice less than a conventional pick. Tubular picks (fig. 15-4d) tend to be more fragile than other types.

The shape of any pick can be easily changed with a hand file or hand grinder, but be judicious in removing metal so that you don't weaken the pick. Consider beveling the top of the pick to aid in removal from the ice. You can also change the tooth pattern of a pick that either sticks too well or doesn't stick well enough. Modifying the angle at the very end of the pick in order to change its clearance will affect its hooking ability; a more pronounced positive clearance should make the pick better for hooking. (Chapter 13 includes a discussion and drawing of positive and negative clearance.)

## Adzes

With the adze of an ice tool, you can chop steps, clear ice to make a good surface for a screw placement, and cut footholds at belay stances. As with picks, adzes come in an array of shapes and sizes (fig. 15-5). Modular ice tools give you the option to replace a broken adze or to change adzes depending on ice conditions. You can even exchange an adze for a hammerhead.

The most common adze is straight, extending perpendicular to the shaft or drooping somewhat downward. The straight adze with its sharp corners is excellent for cutting steps. Some adzes curve downward like the technically curved pick. The very end of the working edge of some adzes curves slightly inward, although this may impede step-cutting because the full force of a swing is diffused. Tubular adzes are available, mainly for use on waterfall ice. Drooped adzes can be used in soft snow. Some adzes and

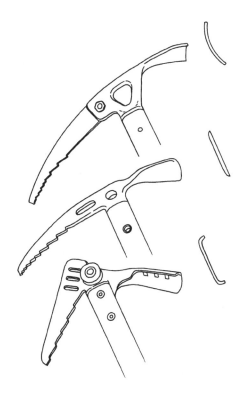

*Fig. 15-5. Side and end views of three adze designs*

hammerheads are now designed so that they can be used for placements in rock.

## Shafts

The shafts of most ice tools are straight, but many models feature bent shafts (fig. 15-6), which are designed to decrease strain in the wrist. Be sure the curve of the bend complements your natural swing. A bent-shaft design will not keep you from bashing your knuckles; this is usually the result of your technique. Bent-shaft designs have some disadvantages: the bend may impede placement of the shaft into snow, the bend makes hammering or chopping somewhat awkward, and a bent-shaft tool may be difficult to remove from a holster. The DMM Predator features a curve with a long radius, a design meant to reduce these disadvantages.

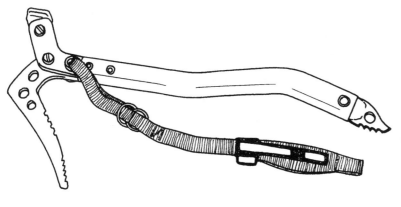

*Fig. 15-6. Bent-shaft ice tool*

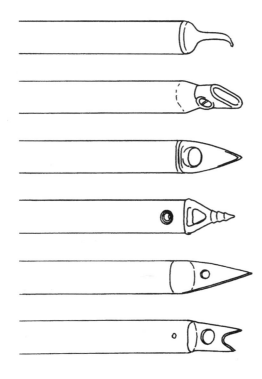

*Fig. 15-7. Various ice-tool spike designs*

The circumference and cross-sectional shape of the shaft will affect your grip. A particular shaft might be too large for your hand. A tool should be comfortable to grip while you're wearing the various glove and mitten combinations that you use while climbing.

## Spikes

To penetrate ice, the spike on an ice tool must be sharp, and the joint between spike and shaft must be smooth. Spikes are solid or tubular. Solid spikes consist of a flat plate or a cone-shaped tip, and cone-shaped spikes point either straight down or somewhat forward. Most spikes have carabiner holes, which you can clip to as a temporary anchor when setting up a belay anchor (fig. 15-7).

## Attachment

A wrist leash from you to each ice tool serves several purposes. The leash secures a dropped tool, helps in the work of swinging the tool, and lets you rest your grip by hanging your weight from it. Manufactured leashes are available with a variety of features designed to increase comfort and security.

A wrist leash is an energy-saving necessity on extremely steep or vertical ice. The leash attached through the carabiner hole at the head of the tool should be just long enough to let you grasp the shaft near the spike. The leash needs an end loop to slip your hand through. You may tie or tape the loop to the shaft at the desired hand position, to help hold your hand in the right spot at all times and to direct the downward pull straight along the shaft (fig. 15-8). Used like this, the leash shares in the work of holding and swinging the ax. The wrist leash also makes it possible to hang from an ice tool without maintaining a forearm-killing grip. To do this, let your arm hang straight, with hand and arm relaxed, and allow your skeletal system to support your body weight.

You can also rest by hanging from a tether (umbilical) that runs from the carabiner hole in the spike

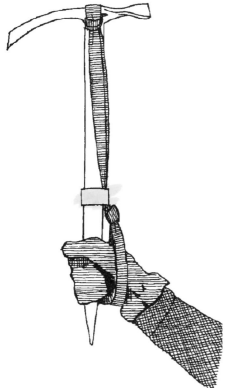

*Fig. 15-8. Wrist leash for ice tools*

to your harness. (Some ice climbers avoid this technique, considering it to be a use of artificial aid.) A tether can be a hindrance; it needs to be long enough so that it won't hamper your swing but short enough so that it doesn't get in the way, perhaps catching on a crampon. Put an ice tool in a holster or tool loop when it's not needed.

## Ice Screws

Ice screws evolved from ice pitons, which were extra-long, blade-type rock pitons with holes, notches, or bulges to increase their grip in ice. After World War II, climbers experimented with new designs that featured a greater shaft area to decrease the load per square inch on the ice and more holes to help the shaft freeze into the slope.

When ice screws first appeared in the early 1960s, enthusiasts claimed they would revolutionize ice climbing, bringing security to the slopes. Critics scoffed that the screws weren't much better than the older ice pitons. This proved particularly true of the lightweight, relatively weak "coat-hanger" ice screw, rarely used today. But ice screws continued to improve and now provide fairly reliable protection.

The modern tubular ice screw (fig. 15-9a) is the strongest and most reliable design. The shape and size of an ice screw have a great bearing on its strength: a large-diameter screw supports more weight than a smaller-diameter screw of the same length. Commonly 7 to 9 inches long (18 to 23 centimeters), this screw works well in temperatures of both winter and summer. It is relatively easy to screw in and to screw out, with some models including a built-in ratchet for faster placement and removal. The hollow design minimizes fracturing of the ice by allowing the displaced ice to work itself out through the core of the screw.

Another type of tubular ice screw is hammered into place but screwed back out (fig. 15-9b). This type was developed in an attempt to make an easy-to-place and easy-to-remove screw. The tubular pound-in, screw-out design, with its fine threads, can be placed with a series of light blows and later removed relatively easily by unscrewing or by levering out with an ax pick. This design works best in hard ice and can be unreliable in temperatures above freezing.

The ice hook, another type of pound-in protection, is designed for thin ice and mixed climbing (fig. 15-9c). The ice hook may also be used to hook features in ice or rock.

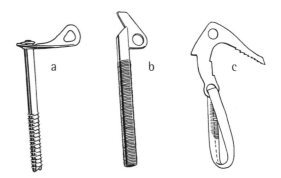

*Fig. 15-9. Ice protection: a, tubular ice screw; b, tubular pound-in/screw-out design; c, ice hook.*

## Other Gear

### Holsters

You can add two holsters or a double-size holster to your seat harness for carrying ice tools. Try out the tools in the holster before you use it. The tools may be hard to remove if the holster was designed for small rock-climbing implements.

### Ropes

Standard single ropes (10 to 11 millimeters in diameter) are the most commonly used for ice climbing, though this depends on the type of climb and the preference of the climbers. Use of a rope longer than the standard 50 meters (165 feet) will permit longer pitches. Double-rope and twin-rope techniques (outlined in Chapter 11) are an option for ice climbing. Some climbers feel more comfortable using two ropes for an activity that puts ropes and sharp implements together; a rope under tension can be cut by even slight pressure from a sharp edge.

Water-repellent ropes are probably worth the extra cost because they retain more strength and won't freeze like untreated ropes–though a "dry" rope can still become ice-coated, and the water repellency may not last the lifetime of the rope.

### Head and Eye Protection

Your head and eyes need protection from the chunks of ice that start flying when climbers begin swinging their tools into ice. Helmets and goggles are both strongly recommended. The helmet should be fitted to accommodate a cap or balaclava. The goggles must fit when your helmet is on, provide protection from ultraviolet rays, and have adequate ventilation to minimize fogging. Sunglasses with side shields are an acceptable substitute.

### Energy-Absorbing Runners

Consider using energy-absorbing runners (also known as load-limiting runners), such as the Yates Screamer or Ice Scream. Combined with a locking carabiner, the runners can provide an extra margin of safety when your screw placement is in ice of questionable quality.

## — TECHNIQUES OF ICE CLIMBING —

Ice climbing is an exhilarating activity, combining an ever-changing medium and a cold environment that challenge both mind and body. A rock climber taking up ice climbing may find striking similarities in the two pursuits. In both, climbers progress by moving their weight from one point of balance to another, supporting themselves as much as possible on their legs; they plan several moves in advance, climbing "with their eyes." On ice, as on rock, climbers use surface features, seeking out pockets, protrusions, and ledges for handholds and footholds, and depressions for ice-tool placements. Of course, the differences are at least as striking. Ice climbers must rely on hand tools and on crampons. They learn to make do with anchors and protection placements that can be uncertain. They work in a medium that changes throughout the day and throughout the season.

### Climbing without Crampons

Alpine climbers often encounter short sections of ice or frozen snow. Negotiating these sections without crampons requires balance climbing, moving up from one position of balance to the next. At each point of balance, your inside (uphill) foot is in front of and above the trailing outside (downhill) foot. To minimize muscle effort, your downhill leg is fully extended so you can put most of your weight on the bone of that leg. The ax, in your uphill hand, moves only after your body and feet are in balance, and your feet move only after the ax has been moved forward. As you climb, look for irregularities in the surface of the ice to use as footholds.

If the slope is too steep for secure balance climbing and you plan to proceed without crampons, you could take another route or try cutting steps. Step-cutting may be the answer if they can be cut quickly and efficiently.

### Step-Cutting

For the earliest alpinists, chopping or cutting steps was the only technique available for climbing steep ice and hard snow. The invention of crampons reduced the need for step-cutting but never eliminated it. Climbers still encounter areas of ice when they are not

*Fig. 15-10. The motion of the ice ax in creating a slash step*

swing. For all step-cutting, attach the ice ax to your wrist with a leash to help support your hard-working hand and to prevent loss of the ax if you drop it.

The most frequently used technique for step-cutting is the slash step, for traversing up or down gentle to slightly moderate slopes (up to 30 degrees). To cut ascending slash steps, stand in a position of balance, holding the ax in the inside (uphill) hand. Swing the adze parallel to your uphill foot and away from your body (fig. 15-11). Swing the ax from your shoulder, cutting with the adze and letting the weight of the ax do most of the work. On harder ice, this takes extra muscle, and two hands may be necessary. With successive swings, slice ice out of the step, starting at the heel end of the new step and working toward the toe. Scoop out chunks of ice with the adze and use the adze and pick to finish the step.

The usual sequence is to cut two steps from a position of balance, place the ax for security, move up to a new position of balance, cut two more steps, and so

carrying crampons or face short ice problems that may not merit taking the time to put on crampons. A broken crampon, or an injured or inexperienced climber, may be reason enough to cut steps. Even if you're wearing crampons, you might welcome a slight step chipped out by the ax for added security or to serve as a small platform to rest on. Just being able to chop out a comfortable belay platform is justification for developing a good working knowledge of the technique.

The adze of the ax can be used in one of two ways for step-cutting. The adze can be used to slash the ice by swinging it in a nearly parallel motion to the surface of the ice to create a slash step (fig. 15-10) or it can be used to chop by swinging it perpendicular to the ice to create a pigeonhole step. In softer conditions, the pick can often aid in creating steps, by using it to slice through snow and ice in one smooth

*Fig. 15-11. Cutting slash steps on a diagonal ascent. The climber works from a position of balance, with the ax in the inside (uphill) hand.*

on. Never swing the ax toward your body because a glancing blow can bounce the adze off the ice and into your leg. A single line of diagonal steps is usually cut up gentle slopes, whereas a double parallel line of diagonal steps is put in on moderate slopes where balance is more of a problem. Pigeonhole steps are used on steeper slopes.

Make each diagonal step slope slightly inward to help keep your boot from slipping out. On gentle slopes, it may be okay if the step holds only a small part of the boot, but steps on steeper slopes should be roomy enough for the entire boot. Space the steps so they are convenient for all members of your party. When you're ready to change the direction of a series of diagonal steps, chop a hold large enough for both feet as a secure position for turning and for switching hands on the ax.

On hard ice that fractures easily, swing the pick horizontally into the ice to define the bottom of the

Fig. 15-13. A pigeonhole step, deep enough for the front half of a boot and with a small lip for a handhold

step so that cutting with the adze doesn't destroy the foothold. If you jerk outward on the ax just as the pick penetrates the ice, the pick should chip out the ice successfully rather than sticking in it.

Pigeonhole steps for the direct ascent of steep ice are placed about a shoulder-width apart and within easy stepping distance of each other (fig. 15-12). Each step functions as both a handhold and foothold, so each should be large enough to hold the front half of a boot and should have a small lip to serve as a handhold (fig. 15-13). Cut the step by starting with a slash step, and then chop to the desired depth. Create the lip with small chops of the adze.

Fig. 15-12. Cutting pigeonhole steps

*Fig. 15-14. Cutting steps on descent*

If you decide to chop steps down an ice slope, the easiest method is to cut ladder steps that descend straight down the hill (fig. 15-14). To cut two steps in sequence, start in a position of balance, facing down the slope. Chop two steps directly below the ones you are standing in. When they are ready, step down with the outside (downhill) foot and then the inside (uphill) foot. To cut just one step at a time, again start in a position of balance. Cut the step for the outside (downhill) foot and move that foot down into the step. Then cut the step for the inside (uphill) foot and move that foot down into it. (Climbers may opt to rappel rather than step-cutting down an icy incline.)

The step-cutter works at a tiring, difficult job on a slippery surface, often in an exposed location, and therefore usually needs to be belayed. The skill of step-cutting can be a life-saver in an emergency, and the only way to gain the skill is to take the time once in a while to practice.

# Climbing with Crampons

## Technique Overview

Ice climbers usually employ features of two basic techniques, depending on steepness of the slope, conditions of the ice, and their ability and confidence level. They are known as the French and German techniques. Although each technique has its own distinct benefits, modern ice climbing melds the two. Mastery of both French and German technique is essential for climbing in the changeable alpine environment.

## French Technique (Flat-Footing)

French technique is the easiest and most efficient method of climbing gentle to steep ice and hard snow—once you learn how to do it. Good French technique demands balance, rhythm, and the confident use of crampons and ax.

## German Technique (Front-Pointing)

Developed by the Germans and Austrians for climbing the harder snow and ice of the eastern Alps, front-pointing can take an experienced ice climber up the steepest and most difficult ice slopes. With this technique, even average climbers can quickly overcome sections that would be difficult or impossible with French technique. Front-pointing, in contrast to the choreography of flat-footing, is straightforward and uncomplicated. The technique is much like step-kicking straight up a snow slope, but instead of kicking your boot into the snow, you kick your front crampon points into the ice and step directly up on them. Just as in French technique, good front-pointing is rhythmic and balanced, with the weight of your body over the crampons. Efficiency of movement is essential, whether it's planting your front points, placing your hand tools, or moving on the ice.

## Modern Technique

Modern crampon technique evolved from the French and German styles. As on rock, climbing on ice involves the efficient and confident use of footwork to maintain balance and minimize fatigue. Flat-footing is generally used on lower-angle slopes and where point penetration is easy; front-pointing is most common on slopes steeper than 45 degrees and on very hard ice. In practice, most climbers blend them into a combination approach, sometimes called the American technique. In any technique, the most important element is confident use of the crampons. Practicing on gentle and moderate slopes helps develop skill, confidence, and the aggressive approach needed at steeper angles.

A skilled ice climber, whether flat-footing or front-pointing, displays the same deliberate movement as a skilled rock climber on a difficult slab. The crampon points must be carefully and deliberately placed on the ice, the weight transferred from one foot to the other smoothly and decisively. Boldness is essential to skillful cramponing. Exposure must be disregarded and concentration focused solely on the climbing. But boldness is not blind bravado. It is confidence and skill born of time and enthusiasm, nurtured in many practice sessions on glacial seracs and on ice bulges in frozen gullies, and matured by ascents of increasing length and difficulty.

## Ice-Climbing Terms

In the box below is an abbreviated list of ice-climbing terms related to crampon and ice-ax technique, along with the approximate steepness of slope for each. French terms are sometimes used and are given here in parentheses. Terms using the French word *pied* refer to the feet; terms using *piolet* refer to the ice ax.

None of these techniques are restricted to any particular set of conditions, and all can be useful in a wide range of snow and ice situations. As you practice these techniques, keep in mind that a sharp crampon is a happy crampon, requiring only your body weight to set it securely in place.

## Gentle to Moderate Slopes

### French Technique (Flat-Footing)

Many climbers find flat-footing awkward and needlessly complicated when they first try it. Proper flat-footing requires you to bend your ankles into

---

## Techniques for Crampons

| | |
|---|---|
| Walking, or marching (*pied marche*) | Gentle, 0 to 15 degrees |
| Duck walk (*pied en canard*) | Gentle, 15 to 30 degrees |
| Flat-footing (*pied à plat*) | Moderate to steep, 30 to 50 degrees and higher |
| Front-pointing | From 45 degrees through vertical and overhanging |

## Techniques for Ice Axes and Ice Tools

| | |
|---|---|
| Cane position (*piolet canne*) | Gentle to moderate, 0 to 40 degrees |
| Cross-body position (*piolet ramasse*) | Moderate, 35 to 50 degrees |
| Anchor position (*piolet ancre*) | Steep, 45 degrees and higher |
| Low-dagger position (*piolet panne*) | Steep, 45 to 55 degrees |
| High-dagger position (*piolet poignard*) | Steep, 50 to 60 degrees |
| Traction position (*piolet traction*) | Extremely steep, 60 degrees through vertical and overhanging |

snagging a crampon point on clothing or on a crampon strap on your other foot. Press all bottom points of each crampon firmly into the ice and walk straight forward. Use the ice ax in the *cane position* (fig. 15-15), holding the ax in the self-belay grasp, with the pick forward and your palm on top of the adze.

As the slope steepens slightly, it will begin to get awkward to keep your toes pointing directly uphill. So splay them outward, in *duck walk* fashion (fig. 15-15). Keep your knees bent and your weight balanced over your feet. Continue to use the ax as a cane.

As the slope gets steeper still, heading straight upward in the duck walk causes severe ankle strain. Then it's time to turn sideways to the slope and ascend diagonally for a more relaxed, comfortable step. Be sure that you are *flat-footing,* with all crampon points weighted into the ice (fig. 15-16). In using this technique for the first time, people have a strong tendency

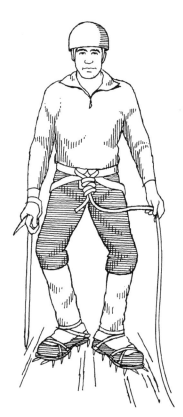

*Fig. 15-15. French technique: duck walk combined with ice ax in cane position*

unnatural positions in order to keep your feet flat on the surface. You must put maximum trust in your crampons—but once this trust develops, flat-footing provides great security because it keeps you in balance over your feet, with maximum penetration of all vertical crampon points. Ankle strain can be eased by pointing your boots downhill more and more as the slope steepens, so that the flex needed to keep your feet flat comes from the more normal forward flex of the ankle and from the knees, which are bent away from the slope and spread well apart. Boots that are flexible at the ankle help with flat-footing, although most climbers now use the more rigid plastic boots when climbing on hard snow and ice.

Walking on gentle slopes with crampons requires little more technique than walking anywhere else. Keep your feet slightly farther apart than normal to avoid

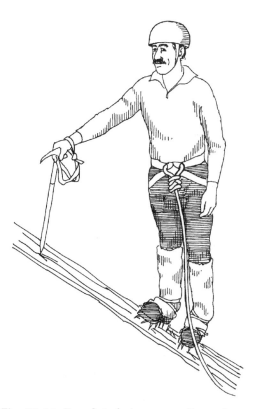

*Fig. 15-16. French technique, on a diagonal ascent: flat-footing combined with ice ax in cane position*

to try to edge with their crampons. Fight this tendency, and keep your crampon points flat against the ice at all times. Start with your feet pointed in the direction of travel. As the slope steepens, you'll have to rotate your feet more and more downward in order to keep them flat. On the steepest slopes they may be pointing downhill.

As the slope angle changes from gentle to moderate, using the ax in the cane position becomes awkward. You can now get greater security by holding the ax in the *cross-body position* (fig. 15-17). Grip the shaft just above the spike with the inside hand and hold the head of the ax in the self-belay grasp, pick pointing forward, with the outside hand. Drive the spike into the ice, the shaft perpendicular to the slope and roughly horizontal across your waist. In the cross-body position, most of the force on the ax should be at the hand on the shaft. The hand on the head stabilizes the ax and is a reminder not to lean into the slope. To keep your body from leaning into the ice you need a full-length ice ax, rather than a shorter ice tool. Even experienced ice climbers have difficulty maintaining proper French technique with a short ax.

Move diagonally upward in a two-step sequence, much the same as ascending a snow slope without crampons. Remember to keep your feet flat at all times (fig. 15-17). Start from a position of balance, your inside (uphill) foot in front of and above the trailing outside (downhill) leg. From this in-balance position, bring the outside foot in front of and above the inside foot, into the out-of-balance position. The outside leg crosses over the knee of the inside leg, because if the cross is made at the ankle, stability is compromised and the next step will be difficult to make. To return to a position of balance, bring the inside foot

*Fig. 15-17. French technique, on a diagonal ascent: flat-footing combined with ice ax in cross-body position (pick forward)*

*Fig. 15-18. French technique, changing direction on a diagonal ascent: flat-footing combined with ice ax in cross-body position*

up from behind and place it again in front of the outside foot. Keep the weight of your body over the crampons. Avoid leaning into the slope and creating the danger of crampon points twisting out of the ice. Step on lower-angled spots and natural irregularities in the ice to ease ankle strain and conserve energy.

During this diagonal ascent, plant the ax about an arm's length ahead of you each time before moving another two steps. Whether you're using the ax in the cane or the cross-body position, plant it far enough forward so that it will be near your hip after you move up to the next in-balance position.

To change direction (switchback) on a diagonal ascent of an ice slope, use the same technique as on a snow slope where you aren't wearing crampons, but keep your feet flat (fig. 15-18). From a position of

balance, place the ax directly above your location. Move your outside (downhill) foot forward, into the out-of-balance position, to about the same elevation as the other foot and pointing slightly uphill. Grasping the ax with both hands, turn into the slope, moving your inside (uphill) foot to point in the new direction and slightly uphill. You are now facing into the slope, standing with feet splayed outward. (If the splayed-foot position feels unstable, you can front-point.) Return to the in-balance position by turning your attention to the foot that is still pointing in the old direction. Move this foot above and in front of the other foot. Reposition your grasp on the ice ax, depending on whether you are using the cane or cross-body method. You're now back in balance and facing the new direction of travel.

## Moderate to Steep Slopes

With steeper ice, other variations of French technique are called for. At some point, the German technique of front-pointing comes into play.

### French Technique (Flat-Footing)

On moderate to steep slopes, you can switch the ax from the cross-body position to what is known as the *anchor position* for more security. Your feet remain flat, with all bottom crampon points weighted into the ice at each step.

To place the ax in the anchor position, begin in a position of balance. Grip the ice-ax shaft just above the spike with your outside (downhill) hand (fig. 15-19a). Swing the ax so that the pick sticks into the ice in front of and above your head, with the shaft parallel to the

slope. With your other hand, take hold of the ax head in a self-arrest grasp. Now pull on the ax as you move two steps forward to a new position of balance (fig. 15-19b–c). A gentle and constant outward pull sets the teeth and keeps the ax locked into the ice. When you're ready to release it, push the shaft toward the ice as you lift the pick up and out.

To keep your feet flat at these angles, your body must lean farther away from the slope, knees and ankles flexed, and the toes of your boots will increasingly point downhill. Try to continue advancing upward in the standard sequence, moving two steps at a time. At the steepest angles, however, your feet will be pointing downhill, and you will have to begin shuffling your feet instead, moving backward up the slope. But continue to plant and remove the pick from a position of balance. The foot that is on the same side

*Fig. 15-19. French technique, on a diagonal ascent: flat-footing combined with ice ax in anchor position*

as your direction of travel should be at least slightly higher than the other foot, allowing the upper body to rotate for a smooth, strong swing of the ax.

You can change diagonal direction when the ax is in the anchor position by using the same sequence as with the cane or cross-body positions. However, on the steepest slopes, where you are shuffling backward,

*Fig. 15-20. French technique: pied assis. The ice climber is using this position for rest and balance.*

you can change direction simply by switching hands on the ax and planting it on your other side. There won't be much diagonal movement at this point, because you'll mainly be moving backward straight up the slope.

The French also devised a position—called *pied assis*—that gives leg muscles a rest and provides more security for replanting the ax (fig. 15-20). From a position of balance, bring your outside (downhill) foot up and beneath your buttocks, with the boot (flat as always) pointing straight downhill. Then sit down on that foot. You'll discover a balanced position, a relatively comfortable one.

The invaluable technique of flat-footing, used with the ice ax in the cane or cross-body positions, will serve an experienced climber for many alpine routes. For short stretches of steeper ice, flat-footing combined with the ice ax in anchor position will often work, but this marks the upper limit of French technique.

### German Technique (Front-Pointing)

On moderate to steep ice slopes, use of the French and German techniques begins to overlap. They both have a place on these slopes.

The French technique (flat-footing) takes a lot of practice to perfect, but most people pick up front-pointing quickly because it feels natural and secure. Unfortunately, this encourages climbers to use it excessively on moderate slopes where flat-footing would be more efficient and just as secure. In flat-footing, most of the strain is on the large, powerful thigh muscles. Front-pointing, however, depends almost solely on the calf muscles, which burn out much faster. Even climbers who strongly prefer front-pointing would benefit from alternating the techniques to give calf muscles a rest.

Plastic boots provide a firm base for crampons and make front-pointing easiest. Full-shank, stiff-soled leather boots also are good. Three-quarter-shank boots can be used in some cases, but require more muscular effort. As for soft-soled boots (fig. 15-21), pioneer ice-climber Yvon Chouinard said it well: "You can't dance on hard ice with soft-soled shoes."

Front-pointing uses not only the two forward points of each crampon, but also the two vertical points immediately behind them. These four points, properly

low the odds are that they are in the correct horizontal position. This is especially important coming over the top of steep ice onto a gentler slope, where the natural tendency is to raise your heels, relax your level of concentration, and hurry. This is a formula for trouble because it could cause the crampon points to shear from the ice. A good way to become comfortable with the essential skills of crampon placement and foot positioning is to practice on a top rope with an experienced ice climber who can critique your style.

In your initial crampon placements on a route, concentrate on determining the amount of force required

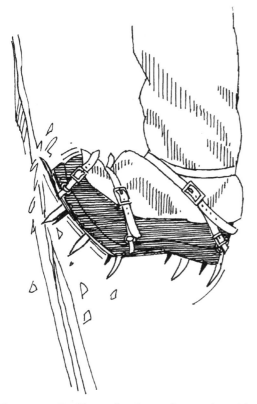

*Fig. 15-21. Problems of trying to front-point with soft-soled boots*

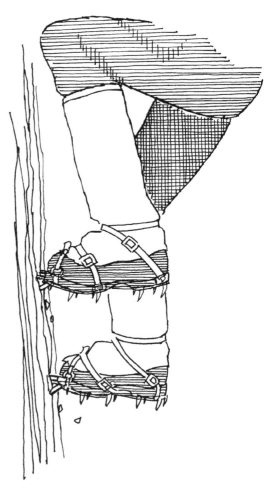

placed, provide a platform to stand on. The best placement of the boot is straight into the ice, avoiding the splayed feet that tend to rotate the outside front points out of the ice. Boot heels need to be level in order to push the first set of vertical points into the ice and complete the four-point platform for standing (fig. 15-22). To provide stability and a balanced platform, try to keep foot placements at least hip width apart. A slight bend at the knee aids in reducing the strain on calf muscles.

Resist the temptation to raise your heels higher. This pulls the stabilizing vertical points from the ice, endangering placement of the front points and fatiguing calf muscles. Your heels will normally feel lower than they really are, so if you think your heels are too

*Fig. 15-22. Correct boot position in front-pointing*

to kick a secure foothold. After that, a single confident kick should be all that's needed. Watch out for two common mistakes: kicking too hard (prematurely fatiguing yourself) and kicking too often in one place (fracturing the ice and making it harder to get a good foothold). After making a crampon placement, avoid foot movement because it can make the points rotate out of the ice.

Front-pointing encompasses a variety of ice-ax positions.

**Low-dagger position:** This position is helpful in tackling a short, relatively steep section that requires only a few quick front-pointing moves. For the low-dagger position, hold the ax by the adze in the self-belay grasp and push the pick into the ice near your

*Fig. 15-24. Front-pointing, with ax in high-dagger position*

*Fig. 15-23. Front-pointing, with ax in low-dagger position*

waist, to aid balance (fig. 15-23). This position tends to hold you away from the slope and out over your feet, the correct stance for front-pointing.

**High-dagger position:** If the slope is a bit too steep to insert the pick effectively into the ice at waist level, in the low-dagger position, move it into the high-dagger position (fig. 15-24). For this method, hold your hand on the ax head the same as if you were in self-arrest and jab the pick into the ice above your shoulder.

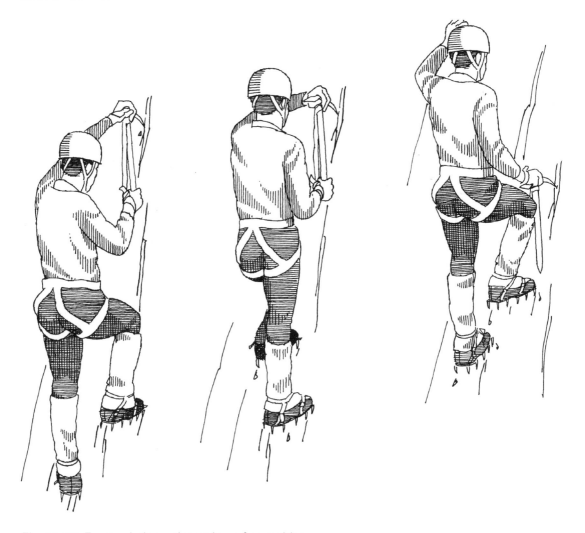

*Fig. 15-25. Front-pointing, using ax in anchor position*

Dagger positions are useful in hard snow and relatively soft ice. They don't work well in hard ice. The jabbing and stabbing motions of placing the pick aren't very powerful, and poor pick penetration into the hard ice could mean an insecure placement. Attempts to force a deeper placement may result in nothing more than a bruised hand.

**Anchor position:** For harder ice or a steeper slope, you can abandon the high-dagger position for the anchor position that is also used in flat-footing. As you stand on front points, hold the ax shaft near the end and swing the pick in as high as possible without overreaching (fig. 15-25). Front-point upward, holding on higher and higher on the shaft as you progress, adding a self-arrest grasp on the adze with the other hand when you get high enough. Finally, switch hands on the adze, converting to the low-dagger position. When the adze is at waist level, it's time to remove it from the ice and replant it higher.

**Traction position:** The steepest and hardest ice calls

*Fig. 15-26. Front-pointing with ax overhead in traction position*

*Fig. 15-27. Front-pointing, using low-dagger position with two tools*

for the ax to be placed in the traction position (fig. 15-26). The ax is held near the spike and planted high; the ice is then climbed by slightly pulling straight down on the ax as you front-point up.

It becomes necessary to use a second ice tool on very hard or extremely steep ice when it gets too difficult to balance on your front points while replanting the ax. It's possible to use two tools at the same time because, except for the anchor position, all ice-ax techniques associated with front-pointing require only one hand.

Using two tools provides three points of support—two crampons and one ice tool—as you replant the other tool. The placements must be secure enough that if one point of support fails, the other two will hold you until the third point is replaced. The legs carry most of the weight, but the arms help with both weight and balance.

In double-tool technique, you can use the same ice-ax method for both hands or a different method for each. For instance, you can climb with both tools in

The three-o'clock position is a potent resource for a direct line of ascent, much less tiring than front-pointing alone. The position lets you distribute the work over more muscle groups by alternating techniques with each leg. As you climb, seek out irregular flatter spots and any pockets or ledges for flat-footing, allowing you to rest calf muscles. With your ice tools, use whatever positions are appropriate to the situation.

Climbers alternate crampon techniques depending on ice conditions. Flat-footing is usually more secure on frozen snow, ice crust over snow, and soft

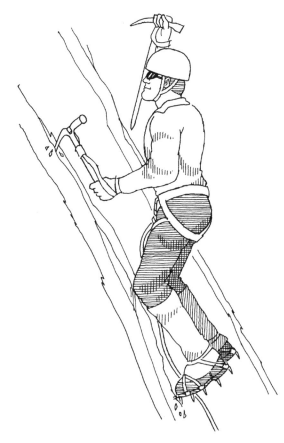

Fig. 15-28. Front-pointing, using traction position with the tool in the left hand and high-dagger with the tool in the right hand

low-dagger position (fig. 15-27). Or you can place one tool in high-dagger position and the other in the traction position (fig. 15-28). The upcoming section on vertical ice spells out details of double-tool technique using traction with both tools.

### Combination Techniques

One fast and powerful technique combines flat-footing and front-pointing. It's called the three-o'clock position, *pied troiséme* (fig. 15-29) because as one foot is front-pointing the other is flat and points to the side (to three o'clock if it's your right foot or nine o'clock if it's your left).

Fig. 15-29. Three-o'clock position for the feet, combining flat-footing and front-pointing

or rotten ice, because more crampon points dig into the surface. For soft snow over ice or hard snow, front-pointing or the three-o'clock position lets you blast through the surface to get points into the firmer layer beneath. Front-pointing is often the most secure technique for the average climber to use with very hard ice on all but gentle slopes. If you are having serious problems on a climb with flat-footing—perhaps due to fatigue, winds, high altitude, or fear—switch to front-pointing or the three-o'clock position.

## Vertical Ice

The basic method of climbing vertical ice is front-pointing combined with use of two ice tools in traction, in which you use both tools as you ascend (fig. 15-30). The standard position for the feet is about a shoulder-width apart and level with each other, a stable and relatively comfortable stance.

Reach up and plant the pick of one ice tool as high as possible—but off to the side a bit so you're not hit by dislodged ice or by a tool that comes loose. Then plant the other tool, in the same manner. Be careful not to overreach for a tool placement because that motion may cause your heels to rise from their position perpendicular to the ice.

From the back, your body at this point resembles an X against the ice wall. Your feet are level with each other, heels slightly down, and your arms are straight. As you pull down on the tools, also pull slightly outward to keep their teeth set in the ice, and apply inward pressure on the crampon points. You can liken this to a mild lieback on rock. To conserve energy, you can now hang your weight from the wrist loops rather than gripping the tools tightly.

To ascend, grasp the tools and pull yourself higher as you step upward on the front points to a new level position. Let your legs do most of the work, however. You don't want to burn your arms out by doing pull-ups as you climb the pitch. You're now ready to replant the ice tools higher, one at a time, returning you to the X body position. Repeat this sequence. Concentrate on efficient, methodical placement of crampon points and hand tools. Rhythm is as important as balance.

Climbers sometimes find themselves "barn-dooring"—swinging out of balance—as they remove one tool in order to place it higher. You can avoid this unsettling experience by centering your balance

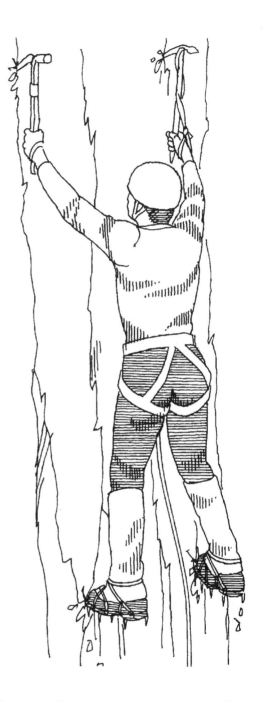

*Fig. 15-30. Front-pointing on vertical ice, in X body position with two tools overhead*

*Fig. 15-31. Staying in balance on vertical ice: a, center body weight on the right-hand tool as the left-hand tool is removed for higher placement; b, then center body weight on the replanted left-hand tool as the right-hand tool is removed.*

around the tool that will remain in the ice as you remove the other tool for higher placement (fig. 15-31). Once that new placement is made, center your body weight about the higher tool and then remove the lower tool, maintaining balance at all times.

To overcome ice bulges and small overhangs, you can try the monkey hang (fig. 15-32). Starting from the X body position, walk your front points up the ice without raising your body. Loosen—but do not re-move—one of the hand tools. Rise to a standing or nearly standing position by pushing with your feet and pulling on the tools. Then in one smooth, continuous motion, remove and replant the loosened tool, while balancing your body weight on the remaining tool

388

horizontal step or ledge. With a secure horizontal section of ice ahead, a climber may tend to relax concentration and forget about good foot placement. At the same time, the climber faces the problem that it's virtually impossible to obtain a confident tool placement by blindly swinging over a ledge.

First you need to move high enough to see onto the ledge. To do this, make shorter tool and foot placements for a slightly exaggerated X body position as you approach the lip of the ledge; then step up to a high-dagger position so you can see onto the ledge and look for a good spot to place an ice tool. You may have to remove snow or rotten ice, which often accumulates on ledges and moderate ice slopes. Then place an ice tool securely into the ledge, followed by placement of your second ice tool; then move your feet up until they are safely over the lip.

## Traversing Steep to Vertical Ice

The principles for traversing are much the same as for front-pointing up steep ice. However, because you're moving to the side instead of straight up, it's more difficult to keep one foot perpendicular to the ice as you replace the front points of the other foot. If the heel rotates, the front points will also rotate and come out of the ice. Hand tools also tend to rotate out in sideways travel.

Start from a secure position—feet on the same level, with front points and hand tools in place. Plant the *trailing tool* at a 45-degree angle to your body; plant the *leading tool* vertically in the ice, but a foot or so to your right (if you are traversing to the right) (fig. 15-33a). This places the leading tool lower than if you were ascending, but not so far to the side that it causes your body to rotate out from the wall when you remove the trailing tool. And it places the trailing tool so that you can pull on it (in a sort of modified lieback) as you traverse to the right, without twisting the tool out of the ice.

You can now shuffle sideways on front points (fig. 15-33b). You also have the option of making a two-step move, crossing the trailing foot over the leading foot, and then bringing the other foot back into the lead. Most climbers prefer the shuffle, which is less awkward and feels more secure. After moving your feet, replant the trailing tool closer to your

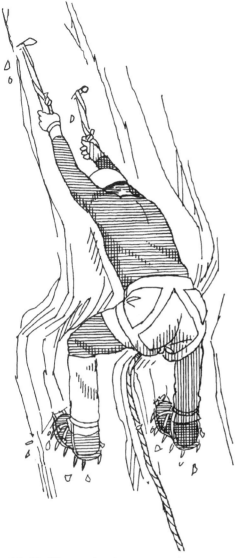

*Fig. 15-32. The monkey hang*

placement. Quickly rest the arm that made the new placement, by relaxing the hand and letting the arm hang from the tool's wrist loop. Loosen and replant the other tool. You're now back in the X body position, ready to repeat the sequence.

Oddly, one of the most challenging sequences involves climbing from a vertical face up onto a

*Fig. 15-33. Traversing to the right on vertical ice: a, in position to begin the traverse; b, moving to the right.*

body at the 45-degree angle, replant the leading tool vertically to your right, and repeat the process.

## Descending

### Flat-Footing

To descend gently sloping ice, simply face directly downhill, bend the knees slightly, and walk firmly downward. Plant all bottom crampon points into the ice with each step. Hold the ax in the cane position.

As the descent angle steepens, bend your knees more and spread them apart, with body weight over your feet so all crampon points bite securely (fig. 15-34). Thigh muscles do the bulk of the work. For greater security, plant the ax perpendicular to the slope in the cross-body position (fig. 15-35).

For the next level of security, use the ax in the *support position* (fig. 15-36). Simply grasp the ax near the middle of the shaft and hold it beside you as you de-

Fig. 15-34. Flat-footing on descent, with ice ax in cane position

Fig. 15-36. Flat-footing on descent, with ice ax in the support position

Fig. 15-35. Flat footing on descent, with ice ax in the cross-body position

scend; the ax head points uphill, with the pick down and the spike downhill.

As the slope steepens, switch the ax to the *bannister position* (fig. 15-37). To do this, grasp the ax near the end of the shaft. Swing the ax to plant the pick as far below as possible. Walk downward, sliding your hand along the shaft toward the head of the ax. It's important to maintain a slight outward pull on the shaft to keep the pick locked in the ice. Keep moving down until you are below the ax head. Then push the

Fig. 15-37. Flat-footing on descent, with ice ax in the bannister position

Fig. 15-38. Flat-footing on descent, with ice ax in the anchor position

shaft against the ice to help release the pick, and re-plant the ax farther down.

On a slope too steep to safely descend facing out-ward, turn sideways and descend diagonally. Your footwork changes to the same flat-foot technique used to ascend diagonally. Use the ax in the anchor posi-tion (fig. 15-38). With your outside arm, swing the ax out in front and plant the pick in the ice, take hold of the head with the other hand in the self-arrest grasp, and then flat-foot diagonally down below the ax. The shaft rotates as you pass below it.

### Front-Pointing

It's often tiring and ineffective to try front-pointing down a gentle to moderate slope. A climber tends to be bent over, facing the moderate slope, and to vacillate between flat-foot and front-point technique.

On steep slopes, front-point and hand-tool tech-niques are generally the same for going down as for going up. But just as on rock, downclimbing is more difficult. There is a tendency to step too low, which keeps the heel too high, so front points may shear out or fail to penetrate in the first place. You don't get a good view of the route on a descent (although descend-ing on a slight diagonal will help). It's awkward to plant the ice tools because they must be placed closer to your body, so you lose the power of a good full swing. On a descent, the only feasible way to get secure placements may be to plant the tools back in the holes that were made on the ascent.

Climbers don't often front-point a descent, but it's still a valuable skill for occasions such as retreating from a route. Downclimbing ability also builds confidence in ascending. Ice climbers usually rappel down steeper routes. Rappelling is discussed near the end of this chapter, in "Roped Climbing Techniques."

## Placing Ice Tools

The objective of placing any ice tool is to establish a solid placement with one swing. Each swing saved during a pitch will mean that much less fatigue at the top. It takes a lot of practice to learn pinpoint placement, especially when you're swinging the tool with your nondominant arm. But with a combination of proper technique and equipment, you should be able to place a tool easily and precisely so that it's secure for as long as it takes you to climb through a particular section.

At the base of your route, try a few tool placements to get a feel for the plasticity of the ice. Plasticity—which determines the ability of the ice to hold and release a tool—varies tremendously with temperature and age of the ice.

As you climb, study the ice for good placements. A slight depression above and slightly to the side is likely to be good. Ice is more compact and holds the pick better in depressions than in bulges, which shatter or break off under the impact of an ice tool. Try to make placements in opaque ice, which is less brittle than clear ice because it has more air trapped inside. Minimize the number of placements by planting the pick as high as possible without lifting the heel of your boot and by moving upward as far as you can with each placement.

Experiment to discover which tools work best for you. You'll find that one tool may be good for a particular type of ice climbing but that different conditions will call for a different tool. Investigate each climb well in advance to decide which tools to use. Halfway up a difficult ice face is not the time to realize you brought the wrong tools. Keep your tools sharp, and protect the pick with a rubber cap when not in use.

Because of differences in climbing ability and background, two climbers may have different experiences even though they are using identical tools. The more experienced climber may climb confidently with only a small bite of the pick into the ice, while the other

climber might not feel comfortable without slamming the tool deep. Novice climbers often overdrive their tools, making it difficult to remove them from the ice. On most tools, only the first few teeth provide any useful bite into the ice, and the upward angle of the pick in the ice provides most of the holding power. Small teeth often perform better than large teeth.

In addition to learning the proper force to use in placing a tool, you also need to learn the best way to remove it (fig. 15-39). Unless it's done right, removing a tool can be as tiring as placing it. Try to remove the tool in reverse of the motion used to set it. First, loosen the placement by rocking the tool back and forth in the same plane as the pick (fig. 15-39, motions 1 and 2). Then try to remove the tool by pulling up and out (motions 3 and 4). If this fails, release your grip on the tool and try to knock it loose by hitting up against the adze with the palm of your hand. Never try to remove a tool by torquing it from side to side because the pick could break. (Tubular-nosed tools take a special removal method; see the section that follows.)

Placement and removal techniques vary somewhat, depending on the type of pick that is on the ice tool, as discussed in the following.

*Fig. 15-39. How to remove an ice tool*

**Technically curved:** These picks, also known as al-pine picks, result in an ice tool that is most like a standard ice ax. However, the picks are curved more than on a regular ax to hold better in ice, and the shaft is shorter to permit an easier swing on steep surfaces. A tool with a technically curved pick requires a natural swing, from the shoulder. The first swing should result in a satisfying, solid "thunk"—the sound and feel

of a well-placed ice tool. This tool is used in conditions ranging from soft serac ice to hard water ice, though you may need to weight a lighter tool (perhaps with lead sheet taped to the head) for good penetration on hard ice. The pick is usually removed from the ice by lifting straight up on the shaft.

**Reverse curved:** While technically curved picks take a natural swing, the sharp angles of the reverse-curved and straight-drooped picks require a shorter, choppy swing. A reverse-curved pick, featuring a drooped pick with a slight upward curve, penetrates waterfall ice with a straight, downward hooking motion. It is usually easy to remove. The reverse-curved pick works well for hooking holes in the ice, a common technique in waterfall ice. Large icicles often form in clusters on vertical sections, creating slots or gaps between them that are ideal for secure hooking placement of the pick (fig. 15-40).

**Straight drooped:** This sharply angled pick requires a decisive downward flick of the wrist at the end of a short swing, making it penetrate well in ice from soft to hard. It is fairly easy to remove by using an up-and-down levering motion. The straight-drooped pick also makes a good hooking tool.

**Tubular:** A tubular-nosed tool works best with a short-arc swing and often grips securely on the first try. A tubular pick is moderately easy to remove by twisting sideways while holding the head (up-and-down levering can fracture the nose). The nose dents easily and is particularly vulnerable if the climb involves ice with sand or rocks close to the surface.

## — ROPED CLIMBING TECHNIQUES —

Climbers usually rope up on ice. The principal exception comes when they decide that overall team safety is served best by climbing unroped. Late on a stormy day or while ascending a couloir threatened by rock-fall, the greater speed of unroped travel might offer relatively more safety than continuing on the rope. It is also sensible to unrope through a section so difficult to protect that a fall by one roped climber would sweep them both away. Ice pitches can be climbed using a standard single rope or by using two ropes (see Chapter 11, Leading on Rock, for details on double-rope and twin-rope techniques).

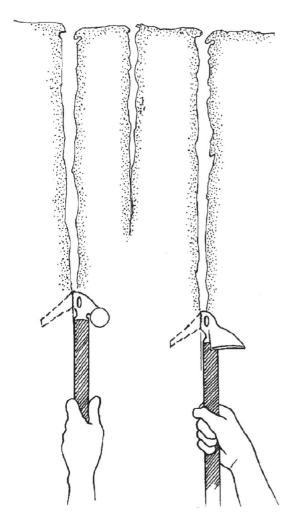

*Fig. 15-40. Hooking gaps in waterfall ice with ice tools*

## Protection on Ice

Modern ice screws offer dependable security on ice climbs. However, there is some sacrifice of safety in the time and energy it takes to put them in place. Leaders, therefore, commonly place fewer points of protection in a rope length on ice than they would in a rock pitch of the same length. Ice climbers also make some use of natural protection.

### Natural Protection

Ready-made natural protection is hard to come by on an alpine ice route. Good natural protection may be available not on the ice itself but in rock bordering the route or protruding through the ice.

Natural protection is often found on frozen waterfalls, where runners can be placed around ice columns. Climbers also devise some slightly unconventional protection points. On frozen waterfalls or high alpine routes, where large ice columns may form only an inch or two apart, an ice screw tied off with webbing can be inserted behind the columns and turned sideways as a deadman. You may find a sheet of ice separated from the underlying rock by an inch or two, leaving a slit that can be enlarged enough to insert a screw tied off with webbing; again, turn the screw sideways to function as a deadman. You can also punch two holes in the sheet of ice, thread a runner through them, and clip the rope into it. On mixed rock and ice climbs, rock-climbing chocks may be wedged into ice holes.

### Ice Screws

A favorable location for an ice-screw placement is the same as for an ice tool. A good choice is a natural depression, where fracture lines caused by the screw are not as likely to reach the surface (fig. 15-41). A screw placed into a bulge in the ice, on the other hand, can cause serious fracturing that weakens the placement or makes it useless. If this happens, move the screw a foot or two and try again. Generally keep screw placements at least 2 feet apart—more in rotten ice—to reduce chances that fracture lines from one placement could reach the other, weakening both.

The procedures for placing a screw vary somewhat with ice conditions, but the basic routine is much the same in any case: punch out a small starting hole with the pick or spike of a hand tool, to give a good grip

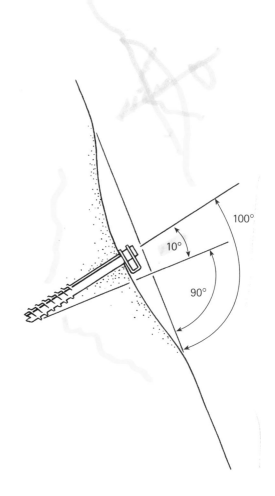

*Fig. 15-41. Ice-screw placement in a solid surface, with the screw angled uphill 10 degrees against the anticipated direction of pull and the screw eye facing the direction of pull*

for the starting threads or teeth of the screw. Make the hole gently, with light taps, to avoid fracturing the ice. Start the screw in the hole, angled uphill 10 degrees against the anticipated direction of pull. (On hard ice, it may take a few light taps to make the threads catch.) The eye of the screw must face in the direction of the anticipated pull.

On ice topped with a layer of soft snow or rotten ice, scrape down with the adze to get to a hard, trustworthy surface before making the starting hole (fig. 15-42a). In extremely rotten ice, make a large horizontal step with a hand tool and place the screw vertically at the back of the step, in a starting hole (fig. 15-42b).

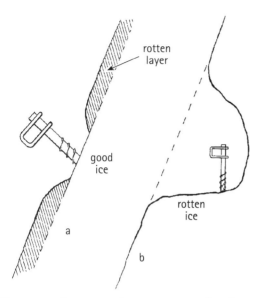

*Fig. 15-42. Ice-screw placements: a, with soft or rotten surface layer; b, in extremely rotten ice.*

Press the screw firmly and twist it into the ice at the same time.

When glacier ice fractures and shatters at the surface, you may still be able to get a secure placement by continuing to install the screw and gently chopping out the shattered ice with sideways strokes of the pick.

A screw with sharp cutting teeth can sometimes be screwed in all the way by hand. If not, do it with the help of a lever through the screw eye; another ice screw or the pick of a hand tool works well (fig. 15-43). Screws with a built-in ratchet are simpler to screw in and out.

Twist the screw all the way until the eye is against the ice, tight and solid. Clip a carabiner into the eye, with the carabiner gate down and out. To slow melt-out in soft summer ice or direct sun, pack ice around the screw head. If the screw doesn't go in all the way, reduce leverage on it by tying it off at the surface of the snow with a runner and then clipping into the runner (fig. 15-44).

The placement considerations that apply to standard ice screws apply equally to the type of ice screw that is hammered into place and then removed by unscrewing. The principal difference is that this device is pounded in with a series of light blows with an ice hammer, rather than being screwed in. Remember that your second will have to unscrew the piece

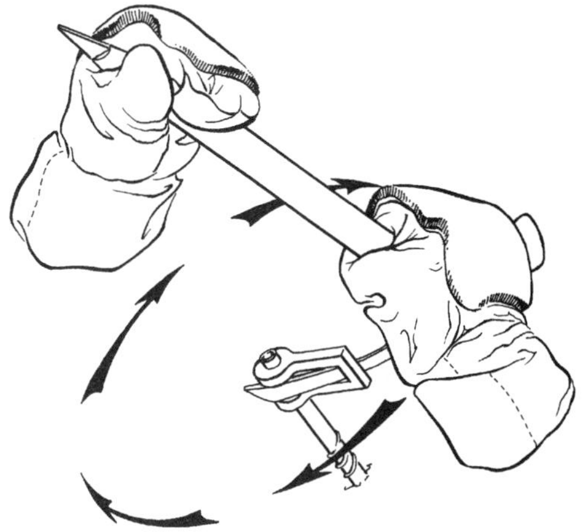

*Fig. 15-43. Screwing in an ice screw with the pick of an ice tool*

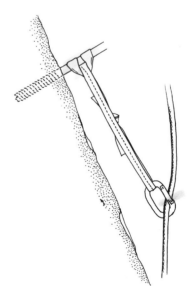

*Fig. 15-44. Tying off a partially placed ice screw with a runner at the surface of the ice*

*[handwritten: hammer in + 2nd must screw out]*

to get it out; provide enough clearance around the piece so that easy removal is possible.

Climbing extremely steep ice is fatiguing, physically and mentally. To conserve energy and keep moving upward efficiently, climbers work to minimize the number of screw placements. If the ice is hard and solid, or the slope not extremely steep, only one or two protection points may be placed on an entire pitch.

Unless the ice is rotten, only one screw is placed at each protection point.

It usually takes two hands to place an ice screw, exacting business on extremely steep, exposed ice. For extra support, you can slip one arm through the wrist loop of a solidly planted hand tool (fig. 15-45a). Or clip a runner from your seat harness to one or two securely placed hand tools (fig. 15-45b).

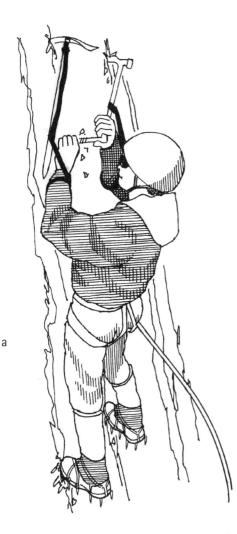

*[handwritten: sling it so don't loose it but also spike hole?]*

Fig. 15-45. Support from hand tools while placing an ice screw: a, through wrist leashes; b, from runners between tools and seat harness.

*which one*

On a moderate to steep slope, it may help to chop a step for standing in as you place the screw. On extremely steep ice, however, it's too difficult a job, so save your energy. When it's time to place an ice screw, do it from your front points, and then continue climbing.

After a screw is removed, ice inside the core must be cleaned out immediately or it may freeze to the interior, making the screw temporarily useless. The interior of some screws is slightly conical, permitting easier ice removal. If ice freezes to the inside, push it out with a smaller-diameter screw, your pick, or a length of stiff wire. You can also try to melt the ice with your breath or with the warmth of your hand as it holds the screw.

## Ice Anchors

Ice climbers have several options for anchors to use in belaying or rappelling, including ice bollards, the Abalakov V-thread, and multiple ice screws. This section discusses bollards and the V-thread, which are used mainly in rappelling. The next section, on the topic of belaying on ice, explains the standard anchor set-up using two ice screws.

### Ice Bollards

A bollard can be among an ice climber's most useful anchors. By linking together two bollards, one cut for an upward pull and the other for a downward pull, you have a multidirectional anchor. The strength of a bollard is proportional to its size and the hardness of the ice. Made of hard, solid ice, it can be stronger than the rope.

A completed ice bollard is teardrop-shaped when viewed from above and horn-shaped when viewed from the side (fig. 15-46). All you need for a bollard is an ice ax and good ice, uniform and without cracks or holes. Cut the outline of the bollard with the ax pick. In hard ice, give it a diameter of 12 to 18 inches across the wide end of the teardrop. Cut a trench around the bollard at least 6 inches deep, working outward from the outline with both the pick and the adze.

Undercut the sides and top half of the bollard to form a horn that prevents the rope from popping off over the top. This is the most sensitive part of the construction because you can easily fracture or break the

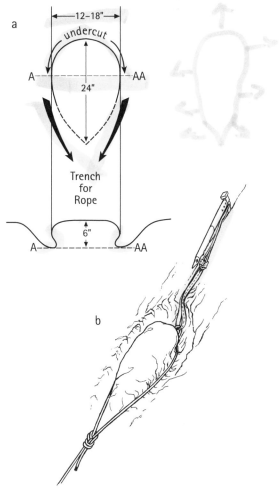

*Fig. 15-46. Ice bollard: a, diagram; b, with backup ice-tool anchor*

bollard if you're careless with the ax. The single largest disadvantage to a bollard is the long time it takes to construct one.

### The Abalakov V–Thread

The V-thread (fig. 15-47) is a popular anchor because of its simplicity and ease of construction. Devised by Vitaly Abalakov, a premiere Soviet alpinist in the 1930s, the V-thread is nothing more than a tiny V-shaped tunnel bored into the ice, with a cord or webbing threaded through the tunnel and tied to form a sling.

Here's how to make this anchor:

1. Screw an 8-inch (22-centimeter) ice screw into the slope. Angle the screw uphill 10 degrees against the anticipated direction of pull; also tilt it about 60 degrees to one side (fig. 15-47a).

2. Back this screw out about halfway, but keep it there as a guide. Insert a second screw into the slope about 6 to 8 inches from the first, angling it to intersect the first hole at its bottom (fig. 15-47b). Remove both screws.

3. Thread a length of 7-millimeter perlon accessory cord or half-inch tubular webbing into the V-shaped tunnel. A V-thread wire—a 12-inch piece of rigid wire with a small hook on the end, available at some

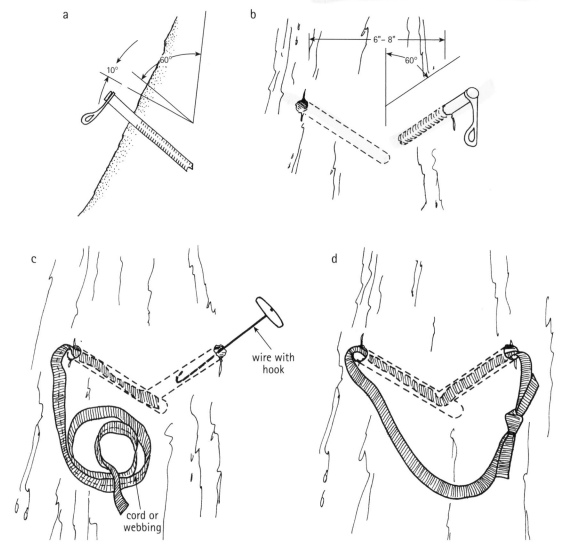

Fig. 15-47. The Abalakov V-thread anchor: a, boring the first hole with an ice screw; b, boring the intersecting hole with another ice screw; c, threading a piece of accessory cord or webbing through the V-shaped tunnel; d, completed anchor, with cord tied to form a sling.

climbing shops—is useful for fishing out the cord from the bottom of the tunnel (fig. 15-47c).

4. Holding both ends of the cord, saw it back and forth in the tunnel in order to break down the sharp edge where the two ice holes intersect. Otherwise, the edge might cut the cord in a fall. Tie the cord or webbing so that it forms a sling (fig. 15-47d). The anchor is now complete.

The V-thread anchor has held up well in testing and in use, but remember that it can only be as strong as the ice in which it is constructed.

## Belaying on Ice

As in other forms of roped climbing, ice climbers have the options of using running belays or fixed belays. They also have the use of boot/ice-screw belay techniques.

### Running Belays

Ice climbers can get a measure of protection that is somewhere between climbing on belay and climbing unroped by setting up a running belay. It's another way for a team to move faster when storms or avalanches threaten and, more than ever, speed is safety. It can also be useful on gentle to moderate terrain where danger of falling is minimal and actual belays would be too time-consuming.

A running belay on ice is created very much the same as a running belay on rock (described in Chapter 11) or snow (described and illustrated in Chapter 13). Members of the team, usually just two climbers, move simultaneously. The leader places protection as they climb and clips the rope through it; the follower removes the protection. The idea is to keep at least two points of protection between them at all times to hold the rope in case of a fall. The protection is usually spaced so that as the leader makes each new placement, the follower is removing the bottom one.

Because the technique of running belays sacrifices much of the safety of true belaying, the decision to use it takes fine judgment, based on extensive experience.

### Fixed Belays

Fixed belaying on ice requires a belayer, belay anchor, and intermediate points of protection, just as it does on snow or rock. A belay anchor is set up and the leader climbs the pitch on belay, sets up another anchor, and then belays the follower up the route. The climbers can either swing leads or have a single climber continue as the leader.

Near the end of a pitch that you are leading, keep an eye out for a good belay spot, perhaps at a slight depression or where the ice is not so steep or an area where a platform can be chopped out quickly. Plant a hand tool off to one side and clip in for temporary protection while you chop a step large enough to permit you to stand facing the ice with both feet flat and splayed. On steep ice you may only be able to chop a simple ledge the width of your foot.

### Belay Anchor

A standard anchor set-up for an ice belay (fig. 15-48) takes two ice screws. (The ice bollard or the Abalakov V-thread also can serve as a belay anchor, but they are

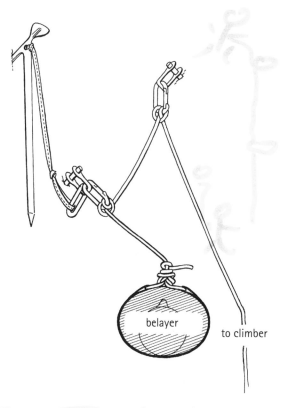

*Fig. 15-48. Anchor set-up for an ice belay*

more time-consuming to set up and therefore are used primarily for rappelling.) Place the first screw in the ice in front of you, a bit to one side, at about waist to chest level. Clip in a carabiner and tie into it with the climbing rope as it comes from your seat harness. Use a clove hitch or figure-8 knot.

Unclip from the hand tool that was placed as a temporary anchor and replant that tool above and to the outside of the ice screw. Clip the tool to the screw (via the wrist leash or a runner) as a backup to the anchor. Then tell your belayer down below that you are off belay.

Now you can place the second ice screw. Put it above you and about 2 or 3 feet higher than the first one

and off to the opposite side. Extend the climbing rope from the first screw to the second screw and tie in with a clove hitch. There should be little or no slack between the two screws. This completes the anchor set-up.

### Belay Methods

You have the choice of using a mechanical belay device, a Münter hitch, or a hip belay. The anchor set-up is the same in any case. Your choice will probably depend on what you're accustomed to and on your degree of confidence in the anchor. The hip belay tends to be somewhat dynamic, with a bit of movement at the belay—resulting in a slower stop to a fall but less force on the anchor and intermediate protection

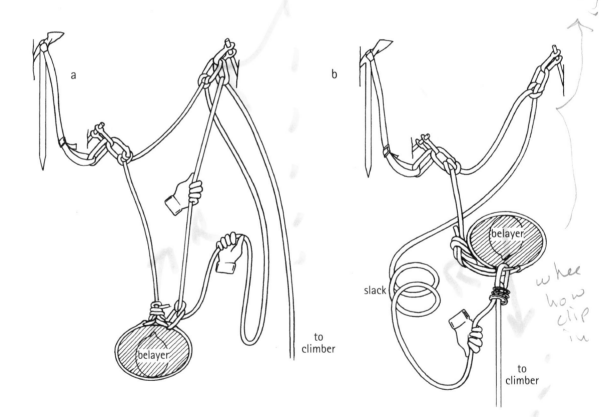

*Fig. 15-49. Ice belay set-up for a mechanical belay device or Münter hitch at the climber's seat harness: a, facing into the ice; b, facing out.*

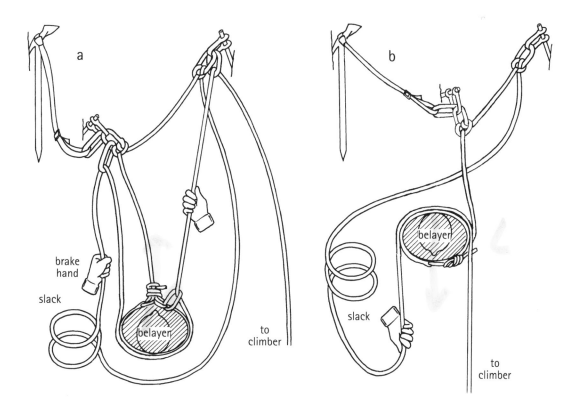

*Fig. 15-50. Ice belay set-up for a hip belay: a, facing into the ice; b, facing out.*

points. Belay devices and the Münter hitch, on the other hand, tend to be less dynamic, stopping a fall faster but putting more force on the anchor and intermediate protection points. (See Chapter 7 for details on the various belay methods.)

**Mechanical devices:** A belay device or a Münter hitch is easy to set up and efficient in use (fig. 15-49). Many ice climbers use such a method as standard procedure. The mechanism is usually situated at your seat harness, though you also have the option of belaying directly from the anchor. The belayer usually faces into the ice to belay a leader but, for belaying a follower, you can either face into the ice or face out.

If you face the ice to belay the follower (fig. 15-49a), the belay rope runs up through the top screw in the anchor set-up, directing the pull from the second climber

through this screw. After the follower ascends to the belay station and starts upward to take the lead, that screw becomes the first piece of protection on the new pitch.

If you face outward to belay the follower (fig. 15-49b), the belay rope runs directly to the device at your harness, and you tie into the anchor much as you would in a fixed belay in rock climbing.

**Hip belay:** You can establish a hip belay as you stand facing the ice by running the belay rope through a control carabiner at your waist, around your back, through an extra carabiner on the first screw, and then into your braking hand (fig. 15-50a). You also have the option of facing outward to belay a follower with a hip belay (fig. 15-50b). The hip belay is especially favored when the rope is stiff and frozen and could jam in belay devices.

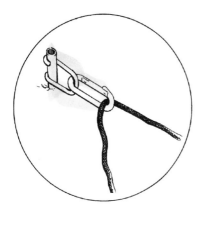

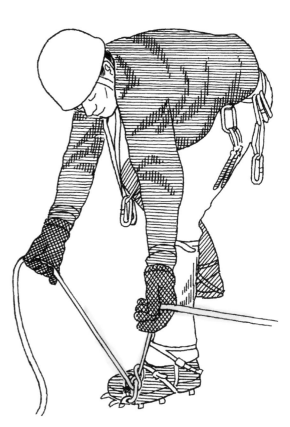

Fig. 15-52. Boot/ice-screw belay using Münter hitch

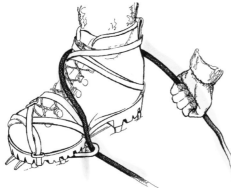

Fig. 15-51. Boot/ice-screw belay

## Boot/Ice-Screw Belay

For flat or gentle ice slopes, the boot/ice-screw belay is very useful (fig. 15-51). Here's how to do it: Start by twisting an ice screw into place, and then clip in a carabiner and run the belay rope through the carabiner. Plant your uphill boot over the screw, perpendicular to the direction of pull. Place the boot so that the inside point of your midboot row of crampons goes through the carabiner. Don't jab the rope. Bring the belay end of the rope over your instep, around the back of your boot ankle, and into your uphill hand.

You control friction on the rope by the amount of wrap on the ankle, much as in a boot-ax belay. You can also adjust the space between the edge of the boot

and the outside edge of the carabiner. If the climber falls, slowly tighten the rope low against the ankle with your uphill hand.

Helpful variations of the boot/ice-screw belay include two that utilize the Münter hitch. Use a large pear-shaped carabiner, which has the correct diameter for the Münter, instead of a standard carabiner. In one method, simply use a Münter hitch at the carabiner instead of running the belay rope around your ankle (fig. 15-52). Another method permits you to operate the belay while standing (fig. 15-53).

## Rappelling

Rappelling is usually the method of choice for descending steep ice. The principal considerations for

party descends. The last person removes the screws and rappels on the anchor with no backup.

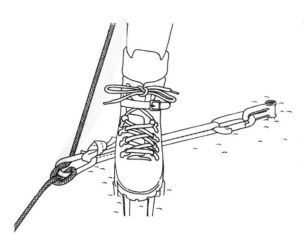

*Fig. 15-53. Boot/ice-screw belay using Münter hitch while standing*

rappelling on ice are the same as for rappelling on rock (see Chapter 8), but there is a big difference in anchor options. On rock, you can often use a natural anchor, such as a rock horn or a tree. On ice, you frequently have to make your own anchors. The two most popular rappel anchors for ice are the bollard and the Abalakov V-thread. Ice screws are commonly used to back up an ice anchor until the last member of the

## THE ICE CLIMBER

To climb steep ice, you'll use a lot of what you learned in rock and snow climbing and add in the special tools and techniques for ice. As an ice climber, you will especially share the joys of snow climbing, along with its perils: avalanches, hazardous couloirs and unstable cornices, ice blocks and icefalls. You can find climbing opportunities year-round, from the winter challenge of waterfall ice on short dark days in cold weather to the summer experience of alpine ice on days that are long and warm.

Skill and confidence in ice climbing come from long practice. If you can link up with a steady partner, so much the better. Practice together often. Work on pinpoint ice-tool and crampon placement, which conserves energy so you can meet the rigors of serious routes. Also work to increase the speed and efficiency of your climbing, gearing it to the conditions of the ice and the current strength of your body. Learn to determine when you and your partner should rope up for protection—and when it's safer not to. An experienced ice climber learns these skills and applies them with confidence and good judgment.

# 16

# Alpine, Winter, and Expedition Climbing

The pursuit of alpine, winter, or expedition climbing brings new demands on you as a mountaineer. These three varieties of climbing are complementary, but each has its own special requirements of equipment, techniques, and mental perspectives.

The weekend alpine climbing practiced by many mountaineers often requires a reasonable level of skill in several disciplines, such as rock and ice climbing, and the ability to shift from one to the other with limited equipment and time. Virtuosity in technique is rarely required. The challenge of alpine climbing often lies in ascending a peak that demands a wide variety of skills while carrying all the things you need and completing the affair before darkness or bad weather catches up with you.

Climbers enter a new world of effort and commitment when they take on winter or expedition climbing. There are big differences between weekend alpine climbing and the winter and expeditionary mountaineering of the serious amateur climber or the professional alpine mountaineer.

Building on the skills of alpine mountaineering, winter climbing can bring severe conditions that require specialized equipment, a high level of skill, and a tremendous will to succeed. Expedition climbing goes a step further, demanding the skills of alpine and winter climbing plus the ability to handle logistics of an extended trip, often in a foreign country.

The subject of weather helps to illustrate the differing levels of commitment needed in each of these types of climbs. On a typical summer alpine climb, weather is seldom a big issue. If the weather is poor, you can cancel the climb and try again when it gets better. If the weather turns poor on the climb, a bit of unpleasantry usually gets climbers down from the route, and a wet walk brings them back to the trailhead. In the winter, however, good weather is harder to come by, and frustrated climbers may give it a try despite a marginal forecast. If the weather does turn poor, descending the route and returning to the cars may turn into a mini-epic, with routefinding difficulties and increased danger from cornices and avalanches. On expeditions, the climbing team rarely has the luxury to choose the weather. Once the team leaves town, the trip schedule grinds on inexorably and weather becomes a condition that must be dealt with like any other obstacle on the trip.

The requirements of acclimatization to altitude can also differ depending on the type of climb. On short-term alpine and winter climbs at moderate elevations, acclimatization is not the critical issue that it is on expeditions to the high mountains of the world. On these expeditions, schedules must match not only your ability to climb the route but also the ability of your body to meet the rigors of living at high altitudes. More than one climber on the "dog" route of a high peak has turned back not because of weather or technical difficulties but because of too rapid an ascent.

Pulling off a successful winter climb or expedition often takes a lot of extra gear that you would not even consider taking on an alpine climb. For a one-day summer rock climb, you may need little more than a rope, rack, lunch, water bottle, and windbreaker. But the pack for even the simplest winter climb is heavier, with more equipment and clothing. The pack for an overnight trip must accommodate a warm sleeping bag for the low temperatures, a comfortable four-season tent for the long nights and more severe weather, and an ample stove and cook kit. An expedition multiplies the amount of food and fuel by the length of the trip. The expedition also may require extra climbing equipment for "fixing" parts of the route, leaving ropes in place for the safety of climbers and porters.

Looking at all the special demands of winter and expedition climbing, it's no surprise you need exceptional endurance. This is different from the intense short-term effort made by weekend alpine climbers, who are accustomed to the early Saturday morning drive to the trailhead and the bleary-eyed drive back home Sunday night or early Monday morning. It's the marathon run compared to the 100-yard dash. On an expedition, bursts of intense effort cannot be sustained, as the body does not heal or recover quickly at high altitudes. Team members need to find levels of physical and mental effort they can sustain for the entire trip. Save the climbing "burnout" of the weekend climb for the final summit push.

Regardless of whether your goal is alpine, winter, or expeditionary, you must be self-sufficient. The climbing team must rely on its own resources to get out of a jam because self-rescue often is the only option when the nearest help may be days or, in the case of expeditions, even weeks away.

------ **WINTER GEAR** ------

## Clothing

Your clothing and equipment should accommodate extremes of weather on any type of climb, whether it's an expedition, an alpine outing to your local peaks, or mountaineering in winter. Climb often enough in the mountains, and even in the summer you will encounter winterlike conditions. Likewise, many of the best winter climbs are done when the weather resembles spring. Clothing decisions are critical: carrying too much clothing does nothing but add weight to your pack and sap your strength; carrying too few clothes or the wrong type may lead to hypothermia or frostbite.

Summer clothing serves as the starting point. Begin with a wicking layer of underwear, followed by whatever layers of insulating clothing the weather dictates, topped off by a windbreaking layer made of a material that is also waterproof. How much extra clothing you bring, and what kind, depends on the conditions you can expect at your destination. Additional layers of synthetics work best in the cold damp of maritime climates. Where the climate is drier and colder, you can take advantage of the lightness and compactness of down, which you must keep dry.

The dangerous chilling effect of wind means you must always pack a complete layer of windproof clothing during the winter. The wind layer needs to fit over all the insulating layers you are likely to wear at one time and should overlay or tuck together for a solid shield against the wind. If you've left any chinks in the armor, the wind will find them. Fabrics vary in their windproofness, so get recommendations from other climbers and from the people at outdoor stores. Laminated materials such as Gore-Tex are among the most windproof.

If you are climbing in winter or are likely to encounter winterlike conditions, carry extra gloves. Once your first pair gets wet, your hands will stay cold until you put on your dry pair. For your head, keep a lightweight balaclava handy and, for very cold conditions, warmer headgear as well. (Chapter 2, Clothing and Equipment, has more information on clothes for mountaineering.)

Your own perspiration can be a danger if it makes your clothes damp. On a hot summer day, a sweaty shirt dries quickly in the sun after you've stopped working. But in wintry conditions, there is little warmth from the sun to dry out wet clothing. The only other source of heat to dry a shirt is your own body, and tremendous amounts of energy are necessary to evaporate water. Wearing damp clothing is the quickest way to chill yourself.

There are two ways to avoid dampening clothing

from perspiration: by regulating your pace, not allowing yourself to overheat; and by adding or removing layers of clothing, wearing lighter items for the approach and heavier layers when you slow down for belayed climbing. If clothes get damp, from either perspiration or precipitation, change as soon as you reach camp. If several layers of clothing are damp, at least change the layer closest to your skin.

## Care of the Feet

Because of their distance from the body core, extremities have the poorest circulation. To make matters worse for your feet, they are often close to snow or ice during alpine, winter, or expedition climbing. The same factors that keep your body warm—adequate insulation and staying dry—will also warm your feet.

The advent of plastic double boots made it much easier than before to keep your feet warm and dry. The plastic shell is an absolute barrier to snow and water, while the inner boot provides the insulation. By contrast, leather boots will absorb water and freeze overnight in cold conditions.

Whenever you climb on snow, you need gaiters to keep snow from entering the boot. Standard gaiters cover the upper boot and lower leg, whereas supergaiters cover the entire boot except for the sole. Overboots go one step further by covering the sole as well. Various brands of supergaiters and overboots offer insulation as well as a snow barrier. When purchasing overboots, be sure they are compatible with your crampon attachment.

In very cold conditions, vapor-barrier socks will keep your feet warmer by preventing perspiration from evaporating. The energy required by evaporation robs warmth from your feet. The vapor barrier also keeps outer socks and boots drier. Vapor-barrier socks are worn over a light pair of liner socks and beneath a heavier pair of insulating socks. The major disadvantage to vapor-barrier socks is the necessity to change the liner socks and dry your feet each night. Apply foot powder and a strong antiperspirant (not merely a deodorant) to help keep feet dry and comfortable—and watch out for blisters on the soft, moist skin.

The right socks are important in keeping your feet warm, but too many socks can do just the reverse. They can make the boot tight, restricting circulation and causing cold feet.

## ALPINE CLIMBING

There's no hard-and-fast definition of an alpine climb, but you can usually count on a venture that requires a variety of climbing techniques in reaching a summit that is at least several miles from the trailhead. Sport-climbing routes, on the other hand, more commonly concentrate on a single activity—face climbing, for example—and often are short ascents within sight of the parking lot. Much of the information in this book can be applied to sport climbing as well as mountaineering. But in this section we'll focus on those trips where you shoulder your pack, leave your cooler of beer behind—your pack is already too heavy—and hike what at times seems an interminable trail to reach your chosen peak. A flexible attitude is one of the most helpful possessions on an alpine climb, where you'll need the toughness to handle adversity and the sense to know when to call it quits.

## Equipment Decisions

One of the first decisions in preparing for an alpine outing is what climbing gear to carry. If the route is a rock climb, should you take your entire rack, or can you get by with a selection of hardware? If a selection, which sizes? Will you need two ropes for the rappels, or will one be enough? If you are climbing ice or snow, how many screws will you need? Are the snow conditions such that pickets or flukes will be helpful?

Mixed climbs involving both snow and rock magnify your decision-making chores as you see your pack gain unwanted weight with every piece of hardware you add. You'll find answers to your gear-selection questions in guidebooks and from talking with climbers who have done the route. Collecting information beforehand means you'll take on the route in less than a pioneering manner, but the alternative is making guesses that may leave you with gear you don't need and without the hardware that's required.

You'll also be deciding what camping equipment to carry. If it's just you and a partner heading into the mountains on a hot July weekend, you won't be packing that big dome tent with expedition fly and vestibule. Perhaps you'll consider a planned bivouac, spending the night with just a minimum of equipment.

Maybe you can do without your candle lantern, down booties, and Crazy Creek chair. What about that sleeping bag? Will your down jacket do just as well? Or maybe you can complete the entire trip in a single day by starting extremely early and coming out in the dark. These are all decisions that you and your partner must make in full light of possible consequences should things go awry.

Clothing selection brings another set of decisions. Chances are you won't need multiple layers of insulation in the Lower 48 states during the summer. Then again you may, if the mountain is high and the weather is questionable.

Carefully consider every item you put in your pack. Whenever you can safely leave something behind, you are lightening your burden and increasing your speed. A lighter load helps extend your range on those few precious weekends you have free for climbing.

## Alpine Dangers

Unlike most of the popular crags that attract sport climbers, alpine routes often have objective dangers such as loose or rotten rock or avalanche hazard. Take the time to study the route for predictable patterns in the falling of rock or ice. If you are climbing an icefall, this may mean observing it from a safe distance for a couple of days to determine when seracs tend to topple. You may discover that by climbing after midnight (or at some other time of day) you can avoid the worst danger. You can also consult others who have done the route to see what patterns they may have observed.

The same goes for routes plagued with rockfall. Perhaps the rockfall is due to melting snow that releases frozen rocks at certain times of day or at certain periods of year. Ask around, and add the observations of others to your own. You may find that a route that is a bowling alley in the fall will be much safer in late spring.

Beware of loose or rotten rock. If a rock sounds hollow when you tap on it, you probably can't trust it. Check all protection placements carefully; your favorite piece of protection may fit perfectly behind a rock flake that could break loose during a leader fall. Many alpine climbers have had rocks the size of backpacks come off in their hands; others have had even larger rocks roll and cut a rope.

## Mixed Terrain

Mixed climbing involves a combination of rock, snow, and ice. Perhaps it's a rock route climbed in the winter, with ice in the cracks and snow on the ledges. Or maybe the route is rock punctuated with icy sections. In its purest form, a mixed route would have the climber with one foot on rock and the other on ice.

You will probably climb most of a mixed route in crampons. Although considerable rock may be showing, the surface could be slick with a veneer of snow or ice. Climb deliberately. Search for small holds or level spots on which the crampon points can rest. You may be surprised at how well you can stand on even the smallest edge. However, crampon points can shear off the rock quite easily, so keep your feet steady once you are in your stance.

Mixed climbing rapidly dulls crampon points, but they should be able to withstand the abuse. Consider carrying a small file to sharpen points if difficult ice climbing is required after the mixed terrain. An option is to use step-in crampons and to remove them when climbing sections of rock. This shouldn't slow you down much because step-ins are relatively quick to remove and to put on.

An ice tool (ax or hammer) is useful even on a rock route. The tool can be placed in occasional ice or snow pockets and can even be hooked over the edge of rock holds. With imaginative use of all the parts of your tool—pick, adze, hammer head, or shaft—you should be able to hook some feature or wedge it in a crack.

When it is not needed, you can holster the tool on your harness (be sure the tool is secured, perhaps by its own leash) or sling it between your back and the pack. In many circumstances, however, you may be better off to let the ice tool simply dangle from your wrist by the wrist loop. This frees both hands for more traditional rock holds or even for grabbing onto an ice column, but when you need the tool again it's readily available with a flick of the wrist. Be sure the wrist loop is secure; no ice tool will do you any good as it bounces down the route below because the wrist loop threaded itself out of its own D-rings. You can prevent this by sewing the loose end of the wrist loop back on itself so it can't slip through the rings.

Above all, when you're climbing mixed terrain, be

creative, using your tools and climbing techniques to best advantage.

## Protection for Mixed Terrain

Previous chapters have detailed the types of protection used on rock, snow, and ice. When you combine them for mixed climbing, there are some additional considerations.

Given a choice between a rock anchor and a snow anchor, the rock anchor is usually the one to use. It's relatively easy to check the soundness of rock anchors; not so with most snow or ice anchors. Even a good anchor in snow or ice has less strength than one well placed in rock.

You may have to do a good bit of digging and grooming to clear away snow and ice in order to place a piece of protection in the rock. Your hands can knock off powdery snow, but it will probably take an ice ax to clear hard snow or ice. If a crack is filled with ice, a piton may be the only possible method of protection. But keep in mind that a piton scar on a mixed climb is just as damaging as one made anywhere else. Always use the least damaging yet secure anchor.

Ice screws and pickets used for protection in mixed terrain sometimes go in only partway because the snow or ice is shallow. In this situation, tie off to the protection at the surface of the snow or ice to minimize the danger that the protection will be levered out (fig. 16-1). Don't try to force an ice screw farther in than it can go, because this useless effort could shatter the ice.

## Use of the Rope

Decisions about rope use on a sport climb are generally quite easy; you rope up at the bottom of the route and stay roped up until you either rappel or walk off. In an alpine setting, things are not so cut-and-dried. The sheer length of many alpine routes requires a selective use of the rope—unless you want to stay roped all the time, with the likely result that your climb will proceed at a glacial pace. Many alpine routes have varied terrain: midlevel fifth-class climbing interrupted by sections of third- or fourth-class, or rock sections interspersed with snow slopes. In such situations it may be desirable to anchor your belays on the more difficult terrain while moving together or unroped on the easier stuff.

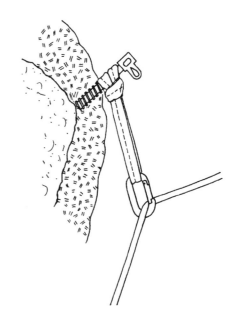

*Fig. 16-1. Ice screw placement in thin ice over rock*

When moving unroped on easy terrain above technical ground, remember that a simple slip could turn into tragedy. Another danger in unroped climbing on easy ground is that you may find yourself getting lured into climbing more difficult terrain. Once you realize your situation, it may be difficult to remove your pack and rope up; retreat to a safer place may be impossible. Always be aware of your surroundings so that you can rope up before you absolutely have to.

One useful technique on moderate terrain is the running belay. You remain roped to your partner, and the leader places occasional pieces of protection on the way up. There is no true belay—you both continue to climb—but the protection that is placed serves to limit the length of any fall. If you find yourself transitioning into difficult climbing, your partner can then set up an anchor for a solid belay. (Chapter 11, Leading on Rock, and Chapter 13, Snow Travel and Climbing, include discussions of running belays.)

Rappelling in an alpine setting requires closer attention to the soundness of anchors than on a typical sport-climbing route. Most of the loose rock has already been knocked off on sport routes, and rappels are often anchored securely to permanent bolts. But alpine routes may be littered with loose rock and questionable anchors, and you certainly shouldn't expect to find any bolts.

On alpine climbs you won't always have the luxury of rappelling in daylight. Again, this requires extra care in choosing anchors. Also be alert that you don't rappel right on past a lower rappel anchor in the dark.

## Bivouacs

Bivouacs, planned and unplanned, are common on alpine climbs. The idea of a planned bivouac—camping with just the minimum of equipment to make it safely through the night—may sound masochistic. However, with a bit of thought and foresight, a planned bivouac can be comfortable, and even an unplanned bivy can be at least bearable. (Chapter 3, Camping and Food, also includes a short section on bivouacs.)

The most comfortable bivouac is the one that is planned. The goal is to travel as light as possible on a route that will require a night out. You'll take minimal camping gear for a reasonably comfortable night: a full sleeping pad, adequate extra clothing, a bivy sack, and perhaps a very light sleeping bag.

Some bivouacs are semi-planned. That is, the route may be doable in a day; then again, it may not, and a bivouac could be necessary. In this case you might consider taking a long sit pad, a bivy sack, and a little extra clothing. You won't slow yourself down with a lot of extra weight, but you'll be prepared to get through the night if you must.

Unplanned bivouacs give you a chance to make the most of the Ten Essentials you always carry, especially the extra food and clothing. Knowing that unplanned bivouacs *do* occur should help you when packing for any alpine climb. Always carry an insulated sit pad. If you carry a space blanket as part of your first-aid kit, it may provide the insulation needed for a night of minimal discomfort. There may be times you'll consider carrying some *extra* extra clothing; perhaps an additional layer of polyester or polypropylene long underwear.

Your pack could see extra duty in an unplanned bivouac. Maybe the pack can double as a half-body bivy sack, with a rain parka for the upper half of your body. And perhaps the pack has some foam in its construction that can serve as ground insulation.

If you must bivouac, try to choose your spot before dark so you have time to prepare the site. Struggling on until last light may get you closer to home, but it also may leave you crouched for the night on a narrow ledge or suspended from an anchor on a steep wall, stuck in a painful stance until daybreak.

In preparing a bivouac site, safety comes first. Study the terrain to be sure you've picked the site with the least danger from falling rock or avalanches. Next in priority are shelter from wind and weather and a level space for sitting or lying down. Perhaps you can remove a few rocks or level the site with your shovel or ice ax. For warmth, the entire party should huddle together.

To keep from losing gear—or climbers—on steep, exposed bivouacs, everything and everybody must be anchored to the mountain. As you remove boots and other clothing items, store them immediately in anchored packs. Despite the inconvenience, all climbers should anchor themselves.

Following are a few ways you can make a bivouac more comfortable.

- Remove wet or damp clothing that is next to your skin (although wet polypro usually will dry from body heat as you prepare your bivouac site).
- Remove wet or damp socks for the night, perhaps replacing them with dry mittens if you're out of dry socks. (It's a good idea to wear vapor-barrier socks while you're climbing, but remove them and your wet liner socks when you bivy.)
- Keep drinking fluids, warm if possible.
- Eat plenty of food.
- Try to exercise before turning in; if you get unbearably cold, exercise off and on through the night.
- If possible, fill water bottles with warm water and sleep with them.

If the bivouac is unplanned, get out to the trailhead as quickly as possible the next day and call home so that an unneeded rescue won't be started.

A final thought on bivouacking: Before you make the final decision to stop for the night, consider not bivouacking at all. Assuming you're carrying a good headlamp with extra batteries, you may be able to travel by its light—and moving slowly will keep you warmer than not moving at all.

## WINTER CLIMBING

Climbing in winter is a natural extension of climbing at other times of year, with a lot of similar techniques and equipment and many of the same goals and rewards. It's just more complicated. Winter makes just about every route harder to climb than in the summer. The first winter outing is usually a humbling experience in comparison to summer expectations. The days are shorter, travel is slower, and routine tasks take more time. Allow for the short days: scale down your goals, get under way at first light, and carry a good headlamp.

You will need skis or snowshoes for support, except during the low snow of early season or the firm snow of late season. Whether you choose skis or snowshoes depends on your ability and the route. Are you a diehard skier who loves skis even if conditions are poor? Are you good enough to ski virtually any slope? Will you be moving along a broad ridge or logging road, which is good terrain for skis, or will you be traveling through forest and brush? Is the approach long but easy, where the speed of skis is a benefit? Will you encounter technical climbing, where skis would be more cumbersome to carry than compact snowshoes? Are you able to ski in a variety of conditions with a heavy pack? Consult specialized texts on skiing or snowshoeing for details on equipment and techniques.

Whether you're on skis or snowshoes or afoot, ski poles are useful for helping you stay in balance and assisting over obstacles. Ski poles beat an ice ax for much winter travel: the poles are longer, serving better as walking sticks, and the basket at the end of each pole provides some support in soft snow. Your hands may stay drier because a ski pole won't plunge so deeply into soft snow that your hands get wet, as an ice ax often will.

An avalanche beacon is an essential item of equipment for winter travel. An optional item that comes in very handy is an insulated water-bottle carrier; your drink won't do you any good if it's frozen.

For additional information applicable to mountaineering in snow, see the three chapters preceding this one, plus Chapter 4, Navigation.

## Routefinding

Winter routefinding gets challenging when bad weather hides the destination or landmarks along the way. Study the map ahead of time and become familiar with the terrain you will cross. Note broad features such as ridges, ravines, streams, and changes in steepness of the slope so that when you encounter them you'll have an idea where you are. You may find that your altimeter and compass are especially useful in winter mountaineering.

When the visibility is good, route features often stand out more clearly than in summer. Ledges and couloirs hold snow and show up sharply against dark surrounding rock features. Ridges or arêtes blown free of snow stand out against the white of a snow face.

Avalanche hazard often dictates changes in the usual summer route, which may lead through an active avalanche path. A rock route that's free of avalanche danger in summer may be topped by cornices in winter. Heavy snowfall, warm temperatures, or wind can increase the hazard of slab and loose-snow avalanches. Ridges are safer from avalanche than gullies and broad open slopes; windward slopes are safer than leeward. Never underestimate the danger of avalanches.

Snow can be deceptively hazardous. A small tree that appears to be a sound rappel anchor may in fact be only a branch from a log buried in the snow. Just as snow bridges over crevasses may collapse, so also may snow bridges over streams.

The conventional wisdom is that loose snow will not stay long on a steep surface. But occasionally you encounter circumstances that seem to defy the rules, such as a short slope with snow well anchored by boulders or by a wind-sculpted snow trough. Normal step-kicking won't work because the snow is too loose, nor is delicate footwork the answer. You must use your whole body to flail your way up the slope. An ice ax placed horizontally may be the only handhold, and you move upward on your knees rather than your feet. Rarely is the effort graceful. At times, it takes a snow shovel to literally dig a path through the snow.

With winter weather always ready to deteriorate, don't let summit lust cloud your ability to reach a sound decision on when to turn back. Wands are a big help in finding the return route during winter's poor weather and limited visibility, and when wind-driven snow covers your tracks. Expect to put your headlamp and extra batteries to use for travel in the dark because of the short days of winter. (For more details on routefinding on snow, see Chapter 13, Snow Travel and Climbing.)

## Health Hazards

Surprisingly, dehydration is a winter hazard. Sweat may not pour from your brow the way it does in summer, but depending on your level of exertion and the dryness of the air, significant moisture loss occurs. Also, fluid intake normally drops because people don't crave cold drinks during the winter. Make a conscious effort to drink enough fluids to keep your urine output copious and clear. This need for fluids highlights the importance of a stove that can dependably melt plenty of snow for drinks.

Hypothermia and frostbite are more traditional winter health hazards. You can prevent both through awareness of the hazards and with adequate clothing, food, and water. Avoid chills by staying as dry as possible and eating and drinking adequately. If you become chilled, do something about it. Put on more clothes or change damp clothes. If your feet are numb, wiggle your toes vigorously in the boot. If these actions don't work, you may need to take a break to warm the numb body parts. Once you establish camp, inspect feet and fingers for frostbite and treat as necessary.

Sunburn and snow blindness are major concerns. Apply sunscreen liberally to all exposed flesh, and always have glacier glasses ready to put on. A good rule of thumb is that if you are squinting, you need to wear your glasses—even if it's foggy.

You're obviously responsible for taking care of your own health and guarding against problems that could jeopardize the climb or endanger fellow climbers. At the same time, keep alert to any health problems of other team members. (See Chapter 19, First Aid, for more information on dehydration, hypothermia, frostbite, sunburn, snow blindness, and other health hazards.)

## Camping

Winter camping can be a difficult business compared with overnighting in summer. The duties of setting up camp, finding water, securing gear, and keeping warm are transformed from simple tasks into significant undertakings in the winter environment.

Turn to Chapter 3, Camping and Food, for a complete discussion of winter camping, including the topics of tents, tent cooking, snow shovels, snow shelters, stoves, and sleeping bags.

## EXPEDITION CLIMBING

Expedition climbing does not represent a different type or standard of climbing as much as an expansion of the time scale for a climb. A weekend trip may involve several hours or a day for the approach to the peak, whereas an expedition can require two or three days of air travel followed by a day or two of land travel, followed by a ten-day hike into base camp. A rest break is not a 10- or 15-minute sit down but may be an entire day spent lounging. The actual climbing is much the same as discussed in earlier chapters and in the alpine climbing section of this chapter. The main differences between expedition climbing and other mountaineering come in the logistics of tackling a remote peak, the more severe weather likely to be encountered, and the difficulties of climbing at high altitude—and often the challenge of dealing with local customs and the daunting red tape of foreign climbing regulations.

The scope of this chapter is expeditions of three to four weeks on relatively accessible 20,000- to 23,000-foot peaks, such as Alaska's Mount McKinley (Denali) or Peru's Huascaran. Many of the techniques and considerations are similar to those of longer expeditions to higher peaks. However, there also are major differences in permits, hiring of porters, medical requirements, extremes of altitude and cold, use of oxygen, and so forth that are beyond the scope of this chapter.

### Planning and Preparation

In deciding what peak to try and which route to climb, you will take a lot of factors into account.

**Difficulty of the route:** It's generally best to choose a route well within your climbing ability because the challenges of remoteness, changeable weather, and

*Local safer context push limits*

routefinding will add to the difficulties. Until you have gone on a few expeditions, think of the trip as an opportunity to apply well-practiced climbing skills in a new environment, rather than to push the limits of your ability.

**Duration of the climb:** Again, be realistic. Don't try to cram a twenty-five-day route into two weeks of annual leave. Remember that the time it takes to arrive at your mountain and later return home can be a significant part of the expedition's schedule.

**Time of year:** Study information on seasonal temperatures, winds, storms, rains, and amount of daylight. Your trip will be planned far in advance, so in choosing your dates you'll have to deal with probabilities and likelihoods in the hope that the realities will measure up when the time comes.

**Costs:** Major costs are equipment for the climb, transportation and other expenses on the way to the peak, and hiring porters and pack animals to haul gear to base camp. In many cases, expenses within a country are minor compared with the cost of getting there. Estimate costs based on research about the peak and/or area.

**Location:** Where to go? Alaska, Mexico, the Andes of South America, Europe, Nepal, Pakistan, India, Russia, Kazakhstan, and areas of Africa all boast difficult, remote peaks. The experience of traveling in a remote or foreign land is often one of the most enjoyable and rewarding aspects of an expedition. After choosing your peak, research the mountain and its routes. Talk to climbers who have been there, look for descriptions in the journals of the American Alpine Club and of climbing organizations in Canada and Europe, and seek out guidebooks, videos, and stories in climbing magazines. Get all possible details on logistics, potential problems, where to buy fuel, what foods are available, objective hazards on the mountain, and so forth.

Have a backup route in mind in case the main objective is scratched because of avalanche hazard, bad weather, inability of some party members to continue, or any other reason. If you've chosen a highly technical route up your mountain, consider acclimating by climbing the standard route first and then taking on the tougher challenge.

Find out what climbing and communication-device permits and approvals are necessary and how long in advance application must be made. It helps to have typewritten itineraries, climbing résumés of party members, equipment lists, and medical information in hand ahead of time and while traveling to the peak. The appearance of good organization impresses bureaucrats the world around.

## Choosing the Team

Choosing a compatible team is the first step toward an enjoyable experience. Expedition climbing is full of stress, and climbers can be taxed to their physical and mental limits. Climbing literature abounds with "climb and tell" accounts of expeditions in which, it seems, team members despised their fellow climbers; you don't want your expedition to end up being another.

The skill of your team must, of course, be equal to the demands of the climb. Climbing with people of similar technical ability may improve compatibility. Team members need personalities that are compatible with each other and must be able to live harmoniously with others in close quarters under stressful conditions. The climbers should agree on the philosophy of the trip in terms of climbing style, environmental impact, and degree of acceptable risk.

It's important to agree on leadership before the trip gets under way. If all climbers are of roughly equal experience, democratic decision-making usually works well. If one climber is clearly more experienced, that person can be given the leadership role. Even with a single leader, functional areas such as finance, food, medicine, and equipment should be delegated to others to lessen the leader's load and to keep everyone involved and informed. This also helps build expedition leaders for the future.

The number of climbers in the expedition depends partly on the route and on the climbing style you've chosen. A party of two or four climbers may be best on technically difficult routes because of the efficiency of two-person rope teams and the limited space at bivouac sites. However, climbing with a very small team means that, if one person becomes ill or cannot continue, the entire team may have to abandon the climb.

When the route itself does not determine the optimum party size, logistics becomes the deciding factor. As the number of climbers increases, issues of transportation, food, lodging, and equipment become more complicated. The advantage is that parties of six or eight have strength and reserve capacity. If one climber doesn't continue, the rest of the party has a better chance to go on with the expedition. And larger parties usually are better able to carry out self-rescue than smaller teams. However, the logistics of an expedition with more than eight members can become more burdensome than many climbers are willing to accept.

## Establishing a Climbing Style

Do you plan to climb "expedition style" or "alpine style" or somewhere in between? There's a big difference, and it's a question you need to resolve early, based on the route, the size and strength of your party, and the preference of the climbers. Your choice will affect the trip length, risks, equipment, and technical gear suitable for the climb.

Traditional expedition climbing style involves multiple carries between camps, during which food, fuel, and supplies are ferried to higher camps. Technically difficult sections of the route are often protected with fixed lines—ropes anchored in place to minimize danger during repeated trips up and down. It's a slow and measured campaign for the summit.

Alpine climbing style usually means moving camps up the mountain in a continuous push so that the route is climbed only once. All equipment and supplies are carried with the team at all times.

Expedition-style ascents take longer because more time is spent hauling loads between camps. They are heavier because more food, fuel, and perhaps fixed line must be carried and more costly because of the greater amounts of time, equipment, and food. There is less margin of safety on alpine-style trips, but there may also be less exposure to such objective hazards as storms and avalanches because the team moves faster.

## The Climbing Itinerary

Once you've researched your mountain, you can set up an itinerary that makes a good estimate of the number of days to allow for the approach to the peak, for carrying loads up the mountain, for climbing, for sitting out storms, and for resting. An average elevation gain of 1,000 feet per day is recommended for acclimatization, and this figure should be correlated where possible with good campsites. Rest days built into the schedule provide time for mental and physical recuperation, equipment sorting, and such. They can also serve as a time buffer for unplanned delays caused by storms, illness, or other problems. If a storm hits, try to reschedule a rest period for the same time, making the best of a bad day.

For moving camps expedition-style up the mountain, double carries are generally adequate on a three-week climb. The first carry hauls food, supplies, and equipment to the site of the next camp. The second carry involves tearing down the current camp and resetting it at the next site. On bigger mountains, camps may need to be stocked pyramid style, with many carries between camps early in the trip and few if any carries between later camps.

When repeated carries are necessary, each load is usually cached at the next camp while the climbers go back down for more. Plan to set up a protected cache to avoid damage from the elements and from animals. Dig a hole, cover it with something an animal can't get through, such as a sled or snowshoes, and pile snow on top. Mark the cache with long wands. But beware. Ravens on popular peaks have learned to identify caches, so place the wands a little distance away and smooth the surface above the cache.

## Guided Expeditions

Guided climbs are available to just about any expedition objective. A guide is worth considering if this is your first expedition, if you lack capable partners, or if the prospect of organizing such a major adventure is overwhelming. Choosing a guided expedition should allow you to spend more time enjoying the experience and less time organizing it. But a guided climb will cost more than a privately organized venture. More importantly, you will lose control over the selection of party members and other decisions that may affect your safety or prospects for the summit. You also may not find the same unity of purpose and caring interdependence that characterize the best expedition experiences.

Some questions to consider if you decide to look for a guide: Is the guide service licensed and insured as required by the governing authority of your destination? What is its safety record and success rate? What are the qualifications of the guide and the other party members? What is the reputation of the service among climbers?

## Food and Equipment

On expeditions to the remote mountains of the world, you either take it with you or you do without it. Having the necessary equipment, in working order, is much more critical than on a weekend climb where home is a short drive away. Your expedition needs a complete equipment list, both group and personal, worked out in discussions with all team members. (See the sample equipment list at the end of this chapter.)

### Supplies for the Group

#### Food

Food constitutes the heaviest single category of weight carried by an expedition. But who's complaining? Food provides the necessary fuel for your body to carry loads and climb the route, and it also can serve as one of the great pleasures of the trip.

Every climber has preferences in food, so conduct a team survey of strong food likes and dislikes before planning menus. Combat the danger of carrying unpopular foods by providing a lot of variety. If some team members don't like one item, there should be several others they will find tasty, or at least palatable. A condiment and seasoning kit with the likes of Tabasco sauce, spices, soy sauce, margarine, and mustard will add interest to bland packaged foods and perhaps salvage the unpopular foods.

Although fats have the highest caloric density (9 calories per gram), carbohydrates (4 calories per gram) are easiest to digest and provide the quickest energy. Proteins have about the same caloric density as carbohydrates but are not as easy to digest and are usually accompanied by substantially more fat. A reasonable expeditionary diet has about 50 to 70 percent of its calories from carbohydrates, 20 to 30 percent from fat, and 15 to 20 percent from protein.

Plan to provide about 35 ounces (roughly 2¼ pounds) of food per person per day. With no waste, 35 ounces would provide more than 5,000 calories. In reality—because of packaging, nonnutritive fiber, and the food's irreducible water—the food will provide only about 3,900 calories per day. Experience will tell whether this is just right, too much, or not enough. Too much food means extra-heavy loads between camps and possibly a slower trip. Too little means you will begin losing weight. On a trip of three or four weeks weight loss shouldn't cause a problem, but on longer expeditions too much weight loss may affect the team's strength and endurance.

Food is your major controllable weight factor. As you sit at home planning menus and calculating energy expenditures, you'll be tempted to throw into the menu an extra cracker at breakfast, an extra candy bar during the day, or an extra cocoa at dinner. Resist this temptation at all cost. Unless the extra food never gets past base camp, it will eventually find its way onto the climbers' backs or into their sleds, slowing their pace while fatiguing them faster. If you are planning a twenty-day trip, take food for twenty days, not twenty-one. On unplanned storm days, you will simply have to stretch your rations. Food can always be stretched on an expedition, and it's easier than suffering the consequences of overloaded packs.

You can plan foods for early in the trip that are different from those for later as you get up on the mountain. Candidates for lower elevations and warmer climes are foods that are time-consuming to prepare, such as pancakes; items that suffer from freezing, such as cheese and peanut butter; and canned foods. Foods carried to higher altitudes should be very light and require a minimum of preparation, such as freeze-dried items, instant noodles, instant rice, and potatoes. Try to eat local food on approach marches and at base camp so you don't tire too early of expedition food.

Packaging and organizing food is an important element of planning. Eliminate as much of the weight and garbage of the commercial packaging as possible by repackaging the food in appropriately sized portions, perhaps adding spices or other ingredients. Use boilable packages for rehydrating food at higher elevations. Keep the preparation instructions from the packaging material. You should prepackage rations into person-days (put in one bag the food for one person for one day), or into group-days (put in one bag the food for the entire group for one day), or into tent-days (put in one bag the food for one tent for one day). However you do it, measure the food into the correct portions and label it. Clear plastic sacks help organize the food while keeping the contents visible.

Adequate hydration is the first line of defense against altitude sickness. Bring a lot of soups, hot drinks, and cold-drink mixes to help motivate you into drinking the necessary fluids. Contaminated water plagues nearly every part of the world. The expedition kitchen must be able to furnish adequate water for everyone through chemical decontamination, filtering, or boiling.

### Fuel

Fuel cannot be carried on airlines so it must be available at your destination. Multi-fuel stoves may be good insurance in foreign countries where white gas is not readily available. Even with a multi-fuel stove, check the fuel's compatibility with the stove before heading into the mountains. If you're using kerosene or a similar low-volatility fuel, be sure to buy alcohol or gas for priming the stove. The cleanliness of fuel in foreign countries is always questionable. Bring a filter, and filter all fuel before using it; clean the stove often. Plan on using between a quarter-pint and a half-pint of fuel per person per day, depending on how much water must be boiled for purification or melted from snow.

Fuel containers are usually supplied in Alaska or Canada, but you must provide your own elsewhere. Aluminum containers as small as 1 liter are fine if you don't need to carry much fuel. For larger quantities, bring 1-gallon gas cans or sturdy approved plastic fuel containers. They should be new, as airlines object to containers with residual fuel vapors. Plastic bottles sold in foreign countries have a reputation for leaking. All fuel containers should be kept separated from other gear, especially food.

### Community Equipment

For communal cooking, take pots large enough for the group meal courses and for melting large amounts of snow. Filling water bottles is a common activity, so pots must be easy to pour from (a 2-quart coffee pot works well). Bring at least one cook pot per stove. Bring a metal gripper to use on pots that lack handles or bails, or use wool gloves as potholders. (Be careful using synthetic gloves, which will melt if they get too hot.)

To save a bit of weight, the party can carry an altimeter and a compass as pieces of group equipment rather than having each climber carry separate ones. Also among group equipment are wands, which are used for marking routes, camp perimeters, gear caches, and snow shelters. Carry long wands if there's a chance of significant snowfall. Tents are also community equipment.

The party may carry communication devices to get weather information, call for emergency help, or communicate between climbers at different locations. The main choices are citizen's band radios, marine band FM radios, and cellular telephones. You will have to do some investigating to determine both the technical feasibility and the legality of their use.

### Community Climbing Gear

The route and your chosen climbing style determine the climbing gear you need. A route that involves only glacier travel may require just the basics: rope, ice ax, and crampons. Technical routes can take the whole gamut of equipment, from ice screws, snow flukes, and pickets to camming devices, nuts, and pitons.

Depending on the style and organization of the trip, climbing gear can be personal or common. On a technical route where climbers operate in self-sufficient pairs, climbing gear should be personal or left to each rope team to work out. In other cases, virtually all climbing gear—carabiners, runners, screws, and so forth—can be treated as group equipment. The choice is up to the team. Certain pieces of climbing gear, such as crampons and ice axes, are indispensable, and a large party may want to carry spares.

The decision on what ropes to take also depends on the route and its difficulty. For technical pitches, you'll use either a single rope (10.5 or 11 millimeters in diameter) or double or twin ropes (each 8 or 9 millimeters). On a glacier route, a single 9-millimeter rope may be adequate. Keep in mind, however, that an expedition can put extraordinary wear and tear on the rope with daily use in bright sunlight. The team also needs to decide how much rope to bring for fixed line along the route. Fixed line is usually a polypropylene braided rope or a nylon kernmantle rope. Polypro is lightest and cheapest, but kernmantle is better for areas of high use.

### Repair Kit

Equipment failure is common under the prolonged and rugged demands of an expedition, so count on needing to repair or substitute for failed gear. Put together a comprehensive repair kit, keeping in mind the relative importance of each piece of equipment to the progress of the group.

Among the repair-kit items should be the following:

- Tape—gray duct tape seems to be the universal repair favorite, but other tapes, such as ripstop fabric tape or filament tape, are useful.
- Sewing kit for permanent repairs or those beyond the capability of tape.
- Extra stove parts and the tools to disassemble the stove.
- Tent-pole splices or extra tent poles. While the tent body or fly can be patched with tape, broken tent poles must be repaired or replaced.
- Extra crampon parts, such as screws, nuts, and connecting bars, and the necessary tools.
- Patch kit for inflatable foam pads that spring leaks.
- Also, a file, pliers, wire, accessory cord, and a pack buckle.

### First-Aid Kit

An expedition usually carries a comprehensive first-aid kit, which is assembled after everyone in the party has had input into the selections. Keep in mind the isolation of the peak, and consider the specific medical conditions of team members and their medical knowledge. Discuss your group's medical needs with a doctor who is familiar with mountaineering.

The first-aid kit may include such specialized or prescription items as a strong painkiller, antibiotics, a dental repair kit, and a suture kit. Be sure to carry a first-aid manual. (For information on general-purpose mountaineering first-aid kits, see Chapter 2, Clothing and Equipment, and Chapter 19, First Aid.)

## Personal Gear

Expedition climbers need clothing and sleeping bags that can stand up to prolonged use under severe conditions. The suggestions on clothing and equipment in the preceding sections of this chapter are generally applicable to expeditions. The desired comfort rating for your sleeping system varies with the climate and season, but a good general rating for expeditions is about minus 30 degrees Fahrenheit (about minus 35 degrees Celsius).

Every person on an expedition team needs a big pack, with a capacity between 5,500 and 7,000 cubic inches, because there are times you will be called on to carry "impossible" loads. The pack also must be comfortable while you are wearing a climbing harness.

You may want mechanical ascenders, rather than prusik slings, both for crevasse rescue and for protection while climbing with a fixed line. The ascenders permit one-way movement by gripping or squeezing the line when your weight is on them but letting you move them when they are unweighted. The ascenders, under such brand names as Jumar, Clog, and Gibbs, are necessary to handle the large, heavy expedition loads involved in any crevasse rescue. On fixed line, the prusik knots are unsafe because of the time required to unfasten and reattach them past each anchor you encounter on the way up or down.

Although two ascenders are the norm, one plus a prusik sling can work if you need to cut down on weight. Regardless of the choice, make sure the system can be operated while you're wearing bulky gloves or mittens.

Other items of personal gear to consider are the following:

- Prescription glasses—carry an extra set of prescription sunglasses.
- Journal—an expedition can make you introspective. A journal made of waterproof paper (look under surveyor supplies at a bookstore or stationery supply store) and some pencils can help pass the time.
- Books—you can catch up on reading while waiting for flights or during rest days and storm days in the field. Coordinate your selection of books with other team members to avoid repetition and provide variety.
- Personal hygiene items—on cold-weather trips where water is at a premium, chemical wash/wipes can provide a refreshing sponge bath and talcum powder can take some of the bite out of the odors that develop over the course of an expedition.
- Pee bottle—during storms and cold nights, the pee bottle eliminates those unpleasant traipses to the latrine. Be sure the bottle has a secure top.

## Physical and Mental Conditioning

Training for an expedition involves both physical and mental preparation. For the body, emphasize both cardiovascular and strength training. Cardiovascular conditioning is important for physical activity at high altitudes. Powerful leg muscles are needed to walk heavy loads up the mountain, and upper-body strength is needed to hoist, carry, and climb with the large expeditionary packs.

Climbing itself is the best training. Climb often and in all weather conditions, carrying a heavy pack. If you can go on a typical two- to three-day climb packing gear for camping and climbing, gaining 3,000 to 5,000 feet per day, and feel you still have plenty of physical reserves, you're probably sufficiently fit for an expedition. An expedition climber needs the endurance to carry packs of 40 to 60 pounds (sometimes in addition to pulling a sled) for an elevation gain of 2,000 to 3,000 feet every day, day after day.

Your mind and spirit also need to get into shape for the rigors of an expedition. Learn about the special challenges of expedition travel and prepare yourself to accept them. Otherwise, you can be overwhelmed by the size and remoteness of the climbing area or lose your good spirits during a long storm or a bout with the flu.

Success on an expedition often goes to the person who has a greater desire or will to succeed, even though he or she may be physically weaker than another climber. It takes more than physical strength to deal with extreme cold, sickness, cramped quarters, poor food, conflict with teammates, the stress of technical climbing, and the lethargy brought on by high altitude.

You can work on both your physical and mental conditioning by seeking out experiences that come as close as possible to what you expect on the expedition. Prepare for the expedition by going on winter climbs and on longer trips. You may not be able to alter such objective conditions as cold or illness, but you can learn to exercise a great deal of mental control over your response and attitude toward them.

### Before You Leave Home

Food and gear must be packed and frequently repacked to accommodate the various transportation modes used to get to the mountain. Become familiar with the requirements that face your expedition, such as airline regulations on bag sizes and weights, or muleteer requirements on load balancing. Keep lists of what went into each bag so any item can be retrieved

readily. Before leaving home, plan travel arrangements for each leg of the journey and make reservations where possible. Try to work with a travel agent who has booked trips to the region before.

Be as healthy as possible when you leave town because, in all likelihood, you won't get better while traveling. For foreign travel, find out well in advance what inoculations are needed. Have a dental exam and leave no dental care pending. To stay healthy once you get to your destination, plan on purifying all water and be cautious about eating unpeeled fresh vegetables or fruit, dairy products, and uncooked food. And through all the complicated hurry and scurry of getting ready for a big expedition, try to remember that your goal is to get away from it all and climb a mountain.

## Expeditionary Climbing Techniques

Expedition mountaineering calls for the rock-, snow-, ice-, alpine-, and winter-climbing techniques that have been covered throughout this book. An expedition can add a couple of new techniques to your climbing repertoire: hauling sleds and using fixed lines.

### Haul Sleds

Expedition members often pull sleds or haul bags behind them on long glacier approaches as a way to move the loads of gear and supplies (fig. 16-2). A climber can transport a normal load in a backpack in addition to pulling a sled with another pack's worth of gear.

Commercial haul sleds are available, with zippered covers to hold the load, a waist harness for you to wear, and rigid aluminum poles connecting the sled to the harness. These poles help control the sled when traversing or going downhill.

A cheaper but usable alternative is a plastic children's sled, with holes punched in the sides as rope attachment points. Load your gear into a duffel bag and tie it to the sled. Perlon accessory cord (5 to 7 millimeters) is used to pull the sled, and most climbers prefer to attach the cord to their pack, not their climbing harness.

A final alternative is to drag a haul bag, constructed of durable, slick material to help it slide over the snow. A swivel connector attaching the haul line to the haul bag will keep the rolling of the bag from putting twists in the line.

*Fig. 16-2. Sled and climber rigged for glacier travel*

As the route steepens, the amount of weight you can pull in a sled decreases, and it can't be used at all on steep technical climbing terrain. Haul bags may then be what you need. (See Chapter 12, Aid Climbing, for techniques for using haul bags on technical routes.)

No special trick is involved in towing a sled behind you. It simply takes steadfast pulling. Where it can get complicated is during roped travel on glaciers, where any fall into a crevasse is made more treacherous by having the sled plunge down behind you. Even if you aren't injured by the plummeting sled, rescue is more difficult with the need to deal with you, your pack (weighing perhaps 60 pounds), and the sled (carrying another 50 pounds or so).

You can minimize the danger of getting hit by the sled during a crevasse fall with a simple preventive technique. Just take your climbing rope where it runs past the sled and tie it snugly with a clove hitch or prusik knot to a carabiner at the rear of the sled. In a crevasse fall, you will drop in, followed by the sled. But the sled will be stopped above you by the tie-in to the climbing rope. If you are using a hauling tether to the sled (instead of rigid aluminum poles), be sure the tether is long enough so you are well beyond the reach of the sled as it hangs from the climbing rope. This technique depends on having a team member behind you on the rope to arrest the fall of both you and the

sled, so it won't work for the last climber on a rope. The last person either assumes the extra risk, or the team can decide to haul only two sleds for each three climbers.

### Crevasse Rescue

If you are hauling a sled, it takes some special procedures for crevasse rescue, beyond those spelled out in Chapter 13, Snow Travel and Climbing. Imagine that you have just fallen into a crevasse. The sled, attached to the climbing rope, dangles above you. Here is how you can help yourself get out.

First of all, get your weight onto the climbing rope. As you dangle in the crevasse, your weight may be on the sled haul line (or towing poles, if you are using a commercial sled). Transfer your weight to the climbing rope by standing in slings attached to your ascending system (mechanical ascenders, prusik slings, or a combination).

Then disconnect the attachment from you to the sled. If you are using a haul line attached to your pack, simply take off the pack and let it hang from the line.

Once free of the sled, you can try to rescue yourself or wait for your climbing mates to get you out. If you start up the climbing rope on your own, the sled probably will cause some complication. You may need to ascend around the climbing rope knot that holds the sled. In this case, remove and reattach your ascenders above the knot, one at a time.

You may also need to untie from the climbing rope in order to move past the sled and reach the lip of the crevasse. To make it easier to disconnect from the climbing rope, many sled-pullers travel with the rope clipped to a locking carabiner on their harness, rather than tying directly to the harness itself. If you must unclip from the climbing rope, use extreme caution to ensure that the ascenders are secure.

Your fall into the crevasse can also mean extra effort for your teammates if they must pull you out. If you can't disconnect yourself from the sled or if there is no extra rescue rope available, they must haul both you and the sled at the same time. They will have to use a Z-pulley system to get the most mechanical advantage in pulling on the climbing rope. Far preferable is to use a spare rope to pull you out and to then pull the sled out on the climbing rope it is already attached to.

## Fixed Lines

A fixed line is simply a rope that is anchored to the route and left in place. It allows safe, quick travel up and down a difficult stretch. Climbers protect themselves by tying into a mechanical ascender on the fixed line, eliminating the need for time-consuming belays. If you fall while climbing next to the fixed line, the ascender cam locks onto the line and holds the fall.

It's also possible in some cases to climb a fixed line directly by hanging from slings attached to two ascenders and moving them methodically upward. However, fixed lines are not generally used for direct aid in the situations discussed in this chapter.

The fixed line simplifies the movement of people and equipment, especially when numerous trips are required, and permits less-experienced climbers to follow a route. Fixed lines have been common on large expeditions to major peaks to provide protection on long stretches of exposed climbing or to protect porters while they make carries from camp to camp in the face of such obstacles as icefalls, glaciers, and steep rock or ice. The lines make it possible for climbers and porters to carry heavier loads than they could safely carry without them.

Fixed lines are sometimes used as a siege tactic on difficult rock and ice faces, with climbers retreating down the lines each night to a base camp and then reascending the next day to push the route a little farther. They also come into play on continuous multiday aid climbs of big walls, where the second climber follows on the line, removing protection and hauling up equipment. The climbers do not retreat down this line but move it upward as they go. Thus it becomes a "moving" fixed line, only one rope length long.

Some climbers argue that fixing ropes is an outmoded technique, no longer required to climb any mountain or route. This is not the majority view, but the technique should not be abused. Fixed lines should not be used to supplement the climbing ability of an expedition team. If many of the climbers don't have the ability to climb a route without help from a fixed line, find an alternate route. Fixed lines should not be added on popular routes or in regions where they are not normally used.

In the past, climbers often abandoned fixed lines when a climb was done. It was not uncommon to find several lines, one on top of the next, frozen into a route. This is no longer acceptable in a time of increasing environmental awareness, and each party needs to make a commitment to remove its fixed lines.

Exercise extreme caution in deciding whether to make use of a fixed line that you find already in place on your route. It's hard to determine the integrity of an existing line and its anchors. The rope may be damaged by age, exposure to weather, or the ice tools or crampons of the climbers who used the line before you.

### Equipment for Fixed Lines

To set up and use fixed lines, you need rope, anchors, and ascenders. Climbing ropes don't make good fixed lines because they are designed to stretch under a load, an undesirable characteristic in a fixed line. What you want is a more static rope, one with low elongation under load. Nylon is the most common material for fixed lines, though polypropylene and Dacron also are used. Kernmantle construction is best, though braided ropes can be used.

The diameter of fixed lines usually varies between 7 and 10 millimeters, with the size depending on the terrain and the amount of use the line is expected to get. Try to carry your fixed line in long lengths. The ropes are usually manufactured in lengths of somewhere between 300 and 1,000 feet, depending on rope diameter.

To anchor the fixed line to the mountain, employ any attachment points that are normally used in belaying and climbing on rock or ice: pitons, chocks, natural outcrops, ice screws, pickets, and snow flukes or other deadman anchors.

A mechanical ascender attached from your harness to the fixed line is the most efficient means of protecting you from a fall as you climb next to the line. Prusik knots can be dangerous because it is so time-consuming to untie and retie them as you move past an anchor, especially while wearing mittens. Prusiks are okay in an emergency or on very short sections of rope.

## Anchors for Fixed Lines

Every fixed line needs an anchor at the bottom to hold the rope in place while climbers ascend and a bombproof anchor at the top. Mark the location of the anchors with wands so you can find them after a snowstorm.

Place a series of intermediate anchors between the bottom and top of the fixed line. The fixed line is tied off at each anchor so that every section of line is independent of the others. This permits more than one climber at a time on the line. In deciding where to place the intermediate anchors, take several considerations into account. Place an anchor at points where you would like to change direction of the line or prevent pendulum falls. An anchor at the top of difficult sections of the route is helpful. If possible, place the intermediate anchors at natural resting spots, making it easier to stand and move the ascenders past the anchor.

Always bury or cover snow and ice anchors and inspect them regularly for possible failure from creep or melting. Also keep a close eye on any rock anchors capable of creeping or loosening. Place anchors at locations that help keep the line from rubbing on rough or sharp surfaces, or pad the line at points of abrasion. Even small amounts of wear can multiply into dangerous weak spots on fixed lines, which usually use lightweight rope. Falls will also damage the line. After any fall on the line, inspect it for damage and check the anchors for any indications of possible failure.

## How to Set up Fixed Lines

There are many variations in how to set a fixed line, each appropriate for certain conditions, climber preferences, types of line, and so forth. The key is to think through a system prior to starting out and, if possible, test and refine it before you actually need it. Here are three possible methods:

- The most common way is for two or three climbers to ascend the route—using a standard climbing rope to belay one another or to establish a running belay—and setting the fixed line as they climb. They can carry the whole spool of line with them and let it out as they ascend, tying it off at

each intermediate anchor along the way. Or they can just pull the end of the line up with them as they ascend, clipping the line into each anchor with carabiners. Then after anchoring the top, they can go back down, tying off the line at each anchor as they go. In either case, it can be a big job. Carrying the spool of line is difficult, but so is pulling up on the end of the line and trying to overcome the tremendous friction that develops as it travels through carabiners and over the route.

- The entire fixed line also can be set on descent. The material for the fixed line must first be carried to the top of the route, of course. Tie the line into a bombproof anchor at the top; then rappel or downclimb to tie the line off at intermediate anchors. These anchors can be the ones that were placed on the earlier ascent of the route, although new ones can be added just for the fixed line.

- You can also use the fixed line as your climbing rope at the same time you are setting it in place.

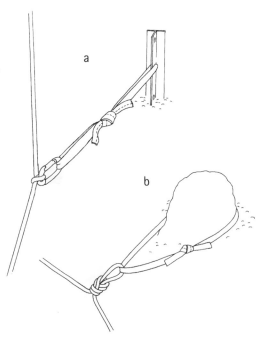

*Fig. 16-3. Intermediate, fixed anchors: a, anchor with carabiner in system; b, anchor without carabiner.*

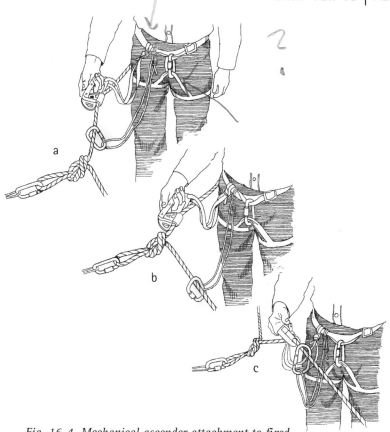

*Fig. 16-4. Mechanical ascender attachment to fixed line: a, set up for normal movement; b, passing an anchor, move the safety carabiner first; c) moving the ascender past the knot.*

For the final tie-off of the fixed line at each intermediate anchor, use a clove hitch or figure-8 knot in the line. Tie a sling directly to the anchor and clip the figure-8 loop or clove hitch into a carabiner attached to that sling (fig. 16-3a). Or better yet, minimize use of carabiners and have one less link in the system by retying the sling directly through the figure-8 loop (fig. 16-3b).

### Ascending

Ascending with a fixed line simply involves climbing as usual, except that your harness is attached by a sling to the mechanical ascender on the line in case you fall (fig. 16-4a).

Start by tying a sling from the ascender to your seat harness where you normally tie in with the climbing rope. (A less desirable way is to clip the sling into a locking carabiner attached to the harness.) Make the sling short so the ascender won't be out of reach if you fall. If you're climbing a near-vertical section or have a heavy pack, you may want to pass the sling through your chest harness as well to prevent tipping upside down in a fall.

Then attach the ascender to the fixed line, following the specific directions for your brand of ascender. The ascender should be oriented so that a fall will cause it to clamp the rope. It should slide easily up the line but lock tight when pulled down. Test it before starting upward and also check the fittings on your seat harness.

You should attach a carabiner from the ascender sling or from a separate sling to the fixed line to serve as a safety link as you move upward. If you fall and the ascender fails, the safety carabiner will slide down the rope but stop at the next anchor below and arrest your fall.

At each intermediate anchor, you have to remove

Use the line just as you would a normal climbing rope, clipping it into anchors as you climb, belayed from below. At the top, tie the fixed line into a bombproof anchor, and then it is ready to be tied off at each intermediate anchor. The problem with this method is that fixed line is usually thinner and has less stretch than climbing ropes. If you fall, there's a bigger chance the line could break. Even if it holds, the limited stretch in the line would make for a hard fall. An additional drawback is that the friction on the line as you pull it up through more and more carabiners will probably limit the maximum length of the run. This method is best saved for short sections of fixed line or for instances where a standard climbing rope is being used as a fixed line.

the ascender from the fixed line and reattach it beyond the knot. This is the most dangerous moment in fixed-line travel, particularly if conditions are severe and you are exhausted. Be sure the safety carabiner stays on the line while the ascender is detached. It's best to first move the safety carabiner and reattach it above the anchor, followed by the ascender. This order offers more security than moving the ascender first. If you are using a separate sling for the safety carabiner, it's easy to move the safety carabiner first (fig. 16-4b), followed by the ascender (fig. 16-4c). Another safety option is to briefly clip yourself into the anchor as you relocate the ascender.

Whatever your procedure, it's urgent that you think it through in advance and practice it on a good day so you can perform it reliably under the worst possible conditions.

More than one climber can use a fixed line at the same time as long as there is at least one anchor between each climber. Also be sure that a fall by any climber would not cause rope movement, rockfall, or other activity that could endanger anyone else.

### Descending

Climbing down with a fixed line is similar to climbing up. Again attach the ascender sling to your harness, and then attach the ascender to the fixed line exactly the same as for ascending. Double-check that the ascender locks onto the rope when you pull down on it and that it will be within reach if you end up hanging from it after a fall. Attach the safety carabiner.

Begin your descent. As you climb downward, you will be moving the ascender down the rope to stay with you. Use a light grip on the ascender release so that you can let go of it instantly to permit the ascender to grab the rope if you fall. It's natural to try to hang onto something if you lose your balance, but the last thing you want to grab hold of at that moment is the ascender release.

Take extreme care as you climb past anchors, removing and reattaching the ascender. As in climbing up, never detach the ascender and the safety carabiner at the same time. Again, you can temporarily clip into the anchor while you relocate the ascender. On steep sections of fixed line, rappelling the fixed line may be a good alternative to downclimbing.

### Removing Fixed Lines

Exhausted mountaineers at the end of a grueling climb often find it easier to abandon gear, garbage, and fixed line to the mercies of the mountain. This kind of behavior has become less and less acceptable, and expeditions now are learning to approach their climbs with a commitment to removing all signs of their passage.

Removing fixed lines will be easier if you keep it in mind as you plan where to put them up in the first place. In some cases you may be able to use a "moving" fixed line, removing it and moving it higher as you ascend the mountain and then descending via a safer route. If you are leaving the mountain and going down a fixed route for the last time, plan a downclimbing or rappelling procedure, or a combination of the two, that will permit the party to remove the fixed line.

What applies to fixed line also applies to all the other odds and ends of the expedition. Everything that goes in has got to come back out. Crevasses can't be used as garbage dumps because between wind and hungry ravens, the contents can end up strewn up and down the glacier. For human waste, set up a group latrine at each camp. In an exception to the use of crevasses, you can line the latrine with plastic garbage bags and then dispose of the waste in a deep crevasse.

## Expedition Weather

You need to become something of an amateur weather forecaster on an expedition because your safety and success are so closely bound to nature's moods. When you get to the climbing area, add to your knowledge of local weather patterns by talking to other climbers and to people who live there. Find out the direction of the prevailing winds. Ask about rain and storms. On the mountain, become a student of weather patterns. Your altimeter can serve as a barometer to signal weather changes.

Take clues from the clouds. Cirrus clouds (such as mare's tails) warn of a front bringing precipitation within the next 24 hours. Lenticular clouds (cloud caps) mean high winds. A rapidly descending cloud cap signals that bad weather is coming. And if you climb into a cloud cap, expect high winds and poor visibility. (For more information on mountain weather, see Chapter 23.) Be prepared for the fact that big mountains typically have storms and winds to match. Wait storms out if you can because of the risk inherent in descending under bad conditions. If it looks like you'll be stuck for some time, start rationing food.

Fair weather poses problems too. If it's hot and solar radiation is intensified by protected glaciers, the result can be collapsing snow bridges, crevasse movement, and increased icefall. Then it's best to climb at night, when temperatures are lowest and snow and ice are most stable.

## Health Hazards at High Altitudes

Expedition climbing and a great deal of other mountaineering takes you to altitudes where your body no longer feels at home. Every climber is affected to one degree or other by the reduced oxygen of higher elevations. It often causes acute mountain sickness (altitude sickness), and it can lead to the life-threatening conditions of high-altitude pulmonary edema and high-altitude cerebral edema. Frostbite is another danger, though it's not limited to high altitudes.

It's important to learn how to prevent these conditions and how to recognize and treat them when they occur. Turn to Chapter 19, First Aid, for a discussion of these problems. Also consult your first-aid manual, specialized texts, or physicians familiar with mountaineering for detailed information.

## Acclimatization

The best way to combat altitude illness is to prevent it in the first place, and the principal way to do this is to ascend slowly. The body needs time to acclimate to higher altitude, though the time it takes varies from person to person.

Ascend at a moderate rate, averaging 1,000 feet a day in net elevation gain. If you are doing double carries, this may mean establishing camps at 2,000-foot intervals, so that you can carry one day and move camp the next, for a net elevation gain of 2,000 feet every two days. If suitable campsites are 3,000 feet apart, you can carry one day, move camp the next, and rest the third day, for a net gain of 3,000 feet every three days. Try not to overdo your efforts until you've become well acclimated, and schedule rest days after big pushes.

Hydration is critical in avoiding altitude sickness. Rather than relying on a specific figure for daily liquid intake, monitor your urine output and color. A good rule of thumb is that urine should be copious and clear; dark urine indicates you're not drinking enough water. The fact that climbers lose their appetites at high altitudes, and find themselves eating and drinking less than they should, points at the importance of a varied menu—one that includes food and drink acceptable to each member of the party. It's best to avoid alcohol because it contributes to dehydration.

Above 18,000 feet, most people begin to deteriorate physically regardless of acclimatization. Minimize the stays at high altitudes, and periodically return to lower altitudes to recover. The old advice is good: Climb high, sleep low. The body acclimates much faster during exertion than during rest and recovers more quickly at a lower altitude. Expedition-style climbing takes advantage of these concepts in carrying loads to a high camp, returning to lower altitude to recover and then ascending again.

## An Expedition Philosophy

Members of an expedition need a common code to live by during the weeks they travel and climb together. A good one is summed up in three promises you and your teammates can make: to respect the land, to take care of yourselves, and to come home again.

Every day, your expedition will have the chance to put the health and beauty of the land ahead of your immediate comfort. The easy way out might be to burn wood fires or set up camp in a virgin meadow or abandon heavy gear. But if you've promised to respect the land, you'll be able to do the right thing.

If you and your partners have promised to take care of yourselves, you've made a commitment to group self-reliance. You may have no choice in the matter, anyway, as you will likely be a long way from rescuers, helicopters, hospitals, or even other climbers. You can prepare by thinking through the emergencies the expedition could face and laying plans for saving the day. You'll be happy the plans are ready if you have to use them and grateful if you don't.

The third promise might be the hardest to keep

# A Sample Expedition Equipment List

## GROUP GEAR

### SHELTER

Expedition-quality tent

Snow stakes and/or tent flukes

Sponge and whisk broom

Snow shelter construction tools: large snow shovel (for moving a lot of snow), small snow shovel (for delicate trimming), snow saw (for cutting blocks)

### GROUP CLIMBING GEAR

Ropes

Hardware: snow and ice gear (pickets, flukes, ice screws), rock gear (pitons, spring-loaded camming devices, chocks), carabiners, runners, fixed line, extra climbing equipment (spare ice ax or tool, spare crampons)

### KITCHEN

Stove gear: stove, wind screen and stove pad, fuel containers and fuel filter, matches and/or butane lighters

Cooking gear: pots, pot cozy, pot gripper, sponge/scrubber, dip cup, cooking spoon, snow sack

### REPAIR KIT

Tent repair kit (pole splices, spare pole)

Stove repair kit

Crampon repair kit (extra screw, connecting bars, straps)

Tape (duct, filament, ripstop fabric repair tape)

Tools (standard, Phillips, and Allen screwdrivers; small pliers; small wire cutter/shear; file)

Sewing kit: assorted needles and thread; assorted buttons, snaps, buckles, and D-rings; Velcro (hook and rug); fabric (Cordura, ripstop); flat webbing

Other: wire, accessory cord, pack buckle, extra ski-pole basket, patch kit for inflatable foam pads

### FIRST-AID KIT

Most expeditions carry a comprehensive group first-aid kit. In addition to normal first-aid items, the kit should include the following drugs, plus others recommended by a physician.

Prescription drugs: vary with the destination but should include antibiotics, strong analgesics, anti-diarrhetic, laxatives, and altitude medication (Diamox, dexamethasone)

Nonprescription drugs: vary with the destination but should include a cough suppressant, decongestant, and mild analgesic (aspirin, ibuprofen)

### OTHER GROUP GEAR

Wands

Altimeter, map, compass

Radio transceiver
Cellular phone

Latrine equipment (plastic sacks, rubber gloves)

---

because it can conflict with that burning desire for the summit. It's really a promise to climb safely and to sacrifice dreams of the summit before laying your life on the line. But expedition climbing is, after all, about pushing limits and testing yourself in a very tough arena. Each person and each team must decide what level of risk they wish to accept. Out of that flows daily decisions on how fast to ascend, what gear to carry, when to change routes, and when to back off. Most climbers would rather return home safely than push for the summit under unsafe conditions. But how do you define "unsafe"? You'll keep the third promise by being sure you find the definition that is just right for your expedition.

# A Sample Expedition Equipment List

## Personal Gear

### CLOTHING

Synthetic fabric underwear

Insulating layers

Down clothing

Wind protection and rain protection garments (top and bottom)

Plastic boots

Supergaiters and/or overboots

Extremities: hands (liner gloves, insulating gloves, mittens), feet (liner socks, insulating socks, vapor-barrier socks), head (balaclavas, sun hats, face masks, wool hat)

Other: bandannas, sun shirt, Polarguard/down booties

Sleeping gear

Sleeping bag

Bivouac sack

Vapor-barrier liner

Inflatable foam pad

Closed-cell foam pad

### CLIMBING GEAR

Ice ax

Second ice tool

Seat harness with ice-tool holster

Chest harness

Crampons

Personal carabiners and slings

Ascenders/prusiks

Ski pole

Helmet

Large-volume pack

Snowshoes or skis

Sled with associated hardware for pulling

Duffel bag

### OTHER GEAR

Avalanche beacon

Sunglasses and goggles

Spare prescription glasses

Swiss/pocket knife

Headlamp

Wide-mouth water bottles

Personal hygiene: toilet paper, pee bottle, toothbrush, comb, chemical wash/wipes, sunscreen, lip balm, foot powder, ear plugs

Personal recreation: camera and film, books, journal, personal stereo, cards

Overleaf: *Cordillera Sarmiento, Chile* ©*Gordon Wiltsie;* overleaf inset: ©*Tom Holt;*

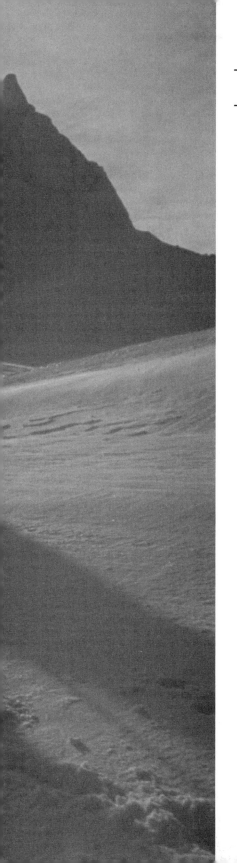

# PART FIVE

# EMERGENCY PREVENTION AND RESPONSE

# 17 LEADERSHIP

*Fail to honor people,*
*They fail to honor you;*
*But of a good leader, who talks little,*
*When his work is done, his aim fulfilled,*
*They will say, "We did this ourselves."*

—Lao-tzu

Just as every climbing party needs map and compass, evey climb needs good leadership—but the style and form of that guidance will vary with the venture. It's one thing to head out with some longtime climbing companions for a sunny weekend of peak bagging, and another to mount an extended technical climb with mountaineers you don't know to a peak none of you has ever seen. You and your pals achieve good leadership very informally, probably without even knowing it; the other trip requires a more formal, structured organization. But in both cases, the substance of leadership is the same, providing a way to put a climb together and make it a safe and enjoyable success.

## THE CLIMB LEADER

A climb leader is someone who has special responsibility for organizing the climb and for making decisions en route. Depending on the nature of the party, the degree of formal organization may vary from highly structured to virtually nonexistent. Nevertheless, certain necessary group functions get performed one way or another. The position of leader may be conferred by a sponsoring organization or may develop informally and spontaneously, but the fact is that most climbs have a leader.

Small, informal parties often do not select a leader. Everyone feels responsible for organizing, sharing work, and team building. It is easy for each member to know what the others are doing, so coordination is not much of an issue. The climb organizer or most experienced party member may be tacitly recognized as leader of such a group but should try not to be too directive.

Large groups, on the other hand, do not lead themselves and usually do better with a designated leader. Party members cannot know what every other person is doing, so someone needs to be chief organizer if only to be sure no critical details are ignored. Large groups may also need more focus on team building, because it is likely that the members do not all know one another.

The leadership structure of most climbing parties tends to fit into one of the following categories.

**Peers:** This is a group of acquaintances who decide to go climbing. Usually there is no designated leader, but members will informally allocate key functions. One may take responsibility for organizing equipment, another for transportation and food, and so forth. Most decisions are made by consensus. Even in this least formal type of organization, one member will usually emerge as "first among equals" and be regarded as leader. It will be the person who displays initiative, good judgment, and concern for the group and who generally inspires the most confidence.

**Climb champion:** This is the person who champions the climb—the one who has the original idea for the venture and then recruits others. The organizer is usually recognized as de facto leader, even if the position is never formalized.

**Most experienced:** A group tends to bestow leadership upon, and to defer to the judgment of, a climber who is clearly the most experienced in the party.

**Climbing clubs and schools:** Leadership is formally conferred by the sponsoring group when a climb is part of an organized program. Often there is an accreditation process for leaders to ensure a certain level of experience and competence. There may even be a hierarchy among the leadership, with an overall leader and assistant instructors to help. There is no doubt who is leader, and it is not up to the party to select one. The leader is expected to research the climb and to take charge of equipment, transportation, and other logistical matters. Such climbs are often teaching situations; students are expected to follow the leader's guidance, but they are also supposed to be learning and gaining in self-sufficiency.

**Guided climbs:** Climbers pay guide services to provide competent leadership. Professional guides are often outstanding climbers and are completely in charge of their groups. Guides make the decisions for their clients and assume responsibility for their safety.

## Roles of the Leader

A leader's goal is to help the party have a safe, enjoyable, successful trip, with minimum impact on the alpine environment. A leader must be experienced, with technical skills appropriate for the climb, but does not necessarily need to be the most experienced in the group or the hottest climber. A leader should be in good enough shape to keep up, but need not be the strongest in the party. A leader does need an abundance of good judgment, common sense, and a sincere interest in the welfare of the entire party. Along the way, a leader simultaneously adopts many roles, such as the following.

**Guardian of safety:** The paramount concern of any party is safety, and it begins with the planning stage. A leader should ensure that everyone has appropriate equipment, experience, and stamina and that the route chosen is reasonable for the party and in safe condition. En route, when climbers are tired, impatient, excited, or inexperienced, they get careless. A leader learns to see these circumstances as red flags and become more alert, watching, gently reminding, even nagging when necessary. When tough decisions have to be made, like turning back due to weather or time, it is often up to the leader to raise the unpleasant topic before the situation becomes critical.

**Planner:** Many details need attention if a group of people is to be at the right place at the right time with the right equipment to mount a successful attempt. A leader does not have to do all the planning personally but does bear responsibility for seeing that all necessary preparations are being attended to by someone in the group.

**Expert:** Giving advice when asked or when needed is an important leadership role. Training, experience, and judgment are the prerequisites for this job. You don't have to be the party's best climber to be an effective leader, but certainly you need enough experience to have developed "mountain sense." A range of skills is needed in addition to technical climbing lore. Leaders should know something about equipment, navigation, first aid, rescue techniques, weather, and in fact the variety of topics treated in the various chapters of this book.

**Teacher:** When less experienced climbers are along, teaching becomes part of the leadership role. Usually this involves nothing more than occasional advice and demonstrations. However, if some members lack techniques required for safe progress, it may be wise to halt and conduct a little school right then and there. Many seasoned mountaineers find that passing along their hard-won knowledge is a fulfilling experience— but it should be done with a careful touch. The novices may be embarrassed by their relative lack of skill, or intimidated by the physical danger. This is no time for bullying. Best avoid the approach that says they are wrong; rather, try "Let me show you what works for me." The exception is when a student is doing something dangerous; then a directive approach is needed.

**Coach:** This is a little different than teacher. The coach helps people over difficulties by adding encouragement and support to a base of knowledge. Who has not had a bad day or come up against an unyielding obstacle? And often the real obstacle is one of confidence. Assisting a companion over some difficulty helps that person and also keeps the entire party moving forward. Coaching effectively, helping people do their best and emerge smiling, can be one of the particular delights of leadership.

**Initiator:** The progress of a climb is a series of decisions: Where shall we camp? Which route do we take? What time should we get up? When do we rope up? Often the decisions themselves are not hard, but they need to be made in timely fashion. The function of leadership is not necessarily to dictate answers but to get the right issues on the table at the appropriate time.

**Arbiter:** Once a discussion is under way, differences of opinion will arise. It is good to collect opinions and get all views out into the open, but this can lead to indecision ("Which course do we select?") or argument ("You're wrong!"). Anyone in a position of leadership, whether or not formally conferred, has some leverage that can be used to advantage here. If the party seems to be making a technically incorrect or dangerous decision, if tempers are rising, or if the discussion is aimlessly wandering, the weight of the leader's opinion will often settle matters and get the climb moving again.

**Guardian of the environment:** Climbers must do their best to leave the alpine environment undisturbed so that future generations may sample the same pleasures. Leaders should set the example by always practicing minimum-impact techniques (see Chapter 3, Camping and Food, and Chapter 24, Minimum Impact). If others fail to follow, they should be reminded, gently at first, insistently if necessary.

## Styles of Leadership

Two broad categories of behavior characterize what leaders do. Goal-oriented behavior has to do with process and structure: what to do, who will do it, and how. Goal-oriented leaders concentrate on making decisions and directing others. Relationship-oriented behavior

has to do with showing consideration and helping a group of people become a supportive, cooperative team. Relationship-oriented leaders take a personal interest in people and their views, consulting with them on decisions and thereby building group cohesion and morale. Most of us lean toward one type or the other, but it is not an either/or choice. Neither can be neglected, and effective leaders balance both styles. The proper balance depends on the nature of the party and the needs of the moment.

Each leader must develop a personal style through a process of learning and discovery: learning the craft of mountaineering, and discovering effective ways of relating to climbing companions to help them become a happy, effective team. There is no simple formula for becoming a leader, but there are guidelines:

- A leader cannot be self-centered; decisions are made for the good of the party, not the leader.
- A genuine interest in every party member will be mirrored in how they care about each other and will strengthen the group.
- Don't pretend and don't show off; be honest about your limitations. If you don't know, admit it—and get the group to help you figure it out.
- A sense of humor helps.

Beyond that, be yourself. Some people are jolly and talkative; some are more reserved. Successful leaders are found in all camps. It is more important to be genuine than to try copying some idealized style.

## Leading in a Crisis

We hope it never happens, but sometimes things go wrong: perhaps conditions turn dangerous or someone is injured. Then the group focus shifts from recreation to safety and survival. The leader's role also changes. If the party has a designated leader, this is the time to switch to a decisive style. The small, informal group may find that a leader emerges. There is a clear need for coordination, and people will tend to look to the most experienced person or the one who, for whatever reason, inspires the most confidence.

When an accident occurs, there is no time for lengthy debate. Prompt, effective action is needed, and it should be directed by someone with training and experience. Nevertheless, the leader should stay "hands off" as much as possible, directing others, maintaining an overview, and thinking ahead to the next steps.

The party should be guided by the three rules of rescue (see Chapter 20, Alpine Rescue) in managing a crisis:

- The safety of the rescuers comes first—even before that of the subject.
- Act promptly, but deliberately and calmly.
- Use procedures you have learned and practiced; this is no time to experiment.

It is easy to think that all climbing mishaps are life-and-death situations and that the outcome depends solely on what the rescuers do. In fact, neither is usually the case. First, most accidents result in cuts and bruises, sprains, sometimes broken bones, but only occasionally anything worse. Second, the outcome is usually determined by factors beyond the rescuers' control. All that can reasonably be expected is that the climb leader draw upon training and experience to devise an appropriate plan and then carry it out as safely and effectively as conditions permit.

The best way to avoid trouble is to anticipate it. Leaders should always be thinking ahead, asking "What if?" In camp, they think of the climb; on the ascent, of the descent; in success, of retreat. They look for early signs of fatigue in companions, mentally record bivouac sites, keep watch on the time, and note any changes in the weather. Everywhere on trips, leaders mentally cross bridges before reaching them; they borrow trouble. Trying to stay a step ahead, they hope to avoid problems or to catch burgeoning ones before they become crises.

Accidents are unexpected, but you can prepare for them by taking courses, reading, and mentally rehearsing. Anyone who proposes doing much climbing should get first-aid training. Chapter 19 describes the prevention and treatment of medical conditions commonly experienced by mountaineers, but it is not a substitute for hands-on training. The American Red Cross and many fire departments offer first-aid courses, and some climbing clubs give mountain rescue training. Also, you can benefit from studying the experiences of other climbers. The American Alpine Club and the Alpine Club of Canada jointly publish *Accidents in North American Mountaineering*. This annual contains detailed descriptions and analysis of mountaineering accidents and is instructive.

## ——— ORGANIZING THE CLIMB ———

Even a simple climb is a complex undertaking. Once you choose an objective, you need to get information on the approach and the climbing route itself. The party must be selected, and decisions must be made regarding what equipment is needed and who will bring it. A schedule should be worked up to assure that enough time is allowed to complete the climb with a margin for contingencies. Everyone needs transportation to the trailhead. And in the days leading up to the climb, snow conditions and weather trends should be monitored. The checklist at the end of this chapter is a useful guide to this process.

### Researching the Climb

Mountaineers like to think of themselves as free spirits, so they sometimes set out with minimal research or use of guidebooks to increase the sense of adventure. This can lead to an enjoyable trip if someone in the group has enough experience to keep them from accidentally getting in over their heads. More often, climbers will research the trip so they know what to expect and can prepare accordingly.

Guidebooks are available covering most popular climbing areas. They usually have written descriptions of approaches and routes, maps, drawings, and sometimes photos. Copy the relevant pages and take them with you for reference. Topographic maps are invaluable—be sure you know how to read them (see Chapter 4, Navigation). An excellent way to study the route at home is to try following it on the map while reading through the description in the guidebook.

Some climbing clubs keep files of trip reports from their outings, and these can be valuable both for themselves and because they will often give the names of those who went on the climb. Firsthand information from someone who has recently done the route can add significantly to what you find in guidebooks. Climbers love to recount their adventures, so a phone call can let loose an avalanche of information.

For peaks on public land, government agencies such as those in charge of national parks or forests can be good sources. Rangers can usually provide information on road and trail conditions. The most popular climbing areas may even have designated climbing rangers who are in the mountains regularly and can give informed and current reports. Check also for permit requirements, access restrictions, and fees.

Interest groups that use the Internet solicit and share information on routes and climbs. Exercise some judgment when using these computer sources, though; there is no accountability on the Internet, and it is difficult to gauge the credentials of those leaving advice there.

Finally, if you think it necessary, you can go and gather information firsthand. Sometimes, climbers will make an exploratory trip to check the approach and inspect the route before actually mounting a climb.

## Equipment

The party will need to make decisions about equipment, both personal and group. Personal equipment is that which each climber must bring—ice ax, pack, clothing, and food, for example. Some personal items, like crampons or avalanche beacons, are useful only if everybody brings them, so coordination is essential. In a large party, someone should take the lead in coordinating equipment.

Group equipment is shared: tents, stoves and pots, ropes, racks, and snow shovels are examples. Someone needs to determine what is needed, survey the climbers to see who owns what, and then decide who will bring which items.

The party can give itself a margin of safety by planning to arrive at the trailhead with a little extra equipment. Surplus gear can be left in vehicles out of view, but if conditions are more severe than anticipated, or if someone forgets an item or fails to show up, then the party may still be adequately equipped.

If you are the leader, double-check your own gear before leaving home. It's embarrassing for the leader to forget some critical piece of equipment.

## Party Strength

A climbing party must have adequate strength in order to have a safe, enjoyable, and successful trip. Strength refers to the group's ability to accomplish the climb and to cope with situations that may arise. The party's strength is determined by the mountaineering proficiency of the members, their physical condition, the size of the party, and their equipment. Intangibles such as morale, the members' degree of commitment to the climb, and the quality of leadership also affect party strength.

A strong party would consist of several experienced, proficient climbers, well equipped and in good condition. What constitutes weakness is not so easy to define because a party is strong or weak only in relation to its goals. On a very challenging climb, the addition of a single ineffective member would make a party too weak. On easier trips, a party may be strong enough if it has only two strong climbers and several weaker ones. In fact, this is common on guided climbs. A party with no experienced members is weak in any situation.

Researching the route will help determine what strength is needed for a particular climb. Is the route or the approach physically arduous? What level of technical challenge does it pose? Is the place so remote that the party will be completely on its own, or are there likely to be many other people in the vicinity?

## Forming the Party

### Who Should Go?

Every member of a climbing party must be up to the challenge, both physically and technically. Some climbers will go only with proven companions when attempting routes near the limit of their abilities. When considering inclusion of a climber you don't know, ask some questions. Experience is the surest indicator of ability; someone who has climbed several times at a given level is probably capable of doing so again. Expeditions sometimes even require written résumés, but for a weekend climb a little probing conversation is probably enough to ascertain a person's fitness. However, when dealing with inexperienced people, be aware they may not realize they are unprepared for the climb you have in mind.

A party that includes novices, or even experienced people who have never before climbed at this level of difficulty, will need veteran climbers who are willing and able to coach. The climb almost surely will take longer, and the chance of success will be reduced. Be sure everyone in the party understands this situation and accepts it.

Fortunately, most people seem to be on their best behavior while on climbs. The unspoken knowledge that your companions will soon be literally holding your life in their hands does much to promote accommodation. Nevertheless, it is well to consider the compatibility factor when forming a climbing party, especially for a long or arduous trip. Expedition literature is filled with engaging tales of squabbling parties. To say the least, dissension in a climbing party is no fun. It may reduce the chance of summiting; it's guaranteed to eliminate much of the enjoyment and can even compromise safety.

People who are known to dislike each other should not be on the same climb. The tensions and close proximity of the climb situation will only exacerbate their animosity. If two people are not getting along during the climb, other party members should do their best to keep the situation from erupting into open conflict.

Often, the group is formed before the objective is selected. Several climbers may decide to "get together and do something." Then the selection process is reversed and it becomes a matter of picking a climb to fit the group. It is important to gauge everyone's skill and stamina and to choose a peak that the party can realistically attempt safely. Usually, the weakest member is the limiting factor.

## How Many Should Go?

The size of the party must be appropriate to the objective. Both strength and speed should be considered—and sometimes they are at odds. The climbing code given in Chapter 1 recommends three as the minimum for safety: if one climber is hurt, the second can go for help while the third stays with the injured person. Another good conservative rule in the code recommends at least two rope teams for safe travel on a glacier: if one team is pinned down holding a colleague who has fallen into a crevasse, the second is there to effect the rescue.

These rules are general guidelines for minimum party size, but the specifics of the proposed trip may introduce other considerations. A prolonged wilderness venture may need a larger group to carry equipment and supplies, as well as to provide better backup in case of emergency. Some rock climbs require double-rope rappels on the descent. This dictates a minimum of two rope teams unless a single team wants to carry two ropes. Technical rock and ice climbs are best done with just two climbers on each rope; for these climbs, whatever the size of party, there should always be an even number.

Maximum party size is determined by considerations of speed and efficiency, by concerns about environmental impact, or by land-use regulations. A large group can carry more gear and offer more helpers in case of emergency, but it is an error to think that a bigger party is necessarily a safer one. A larger party tends to get more spread out, can start bigger avalanches, and may kick down more loose rock.

Sometimes speed is safety, and experienced alpinists know that a larger group is always slower. On certain routes, for example, the climbers must move smartly to ensure finishing before dark or to be past an exposed area before the afternoon sun starts dangerous rockfall. As a general rule, the more difficult the route, the smaller the group should be. In the extreme case, some long technical climbs are often done by parties of just two fast, experienced people, despite the general rule that three is the minimum safe party size.

As climbing areas become more popular, large groups are considered unacceptably damaging to fragile alpine environments. They also erode the wilderness experience. Park and wilderness areas typically have party size limits to reduce impact and preserve esthetic values. At the very least, these limits must be respected. Responsible mountaineers may even choose to impose tighter restrictions on themselves in particularly fragile places.

## Time Management

We can never be more than visitors to the alpine world. On every trip there comes a time when we run out of daylight, or supplies, or good weather; then we must return to our lowland homes. Time has to be carefully rationed on a climb, and the important thing is not how fast we go but how wisely and well we use our time.

Establish a schedule before the climb. Estimate the

length of each segment and allow some extra time for the unexpected. A typical estimate might go like this:

| | |
|---|---|
| Hike up the trail | 2 hours |
| Cross-country approach | 1 hour |
| The climb itself | 4 hours |
| Time on the summit | 1 hour |
| Descent time | 2 hours |
| Return to the trail | 1 hour |
| Hike out | 1.5 hours |
| **Total time estimate** | **12.5 hours** |
| Contingencies | 2 hours |
| **Total time allowance** | **14.5 hours** |

If it gets dark at 9:00 P.M. and the climbers want to be back by 8:00 P.M., they must start at 5:30 A.M.

Setting a turnaround time is a good practice. In the example just given, the party estimates 4.5 hours from summit to trailhead, with no margin for the unexpected. They might decide it is reasonable to allow 5.5 hours. This means they must be descending by 3:30 P.M. or risk walking out in the dark.

Most guidebooks give times for popular climbs and sometimes for the approaches, as well. Keep in mind, though, that times vary greatly from party to party. Experience with a particular guidebook will tell you whether its estimates tend to be faster or slower than your personal times; then you can adjust accordingly. Another good source is to find someone who has done the climb. If no information is available, use rules of thumb based on experience. For example, many climbers have found they can average 3 miles per hour on an easy trail and 1,000 vertical feet per hour on a non-technical approach with light packs.

Avoid scheduling important business meetings, airplane flights, or social events for several hours after the scheduled end of a trip. Climbs frequently take significantly longer than expected. Your companions will not thank you if they have to turn back short of the summit or stumble out in the dark because you have a plane to catch.

## Planning for Self-Reliance

When is it enough? When should the climb organizers allow themselves to feel that their preparation is adequate? A good way to gauge is to ask whether

the party has the people, proficiency, and equipment it needs to be self-reliant under normal circumstances. In the event of a serious accident, nearby climbers should be called upon, and mountain rescue groups should be requested when needed (see Chapter 18, Safety). However, any climbing party should be prepared to take care of itself in case of minor mishap or downturn in the weather. In practice, this means having "a little extra" to provide a margin of safety: extra time, extra clothing, extra food, extra flashlight batteries, extra climbing hardware, and, above all, reserves of strength. Balancing the benefit of extra supplies against the drag of their weight is an art every climber must develop.

Leave a copy of the climb itinerary with a responsible person, specifying when you expect to return and how long the person is to wait before notifying the authorities if you are overdue. Be realistic when estimating how long your climb will take. Specify which authorities are to be notified if you're overdue. For example, in the United States, the National Park Service has responsibility for mountain rescue in national parks; in most other areas of the United States, it is the county sheriff.

Cellular telephones are becoming more popular among mountaineers as technology improves while weight and cost decline. They can dramatically shorten the time taken to summon rescuers. The devices are also useful for telling the people back home that the party will be late but is not in trouble and, thus, can be used to avoid unnecessary rescue efforts. Understanding the limits of cellular phones is as important as understanding their usefulness: the batteries can deplete, and they are unable to transmit or receive in many mountain locations. Cell phones should be viewed as an adjunct to, not a substitute for, self-reliance. No party should set out ill-prepared, inadequately equipped, or attempting a route beyond the ability of its members, with the notion that they will just call for help if needed. They will imperil themselves and the rescuers who may have to bail them out.

## On the Climb

Before leaving the trailhead, take a few minutes to check that all necessary equipment and supplies are aboard. Anyone who has been climbing very long has had a weekend ruined by a missing but critical item.

Some even use a written inventory checklist as an aid to memory while packing.

On the approach and on the climb, it is important to set a steady pace, which does not necessarily mean a fast one. In the long run, the party cannot move faster than its slowest member; progress may even be retarded if that person is reduced to exhaustion. The important thing is to keep moving steadily. Periodic rest stops for the whole party are more efficient than random halts whenever someone decides to stop.

A climbing party should stay together—not necessarily in a tight knot, but at least close enough to be in communication. After all, we climb in groups partly because there is some safety in numbers. That safety is compromised when the party splits. Typically, the stronger members will forge ahead, leaving those most likely to need help isolated from those best able to give it. The danger of getting separated is greatest on the technical portions of a climb, where the more skilled climbers move much faster, or on the descent, where some want to sprint out while others may be dragging a burden of fatigue.

A small party of friends will naturally tend to stick together. It is with larger groups that problems are more likely. A large party usually benefits from having a designated leader, and one reason is that the leader can coordinate its movement. Climbers should be free to hike up the trail at their own pace, but ought to regroup at designated rendezvous points, especially at:

- Trail junctions—to make sure everyone goes the right way.
- Danger spots (such as hazardous stream crossings)—in case anyone needs help.
- The bottom of glissades—because they naturally tend to split the party.

It may be wise to appoint a strong member as trail sweep, especially on the descent, to ensure there are no stragglers.

A leader need not be at the front of the party. In fact, many prefer to lead from the middle, the better to keep an eye on the whole group. However, the leader should be ready to swing into the lead when there is some difficulty, such as a routefinding puzzle or a patch of difficult technical terrain.

A leader's responsibility is to get things done but not necessarily to do them. Delegation gets tasks performed

and has a host of other benefits as well. It allows the leader to maintain an overview of the entire trip, rather than being tied down by every little problem and decision. It builds a team feeling by giving people a chance to get involved and be useful. Also, delegation fosters individual responsibility by clearly demonstrating that doing and deciding are not the task of the leader alone. If someone is having difficulty and needs special help, a strong, experienced climber might be delegated the role of personal coach. In a larger group, especially in a teaching situation, the leader should appoint an assistant who can help keep things moving and who can take over if the leader is incapacitated.

## BECOMING A LEADER

The responsibility of leadership is a burden, but the job can have great rewards. It gives the experienced alpinist an opportunity to pass along all the things learned over the years: how to set a measured pace, how to read terrain and pick out a route, how to deal with difficulties of many sorts. We do not climb because we must; we climb because we love mountains. Climb leaders help others enjoy the sport, and that can be deeply satisfying.

You may never want to take on the role, but you will find that a certain degree of leadership is almost inevitable as you gain experience. A party naturally tends to look to its more seasoned members for guidance, especially in a crisis situation. Therefore, you should give some forethought to what you would do if suddenly expected to take charge.

If you do aspire to leadership, make it your business to climb with people you regard as capable leaders. Study them; observe how they organize the trip, make decisions, and work with people. Offer to help so you can participate in some of these activities. Veteran leaders report that they think ahead, anticipating problems that might arise and concocting solutions. This type of mental rehearsing is excellent training for future leaders. Develop the habit of thinking about the entire climb and the whole party, not just your part of it. This is the first step toward thinking like a leader.

Studying respected leaders is always worthwhile,

but it may be a mistake to copy anyone else too closely. A group must believe that its leader is genuine, and therefore every leader must develop his or her own style. Leadership is not always easy, but it should be natural. Do not strain to be outgoing if you are a reserved type. Anyone who has technical skill, confidence, and a sincere interest in the party's welfare can succeed as a leader.

For your first time out as leader, choose a climb comfortably within your abilities. Perhaps invite a proficient friend, someone you can rely on. Spend some extra time organizing, and seek input from the more experienced members of the party. Be sure to delegate so you are taking advantage of their skills. Do not make an issue of the fact that this is your leadership debut; that will only undermine the group's confidence.

The climbing code in Chapter 1 is a sound set of guidelines for making leadership decisions. It is deliberately conservative. Following the code may cost some summits, but it is unlikely to cost a life. Seasoned leaders may draw on experience to safely modify some of the rules, but they are not likely to depart from it radically because the code embodies a commonsense approach to safe mountaineering.

## Everyone a Leader

Everyone on a climb needs to be a full partner in the twin tasks of moving the group safely toward its goal and of building group cohesion. In other words, each individual must share leadership responsibility. Individual leadership means, for example, being aware of the group and its progress. Is someone lagging behind? Ask whether there is a problem, offer encouragement, and look for ways to help. Everyone should participate in group decision-making. Each person's experience is an asset to the party, but it goes untapped if he or she fails to speak up.

Establishing a supportive atmosphere is one very important role of leadership. People need to know that their companions care about them and will help them. Be part of this effort: help set up a tent, fetch water, carry the rope, share a cookie. Morale is intangible, but it makes a party stronger. Morale is often the deciding factor in party success, and it is always the deciding factor in making the climb enjoyable. And morale is everybody's job.

A group of climbers is weakened whenever they become separated. Work at being aware of where your companions are at all times, and make it your business to help keep the party together. If you are out front and moving fast, remember to look over your shoulder from time to time. If you are too far ahead, stop and let the group catch up—then be nice, and let them have a breather before starting off again.

Take part in routefinding. Study guidebooks and maps so you are familiar with the approach and the climbing route. Your party is much less likely to get lost if everyone is actively involved in navigation. Make it your business to use map, compass, and route description frequently so that you are always oriented and know where you are.

Assume responsibility also for your own knowledge, skill, and preparedness. Research the climb before committing yourself to it; make sure it is within your abilities. Be properly supplied and equipped. If you have questions about whether the climb is appropriate for you, or about what gear to take, ask your companions in advance. If ever you think you are getting in over your head, speak up. Better to get some help over a rough spot or even quit the climb than to create an emergency. Thinking about the party, its welfare, and how you can contribute is in itself a preparation, perhaps the very best preparation, for leadership.

# Checklist for Organizing and Leading a Climb

## BEFORE THE CLIMB

Research the route.
> *Review guidebooks and maps.*
> *Talk with others who have done the route.*
> *Determine the technical level and any special problems of the route.*
> *Estimate the levels of climbing skill and physical condition required.*
> *Determine optimum party size.*

Determine equipment needs.
> *Personal equipment: clothing, boots, food, camping equipment, crampons, ice ax, helmet, other technical gear.*
> *Shared equipment: tents, stoves, ropes, hardware.*

Make arrangements for sharing tents, cooking equipment, and climbing gear.

Research the approach.
> *Driving route: check to be sure backcountry roads are open.*
> *Hiking route: check trail conditions.*
> *Determine whether wilderness permits or reservations are required.*

Develop a trip itinerary.
> *Estimate:*
> > *Miles/hours of driving.*
> > *Miles/hours of hiking to high camp or start of climb.*
> > *Hours to summit.*
> > *Hours back to cars.*
> *Check weather forecast and avalanche conditions.*
> *Leave trip itinerary with a responsible person.*

## ON THE WAY

Make a final check of weather forecast and avalanche conditions.

Register with park or forest agencies if required.

## AT THE TRAILHEAD

Check equipment.
> *Personal equipment: make sure everyone has enough food, clothing, and essential equipment; inadequately equipped climbers should not continue.*
> *Shared equipment: inventory tents, stoves, ropes, and hardware.*
> *Redistribute group equipment, if necessary, to equalize loads.*
> *Discuss the plan: route, campsites, time schedule, expected hazards.*

## ON THE APPROACH

Keep the party together. Agree to regroup at specified times or places—especially at trail junctions.

Decide on formation of rope teams.

## ON THE CLIMB

Establish a turnaround time.

Keep rope teams close enough to be in communication.

## ON THE WAY OUT

Assign a "trail sweep."

Regroup periodically.

Be sure that no one leaves the trailhead until everyone is out and all cars have been started.

*[handwritten margin notes: Mot a leader / med info; save things / current conditions; immediate review + current best team based on approach experience + observation]*

# 18

# SAFETY

Every mountaineering accident is a little different from every other one, but the contributing factors are often the same. Commonly, inadequate experience and skill lead to errors in judgment, poor techniques, and improper use of equipment. However, even mountaineers of superior experience and skill have been injured or killed. In this chapter you will become acquainted with principles of mountaineering safety and ways to incorporate them into your climbing. (Also see the climbing code presented in Chapter 1, First Steps.)

## SELF-RELIANCE

Climbers recognize that responsibility for safety in the mountains rests with the individual, and they understand the concept of relying on one's self. Climbers have developed strong ethics about avoiding dependency on resources other than the skills, knowledge, and equipment they carry into the mountains.

Issues of personal challenge, ethics, and aesthetics arise when you try to determine the acceptable limits of safety preparation for a wilderness adventure. Cellular phones are the latest technological development causing debate. In addition to being an annoyance to those who want to leave behind the distractions of daily life, the cellular phone can sometimes represent an attempt to substitute for lack of preparation and self-sufficiency. On the other hand, an emergency call on a cellular phone or two-way radio can speed a

mountain rescue while allowing all team members to stay put, eliminating the delay and danger of sending someone for help. In the case of a party that is simply overdue but not in trouble, a call to family or friends can put an end to worry and avoid an unnecessary search.

Debate on such issues is ongoing. The discussions are beneficial in helping climbers to evaluate their accomplishments and understand the role that self-reliance plays in mountaineering.

## MOUNTAINEERING INCIDENTS

Mountaineers try to avoid accidents; good mountaineering safety also means studying and avoiding the broader range of general mountaineering incidents. These include all undesirable events that could have led to accident: an emergency bivouac, a lost route, a "close call." An incident without injury or serious consequence can offer valuable insight into the most common factors that lead to accidents.

For instructive reports and analysis of actual accidents, climbers can turn to publications such as *Accidents in North American Mountaineering,* prepared annually by the American Alpine Club and the Alpine Club of Canada. These reports do not necessarily address the root causes of accidents, but they do indicate the elements of danger in climbing and show basic recurring patterns. For example, the most common immediate causes of mishaps reported in *Accidents in*

*North American Mountaineering* have been (1) fall or slip on rock, (2) slip on snow and ice, and (3) falling rock or other object. The most common contributing causes were (1) climbing unroped, (2) attempting a climb that exceeded abilities (inexperience), and (3) being inadequately equipped for the conditions or climbing situation.

It's important to note that incidents do not "just happen." Careful review of reported accidents and of other mountaineering incidents reveals human error in most cases. Even the most competent climbers have accidents, a fact that reminds us of how small we are before the forces of nature.

# CLIMBING HAZARDS

The hazards of mountaineering fall into two broad categories, and an understanding of each is essential for accurate risk assessment. The most easily recognized are the *objective hazards*. These are the physical dangers inherent in the very structure of the mountains and their environment. Equally important are the *subjective hazards*. These are the dangers created by humans themselves when they are physically or psychologically unprepared for the challenge of the mountains. Mountaineering incidents almost always involve both objective and subjective hazards.

## Objective Hazards: The Mountain

Objective hazards are natural processes and conditions that exist whether or not humans are involved. Mountain environments are turbulent places, full of swift change and powerful forces that dwarf the human presence. Snowstorms, lightning, extremes of temperature, gravity, darkness, wind, rain, fog, avalanches, rockfall, high altitude, crevasses, cliffs, cornices, "acts of God"—all such impersonal dangers fall into the category of objective hazards.

## Subjective Hazards: The Climber

Subjective hazards exist any time a climber lacks the physical or mental preparedness to face the objective hazards of the mountains. The climber who is out of shape may not be able to complete a route before darkness sets in. The climber who is overconfident

may try a steep ice route that is beyond his or her ability. Subjective hazards that climbers may bring into the mountains include ignorance, improper training, poor judgment, inadequate equipment, and poor conditioning, along with such psychological traits as overconfidence, false pride, apprehension, or fear.

This book is filled with useful information to prepare you for the mountains so that you don't carry along the dangerous baggage of these subjective hazards. Instead of ignorance and inexperience, you will bring knowledge and skill in confronting objective hazards. You will learn to recognize rockfall danger areas and to then wear a hard hat; to tread lightly to avoid knocking down loose rocks, perhaps onto your climbing companions. You will learn to choose glacier routes that minimize the possibility of falling into a crevasse—and the rescue techniques to use in case someone does fall in. You will learn to recognize avalanche-prone slopes and what to do in the event you're caught in an avalanche.

Individual psychological characteristics such as fear or pride can express themselves in dangerous ways. A climber with a need to show off may be driven by ego to exceed the margins of safety. A more subtly dangerous form of overconfidence is demonstrated by the leader who is so familiar with a particular climb that he can't realistically assess its problems for a first-time party. A lack of confidence can be as hazardous as overconfidence, perhaps resulting in debilitating fear or an overdependence on others. False pride can prod a climber into persisting on a climb despite the fact that it's an "off day" due to fatigue, altitude sickness, or inadequate conditioning.

Some subjective hazards develop out of the psychology of groups. Group overconfidence is the illusion that you are safer because there are other people around. There's also the condition that might be termed "groupthink," in which some individuals defer uncritically to team decisions.

A common characteristic of subjective hazards is that they contribute to poor judgment, which can in turn lead to accidents.

## Special Hazard Considerations

As climbing has evolved into several distinct forms in addition to traditional alpine mountaineering, new safety considerations have emerged. The activity—now encompassing such varieties as competitive climbing, sport climbing (short, tough routes), indoor climbing on artificial walls, and bouldering—is drawing many new adherents, including children. Some problems develop as climbers trained in one type of climbing cross over into another.

Among the special problems of the modern era of climbing is overcrowding at practice areas. A belayer must be especially attentive to overcome the distraction of spectators and other climbers. Even alpine routes can get crowded. Belayer and climber can help sort out the profusion of commands being heard on the route by prefacing each command with their partner's name.

Differences between sport and alpine climbing can create confusion. If you're accustomed to alpine climbing, learn the special commands and techniques of sport climbing before trying it, and vice versa.

If you have a very young climber in the family, remember that children have special needs. Children have a high strength-to-weight ratio, so they can climb surprisingly hard problems. But because they have practically no hips, they could fall right out of a conventional harness. Full-body harnesses designed for young people are available through climbing equipment retailers. Climbing is great for kids, but they need constant attention. If a young person wants down from a climb, honor the request. Consider enrolling the child in formal climb training.

*chest harness*

## RISK

Climbers manage risks. Indeed, many of your more memorable climbs may be those that were the most challenging and the ones where nobody knew whether the climb would succeed until the final moment. Unlike some fictional accounts where daredevils force their way up the mountain with brute strength, good climbers think their way up the mountain, analyzing and evaluating, basing decisions on sound reasoning and mountaineering principles, continually probing for peril and planning ahead to meet it. Clearheaded thinking and appropriate technique are the keys to successful climbing.

## Risk Assessment

You can look at risk assessment as a kind of formula. It can be helpful to think of it something like this:

$$\text{risk} = \text{severity} \times \text{probability} \times \text{time}$$

This simply means that your risk is multiplied when there is an increase in any of the three risk variables: the likely *severity* of any accident, the *probability* an accident will occur, and the length of *time* at risk.

Consider this situation: You're planning to climb a 200-foot rock face as part of the weekend ascent of an alpine peak. The rock is clean, and the route is only fourth class, far below the difficulty standards that you've mastered. You're thinking of climbing the face unroped. What is your risk of accident?

Work out the risk formula:

- **Severity:** A fall high on the face would have very serious consequences: you would be badly injured or killed. Severity is high.
- **Probability:** It's unlikely that you would fall: you've climbed much harder faces many times on belay, with no difficulty whatsoever. Probability is low.
- **Time:** The face is fairly high, and you will be on it for some time. Working through the crux moves will be tiring. Time at risk is moderately long.

As you can see, the risk formula gives no simple, mathematical answer. But it does point to a solution.

- **Probable solution:** Rope up.

By using this formula, a climber should be able to roughly calculate the *real risk* of an undertaking. But practically speaking, a climber's evaluation of risk really amounts to *perceived risk*—which may have little to do with real risk calculated by working out some sort of precise formula.

Perceived risk is affected by subjective variables, most importantly the accuracy of the climber's perceptions of the hazard and of his or her skill and experience in dealing with it. Aspects of a climber's psychology, such as overconfidence, can allow a climber to accept higher levels of real risk without even realizing that these levels have in fact increased. A miscalculation by the climber can lead to a growing difference between the calculated *real risk* and the climber's *perceived risk.* (This chapter's material on the subject of risk owes much to an unpublished paper by J. M. Helms; see Appendix B, Supplementary References.

## Your Sphere of Acceptable Risk

The objectives for risk assessment are, first, to keep perceived risk in line with real risk and, second, to establish a personal *sphere of acceptable risk.* This sphere is the intersection of all of the climber's protective measures (equipment such as helmet, special clothing, and rope, plus training and experience) with the possible hazards of the mountain (such as bad weather, rockfall, and avalanches). If you understand this intersection accurately, you'll have a good idea of the sphere of acceptable risk that is right for you. But if your understanding is clouded, perhaps by overconfidence or wishful thinking, you'll create a dangerously large sphere of acceptable risk.

The late Willi Unsoeld, a pioneer Mount Everest climber, gave a good example of how climbers can let perceived risk get out of balance with real risk and thus end up accepting higher levels of real risk. In "The Changing Expedition Game" (in the 1977 edition of *The Mountaineer,* published by The Mountaineers, Seattle, Washington), Unsoeld wrote:

> Eventually we felt confident enough about our familiarity with the weather and slope conditions that we were willing to venture out into the upper slopes provided everything felt right to us. Later on, we operated with increased boldness although we did not feel that we were aware the avalanche danger had decreased all that much.
>
> Some murmurs were heard about familiarity breeding contempt, but most of us felt that we had simply adjusted to the state of our mountain and had developed sufficient sensitivity to her moods to work between the storms with equanimity. However, if we had been operating in the North Cascades, it is virtually certain that we would have tossed it in and planned on returning either later in the season or next year.

The members of Unsoeld's party slowly let their perception of risk get out of balance with real risk; they enlarged their sphere of acceptable risk to a degree they wouldn't normally accept.

Any number of factors can subconsciously cause you to enlarge your sphere of acceptable risk. If you've spent a lot of time and money to mount a particular climb, you may be willing to accept more risk—especially if you're going for the glory of a first ascent. A group decision can sometimes result in more real risk than an individual decision if no one in a group wants to be a spoilsport by urging caution.

## Nonevent Feedback

You can be misled into accepting dangerous levels of risk by a simple phenomenon that might be termed *nonevent feedback:* nothing bad happened last time; therefore, nothing bad will happen this time. Nonevent feedback occurs when we do not experience the potential consequences of our actions. It can desensitize us to hazard. Willi Unsoeld and his group of climbers acted partly on this type of feedback.

If you've climbed the same route or the same mountain several times without incident, you may make the dangerous assumption that you can deal safely with all conditions you'll run across this time. Or you may chalk up a close call to simple chance rather than interpreting it as the danger signal that it probably is. A climber can even experience a near miss without knowing it. You might glissade a slide-prone slope without triggering an avalanche—a nonevent that produces erroneous feedback. This experience may then be incorrectly used as a standard of safety to evaluate similar slopes.

The phenomenon can take on additional dimensions in groups. For example, the leader of an inexperienced party may mentally conduct a flawless evaluation of a hazard and determine that conditions are safe. But unless the leader shares the thinking that went into this decision, the members of the party may falsely assume that similar situations are always without hazard.

There also are other, less-obvious sources of nonevent feedback. Guidebooks can't be expected to mention all hazards, so a reader may be subtly but erroneously led to believe that dangers not mentioned do not exist. Photos and films may offer up dramatic scenes of expert climbers on extreme climbs but fail to show the protection placements the climber is depending on for safety. Finally, climbers who haven't yet had to pay for their errors may try to pass on to you their own false picture of climbing safety.

## DECISION-MAKING STRATEGIES

The decisions we make today can be traced to the way we have made decisions in the past. Over time, we develop habits and strategies that guide our decision-making. By understanding the various strategies that can be used to make decisions, we may be able to identify faulty patterns in ourselves that lead to poor decisions. (Two publications by Craig Geis provided much of this chapter's information on the decision process; see Appendix B, Supplementary References.)

The following three strategies are generally associated with bad decisions.

**Minimizing:** The climber selects the first course of action that satisfies minimum requirements. Decisions are not reconsidered, and additional information is not processed.

For example, Bill wondered whether he needed crampons on the climb he and Jim were planning. Jim said no. Bill didn't look into the question any further or ask for anyone else's advice. On the climb, both men found themselves on hard ice without crampons.

**Muddling:** The climber works at reaching a decision in small starts and stops, sometimes letting small bad decisions snowball into one big mistake.

For example, from the start of the roped pitch, Shawn felt she was off route, but she kept muddling her way forward. Eventually she ended up at a point where she could not climb any higher nor fashion a rappel anchor for safe descent.

**Denial:** The climber attempts to mentally eliminate the problem, focusing on stress reduction, not problem-solving. The decision that is made cuts off all additional information that increases stress.

For example, Both Fred and Bill felt Stan was suffering from severe altitude sickness, but Stan insisted that he was just feeling a little weak and would wait for them while they went on to the summit. Despite

their fears, Fred and Bill did just that. By the time they returned from the summit and rejoined Stan, he was a very sick man, needing a great deal of help in getting safely down the mountain.

**Optimizing:** In contrast to the three preceding strategies that lead to bad decisions is the effective strategy of optimizing choices and information. The climber considers a wide range of choices and weighs each of the consequences. Information is processed fully and effectively. Instead of minimizing, Bill would do some research and talk to other climbers before deciding to leave his crampons at home. Instead of muddling, Shawn would either abandon the pitch at the start or make sure she always had an escape route. Instead of denial, Fred and Bill would deal forthrightly with the medical emergency that they knew existed.

## TOWARD SAFER CLIMBING

As mountaineers, we can promote safer climbing by remaining constantly aware of our situation and avoiding chains of error in judgment.

### Situational Awareness

Situational awareness is the accurate perception of the factors affecting your climb at a particular moment. More simply, it is knowing what is going on around you. For safety's sake, keep alert to the clues that you may be losing full awareness of your situation.

**Failure to meet planned targets:** Climbing parties set up expectations for starting time, rate of climb, turnaround time, and so forth. If some of these aren't met, find out why.

**Fixation or preoccupation:** When we fixate on one aspect of the climb, we may lose the ability to detect important changes, such as a partner's health problem or increased risk because of changing weather.

**Violating your sphere of acceptable risk:** When you find yourself doing something that you would normally consider unacceptably risky, you have lost your situational awareness.

**Unresolved discrepancies:** Two or more pieces of information may not agree: the map says the terrain should be flat, but it's actually vertical; the climb is rated class 3, but you are roped up and wishing you could place protection. Work to figure out what went wrong.

**Gut feeling or confusion:** This is one of the most reliable clues that something is wrong—that you're no longer safely aware of the full situation. The body is sometimes able to draw its own conclusions long before we have consciously put it all together. Trust your feelings.

If any of these clues tell you that you're not fully on top of the situation, look for ways to put things right. Take whatever action is needed to give you and your fellow climbers a clear-headed view of your status, even if it means aborting the climb.

## Breaking the Poor-Judgment Chain

Most climbing accidents result from a combination of circumstances rather than from a single cause. Often these circumstances include a series of errors in judgment. Breaking this chain of errors is essential to climbing safety.

By understanding the principles of the poor-judgment chain, we can identify when a chain is building and take appropriate action. The principles are as follows.

**One follows the other:** One poor judgment increases the probability that another will follow.

For example, climbing beyond an agreed turnaround time increases the chances that you will unsafely rush your climbing or end up enduring an unplanned bivouac.

**False information increases:** Each error in judgment provides false information that can be used to make additional judgment errors.

For example, concluding that snow conditions are good, when they really are not, can lead to a bad decision on route selection.

**Alternatives decrease:** As the poor-judgment chain grows, alternatives for a safe outcome decrease.

For example, in his book *The Endless Knot* (Seattle: The Mountaineers, 1991), Kurt Diemberger explains how a chain of decisions led to deadly results on K2:

> It was a diabolic machinery, into the cogwheels of which all of us were imperceptibly but irretrievably being sucked—the mechanism being so complicated that it was not recognizable to the individual; every way that might have led us out

> eventually became blocked by the taking of single decisions, which by themselves would never have been so critical, but in their conjunction opened the death trap for seven people up at 8,000 meters. (p. 152)

Five principal steps lead to breaking the poor-judgment chain:

1. Be willing to recognize your own poor judgment. Seek feedback on your decisions—from your own senses and from the climbers around you. For this process to work, there must be open communication among climbing partners and teams.
2. Check for stress. A moderate level of stress sharpens your ability to make good decisions while climbing. A very low level of stress breeds complacency and inattention; too much stress brings panic.
3. Apply structured decision-making. Use a strategy that optimizes choices and information from which decisions are made.
4. Be alert for groups of poor judgments. If one poor judgment is recognized, look for others before you decide that only the first one is affecting the situation.
5. Review your original poor judgment as soon as you have broken the poor-judgment chain. This review provides the feedback you need to avoid beginning a similar poor-judgment chain in the future.

## ——— THE MASTER WARNING ——— PANEL

Imagine a master warning/caution panel in your mind (fig 18-1). The panel is connected to your senses, to your brain, and to some place deep down in your stomach. This last connection, in your gut, is so critical that you have two lines going there in case one comes loose.

So what turns on the caution and warning lights? It's up to you. Are you out of shape, hung over, or fatigued from work? The yellow warning lights should go on. Are some members of your party inexperienced, or has your climbing partner seemed inattentive while belaying? Expect yellow lights, which could easily turn

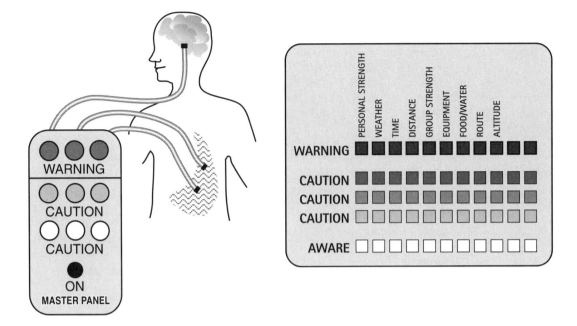

*Fig. 18-1. Examples of master warning/caution/status panels*

to red. Uncertain avalanche conditions usually will turn on at least one red light, as will continuation of the climb beyond the turnaround time. The caution lights will usually go on whenever a party is short on equipment, water, or food. And as for those connections to your stomach: pay closest attention anytime you have a gut feeling that sets off a light.

As you visualize your master warning/caution panel, think back to your last climb. At any point in that climb, would your panel have shown red or yellow lights? Would enough of them have lit up to indicate that you're moving outside your sphere of acceptable risk?

A warning panel bright with lights is a signal to end the climb before an accident happens. Yet most of us have read accounts of climbs where our personal panel would have been lit up like a Christmas tree.

Give the warning panel a try on your next climb. First decide just how your panel will look, and what lights and gauges you want it to display. Then think about which red or yellow lights you would be willing to continue the climb with. Your warning panel, activated by an understanding of the many factors contributing to mountaineering safety, will help you in making good decisions as you climb.

*Good — combine @ Risk Assesst*
*do exercise scenarios*
*Mtn (exp, lineup*
*also like avalan List.*

# 19

# FIRST AID

Accidents and illness can strike mountaineers, just as they can hit urban dwellers at home. However, the mountaineer must be able to manage the situation far from expert help, providing the *first* aid to the victim. In addition to everyday injuries and ailments, the mountain environment and the physical demands of wilderness travel introduce new hazards to the mountaineer's well-being.

The most artful mountaineers grow adept at minimizing the hazards of life in the mountains, preventing exposure to risk whenever possible. For the members of a mountaineering party, skillful prevention of *becoming* victims is vastly preferable to being mere experts at treating injuries after they occur.

Despite prevention awareness, any mountaineer could become the individual who requires first-aid help: the first-aid expert of the group could become the victim. Therefore, it's best for *all* members of the party to train in first aid, through mountaineering-oriented first-aid courses such as those offered by the American Red Cross. Cardiopulmonary resuscitation (CPR) is among the essential first-aid skills in the mountains. Because CPR is learned best through competent hands-on instruction, this chapter does not address CPR procedures. The Red Cross and other organizations teach CPR.

Periodic refresher courses are essential to keep first-aid skills sharp and knowledge current. *This chapter cannot substitute for current first-aid training.* Appendix B, Supplementary References, includes a list of suggested references for more in-depth treatment of first-aid topics.

## MOUNTAIN MALADIES

The mountain environment presents hazards that are, for the most part, predictable. Figure 19-1 lists some of the conditions that can arise from the stress these hazards apply to the human body.

### Dehydration

Individuals vary in the rate at which their body loses water. Water loss occurs through sweating, respiratory loss, urination, and diarrhea. You may not be aware how much water your body is losing; for instance, winter mountaineers can experience substantial fluid loss from sweating and other causes while feeling that they are not sweating much at all. Conditioning can play a minor role in the body's efficient maintenance of water balance. Various medications can influence your body's ability to maintain water balance, by altering sweating, thirst, or urine output.

Maintaining good hydration is important in reducing your risk of heat-related illness, cold-related illness (including frostbite), and altitude illness. Your

| ENVIRONMENTAL STRESSOR | GENERALIZED CONDITIONS (POTENTIALLY AFFECTING ENTIRE BODY) | LOCALIZED CONDITIONS (AFFECTING ONLY PORTION OF BODY) |
|---|---|---|
| Heat | Heat exhaustion<br>Heat stroke* | Heat cramps |
| Cold | Hypothermia* | Frostbite<br>Immersion foot |
| Ultraviolet radiation | | Sunburn<br>Snow blindness |
| High altitude | Acute mountain sickness<br>High-altitude pulmonary edema*<br>High-altitude cerebral edema* | |
| Lightning | Cardiopulmonary arrest*<br>Shock*<br>Coma* | Burns<br>Eye or ear injuries<br>Nerve damage |
| Insect bites and stings | Sting-induced allergic response*<br>Tick-introduced illness | Localized pain and swelling |
| Snake bites | Generalized envenomation reaction* | Localized tissue damage |

*Indicates urgent or life-threatening condition.

Fig. 19-1. *Environmental injuries and conditions*

overall physical performance is improved dramatically, as well.

It is important to begin mountaineering outings well hydrated. You should drink a cup of water or its equivalent 15 minutes before starting out. Once under way, continue drinking fluids at a rate of 1 to 1½ cups every 20 to 30 minutes. This rate of drinking will help maintain hydration while avoiding making your stomach distended from the volume taken in. Do not rely on your sense of thirst as a gauge of when to drink; drink more *before* you feel thirsty. If you do not need to urinate periodically during the day, or if your urine color becomes unusually dark, you are not drinking enough fluids.

Commercial sports drinks are not usually necessary in a mountaineering setting, although they can help in making the fluid replacement project more palatable. Juices, if used, should be diluted by at least 50 percent in order to prevent diarrhea. You can replace electrolytes—body salts—lost through sweating by including snacks that have some salt content to them.

## Heat Cramps

Muscle cramps can develop if you become dehydrated or electrolyte-imbalanced during sustained exertion. Rest, massage, and gentle slow stretching of the affected muscles usually helps. Replacing water and electrolytes is the most important treatment. Heat cramps are avoidable if you replenish fluid and electrolytes throughout the climb.

## Heat Exhaustion

If you build up more heat than your body can lose, heat-related illness can strike. For mountaineers, heat builds up by extreme exertion or by exposure to a hot environment.

Heat exhaustion is the milder of the two major kinds of heat illness. (The more serious, heat stroke, is discussed in the next section.) In the effort to reduce body temperature, blood vessels in the skin become so dilated (and sweating-related moisture loss is so pronounced) that circulation to the brain and other vital organs is reduced to inadequate levels. The result is an effect similar to fainting. All or some of the following symptoms may be present: cool and clammy skin, faintness, weakness, nausea, and perhaps a rapid pulse.

Treatment consists of rest (feet up, head down a bit), preferably in the shade, and drinking plenty of liquids and electrolytes.

The following people appear particularly susceptible to heat exhaustion: the elderly, individuals on medications that interfere with sweating, people inadequately acclimatized to a hot climate, and individuals who are dehydrated or salt-depleted.

## Heat Stroke

Heat stroke, which is sometimes called sunstroke, represents an emergency situation. The body's heat gain, in heat stroke, is so substantial that body core temperature rises to dangerous levels (105 degrees Fahrenheit, or more).

Symptoms of heat stroke include the following:

- Altered mental state (confusion or uncooperativeness, advancing toward unconsciousness)
- Rapid full pulse
- Headache
- Weakness
- Flushed hot skin (sometimes, but not always, dry)

The most reliable symptom is altered mental state. Treatment must be immediate, despite the victim's potential inability to cooperate. Get the victim into shade. Cool the head and body by packing in snow or through evaporative cooling with splashed-on water and vigorous fanning. Once body temperature has declined to 102 degrees, the cooling efforts can be stopped. However, continue to monitor the person's temperature and general condition, because temperature instability may continue for some time and body temperature could climb again, necessitating recooling. If the person's gag reflex and swallowing ability are intact, cold drinks may be provided.

It's doubtful that an individual with heat stroke will recover quickly enough, with restored temperature regulation stability, to continue full participation in a climbing or hiking trip.

## Hypothermia

In contrast to heat exhaustion or heat stroke, if you lose more body heat than your body can restore, cold-related illness can strike. Hypothermia exists when the body's core temperature drops to 95 degrees Fahrenheit (35 degrees Celsius) or less. As with heat stroke, hypothermia is an emergency condition that must be treated immediately to avoid the death of the victim.

Hypothermia occurs as blood is shunted away from the skin surface and from extremities in an attempt to preserve the core temperature. Body heat is lost to the environment through evaporation, radiation, convection, and conduction. Wet clothing and exposure to wind greatly increase the risk of excessive heat loss. Dehydration also can be a risk factor.

Usually, hypothermia occurs after prolonged exposure to chilly environs rather than being the result of extreme cold. A drizzly day with the temperature around 50 degrees Fahrenheit and a strong breeze is more typically the setting for hypothermia than an obvious risk situation such as exposure to a minus 30 degree cold snap at the ice cliffs.

Hypothermia symptoms change dynamically with the severity of the loss in body core temperature. For example, shivering appears in mild hypothermia (body temperatures of 90 to 95 degrees Fahrenheit) as the body attempts to heat back up through the muscular work involved in the shivering. As hypothermia progresses to a more severe level, shivering ceases. In mild hypothermia, symptoms include the following: intense shivering, fumbling hand movements, stumbling, dulling of mental functions, and uncooperative or isolative behavior. Typically, the hypothermia victim will not notice these early signs. If in doubt about the presence of mild hypothermia, have the person walk an imaginary tightrope for 15 feet, heel to toe. Loss of coordination will tend to show up in this test.

In severe hypothermia (body temperatures below 90 degrees), shivering stops, but the decline in muscle and nervous system functioning becomes more obvious. The victim may not be able to walk although may still be able to maintain posture. Muscles will be stiff and movements uncoordinated. Behavior will be confused or irrational, unless stupor or actual unconsciousness has appeared. As hypothermia progresses, it may become extremely difficult to observe a pulse or respiration. The person's pupils may dilate.

Because a severely hypothermic person may appear dead, it is essential to not give up on resuscitation efforts until the victim is *warm,* has had apparently adequate CPR, and still is without signs of life. Keep in mind the saying "No one is dead until warm and dead." Careful rewarming is accompanied or followed by CPR or assisted ventilation, as circumstances dictate.

Treatment of hypothermia begins with *termination of further heat loss* by stopping exposure. Get the victim out of the wind and wet, and remove wet clothing. In mild hypothermia cases, supplying dry clothing and shelter may suffice. If the person's gag reflex and swallowing are intact, he or she can be offered liquids and, later, sugar-based foods. Despite mountain lore to the contrary, supplying warm drinks is not as important in mild hypothermia as is simply replenishing fluids. (Consider this: Pouring a teaspoonful of warm water into a cup full of ice water would not be an effective method for warming up the cup.) Dehydration should be treated until urine output is restored. In some cases, the victim may not be able to warm back up with these measures alone, and direct body contact with a (warm) party member may be needed.

In severe hypothermia, *gentle rewarming* is necessary. If possible, evacuate the individual promptly for rewarming at a hospital. The hypothermia victim must be handled very gently, to avoid inadvertently sending a spurt of cold blood from the surface circulation back to the heart; this could cause another problem in the form of heart rhythm abnormalities. Rewarming shock also is a danger.

If field rewarming is necessary, hot water bottles wrapped in mittens or socks can be placed at the person's armpits and groin, where large blood vessels are near the body surface. Body-to-body contact inside a sleeping bag (or other dry insulation) with a warm party member may be necessary. Do not offer oral liquids to a semiconscious victim. As in heat stroke, the severe hypothermia victim, once back to normal core temperature, must still be monitored

because temperature-regulating mechanisms may not be stable for a considerable period of time.

Prevention of hypothermia involves the following bits of common sense:

- Avoid or terminate being wet.
- Avoid or terminate wind exposure.
- Avoid or terminate dehydration. (In cold conditions, the body may jettison some of its fluids by sending more water out through urination, resulting in dehydration.)
- Have adequate insulation.

The party's members must know when to call off the summit quest. Shivering must never be ignored. Because hypothermia interferes with a mountaineer's judgment and perception, typically you must be annoyingly persistent about getting the shivering party member to don warmer gear. Exhaustion can be forestalled by keeping tabs on the condition of each person.

In contrast to hypothermia, which is a cold-related illness affecting the entire body, the other cold-related illnesses (frostbite and immersion foot, which are covered in the next two sections) are localized in their effects. In *triage* of a victim with hypothermia and frostbite (that is, deciding which condition to treat first), the potentially deadly generalized condition of hypothermia must be treated and stabilized adequately before you devote energy to treating the localized injury of frostbite.

## Frostbite

Frostbite involves actual freezing injury to the blood vessels and surrounding tissues of a body part. Blood vessels can be severely and even permanently damaged. Early on, blood cells clump in the tissue's vascular bed in a reversible fashion, but later these clumps may convert to permanent plugs in the small vessels that nourish the tissue. Skin injury is common, with a separation of epidermis from deeper dermis. Frostbitten tissue is cold, hard, and pale or darkly discolored. Blisters may appear on the skin. Frostbitten tissue is fragile and never should be massaged or mashed.

Intervention with frostbite starts with treatment of any hypothermia. Following that, the party must assess whether field rewarming is appropriate or desirable. Usually, it is not. *If there is any likelihood that a frostbitten part, once thawed, might refreeze during the trip, the victim should be evacuated instead so that rewarming can be accomplished in a medical setting. If the body part is thawed and then refreezes, the line of tissue death probably will extend to the refreeze line.*

If a person has a frostbitten foot, it is important to keep the foot frozen. Once the foot has thawed, it will be impossible to walk on, and the person will have to be carried out.

In the rare instance that field rewarming is considered advisable, the frostbitten part should be rewarmed in a water bath that is 100 to 108 degrees Fahrenheit, never warmer. Don't use hot water; the frostbitten part is extremely susceptible to thermal injury. The person with frostbite should lie down, with the injured part elevated.

Blisters often emerge during rewarming. Management of blisters in frostbite is controversial. Black or blue blisters definitely should be left alone. Sterile drainage of pink or white blisters is advocated by some due to the presence of thromboxane (a tissue-damaging substance) in such blisters; others insist that the safer course is to leave these blisters alone as well, in order to reduce infection risk. Any open wounds or blisters should be washed gently with a skin antiseptic and covered with sterile dressings. Aspirin or ibuprofen may be administered, if the person is not allergic to these, to relieve pain and counteract the thromboxane.

More definitive treatment of frostbite should be reserved for competent medical care.

## Immersion Foot

Immersion foot strikes when your feet have been wet and cool, but not freezing cold, for long periods of time. Climbers on Mount McKinley (Denali) who wear vapor-barrier socks but neglect to dry and warm their feet each night are prime targets for this condition. Similarly, tundra hikers who clamber through the muskeg day after day but never dry their feet at night can be affected. The injury mechanism appears to be a kind of trauma to nerves and muscles caused by diminished oxygen distribution (hypoxia), rather than representing vascular and skin freezing injury as with frostbite.

Immersion foot reveals its presence with pale, pulseless, tingling feet. Typically, these symptoms are discovered in the tent, at night, by the unhappy mountaineer. Very careful rewarming is needed—in a water bath just slightly warmer than body temperature—or gangrene can occur. During rewarming, the affected feet shift to a painful *hyperemic* phase: reddened, swollen feet with a bounding pulse. It may be necessary to slightly cool the feet in order to tone down the intensity of this hyperemic phase. During the subsequent days of the recovery period, the feet may be at risk for recurrence of immersion foot.

*continue or immobile.*

## Sunburn

Intense ultraviolet (UV) radiation from the sun, particularly when reflected off snow and ice, can burn an unprepared mountaineer at high altitudes. Burn injuries from overexposure to UV radiation are potentially serious but preventable. Certain medications (such as tetracycline and oral medicines for diabetes) can increase the sun sensitivity of skin and thus the danger of burning.

Prevention of sunburn requires an awareness of the risk for getting burned. UV radiation is not filtered out effectively by cloud cover, so you must maintain skin protection even on an overcast day.

The most effective prevention involves covering exposed skin with clothing. Some clothing, depending on weave and fiber, screens UV radiation better than other clothing. A tighter weave works better, though it's hotter to wear. Lightweight garments have been specifically developed for their sunscreening capability (an example is the material sold under the name Frogwear). Hats should include a wide brim to protect the back of your neck as well as face and ears.

When skin must be exposed, sunscreen products extend the time you can spend in the sun before burning. These usually are marketed with sun protection factor (SPF) ratings, which provide an estimate of their relative effectiveness at delaying sunburn. For example, a product with SPF 40 supposedly allows a person to remain in the sun 40 times longer than usual before beginning to burn.

The best choice of SPF depends on your individual sensitivity and the severity of environmental exposure. Sunscreens usually contain a compound (para-aminobenzoic acid [PABA] or benzophenones) that absorbs UV to prevent burning. Sun-block agents also are useful; these contain materials such as zinc oxide that reflect UV radiation. Typically, you might restrict the sun block to particularly sensitive areas, such as nose or ears, and use the less abrasive sunscreen for broader coverage. Any of these agents may require reapplication if you are sweating.

Some sunscreens can be difficult to extract from their containers in cold conditions, so assess this potential problem with your favorite sunscreen before your next chilly glacier morning. Sunscreens with PABA have a limited shelf-life for effectiveness, so check the expiration date on the container at purchase and when packing for a trip. (Chapter 2, Clothing and Equipment, includes additional information on sunscreens, in the section on sun protection.)

## Snow Blindness

Snow blindness is a potentially serious problem that results when the outer layers of the eyes become burned by UV radiation. The cornea (the clear layer at the front of the eye) is most easily burned. Its surface can become roughened and blistered. With further radiation, the lenses of the eyes can become burned, as well. Snow blindness sets in 6 to 12 hours after the radiation exposure. The first symptoms, therefore, do not appear until after the damage is done. Dry, sandy-feeling eyes become light-sensitive, then reddened and teary, and then extremely painful. Recovery takes one to several days.

Treatment of snow blindness includes pain relief and prevention of further injury. Contact lenses must be removed, and protection from bright light is needed. Advise the person with snow blindness to avoid rubbing the eyes and to try to rest. To prevent irritation from eyelid movement, cover the eyes with sterile dressings and padding. Recheck for light sensitivity at half-day intervals. When the eyes are no longer extremely light-sensitive, dressings can be removed, but protective sunglasses should be worn.

Prevention of snow blindness is straightforward. In high-UV environs, you must wear either goggles or sunglasses with side shields. This eyewear needs to filter out 90 percent of the UV wavelength that burns. Glare can be filtered out with a darkly tinted lens, but the tint itself will not filter out the burning UV light.

Polarizing layers on the lenses can help in settings where reflection is especially intense. If you lose your eye protection, emergency goggles can be fashioned out of duct tape or cardboard with narrow horizontal slits for each eye. (Chapter 2, Clothing and Equipment, includes additional information on sunglasses, in the section on sun protection.)

## High-Altitude Conditions

As the mountaineer climbs to higher elevations, the altitude begins to force changes in body functioning. As the air gets thinner, the amount of available oxygen in each breath decreases. Just as importantly, the *oxygen tension* instrumental in permitting the body to absorb oxygen from the lungs also decreases. The body's tissues have a harder time getting the oxygen needed for metabolism, entering the state of reduced oxygen called *hypoxia*.

The body attempts to adapt to this drastic environmental change, but adaptation (acclimatization) takes time. There is great variation in how rapidly and how completely different individuals acclimatize. The following provides a rough guideline for rate of ascent:

1. Limit increases in sleeping elevation to 1,000 feet per day, above 10,000 feet.
2. Two or three times a week, allow an additional night at the same elevation as the night before.

One adaptation to high-altitude hypoxia is an increase in the rate of breathing. After ascending to high altitude, your breathing rate continues to increase for several days. As this occurs, dissolved carbon dioxide in the bloodstream decreases (as you exhale carbon dioxide). Another normal adaptation to high-altitude hypoxia is that the kidneys send more water on to the bladder as urine, ridding the body of more fluid. This *diuresis* makes the blood slightly thicker. This change begins promptly upon ascent and continues for several weeks. Eventually, the body produces a greater number of red blood cells, in an effort to increase oxygen-carrying capacity despite the weaker oxygen-loading of hemoglobin caused by low oxygen tension. This change, called *polycythemia* (many cells in the blood), makes the blood considerably thicker and can even interfere with circulation to some tissues.

It is difficult to work as efficiently or powerfully at

high altitude as at lower elevations, due to the effect of hypoxia and the related changes in body functioning. *Maintaining adequate fluid intake* amid these physiologic changes appears critical to good acclimatization.

A climber's ability to sleep soundly deteriorates at high altitude. At altitude, most mountaineers have insomnia, with more awakenings during the night and less deep sleep. Commonly, an irregular rhythm to breathing appears during sleep and sometimes during wakefulness, too: machinelike cycles of alternation between very slow breathing rates and hyperventilation. (This alternating rhythm is known as Cheyne-Stokes respiration.) The low carbon dioxide content of the blood appears to drive this odd change in breathing rate. Opinion is divided on using sleeping pills to relieve climbers' insomnia, because it is not clear whether sleeping pills might worsen the irregular breathing pattern of high altitude.

## Acute Mountain Sickness

At least half of the sea-level residents who travel rapidly to moderate altitude (8,000 to 14,000 feet) experience some degree of acute mountain sickness (AMS). This is a collection of nonspecific symptoms that can resemble a case of flu, carbon monoxide poisoning from stove use inside an inadequately ventilated shelter, or a hangover. AMS can vary widely in severity, and it is important to differentiate AMS from more ominous related conditions: high-altitude pulmonary edema (HAPE) and high-altitude cerebral edema (HACE). All three conditions seem to involve abnormal shifts in body fluids caused by the stress of high altitude.

Signs of acute mountain sickness are the following:

- Headache
- Insomnia
- Listlessness
- Loss of coordination
- Puffiness around eyes and face
- Cough
- Shortness of breath
- Fullness or tightness in chest
- Irregular breathing
- Loss of appetite
- Nausea

- Vomiting
- Reduced urine output
- Weakness
- "Heavy" feeling in legs

AMS settles in within a day of the initial ascent, and when mild it lasts only a day or so; however, it can progress in severity. In cases where symptoms (such as headache and nausea) progress, a descent of 2,000 to 3,000 feet of elevation is the best treatment. Improvement upon descent is confirmation of the AMS diagnosis.

Some medicines are used in dealing with altitude-related health problems; you can ask your physician about the appropriateness of such drugs for your situation. For example, some mountaineers use acetazolamide (Diamox) for several days prior to ascent and through the first 48 hours at high altitude in order to prevent AMS or block recurrence. Potential problems with this medication are tingling of extremities, ringing in the ears, and a change in taste; individuals with sulfa allergies must not take it at all. However, it does appear to have a role in prevention and treatment of AMS as well as irregular breathing.

## High–Altitude Pulmonary Edema

In HAPE, body fluids leak into the lungs to a degree that interferes with respiratory function. HAPE is a potentially fatal condition, and survival depends on a rapid response to its emergence.

Early signs may overlap with more benign problems, such as the persistent cough caused by simple bronchial irritation from dry high-mountain air. Decreasing ability to exercise, accompanied by breathlessness and a hacking cough, appears in HAPE as it develops. Rates of breathing and pulse increase. If the party has brought along a stethoscope, a fine crackling sound may be heard over the lung fields during breathing. This crackling noise is the result of increased fluid in the lungs.

If HAPE is allowed to advance, bubbling noises during breathing effort will be evident even without use of a stethoscope. Lips and nail beds may appear dusky or tinged with blue, reflecting the body's inability to transfer oxygen into arterial blood due to the water barrier in the lungs. Some affected people also may have a fever, making it difficult to distinguish HAPE from pneumonia; one clue to HAPE is how rapidly it worsens with continued ascent.

*The key aspect of treatment of HAPE is descent.* A descent of 3,000 feet will resolve nearly all HAPE cases that are caught early. In some expedition situations, portable hyperbaric chambers (such as the Gamow bag) are used to create a temporary artificial "descent" environment in the effort to stabilize the affected climber for a few hours. Supplemental oxygen can also be helpful in temporary stabilization. Ultimately, however, real descent must occur. Some mountaineers use a drug, nifedipine, as one preventive measure for HAPE if they have a prior history of the condition.

### High-Altitude Cerebral Edema

Vessels in the brain may respond to the stress of high altitude by becoming leaky, resulting in brain tissue turning boggy with increased fluid. Ultimately the brain swells inside its rigid container of cranial bones.

Early signs of this deadly condition include deteriorating coordination (*ataxia*), headache, and loss of energy. The coordination test in which a person is asked to walk an imaginary tightrope for 15 feet, heel to toe, is a useful screen for ataxia. Nausea and forceful vomiting may be present.

As HACE advances (which can occur rapidly), the victim's thinking processes become clouded and there may be an onset of various neurologic problems, such as loss of muscular control of one side of the body. HACE can strike at elevations as low as 10,000 feet. Descent is critical to survival. Drugs such as Decadron are used by some expeditions as an additional part of the treatment for a stricken individual.

## Head, Neck, and Back Injuries

Head and spine injuries are common causes of death in alpine wilderness accidents. Any injury to the head or spine is potentially life-threatening. Such injuries often are caused by falling objects, such as rock or ice, or by a fall taken by the mountaineer in which the head or back strikes a hard object. Deceleration injuries also can injure the spine, even if the person does not actually strike anything during a fall.

The head and spine are so delicate that the slightest mistake in first-aid response may cause further injury or death, yet symptoms of injury are often so nonspecific that it can be difficult to choose a course of ac-

tion. The indecision usually involves the question of whether the injured person can be moved safely or treatment on the spot is essential. For all head injuries, a cervical spine injury (neck injury) must be assumed until thorough examination proves otherwise. For all cervical spine injuries, the person must be monitored for potential head and brain injury.

Indicators of possible head injuries include the following:

- Unconsciousness
- Drainage of blood or clear fluid from the ears, nose, or eyes
- Unequal eye pupil size or unequal constricting response of the pupils to light
- A very slow pulse or noticeable fluctuations in respiratory (breathing) rate
- A headache generalized over the entire head
- Disorientation and confusion

## Lightning Injuries

The high-mountain environment receives five times as many thunderstorms each year as coastal areas do, according to at least one study. Summer afternoons are the most likely time for thunderstorms, and therefore lightning, to present danger to the mountaineer. Lightning strikes can emanate from several miles away toward high points ahead of or, less frequently, behind the main thunderhead cloud formation ("out of a clear blue sky"). Therefore, you can be in danger of a lightning strike at times other than when the storm is directly overhead.

There are various ways for lightning strikes to injure a person: *direct strike* of the mountaineer in the open who could not find shelter; *splash strike,* where the lightning current jumps from an object it initially hit onto the mountaineer who had sought shelter nearby; *contact injury,* from holding an object that lightning hits; *step voltage,* transmitted along the ground or an object nearby to the mountaineer; and *blunt trauma,* created by the shock wave from a nearby strike.

The most immediate danger from being struck by lightning is cardiopulmonary arrest. After the lightning strike, the victim does *not* present an electrical hazard to rescuers, and first aid should proceed promptly with assessment of airway, breathing, and

*Fig. 19-2. Preferred body position and location in an electrical storm*

electrical current and can be damaged in a lightning strike. Ear damage also may occur; a person might not respond to a first-aider's questions because of a loss of hearing caused by the strike.

You can help prevent lightning injury by checking, before your trip, into anticipated weather conditions, so that you can avoid climbing in high-risk situations. If you are caught out in the open during a thunderstorm, try to seek shelter. Unfortunately, tents are poor protection. Metal tent poles may function as lightning rods; stay away from poles and wet items inside the tent. Do not touch metal objects, such as an ice ax or carabiners, and don't wear metal items, such as crampons. Avoid standing near lone tall trees, on ridge tops, or at lookout structures. Do not stand in the middle of a clearing; you'll become the tallest object in the vicinity and thus you'll be a lightning rod. In forested areas, shelter yourself by crouching down or kneeling in lower, dry areas amid clumps of smaller trees or bushes. Crouching on top of your pack may provide added protection against step-voltage transfer of the lightning strike from the ground (fig. 19-2). (Chapter 23, Mountain Weather, includes further information on thunderstorms.)

## Intestinal Disorders

Fecal–oral contamination is the most common cause of gastrointestinal infections, causing diarrhea and abdominal cramping, on mountaineering trips. Most often, the source of the feces is mountaineers themselves. Inadequate handwashing after a toilet break is the typical problem. Some rock-climbing routes may be contaminated with feces from previous parties. On glacier routes, handling ropes that have dragged through soiled snow and ice can lead to contamination. Water bottles as well as food can become contaminated from the mountaineer's unwittingly fouled hands. Climbers often are gregarious at rest stops—but think twice before offering your snack bag for each person to plunge a hand into; pouring some contents into each person's hands would be less risky. For situations where soap and water are inconvenient luxuries, hand cleansers and towelettes can be used to reduce hand contamination.

Animal wastes also present a risk. Many small rodents live in the same crags we climb, and your hands may rest on mouse scat on your way up a cliff. Clean

circulation. CPR must be initiated if these functions have been interrupted. It's important to get the lightning victim to a medical facility, because vital body functions may remain unstable for a considerable time after resuscitation.

Lightning burns often take several hours to develop after the strike. These burns don't usually require treatment, because of their superficial location on the body. The eyes, however, are a vulnerable port of entry for

your hands before eating, and avoid camping near rodent burrows. Cover foods and water so that these are secure from rodent invasion during the night.

Giardiasis, caused by a waterborne protozoan (*Giardia lamblia*) traveling in cyst form from an infected animal host's feces, is prevalent in the United States, particularly in the West. Giardia infection has a long incubation period, ranging from one to three weeks (and averaging a week and a half) after the organism is swallowed. Usually you will not develop symptoms until after you've returned from your wilderness outing. Watery, explosive diarrhea may erupt, accompanied by cramps, flatus, and vomiting. After three or four days, the condition simmers down into an unpleasant subacute phase marked by greasy, mushy stools, mild abdominal cramping, belching, and so on. Treatment for this ailment generally follows laboratory diagnosis. Tinidazole is the treatment of choice in countries other than the United States, where it has not yet received government approval. Various other drugs, such as quinacrine or metronidazole, are used for giardiasis treatment in the United States.

Prevention of giardiasis and other waterborne diarrheas involves sanitation of water. All ingested water, including that used in dishwashing and toothbrushing, must be purified. (See the section on purification techniques in Chapter 3, Camping and Food, for details on the various methods.)

Travelers heading into regions with questionable hygiene and water disinfection practices are encouraged to seek medical advice on antibiotics that can be taken to help ward off infection and on antimotility ("antidiarrheal") drugs. However, taking drugs is not a substitute for dietary discretion. Avoid eating raw vegetables, raw meat, raw seafood, uncooked fruits or vegetables, tap water, and ice. Instead, stick to boiled water, properly cooked meat and vegetables, bottled beverages, and reputable eating establishments.

For most intestinal infections associated with diarrhea, treatment during your trip will consist of maintaining adequate replacement of fluids and electrolytes. This can be challenging if you're also nauseated. Packets of replacement electrolytes can be mixed into a liter of water and provided to the diarrhea sufferer. If these aren't available, simple replacement of fluids is the key. Provide palatable foods and broths with a substantial salt content.

# Blisters

Blisters are dreaded by all wilderness travelers. These bubbles under the skin, filled with clear or blood-tinged fluid, probably represent the most common illness-related reason for ending outings. Small blisters generally are a source of minor irritation and discomfort. Larger blisters can cause significant pain and, if ruptured, can lead to serious infection and ulceration.

Often, blisters are caused by new or poorly fitted boots. Blisters result from your skin rubbing against socks and the inner lining of your boot. This happens when the boots are too large or too loosely laced, or when socks are lumpy or wrinkled. Any irregularity on the inner surface of the boot, or any twig or pebble that falls inside the boot, may create a point of constriction and friction. Moisture tends to soften the skin, so that wet boots or socks promote blister formation.

To prevent blisters, fit your boots properly. Break them in slowly and thoroughly before launching into any extended hikes. The areas most prone to blistering are over the heel or Achilles tendon (at the back of the ankle), or on the toes. If you tend to blister easily, pad the blister-prone areas with moleskin or other adhesive foam (but don't pad so much that you create a new pressure point). Keep your feet dry, wearing adequate and well-fitting socks.

Blisters usually become noticeable first as a hot spot, a localized sensation of heat that increases in size and intensity over time. Inspect such spots immediately, and take preventive measures. Place a generous strip of waterproof, plastic adhesive tape or moleskin over the spot (fig. 19-3a). (Other suitable products include Second Skin and Dr. Scholl's Molefoam.) Avoid using adhesive bandage strips (such as Band-Aids) for covering hot spots; these strips seem to promote blister formation because the nonadhesive dressing pad balls up and rubs against the already sensitive skin.

Once a blister has formed, avoid opening it unless absolutely necessary, to prevent introducing infection to the blistered area. Your body will reabsorb the blister fluid after several days, and healing will occur. If it's necessary to continue your hike or whatever activity caused the blister in the first place, pad the blister and protect it from rupture (fig. 19-3b). Layer a

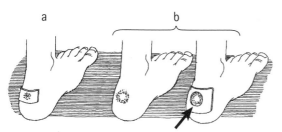

*Fig. 19-3. Blisters: a, tape a hot spot; b, doughnut-cushion a blister.*

"doughnut" of padding until the proper depth is reached so that the blister itself doesn't receive pressure. The padding doughnut must be deeper and wider than the blister. Tape the padding well to prevent displacement.

In rare circumstances, you might decide to drain the fluid from a blister. This might occur if you are unable to wear your boot because of the padding doughnut's bulk or if you're feeling excessive pain from the pressure of the engorged blister. If drainage must be done, wash the area first with soap and water. Sterilize a needle with a burning match, and then insert the needle tip under the blister's edge. Press the blister fluid out gently, and then apply a sterile pad. If the blister already ruptured by itself, wash the area, bandage it, and watch carefully for signs of infection.

## Panic

Mountaineering outings can be refreshing and rejuvenating experiences. They also can induce stress responses in the participants. In extreme situations, such as a serious accident, nearly everyone will have to deal with their own and each other's anxiety or even panic. You may discover that a challenging situation or a difficult performance demand evokes a more intense anxiety response than you had anticipated. This is unpleasant, especially if it occurs as you are halfway up a cliff. You must be able to manage these responses without becoming disabled by them.

Some people have a tendency toward intense anxiety in response to certain physical situations in climbing, such as exposure to heights or to enclosed spaces. This tendency can erupt in a panic response during a step-across move on a cliff face or while squeezing up a rock chimney. If you are affected, you may freeze and refuse to go on. You may hyperventilate (breathe rapidly) or be unable to recognize the safe movements that are actually available to you. Your ability to assess the full situation will be blocked temporarily; your physical movements will be clumsy and fearful, raising the risk of a mishap.

Self-calming techniques are helpful in such situations. One approach involves a five-step process:

1. Identify the panic response for what it is (simply a physical adrenaline reaction to perceived risk).
2. Decide to deal with the panic response effectively.
3. Refocus on *slow, steady, deep breathing* (perhaps enhanced with a mental image of exhaling out the worry with each breath).
4. Identify, systematically, your options for safe movement.
5. Carry out one of these options.

If hyperventilation is a problem, try the old trick of breathing into a bag to increase the carbon dioxide concentration of the air you inhale, which can slow down the hyperventilation trend. Redirecting your focus onto a useful physical task can be an excellent strategy for interrupting the snowballing effect of panic. Your fellow climbers can be most helpful by calm and matter-of-fact prompting toward the self-calming skills, by maintaining an atmosphere of confident acceptance and support, and by pointing out an option for retreat if appropriate.

## ACCIDENT RESPONSE

An orderly reaction to an emergency can make all the difference in how party members translate their first-aid knowledge into effective action. Before leaving the trailhead, a mountaineering party should have a designated first-aid leader, as well as a clearly identified trip leader. The party leader is responsible for the welfare of the entire party; the first-aid leader assumes leadership of any first-aid scenario in the field. If evacuation of a victim becomes necessary, the party leader—not the first-aid leader—orchestrates those plans.

The trip leader and first-aid leader should check with party members to learn of any relevant medical conditions, such as allergy to bee stings, or medication needs, such as use of insulin. Opinions differ on the best format for gathering this information. Some trip leaders like to ask for medical information individually from each party member in advance of the trip. The information is then shared with any assistant trip leader and with the first-aid leader. This approach supports individual privacy, but it has the disadvantage of not alerting other party members to information they might need in order to be most helpful to a stricken person. Thus another approach would be to ask for this information from the group as a whole, at the trailhead.

## The Seven Steps

The effective response to an accident situation in the mountains can be simplified into seven steps (fig. 19-4).

### Step 1: Take Charge of the Situation

Establish the leadership roles that you planned at the trailhead for such a situation. Survey the accident scene, noting all victims, current objective hazards, and the likely cause of the accident. See whether anyone can provide an account of what happened and when.

If there are several victims, *triage* decisions (a battlefield concept) are needed in order to direct the party's limited resources toward actions likely to have the most benefit and away from actions that are either trivial or hopeless. Triage decisions are modified as victims' conditions and status change. In a serious accident with numerous victims, triage decisions result in sorting victims into groupings, based on priority in receiving assistance. First priority goes to seriously injured people with a good chance of survival if given immediate help; second priority is the group of seriously injured people whose conditions are stable and who can wait perhaps an hour or two for first aid; third priority is the group of people with minor injuries who can wait for simple first aid or can administer it themselves with a little help; the final group consists of critically injured people with very little chance of survival no matter what treatment is attempted. Making decisions about who receives care first is a wrenching task, but it is essential to using your party's efforts to best effect. A triage viewpoint also helps in evaluating which victims are most in need of evacuation to outside medical help.

### Step 2: Approach the Victim or Victims Safely

Don't endanger uninjured party members, perhaps extending the disaster, in an effort to reach an injured person. If avalanche or rockfall is a danger, the leader can designate a lookout to keep watch while the first-aid effort proceeds.

### Step 3: Begin Critical First Aid

Note the victim's body position, and decide whether there is a likelihood of back or neck injury. If so, provide support and immobilization for the injured area

---

**1. Take charge of the situation.**

The party leader is in charge of the entire group's welfare and any evacuation efforts; the first-aid leader is in charge of the first-aid effort.

**2. Approach the victim safely.**

Protect the victim from further injury, and protect the party.

**3. Begin critical first aid.**

Move the injured person to a safer location if necessary. Conduct a primary examination to identify and treat potentially fatal conditions. Check ABCD: Airway + Breathing + Circulation + Deadly bleeding. Administer CPR if needed.

**4. Treat for shock.**

Be alert to the signs and symptoms of shock. Provide insulation, dry clothing, pain management, and psychological support, including reassurance and sensitive care.

**5. Check for other injuries.**

Conduct a thorough secondary examination. Record findings on an accident report form.

**6. Make a plan.**

Decide how best to evacuate the injured person.

**7. Carry out the plan.**

*Fig. 19-4. The seven steps in accident response*

as further measures are carried out. If the person must be moved out of a danger zone, do so swiftly, safely, and without causing further injury.

Conduct a *primary examination,* aimed at recognizing and treating any potentially fatal conditions. Quickly note the victim's level of consciousness. The four levels of consciousness, in decreasing order of responsiveness, are:

1. Alert
2. Responsive to vocal stimuli
3. Responsive to painful stimuli
4. Unresponsive

Now look for the person's ABCD indicators:

**A** irway is clear of obstruction.

**B** reathing is spontaneous and adequate.

**C** irculation of blood is adequate, indicated by a beating heart and enough blood pressure to supply a pulse.

**D** eadly hemorrhaging is absent.

Clear the airway if it is blocked. If breathing or circulation are not adequate, start CPR.

Control dangerous blood loss with *direct pressure* over the site of hemorrhage; this almost always is effective. The artery supplying the injury site can be compressed as a second-level effort to stop serious bleeding.

Do not use pressure dressings as a substitute for direct pressure. Limb tourniquets should be used only in a situation where neither direct pressure nor compression of the relevant arterial pressure point have stemmed a life-threatening hemorrhage and where you are prepared for the likelihood that the affected limb will be lost. In such a rare situation, label the tourniquet with the time it was applied, and mark the victim clearly as being someone with a tourniquet in place.

## Step 4: Treat for Shock

Among the goals of the primary examination—along with maintaining adequate breathing and blood circulation and controlling blood loss—is to prevent or limit shock. *Shock* is the simultaneous depression of vital body processes, including blood pressure. Ultimately, blood circulation collapses. Shock is progressive and potentially fatal.

Be aware of the following signs and symptoms of shock:

### Signs That May Be Noted by Observers

- Skin cool and clammy
- Eyes dull
- Pupils dilated
- Face pale
- Lips and nail beds blue
- Pulse rapid but weak
- Breathing rapid and shallow
- Restlessness
- Unresponsiveness (a late sign)

### Symptoms That May Be Experienced by the Victim

- Nausea
- Thirst
- Weakness
- Fear

Shock can be limited by offering the following to the victim: *prevention of body heat loss* by providing insulation, particularly under the injured person, and by replacing wet garments with dry ones; *pain management;* and *reassurance* and *orientation to circumstances and surroundings.* Provide fluids, but be sure the person's gag reflex is intact. Remain vigilant to the emergence of shock later in the course of care; a victim who becomes more withdrawn and less responsive could well be drifting into shock.

At this stage, psychological support becomes important for the victim, response party members, and any bystanders. Response party members should keep an eye out for anyone behaving irrationally or in an agitated or dazed fashion. Often such an individual can be assigned a simple task that will refocus him or her on the work of the group. If you're a member of the accident response party, learn the names of each victim, use the names when you talk to them, and tell them your name. Give the victims reasonable updates about how each person is doing and about the overall plan in progress. It is not reassuring to keep a victim "in the dark," and empty statements that "everything's going to be fine" tend to be alienating and unsettling. Keep in mind the vantage point of each victim: never step over an injured person as if he or she were a piece of wood as you maneuver around the first-aid scene.

## Step 5: Check for Other Injuries

Once the person has been stabilized and treated initially for life-threatening conditions, check for other injuries. Conduct a systematic head-to-toes *secondary examination,* so that no injury goes undiscovered. The secondary examination can bring into view less severe injuries and problems that, if untreated, may turn critical. The examination should be performed by only one person, as more than one set of hands on a victim may result in misleading findings, plus anxiety for the injured person. It is important to examine bare skin while performing this complete look for possible injuries. Protect the victim from environmental exposure, and replace clothing after examining any area of the body.

Specific clues of injury that may be noted during this examination include the following:

- Deformity compared with another body part
- Discoloration or bruising
- Bleeding or loss of other fluids
- Swelling
- Pain or tenderness
- Limited range of motion
- Victim guarding a particular body part

The person conducting the examination should use an accident report form, such as the one shown in Figure 19-5, to help guide the exam. All findings must be recorded in detail on the form. The report will provide essential information in the event of a change in the victim's condition or in case evacuation becomes necessary and the injured person is turned over to others for treatment.

## Step 6: Make a Plan

After the victim's injuries have been treated and stabilized, party members must decide how best to get the person out of the mountains to receive further care. The injured person may be able to walk out with a little help. If not, the party might decide to attempt carrying the person out, though this is usually a poor option for a small party or one untrained in evacuation procedures. If there is any doubt about the party's capacity to self-evacuate, the group must make a plan to get outside help to the accident scene. The decision will be based on an assessment of many factors, including the victim's condition, the strength of the party, available equipment and supplies, and the weather and terrain.

## Step 7: Carry Out the Plan

The trip leader is in charge of carrying out the rescue plan. Party members will move ahead with self-evacuation, if that is the plan. On the other hand, if the plan is to seek outside help, preparations must be made for spending time where they are: setting up a shelter, heating water, and getting ready for another night in the wilderness. In all the preparations, keep the needs of the victim in mind. When dispatching people to find help, try to send at least two of the party's stronger members, along with a completed accident report form with information on the victim's condition, the condition of the rest of the party, and their specific location. (See Chapter 20, Alpine Rescue, for details on rescue and evacuation methods.)

## INJURIES

Immediate application of skillful and caring first aid is critical in minimizing injuries from a mountaineering accident. Specific treatments for injuries are beyond the scope of this book. Hands-on instruction in mountaineering first aid is essential. (See Appendix B, Supplementary References, for the titles of detailed first-aid texts.)

## FIRST-AID KIT

In a mountaineering party, each member must carry a basic personal first-aid kit. In addition, the party will often bring group first-aid supplies, depending on the nature and duration of the outing. Many parties carry a compact splint (such as an inflatable plastic splint), an oral antihistamine, and a pair of bandage scissors.

Suggested contents of a basic personal first-aid kit are given in the list that follows. On trips where dampness is a possibility, it's wise to put the kit in a plastic bag to keep the bandaging materials dry.

| Item | Quantity/Size | Use |
|---|---|---|
| Band-Aids | Six 1-inch | To cover small minor wounds |
| Butterfly bandages | Three, in various sizes | To close minor lacerations |
| Sterile gauze pads | Four 4-inch by 4-inch | To cover larger wounds |
| Carlisle dressing or sanitary napkin | One 4-inch | To absorb and control severe bleeding |
| Nonadherent dressings | Two 4-inch by 4-inch | To cover abrasions and burns |
| Self-adhering roller bandages | Two rolls, 2-inch width by 5 yards | To hold dressings in place |
| Athletic tape | One roll, 2-inch width | Multiple uses |
| Triangular bandages | Two 36-inch by 36-inch by 52-inch | Sling; cravat |
| Moleskin or Molefoam | 4-inch to 6-inch square | To cushion blister areas |
| Tincture of Benzoin | Half-ounce bottle | To aid in adherence of adhesive tape; to protect skin |
| Povidine iodine swabs | Two packages | Antiseptic for surface wounds |
| Alcohol or soap pads | Three packages | To cleanse skin |
| Thermometer | Range of 90 to 105 degrees Fahrenheit (30 to 41 degrees Celsius) | To measure body temperature |
| Sugar packets | Four packets | Diabetes: hypoglycemia intervention |
| Aspirin | Six tablets | Headache; pain; if the party includes children bring acetaminophen tablets instead of aspirin |
| Elastic bandage | One 2-inch width | Sprains: compression of injured area |
| Latex gloves | Two pairs | Infection barrier |
| Safety pins | Two | Multiple uses |
| Tweezers | One pair | To remove splinters, ticks, wound debris |
| Plastic bag | One 12-inch by 18-inch | To hold contaminated materials |

Fig. 19-5. Accident report form

# FIRST AID/ACCIDENT REPORT FORM

## RESCUE REQUEST

Fill Out One Form Per Victim

TIME OF INCIDENT

A.M.    P.M.    DATE

NATURE OF INCIDENT

FALL ON   ❑ ROCK   ❑ SNOW   ❑ FALLING ROCK

     ❑ CREVASSE   ❑ AVALANCHE

     ❑ ILLNESS   ❑ EXCESSIVE   ❑ HEAT   ❑ COLD

BRIEF DESCRIPTION OF INCIDENT

INJURIES      FIRST AID GIVEN
(List Most Severe First)

SKIN TEMP./COLOR:

STATE OF CONSCIOUSNESS:

PAIN (Location):

RECORD:

| | Initial | When leave scene |
|---|---|---|
| Time | | |
| Pulse | | |
| Respiration | | |

VICTIM'S NAME      AGE

ADDRESS

NOTIFY (Name)

RELATIONSHIP      PHONE

OTHER COMMENTS:

DETACH HERE–SEND OUT WITH REQUEST FOR AID

- - - - - - - - - - - - - - - - - - - - - - - - - - - - - - - - - - - - - - - - -

TEAR HERE–KEEP THIS SECTION WITH THE VICTIM

## START HERE    FINDINGS    FIRST AID GIVEN

Airway, Breathing, Circulation
Initial Rapid Check
(Chest Wounds, Severe Bleeding)

ASK WHAT HAPPENED:

ASK WHERE IT HURTS:

TAKE PULSE AND RESPIRATIONS   PULSE   RESPIRATIONS

### HEAD-TO-TOE EXAMINATION

HEAD:   Scalp–Wounds

     Ears, Nose–Fluids

     Eyes–Pupils

     Jaw–Stability

     Mouth–Wounds

NECK:   Wounds, Deformity

CHEST:   Movement, Symmetry

ABDOMEN:   Wounds, Rigidity

PELVIS:   Stability

EXTREMITIES:   Wounds, Deformity

     Sensations & Movement

     Pulses Below Injury

BACK:   Wounds, Deformity

SKIN:   Color

     Temperature

     Moistness

STATE OF CONSCIOUSNESS

PAIN (Location)

LOOK FOR MEDICAL ID TAG

ALLERGIES

VICTIM'S NAME      AGE

COMPLETED BY      DATE      TIME

## VITAL SIGNS RECORD

| Record TIME | BREATHS | | PULSE | | PULSES BELOW INJURY | PUPILS | SKIN | STATE OF CONSCIOUSNESS | OTHER |
|---|---|---|---|---|---|---|---|---|---|
| | Rate | Character | Rate | Character | | | | | |
| | | Deep, Shallow, Noisy, Labored | | Strong, Weak, Regular, Irregular | Strong, Weak, Absent | Equal size, React to Light, Round | Color, Temp, Moistness | Alert, Confused, Unresponsive | Pain, Anxiety, Thirst, Etc. |
| | | | | | | | | | |
| | | | | | | | | | |
| | | | | | | | | | |
| | | | | | | | | | |
| | | | | | | | | | |
| | | | | | | | | | |
| | | | | | | | | | |

Other Observations:

---

## SIDE 2 RESCUE REQUEST

EXACT LOCATION (Include Marked Map If Possible)
QUADRANGLE:      SECTION:
AREA DESCRIPTION:

TERRAIN:
- ❑ GLACIER
- ❑ BRUSH
- ❑ FLAT
- ❑ OTHER: (Describe)
- ❑ SNOW
- ❑ TIMBER
- ❑ MODERATE
- ❑ ROCK
- ❑ TRAIL
- ❑ STEEP

ON SITE PLANS:
- ❑ Will Stay Put
- ❑ Will Evacuate To
Can Stay Overnight Safely   ❑ Yes   ❑ No
On Site Equiment:
- ❑ Tent
- ❑ Flares
- ❑ Ropes
- ❑ Sleeping Bags
- ❑ Saw
- ❑ Stoves
- ❑ Ground Insulation
- ❑ Hardware
- ❑ Fuel

Other:

LOCAL WEATHER:

SUGGESTED EVACUATION:
- ❑ Carry-Out
- ❑ Lowering
- ❑ Helicopter
- ❑ Raising

EQUIPMENT NEEDED:
- ❑ Rigid Litter
- ❑ Other
- ❑ Water
- ❑ Food

PARTY MEMBERS REMAINING (Indicate Numbers):
___ Scrambling Students   ___ Basic Students   ___ Basic Grads
___ Intermediate Students   ___ Intermediate Grads

ATTACH THE PRE-TRIP LIST OF PARTY MEMBERS, including names, addresses, and phone numbers. Update the list to accurately reflect party membership and persons to notify in case of delays.
PARTY LEADERS:

NAMES OF MESSENGERS SENT FOR HELP:

WHOM TO NOTIFY TO INITIATE THE RESCUE:
    IN NATIONAL PARK: Notify the Park Ranger
    OUTSIDE NATIONAL PARK: Sheriff/County Police (Call 911)
    IN CANADA: RCMP

# 20
# ALPINE RESCUE

Mountaineering training emphasizes techniques for staying safe and healthy. However, the dangers inherent in mountaineering can result in illness or injury even in the best-prepared party. At such a time, help can be hours or days away, and that help usually comes from other climbers who volunteer despite the risk and sacrifice. Every mountaineer should be ready to render aid when needed. Thankfully, mountaineers have a proud tradition of going to the rescue of their own.

It's possible for a handful of climbers to effect a difficult rescue quickly and efficiently, aided only by such gear as can be improvised from normal climbing equipment. This chapter focuses on efforts that can be mounted by a small climbing party without specialized rescue equipment and on some of the decisions this group will have to make.

The skills of mountain rescue are akin to those of first aid: we all must learn these skills, but we hope we never need to use them. The time could come, however, when the life of an injured or ill climber depends upon the rescue skills of yourself and other members of your party. With a knowledge of basic rescue techniques coupled with judgment and experience, you can turn a traumatic situation into an example of safe and successful teamwork.

## — WHEN AN ACCIDENT HAPPENS —

The immediate aftermath of a serious mountaineering incident is the most stressful time you're likely to experience in your climbing career. In the middle of an enjoyable outing, a friend, partner, or loved one is suddenly stricken by illness or injury or is missing.

The decisions that are made immediately following an incident can set the course for its final outcome. The first action is an assessment of the situation. Evaluate any injury or illness and begin treatment. Protect an injured person from further harm posed by such dangers as rockfall, shock, hypothermia, or dehydration. If a party member is missing, prepare for a search. Also assess the remaining climbers for any unreported injuries, and judge their mental state and their ability to handle the tasks that face them. (Study the seven steps in accident response that are described in Chapter 19, First Aid.)

Organized climbing parties may already have a designated first-aid leader to direct the medical efforts and a designated trip leader in charge of overall group welfare and any evacuation plans. If your party has no recognized leader, you can select one—or a leader may evolve from within the group. It may be a person with experience in mountain rescue or wilderness medicine. Other times it may simply be the strongest climber or the strongest personality (though personality is not a good measure of leadership potential). A good leader will listen to suggestions from the group but, in the end, the leader's decisions should be accepted without argument (except in the interest of safety).

After the initial assessment of the situation comes the most important step: deciding what course of action to take in order to get all members of the party home safely. Before settling on a plan, thoroughly evaluate several factors:

- The condition of the ill or injured climber. What treatment is needed? Is it safe to move the person?
- The skills of the other climbers. Do they have rescue experience? Are their climbing skills high?
- The hazards of the mountain. Judge such elements as steepness of the terrain, distance to the trailhead, weather conditions, and time of day.

## The Rules of Rescue

Chances for a successful outcome to an emergency situation are greatly improved when you follow these three rules of rescue:

1. The safety of the rescuers comes before the welfare of the subject. It's unfortunate when an accident happens and someone is injured, but the situation is profoundly worsened if rescuers are hurt too. A crisis is a time for the highest standards of safety, not risky heroics.
2. Don't rush. Everyone experiences a surge of adrenaline when an accident happens, but giving in to the urge to rush—to respond hastily and thoughtlessly—leads to bad decisions and mistakes. Act promptly, but calmly. Rescuers who are prompt, calm, caring, and competent give an injured person the confidence to avoid panic and help in the rescue.
3. Do only what your training and experience have taught you to do, because we make fewer mistakes doing things we have already done in the past. An accident is not the time to experiment with new techniques. If you stick to procedures that you know well and that are commonly taught and practiced, other team members will understand what is going on and be able to help effectively.

## Search

Occasionally a climbing party will have to search for one of its own members—either an unroped climber who has fallen out of sight during an accident, or one who has simply become separated from the party during its travels. Although a small party has a limited capability for conducting a search, much can be accomplished by even two or three climbers.

When a climber falls out of sight, you can send a belayed climber to the point where the fall began, in order to look below. If the missing climber is spotted, rescue efforts can begin. If not, mark the start of the fall with a piece of bright cloth that can be spotted from below. The belayed climber can then descend the fall line, taking care to avoid knocking rocks loose. If this descent doesn't reveal the climber, examine the ground at the bottom of the fall line for signs of a falling object. Search any moat that may separate the base of the fall line from an adjoining snowfield.

In the case of a climber who has become separated from the party but is presumed to be uninjured, the first thing to consider is whether the missing person actually needs help. If this climber is well-equipped and experienced, and missing on easy terrain, you may simply decide to wait at the trailhead for the person, deferring any search until the next morning.

Start the search immediately, however, if bad weather, difficult terrain, or medical considerations indicate the climber could use help. The most effective search method usually is to return to the point where the missing person was last seen and retrace the party's route. Look for places where the climber might have left the route; try to visualize errors the person might have made. Look for clues, such as footprints in mud, sand, or snow. If no signs are found after several hours of searching, it's probably time to go for outside help.

## Evacuation by the Climbing Party

A climbing party can sometimes evacuate an ill or injured climber with no outside help. If the injured person can walk and the injuries are relatively minor, a lightened pack and moral support may be all that is required. The party will usually be able to evacuate a climber who has minor but disabling injuries such as a sprained ankle or knee.

An injured person generally benefits from a period of rest following an accident. Because the further trauma of an immediate evacuation is seldom justified, delay the move until the patient's condition has stabilized. The injured person can probably offer the best indications of whether and when to begin the evacuation. Consult the victim and monitor the injuries closely, before and throughout the evacuation, and always keep the person's comfort in mind.

Some medical conditions require immediate evacuation, among these are pulmonary or cerebral edema and progressively deteriorating conditions such as appendicitis. Immediate evacuation is also necessary if circumstances of weather or terrain are life-threatening. Certain other conditions require that evacuation be delayed until trained medical help arrives: head injuries, neck or spinal injuries, heart attack, stroke, and internal injuries. Evacuation is required but not urgent for all other serious injuries or illnesses. (Consult Chapter 19, First Aid, for further information.)

## Outside Help

There are times when a party cannot cope with its own emergency. Outside help will be needed if a climber's injuries are severe, if the evacuation requires long stretches of raising or lowering, or when other circumstances—party size, condition or skill of the party, terrain, or distance to the trailhead—combine to make evacuation by a small climbing party impossible. Thirty or more rescuers can be required to carry an injured climber more than 2 or 3 miles on even the best of trails.

After your party decides that outside help is needed, send for help as soon as the injured climber is stabilized and the persons going for aid are no longer needed at the accident site. If your party needs immediate assistance, don't hesitate to ask for it from climbers on neighboring peaks, from people living or working in the area, or from local authorities. A climbing party should know in advance where to turn for help should its own efforts fail, as well as how to cooperate with rescuers and authorities.

In many areas, help by helicopter may be only an hour away once word gets to the proper authorities, although this will depend on availability, weather, terrain, local politics, and the accuracy of the information carried by the messengers. Ground rescuers often can be at the accident scene within 4 to 12 hours after they get the call for help. If your climbing party is in a sheltered area accessible by helicopter and the weather is good, don't move the victim unless

the injuries require doing so. But if you have to change location after the messengers have gone for help, make sure rescuers know: send another messenger or leave a party member or message at the original site.

Sometimes it's not possible to send anyone from your party for help. Your only alternative then is to try to signal potential rescuers with noise or visual signals and wait to be declared overdue. Such a situation dramatizes the need to leave information about your intended route and your estimated time of return with a responsible person who will notify the proper agency if you don't show up. Obviously it's also vital that you stick to your intended route.

## Going for Help

Whenever possible, send two climbers out together for help—partly for their own safety and partly because two people can do a better job of obtaining aid. Be sure they have a clear understanding of the party's situation and requirements so they will know exactly what aid to request. They should take with them the names and phone numbers of everyone in the party, a completed accident report form for each injured person (such as the form shown in Figure 19-5 in Chapter 19, First Aid), and a marked map or other means of showing the precise location of the party.

Messengers need to carry enough gear to handle their own journey, including emergencies, but not so much that they cannot travel swiftly. However, the certainty, not the swiftness, of getting the message out is the most important consideration. The messengers must travel in a safe manner. The victim and other party members are relying solely upon them, assuming the authorities will get the word and help will soon be on the way. If the messengers are not traveling an established route, they should mark the way, perhaps with flagging tape or cairns, to help rescuers find the climbers.

The messengers have several vital responsibilities once they are out of the wilderness. First, they must contact the appropriate local authorities, such as the county sheriff or park personnel, and request help. If evacuation is to take place over technical terrain, the authorities must know this from the start so they will dispatch rescuers with the appropriate skills.

The messengers then must make certain that the

information is relayed at once, accurately, and to the right people. Often the initial organization of a rescue depends on a chain of communication, messages relayed from a dispatcher to an officer or ranger until a rescue leader is reached by phone, radio, or pager. Along the way, vital information may be lost or ignored by nonmountaineers who don't understand the meaning and importance of words they are asked to convey. If the messengers are unable to immediately speak with the rescue leader, they must be insistent with intermediaries—to the point of being obnoxious—to assure that a garbled message does not result in a tragically failed rescue.

The messengers then wait at the phone or appointed place to meet with the rescue team or authorities. The messengers will turn over the accident report forms, map, list of names, and any other information to the rescue coordinator and assist in devising the rescue plan. The messengers should be prepared to be asked the same questions by a number of different people in the rescue organization. If the messengers are not injured or extremely fatigued, they may be asked to lead the rescue party back to the climbers.

The messengers also can notify relatives of the climbers about the situation. Because of the urgency of getting the rescue organized and the need to keep phone lines available, this task will probably have to await the arrival of the rescue coordinator, who usually has considerable experience in working with concerned relatives.

## Electronic Communications

A trend in backcountry rescue is the use of cellular phones and ham radios to call for help. The devices have some limitations. Climbers often are too far from a cellular relay site to use the phones; ham operators sometimes must go through a complex chain of operators to connect with the proper authorities.

Once your emergency call gets through, give precise details about the accident, location, and patient injuries and conditions. If possible, give the information directly to the rescue leader. Be sure to provide your cellular phone number. If you're using a ham radio, be aware that many rescue units don't have such radios and will not be able to talk to you directly.

# TRANSPORT OVER TECHNICAL TERRAIN

On steep terrain that requires technical climbing, even a minor illness or injury can make a person unable to travel without help. The party may have to raise or lower the disabled person—a procedure more dangerous than simply climbing over the same ground because attention is now focused on the victim instead of on the climbing. Most of the added safety concerns can be alleviated by a few simple steps:

- Assign specific duties to rescuers. Have one person responsible for belaying, another for construction of anchors, another for continuing first aid, and so forth. This system will get the jobs done more thoroughly and consistently than if several people had their hands in on each task.
- Wear a helmet. Everyone in the party should wear a helmet at all times.
- Wear leather gloves when handling belay and rescue ropes.
- Tie in to an anchor. Everyone in the party should be linked to an anchor (even if this might not be necessary in a normal climbing situation).
- Climb only when you're on belay or are attached to a fixed line by a prusik sling or ascender (even if these precautions wouldn't normally be necessary).
- Pad a belay or rescue rope anywhere it runs over a rock edge. Clothing, backpacks, and ensolite pads work well. Even a rounded rock edge—if it's not padded—can cut through a rope during a severe fall. Monitor ropes closely for abrasion.
- Consolidate any gear that is not in use, putting it a short distance from the main rescue effort so that it's accessible if needed. Secure the gear to keep it from falling down the mountain.
- Inspect any anchor and rope system before it's weighted. Both the leader and anyone going over the edge need to inspect the entire system from the anchor to the tie-in at the climber's harness.
- Avoid rockfall by moving loose rock away from where it may be knocked over an edge or dislodged by the rope. Watch your footing closely.

# Anchors

In technical rescues, anchors are the most important part of the system. It is in anchor systems and their use that most of the differences between climbing techniques and the rescue techniques described in this chapter are found. Rescue anchors must bear the weight of up to three people instead of the one-person load normally applied to climbing anchor systems.

Some basic points to keep in mind are:

- Back up every anchor, no matter how strong it may appear.
- Don't overlook natural anchors; solid rock formations or well-rooted trees make outstanding anchors for rescue loads.
- Use a cordelette to distribute the load between multiple anchor points, creating a *load-distributed anchor*. The cordelette is preferred over self-equalizing anchors (in which a sliding carabiner attempts to keep the load equal on all anchors) because failure of one of the anchors in a self-equalizing setup results in shock-loading the remaining anchors. (Chapter 7, Belaying, explains and illustrates how to use the cordelette in distributing the load among three anchor points. The cordelette can also be used to distribute the load between two anchor points, as shown in Figure 20-1 in this chapter.)

## The Rescue Belay

The belay is an important component of the system of raising or lowering persons who are ill or injured. Whenever possible, the person being moved should be on a belay that is independent of the mechanism being used for raising or lowering (fig. 20-1). With this independent belay, the victim is safeguarded in case of any disaster to the raising/lowering system, such as failure of the main anchor, rockfall damage to the rope, loss of the lowering brake or raising system pulley, or sudden injury to anyone operating the system. The belay anchor, independent of the main system anchor, should be constructed of multiple placements, preferably equalized with a cordelette.

For belaying one person who is being raised or lowered, the belayer can use any standard belay device (not a hip belay), maintaining it in a position that ensures maximum friction. For belaying a two-person load, the only normal belay method that provides a safe enough level of friction is the Münter hitch (explained and illustrated in Chapters 6 and 7). The belay device or Münter hitch should be attached directly to an anchor system, not to the belayer's harness. This will prevent the large forces generated by rescue-load falls from hitting the belayer's body via the harness; also, it is easier for the belayer to tie off the belay line and move around if necessary.

The belayer should have the ability to continue lowering the victim if the original lowering system fails. The belayer should also be able to safely carry out a knot bypass of the belay device (described later in this chapter) if two or more ropes must be tied together for lowering.

# Lowering

There are several possibilities for getting the affected person down the mountain, depending on the extent of illness or injuries.

**Downclimbing:** An injured person may be able to climb down under tension from a taut belay, perhaps assisted by a belayed companion who can give guidance and encouragement—even helping with placement of hands and feet. On snow or ice slopes, large handholds and footsteps can be chopped.

**Rappelling:** If the victim has no head injury or bad leg injury, is showing no symptoms of shock, and is not otherwise seriously hurt, a rappel is possible. Belay the rappel from above with a separate rope and anchor. Alternatively, you can offer a belay from below by putting tension on the rope strands below the victim's rappel device. (However, don't pull down on the rope unless the injured person has lost control of the rappel. Otherwise, you will interfere with the rappel, especially if the person is using a hip wrap for additional friction.)

**Lowering in the seat harness:** It is possible to lower the victim in his or her seat harness if neither downclimbing nor rappelling is possible. The victim must have no serious leg or upper-body injuries. Use an anchored rope with a lowering device (such as the doubled carabiner brake system described in the next section) to lower the victim, who can use feet and hands to help guide the way down. The most stable stance will be just as in rappelling: feet shoulder-width apart and body perpendicular to the slope. The injured person will stay upright more easily by wearing a chest

*Fig. 20-1. Typical lower with belay*

harness with the rescue rope going up through a carabiner on that harness. The person should also be on an independent belay.

**Lowering with an attendant:** Someone with an injury to one leg but no other serious lower-body injury may simply need a person alongside to be lowered simultaneously in order to provide support and protection. Lowering two people on the same system requires the use of independently anchored belay and lowering ropes. The two climbers each must be attached to both ropes.

Here is an effective procedure for lowering the victim and an attendant side by side.

With the rescue rope (the lowering rope), the attendant ties in at the very end. The victim is attached to the rescue rope with a prusik sling attached to his or her seat harness, with the sling adjusted to place the victim alongside the attendant.

With the belay rope, the attendant ties in about 10 feet from the end. The victim is tied in to the end of the belay rope.

Both people are now firmly attached to both the rescue and belay systems. As they are lowered together, the attendant's chest should be even with the victim's back, putting the attendant in position to help support and stabilize the injured climber.

**Back carry:** This is a good technique if the victim has relatively minor lower-body injuries but is unable to be lowered in tandem with an attendant. Keep in mind that the rescuer must be strong enough to take the entire weight of the injured person and still be able to maneuver—especially difficult on lower-angle rock.

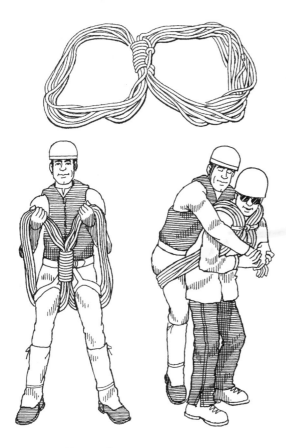

Fig. 20-2. Rope coil carry

sternum to keep the coils from slipping off the rescuer's shoulders. Run a prusik loop from the lowering rope to the injured person's chest harness to take some of the weight off the rescuer's shoulders and help keep the victim upright.

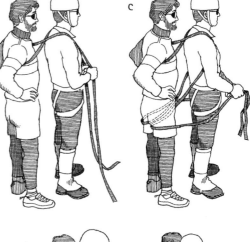

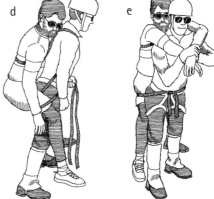

Fig. 20-3. Nylon-webbing carry

Connected like this to the victim, the rescuer will find it almost impossible to give first aid if medical problems arise. Do not use a back carry in cases where you suspect back or neck injuries, internal injuries, serious head injuries, or other conditions that require constant monitoring. For these injuries, a rigid litter and trained rescue personnel are required.

Two common methods of the back carry are the *coil carry* and the *nylon-webbing carry*. For either method, have rescuer and victim tied in to an independent belay.

In the coil carry, the rescuer slips half the loops of a coiled rope over one shoulder and half over the other, with the coils looping down the back to form a seat for the victim (fig. 20-2). You can pad this seat to help make the injured person more comfortable. Tie a short piece of webbing around both loops at the rescuer's

*@ doubled Perlon*

The nylon-webbing carry employs nylon webbing to support and distribute the victim's weight (fig. 20-3). The webbing should be extremely well padded, especially under the victim's thighs and at the rescuer's shoulders, to prevent concentrated pressure that will cause a loss of circulation.

## The Lowering Device

The best lowering device for use by a small party without specialized rescue gear is the standard carabiner brake system, as used in rappelling—but doubled (fig. 20-4). Simply construct two carabiner brakes, and join them with a locking carabiner, gate up. (Chapter 8, Rappelling, gives details on putting together a carabiner brake.) Each brake should include two braking carabiners (the crosswise carabiners).

The rescue rope runs through both brakes, providing increased friction for holding weight during lowering. The use of a standard belay device or a single carabiner brake for technical lowering is not recommended because these devices were designed for single-person loads and will not provide sufficient friction for all conditions of lowering. A doubled carabiner brake, on the other hand, provides enough friction for lowering two people at once.

Please note that the doubled carabiner brake system calls for a locking carabiner—not a pair of opposed regular carabiners—to join the two carabiner brakes. The single locking carabiner eliminates the possibility the rope could be pinched between a pair of carabiners. For the brakes themselves, standard symmetrical oval carabiners work best.

## Passing the Knot

On a long lower, you may want to tie two or more ropes together to permit a long uninterrupted descent for the injured person. As the knot approaches the lowering device (the doubled carabiner brake), it's necessary to stop lowering and perform a careful procedure to pass the knot safely through the device (fig. 20-4). Otherwise, the knot will jam solidly against the device.

It usually takes at least two people to carry out this procedure. Stop the descent when the knot gets to within 2 feet of the braking device. The person attending the lowering system holds the lowering rope while a second rescuer attaches a long prusik sling to the lowering rope just below the brake. (Make the prusik

sling out of a piece of 7- or 8-millimeter perlon accessory cord, 15 to 20 feet long, tied into a loop.) Then use a Münter hitch to attach the prusik sling to a carabiner that is connected to an anchor. For additional friction, the free end of the prusik sling can be wrapped several times around the doubled perlon between the prusik knot and the Münter hitch.

The second rescuer holds tight to the prusik sling while the first person eases the load onto the prusik by slacking off on the lowering rope. The first person then passes the knot through the braking system one brake at a time: the upper brake is disassembled, the knot brought through, and the brake reassembled; then the same procedure is followed with the bottom brake. In this way, one part of the brake is attached to the rope at all times.

Once the knot has been passed through the entire system and the brakes are reset, the second rescuer transfers the victim's weight back onto the lowering rope by slowly releasing the weighted prusik sling through its Münter hitch. As soon as full weight is back on the lowering rope and its brake system, the prusik sling can be removed and the first rescuer can resume lowering the victim.

## Raising

Lowering a person puts the force of gravity on the side of the rescuers, and therefore it's the preferred way to go, but sometimes there is no alternative to raising an injured climber up a steep face. Rescuers have a choice of two general methods: a prusik (or ascender) system, which depends on the victim's own efforts, and a pulley system, in which the rescuers do the raising with the help of the mechanical advantage afforded by pulleys.

These systems work on steep rock, snow, or ice, but they are usually associated with crevasse rescue (several versions of these systems are described in full in Chapter 14). The same safety precautions that apply to lowering injured climbers also apply to raising them. Whenever possible, safeguard the injured person with the use of backup anchors, safety prusiks, independent belays, and padding or other measures to prevent ropes from being cut on sharp edges.

In the prusik system, the climber carries out a self-rescue by ascending the rope in slings that are attached to the climbing rope with prusik knots or other

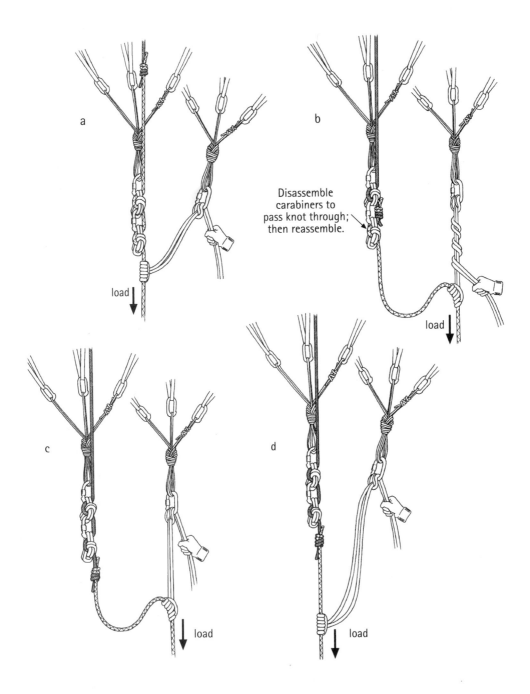

Disassemble
carabiners to
pass knot through;
then reassemble.

load

load

load

load

*Fig. 20-4. Passing the knot in a two-rope lower through a doubled carabiner brake system*

friction knots, or with mechanical ascenders. This can be an exhausting technique, with limited use for evacuating a seriously ill or injured climber.

For a pulley system, rescuers usually use the Z-pulley, the most efficient of the simple raising systems. There are some precautions to observe when using a Z-pulley: establish a main anchor system that is bombproof, keep extra prusik slings handy for replacements if a sling jams or shows signs of wear, and know how to free and replace a jammed prusik without resorting to a knife.

Be careful that haulers don't pull too zealously on the rope. A fast, jerky rise makes it difficult for the victim to negotiate broken terrain and maintain a stable position. If the rope jams and the haulers keep pulling, the Z-pulley then applies its powerful 3-to-1 mechanical advantage to the anchors instead of the injured climber, possibly yanking out the anchors.

Use prusik slings, not mechanical ascenders, in a Z-pulley or other raising system. The use of ascenders instead of prusik slings is a dangerous substitution because, by their design, ascenders pinch the rope. When the great forces of a rescue load are applied to the system, it is possible for the ascenders to fail or to cut the rope. Give the prusik at least three wraps around the rope, for ease of resetting. Each time you reset the Z-pulley, inspect the prusik knot for signs of wear and check that the prusik is holding securely.

An attendant can be raised along with the injured climber, just as an attendant can accompany a person who is being lowered. Both attendant and victim must be tied to the rescue and belay ropes.

## TRANSPORT OVER NONTECHNICAL TERRAIN

In many rescues, the hardest work begins when the steep terrain is past and the ropes are packed away. No longer aided by gravity, the party must carry its burden, very fatiguing work over rough ground. Under some conditions, however, a few simple techniques extend the capabilities of the small party so that it may not need to call for help.

**Four-hand seat:** This technique, useful only for very short distances, requires two carriers who are

approximately the same height. The carriers grab their own right wrist with their left hand, palms down. With the right hand, they grab their partner's left wrist, forming a seat for the incapacitated person (fig. 20-5).

**Back carries:** A strong climber can carry a person on his or her back for a considerable distance if the weight is distributed properly. The two back carries

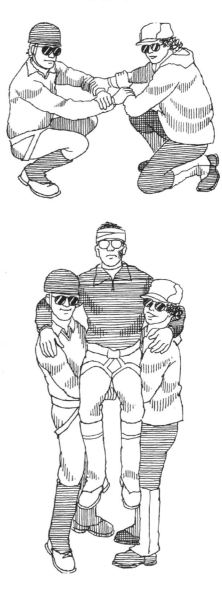

*Fig. 20-5. Four-hand seat carry*

described earlier in this chapter—using webbing or a coiled rope—work well. The carrier can be replaced as often as necessary to prevent exhausting any member of the party. The rucksack carry is another useful type of back carry. In this method, a large backpack is slit on the sides near the bottom so the carried person can step into it like a pair of shorts.

While it is possible to build a rudimentary litter out of a climbing rope, consider the patient's condition before attempting to use one. If a back carry is impossible and a litter is required, perhaps it's time to reevaluate the decision to evacuate the injured person without outside help.

## Snow Evacuations

On snow, it's particularly urgent to protect an injured person from heat loss while you give first aid and plan the evacuation. Wrap the person in extra clothing. Use pads, packs, or ropes as insulation from the snow. If the patient cannot be moved quickly, build a trench or low wall as a temporary wind shield. Of course, if you must stay overnight, the party will put up a tent or dig a snow cave.

If possible, move the patient to a sheltered location, preferably below timberline. Do this as soon as you have given first aid, stabilized the victim's condition, and prepared the person for travel.

An ill or injured climber may be able to get down a snow slope by using some form of assisted sitting glissade. Sometimes the climber can be lowered in a sitting glissade position. Or a rescuer can sit in front of the victim, smoothing the track, both tied together and on belay. A victim in relatively good condition can be roped in with two or three companions who then glissade slowly as a team, constantly under control. An injured climber who is unable to glissade can be put into a bivy sack, insulated with pads or clothes, and carefully slid down the slope.

Rescuers can set up anchors for belays and braking devices by using pickets, flukes, bollards, or improvised deadman anchors (such as a buried ice ax). The boot-ax belay is not strong enough for use in rescues. Moats often provide superb anchor locations for lowering.

Snow evacuations often involve climbers rescued from an avalanche or a crevasse, though they also occur during rescues from rock climbs on peaks above snow-filled basins. (Techniques of avalanche rescue are covered in Chapter 13, and crevasse rescue is explained in Chapter 14.)

# ORGANIZED RESCUE

Alpine and backcountry rescues are sometimes mounted by professional rescue agencies or the military but are most frequently performed by teams of highly trained volunteers. This chapter has emphasized rescue efforts that can be undertaken by small climbing parties with limited equipment. Organized rescue groups bring to the scene the benefits of extensive training and experience, combined with specialized equipment and techniques, including helicopter rescue.

In the Alps, with its large corps of guides and professional rescue companies (the famed Swiss Air Rescue Service is the best-known), organized rescue is all part of the business. In North America, though, where official responsibility for rescues rests with agencies such as the county sheriff's department or National Park Service, mountain rescues are usually carried out by volunteer organizations working closely with these authorities.

Members of volunteer mountain rescue teams draw upon their climbing skills, training, and knowledge of the local mountains to analyze a situation, decide on a course of action, and carry it through. Rescue evacuations usually require a leader and twelve to thirty litter bearers, unless a helicopter is available.

## Specialized Equipment

Rescue teams use equipment specially designed to make their task easier and safer for both themselves and the injured climber. Although many of these items are not standard climbing equipment, every climber should know what they are and what can be done with them.

Most important is a rigid two-piece fiberglass litter. This litter is lighter than the well-known Stokes metal litter and can be broken down into sections for ease of carrying, especially valuable attributes for technical alpine rescues. These litters are also widely used in snow rescues because they slide so well. Many can be fitted with a wide tire for trail carry-outs or with long handles for use as a sled in the snow.

Most rescue teams carry low-stretch ropes that are as long as 600 feet, enabling them to raise or lower an injured climber a considerable distance without having to pass knots through the braking device or set up new anchor stations. The teams use two-way radio equipment to keep in contact with rescue coordinators, medical personnel, and rescue helicopters and to communicate within the team.

## Working with the Team

When a mountain rescue team arrives to aid an injured person in your party, you can help by cooperating closely with the team. The rescue leader will start with an assessment of the situation, concentrating on the status of the injured climber. You can help by also making the rescue leader aware of any climbers who have become exhausted, dehydrated, or hypothermic in the aftermath of the accident or who are feeling shaky on the terrain where rescue efforts are taking place.

The original climb leader will continue in charge of the climbing party while the rescue leader takes over treatment and evacuation of the injured person. However, the climb leader should be prepared to turn over all authority to the rescue leader if requested. The rescue leader will look to members of the rescue team—rather than the climbing party—to perform most of the vital tasks because the team has trained and climbed together. Be prepared to lend a hand if the rescue leader specifically asks for help. *otherwise stay*

## Helicopter Rescue *out of way,*

Helicopters have revolutionized mountain rescue with their ability to insert rescue teams into remote areas or to pluck climbers from cliffs and glaciers and deliver them to the hospital in hours rather than the days sometimes required by ground transport. Rescue helicopters load and transport an injured person in one of three ways. They can land and take the victim aboard. Or they can hover while the injured person, safely attached to a steel cable, is winched aboard. Or

they can fly the injured person to safety as he or she dangles from a cable beneath the helicopter, tied into a harness or litter.

Don't base your rescue plans on an immediate helicopter rescue just because you know helicopters are used in your area. A helicopter or a crew to fly it may not be available exactly when you need help. Helicopter operation will be limited by bad weather, poor visibility, hot temperatures, or high altitude. *Glacier surface*

The following are safety precautions to take during a helicopter rescue:

- Secure loose items to keep them from being blown away or pulled up into the helicopter's rotors. Put gear in packs or weight it down with rocks. Remove caps unless they are secured by a helmet or chin strap. Tuck away any loose straps.
- Stay out from under cliffs where the helicopter's rotor wash could cause rockfall. In such an area, wear helmets and eye protection and use safety lines.
- Never approach the helicopter unless signaled to do so by a crew member.
- Always approach from the front of the ship. The crew cannot see you if you approach from the rear, and you may be in danger from the tail rotor, which spins too fast to see.
- Approach the helicopter from the downhill side—not from uphill, where the main rotor blades can spin quite close to the ground.

Your main concern should be the safety of yourself and the injured person. Don't rush just because the helicopter is waiting, and always bear in mind where you are in relation to it. Protect the injured climber from the rotor wash and flying debris, and explain what is going on before moving that person to the helicopter. With proper safety precautions, a helicopter can bring a speedy conclusion to what may have been an exhausting and dangerous rescue operation.

Overleaf: *Cordillera Sarmiento, Chile* ©*Gordon Wiltsie; overleaf inset:* ©*Roman Dial/Adventure Photo*

# PART SIX

# THE MOUNTAIN ENVIRONMENT

# 21
# MOUNTAIN GEOLOGY

Geology casts the template for mountaineering. It molds landscapes, caps peaks, dictates summit routes and descents, engineers handholds, and deposits rocks that crumble.

Understanding geology requires little more than applying physics and chemistry to the processes that shape the earth. Minerals are chemical compounds like salt or sugar. And rocks are combinations of minerals, just as a chocolate chip cookie is a combination of chemical compounds—some fused together and others discrete chunks. Folds and faults are simply the earth's way of bending and stretching. Geology from this perspective is not so mysterious. We are surrounded, supported, and involved with it every day.

## GEOLOGIC SCALES

Climbers can gain a better understanding of mountains by examining them on three scales: as a landscape, as solitary outcrops, and as individual rocks. Each scale contributes to our overall comprehension.

The first, wide-angle view of geology is the "landscape" perspective: a view of the mountains or range as a whole from several miles away. Observing geology at this scale helps the climber anticipate climbing routes, looking for strong, supporting formations, areas where rock may be weak or unreliable, places to trust, and places for caution. Ridges may follow a resistant bed or volcanic dike. Sharp canyons may suggest a fault or an abrupt change in rock type. Flat-topped plateaus often denote volcanic flows. The overall form of the mountain provides information about its history.

The second scale focuses on specific outcrops. If you examine an outcrop from 10 to 100 feet away, you'll find features that could help—or hinder—an ascent: a regular pattern of cracks that are good bets for chocks, or a resistant dike that provides an avenue upward. At this scale, you can often see structure—folds and faults—that is not evident at larger or smaller scales.

The third scale is a close-up view. With your nose close to the outcrop, the details of rocks are more apparent. At this scale you can recognize what type of rock it is—basalt or granite or something else—and anticipate its particular climbing problems or advantages.

## MOUNTAIN MATERIALS

The rocks that compose mountains are the foundation of the climbing experience. Each type of rock hosts different joint patterns or cleaves in a different manner. The minerals that compose a rock determine how quickly it decomposes or how resistant and reliable its support may be.

### Minerals

Only seven minerals compose most rocks of the earth's crust. Six of these are silicate minerals: feldspar, quartz, olivine, pyroxene, amphibole, and biotite. These silicates are generally hard and resistant to weathering. Only one common rock-forming mineral, calcite, is soft and soluble. Calcite is a carbonate, composed of calcium carbonate (the major ingredient in many antacid tablets). It is resistant and stable in arid climates but dissolves readily in the water (and acid rain) of more humid climates.

Of the seven minerals, feldspar and quartz are the most resistant to decay under the constant assault of nature. They are also the most abundant rock-forming minerals. They compose most granites and sandstones. The other silicates (olivine, pyroxene, amphibole, and biotite) are dark, iron-rich minerals. Abundant fine-grained olivine and pyroxene create the dark color of basalt. Amphibole and biotite are most familiar as the black specks in granite.

## Rocks

Of all life's common things, we probably know the least about rocks. Rocks are merely aggregates of minerals. But their bewildering variety makes them confusing. Plants and animals are one species or another, defined by a DNA recipe. An animal is either a horse or an eagle or a boa constrictor, but it cannot be a cross among them. Rocks have no such limitations. They are a continuous spectrum of color, content, form, and composition. Classification systems help, but many rocks lap over the edges between categories.

Rocks are like a box of chocolates. You can't tell what flavor they are until you look inside each one. Weathered surfaces are deceptive. To identify a rock's true color and appearance, you often have to break it open and look at a fresh surface. Beneath the weathered, brown exterior you may find a black basalt, or a white rhyolite, or even a glassy obsidian.

The best way to understand rocks is to consider the processes that form them (a sort of geological genetic system). Rocks are subdivided into three "genetic" categories: igneous (cooled from molten lava), sedimentary (deposited by water or wind), and metamorphic (changed from one of the other two categories by heat and/or pressure).

### Igneous Rocks

The most fundamental rocks are igneous, a word with roots in Greek meaning fire. Igneous rocks (fig. 21-1) cool from fluid, molten material (magma). There are two broad categories of igneous rock: volcanic (extrusive) and plutonic (intrusive).

**Volcanic rocks (extrusive rocks):** These erupt on the surface as molten lava and cool quickly with little time for crystals to grow. They are usually fine-grained. They may also display small holes where gas bubbles collected as the lava flowed and chilled.

Common volcanic rocks include dark-colored basalt, gray andesite (named after the Andes volcanoes), lighter-colored rhyolite and dacite, and their dark, glassy twin, obsidian. Basalt and andesite are abundant in the volcanic High Cascades of the western United States: in Oregon, basalt forms North Sister, while andesite dominates Mount Jefferson. Dacite and rhyodacite, which, like rhyolite and obsidian, are viscous and cannot flow very far, often compose domes—piles of lava built atop the vent—high on volcanic peaks. In the Cascades, Crater Rock on Mount Hood and the ridge just east of Clark Glacier on South Sister are dacite domes.

Volcanic rocks that are produced by explosive (pyroclastic) eruptions are composed of ash rather than lava. Volcanic ash that is compressed into rock is known as tuff. A rock called welded tuff forms when very hot, nearly molten ash literally sticks or welds together. The popular routes at the Smith Rock climbing area in the state of Oregon ascend vertical walls of welded tuff. Volcanic mudflows (or *lahars*) are considered both volcanic and sedimentary in nature.

**Plutonic rocks (intrusive rocks):** These form from lava (or magma) that never reaches the surface. These rocks slowly solidify underground.

Because there is time for crystals to grow as the rock solidifies, plutonic rocks are coarse-grained. The rocks have a salt-and-pepper appearance. Plutonic rocks include gabbro, a dark-colored equivalent of basalt; diorite, which looks like granite; and everybody's favorite, real granite, which tends to be white, although there are dark pink or red granites in the Rocky Mountains of Colorado and Wyoming.

Most people use the term *granite* for any coarse-grained, light-colored igneous rock, but many rocks that look like granite are not granite by geologists' definition. They do not have the right percentages of minerals to qualify as pedigreed granite. Granite look-alikes include granodiorite and diorite, which form the heart of California's Sierra Nevada range and the Mount Stuart area of the northern Cascades.

The cooled bodies of plutonic rocks come in many

different sizes and shapes. The largest bodies, by definition greater than 100 square kilometers in area, are known as batholiths. Smaller bodies are known as stocks. The narrow conduits of magma that slice through rock are known as dikes. On rare occasions dictated by the right tectonic circumstances, fragments of the earth's mantle arrive on mountaintops. In the North Cascades, a scrap of mantle rock called the Twin Sisters Dunite forms the top of Twin Sisters peaks.

## Sedimentary Rocks

Sedimentary rocks (fig. 21-2) are the earth's history book. Their fossils reveal primeval ecosystems; their textures evoke ancient seas. Most sedimentary rocks are deposited in layers, or beds, and can be distinguished from igneous or metamorphic rocks by this feature.

Most sedimentary rocks are classified according to grain size. Fine-grained rocks, including thinly bedded shales, are the scions of quiet, low-energy water. Coarse-grained rocks, including sandstones and conglomerates, are transported and deposited by higher-energy, turbulent flow. Limestones, composed of coral and sea shells, develop in tropic waters.

Sedimentary rocks are the repository of fossils, and fossils are usually the only guide to their age. In fine-grained rocks, microscopic fossils of one-celled plants or animals provide clues to the age of the ancient seafloor. These fossils and sedimentary rocks also help us understand how far-dispersed the earth's plates have become: fossils of an Asiatic sea cap, the Matterhorn in the Swiss Alps, corals rim Alaska's Brooks range, and sediments of a subtropical seafloor grace the summit of Mount Everest.

## Metamorphic Rocks

Metamorphic rocks are merely igneous or sedimentary rocks that have been changed by heat and pres-

| COLOR/MINERAL CONTENT: | VOLCANIC (EXTRUSIVE):  fine-grained rock erupted as lava or ash; cools quickly; may contain small holes or crystals | PLUTONIC (INTRUSIVE): 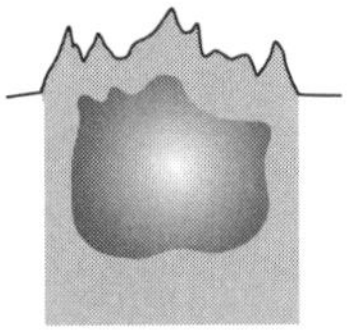 coarse-grained rock that cools and crystallizes slowly underground |
|---|---|---|
| LIGHT–COLORED; VERY LITTLE IRON IN ROCK | Rhyolite or Dacite (black, glassy = Obsidian) | Granite or Granodiorite |
| USUALLY GRAY; MODERATE IRON IN ROCK | Andesite | Diorite |
| DARK: BLACK TO GREEN–BLACK; HIGH IRON CONTENT | Basalt | Gabbro or Peridotite (rare) |

*Fig. 21-1. Classification of igneous rocks*

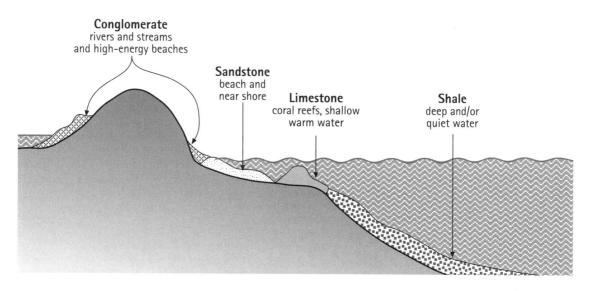

*Fig. 21-2. Sedimentary rock types*

sure. These changes vary from barely discernible meta-morphism of the Precambrian sediments exposed in Glacier National Park in the United States to the high-temperature metamorphism that created the granite-like rocks of Nanga Parbat in Pakistan.

Generally six kinds of metamorphic rock can be easily identified: slate, schist, gneiss, amphibolite, marble, and greenstone.

**Slate:** This is basically a harder, shinier shale, a clay-rich sedimentary rock that has been slightly heated and compressed.

**Schist:** Produced at greater metamorphic intensity, schist is a flaky (friable) rock with thin layers of mica and other shiny minerals.

**Gneiss:** Produced at a still-higher level in tempera-ture and pressure, gneiss looks like a granite with rac-ing stripes. Gneiss is a hard, banded rock.

**Amphibolite:** This is a dark rock similar to gneiss but lacking the exuberant banding. Amphibolite forms much of the North Cascades and the Teton Range in the state of Wyoming.

**Marble:** Heated and recrystallized limestone, marbles can be extremely hard, resistant rocks—espe-cially in arid areas—or they may be crumbly and ex-tremely difficult to climb, with large calcite crystals and a texture like coarse granulated sugar.

**Greenstone:** This is a catch-all term for a metamor-phosed basalt.

Serpentine is a rare, shiny green or black rock sometimes associated with greenstones and dark ig-neous rocks like gabbro and peridotite. It can be found on the Twin Sisters peaks in Washington state. It is a slippery, highly fractured rock that presents a haz-ard for climbers in the few alpine locations where it occurs.

Migmatite is the ultimate in recycling: metamor-phic rocks heated to the melting point. The upper slopes of Nanga Parbat in the Himalayas expose migmatite. Migmatites that melt become magmas and begin the whole rock cycle over again.

## ── MOUNTAIN OUTCROPS: THE ── STRUCTURE OF THE MOUNTAIN

If rocks and minerals are the building blocks of moun-tains, then structure—the folds and joints and faults that shape the rocks—are the architect's plans. While these features come in all sizes, they are easiest to rec-ognize at "outcrop" scale.

## Folds

Folding is a rock's most graceful—and plastic—response to stress. Consider a sheet of plywood. If you push gently and persistently on this thin, seemingly brittle material, the plywood will bend or fold slowly, over a long period of time. Folds in rock, as well as plywood, are the result of long-term compression, of pushing together.

Mountain ranges created by compression and collision, including the Alps, Appalachians, and Himalayas, commonly contain folds. Upfolds are called anticlines; downfolds are called synclines. Folds appear on all scales, from a single fold the size of a mountain to wrinkles visible only under a microscope. Everest's Nuptse-Lhotse Wall displays intricate anticlines and synclines more than a hundred meters high.

## Joints

Like any brittle solid, rocks tend to crack when they are deformed. Geologists refer to these cracks as joints. Joints occur in more or less regular, geometric patterns. They develop at all scales, from microscopic to mountain-size. On a large scale, these cracks may provide the dominant fabric of the rock upon which a climber relies for holds and rests.

In igneous rocks, joints are related to the rock's cooling history. Basalts develop columns; granites produce several sets of joints, including exfoliation joints as pressure is released.

In sedimentary and metamorphic rocks, joints are usually produced by stress—folding and faulting. These joints may be related to folds or other structures in the rock. Such small-scale joints often cut through sedimentary rock bedding, creating rocks that break easily and provide risky climbing conditions.

## Faults

A fault is a break in the rock along which some tectonic movement has occurred. Faults of interest to climbers range from those that uplift entire mountain ranges—like the Wasatch fault that uplifts the mountains from Salt Lake City to Provo, Utah—to unnamed fractures that offset bedding a few inches. Faults may present climbing hazards due to the broken rock (breccia) that occupies a fault zone.

Faults that mountaineers may encounter come in four varieties: reverse faults, thrust faults, normal faults, and strike-slip faults. Each type represents a different kind of tectonic movement. Some of each of these types of faults are active today. Movement along an active fault produces earthquakes.

Reverse faults and thrust faults are produced when continents collide. They are most common in mountains like the Alps or Himalayas. The Himalayas are being upthrust rapidly along these faults, creating thousands of small earthquakes each year. Normal faults pull rocks apart. They occur when the earth's brittle crust is stretched too far and breaks. Normal faults created the fault block mountains of Nevada's Basin and Range. Southern Nevada ranks among North America's most active seismic regions. Strike-slip faults, like California's San Andreas, are the least significant to mountaineers. They permit movement in a horizontal plane, rather than up and down.

---

## MOUNTAIN LANDSCAPES: HOW MOUNTAINS ARE FORMED

---

Until we begin to scrutinize the details, most mountain ranges seem similar, but not all mountains are created equal. The solitary peaks in Oregon's High Cascades and the Rockies of Montana are barely geologic cousins. The first is a chain of young volcanoes; the second is a folded layer cake of ancient sediments.

Three major types of mountain ranges provide habitat for climbers: volcanic ranges, such as the Andes and High Cascades; folded (compressional) ranges, like the Rockies and Himalayas; and fault-block (extensional) ranges, such as the Sierra Nevada.

### Volcanic Mountain Ranges

Mountains created by volcanic action are epitomized by solitary peaks. Volcanic mountains can be categorized into three basic types: shield volcanoes, stratovolcanoes (fig. 21-3), and calderas.

**Shield volcanoes:** These volcanoes erupt mostly lava and develop gently sloping sides. Mauna Loa in Hawaii and Newberry Crater in Oregon are examples. The subdued topography of most shield volcanoes provides minimal climbing opportunities.

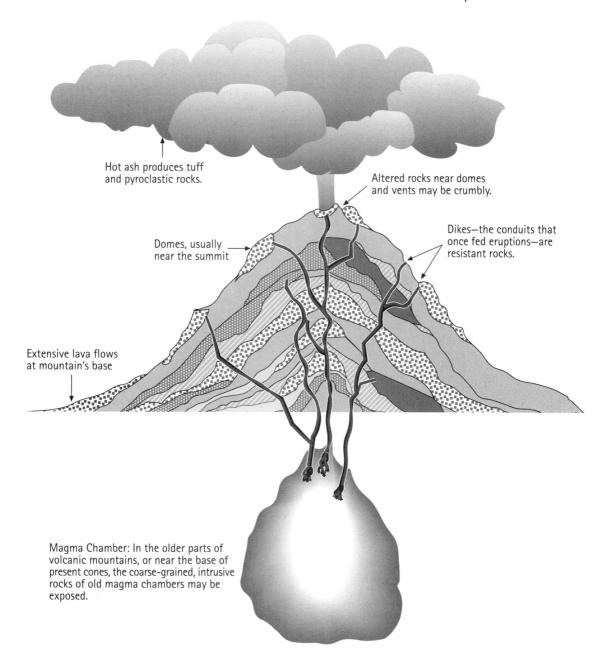

Hot ash produces tuff and pyroclastic rocks.

Altered rocks near domes and vents may be crumbly.

Domes, usually near the summit

Dikes—the conduits that once fed eruptions—are resistant rocks.

Extensive lava flows at mountain's base

Magma Chamber: In the older parts of volcanic mountains, or near the base of present cones, the coarse-grained, intrusive rocks of old magma chambers may be exposed.

*Fig. 21-3. Volcanic mountains are layer cakes of lava and ash. Most volcanic mountains that interest climbers are the lofty stratovolcanoes (built of ash, lava, and mudflows), like Mount Hood, Mount Rainier, and Mount Fuji.*

**Stratovolcanoes:** Also called composite cones, stratovolcanoes erupt ash, cinders, and lava. Much of the Cascade Range that interests climbers consists of young volcanoes known to geologists as the High Cascades. These peaks, including Shasta, Three Sisters, Jefferson, Hood, Adams, Rainier, and Baker, are all stratovolcanoes less than 700,000 years old. These volcanoes are built on older rocks, including those that form the North Cascades. Worldwide, other stratovolcanoes appear generally along coastlines where the seafloor dives beneath the continent, and include Mount Fuji in Japan and the volcanoes of Central and South America. The combination of crumbly cinders and brittle, often glassy, volcanic rock found in stratovolcanoes can produce hazardous climbing conditions.

**Calderas:** In most cases, calderas are difficult to recognize as anything more than flat plains surrounded by a few hills. These volcanoes erupt explosively, sending thin sheets of ash tens or hundreds of miles from the vent. Their eruptive products—welded tuffs—often erode into a climber's nirvana of cliffs, like the yellow rocks of Oregon's Leslie Gulch.

There are other kinds of volcanic mountains. Some are eroded relics of volcanic conduits or near-surface magma chambers. These mountains rise as sharp, isolated peaks, and include Ship Rock in New Mexico and the Henry Mountains in Utah. Tuff cones and tuff rings provide soft, rough rock like Smith Rock, ideal for technical climbs.

Volcanic mountains were built by eruptions, and many are still under construction. Several Cascade peaks—especially Mount Hood, Mount Rainier, and Mount Baker—will erupt again.

## Folded (Compressional) Mountain Ranges

Where the major plates of the earth's crust collide, mountain ranges are built by folding and compression (fig. 21-4). The Himalayas have been uplifted by the collision of India and Asia. The Alps were created by Africa's northward push into Europe.

In these compressional ranges, folding and faulting may combine to thrust one part of the range over another. These huge thrust-faulted structures, known as *knapps,* are well exposed in the Alps.

As faulting, folding, uplift, and erosion expose deeper levels of a compressional range, metamorphic rocks are exposed. The schist of Mount Shuksan in the North Cascades, for example, was clay and silt on the seafloor 250 million years ago. Folding and burial to

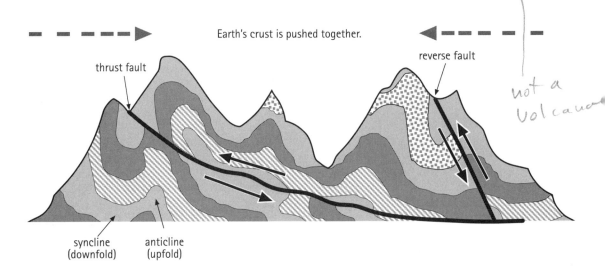

*Fig. 21-4. Folded (compressional) mountain ranges, including the Alps, Himalayas, and Rocky Mountains, are thrust and folded upward, where two plates collide.*

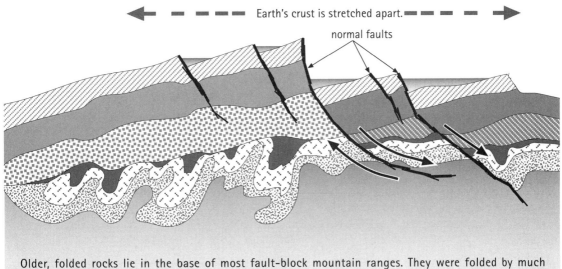

Older, folded rocks lie in the base of most fault-block mountain ranges. They were folded by much earlier compression. In the Sierra Nevada, most of the young rocks have been removed by erosion, leaving the older granites and metamorphic rocks to form the summits.

*Fig. 21-5. Fault-block (extensional) mountain ranges develop where the earth's crust is pulled apart. Huge blocks of crust drop down on one side and tilt up on the other. Examples include the Sierra Nevada and Wasatch Mountains.*

depths of almost 7 miles beneath the earth's surface supplied heat and pressure, transforming soft seafloor sediments into shale and then schist. Continued folding, faulting, and plate tectonic activity has uplifted the Shuksan schist formation to the flanks of one of Washington state's highest peaks. To the south, the eroded remnants of these rocks provide a foundation for the volcanoes of the High Cascades, including Mount Rainier and Mount Adams.

## Fault–Block (Extensional) Mountain Ranges

In some places, like the Himalayas, the earth's crust is pushed together. But in others the crust is stretched and pulled apart. Where the brittle crust is stretched, it ultimately breaks, like pulling cold taffy too quickly. Faults break the crust into huge blocks. In these fault-block mountains (fig. 21-5), one side of the entire fault block rises and the other end sinks deeper into the earth's mantle. This process creates huge block-shaped mountains with nearly vertical faces on one side and more gentle slopes on the other. The mountains in the Basin and Range, including the Wasatch Range and the Sierra Nevada, are fault-block ranges. Streams and glaciation have chiseled peaks and valleys from a fairly solid block.

Fault-block (extensional) mountains are more rare and generally less extensive than ranges where compression squeezes rocks to great height, but not always. Mount Whitney, part of the Sierra Nevada fault-block range, is the highest peak in the contiguous United States (14,494 feet); Wheeler Peak of the Snake Range in eastern Nevada rises above 13,000 feet.

In a world composed of rocks, knowing a little about geology can help us climb them. And maybe help us appreciate where we are going, and where we—and the mountains—have been.

# THE CYCLE OF SNOW

Snow crystals form in the atmosphere as water vapor condenses at temperatures below freezing. They form around centers of foreign matter, such as microscopic dust particles, and grow as more atmospheric water vapor condenses onto them. Tiny water droplets also may contribute to snow crystal growth. The crystals generally are hexagonal, but variations in size and shape are almost limitless and include plates, columns, and needles (fig. 22-1). The particular shape depends on the air temperature and the amount of water vapor available.

When a snow crystal falls through air masses with different temperature and water-vapor conditions, more complex or combined types may develop. Crystals in air that have a temperature near freezing stick together to become snowflakes, aggregates of individual crystals. When snow crystals fall through air that contains water droplets, the droplets freeze to the crystals, forming the rounded snow particles called *graupel* (soft hail).

The density of new-fallen snow depends on weather conditions. The lowest-density snow (lightest and driest) falls under moderately cold and very calm conditions. At extremely low temperatures, the new snow is fine and granular, with somewhat higher densities. The general rule is that the higher the temperature, the more dense (heavier and wetter) the snow, though density varies widely in the range of 20 to 32 degrees Fahrenheit (minus 7 to 0 degrees Celsius). The very highest densities are associated with graupel or needle crystals falling at temperatures near freezing. The percentage of water in new-fallen snow ranges from 1 to 30 percent, sometimes even higher, with the average for mountain snowfall being 7 to 10 percent. Wind affects snow density, for high winds break up falling crystals into fragments that pack together to form dense, fine-grained snow. The stronger the wind, the denser the snow.

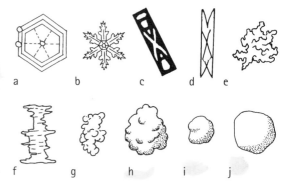

*Fig. 22-1. Snow crystal forms: a, plates; b, stellar crystals; c, columns; d, needles; e, spatial dendrites (combinations of feathery crystals); f, capped columns; g, irregular particles (compounds of microscopic crystals); h, graupel (soft hail); i, sleet (icy shell, inside wet); j, hail (solid ice).*

## SURFACE FORMS OF SNOW COVER

Snow and ice undergo endless surface changes as they are worked on by wind, temperature, sun, freeze-and-thaw cycles, and rain. Following is a rundown on most of the surface permutations mountaineers typically encounter. See Figure 22-2 for a summary of the dangers and travel considerations associated with these various forms of snow.

**Rime:** This is a type of snow that forms right at ground level. It is the dull white, dense deposit formed from the freezing of droplets of water on trees, rocks, and other objects exposed to the wind. Rime deposits build up toward the wind. Rime may form large feathery flakes or a solid incrustation, but it lacks regular crystalline patterns.

**Hoarfrost:** Hoarfrost is another type of snow that forms at ground level. Unlike rime, hoarfrost displays distinct crystalline shapes: blades, cups, and scrolls. Hoarfrost forms on solid objects by the process of sublimation—the direct conversion of atmospheric water vapor to a solid. Deposited on top of snow, it is known as surface hoar and is generally produced during a cold, clear night. The crystals appear fragile and feathery and sparkle brilliantly in sunlight. A heavy deposit of surface hoar makes for fast, excellent skiing with fun, crinkly sounds.

**Powder snow:** This is a popular term for light, fluffy new-fallen snow. Powder snow, however, is more specifically defined as new snow that has lost some of its cohesion due to the recrystallizing effects of large temperature differences between the pits and peaks of a feathery dendrite crystal. The changed snow is loose and powdery, commonly affords good downhill skiing, and may form dry loose-snow avalanches. It is difficult to climb or walk through powder because it is mostly air, and any weight on it will readily sink.

**Corn snow:** After the advent of melting in early spring, a period of fair weather may be followed by formation of coarse, rounded crystals on the snow surface, often called corn snow. The crystals are formed from the daily melting and refreezing of snow. Only when the same surface layer continues to melt and refreeze does true corn snow develop. When corn snow thaws each morning after the nighttime freeze, it is great for skiing and stepkicking. Later in the day, after thawing has continued, corn snow can become too thick and gooey for easy travel. During the afternoon, the associated meltwater also may contribute a type of lubrication to the underlying snow and promote wet loose-snow avalanches, especially if the snow is stressed by glissading or by the sliding and turning of skis, snowboards, and snowmobiles.

**Rotten snow:** Rotten snow is a spring condition characterized by soft, wet layers that offer little support to the firmer layers above. In its worst forms, it will not support even the weight of a skier. Snow that promises good spring skiing in the morning, while there is some strength in the crust, may deteriorate to rotten snow later in the day. Rotten snow forms when lower layers of the very weak type of snow known as depth hoar become wet and lose what little strength they have. It is a condition that often leads to wet loose-snow or slab avalanches running clear to the ground. Continental climates, such as those of the American Rockies, often produce rotten snow. Maritime climates, like the Pacific coastal ranges, which usually have deep, dense snow covers, are less likely to produce rotten snow conditions.

**Meltwater crust:** This is a snow crust formed when water melted at the surface is refrozen and bonds snow crystals into a cohesive layer.

*Sun crust* is a common variety of meltwater crust, getting its name from its main source of heat for melting. Heat to permit meltwater crusts also comes from warm air or condensation at the snow surface. In winter and early spring the thickness of a sun crust usually is determined by the thickness of the surface layer where meltwater is formed in otherwise dry snow. Often it is thin enough to break through, making skiing and walking very uncomfortable. In later spring and summer when free water is found throughout the snow cover, the thickness, usually less than about 2 inches, depends on how cold it gets at night.

*Rain crust* is another type of meltwater crust; it forms after rainwater has percolated into the surface layers of snow. The rainwater often follows preferred paths as it percolates through the snow and creates fingerlike features that act as pinning points and hold the crust to the underlying snow after it refreezes. This pinning feature of many rain crusts helps to stabilize

| SNOW CONDITION | TRAVEL | PROTECTION | DANGER |
|---|---|---|---|
| Rime | Breakable; can trap | – | – |
| Hoarfrost | Fun skiing | – | If hoarfrost buried, potential avalanche danger |
| Powder snow | Difficult walking, good skiing | Ropes cut through; axes don't hold; clogs crampons; "deadmen" need reinforcing with buried packs, etc. | Potential avalanche danger |
| Corn snow | Best walking in morning; best skiing in afternoon | Bollards must be large to hold | Avalanche potential low when frozen and depends on water content and underlying layer strengths when melted |
| Rotten snow | Difficult traveling | Ropes cut through; axes don't hold; clogs crampons; "deadmen" need reinforcing with buried packs, etc. | Potential avalanche danger |
| Meltwater crust | Breakable; can trap feet if thin crust; good walking if thick; skis require edges | May require crampons | Slippery |
| Wind slab | Good walking | – | Potential avalanche, especially on leeward slopes |
| Firnspiegel | Breakable | – | – |
| Verglas | Breakable; can trap feet | – | Slippery |
| Sun cups | Uneven, but solid walking or skiing | – | Low danger; usually form in old, stable snow |
| Nieve penitentes | Difficult to negotiate | Ropes catch | Low danger; usually form in old, stable snow |
| Drain channels | Uneven, but solid walking or skiing | – | Avalanche potential depends on underlying layer strengths |
| Sastrugi | Uneven, but solid walking or skiing | Ropes catch | Is a sign of wind transport and potential slab formation; also, ski edges may catch |
| Cornices | Difficult to negotiate; best to avoid | Ropes cut through | Can break away |
| Crevasses | Difficult to negotiate; may be hidden by snow; best to avoid | Require rope protection | Easy to fall into, especially if hidden |
| Seracs | Difficult to negotiate; best to avoid | Ropes catch | Very unstable; can break catastrophically |
| Avalanche paths | Hard surface, good walking | – | Slippery; relatively free from avalanche danger unless portion of slab remaining or recharged by new snow |
| Avalanche debris | Difficult to negotiate | – | Relatively free from avalanche danger unless portion of slab remaining or recharged by new snow |

*Fig. 22-2. Snow conditions and their related travel considerations and dangers*

the snow against avalanching and makes for strong walking surfaces, especially in the coastal mountain ranges where heavy winter rainfall is not uncommon, even at high elevations. Glazed crusts can be extremely slippery and dangerous.

**Wind slab:** After surface snow layers are disturbed by the wind, age-hardening takes place. Fragments of snow crystals broken by the wind are compacted together when they come to rest, adding to the process. The hardening is compounded when the wind provides heat, particularly through water-vapor condensation. Even when there is not enough heat to cause melting, the warming of the disturbed surface layer, followed by cooling when the wind dies, provides additional metamorphic hardening. Traveling usually is fast and easy on hard wind slabs, but the slabs can break in long-running fractures and, if overlying a weak layer, added stress causes avalanching.

**Firnspiegel:** The thin layer of clear ice sometimes seen on snow surfaces in spring or summer is called firnspiegel. In the right conditions of sunlight and slope angle, its reflection produces the brilliant sheen of "glacier fire." Firnspiegel forms when solar radiation penetrates the snow and causes melting just below the surface at the same time that freezing conditions prevail at the surface. Once formed, it acts like a greenhouse, allowing snow to melt beneath while the transparent ice layer remains frozen at the surface. Firnspiegel usually is paper thin and quite breakable. Unlike sun crusts, breaking through firnspiegel while traveling causes little discomfort.

**Verglas:** This is a layer of thin, clear ice formed from water freezing on rock. It is most commonly encountered at higher elevations in the spring or summer when a freeze follows a thaw. The water comes from rainfall or melting snow. Verglas also may be formed directly by supercooled raindrops freezing as they fall onto exposed objects ("freezing rain," also sometimes inaccurately called "silver thaw"). Verglas forms a very slippery surface and, like "black ice" on a roadway, it can be difficult to anticipate.

**Sun cups:** Sun cups (ablation hollows) can vary in depth from 1 inch to 2 feet or more (fig. 22-3a). Cup depths usually increase with increasing elevation and decreasing latitude where sunshine is intense and the air is relatively dry.

On the ridges of each cup, sun-heated water

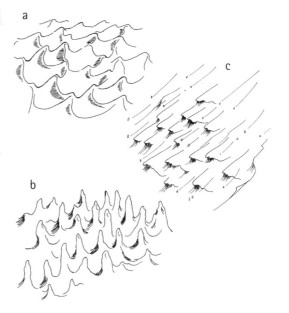

Fig. 22-3. Surface features on snow: a, sun cups; b, nieve penitentes; c, sastrugi.

molecules evaporate away from the snow surface. In the hollows, water molecules released by solar heating are trapped near the snow surface, forming a liquid layer that promotes further melt. Because melting can occur with only one-seventh of the heat that is required for evaporation, the hollows melt and deepen faster than the ridges evaporate. The hollows are further deepened by differential melting when dirt in the hollows absorbs solar radiation. The sun cups melt faster on the south (sunny) side in the Northern Hemisphere, so the whole sun cup pattern gradually migrates northward across its snowfield.

Warm, moist winds tend to destroy sun cups by causing faster melt at the high points and edges. A prolonged summer storm accompanied by fog, wind, and rain often will erase a sun cup pattern completely, but they start to form again as soon as dry, fair weather returns.

It is easy to catch an edge while skiing over sun cups, especially if they are hard and frozen from nighttime cooling. The unevenness of sun-cupped surfaces makes walking uphill tedious, but traveling downhill is made a little easier by "skating" into each hollow.

**Nieve penitentes:** When sun cups grow up, they become *nieve penitentes* (Spanish for "penitent snow"). They are the pillars produced when sun cups intersect to leave columns of snow standing between the hollows (fig. 22-3b). They are peculiar to snowfields at high altitudes and low latitudes, where radiation and atmospheric conditions conducive to sun cups are intense. Nieve penitentes reach their most striking development among the higher peaks of the Andes and the Himalayas, where they may become several feet high and make mountain travel very difficult. The columns often slant toward the midday sun.

**Drain channels:** After melting has begun in spring, drainage patterns formed by the runoff of water appear on snowfields. The actual flow takes place within the snowpack, however, not on the surface. As snow melts at the surface, the water formed percolates downward until it encounters impervious layers, which deflect its course, or highly permeable layers, which it can easily follow. Much of the water also reaches the earth beneath. Water that flows within the snow often causes a branching pattern of channels that appear on the surface. This happens because the flowing water accelerates the snow settlement around its channels, which are soon outlined by depressions at the surface. The dirt that collects in these depressions absorbs solar radiation and accentuates them further by differential melting.

On a sloping surface, drain channels flow downhill and form a parallel ridge pattern that can make turning while glissading or skiing a little difficult. On flat surfaces, drain fields create a dimply looking surface, similar to sun cups but more rounded. The appearance of dimples or drain channels suggests that significant water has percolated into the snow cover. If these dimples or channels are frozen, it can be a good sign of stability against avalanches. However, if they are newly formed and still soft with liquid water, snow stability may be compromised by meltwater that has percolated into a susceptible buried layer and weakened it.

**Sastrugi:** The surface of dry snow develops a variety of erosional forms from the scouring of wind, such as small ripples and irregularities. On high ridges and treeless arctic territory, under the full sweep of the wind, these features attain considerable size. Most characteristic are the wavelike forms, with sharp prows directed toward the prevailing wind, known as sastrugi (fig. 22-3c). A field of sastrugi—hard, unyielding, and as much as several feet high—can make for tough going. High winds over featureless snow plains also produce dunes similar to those found in desert sand, with the crescent-shaped dune, or barchan, being most common. These stiff, uneven features cause difficult traveling, especially when ice or rocky ground is exposed between each.

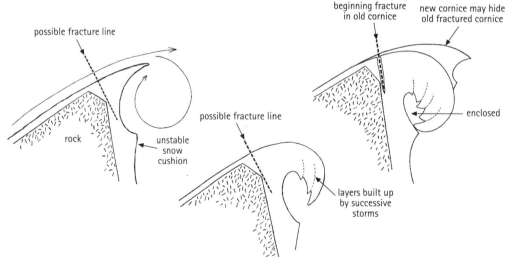

*Fig. 22-4. Formation of cornices*

**Cornices:** Cornices are deposits of snow on the lee edge of ridges or other features (fig. 22-4). They offer a particular hazard because they overhang, forming an unstable mass that may break off from human disturbance or natural causes. Falling cornices are dangerous in themselves and also can set off avalanches. During storms, the precipitated snow furnishes material for cornice formation. Cornices also are formed or enlarged by material blown in from snowfields that lie to windward. As a general rule, cornices formed during snowstorms are softer than those produced by wind drift alone.

## AGING OF THE SNOW COVER

Snow that remains on the ground changes with time. The crystals undergo a process of change—metamorphism—that usually results in smaller, simpler forms and a snowpack that shrinks and settles. Because the snowpack continually changes over time, mountaineers find it useful to know the recent history of weather and snow conditions in an area.

Metamorphism begins the moment that snow falls and lasts until it melts. The equilibrium growth process gradually converts the varied original forms of the crystals into homogeneous rounded grains of ice (old snow) (fig. 22-5). Both temperature and pressure affect the rate of change. When temperature within the snow is near the freezing point (32 degrees Fahrenheit [0 degrees Celsius]), change is rapid. The colder it gets, the slower the change, and it virtually stops

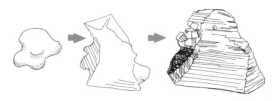

*Fig. 22-6. Kinetic metamorphism of a snow crystal*

below minus 40 degrees Fahrenheit (minus 40 degrees Celsius). Pressure from the weight of new snowfall over an older layer speeds changes within the layer. Snow that has reached old age—surviving at least one year and with all original crystals now converted into grains of ice—is called firn (or névé). Any further changes to firn snow lead to formation of glacier ice.

Another type of metamorphism takes place when water vapor is transferred from one part of the snowpack to another by vertical diffusion and is deposited in the form of ice crystals with characteristics different from those of the original snow. This kinetic growth produces faceted crystals (fig. 22-6). When the process is carried to completion, the crystals often have a scroll or cup shape, appear to be layered, and may grow to considerable size. They form a fragile structure that loses all strength when crushed and becomes very soft when wet. This weak and unstable snow form is depth hoar, popularly referred to as sugar snow. The necessary conditions for its formation are a large difference in temperature at different depths in the snow and

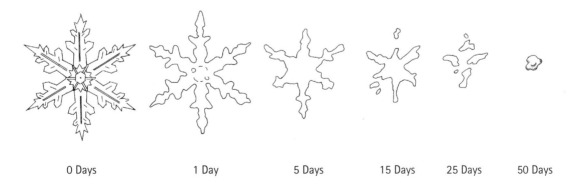

| 0 Days | 1 Day | 5 Days | 15 Days | 25 Days | 50 Days |

*Fig. 22-5. Equilibrium metamorphism of a snow crystal*

sufficient air space so that water vapor can diffuse freely. The conditions are most common early in winter when the snowpack is shallow and unconsolidated.

Variations in the strength of snow are among the widest found in nature, with strength continually changing due to metamorphism, temperature differences, and wind. The hardness of wind-packed old snow may be 50,000 times that of fluffy new snow. An increase in hardness is always associated with wind-drifted snow, or snow mechanically disturbed in any fashion, which undergoes a process known as age-hardening for several hours after it is disturbed. This hardening is what makes it easier to travel in snow if you follow previously set foot, ski, snowshoe, or snowmobile tracks.

## — THE FORMATION OF GLACIERS —

Glaciers form for a rather simple reason. Snow that does not melt or evaporate during the year is carried over to the next winter. If snow continues to accumulate year after year, eventually consolidating and beginning a slow downhill movement, a glacier is formed. (For information on mountaineering involving glaciers, see Chapter 14, Glacier Travel and Crevasse Rescue.)

Within the old snow (the firn, or névé), the metamorphic conversion of snow crystals into grains of ice has been completed. Now the grains of ice are changed into glacier ice in a process called firnification. Firn turns into glacier ice when the air spaces between the grains become sealed off from each other so that the mass becomes airtight (fig. 22-7).

Part of the glacier ice is formed by refreezing of percolating meltwater each spring when the lower snow layers are still at temperatures below freezing. This refrozen meltwater forms ice layers within the firn. Therefore, by the time compaction and metamorphism have prepared an entire area of firn for conversion to glacier ice, it may already contain irregular bodies of ice.

Once glacier ice has formed, metamorphism does not cease. Through crystallographic changes, some of the ice grains continue to grow at the expense of their neighbors, and the average size of the ice crystals increases with age (fig. 22-8). Large glaciers, in which

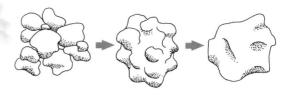

Fig. 22-7. Rounded snow grains pressed and squeezed together, forming large glacier ice crystals

the ice takes centuries to reach the terminus, may produce crystals more than 1 foot in diameter, gigantic specimens grown from minute snow particles.

In our imagination, we can follow the birth of a simple valley-type alpine glacier. Picture a mountain in the Northern Hemisphere that has no glaciers. Now suppose climatic changes occur that cause snow to persist from year to year in a sheltered spot on a northern exposure. From the beginning, snow starts to flow toward the valley in the very slow motion called creep. New layers are added each year, the patch of firn snow grows deeper and bigger, and the amount of snow in motion increases. The creeping snow dislodges soil and rock, while the melting, refreezing, and flow of water

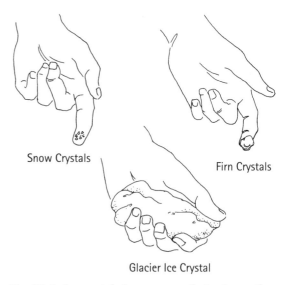

Snow Crystals

Firn Crystals

Glacier Ice Crystal

Fig. 22-8. Ice crystals increase greatly in size as they transform from snowflakes and firn into glacier ice.

around and under the snow patch additionally impact the surroundings. This small-scale process of erosion eventually leads to formation of a hollow where the winter snows are deposited in deeper drifts. After the snow deepens beyond 100 feet or so, the increasing pressure of the many upper layers of firn causes the lower layers to begin turning to glacier ice. A glacier is born.

With continued nourishment from heavy winter snows, the glacier flows toward the valley as a stream of ice. At some point in its descent, the glacier reaches an elevation low enough and warm enough that no new snow accumulates. The glacier ice begins to melt. Eventually the glacier reaches the point, even lower and warmer, at which all ice carried down from above melts each year. This is the lower limit of the glacier.

Glaciers vary from stagnant masses with little motion to vigorously flowing rivers of ice that transport large masses each year from higher to lower elevations. Glaciers in relatively temperate climates flow both by internal deformation and by sliding on their beds. Differences in speed within the glacier are somewhat like that in a river, fastest at the center and surface and slower at the sides and bottom where bedrock creates a drag. Small polar glaciers present a striking difference in appearance from their temperate cousins, for they are frozen to their beds and can flow only by internal deformation. The polar glaciers look much like flowing molasses, while temperate glaciers are rivers of broken ice.

## Crevasses

Crevasses are important features of glaciers. Crevasses are fractures that occur when ice encounters a force greater than it can bear. Near the surface of a glacier, where ice is just beginning to form, the ice is full of tiny flaws and weakly bonded crystals. When it stretches or bends too fast, it can break apart in a brittle manner, like glass. The result is a crevasse.

Crevasses typically are 80 to 100 feet deep. Deeper than that, ice layers become stronger, with increasingly large and well-bonded crystals. When stresses try to pull this deeply buried ice apart, overlying pressure further squeezes it together, causing it to flow and deform like thick, gooey honey. In colder glaciers—at high elevations or in polar climates—crevasses can penetrate

somewhat deeper because colder ice is more brittle and tends to break more easily.

Temperate glaciers normally have more (and shallower) crevasses than polar glaciers because the temperate glaciers usually move faster. When glaciers move very fast, such as over icefalls, extensive fracturing occurs. The numerous crevasses link together, isolating columns of ice called seracs.

## Ice Avalanches

Glaciers are breeding grounds for ice avalanches, which can pour from hanging glaciers, icefalls, and any serac-covered portion of a glacier. They are caused by a combination of glacier movement, temperature, and serac configuration. On warm, low-elevation glaciers, ice avalanches are most common during late summer and early fall when meltwater has accumulated enough to flow underneath the glacier and increase its movement. The avalanche activity of high-elevation glaciers and cold glaciers that are frozen to the bedrock has no such seasonal cycle.

There are differing reports on the most active time of day for ice avalanches. Field observers suggest they are most common during the afternoon. This may be possible in a snow-covered serac field if daytime heating loosens snow enough to avalanche into seracs and cause them to fall, creating an ice avalanche. However, scientists have discovered an increase in activity during the early morning hours when the ice is cold and most brittle. Though their frequency varies, ice avalanches can occur any time of year and any time of day or night.

## THE FORMATION OF SNOW AVALANCHES

Numerous combinations of snow patterns cause avalanches. With every snowstorm, a new layer of snow is deposited. Even during the same storm, a different type of layer may be deposited each time the wind shifts or temperatures change. After deposition, the forces of wind, temperature, sun, and gravity continue to alter the character of the layers. Each layer is composed of a set of snow crystals that are similar in shape to each other and that are bonded together in similar ways. Because each layer–each set of crystals–is different, each reacts differently to the various forces. Knowing something about these differences and about the special characteristics of snow can help mountain travelers understand and avoid avalanches. (Also see the section on avalanche safety in Chapter 13, Snow Travel and Climbing, for information on avalanche hazard evaluation and rescue.)

Snow avalanches usually are categorized by their release mechanism: *loose avalanches* (sometimes called loose-snow avalanches) start at a point; *slab avalanches* begin in blocks. Slab avalanches usually are much larger and involve deeper layers of snow. Loose avalanches can be equally dangerous, however–especially if they are wet and heavy, if they catch victims who are above cliffs or crevasses, or if they trigger slab avalanches or serac falls.

## Loose Avalanches

Loose avalanches can occur when new snow builds up on steep slopes and loses its angle of repose. The snow rolls off the slope, entraining more snow as it descends. Sun and rain also can weaken the bonds between snow crystals, especially if they are newly deposited, causing individual grains to roll and slide into loose avalanches. These slides also can be set off by skiing, glissading, and other human activities.

## Slab Avalanches

Slab avalanches are more difficult to anticipate than loose avalanches because they involve buried layers of snow that often cannot be detected from the surface. Usually a *buried weak layer* or weak interface is sandwiched between a *slab layer* and a *bed layer* (fig. 22-9). The buried weakness is disturbed in a way that causes it to reduce its frictional hold on the overlying slab.

### The Buried Weak Layer

Depth hoar and buried surface hoar (hoarfrost) are the most notorious weak layers. They can withstand a significant amount of vertical load but have little or no shear strength; they may collapse like a house of cards, or their structure may give way like a row of dominoes. In addition, depth hoar and buried surface

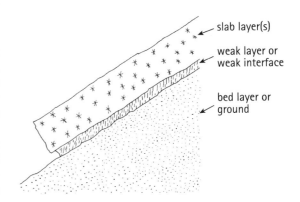

Fig. 22-9. Typical snow layering in a slab avalanche

hoar can survive weeks to months with little change in their fragile structure.

Surface hoar can form all across the snow cover, persisting most in shaded places that are protected from wind. Buried by subsequent snowfall, it becomes a weak layer that can promote avalanching. It becomes most dangerous if the first storm following hoarfrost formation begins with cool, calm conditions.

Depth hoar matures fastest in the shallow snow of early winter, especially in continental regions, but can develop anytime or anywhere there are large temperature gradients within the snow. Weakness begins as soon as temperature and associated vapor-pressure gradients cause molecules to move onto facets instead of into bonds between crystals. Therefore, immature depth hoar (solid, faceted shapes) may be just as weak as mature depth hoar (open, cup, and scroll shapes).

Buried graupel (soft hail) is another classic weakness within the snowpack because it can act like ball bearings if disrupted. Other weaknesses that can make it easier for slabs to avalanche include slightly rounded new-snow crystals and plate-shaped crystals.

### The Slab Layer

Once the underpinning of a snowpack is sufficiently weakened, the overlying snow (either a single layer or group of layers) begins to slide. If the overlying snow is cohesive enough to develop some tension as sliding begins—that is, if it is a slab—it may break in long fractures that propagate across the slope. Lengthy fractures can result in large, heavy blocks that easily pull away from the rest of the slope, such as along the side and bottom of a slope where more stable snow may exist.

Brittle, wind-deposited snow layers are common slabs. Wind often deposits snow in pillowlike patterns on the leeward side of ridges, thickest in the middle of the slope (where most weight of the slab and thus the greatest avalanche danger exists) and thinner on the edges. Wind slabs can maintain their blocky integrity throughout a slide, thrusting powerful masses downslope.

Layers of needle-shaped crystals deposited like a pile of pickup sticks and layers of dendrite crystals with many interlocking arms also are common slabs, often pulverizing immediately after release to form fast-moving powder avalanches.

Thick rain crusts often bridge over weakened surfaces and are rarely involved in avalanches until they begin to melt in spring. Sun crusts, on the other hand, usually are thinner and weaker than rain crusts and can be incorporated in a group of slab layers.

If the overlying snow is too warm or too wet compared to the underlying weakness, it may not break—just deform slightly in response to the change in basal friction and stay on the slope. But if the underlying weak layer fails quickly and initial movement is significant, even this wet and pliable slab can avalanche. This scenario occurs commonly during spring when thick layers of old depth hoar are weakened by percolating meltwater. The resulting collapse of the depth hoar can cause a bending motion, like a whip, that overstresses the slab and causes it to fracture and slide. This whiplike effect also can occur in dry snow.

If the overlying snow is fragile and noncohesive—technically not a slab—the failure of a weak layer may simply result in snow grains in the overlying snow collapsing over each other but remaining in place. But if the weakness is buried surface hoar or slightly rounded dendrite or plate crystals, the failure can be so rapid that even the most fragile snow layers can turn into slab avalanches.

## The Bed Layer

A bed layer provides the initial sliding surface of avalanches. Common bed layers are the smooth surfaces of old snow, crust, glaciers, bedrock, or grass. The interface of these smooth surfaces and the snow above can be further weakened if temperature gradients promote depth hoar formation or if the interface is lubricated by meltwater or percolating rainwater. The bed layer can also be the collapsed fragments of old depth hoar.

# Avalanche Triggers

Humans are efficient trigger mechanisms for avalanches. Stomping snowshoers and ascending skiers, especially during kick-turns, easily disturb layers of depth hoar or buried surface hoar. The sweeping turns and traversing motions of downhill skiers and snowboarders are efficient at releasing loose-snow avalanches and fragile but fast-moving soft-slab avalanches. Skiers in snowplow turns or sliding downhill, snowboarders, and glissaders efficiently release wet loose and wet slab avalanches. It's even possible to initiate an avalanche by traveling below a slope, especially if the buried weakness is surface or depth hoar, because a domino effect as the delicate crystal structure collapses can propagate uphill. Because of their weight and vibration, snowmobiles can set off avalanches in places that nonmotorized travel does not.

Storms also trigger avalanches. Many types of buried layers (such as thin layers of slightly rounded dendrites and platelike crystals) fail when a force is applied evenly over a broad surface, as occurs when storms deposit layers of new snow. Earthquakes, cornice and serac falls, and other internal and external effects on the snow can cause avalanches at times and places that are unpredictable.

# 23

# MOUNTAIN WEATHER

A trip into the mountains can leave you more exposed to dangerous weather than in any other environment on earth. Refuge can be harder to find, and changes in the atmosphere more difficult to detect. Despite improvements in weather forecasting, knowledge of exactly how the atmosphere works is still inexact, particularly in mountainous regions. Given the ability of the mountains to literally create their own weather, the wise climber carefully checks forecasts and reports before a trip but also develops an ability to assess the weather in the field.

## MOUNTAIN WEATHER: AN OVERVIEW

The sun does far more than simply illuminate our home planet. It is the engine that drives our atmosphere, providing the heating that, along with other factors, creates the temperature variations that are ultimately responsible for wind, rain, snow, thunder, and lightning—everything we call weather.

The key to the sun's impact is that the intensity of the sun's radiation varies across the earth's surface. The closer you are to the equator, the more intense the sun's heat. The extremes in temperature between the equator and the poles come as little surprise. But as large as those extremes can be, they are limited by the movement of air. Differences in air temperature lead to air movement, which prevents runaway heating or cooling.

The sideways movement of air (wind) is all too familiar to anyone who has pitched a tent in the mountains, but air also rises and descends, movements that can generate or dissipate clouds. When air cools, it becomes more dense and sinks. The air pressure increases. When air warms, it becomes less dense and rises. The air pressure decreases. These pressure differences, the result of temperature differences, produce moving air—what we call wind. Air generally moves from an area of high pressure to one of low pressure (fig. 23-1).

Air moving from high to low pressure carries moisture with it. As that air rises and cools, the moisture condenses into clouds or fog. This occurs because, as air cools, its capacity to hold water vapor is reduced. The process of cooling and condensation operates on a large scale in the atmosphere as air moves from high pressure into low-pressure systems and is lifted.

Because polar and arctic air is colder and therefore more dense than air farther south, it sinks. The zone where it sinks and piles up is a region of high pressure. As the air sinks and its pressure increases, its temperature also increases. The effect is similar to what happens to football players caught at the bottom of a pile: they get squeezed the most, and their temperature (and possibly temperament) heats up. In the atmosphere, this warming within a high tends to evaporate the little moisture present. This is why the Arctic receives very little precipitation.

If our planet didn't rotate, this cold air would just continue to slide southward to the equator. Intense solar heating near the equator forces air to

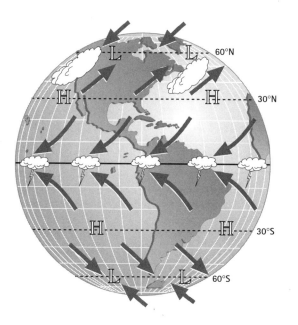

Fig. 23-1. *Air circulation patterns: movement from areas of high pressure to areas of low pressure*

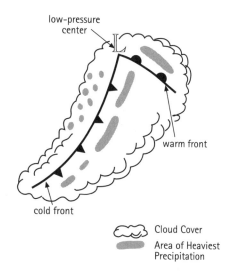

Fig. 23-2. *Precipitation pattern from cold front, overview (courtesy Department of Atmospheric Sciences, Cloud Physics Group, University of Washington)*

rise, creating a region of low pressure that rings the globe. Because air within this band rises, it also cools, which tends to condense water vapor into liquid water droplets that form clouds.

But the air sinking and moving south from the pole and that rising from the equator don't form a simple loop moving from north to south and back again. The rotation of the earth is responsible for deflecting this air. Some of the air rising from the equator descends over the subtropics, creating a region of high pressure. In turn, part of the air moving from these subtropical highs moves north to the air moving from the poles. The boundary between these two very different air masses is called the polar front. When this boundary doesn't move, it's called a stationary front. It often serves as a nursery for the development of storms.

Because of the great contrast in temperatures across the polar front, together with imbalances caused by the rotation of the earth and differing influences of land, sea, ice, and mountains, some of the cold, dry air from the north slides south. That forces some of the warm air to rise. The zone where cold air

is replacing warm air is referred to as a cold front; the zone where warm air is gradually replacing cooler air is referred to as a warm front (fig. 23-2). Both are marked by unique clouds (fig. 23-3), which help the mountaineer distinguish one type of front from the other. The "wave" or bend that develops along what started out as a stationary front may develop into a low-pressure system, with air circulating counterclockwise around the low (the opposite direction of air moving around a high)—again a consequence of the earth's rotation and friction.

## —— THUNDER AND LIGHTNING ——

Thunderstorms in the mountains can and do kill. An average of 200 people die from lightning strikes in the United States each year, some in the mountains. A single lightning bolt can heat the surrounding air up to 50,000 degrees Fahrenheit. That heating causes the air to expand explosively, generating earsplitting thunder. Even a moderate thunderstorm can produce up to 125 million gallons of water. This heavy discharge of

*Fig. 23-3. Cloud types*

Halo: commonly seen 24–48 hours ahead of precipitation

## CLOUDS SEEN AHEAD OF OR ALONG A COLD FRONT

Cumulus: with continued upward growth these suggest showers later in the day

Altocumulus: high-based clouds often indicating potential for thunder, rain showers

Cumulonimbus: cumulus producing rain, snow, or thunder and lightning

Stratocumulus: lumpy, layered clouds often following a cold front, suggesting showers

## CLOUDS SEEN AHEAD OF OR ALONG A WARM FRONT

◄

Lenticular: wavelike clouds over mountains often suggesting precipitation within 48 hours

►

Stratus: layerlike clouds associated with widespread precipitation or ocean air

### Cirrus Types

◄

Cirrocumulus

►

Cirrostratus

◄

Altostratus: when part of approaching warm front, follows cirrostratus

►

Nimbostratus: stratus clouds producing widespread precipitation and low visibility

rain can quickly flood streambeds and small valleys, sweeping away entire campgrounds.

Thunderstorms (fig. 23-4) can be set off by the passage of fronts or by the rapid heating of air in contact with mountain slopes. Once this air is warmed, it becomes buoyant and tends to rise. If the atmosphere above is cold enough, the air will tend to keep rising, producing what are called air mass thunderstorms. With a few precautions, most accidents caused by mountain thunderstorms could be avoided. (See Chapter 19, First Aid, regarding prevention and treatment of lightning injuries.)

The following are guidelines concerning thunderstorms:

### IF THUNDERSTORMS ARE FORECAST

- Do not camp or climb in a narrow valley or gully.
- Do not plan to climb or hike in high, exposed areas.
- Watch small cumulus clouds for strong, upward growth; this may signal a coming thunderstorm.
- Keep track of weather reports.

### IF YOU SPOT A THUNDERSTORM

- Get away from water.
- Seek low ground in an open valley or meadow.
- Move immediately if your hair stands on end.
- Do not stand under trees, especially in open areas.
- Do not remain near or on rocky pinnacles or peaks.
- Do not remain near metal or graphite equipment, such as ice axes, crampons, climbing devices, and frame packs.
- Insulate yourself from the ground if possible; sit on a soft pack or foam pad.
- Crouch to minimize your profile.
- Do not lie down.
- Gauge the movement of the thunderstorm.

As for that last point, how do you gauge the movement of a thunderstorm? It's easy if you have a watch. The moment you see lightning, start counting the seconds. Stop timing once you hear thunder. Divide the number of seconds by five; the result is the distance of the thunderstorm from you in miles. Continue to time lightning and thunder discharges to judge whether the thunderstorm is approaching, remaining in one place, or receding. If the time interval between the lightning

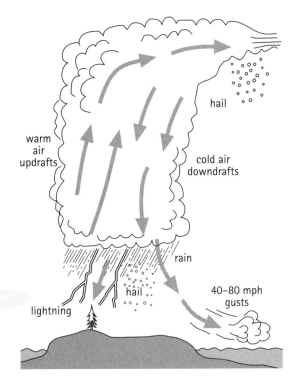

*Fig. 23-4. Thunderstorm hazards*

and thunder is decreasing, the thunderstorm is approaching; if the interval is increasing, it's moving away.

This technique works because the light from the lightning moves much faster than the sound from the thunder. Although the thunder occurs at virtually the same instant as the lightning, its sound travels to you at only about a mile every 5 seconds while the lightning flash, traveling at 186,000 miles per second, arrives essentially instantaneously. That's why you see the lightning before you hear the thunder, unless you're very close to the thunderstorm—too close.

## LOCALIZED WINDS

Large-scale wind patterns are important, both at the surface and in the upper atmosphere. But mountains, by their very nature, alter wind considerably.

Understanding localized patterns is very important to the mountaineer.

## Gap Winds

Winds are often channeled through gaps in the terrain such as major passes or even between two peaks. Wind speeds can easily double as they move through such gaps (fig. 23-5).

Mountaineers can use this information to their advantage. If possible, gauge the surface winds upwind of a gap or pass before you travel into the vicinity of these terrain features. Knowing the upwind conditions, you can be prepared for gap winds that may be twice as strong. You can also find lighter winds a few miles downwind of a major peak.

## Valley and Gravity Winds

Differences in the heating of bare ground or rock, as opposed to ground covered by vegetation or trees, can produce valley winds. As the ground heats during the day, the air close to the earth also heats and rises, moving up either side of a valley and spilling over adjoining ridge tops. Such uphill breezes can reach 10 to 15 miles per hour, attaining peak speed during the early afternoon and dying out shortly before sunset.

At night the land cools, and the cool air flows downslope in what is called a gravity wind. Such downslope breezes reach their maximum after midnight, dying out just before sunrise. Camping at the base of a cliff, then, may result in an uncomfortably breezy evening.

## Foehn or Chinook Winds

When winds descend a slope, air temperatures can sometimes increase dramatically in what is called a foehn wind or, in the western United States, a chinook

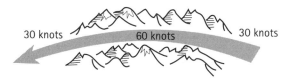

*Fig. 23-5. Wind acceleration through gaps and passes*

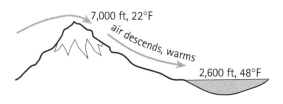

*Fig. 23-6. Foehn (chinook) winds*

(fig. 23-6). These winds are significant because of their potential speed, the rapid rise in air temperature associated with them, and the potential they create for rapid melting of snow and flooding. The air heats as it sinks and compresses on the leeward side of the crest, sometimes warming 30 degrees Fahrenheit in minutes, melting as much as a foot of snow in a few hours. Such winds can increase the risk of avalanches, weaken snow bridges, and lead to sudden rises in stream levels.

There are warning signs of a potentially dangerous foehn or chinook. You can expect such a wind with warming as much as 6 degrees Fahrenheit per 1,000 feet of descent if these three conditions are met:

- You are downwind of a major ridge or crest, primarily to the east of mountains.
- Wind speeds across the crest or ridge exceed 30 miles per hour.
- Precipitation is observed over the crest.

The opposite of a chinook is a bora or, as it's called in Alaska, a taku. A bora is simply wind bringing air that is so cold that its sinking, compressing motion as it flows downslope fails to warm it significantly. Such winds are most common downslope of large glaciers. Their speeds can easily exceed 50 miles per hour.

## FIELD FORECASTING IN THE MOUNTAINS

Weather-related accidents in the mountains rarely occur without warning. At times the clues can be subtle, and sometimes they're as broad as daylight. The process of gathering and evaluating weather data

## Cloud-Cover Clues (refer to Figure 23-3)

| IF | THEN | CHECK FOR |
|---|---|---|
| High cirrus clouds forming loose halo around sun /moon | Precipitation possible within 24 to 48 hours | Lowering, thickening clouds |
| High cirrus clouds forming tight ring or corona around sun/moon | Precipitation possible within 24 hours | Lowering, thickening clouds |
| "Cap" or lenticular clouds forming over peaks | Precipitation possible within 24 to over 48 hours, and strong winds possible near summits or leeward slopes | Lowering, thickening clouds |
| Thickening, lowering, layered flat clouds | Warm or occluded front likely approaching within 12 to 24 hours | Wind shifts, pressure drops |
| Breaks in cloud cover closing up | Cold front likely within 12 hours | Wind shifts, pressure drop |

## Wind Direction/Speed Clues (Northern Hemisphere)

| IF | THEN | CHECK FOR |
|---|---|---|
| Winds shift to E or SE | Low-pressure system approaching; precipitation possible | Lowering, thickening clouds; pressure drops |
| Winds shift to SW or NW | Cold front passage, drying likely | Rising pressure, clearing; possible showers windward slopes, especially along the U.S. or Canadian West Coast |
| Increasing winds from SE to E | Low-pressure system approaching; continued pressure drop | Accelerating increase in wind speed |
| Increasing winds from SW to W | High-pressure system approaching; gusty winds will gradually decrease | Accelerating pressure rise |

## Air Pressure/Altimeter Changes over 3 Hours

| PRESSURE DECREASE | ALTIMETER INCREASE | ADVISED ACTION |
|---|---|---|
| 0.02–0.04 inches (0.6–1.2 millibars) | 20–40 feet | None. Continue to monitor. |
| 0.04–0.06 inches (1.2–1.8 millibars) | 40–60 feet | Clouds lowering/ thickening? If so, begin checking pressure changes hourly. |
| 0.06–0.08 inches (1.8–2.4 millibars) | 60–80 feet | Winds ranging 18–33 knots (21–38 miles per hour) are likely. |
| More than 0.08 inches (more than 2.4 millibars) | More than 80 feet | Winds of 34 knots (40 miles per hour) or greater are likely. Immediate movement to protected area advised. |

shouldn't end at the beginning of the trailhead or climbing route.

There are four major indicators of an approaching storm: changes in cloud cover, changes in air pressure, changes in wind speed, and changes in wind direction. No single factor will tell you all you need to know; each should be examined carefully. The charts on page 502 show some guidelines for evaluating these elements that can enhance the weather reports and forecasts obtained before leaving home.

## Air-Pressure Clues

A barometer or barometer/altimeter can give excellent warning of an approaching weather system. A barometer measures air pressure directly; an altimeter measures air pressure indirectly by indicating elevation. A decrease in air pressure shows on an altimeter as an increase in elevation—even though you haven't changed location—while an increase in air pressure shows as a decrease in elevation.

The chart at left evaluates a developing low-pressure system, but rapidly building high pressure also can have its troublesome effects, principally strong winds.

# FREEZING LEVEL AND SNOW LEVEL

It can be useful to estimate the freezing level and snow level (see chart below). Such estimates are subject to error because they are based on the average decrease in temperature as altitude increases: 3.5 degrees Fahrenheit per thousand feet. Still, such estimates are usually better than the alternative, no estimate.

# CREATING YOUR OWN WEATHER BRIEFINGS

The mountaineer has a rich supply of weather information sources available to him or her before departure. But information by itself is of limited use; information gathered with a purpose is of great value. Consider gathering weather information at least one day, and preferably two days, before your planned departure. That gives you a chance to verify

## Estimating the Freezing Level and Snow Level

To estimate the freezing level—the elevation at which the temperature drops to 32 degrees Fahrenheit—you simply need to know your elevation and the temperature:

$$\frac{\text{your elevation} + (\text{Fahrenheit temperature} - 32) \times 1{,}000}{3.5} = \text{estimated freezing level}$$

Once you have estimated the freezing level, use the following guidelines to estimate the snow level:

| If | And If | Then |
|---|---|---|
| Stratus clouds or fog present | Steady, widespread precipitation | Expect to find the snow level 1,000 feet below the freezing level. |
| Cumulus clouds present or cold front approaching | Locally heavy precipitation, varying from time to time or place to place | Expect to find the snow level as much as 2,000 feet below the freezing level. Snow will stick 1,000 feet below the freezing level. |

the forecasts with observed conditions. If the forecasts are pretty close to what you actually see, planning can proceed with more confidence than if the forecast and observed weather conditions are 180 degrees apart. Here's a suggested sequence for gathering information:

### TWO DAYS BEFORE THE TRIP

- Check the overall weather pattern: the positions of highs, lows, and fronts.
- Check the projected weather for the next two days.

### ONE DAY BEFORE THE TRIP

- Check the current weather to evaluate the accuracy of the previous day's forecasts.

- Again check the overall weather pattern.
- Check the projected weather for the next two days.
- If the possibility of strong winds, thunderstorms, or significant snow or rain is mentioned, plan on checking for updates every 6 to 8 hours. The lead time on such forecasts is short because of the rapid changes that sometimes occur.

### DAY OF THE TRIP

- Check the current weather to evaluate the previous day's forecasts.
- Check the projected weather for the trip.
- Make a go/no go decision based on current forecasts, the track record of earlier forecasts, your personal experience, and the demands of the trip.

# 24
# MINIMUM IMPACT

Climbers seek many experiences in the mountains. We look for challenge, both physical and mental, and we pursue the beauties of the outdoors: spectacular summit views, a cold mountain stream, meadows ablaze with color, and the songs of birds. We gain precious experiences that give us every reason to help in the preservation of wild places.

These experiences are becoming elusive as the mountains fill with people. The granite walls of Yosemite Valley host crowds of climbers, and hidden corners of the Himalayas attract large numbers of trekkers. The popular spots are crowded, wild places that don't regularly receive human visitors are becoming a rarity, and fewer truly wild areas remain.

So many people are heading into the mountains nowadays that we may be in danger of loving some areas to death. You don't have to look far for examples. A meadow is veined with parallel paths where hikers over the years chose to walk side by side instead of staying in single file—and killed the grass and heather as they did so. These "social trails" cause erosion both in the backcountry and at local climbing crags. A bivy site high on a popular peak is littered with garbage left by climbers. Routefinding up the flanks of a major glaciated peak is simplified by merely following the mounds of decaying human excrement.

But today, more and more people are striving for minimum impact in the mountains and observing the simple rule that what you pack in, you pack out. Climbers on some standard glaciated routes are confronting the problem of human waste by using the "blue bag" system, toting their own feces off the mountain in special plastic pouches. It may have been common in the past to abandon gear when things got tough or turn a blind eye to trash along the trail or remodel the landscape to make a more comfortable camp. Increasingly, this is no longer acceptable. One way to do the right thing is to practice a kind of mountaineering "golden rule": Consider the experiences you like to have in the mountains—then do whatever you can to preserve these experiences for the next person.

For mountaineers, minimum-impact travel is sometimes a balance between doing what is necessary to conduct a technical climb safely and avoiding harmful actions. Some impacts seem unavoidable—it's hard to climb a route without knocking lichen off the rocks or to descend without leaving a couple of rappel slings behind—but the main thing is to do what we can to mitigate these effects. Reducing the number of climbers in popular areas can help spare the vegetation; using dark-colored slings can limit their visual impact.

## STANDARDS OF MINIMUM IMPACT

Everyone who uses the out-of-doors can help promote the values of minimum impact. Chapter 3, Camping and Food, looked closely at techniques for leave-no-trace camping, and a strong theme of caring for the wilderness runs throughout the book. This chapter reviews some of the earlier material while outlining standards of minimum-impact travel that have developed over the years.

You can stand up for the wilderness even before you leave home. Wherever you're headed, there's undoubtedly a park office or some agency that keeps track of camping, mountaineering, and waste management. Drop them a line or give them a call to get information on local conditions and whatever rules and recommendations they may have.

You can support minimum impact, in addition to safety, by planning a climb that's appropriate for your group. A party that stretches itself to the limit, and perhaps gets into trouble, will no longer care about minimum impact. If rescuers have to go in and pluck someone off a precarious perch, safety comes first, regardless of environmental damage. And anyone who has survived an epic retreat from a climb gone wrong knows that you'll abandon heavy gear or call in rescuers or do whatever it takes to get out. Realistic planning can often prevent the epic in the first place.

Also before leaving home, take a look at your gear and see that it's clean of the mud or vegetation you might have picked up on your last trip. You don't want to take a chance of accidentally spreading unwanted or noxious plant life from one wilderness area to another or bringing it home.

The fundamental principle of minimum-impact travel is to pass through an area without disturbing it and to leave the place with no evidence you were ever there. Following is a list of some standards of minimum impact that flow naturally from this principle; you may recognize most of them from Chapter 3.

### TRAVEL

- Stay on trails where they exist. Don't cut switchbacks; it causes erosion.
- Stay in single file on existing meadow trails, and walk through—not around—muddy areas. You'll be helping to reduce the widening and multiplication of trails (trail braiding).
- Tread lightly in trailless areas, looking for routes on durable surfaces that minimize damage to vegetation.
- Spread the hiking party out if the route must go through a vegetated area with no trail, rather than walking single file. This is less damaging and less likely to start erosion.

### CAMPSITES

- Camp in fully established campsites when they're available, on barren ground.
- Camp on snow or rock as a second choice if there is no well-established campsite.
- Avoid camping in a meadow; if you must stay there, keep in mind that sedge grasses are hardier than woody plants.
- Be very gentle if you must camp in a meadow; stay no more than a night or two in one spot. (Chapter 3 has more details on preferred campsites.)

### CAMP STOVES

- Use a camp stove instead of a fire; firewood gatherers trample the terrain, create unwanted trails, and rob the area of biological material.

### WASHING

- Wash well away from camps and water sources.
- Use biodegradable soap sparingly, if at all.
- Do not wash directly in a stream.
- Minimize erosion around watercourses; use of a water bag reduces the number of trips to a stream and the accompanying erosion and impact.

### ANIMALS

- Do not feed wildlife, either deliberately or by leaving food waste.
- Leave pets at home.

### WASTE

- Pack out your garbage, plus any litter left by previous parties.
- Dispose of human waste in a proper manner (see the next section in this chapter).

Arctic environments need special consideration beyond the minimum-impact techniques for alpine zones, because they may take decades—even centuries—to recover from damage. If you're planning a trip to the arctic, seek out information on ways to help preserve this immense wild area.

# DISPOSAL OF HUMAN WASTE

Like most aspects of wilderness travel, going to the "bathroom" is no longer such a simple matter. As the number of mountaineers grows, problems associated with human waste increase: threats to water purity, disrupted terrain and damaged vegetation, toilet-paper litter, and the decided unpleasantness of stumbling across deposits as you camp or climb. The problems are magnified in arctic and high alpine areas, where waste breaks down very slowly or not at all.

Whenever possible, travelers should use an outhouse or wait until returning from the backcountry. But because these usually aren't options, the general rule is to use an area at least 200 feet from watercourses, away from trails and camp areas. Other methods are coming into use, including ways for people to pack their own waste out of the wilderness. The following section outlines some suggested methods of disposal; which you use will depend on the area.

## Toilet Paper

Ideally, toilet paper should be carried out. In forested areas with organic soil, it may be acceptable to bury toilet paper along with feces, though even here it can take a long time for the paper to break down. Mountaineers are asked to get in the habit of carrying plastic bags designated for packing out soiled toilet paper. Also consider using alternatives to toilet paper, such as rocks, leaves, or snow.

## Urine

Urinate on bare ground or rocks, not on vegetation. The salt in urine will attract animals that might then damage vegetation. On snow or ice, concentrate urine at designated locations in camp or at rest stops, rather than creating a proliferation of pee holes. On steep rock or ice faces, wait until you are at a place where urine can be streamed away from the climbing route. A pee bottle is useful on climbing routes or in tents for collecting urine for later disposal at a better place.

## Feces

### Cat-Hole Burial

At lower elevations, in forests and other areas with organic soils, you can dig a "cat hole" for burying solid waste. Find a place at least 200 feet from watercourses or from where it's likely that water sometimes runs. Stay the same distance from trails, campsites, and other places people are likely to gather.

Prepare a hole by digging 6 to 8 inches into this organic layer. After defecating, cover the feces with soil, leaving the area looking as close to natural as possible. The feces will decompose in this organic soil. Burying solid waste is not recommended in the thin mineral soil or rocks of high alpine areas, where the waste will not readily break down.

### Packing It Out

The preferred minimum-impact method of disposal is to simply pack it out, especially from popular glacier routes, alpine areas with thin mineral soils, and steep rock and ice routes. Two techniques now in use are the blue-bag system and the poop tube.

#### The Blue-Bag System

This system gets its name from a method employed in some national parks in the United States on heavily used glacier routes. Climbers are provided with sets of sealable plastic bags. Each set has two bags: an outer bag and a blue inner bag. Like an urban dog owner following his pet around the neighborhood, the climber puts the blue bag over one hand as a kind of glove and scoops up the solid waste. Then the user turns the bag inside out to envelop the waste, seals this bag, places it inside the second bag, seals that bag—and it's ready to carry down the mountain to the disposal site specified by the park authorities.

Climbers can help expand this system to other areas by packing along their own plastic bags for waste storage. However, after the climb, the waste must be disposed of. The bags shouldn't go into a sewer system or even into a vault toilet (outhouse). The contents can be dumped into either, but then you're still left with the soiled bags, which can be disposed of in the same manner as disposable diapers. The poop-tube

*35 – 150'/yr*

system, described in the next section, might be a good alternative.

### The Poop Tube

The poop-tube disposal system offers a good do-it-yourself way to pack out solid waste. The system was developed in Yosemite National Park for use on big-wall climbs. You'll need to carry some small paper bags (lunch-sack size), a sturdy plastic container with a tight-fitting lid, and a bit of kitty litter (or chlorinated lime).

The climber defecates into a bag, adds a bit of kitty litter for smell and moisture control, closes up the bag, and puts it into the plastic container. The container, more rugged than a plastic bag, offers a practical way to carry the waste beneath big-wall haul bags or on backpacks. You can construct your own container out of commercially available 4-inch-diameter plastic tubing (plastic pipe). Cut the tube to the length you want, then glue a solid cap at one end and a screw-type cap at the other. At the end of the trip you can throw the paper bags into a vault toilet (outhouse) and clean the plastic container for future use.

### The Smear Technique

This method can be considered for remote areas, well away from climbing routes or likely gathering places. Feces is deposited on rock or hard snow that has good exposure to the sun, then smeared out with a rock to reduce thickness of the deposit and create a large surface area. The feces now can dry and disintegrate much more quickly than if it were left in a pile. There may even be some decontaminating benefit from the sun's ultraviolet radiation. Check with local land managers before using this technique, as questions have been raised about possible health hazards, even in remote areas.

### On Glaciers and Snow Climbs

The best minimum-impact solution for human waste on glaciers or snow climbs is to pack it out in a "blue bag" or poop tube, especially on crowded routes. In more remote and distant areas, a second choice is the smear technique. In some glaciated areas, disposal in crevasses is the accepted and recommended practice. In this case, feces is collected together in a plastic garbage sack and then thrown into a deep crevasse when the party breaks camp.

### On Rock and Ice Routes

The most suitable method of waste disposal for big-wall climbs in popular areas is the poop tube. This system is mandatory on big-wall routes in Yosemite.

Use of a poop tube is also the preferred minimum-impact method for steep rock and ice routes in remote areas. A less desirable solution is to deposit feces on a rock or block of snow, which is then thrown off and away from the climbing route. But first, be sure your party has that section of the mountain to itself. Then before making the toss, yell out a warning—"Rock! Rock!" or some other appropriate cry—just in case you missed seeing or hearing someone below.

The most undesirable situation is leaving human waste right on the route, but sometimes this is the only option. Give a little thought to the next folks who will climb the route. If you can thoroughly cover the feces, do so. If not, leave it out in the open so it can be seen. It's better to see and avoid a deposit than to make an unwitting discovery as you're going for your next handhold or foothold.

## MINIMUM-IMPACT MOUNTAINEERING

There are any number of ways to practice minimum-impact mountaineering while enjoying the excitement and challenge of ascending the peaks. Here are some of them:

- Remove climbing litter of any kind—yours and that left by people before you.
- Avoid leaving cairns, flagging, wands, or any other markers that you have placed.
- Keep track of gear and maintain a tidy camp so that equipment and camp goods are not lost or forgotten if it snows.
- Break down camp areas and snow structures before you leave a camp set up on snow, to reduce visual impact.
- Watch for nesting birds on rock routes so that you

won't disturb them. Some birds, including raptors, make their nests on the same cliffs enjoyed by climbers.

- Avoid disturbing vegetation or rocks on a climbing route. On an alpine climb, try to adjust loose rocks in order to make them stable, rather than just pushing them off. At popular sport-climbing crags, on the other hand, it's better to remove loose rocks because of the danger they pose in crowded areas.
- Leave untouched any area with evidence of archeological artifacts, such as those left by prehistoric or native populations. Report findings to land managers. Don't climb near indigenous rock artwork.
- Use natural-color webbing at rappel points. Remove and pack out old or deteriorated webbing from rappel points.
- Avoid setting up new, permanent fixed anchors and rappel points or reinforcing existing ones, unless it's absolutely necessary for safety.
- Never chip holds or alter the rock structure for climbing purposes.
- Avoid using pitons or other hardware that mar or fracture the rock or that remain permanently in place. The huge array of hammerless nuts, cams, and other pieces of protection that are easy to place and remove has largely eliminated the damaging practice of using pitons. Pitons are appropriate for winter climbing when otherwise usable cracks are filled with ice and for some aid climbing. The use of bolts should be considered only when no other protection is possible and when they are needed to provide a margin of safety. Because bolts are permanent, think it through carefully before deciding to place one.
- Follow the local practices and rules at climbing crags. In one area, the local climbers may use only camouflaged bolt hangers (painted so that they aren't shiny); in another area, the bolting of new routes may be illegal.
- Respect the customs and culture of foreign areas. Pack in your own fuel so you don't have to despoil these areas in the search for firewood. Just as you would at home, pack your garbage out.

We who seek the beauty and challenge of wild places have an obligation to treat the mountains with respect. Practicing minimum-impact values is one way to do this. Mountaineers also have many opportunities to become active stewards of the land, perhaps by helping with trail maintenance or working on a meadow restoration project. Pick a favorite area and become involved.

# A: RATING SYSTEMS

The development of rating systems for climbing began in the late nineteenth and early twentieth centuries in Britain and Germany. In the 1920s, Willo Welzenbach defined a rating system, using roman numerals and the British adjectival system to compare and describe routes in the Alps, which today forms the basis of the UIAA (Union Internationale des Associations d'Alpinisme) system of rating. Rating systems have proliferated. Ratings used internationally today include no less than seven systems for rock, four for alpine climbing, four for ice, and two for aid climbing. This appendix will briefly describe and compare some of these systems.

A rating system is a tool that helps a climber choose a climb that is challenging and within his or her ability. In some circumstances a rating will indicate the amount and type of equipment needed. Unfortunately, the rating of a climb is sometimes translated into the rating of a climber (as in, "he's only a 5.7 climber" or "she's only a 5.12c climber").

Rating climbs is a subjective task, which makes consistency between climbing areas elusive. The rating of climbs assumes good weather and the best equipment available. Variables that affect the rating include the size, strength, and flexibility of the climber and the type of climb (for instance, face, crack, or friction rock climbing).

Ideally a route is rated by consensus in order to reduce personal bias, though climbs often are rated by the first-ascent party. This can lead to some awkward situations. There have been instances in which a first-ascent party, criticized for rating a climb harder than it really is, gets its revenge by "sandbagging"—underrating subsequent first ascents. A guidebook author typically does not climb every route in the guidebook and therefore has to rely on the opinions of others. In some cases a route may have been completed only once.

Ratings described as "stiff" indicate that the climb is harder than it is rated, whereas a description of "soft" indicates it is easier than it is rated. Of course, evaluation of a rating system is no more precise than the rating system itself. Whenever you climb in an area for the first time, it's a good idea to start out at a lower level than your usual ability until you can evaluate the local ratings and the nature of the rock.

## ALPINE CLIMBING

The National Climbing Classification System (NCCS), developed in the United States, describes the overall difficulty of a multipitch alpine climb or long rock climb in terms of time and technical rock difficulty. It takes the following factors into account: length of climb, number of hard pitches, difficulty of hardest pitch, average pitch difficulty, commitment, routefinding problems, and ascent time. The approach and remoteness of a climb might or might not affect the grade given, depending on the guidebook and area. It should be emphasized that with increasing grade, an increasing level of psychological preparation and commitment is necessary. This system assumes a competent party for the level of climbing expected.

**Grade I:** Normally requires several hours; can be of any technical difficulty.

**Grade II:** Requires half a day; any technical difficulty.

**Grade III:** Requires a day to do the technical portion; any technical difficulty.

**Grade IV:** Requires a full day for the technical portion; the hardest pitch is usually no less than 5.7 (in the Yosemite Decimal System for rating rock climbs).

**Grade V:** Requires a day and a half; the hardest pitch is usually 5.8 or harder.

**Grade VI:** A multiday excursion with difficult free climbing and/or aid climbing.

Like other rating systems, the grade is subjective. For example, the Nose on El Capitan in Yosemite is rated Grade VI. Warren Harding and companions took forty-five days for the first ascent, in 1958. John Long, Billy Westbay, and Jim Bridwell made the first one-day ascent in 1975. Hans Florine and Peter Croft cut the time to under $4^{1}/_{2}$ hours in 1992, and Lynn Hill (accompanied by a belayer) led the first free ascent in 1993 and the first one-day free ascent in 1994. The time needed is as relative as the abilities and technologies of the climbers. The type of climb affects what factors of the given grade are to be emphasized. Proper planning, including study of a route description, are more valuable in estimating your time than the given grade.

## —— ROCK CLIMBING ——

### Free Climbing

In 1937, a modified Welzenbach rating system was introduced in the United States as the Sierra Club System. In the 1950s, this system was modified to more accurately describe rock climbing being done at Tahquitz Rock in California by adding a decimal to the Class 5 rating. This is now known as the Yosemite Decimal System (YDS). This system categorizes terrain according to the techniques and physical difficulties

encountered when rock climbing. (See Figure A-1 for a comparison of the YDS with other international rating systems.)

**Class 1:** Hiking.

**Class 2:** Simple scrambling, with possible occasional use of the hands.

**Class 3:** Scrambling; a rope might be carried.

**Class 4:** Simple climbing, often with exposure. A rope is often used. A fall on Class-4 rock could be fatal. Typically, natural protection can be easily found.

**Class 5:** Where rock climbing begins in earnest. Climbing involves the use of a rope, belaying, and protection (natural or artificial) to protect the leader from a long fall.

The decimal extension of Class-5 climbing originally was meant to be a closed-end scale of 5.0 to 5.9. Up until 1960 or so, a climb that was the hardest of that era would be rated 5.9. The rising standards in the 1960s, however, led to a need for an open-ended scale. Strict decimal protocol was abandoned, and 5.10 (pronounced "five-ten") was adopted as the next highest level. As the open-ended system let the decimal numbers go up to 5.11, 5.12, and ever higher, not all climbs were rerated, leaving a disparity between the "old-school ratings" and the new ratings.

The YDS numbers reached 5.14 in the 1990s. The ratings from 5.10 to 5.14 are subdivided into a, b, c, and d levels to more precisely state the difficulty. The most difficult 5.12 climb, for instance, is rated 5.12d. A plus sign or a minus sign is occasionally used as a more approximate way to refine a classification. Sometimes a plus sign will be added to indicate that the pitch is sustained at its particular rating, while a minus sign might indicate that the pitch has only a single move at that level.

The extended numbers of the fifth-class rating system can't be defined precisely, but the following descriptions offer general guidelines.

**5.0–5.7:** Easy for experienced climbers; where most novices begin.

**5.8–5.9:** Where most weekend climbers become comfortable; employs the specific skills of rock climbing, such as jamming, liebacks, and manteling.

**5.10:** A dedicated weekend climber might attain this level.

| UIAA | French | Yosemite Decimal System | Australian | Brazilian | British | |
|---|---|---|---|---|---|---|
| I | 1 | 5.2 | | | 3a | VD |
| II | 2 | 5.3 | 11 | | 3b | |
| III | 3 | 5.4 | 12 | II | 3c | HVD |
| IV | 4 | 5.5 | | IIsup | 4a | MS / S / HS |
| V– | | 5.6 | 13 | III | 4b | |
| V | 5 | 5.7 | 14 | IIIsup | | VS |
| V+ | | | 15 | | 4c | |
| VI– | | 5.8 | 16 | IV | | HVS |
| VI | | 5.9 | 17 | IVsup | 5a | |
| VI+ | 6a | 5.10a | 18 / 19 | V | | E1 |
| VII– | 6a+ | 5.10b | 20 | Vsup | 5b | E2 |
| | 6b | 5.10c | 21 | VI | | E3 |
| VII | 6b+ | 5.10d | 22 | VIsup | 5c | |
| VII+ | 6c | 5.11a | 23 | VII | | E4 |
| | 6c+ | 5.11b | 24 | | 6a | |
| VIII– | 7a | 5.11c | 25 | VIIsup | | E5 |
| VIII | 7a+ | 5.11d | | VIII | 6b | |
| VIII+ | 7b | 5.12a | 26 | VIIIsup | | E6 |
| | 7b+ | 5.12b | 27 | | 6c | |
| IX– | 7c | 5.12c | | | 7a | E7 |
| IX | 7c+ | 5.12d | 28 | | | |
| IX+ | 8a | 5.13a | 29 | | | |
| X– | 8a+ | 5.13b | 30 / 31 | | | |
| X | 8b | 5.13c | 32 | | | |
| | 8b+ | 5.13d | | | | |
| X+ | 8c | 5.14a | 33 | | | |
| | | 5.14b | | | | |
| | | 5.14c | | | | |
| | | 5.14d | | | | |

*Fig. A-1. Rating systems*

**5.11–5.14:** The realm of true experts; demands much training, often repeated working of a route, and much natural ability.

The YDS rates only the hardest move on a pitch and, for multipitch climbs, the hardest pitch on a climb. The YDS gives no indication of overall difficulty, protection, exposure, run-out, or strenuousness. Some guidebooks, however, will rate a pitch harder than the hardest move if it is very sustained at a lower level. A guidebook's introduction should explain any variations on the YDS that may be used.

Because the YDS does not calculate the potential of a fall, but only the difficulty of a move or pitch, a seriousness rating has been developed. This seriousness rating (introduced by James Erickson in 1980) appears in guidebooks in a variety of forms; read the introduction to any guidebook for an explanation of its particular version.

**PG–13:** Protection is adequate; if it is properly placed, a fall would not be long.

**R:** Protection is considered inadequate; there is potential for a long fall, and a falling leader would take a real whipper, suffering injuries.

**X:** Inadequate or no protection; a fall would be very long with serious, perhaps fatal, consequences.

Ratings of the quality of routes are common in guidebooks. If anything, they are even more subjective than the basic climb ratings as they attempt to indicate aesthetics. The number of stars given for a route indicates the quality of the route in the eyes of the guidebook writer. A standard number of stars for the very best climbs has not been established. A climb with no stars does not mean the climb isn't worth doing, nor does a star-spangled listing mean that everyone will like the route.

## Aid Climbing

Rating aid moves or aid climbs is different than rating free climbs in that the rating system is not open-ended like the YDS. An aid-climbing rating indicates the difficulty of placing protection and the quality of that protection.

The scale is from A0 to A5 or from C0 to C5. The A refers to aid climbs in general, which may utilize pitons, bolts, or chocks. The C refers to clean aid climbing,

using only chocks, which do not mar the rock. It's sometimes possible to clean-climb a route that is rated with the A0–A5 system. For a climb rated with the C0–C5 system, subsequent climbers are expected to honor the clean style that has been established.

The following rating system is used worldwide except in Australia, which uses M0 to M8; the M stands for mechanical:

**A0 or C0:** Fixed protection is in place.

**A1 or C1:** Easy aid placements, where virtually every placement is capable of holding a fall. Often climbed "French free," simply grabbing the fixed gear.

**A2 or C2:** Placements are fairly good, but may be tricky to place. There may be a couple of bad placements between good placements.

**A2+ or C2+:** Same as A2, though with increased fall potential—perhaps 20 to 30 feet.

**A3 or C3:** Hard aid. Several hours to lead a pitch, with the potential of 60- to 80-foot falls, but without danger of grounding or serious injury. Requires active testing of placements.

**A3+ or C3+:** Same as A3, but with the potential of serious injury in a fall. Tenuous placements.

**A4 or C4:** Serious aid. Fall potential of 80 to 100 feet, with very bad landings. Placements hold only body weight.

**A4+ or C4+:** More serious than A4. More time on the route, with increased danger.

**A5 or C5:** Placements hold only body weight for an entire pitch, with no solid protection such as bolts. A leader fall at the top of an A5 pitch means a 300-foot fall.

**A5+:** A theoretical grade; A5, but with bad belay anchors. If you go, you go until you hit the ground.

Aid ratings are always subject to change. What was once a difficult A4 seam may have been beaten out with pitons to the point that it will accept large chocks, rendering it C1. Camming devices and other examples of newer technology can sometimes turn difficult climbs into easy ones. Some climbs once considered A5 might now be rated A2 or A3 by today's standards.

## Bouldering

Bouldering—climbing on large rocks, fairly close to the ground—has gained popularity. Though once a game played by alpinists in mountain boots on days too rainy to climb, bouldering has become an all-out pursuit of its own. John Gill created his B-scale to rate boulder problems:

**B1:** Requires moves at a high level of skill—moves that would be rated 5.12 or 5.13.

**B2:** Moves as hard as the hardest climbs being done in standard rock climbing (5.14 as of 1996).

**B3:** A successful B2 climb that has yet to be repeated. Once repeated, the boulder rating automatically drops to B2.

John Sherman created the open-ended V-scale, which gives permanent ratings to boulder problems (unlike Gill's scale, with its floating ratings). As shown in Figure A-2, Sherman's scale starts at V0-minus (comparable to 5.8 YDS); it moves up through V0, V0+, V1, V2, and so on, with V11 being comparable to 5.14 YDS. Neither the B nor V scale takes into account the consequences of a rough landing on uneven terrain.

## ICE CLIMBING

The variable conditions of snow and ice climbing make rating climbs difficult. The only factors that usually do not vary throughout the season and from year to year are length and steepness. Snow depth, thickness of the ice, and temperature affect the conditions of the route; these factors plus the nature of the ice and its protection possibilities determine its difficulty. These rating systems apply mainly to waterfall ice and other ice formed by meltwater (rather than from consolidating snow, as on glaciers).

### Commitment Rating

The important factors in this ice-climbing rating system are length of the approach and descent, length of the climb itself, objective hazards, and the nature of the climbing. (The roman-numeral ratings used in this system have no correlation to the numerals used in the grading system for alpine climbs.)

**I:** A short, easy climb near the road, with no avalanche hazard and a straightforward descent.

**II:** A route of one or two pitches within a short distance of rescue assistance, with very little objective hazard.

| Yosemite Decimal System | Sherman V-Scale (Bouldering) |
|---|---|
| 5.8 | V0– |
| 5.9 | V0 |
| 5.10a/b | V0+ |
| 5.10c/d | V1 |
| 5.11a/b | V2 |
| 5.11c/d | V3 |
| 5.12– | V4 |
| 5.12 | V5 |
| 5.12+ | V6 |
| 5.13– | V7 |
| 5.13 | V8 |
| 5.13+ | V9 |
| 5.14– | V10 |
| 5.14 | V11 |
| 5.14+ | V12 |
| | V13 |
| | V14 |
| | V15 |

*Fig. A-2. The Sherman V-scale for rating boulder problems compared with the Yosemite Decimal System for rating rock climbs*

**III:** A multipitch route at low elevation, or a one-pitch climb with an approach that takes an hour or so. The route requires from a few hours to a long day to complete. Descent may require building rappel anchors, and the route might be prone to avalanche.

**IV:** A multipitch route at higher elevations; may require several hours of approach on skis or foot. Subject to objective hazards; possibly with a hazardous descent.

**V:** A long climb in a remote setting, requiring all day to complete the climb itself. Requires many rappels off anchors for the descent. Sustained exposure to avalanche or other objective hazard.

**VI:** A long ice climb in an alpine setting, with sustained technical climbing. Only elite climbers will complete it in a day. A difficult and involved approach and descent, with objective hazards ever-present, all in a remote area far from the road.

**VII:** Everything a grade VI has, and more of it. Possibly days to approach the climb, and objective hazard rendering survival as certain as a coin toss. Needless to say, difficult physically and mentally.

## Technical Rating

The technical grade rates the single most difficult pitch, taking into account the sustained nature of the climbing, ice thickness, and natural ice features, such as chandeliers, mushrooms, or overhanging bulges.

**1:** A frozen lake or streambed (the equivalent of an ice rink).

**2:** A pitch with short sections of ice up to 80 degrees; lots of opportunity for protection and good anchors.

**3:** Sustained ice up to 80 degrees; the ice is usually good, with places to rest, but it requires skill at placing pro and setting anchors.

**4:** A sustained pitch that is vertical or slightly less than vertical; may have special features such as chandeliers and run-outs between protection.

**5:** A long, strenuous pitch—possibly 50 meters of 85- to 90-degree ice with few if any rests between anchors. Or the pitch may be shorter, but on featureless ice. Good skills at placing protection are required.

**6:** A full 50-meter pitch of dead-vertical ice, possibly of poor quality; requires efficiency of movement, and ability to place protection while in awkward stances.

**7:** A full pitch of thin vertical or overhanging ice of dubious adhesion. An extremely tough pitch, physically and mentally, requiring agility and creativity.

**8:** Simply the hardest ice climbing ever done, extremely bold and gymnastic.

These ratings describe a route in its typical condition. A route that is usually rated a 4 might be a 5 in a lean year for ice, but only a 3 in a year with thick ice. These ratings have been further subdivided, with a plus added to grades of 4 and above if the route is usually more difficult than its stated numerical grade.

The numerical ice ratings are often prefaced with WI (water ice, or frozen waterfalls); AI (alpine ice); or M (mixed rock and ice). (Mixed climbs can also be described with the Yosemite Decimal System.)

## New England Ice Rating System

This system was developed for the water ice found in New England. It applies to normal winter ascent of a route in moderate weather conditions.

**NEI 1:** Low-angle water ice of 40 to 50 degrees, or a long moderate snow climb requiring a basic level of technical expertise for safety.

**NEI 2:** Low-angle water ice with short bulges up to 60 degrees.

**NEI 3:** Steeper water ice of 50 to 60 degrees, with bulges of 70 to 90 degrees.

**NEI 4:** Short vertical columns, interspersed with rests, on 50- to 60-degree ice; fairly sustained climbing.

**NEI 5:** Generally multipitch ice climbing with sustained difficulties and/or strenuous vertical columns, with little rest possible.

**NEI 5+:** Multipitch routes with a heightened degrees of seriousness, long vertical sections, and extremely sustained difficulties; the hardest ice climbing in New England to date.

# OTHER MAJOR RATING SYSTEMS

A variety of rating systems are used throughout the world. Figure A-1 compares the principal systems.

## Rock Climbing

**Australian:** The Australian system uses open-ended numerics. The Australian number 33, for example, is equivalent to 5.14a in the Yosemite Decimal System.

**Brazilian:** The rating of climbs in Brazil is composed of two parts. The first part gives the general level of difficulty of the route as a whole, ranging from first to eighth grade (or degree). The second part gives the difficulty of the hardest free move (or sequence of moves without a natural rest), expressed in roman numerals; the designation "sup" (for superior) can be added to a numeral in order to refine the accuracy of the rating. (Figure A-1 shows only the roman numeral portion of the Brazilian system, which is the part that is most comparable to the other systems shown.)

**British:** The British system is composed of two elements, an adjectival grade and a technical grade.

The adjectival grade (such as Very Difficult or Hard Severe) describes the overall difficulty of a route, including such factors as exposure, seriousness, strenuousness, protection, and run-outs. The list of adjectives to describe increasingly difficult routes became so cumbersome that the British finally ended it at Extremely Severe, and now simply advance the listing with numbers: E1 for Extremely Severe 1; E2 for Extremely Severe 2; and so forth.

| Easy | E |
| Moderate | M |
| Difficult | Diff |
| Very Difficult | V. Diff |
| Hard Very Difficult | HVD |
| Mild Severe | MS |
| Severe | S |
| Hard Severe | HS |
| Very Severe | VS |
| Hard Very Severe | HVS |
| Extremely Severe 1 | E1 |
| Extremely Severe 2 | E2 |
| Extremely Severe 3 | E3 |
| Etc. | |

The technical grade is defined as the hardest move on a particular route. This numeric component of the British system is also open-ended and is subdivided into a, b, and c.

The two grades are linked to each other. For example, the standard adjectival grade for a well-protected 6a, which is not particularly sustained, is E3 (and the combined rating would be expressed as E3 6a). If the route is a bit run out, it would be E4; if it is really run out, it would be E5.

**French:** In the French open-ended system, ratings of 6 and above are subdivided into a, a+, b, b+, c, and c+. The French rating of 8c is comparable to 5.14a.

**UIAA:** The UIAA open-ended rating system uses Roman numerals. Beginning with the fifth level (V), the ratings also include pluses and minuses. The UIAA rating of X+ is comparable to 5.14a. German climbers use the UIAA system.

# Alpine Climbing/Ice Climbing

The International French Adjectival System (IFAS) is an overall rating of alpine and ice climbs used primarily in the Alps. The system is utilized by several countries, including France, Britain, Germany, Italy, and Spain. It expresses the seriousness of the route, including factors such as length, objective danger, commitment, altitude, run-outs, descent, and technical difficulty in terms of terrain.

The system has six categories that are symbolized by the initials of the French adjectives used. It is further refined with the use of plus or minus signs, or the terms "sup" (superior) or "inf" (inferior). The ratings end with an adjective readily understood in English.

**F:** *Facile (easy).* Steep walking routes, rock scrambling, and easy snow slopes. Crevasses possible on glaciers. Rope not always necessary.

**PD:** *Peu difficile (a little difficult).* Rock climbing with some technical difficulty, snow and ice slopes, serious glaciers, and narrow ridges.

**AD:** *Assez difficile (fairly difficult).* Fairly hard climbs, steep rock climbing, long snow/ice slopes above 50 degrees.

**D:** *Difficile (difficult).* Sustained hard rock and snow/ice climbing.

**TD:** *Tres difficile (very difficult).* Serious technical climbing on all kinds of terrain.

**ED:** *Extremement difficile (extremely difficult).* Extremely serious climbs with long, sustained difficulties of the highest order.

**ABO:** *Abominable.*

# B: Supplementary References

## Chapter 3: Camping and Food

Axcell, Claudia, Diana Cooke, and Vikki Kinmont. *Simple Foods for the Pack: The Sierra Club Guide to Delicious Natural Foods for the Trail.* San Francisco: Sierra Club Books, 1986.

Gunn, Carolyn. *The Expedition Cookbook.* Evergreen, Colo.: Chockstone Press, 1988.

Latimer, Carole. *Wilderness Cuisine: How to Prepare and Enjoy Fine Food on the Trail and in Camp.* Berkeley: Wilderness Press, 1991.

McHugh, Gretchen. *The Hungry Hiker's Book of Good Cooking.* New York: Alfred A. Knopf, 1982.

Prater, Yvonne, and Ruth Dyar Mendenhall. *Gorp, Glop & Glue Stew: Favorite Foods from 165 Outdoor Experts.* Seattle: The Mountaineers, 1982.

## Chapter 4: Navigation

Letham, Lawrence. *GPS Made Easy: Using Global Positioning Systems in the Outdoors.* Seattle: The Mountaineers, 1995.

## Chapter 7: Belaying

Mauthner, Kirk and Katie. *Gripping Ability on Rope in Motion.* British Columbia Council of Technical Rescue, 1994.

## Chapter 9: Rock–Climbing Technique

Goodard, D., and U. Neumann. *Performance Rock Climbing.* Mechanicsburg, Pa.: Stackpole Books, 1993.

Long, John. *Sport and Face Climbing: How to Rock Climb.* Evergreen, Colo.: Chockstone Press, 1991.

———. *Rock Climb!,* 2d ed. Evergreen, Colo.: Chockstone Press, 1993.

Long, John, and John Middendorf. *Big Walls! How to Rock Climb.* Evergreen, Colo.: Chockstone Press, 1994.

Loughman, Michael. *Learning to Rock Climb.* San Francisco: Sierra Club Books, 1981.

## Chapter 13: Snow Travel and Climbing

Armstrong, Betsey R., and Knox Williams. *The Avalanche Book.* Golden, Colo.: Fulcrum Publishing, 1992.

Atkins, Dale. *Avalanche Rescue Beacons: A Race against Time.* Boulder, Colo.: People Productions, 1995. Video: 38 minutes.

Fredston, Jill A., and Doug Fesler. *Snow Sense.* Anchorage: Alaska Mountain Safety Center, 1994.

LaChapelle, E. R. *ABC of Avalanche Safety,* 2d ed. Seattle: The Mountaineers, 1985.

McClung, David, and Peter Schaerer. *The Avalanche Handbook.* Seattle: The Mountaineers, 1993.

Prater, Gene (Edited by Dave Felkley). *Snowshoeing,* 4th ed. Seattle: The Mountaineers, 1997.

Wasatch Interpretive Association. *Winning the Avalanche Game.* Salt Lake City, 1993. Video: 60 minutes.

Westwide Network: Avalanche forecasts and safety information. Website: http://www.avalanche.org

## Chapter 14: Glacier Travel and Crevasse Rescue

Barry, John. *Snow and Ice Climbing.* Seattle: Cloudcap Press, 1987.

Cinnamon, Jerry. *Climbing Rock and Ice: Learning the Vertical Dance.* Camden, Maine: Ragged Mountain Press, 1994.

Ferguson, Sue. *Glaciers of North America*. Golden, Colo.: Fulcrum Publishing, 1992.

Fyffe, Allen, and Iain Peter. *The Handbook of Climbing*. London: Pelham Books, 1990.

Hambrey, Michael, and Jurg Alean. *Glaciers*. Cambridge, England: Cambridge University Press, 1992.

March, Bill. *Modern Snow and Ice Techniques*. Milnthorpe, Cumbria, England: Cicerone Press, 1984.

McMullen, John. *The Basic Essentials of Climbing Ice*. Merrillville, Ind.: ICS Books, 1992.

Powers, Phil. *NOLS Wilderness Mountaineering*. Mechanicsburg, Pa.: Stackpole Books, 1993.

Schubert, Pit. *Modern Alpine Climbing, Equipment, and Techniques*. Translated by G. Steele and M. Vapenikova. Milnthorpe, Cumbria, England: Cicerone Press, 1991.

Selters, Andy. *Glacier Travel and Crevasse Rescue*. Seattle: The Mountaineers, 1990.

Shirahata, Shiro. *The Karakoram: Mountains of Pakistan*. Seattle: Cloudcap Press, 1990.

## Chapter 15: Ice Climbing

Barry, John. *Alpine Climbing*. Seattle: Cloudcap Press, 1988.

Chouinard, Yvon. *Climbing Ice*. San Francisco: Sierra Club Books, 1978.

Cliff, Peter. *Ski Mountaineering*. Seattle: Pacific Search Press, 1987.

Fawcett, Ron, Jeff Lowe, Paul Nunn, and Alan Rouse. *The Climber's Handbook*. San Francisco: Sierra Club Books, 1987.

Lowe, Jeff. *The Ice Experience*. Chicago: Contemporary Books, 1979.

——. *Ice World: Techniques and Experiences of Modern Ice Climbing*. Seattle: The Mountaineers, 1996.

Raleigh, Duane. *Ice: Tools & Techniques*. Carbondale, Ind., 1995.

## Chapter 16: Alpine, Winter, and Expedition Climbing

Bearzi, Michael. "Doing the Mixed Thing." *Climbing* 130 (February/March 1992): 101–3.

Clark, Nancy, "Expedition Nutrition: Tips for Menu Planning." *Climbing* 97 (August/September 1986): 66–69.

Fyffe, Allen, and Iain Peter. *Handbook of Climbing*. London: Pelham Books, 1990.

Houston, Charles S. *Going Higher: The Story of Man and Altitude*. Boston: Little, Brown and Company, 1987.

Jenkins, Mark, and Dan Moe. "Adventures in the Refrigerator Zone: 30 Tips for Successful Winter Camping." *Backpacker,* (October 1993): 42–43.

## Chapter 17: Leadership

Bass, Bernard M., and Ralph Melvin Stogdill. *Bass & Stogdill's Handbook of Leadership*, 3d ed. New York: Free Press, 1990; and London: Collier Macmillan, 1990.

Petzoldt, Paul. *The New Wilderness Handbook*. New York: W. W. Norton, 1984.

## Chapter 18: Safety

The American Alpine Club and The Alpine Club of Canada. *Accidents in North American Mountaineering*. Golden, Colo., annual.

Geis, Craig. *Breaking the Poor Judgment Chain*. Napa, Calif.: Geis-Alvarado & Associates, 1990.

——. *Decision Making*. Napa, Calif.: Geis-Alvarado & Associates, 1990.

Helms, J. M. "The Perception of Risk in Mountaineering." The Evergreen State College, Daniel J. Evans Library, Olympia, Wash., 1981.

## Chapter 19: First Aid

Auerbach, Paul S., ed. *Wilderness Medicine: Management of Wilderness and Environmental Emergencies,*. 3d ed. St. Louis: Mosby, 1995.

Bergeron, J. David, and Gloria Bizjak. *First Responder,* 4th ed. Englewood Cliffs, N.J.: Brady/Prentice Hall, 1996.

Bezruchka, Stephen. *Altitude Illness: Prevention and Treatment*. Seattle: The Mountaineers, 1994.

Carline, Jan D., Martha J. Lentz, and Steven C. Macdonald. *Mountaineering First Aid: A Guide to Accident Response and First Aid Care,* 4th ed. Seattle: The Mountaineers, 1996.

Christensen, Anna, ed. *Wilderness First Aid: A Resource Manual for Outdoor Leaders in British Columbia*. Vancouver, B.C.: Wilderness First Aid and Safety Association of British Columbia, 1986.

Darville, Fred T., Jr. *Mountaineering Medicine: A Wilderness Medical Guide*, 12th ed. Berkeley: Wilderness Press, 1989.

Drummond, Roger. *Ticks and What You Can Do about Them*. Berkeley: Wilderness Press, 1990.

Dubas, Frédéric, and Jacques Valloton, eds. *Color Atlas of Mountain Medicine*. St. Louis: Mosby, 1991.

Forgey, William W., ed. *Wilderness Medical Society Practice Guidelines for Wilderness Emergency Care*. Merrillville, Ind.: ICS Books, 1995.

Forgey, William W. *Wilderness Medicine: Beyond First Aid*, 4th ed. Merrillville, Ind.: ICS Books, 1994.

Hackett, Peter H. *Mountain Sickness: Prevention, Recognition, and Treatment*. Golden, Colo.: The American Alpine Club, 1980.

Houston, Charles. *High Altitude: Illness and Wellness*. Merrillville, Ind.: ICS Books, 1993.

Isaac, Jeff, and Peter Goth. *The Outward Bound Wilderness First-Aid Handbook*. New York: Lyons & Burford, 1991.

Weiss, Eric A. *A Comprehensive Guide to Wilderness and Travel Medicine*. Berkeley: Adventure Medical Kits, 1992.

Wilkerson, James A., ed. *Medicine for Mountaineering and Other Wilderness Activities*, 4th ed. Seattle: The Mountaineers, 1992.

Wilkerson, James A., ed., Cameron C. Bangs, and John S. Hayward. *Hypothermia, Frostbite, and Other Cold Injuries: Prevention, Recognition, and Prehospital Treatment*. Seattle: The Mountaineers, 1986.

## Chapter 20: Alpine Rescue

Fasulo, Jeff. *Self Rescue: How to Rock Climb*. Evergreen, Colo.: Chockstone Press, 1996.

Long, John. *Climbing Anchors: How to Rock Climb*. Evergreen, Colo.: Chockstone Press, 1992.

Long, John, and Bob Gaines. *More Climbing Anchors: How to Rock Climb*. Evergreen, Colo.: Chockstone Press, 1996.

May, W. G. *Mountain Search and Rescue Techniques*. Boulder, Colo.: Rocky Mountain Rescue Group, 1973.

Setnica, Tim. *Wilderness Search and Rescue*. Boston: Appalachian Mountain Club, 1980.

## Chapter 23: Mountain Weather

LaChapelle, Edward R. *Field Guide to Snow Crystals*. Seattle: University of Washington Press, 1969.

Renner, Jeff. *Northwest Mountain Weather*. Seattle: The Mountaineers, 1992.

Williams, Jack. *The Weather Book*. USA Today, 1992.

## Chapter 24: Minimum Impact

Hampton, Bruce, and David Cole. *Soft Paths*. National Outdoor Leadership School. Mechanicsburg, Pa.: Stackpole Books, 1988.

National Outdoor Leadership School. *Leave-No-Trace Skills and Ethics Series*. Volumes covering various parts of the United States. Information: 1-800-332-4100.

Strauss, Robert. *Adventure Trekking: A Handbook for Independent Travelers*. Seattle: The Mountaineers, 1995. Includes chapters on minimum impact and foreign cultures.

# INDEX